# DIGITAL DESIGN AND COMPUTER ORGANISATION

# DIGITAL DESIGN AND COMPUTER ORGANISATION

*(For B.E./B.Tech., B.Sc., B.C.A., B.I.T., M.C.A., M.Tech./M.E./M.S., M.Sc. and Other Computer Courses)*

*By*


**Dr. NASIB S. GILL**
*Commonwealth Fellow (CSFPAA, U.K.)*
*Ph.D. (Computer Sc.), PDS (Brunel, U.K.),*
*Head, Department of Computer Science & Applications,*
*M.D. University, Rohtak*
*Haryana*

**J.B. DIXIT**
*M.Sc. (Applied Mathematics)*
*Post M.Sc. Diploma in Computer Science,*
*Kurukshetra University, Kurukshetra*
*Haryana*



UNIVERSITY SCIENCE PRESS
(An Imprint of Laxmi Publications Pvt. Ltd.)
An ISO 9001:2015 Company
BENGALURU • CHENNAI • GUWAHATI • HYDERABAD
KOCHI • KOLKATA • LUCKNOW • RANCHI
NEW DELHI

**DIGITAL DESIGN AND COMPUTER ORGANISATION**



Printed and bound in India
*Typeset at* : Kalyani Computer Services, New Delhi.
*First Edition* : 2008, *Reprint* : 2009, 2010, 2016, 2023, 2024, *Edition* : 2025
*ISBN* : 978-81-318-0345-5



**Branches**

|  |  |
|---|---|
| Bengaluru | 080-26 75 69 30 |
| Chennai | 044-24 34 47 26 |
| Guwahati | 0361-254 36 69 |
| Hyderabad | 040-27 55 53 83 |
| Kochi | 0484-405 13 03 |
| Kolkata | 033-40 04 77 79 |
| Lucknow | 0522-430 36 13 |
| Ranchi | 0651-224 24 64 |

PUBLISHED IN INDIA BY

UNIVERSITY SCIENCE PRESS
(An Imprint of Laxmi Publications Pvt. Ltd.)
An ISO 9001:2015 Company
113, GOLDEN HOUSE, GURUDWARA ROAD, DARYAGANJ,
NEW DELHI - 110002, INDIA
Telephone : 91-11-4353 2500, 4353 2501
www.laxmipublications.com
info@laxmipublications.com

C—00729/024/012
*Printed at* : Ajit Printing Press, Delhi.

*Dedicated to*

*All Beloved Readers, Friends*
*and Family Members*

# CONTENTS

# Preface to the First Edition

We are highly delighted to place the book titled **"Digital Design and Computer Organisation"** in the hands of our esteemed readers.

This book has been written for B.E./B.Tech, M.Tech./M.E./M.S., M.C.A., M.Sc., B.I.T., B.C.A., B.Sc.(Comp.Sc.)/B.Sc.(IT) and other computer programmes' students keeping in view the following special points:

- Conceptual clarity and practical orientation.
- To learn the basic concepts used in the design and analysis of digital systems.
- Introduces the principles of digital computer organization.
- Provides various methods and techniques suitable for a variety of digital system design applications.
- Covers all aspects of digital systems from the basic concepts of Boolean algebra, combinational logic and sequential logic circuits to the complex structure of microcomputer systems.
- Covers abundance of examples and their solutions.

We have put our sincere efforts and knowledge to make you understand the subject matter in simplest and easiest way. Valuable suggestions are always welcome.

**—Authors**

# ACKNOWLEDGEMENT

It is our pleasure to take this opportunity to thank all those who helped us directly or indirectly in the preparation of this book. The writing of a book of this nature would not have been possible without consulting the writings of many other learned authors, researcher and practitioners in this field, and we are indeed indebted to all of them.

We are quite thankful to all our readers who always expected of us to write a simple book that enables them to comprehend the concepts in a simplified manner.

Besides, we are also very thankful to all our friends at all Universities, Engineering Colleges/Institutes, and Colleges of the region, and MDU staff, who encouraged and inspired us directly or indirectly to write a very different and unique kind of book that could serve purpose for all those readers who might be new or an experienced hand in the field of Digital Design, Digital Electronics, Computer Design, Computer Organisation and Computer Architecture.

We owe a sincere debt of gratitude to all our students from whom we have learnt more than we have given and to all those researchers and practitioners of the discipline whose ideas, work and techniques find a place in this book.

Finally, we wish to express our sincere thanks to all our family members and relatives for their moral support. In particular, we are grateful to our parents, spouses and children, who never minded stealing of their home time, which otherwise we would have enjoyed with them rather than spending in writing this book.

Lastly, we thank everyone at Laxmi Publications (P) Ltd. for their efforts in making this book a reality and that too in such a nice getup.

**—Authors**

Chapter 1

# Number Systems and Data Representation

## 1.1 INTRODUCTION

A digital computer is an electronic machine that accepts a stream of symbols as its input, stores them, processes them according to precise rules and produces meaningful output. Computers are used in scientific calculations, commercial and business data processing, air traffic control, space guidance, the educational field, and many other areas. The most important characteristic of a digital computer is its generality. It can follow a sequence of instructions, called a *program,* that operates on given data.

In this Chapter, we will discuss the Number Systems and representation of data in digital systems. There are two main categories of data:

(*i*) Numbers, and

(*ii*) Characters.

As mentioned earlier that internally in a digital system all data is represented by sequence of symbols where each symbol, called a bit, is either a 0 or a 1. The general properties of number systems, methods of their inter-conversions, complements and other data representation techniques are also discussed in this Chapter.

## 1.2 BASIC FEATURES OF DIGITAL SYSTEMS

Few basic features which are common to all digital systems are as under:

- All streams of input symbols to a digital system are encoded with two distinct symbols 0 (zero) and 1 (one), known as *binary digits* or *bits*. Bits can be stored and manipulated reliably and inexpensively using electronic circuits.
- The instructions for manipulating the symbols are to be properly specified so that a machine can be built to execute these. The instructions for manipulation are also encoded using *bits.*
- A digital computer has a storage unit which stores the symbols to be manipulated and the encoded instructions for manipulation of the symbols.
- Bit manipulation instructions are realized by electronic circuits.

## 1.3 NUMBER SYSTEMS

Number systems are very important to understand because the design and organisation of a computer depends on the number systems. The modern civilization is familiar with ***Decimal Number System,*** in which ten digits, namely 0 to 9 are used to represent any number. Now the *decimal number system* is used frequently in the field of Science and Technology. Once the famous Mathematician Laplace stated, "It is India that gave us the ingenious method of expressing all numbers by means of ten symbols, each symbol receiving a value of position as well as an absolute value, a profound and important idea which appears so simple to us now that we ignore its true merit."

Thus, the importance of a number system does not lie in the number of symbols used in it but what is important in it is the concept of face value (absolute value) and the place value (value of position) of a symbol. However, if instead of decimal system the binary number system, using two digits namely, 0 and 1, had been popular everywhere, the understanding of computer working would have been much easier. The binary number system is the one which is used in computers and is based on the fundamental concept of decimal number system. Various other number systems such as Octal System and Hexadecimal System (popularly known as Hex system) also use the fundamental concept of face value and place value.

The knowledge of number systems is essential for understanding of computers. The useful number systems discussed are:

- Binary Number System.
- Octal Number System.
- Decimal Number System.
- Hexadecimal Number System.

### 1.3.1 Binary Number System

The **Binary Number System,** as the name suggests, consists of two digits namely, 0 and 1. These binary digits are called BITS. Thus, the word **BIT** stands for either of the binary digits, namely 0 or 1. Since this system uses two digits only, it has the **base** or **radix 2.** It may be noted that the base digit namely 2, is not the fundamental or basic digit of the system. Thus, all the numbers in binary system are written with the help of these two digits namely, 0 and 1. The positional value or place value of each digit in a binary number is twice the positional value of the digit on its right. This number system is identical to decimal number system with the base replaced by 2. The binary numbers are usually written with the base indicated as a subscript on the least significant digit (LSD). For example,

$$(101101.1011)_2$$

It can be represented as shown in Figure 1.1:

Here, the places to the left of the binary point are positive powers of 2 and places to the right are negative powers of 2.

The commonly used terms in coding of data in computer terminology are:

**BIT (BInary digiT):** A binary digit is logical 0 or 1.

**Nibble:** A group of four bits (binary digits) is called a Nibble. It is useful in coding the numeric data to hexadecimal form.

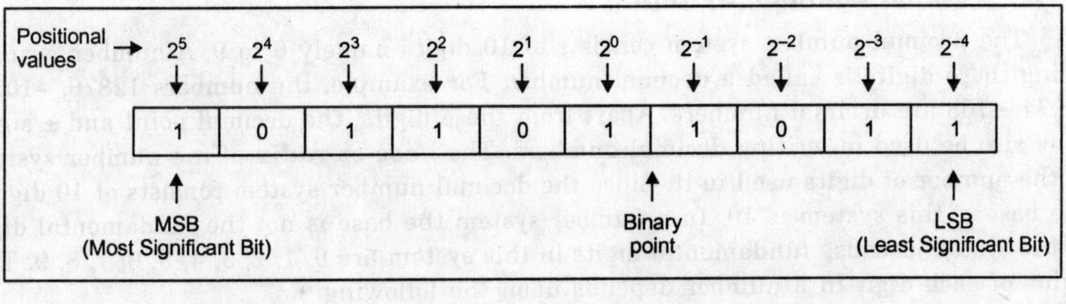


**Fig. 1.1:** Binary number shown with positional values.

**Byte:** A group of 8 bits make a byte. A byte is the smallest unit which can represent a data item or a character.

**Computer Word:** A computer word, like a byte, is a group of fixed number of bits which varies from computer to computer but is fixed for each computer. The number of bits in a computer word is known as the **word size** or **word length.**

**Why is Binary Number System used in Computers?**

*(i)* The circuits and switches in a computer have only two states, either on or off, which are represented by 1 and 0.

*(ii)* Handling of two digits, that is, 1 and 0 is simpler, cheaper and more reliable.

*(iii)* Every operation or activity that can be performed by decimal number system can also be done using binary number system, so it does not create any problem.

## 1.3.2 Octal Number System

This number system has **base** or **radix** 8. The basic digits of this system are 0, 1, 2, 3, 4, 5, 6 and 7. It may be noted that the base 8 is not the basic digit of the system. It is commonly used as a shorthand way of expressing binary quantities. Also the numbers represented in octal number system can be used directly for input and output operations.

The octal number system is also a positional value system, wherein each octal digit has its own value or weight expressed as a power of 8. For example,

$$(157246.3174)_8$$

It can be represented as shown in Figure 1.2:

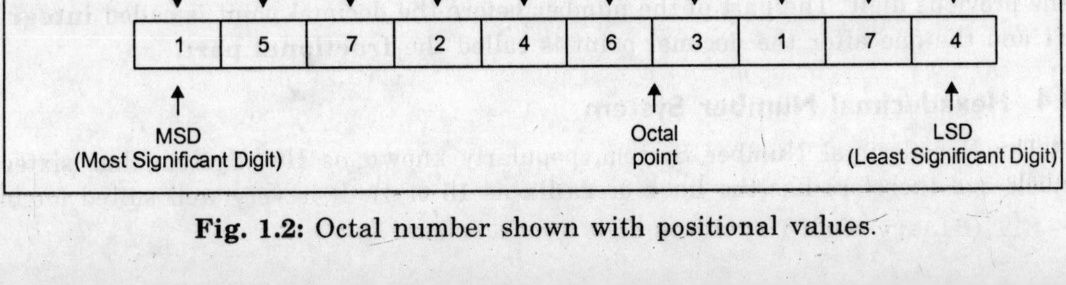


**Fig. 1.2:** Octal number shown with positional values.

Here, the places to the left of the octal point are positive powers of 8 and places to the right are negative powers of 8.

### 1.3.3 Decimal Number System

The decimal number system consists of 10 digits namely 0 to 9. A number written using these digits is called a decimal number. For example, the numbers 12876, –1024, 58.74, +768 are decimal numbers. Apart from these digits, the decimal point and ± signs may also be used in writing decimal numbers. The **base** or **radix** of the number system is the number of digits used in it. Since the decimal number system consists of 10 digits, the base of this system is 10. In a number system the base is not the fundamental digit of the system because fundamental digits in this system are 0, 1, 2, 3, 4, 5, 6, 7, 8, 9. The value of each digit in a number depends upon the following:

(*i*) The face value of the digit, that is, the digit itself.

(*ii*) The base of the system.

(*iii*) The position of the digit in the number.

Thus, the magnitude of a number depends upon the digits of which it is made, position of the digits and base of the system. For example,

351479.8265

Since no base is mentioned, the base is taken as 10.

It can be represented as shown in Figure 1.3:

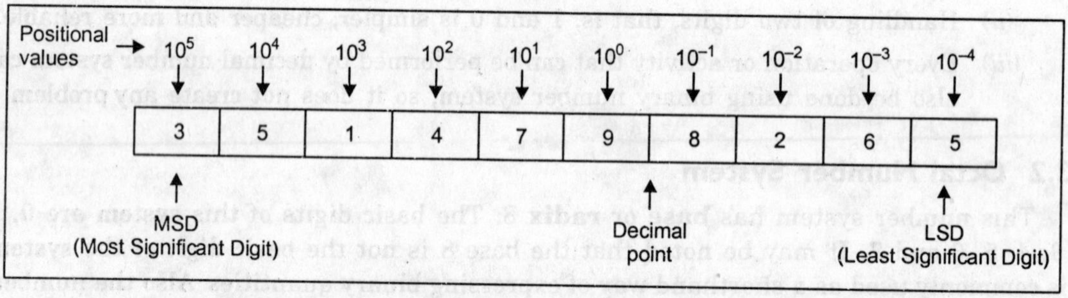


**Fig. 1.3:** Decimal number shown with positional values.

Here, the places to the left of the decimal point are positive powers of 10 and places to the right are negative powers of 10.

In a decimal number as we move from right to left (starting with the digit before decimal point) the positional or place value of each digit is 10 times the positional value of the digit to its right and as we move from left to right (starting with the digit after decimal point) the positional value of each digit becomes one-tenth of the positional value of the previous digit. The part of the number before the decimal point is called **integral part** and the one after the decimal point is called the **fractional part.**

### 1.3.4 Hexadecimal Number System

The Hexadecimal Number System, popularly known as Hex System, has sixteen symbols and therefore has the **base** or **radix** as 16 or H. It is very well suited for big computers. The hexadecimal number system represents an information in the concise form. The sixteen symbols used in this system are:

0, 1, 2, 3, 4, 5, 6, 7, 8, 9, A, B, C, D, E, F

The equivalence between hex-numbers (hexadecimal numbers) and decimal numbers is given below:

| *Decimal* | 0 | 1 | 2 | 3 | 4 | 5 | 6 | 7 | 8 | 9 | 10 | 11 | 12 | 13 | 14 | 15 |
|---|---|---|---|---|---|---|---|---|---|---|---|---|---|---|---|---|
| *Hexadecimal* | 0 | 1 | 2 | 3 | 4 | 5 | 6 | 7 | 8 | 9 | A | B | C | D | E | F |

Hexadecimal number system is also a positional value system, wherein each hexadecimal digit/letter has its own value or weight expressed as a power of 16. For example,

$$(6A9E83.C5BD)_{16}$$

It can be represented as shown in Figure 1.4:

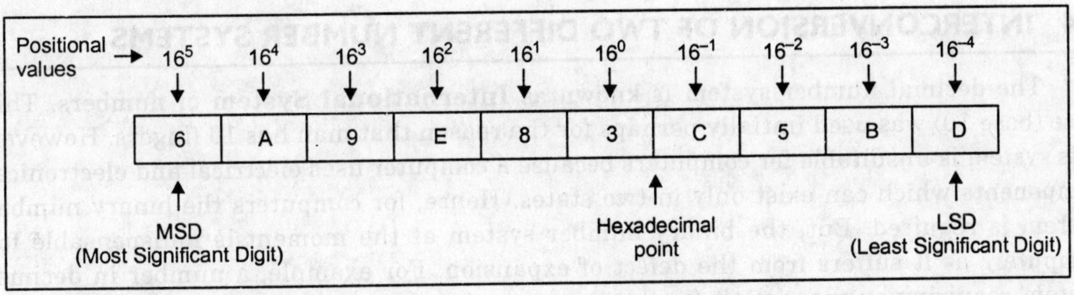


**Fig. 1.4:** Hexadecimal number shown with positional values.

Here, the places to the left of hexadecimal point are positive powers of 16 and places to the right are negative powers of 16.

Table 1.1 illustrates the relation between binary, octal, decimal and hexadecimal number systems:

**Table 1.1: Numbers with Different Bases**

| *Binary (base 2)* | *Octal (base 8)* | *Decimal (base 10)* | *Hexadecimal (base 16)* |
|---|---|---|---|
| 0000 | 0 | 0 | 0 |
| 0001 | 1 | 1 | 1 |
| 0010 | 2 | 2 | 2 |
| 0011 | 3 | 3 | 3 |
| 0100 | 4 | 4 | 4 |
| 0101 | 5 | 5 | 5 |
| 0110 | 6 | 6 | 6 |

| | | | |
|---|---|---|---|
| 0111 | 7 | 7 | 7 |
| 1000 | 10 | 8 | 8 |
| 1001 | 11 | 9 | 9 |
| 1010 | 12 | 10 | A |
| 1011 | 13 | 11 | B |
| 1100 | 14 | 12 | C |
| 1101 | 15 | 13 | D |
| 1110 | 16 | 14 | E |
| 1111 | 17 | 15 | F |

## 1.4 INTERCONVERSION OF TWO DIFFERENT NUMBER SYSTEMS

The decimal number system is known as **International System** of numbers. This base (base 10) was used initially perhaps for the reason that man has 10 fingers. However, this system is unsuitable for computers because a computer uses electrical and electronical components which can exist only in two states. Hence, for computers the binary number system is required. But, the binary number system at the moment is indispensable for computers as it suffers from the defect of expansion. For example, a number in decimal system requiring only one digit for its representation may require more than one bits in binary form.

To overcome this problem various other number systems such as Octal (base 8) and Hexadecimal (base 16 or H) were developed. A base greater than 10 is preferred because it will require even lesser number of digits. The choices of bases 8 and 16 are useful because of their being multiple of two.

### 1.4.1 Binary to Decimal

A binary number can be converted to its decimal equivalent by adding the weights of the various positions in it which have a 1.

**Example 1.** *Find the decimal equivalent of the following binary numbers:*

*(i) 10110 (ii) 101011 (iii) 11011100.*

**Solution.** (*i*)

$$(10110)_2 = 1 \times 2^4 + 0 \times 2^3 + 1 \times 2^2 + 1 \times 2^1 + 0 \times 2^0$$
$$= 16 + 0 + 4 + 2 + 0$$
$$= (22)_{10}.$$

It must be noted that the binary number 10110 has five digits in all. The most significant digit (MSD) has the fifth position (starting from rightmost digit) so it is multiplied by $2^4$ and each digit on its right will be half of it in its positional value, so these are multiplied by $2^3$, $2^2$, $2^1$, $2^0$ respectively and the products so obtained are added to get the required decimal equivalent.

*(ii)* $(101011)_2 = 1 \times 2^5 + 0 \times 2^4 + 1 \times 2^3 + 0 \times 2^2 + 1 \times 2^1 + 1 \times 2^0$

$= 32 + 0 + 8 + 0 + 2 + 1$

$= (43)_{10}$

$= 43.$

*(iii)* $(11011100)_2 = 1 \times 2^7 + 1 \times 2^6 + 0 \times 2^5 + 1 \times 2^4 + 1 \times 2^3 + 1 \times 2^2 + 0 \times 2^1 + 0 \times 2^0$

$= 128 + 64 + 0 + 16 + 8 + 4 + 0 + 0$

$= (220)_{10}$

$= 220.$

**Example 2.** *Convert the following binary fractions to their decimal equivalents: (i) $(0.111)_2$ (ii) $(0.1010111)_2$ (iii) $(0.1011)_2$.*

**Solution.** *(i)* $(0.111)_2 = 1 \times 2^{-1} + 1 \times 2^{-2} + 1 \times 2^{-3}$

$= 1/2 + 1/4 + 1/8$

$= 0.5 + 0.25 + 0.125$

$= (0.875)_{10}$

$= 0.875$

$\therefore \quad (0.111)_2 = (0.875)_{10}$

*(ii)* $(0.1010111)_2 = 1 \times 2^{-1} + 0 \times 2^{-2} + 1 \times 2^{-3} + 0 \times 2^{-4} + 1 \times 2^{-5} + 1 \times 2^{-6} + 1 \times 2^{-7}$

$= 1/2 + 0 + 1/8 + 0 + 1/32 + 1/64 + 1/128$

$= 0.5 + .125 + 0.03125 + 0.015625 + 0.0078125$

$= (0.6796875)_{10}$

$= 0.6796875$

$\therefore \quad (0.1010111)_2 = (0.6796875)_{10}$

*(iii)* $(0.1011)_2 = 1 \times 2^{-1} + 0 \times 2^{-2} + 1 \times 2^{-3} + 1 \times 2^{-4}$

$= 1/2 + 0 + 1/8 + 1/16$

$= 0.5 + 0.125 + 0.0625$

$= (0.6875)_{10}$

$= 0.6875$

$\therefore \quad (0.1011)_2 = (0.6875)_{10}$

**Example 3.** *Find the decimal equivalent of the following binary numbers: (i) $(110010.1011)_2$ (ii) $(1110.1001)_2$.*

**Solution.**

*(i)* $(110010.1011)_2 = (1 \times 2^5) + (1 \times 2^4) + (0 \times 2^3) + (0 \times 2^2) + (1 \times 2^1) + (0 \times 2^0) + (1 \times 2^{-1}) + (0 \times 2^{-2}) + (1 \times 2^{-3}) + (1 \times 2^{-4})$

$= 32 + 16 + 0 + 0 + 2 + 0 + 0.5 + 0 + 0.125 + 0.0625$

$= (50.6875)_{10}$

$$= 50.6875$$

$$\therefore \quad (110010.1011)_2 = (50.6875)_{10}.$$

(*ii*)

$$(1110.1001)_2 = 1 \times 2^3 + 1 \times 2^2 + 1 \times 2^1 + 0 \times 2^0 + 1 \times 2^{-1} + 0 \times 2^{-2} + 0 \times 2^{-3} + 1 \times 2^{-4}$$

$$= 8 + 4 + 2 + 0 + 1/2 + 0 + 0 + 1/16$$

$$= 14 + 0.5 + 0.0625$$

$$= 14.5625.$$

**Example 4.** *Provide the missing number* $(11001.1101)_2 = (\ldots\ldots\ldots\ldots)_{10}$.

**Solution.** Let us find the decimal equivalent of the binary number.

$$(11001.1101)_2 = 1 \times 2^4 + 1 \times 2^3 + 0 \times 2^2 + 0 \times 2^1 + 1 \times 2^0 + 1 \times 2^{-1} + 1 \times 2^{-2} + 0 \times 2^{-3} + 1 \times 2^{-4}$$

$$= 16 + 8 + 0 + 0 + 1 + 1/2 + 1/4 + 0 + 1/16$$

$$= 25 + 0.5 + 0.25 + 0.0625$$

$$= (25.8125)_{10}$$

$$= 25.8125$$

Hence, the missing number is 25.8125.

## 1.4.2 Decimal to Binary

A positive decimal integer can be converted to binary form by successive division by 2. The procedure is given below:

Divide the given number N by 2 and let the quotient be $q_1$ and the remainder be $R_1$. Again divide the quotient $q_1$ by 2 and let the remainder be $R_2$. Continue the procedure of division till the quotient becomes 0 and in this case let the remainder be $R_n$.

Then, the binary representation by N is given as

$$N = R_n\, R_{n-1} \ldots\ldots R_3\, R_2\, R_1,$$

where each of the R's is either 0 or 1.

**Example.** *Convert the following decimal integers into their binary equivalents:*

*(i) 25 (ii) 283 (iii) 5280.*

**Solution.** (*i*) Start dividing 25 by 2 and continue the procedure till the quotient is 0. The procedure is shown below:

| | | |
|---|---|---|
| 2 | 25 | |
| 2 | 12 – 1 | (=$R_1$) ↑ |
| 2 | 6 – 0 | (=$R_2$) |
| 2 | 3 – 0 | (=$R_3$) |
| 2 | 1 – 1 | (=$R_4$) |
| | 0 – 1 | (=$R_5$) |

The required number in the binary number system

$= R_5\ R_4\ R_3\ R_2\ R_1$

$= 11001$

Thus, $(25)_{10} = (11001)_2$

(*ii*) Start dividing 283 by 2 and continue the procedure till the quotient becomes 0.

| | | |
|---|---|---|
| 2 | 283 | |
| 2 | 141 – 1 | (=$R_1$) |
| 2 | 70 – 1 | (=$R_2$) |
| 2 | 35 – 0 | (=$R_3$) |
| 2 | 17 – 1 | (=$R_4$) |
| 2 | 8 – 1 | (=$R_5$) |
| 2 | 4 – 0 | (=$R_6$) |
| 2 | 2 – 0 | (=$R_7$) |
| 2 | 1 – 0 | (=$R_8$) |
| | 0 – 1 | (=$R_9$) |

The required binary equivalent of 283

$= R_9\ R_8\ R_7\ R_6\ R_5\ R_4\ R_3\ R_2\ R_1$

$= (100011011)_2$

Thus, $(283)_{10} = (100011011)_2$

(*iii*) Start dividing 5280 by 2 and continue the procedure till the quotient becomes 0.

| | | |
|---|---|---|
| 2 | 5280 | |
| 2 | 2640 – 0 | (=$R_1$) |
| 2 | 1320 – 0 | (=$R_2$) |
| 2 | 660 – 0 | (=$R_3$) |
| 2 | 330 – 0 | (=$R_4$) |
| 2 | 165 – 0 | (=$R_5$) |
| 2 | 82 – 1 | (=$R_6$) |
| 2 | 41 – 0 | (=$R_7$) |
| 2 | 20 – 1 | (=$R_8$) |
| 2 | 10 – 0 | (=$R_9$) |
| 2 | 5 – 0 | (=$R_{10}$) |
| 2 | 2 – 1 | (=$R_{11}$) |
| 2 | 1 – 0 | (=$R_{12}$) |
| | 0 – 1 | (=$R_{13}$) |

The required binary equivalent of 5280

$= R_{13}\ R_{12}\ R_{11}\ R_{10}\ R_9\ R_8\ R_7\ R_6\ R_5\ R_4\ R_3\ R_2\ R_1$

$= (1010010100000)_2$

Thus, $(5280)_{10} = (1010010100000)_2$

The decimal digits and their binary equivalents are given below:

| *Decimal Digit* | *Binary Equivalent* | |
|---|---|---|
| 0 | 0 | $(0 \times 2^0)$ |
| 1 | 1 | $(1 \times 2^0)$ |
| 2 | 10 | $(1 \times 2^1 + 0 \times 2^0)$ |
| 3 | 11 | $(1 \times 2^1 + 1 \times 2^0)$ |
| 4 | 100 | $(1 \times 2^2 + 0 \times 2^1 + 0 \times 2^0)$ |
| 5 | 101 | $(1 \times 2^2 + 0 \times 2^1 + 1 \times 2^0)$ |
| 6 | 110 | $(1 \times 2^2 + 1 \times 2^1 + 0 \times 2^0)$ |
| 7 | 111 | $(1 \times 2^2 + 1 \times 2^1 + 1 \times 2^0)$ |
| 8 | 1000 | $(1 \times 2^3 + 0 \times 2^2 + 0 \times 2^1 + 0 \times 2^0)$ |
| 9 | 1001 | $(1 \times 2^3 + 0 \times 2^2 + 0 \times 2^1 + 1 \times 2^0)$ |

## 1.4.3 Decimal Fractions to Binary Fractions

While converting decimal fractions to binary fractions, instead of dividing by 2, multiply successively by 2 and instead of noting the remainders as in case of integers, keep track of the overflow. If overflow digits are $f_1, f_2, f_3, \ldots, f_n$ then the equivalent binary fraction is

$$0 . f_1 f_2 f_3 \ldots\ldots f_n$$

while multiplying by 2, it must be noted that every time only fractional part is to be multiplied and not the integral part. The following examples illustrate the procedure.

**Example 1.** *Convert the decimal fractional number 0.8125 into its binary equivalent.*

**Solution.**

$$\begin{array}{lr} & 0.8125 \\ & \times\ 2 \\ \hline f_1 & \leftarrow \boxed{1}.\ 6250 \\ & \times\ 2 \\ \hline f_2 & \leftarrow \boxed{1}.\ 2500 \\ & \times\ 2 \\ \hline f_3 & \leftarrow \boxed{0}.\ 5000 \\ & \times\ 2 \\ \hline f_4 & \leftarrow \boxed{1}.\ 0000 \end{array}$$

(Multiply only the fraction part)

Further multiplication gives only zero digits as overflow.

Thus, $(0.8125)_{10} = 0.\, f_1\, f_2\, f_3\, f_4$

$= (0.1101)_2$

**Example 2.** *Convert 0.33 into its binary equivalent.*

**Solution.**

| | | |
|---|---|---|
| | 0.33 | |
| | × 2 | |
| $f_1$ | ← [0]. 66 | |
| | × 2 | |
| $f_2$ | ← [1]. 32 | |
| | × 2 | (Multiply only the fraction part) |
| $f_3$ | ← [0]. 64 | |
| | × 2 | |
| $f_4$ | ← [1]. 28 | |
| | × 2 | |
| $f_5$ | ← [0]. 56 | |
| | × 2 | |
| $f_6$ | ← [1]. 12 | and so on. |

Thus, $(0.33)_{10} = 0.f_1\, f_2\, f_3\, f_4\, f_5\, f_6\ldots\ldots$

$= (0.010101\ldots)_2$

**Note.** *The conversion in the above examples is not exact. However, it is correct only to six places of binary. By considering more digits in binary a still better and closer approximation can be obtained. It may be noted that if a decimal fraction is an exact combination of the fraction such as 1/2, 1/4, 1/8, 1/16 etc., the conversion of the decimal fractions to equivalent binary will be exact i.e., the number of digits is exact in equivalent binary fraction otherwise the binary fraction will be infinite in length.*

### 1.4.4 Mixed Decimal Numbers to Binary

A mixed number consists of an integral part as well as a fractional part. For example, 38.625 is a mixed number. A mixed number in decimal system can be converted to its binary equivalent by converting the integral and fractional parts separately into their binary equivalent.

The following example illustrates this concept:

**Example.** *Convert the decimal number 38.625 into its binary equivalent.*

**Solution.** The given decimal number has two parts, namely an integral part 38 and a fractional part 0.625. These are to be converted into their binary equivalents separately, as follows:

| | | |
|---|---|---|
| 2 | 38 | |
| 2 | 19 – 0 | (=$R_1$) ↑ |
| 2 | 9 – 1 | (=$R_2$) |
| 2 | 4 – 1 | (=$R_3$) |
| 2 | 2 – 0 | (=$R_4$) |
| 2 | 1 – 0 | (=$R_5$) |
| | 0 – 1 | (=$R_6$) |

Thus, the binary equivalent of $(38)_{10} = R_6\ R_5\ R_4\ R_3\ R_2\ R_1$

$= (100110)_2$

Also

$$\begin{array}{lr} & 0.625 \\ & \times\ 2 \\ \hline f_1 & \leftarrow \boxed{1}.\ 250 \\ & \times\ 2 \\ \hline f_2 & \leftarrow \boxed{1}.\ 500 \\ & \times\ 2 \\ \hline f_3\ \downarrow & \leftarrow \boxed{1}.\ 000 \end{array}$$

(Multiply only the fraction part)

Further multiplication gives only zero digits as overflow.

Thus, $(0.625)_{10} = 0.f_1\ f_2\ f_3$

$= (0.101)_2$

Hence, $(38.625)_{10} = (100110.101)_2$

## 1.4.5 Decimal Numbers to Octal Numbers

For converting integer decimal numbers into their equivalent octal numbers, divide the given number repeatedly by 8 till the quotient obtained is zero. The following example illustrates this concept:

**Example 1.** *Convert the following Decimal numbers into their Octal equivalents:*

*(i) 759* *(ii) 1598.*

**Solution.** (*i*) Start dividing 759 by 8 and continue the procedure till the quotient is 0. The procedure is shown below:

| | | |
|---|---|---|
| 8 | 759 | |
| 8 | 94 – 7 | ↑ LSD |
| 8 | 11 – 6 | |
| 8 | 1 – 3 | |
| | 0 – 1 | MSD |

Thus, $(759)_{10} = (1367)_8$

(*ii*)

$$\begin{array}{r|l} 8 & 1598 \\ \hline 8 & 199-6 \quad \uparrow \text{LSD} \\ \hline 8 & 24-7 \\ \hline 8 & 3-0 \\ \hline & 0-3 \quad \text{MSD} \end{array}$$

Thus, $(1598)_{10} = (3076)_8$

For converting decimal fractions into their equivalent octal fractions, multiply the fractional part repeatedly by 8 and keep track of the overflow. The process of multiplication continues till the fractional part becomes zero or upto required number of digits.

The following example illustrates this concept:

**Example 2.** *Convert the following decimal fractions to their equivalent Octal fractions:*

*(i)* $(0.125)_{10}$ *(ii)* $(0.175)_{10}$.

**Solution.** (*i*)

$$\begin{array}{r} 0.125 \\ \times\, 8 \\ \hline \boxed{1}.000 \end{array}$$

Thus, $(0.125)_{10} = (0.1)_8$

(*ii*)

$$\begin{array}{lr} & 0.175 \\ & \times\, 8 \\ \hline f_1 & \leftarrow \boxed{1}.400 \\ & \times\, 8 \\ \hline f_2 & \leftarrow \boxed{3}.200 \\ & \times\, 8 \\ \hline f_3 & \leftarrow \boxed{1}.600 \\ & \times\, 8 \\ \hline f_4 & \leftarrow \boxed{4}.800 \\ & \times\, 8 \\ \hline f_5 & \leftarrow \boxed{6}.400 \\ & \times\, 8 \\ \hline f_6 & \leftarrow \boxed{3}.200 \\ & \times\, 8 \\ \hline f_7 & \leftarrow \boxed{1}.600 \\ & \times\, 8 \\ \hline f_8 & \leftarrow \boxed{4}.800 \\ & \times\, 8 \\ \hline f_9 & \leftarrow \boxed{6}.400 \end{array}$$

(Multiply only the fraction part)

and so on.

Thus, $(0.175)_{10} = (0.1\,\overline{3146})_8$ recurrence

Here, the bar shows that these digits will be repeated infinitely.

For converting the decimal mixed numbers into their equivalent octals, integral and fractional parts are treated separately. Each part is converted to octal separately.

The following example illustrates this concept:

**Example 3.** *Convert the following mixed decimal numbers to their equivalent octals:*

*(i) 22.21875* *(ii) 79.4375.*

**Solution.** *(i)* $(22.21875)_{10}$

Integral part

| | | |
|---|---|---|
| 8 | 22 | |
| 8 | 2 – 6 | ↑ LSD |
| | 0 – 2 | MSD |

Fractional part

$$\begin{array}{r} 0.21875 \\ \times 8 \\ \hline \boxed{1}.75000 \\ \times 8 \\ \hline \boxed{6}.00000 \end{array}$$

(Multiply only the fraction part)

Thus, $(22)_{10} = (26)_8$ Thus, $(0.21875)_{10} = (0.16)_8$

Hence, $(22.21875)_{10} = (26.16)_8$

*(ii)* $(79.4375)_{10}$

Integral part

| | | |
|---|---|---|
| 8 | 79 | |
| 8 | 9 – 7 | ↑ LSD |
| 8 | 1 – 1 | |
| | 0 – 1 | MSD |

Fractional part

$$\begin{array}{r} 0.4375 \\ \times 8 \\ \hline \boxed{3}.5000 \\ \times 8 \\ \hline \boxed{4}.0000 \end{array}$$

(Multiply only the fraction part)

Thus, $(79)_{10} = (117)_8$ Thus, $(0.4375)_{10} = (0.34)_8$

Hence, $(79.4375)_{10} = (117.34)_8$

> **Note.** *It may be noticed that when a decimal number is converted to its binary equivalent, a long string of binary digits, namely 0 and 1 is obtained. On the other hand, if the same decimal number is converted to its octal equivalent, the number so obtained contains less number of digits compared to binary. In fact, this was the reason for the development of Octal Number System. It must be remembered that computers still work in binary and all these number systems (except binary) are for users' convenience.*

### 1.4.6 Octal Numbers to Decimal Numbers

A mixed octal number can be converted to decimal number by the formula given below:

$$M = d_{n+1}8^n + d_n8^{n-1} + d_{n-1}8^{n-2} + \ldots\ldots d_38^2 + d_28^1 + d_18^0 + d_{-1}8^{-1} + d_{-2}8^{-2} + d_{-3}8^{-3} + \ldots + d_{-n}8^{-n}$$

Here, M is the mixed number

$d_{n+1}$ is the digit in the $(n + 1)$th position of the integral part

$d_{-1}$ is the digit immediately after the octal point.

The following examples illustrate this concept:

**Example 1.** *Convert the following octal numbers into their decimal equivalents:*

*(i)* $(47)_8$ *(ii)* $(564)_8$.

**Solution.** *(i)*

$$(47)_8 = 4 \times 8^1 + 7 \times 8^0$$
$$= 32 + 7 = 39$$

Thus, $(47)_8 = (39)_{10}$

*(ii)*

$$(564)_8 = 5 \times 8^2 + 6 \times 8^1 + 4 \times 8^0$$
$$= 5 \times 64 + 6 \times 8 + 4 \times 1$$
$$= 320 + 48 + 4$$
$$= 372$$

Thus, $(564)_8 = (372)_{10}$

**Example 2.** *Convert the following octal fractions to their decimal equivalents:*

*(i)* $(0.34)_8$ *(ii)* $(0.542)_8$.

**Solution.** *(i)*

$$(0.34)_8 = 3 \times 8^{-1} + 4 \times 8^{-2}$$
$$= 3 \times 1/8 + 4 \times 1/64$$
$$= 3 \times 0.125 + 4 \times 0.015625$$
$$= 0.375 + .062500$$
$$= (0.4375)_{10}$$

*(ii)*

$$(0.542)_8 = 5 \times 8^{-1} + 4 \times 8^{-2} + 2 \times 8^{-3}$$
$$= 5 \times 0.125 + 4 \times .015625 + 2 \times .001953125$$
$$= 0.625 + 0.062500 + .003906250$$
$$= (0.691406250)_{10}$$

### 1.4.7 Octal to Binary

The octal number system is widely used as a shorthand way of expressing binary values. The octal number system groups three binary bits together into one digit (0 to 7) as given below:

| *Octal* | *Binary Equivalent* |
|---|---|
| 0 | 000 |
| 1 | 001 |
| 2 | 010 |
| 3 | 011 |

| | |
|---|---|
| 4 | 100 |
| 5 | 101 |
| 6 | 110 |
| 7 | 111 |

To convert an octal number to its binary equivalent, each digit of the octal number is converted to its 3 bits binary equivalent.

The following examples illustrate this concept:

**Example 1.** *Convert the following octal numbers into their binary equivalents:*
*(i)* $(746)_8$ *(ii)* $(5043)_8$.

**Solution.** *(i)*

$$(746)_8 = \frac{111}{7}\ \frac{100}{4}\ \frac{110}{6} \quad \text{(Replace each octal digit by its 3 bits binary equivalent)}$$

$$= (111100110)_2$$

Thus, $(746)_8 = (111100110)_2$

*(ii)*

$$(5043)_8 = \frac{101}{5}\ \frac{000}{0}\ \frac{100}{4}\ \frac{011}{3}$$

$$= (101000100011)_2$$

Thus, $(5043)_8 = (101000100011)_2$

**Example 2.** *Convert the following octal numbers into their binary equivalents:*
*(i)* $(35.216)_8$ *(ii)* $(417.25)_8$.

**Solution.** *(i)*

$$(35.216)_8 = \frac{011}{3}\ \frac{101}{5}\ .\ \frac{010}{2}\ \frac{001}{1}\ \frac{110}{6}$$

$$= (11101.01000111)_2$$

(Discarding the leftmost and rightmost zero)

Thus, $(35.216)_8 = (11101.01000111)_2$

*(ii)*

$$(417.25)_8 = \frac{100}{4}\ \frac{001}{1}\ \frac{111}{7}\ .\ \frac{010}{2}\ \frac{101}{5}$$

$$= (100001111.010101)_2$$

Thus, $(417.25)_8 = (100001111.010101)_2$

### 1.4.8 Binary to Octal

For converting a binary number into its octal equivalent the following steps are followed:

*(i)* Divide the given binary number before the binary point into groups of three bits each (from right to left) and after the binary point into groups of three bits each (from left to right) by adding 0 bits for completing the groups (if needed).

*(ii)* Replace each group by its octal equivalent.

The following examples illustrate this concept:

**Example 1.** *Convert the following binary numbers into their octal equivalents:*

*(i)* $(11101)_2$ *(ii)* $(101010011011.10100011)_2$.

**Solution.** *(i)* $(11101)_2 = \underbrace{011}_{3}\ \underbrace{101}_{5}$ (Replacing each group by its octal equivalent, 0 added on leftmost position for completing the group)

Thus, $(11101)_2 = (35)_8$

*(ii)* $(101010011011.10100011)_2 = \underbrace{101}_{5}\ \underbrace{010}_{2}\ \underbrace{011}_{3}\ \underbrace{011}_{3}\ .\ \underbrace{101}_{5}\ \underbrace{000}_{0}\ \underbrace{110}_{6}$

(Replacing each group by its octal equivalent, 0 added on rightmost position for completing the group).

Thus, $(101010011011.10100011)_2 = (5233.506)_8$

**Example 2.** *Convert the following binary numbers into their octal equivalents:*

*(i)* $(10110101.11001)_2$ *(ii)* $(11110011.0001)_2$.

**Solution.** *(i)* $(10110101.11001)_2 = \underbrace{010}_{2}\ \underbrace{110}_{6}\ \underbrace{101}_{5}\ .\ \underbrace{110}_{6}\ \underbrace{010}_{2}$

(Replacing each group by its equivalent, 0 added on leftmost and rightmost position for completing the group).

Thus, $(10110101.11001)_2 = (265.62)_8$

*(ii)* $(11110011.0001)_2 = \underbrace{011}_{3}\ \underbrace{110}_{6}\ \underbrace{011}_{3}\ .\ \underbrace{000}_{0}\ \underbrace{100}_{4}$

(Replacing each group by its equivalent, 0 added on leftmost and two 0's added on rightmost position for completing the group).

Thus, $(11110011.0001)_2 = (363.04)_8$

## 1.4.9 Decimal Numbers to Hexadecimal Numbers

For converting integer decimal numbers into their equivalent hexadecimal numbers, divide the given number repeatedly by 16 (if the remainder is greater than or equal to 10 then write its symbol, that is, A to F, otherwise the digit 0 to 9) till the quotient obtained is zero.

The following examples illustrate this concept:

**Example 1.** *Convert the following Decimal numbers into their Hexadecimal equivalents:*

*(i)* $(28)_{10}$ *(ii)* $(1795)_{10}$.

**Solution.** *(i)* Start dividing 28 by 16 and continue the procedure till the quotient is 0. The procedure is given below:

| | |
|---|---|
| 16 | 28 |
| 16 | 1 – C |
| | 0 – 1 |

(read remainders upward ↑)

Thus, $(28)_{10} = (1C)_{16}$

*(ii)*

| | |
|---|---|
| 16 | 1795 |
| 16 | 112 – 3 |
| 16 | 7 – 0 |
| | 0 – 7 |

(read remainders upward ↑)

Thus, $(1795)_{10} = (703)_{16}$

For converting decimal fractions into their equivalent hexadecimal fractions, multiply the fractional part repeatedly by 16 and keep track of the overflow. If the overflow is greater than equal to 10 then write its symbol, that is, A to F, otherwise the digit 0 to 9. The process of multiplication continues till the fractional part becomes zero or upto required number of digits.

The following example illustrates this concept:

**Example 2.** *Convert the following decimal functions to their equivalent hexadecimal fractions:*

*(i)* $(0.875)_{10}$ *(ii)* $(0.28125)_{10}$.

**Solution.** *(i)*

$$\begin{array}{r} 0.875 \\ \times\ 16 \\ \hline \boxed{14}.\ 000 \\ = \text{E} \end{array}$$

Thus, $(0.875)_{10} = (0.E)_{16}$

*(ii)*

$$\begin{array}{rl} 0.28125 & \\ \times\ 16 & \\ \hline \boxed{4}.\ 50000 & \\ \times\ 16 & \text{(Multiply only the fractional part)} \\ \hline \boxed{8}.\ 00000 & \end{array}$$

(read digits downward ↓)

Thus, $(0.28125)_{10} = (0.48)_{16}$

For converting a mixed decimal number to its hexadecimal equivalent, the integral and fractional parts are converted separately into their hexadecimal equivalents.

The following example illustrates this concept:

**Example 3.** *Convert the following mixed decimal numbers to their equivalent hexadecimals:*

*(i)* $(47.375)_{10}$ *(ii)* $(835.390625)_{10}$.

**Solution.** *(i)* $(47.375)_{10}$

Integral part

| | |
|---|---|
| 16 | 47 |
| 16 | 2 – 15 = F ↑ |
| | 0 – 2 |

Thus, $(47)_{10} = (2F)_{16}$

Fractional part

$$\begin{array}{r} 0.375 \\ \times\ 16 \\ \hline \boxed{6}.\ 000 \end{array}$$

Thus, $(0.375)_{10} = (0.6)_{16}$

Hence, $(47.375)_{10} = (2F.6)_{16}$

*(ii)* $(835.390625)_{10}$

Integral part

| | |
|---|---|
| 16 | 835 |
| 16 | 52 – 3 ↑ |
| 16 | 3 – 4 |
| | 0 – 3 |

Thus, $(835)_{10} = (343)_{16}$

Fractional part

$$\begin{array}{r} 0.390625 \\ \times\ 16 \\ \hline \boxed{6}.\ 250000 \\ \times\ 16 \\ \hline \boxed{4}.\ 000000 \end{array}$$

Thus, $(0.390625)_{10} = (0.64)_{16}$

Hence, $(835.390625)_{10} = (343.64)_{10}$

## 1.4.10 Conversion of Hexadecimal Numbers to their Decimal Equivalents

The conversion of hexadecimal numbers to their decimal equivalents is performed by using the concept of the positional value of each digit in the number, whether it is an integer, a fraction or a mixed number. The following examples illustrate this concept:

**Example 1.** *Convert the following hexadecimal numbers to their decimal equivalents:*

*(i)* $(9D)_{16}$ *(ii)* $(517)_{16}$.

**Solution.** *(i)*

$$\begin{aligned} (9D)_{16} &= 9 \times 16^1 + D \times 16^0 \\ &= 144 + 13 \times 1 \qquad (\because D = 13) \\ &= 144 + 13 \\ &= 157 \end{aligned}$$

Hence, $(9D)_{16} = (157)_{10}$

*(ii)*

$$\begin{aligned} (517)_{16} &= 5 \times 16^2 + 1 \times 16^1 + 7 \times 16^0 \\ &= 5 \times 256 + 1 \times 16 + 7 \times 1 \\ &= 1280 + 16 + 7 \\ &= 1303 \end{aligned}$$

Hence, $(517)_{16} = (1303)_{10}$

**Example 2.** *Convert the following hexadecimal fractions into their decimal equivalents:*

*(i)* $(0.48)_{16}$ *(ii)* $(0.125)_{16}$.

**Solution.** (*i*)

$$(0.48)_{16} = 4 \times 16^{-1} + 8 \times 16^{-2}$$
$$= 4 \times 1/16 + 8 \times 1/16^2$$
$$= 4 \times .0625 + 8 \times 0.00390625$$
$$= 0.2500 + .03125000$$
$$= 0.28125000$$

Hence, $(0.48)_{16} = (0.28125)_{10}$

(*ii*)

$$(0.125)_{16} = 1 \times 16^{-1} + 2 \times 16^{-2} + 5 \times 16^{-3}$$
$$= 1 \times 0.0625 + 2 \times 0.00390625 + 5 \times 0.00024414$$
$$= 0.0625 + 0.00781250 + 0.00122070$$
$$= 0.07153320$$

Hence, $(0.125)_{16} = (0.0715332)_{10}$

### 1.4.11 Hexadecimal to Binary

For converting a hexadecimal number to its binary equivalent, each digit of the hexadecimal number is converted to its 4-bits binary equivalent. For reading convenience, usually each nibble (4-bit binary equivalent) is written with a little space in between. The following examples illustrate this concept:

**Example 1.** *Convert the following hexadecimal numbers into their binary equivalents:*
*(i)* $(B9F)_{16}$ *(ii)* $(8796)_{16}$.

**Solution.** (*i*)

$$(59F)_{16} = \frac{0101}{5}\ \frac{1001}{9}\ \frac{1111}{F}$$ (Replace each hexadecimal digit by its 4 bits binary equivalent)

$$= (0101\ 1001\ 1111)_2$$

Thus $(59F)_{16} = (0101\ 1001\ 1111)_2$

(*ii*)

$$(8796)_{16} = \frac{1000}{8}\ \frac{0111}{7}\ \frac{1001}{9}\ \frac{0110}{6}$$ (Replace each hexadecimal digit by its 4 bits binary equivalent)

$$= (1000\ 0111\ 1001\ 0110)_2$$

Thus, $(8796)_{16} = (1000\ 0111\ 1001\ 0110)_2$

**Example 2.** *Convert the following hexadecimal numbers into their binary equivalents:*
*(i)* $(F3A.CB)_{16}$ *(ii)* $(5D.8F)_{16}$.

**Solution.** (*i*)

$$(F3A.CB)_{16} = \frac{1111}{F}\ \frac{0011}{3}\ \frac{1010}{A}\ .\ \frac{1100}{C}\ \frac{1011}{B}$$ (Replace each hexadecimal digit by its 4 bits binary equivalent)

$$= (1111\ 0011\ 1010\ .\ 1100\ 1011)_2$$

Thus, $(F3A.CB)_{16} = (1111\ 0011\ 1010\ .\ 1100\ 1011)_2$

*(ii)* $(5D.8F)_{16} = \frac{0101}{5}\frac{1101}{D}.\frac{1000}{8}\frac{1111}{F}$ (Replace each hexadecimal digit by its 4 bits binary equivalent)

$= (0101\ 1101\ .\ 1000\ 1111)_2$

Thus, $(5D.8F)_{16} = (0101\ 1101\ .\ 1000\ 1111)_2$

> **Note.** *It must be remembered that whatever number system one may use, the information stored in the computer is always in terms of binary digits. It is only for our convenience that we use octal or hexadecimal numbers.*

## 1.5 COMPLEMENTS

Complements are used in digital computers for simplifying the subtraction operation and for logical manipulations. There are two types of complements for each number system of base-*r*: the *r*'s complement and the $(r - 1)$'s complement. When we deal with binary system the value of *r* is 2 and hence the complements are 2's and 1's complements. Similarly for decimal system the value of *r* is 10 and we get 10's and 9's complements. With the same logic if the number system is octal we get 8's and 7's complement, while it is 16's and 15's complements for hexadecimal system.

### 1.5.1 The *r*'s Complement

If a positive number *N* is given in base *r* with an integer part of *n* digits, the *r*'s complement of *N* is given as $r^n - N$ for $N \neq 0$ and 0 for $N = 0$. The following examples will clarify the definition.

The 10's complement of $(23450)_{10}$ is $10^5 - 23450 = 76550$.

The number of digits in the number is $n = 5$.

The 10's complement of $(0.3245)_{10}$ is $10^0 - 0.3245 = 0.6755$.

Since the number of digits in the integer part of the number is $n = 0$, we have $10^0 = 1$.

The 10's complement of $(23.324)_{10}$ is $10^2 - 23.324 = 76.676$.

The number of digits in the integer part of the number is $n = 2$.

Now if we consider binary system, then $r = 2$.

The 2's complement of $(10110)_2$ is $(2^5)_{10} - (10110)_2 = (100000 - 10110)_2 = 01010$.

The 2's complement of $(0.1011)_2$ is $(2^0)_{10} - (0.1011)_2 = (1 - 0.1011)_2 = 0.0101$

Now if we consider octal system, then $r = 8$.

The 8's complement of $(2450)_8$ is $(8^4)_{10} - (2450)_8$

$= (4096_{10} - 2450_8)$

$= (4096_{10} - 1320_{10})$

$= 2776_{10}$.

$= 5330_8$.

Now if we consider hexadecimal system, then $r = 16$.

The 16's complement of $(4A30)_{16}$ is $(16^4)_{10} - (4A30)_{16}$

$= (65536_{10} - 4A30_{16})$

$= (65536_{10} - 18992_{10})$

$= 46544_{10}$

$= B5D0_{16}$.

From the above examples, it is clear that to find the 10's complement of a decimal number all of the bits till the first significant 0 are left unchanged and the first non-zero least significant digit is subtracted from 10 and the rest of the higher significant digits are subtracted from 9. With a similar reasoning the 2's complement of a binary number can be obtained by leaving all of the least significant zeros and the first non-zero digit unchanged, and then replacing 1's by 0's and 0's by 1's. Similarly the 8's complement of an octal number can be obtained by keeping all the bits till the first significant 0 unchanged, and the first non-zero least significant digit is subtracted from 8 and the rest of the higher significant digits are subtracted from 7. Similarly the 16's complement of a hexadecimal number can be obtained by keeping all the bits till the first significant 0 unchanged, and the first non-zero least significant digit is subtracted from 16 and the rest of the higher significant digits are subtracted from 15.

Since $r$'s complement is a general term, hence $r$ can take any value *e.g.*, $r = 11$. Then we will have 11's complement for $r$'s complement case and 10's complement for $(r - 1)$'s complement case.

## 1.5.2 The (*r* – 1)'s Complement

If a positive number $N$ is given in base $r$ with an integer part of $n$ digits and a fraction part of $m$ digits, then the $(r - 1)$'s complement of $N$ is given as $(r^n - r^{-m} - N)$ for $N \neq 0$ and 0 for $N = 0$. The following examples will clarify the definition.

The 9's complement of $(23450)_{10}$ is $10^5 - 10^0 - 23450 = 76549$.

Since there is no fraction part, so $10^{-m} = 10^0 = 1$.

The 9's complement of $(0.3245)_{10}$ is $10^0 - 10^{-4} - 0.3245 = 0.6754$.

Since there is no integer part, so $10^n = 10^0 = 1$.

The 9's complement of $(23.324)_{10}$ is $10^2 - 10^{-3} - 23.324 = 76.675$.

Now if we consider binary system, then $r = 2$, *i.e.*, $(r - 1) = 1$.

The 1's complement of $(10110)_2$ is $(2^5 - 1)_{10} - (10110)_2 = 01001$.

The 1's complement of $(0.1011)_2$ is $(1 - 2^{-4})_{10} - (0.1011)_2 = 0.0100$

Now if we consider octal system, then $r = 8$, *i.e.*, $(r - 1) = 7$.

The 7's complement of $(2350)_8$ is $8^4 - 8^0 - 2350_8$

$= 4095_{10} - 1256_{10}$

$= 2839_{10}$

$= 5427_8$

The 15's complement of $(A3E4)_{16}$ is $16^4 - 16^0 - A3E4_{16}$

$$= 65535_{10} - 41956_{10}$$
$$= 23579_{10}$$
$$= 5C1B_{16}$$

From the above examples, it is clear that to find the 9's complement of a decimal number each of the digits can be separately subtracted from 9. The 1's complement of a binary number can be obtained by changing 1's into 0's and 0's into 1's. Similarly to find the 7's complement of a decimal number each of the digits can be separately subtracted from 7. Again to find the 15's complement of a decimal number each of the digits can be separately subtracted from 15.

**Example.** *Find out the 11's and 10's complement of the number $(576)_{11}$.*

**Solution.** The number in base is 11. So to find 11's complement we have to follow the $r$'s complement rule and in order to get 10's complement the $(r - 1)$'s complement rule is to be followed.

11's complement:

$$r^n - N = 11^3 - 576_{11}$$
$$= (1331)_{10} - (576)_{11}$$

Now, $576_{11} = 5 \times 11^2 + 7 \times 11^1 + 6 \times 11^0$

$$= 605 + 77 + 6$$
$$= 688_{10}$$

Therefore, 11's complement is $1331_{10} - 688_{10} = 643_{10}$

Now, the decimal number has to be changed in the number system of base 11.

| | |
|---|---|
| 11 | 643 |
| 11 | 58 – 5 |
| 11 | 5 – 3 |
| | 0 – 5 |

Hence the 11's complement number is $(535)_{11}$

10' complement :

$$r^n - r^{-m} - N = 11^3 - 11^0 - 576_{11}$$
$$= (1331)_{10} - (1)_{10} - (576)_{11}$$

Therefore, 10's complement is $1331_{10} - 1_{10} - 688_{10} = 642_{10}$

Now, the decimal number has to be changed in the number system of base 11.

| | |
|---|---|
| 11 | 642 |
| 11 | 58 – 4 |
| 11 | 5 – 3 |
| | 0 – 5 |

Hence the 10's complement number is $(534)_{11}$.

## 1.6 REPRESENTATION OF INFORMATION

We are familiar with different types of number systems. In order to talk to computers one has to convert the information, numeric or non-numeric, into binary form. Therefore, one must know how the information is stored in computer memory.

### 1.6.1 Binary Representation of Integers

The different ways of integer representation in computer memory are:

(*i*) Sign and Magnitude representation

(*ii*) One's complement representation

(*iii*) Two's complement representation

#### *1.6.1.1 Sign and Magnitude Representation*

It is the conventional form for number representation. Every integer has a sign (+ or –) and a string of digits representing the magnitude.

For example,

+ 241 or 745 are positive integers (+ sign may be omitted)

– 127, – 82 are negative integers

The sign of a number is represented by the MSB (Most Significant Bit). If it stores value 0, the sign is +, and if stores 1, the sign is –.

Let us assume that the word size of the computer is 16 bits, then +93 will be represented as given below:

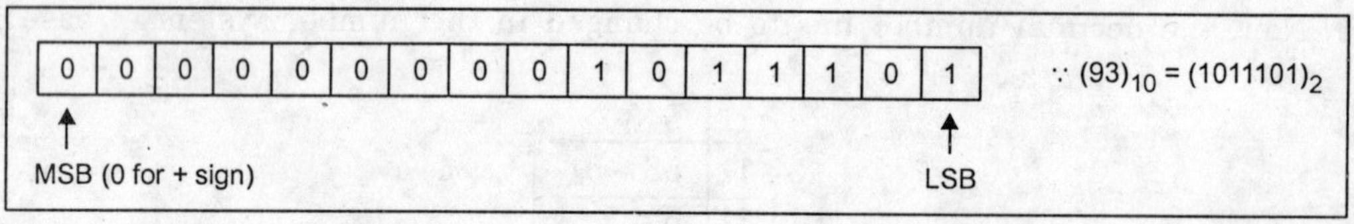


**Fig. 1.5:** Representation of Integer Number in binary form.

Since, bit pattern of 93 consists of 7 bits, it is expanded to 15 bits by adding the required number of zeros to the left as 000000001011101.

–33 will be represented as given below:

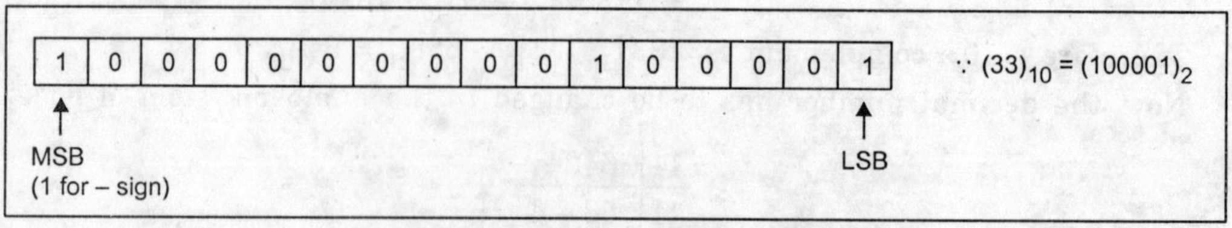


**Fig. 1.6:** Number in binary form.

Since bit pattern of 33 consists of 6 binary digits, it is expanded to 15 bits by adding the required number of zeros to the left as 000000000100001.

**Integer Range for N Bit Word.** The range for integer numbers using sign and magnitude representation is given by the formula:

$$-2^{N-1} \quad \text{to} \quad 2^{N-1}-1$$

as 1 bit is used for sign notation so (N–1) bits represent the magnitude.

For N = 16, the range is

| | | | |
|---|---|---|---|
| | $-2^{16-1}$ | to | $2^{16-1}-1$ |
| that is | $-2^{15}$ | to | $2^{15}-1$ |
| or | –32768 | to | 32767 |

> **Note.** *In this method of representation, we obtain two representations for 0, one for +0 and other for –0.*

The number + 0 is represented as given below:

| | | | | | | | | | | | | | | | |
|---|---|---|---|---|---|---|---|---|---|---|---|---|---|---|---|
| 0 | 0 | 0 | 0 | 0 | 0 | 0 | 0 | 0 | 0 | 0 | 0 | 0 | 0 | 0 | 0 |

↑ MSB (0 for + sign) ↑ LSB

The number – 0 is represented as given below:

| | | | | | | | | | | | | | | | |
|---|---|---|---|---|---|---|---|---|---|---|---|---|---|---|---|
| 1 | 0 | 0 | 0 | 0 | 0 | 0 | 0 | 0 | 0 | 0 | 0 | 0 | 0 | 0 | 0 |

↑ MSB (1 for – sign) ↑ LSB

#### *1.6.1.2 One's Complement Representation*

Using one's complement positive numbers are represented by their binary equivalents (also known as true forms) and negative numbers by their 1's complements (also known as 1's complement forms). For an $n$-bit number, the maximum positive number which can be represented in 1's complement form is $(2^{n-1}-1)$ and the minimum negative number is $-(2^{n-1}-1)$.

> 1's complement of a binary number is found by replacing every 0 with 1 and every 1 with 0.

For example,

1's complement of binary number 100111 will be 011000

The number – 45 using a 16-bit word is represented as given below:

$\because \quad (45)_{10} = (101101)_2$

Now the 16-bit pattern is 0000000000101101

1's complement of the above pattern is 1111111111010010, which is stored as:

| | | | | | | | | | | | | | | | |
|---|---|---|---|---|---|---|---|---|---|---|---|---|---|---|---|
| 1 | 1 | 1 | 1 | 1 | 1 | 1 | 1 | 1 | 1 | 0 | 1 | 0 | 0 | 1 | 0 |

**Note.** *In this method of representation, like sign bit magnitude representation, we obtain two representations of 0, one for + 0 and other – 0. These representations are:*

| | | | | | | | | | | | | | | | |
|---|---|---|---|---|---|---|---|---|---|---|---|---|---|---|---|
| 0 | 0 | 0 | 0 | 0 | 0 | 0 | 0 | 0 | 0 | 0 | 0 | 0 | 0 | 0 | 0 |

*Representation of + 0*

| | | | | | | | | | | | | | | | |
|---|---|---|---|---|---|---|---|---|---|---|---|---|---|---|---|
| 1 | 1 | 1 | 1 | 1 | 1 | 1 | 1 | 1 | 1 | 1 | 1 | 1 | 1 | 1 | 1 |

*1's complement representation of – 0*

### 1.6.1.3 Two's Complement Representation

Using two's complement positive numbers are represented by their binary equivalents (also known as true forms) and negative numbers by their 2's complement form. For an $n$-bit number, the maximum positive number which can be represented in 2's complement form is $(2^{n-1}-1)$ and the minimum negative number is $-2^{n-1}$.

2's complement of a number is found by adding 1 to its 1's complement.

**or**

For finding the 2's complement of a number, start from the LSB and write the bits as it is till the first 1 appears (**do not** change the first 1 to 0), then write the 1's complement of the remaining bits to the left side of it.

For example, 2's complement of binary number 1110001 will be calculated as given below:

1's complement of 1110001 = 0001110

+1

2's complement of 1110001 = 0001111

**Note.** *Rules for binary addition are:*

$0 + 0 = 0$

$0 + 1 = 1$

$1 + 0 = 1$

$1 + 1 = 10$

The number – 45 using a 16-bit word is represented as given below:

$\because \quad (45)_{10} = (101101)_2$

Now the 16-bit pattern is 0000000000101101

1's complement of the bit pattern is 1111111111010010

The 2's complement is obtained as under:

1's complement is 1111111111010010

+1

2's complement is 1111111111010011

The above shown pattern is stored as:

| | | | | | | | | | | | | | | | |
|---|---|---|---|---|---|---|---|---|---|---|---|---|---|---|---|
| 1 | 1 | 1 | 1 | 1 | 1 | 1 | 1 | 1 | 1 | 0 | 1 | 0 | 0 | 1 | 1 |

**Note.** *Unlike sign-bit magnitude and 1's complement representation, both + 0 and – 0 have the same representation under 2's complement method.*

In general, the negative numbers are stored in the computer memory in 2's complement form and positive numbers in sign and magnitude form.

### *Comparison between 1's and 2's Complements*

A comparison between 1's and 2's complements reveals the advantages and disadvantages of each.

(*i*) The 1's complement has the advantage of being easier to implement by digital components (*viz.* inverter) since the only thing to be done is to change the 1's to 0's and vice versa. To implement 2's complement we can follow two ways:

- by finding out the 1's complement of the number and then adding 1 to the LSB of the 1's complement, and
- by leaving all leading 0's in the LSB positions and the first 1 unchanged, and only then changing all 1's to 0's and vice versa.

(*ii*) During subtraction of two numbers by complement method, the 2's complement is advantageous since only one arithmetic addition is required. The 1's complement requires two arithmetic additions when an end-around carry occurs.

(*iii*) The 1's complement has an additional disadvantage of having two arithmetic zeros: one with all 0's and one with all 1's. The 2's complement has only one arithmetic zero. The fact is illustrated below:

We consider the subtraction of two equal binary numbers 1010 – 1010.

Using 1's complement:

```
    1010
  + 0101   (1's complement of 1010)
  ------
  + 1111   (negative zero)
```

We complement again to obtain (–0000) (positive zero).

Using 2's complement:

```
                 1010
               + 0110   (2's complement of 1010)
               ------
(Carry over)   [1] 0000
```

After dropping the carry over, the result is +0000.

In this 2's complement method no question of negative or positive zero arises.

### 1.6.2 Fixed-point Representation of Numbers

In a fixed-point system of number representation all numbers are represented as integers or fraction. Signed integer or BCD numbers are known as fixed-point numbers because they contain no information about the binary point or decimal point. The binary or decimal point is assumed at the extreme right or left of the number. If the binary or decimal point is at the extreme right or left of the computer word, all numbers are positive or negative numbers. If the radix point is assumed to be at the extreme left, all numbers are positive or negative fraction. Suppose one has to multiply 7.35 × 80.64. This will be represented as 735 × 8064. The result will be 5927040. The decimal point has to be placed by the programmer to get the correct result, that is 592.7040. Thus in fixed-point of representation the user has to keep the track of radix point which is a tedious (very difficult) job.

In scientific applications of computers fractions are frequently used. So a system of representation which automatically keeps track of the position of the binary or decimal point is needed. Such a system of representation is known as floating point representation of numbers. It is discussed in the next section. Many computers and all electronic calculators use floating-point arithmetic operations. The computers which do not have internal circuitry for floating-point operations can solve the scientific problems involving fractions with the help of floating-point software.

### 1.6.3 Floating-Point Representation of Real Numbers

A number having both integer part as well as a fractional part is called real number or floating point number. It may be either positive or negative. For example, 975.88, 0.586, – 0.866 represent real decimal numbers and 1101.001, 0.0101, – 100.1001 represent binary real numbers.

Real numbers are represented in the memory of the computer by their **mantissa** and **exponent.** In the general form,

$$N = M \times R^e$$

The mantissa M and the exponent $e$ are actually stored in a register of a computer. But, the base or radix R and the radix-point (decimal or binary point) are not present in the register. An assumption is made about these and the electronic circuitry taking these things into account performs the computation and manipulation.

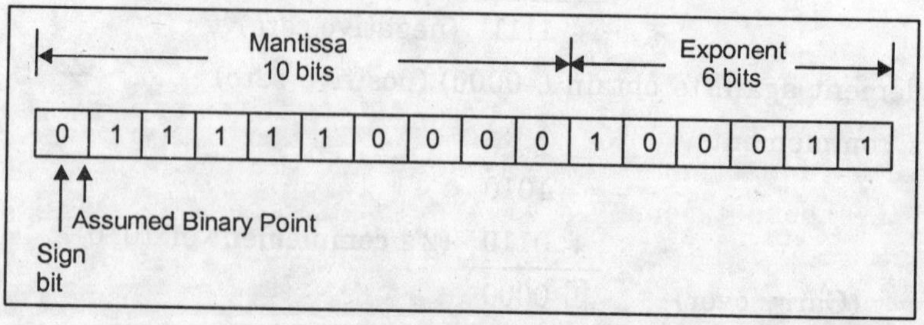


**Fig. 1.7:** Floating point format.

Let us assume a 16-bit word for a computer having two parts : a 10-bit mantissa and a 6-bit exponent. The mantissa is in two's complement form ; the left most bit represents a sign bit. The binary point is assumed to be to the right of the sign bit.

The 6 bits of the word store the exponent without any sign. The reason for not having the place for storage of the sign of exponent is that the exponent is represented in **biased** form.

Now, let us understand the meaning of biased form of the exponent.

The minimum number represented by 6 bits is ($-2^5$), that is, –32. While representing align the floating point numbers, this number 32 is added to the actual exponent, thus leaving no space for negative exponent. The new exponent (after adding 32 to the actual exponent) is called **Biased Exponent.** This code for floating point representation is called as the base 2 excess 32 code.

Some examples of this system for exponent part are given in Table 1.2 given below:

**Table 1.2: Illustration of Biased Exponents**

| *Actual Exponent* | *Binary Representation (Biased Exponent)* |
|---|---|
| –32 | 0 0 0 0 0 0 |
| –2 | 0 1 1 1 1 0 |
| 0 | 1 0 0 0 0 0 |
| +5 | 1 0 0 1 0 1 |
| +31 | 1 1 1 1 1 1 |

Now, using the above definitions, the floating point number in Figure 1.2 is:

Mantissa part is + 0.111110000

Exponent part is 100011

Subtracting 100000 from exponent

($\because$ $(100000)_2 = (32)_{10}$ was added to it)

The value of the number is

$$N = +(0.11111)_2 \times 2^3 \quad (\because N = M \times R^e)$$

$$= (111.11)_2$$

$$= 7.75$$

There are many formats of storage of floating point numbers on different computers. Some use two words for the mantissa and one for the exponent; others use one and one-half word for the mantissa and one-half word for the exponent. Few systems even allow to select a format out of many, depending on the accuracy desired. Some use excess-n notation for the exponent; some use 2's complement. Some even use signed magnitude for both the mantissa and the exponent.

Floating point numbers are used to express very large and very small numbers. Using above mentioned system of storage for numbers, we can have 9-bit accuracy (1 bit allowed for sign of mantissa). The exponent bits add nothing to accuracy, only to magnitude. The accuracy of fixed point 2's complement numbers expressed in 16 bits is of 15 bits. So, the floating points are less accurate than an equivalent length fixed point number.

For achieving the full 10 bits of accuracy in the floating point number, the most significant bit of the mantissa is made non-zero and the number so obtained is said to be in the **normalized** (or standard) form. The process of shifting of mantissa left to make the most significant bit non-zero is called **normalization**.

## SUMMARY

- Numbers are represented by a string of digit symbols.
- The binary number system has the base or radix 2, the octal 8 and hexadecimal 16.
- Complements are used in digital systems for simplifying the subtraction operation and for logical manipulations.
- Codes are used to represent information, error detection and error correction.
- Integers can be represented in computer memory using sign and magnitude, 1's complement and 2's complement forms.
- In general, the negative numbers are stored in the computer memory in 2's complement form and positive numbers in sign and magnitude form.
- Arithmetic operations are possible on binary numbers.
- Booths multiplication method deals with operands in 2's complement form.

## REVIEW QUESTIONS AND EXERCISES

1. What is a Number System ? State the utility of Number Systems.
2. Why do digital computers use binary numbers for their operation?
3. Convert the following binary numbers to equivalent decimal numbers:
   (*i*) 11011 (*ii*) 10011010
4. Convert the following decimal numbers to equivalent binary numbers:
   (*i*) 44 (*ii*) 155
5. Convert the following real binary numbers to equivalent decimal numbers:
   (*i*) 1101.11 (*ii*) 101001.1101
6. Convert the following decimal numbers to equivalent binary numbers:
   (*i*) 18.71875 (*ii*) 75.6875
7. Convert the following octal numbers to equivalent binary numbers:
   (*i*) 534 (*ii*) 647
8. Convert the following binary numbers to equivalent octal numbers:
   (*i*) 1100110 (*ii*) 10111101
9. Convert the following hexadecimal numbers to equivalent binary numbers:
   (*i*) 6BC (*ii*) 4C3F
10. Convert the following binary numbers to equivalent hexadecimal numbers:
    (*i*) 10110110111 (*ii*) 1101001100
11. Convert the binary number 101101.101101 into octal and hexadecimal number system.

12. The roots of the quadratic equation $x^2 - 12x + 37 = 0$ are 5 and 8. Find the base in which this equation is written.
13. What are complements? Why are these used ? Given their types.
14. Write the 10's and 9's complements of the following numbers:
    (i) $(52520)_{10}$ (ii) $(0.3267)_{10}$ (iii) $(25.639)_{10}$
15. Write short notes on the following:
    (i) Binary representation of integers
    (ii) Fixed-point representation of numbers.
    (iii) Binary representation of floating point numbers.
16. Compare the 1's and 2's complements.
17. What is normalized floating point representation for real numbers ?
18. Write the 1's complement of the binary numbers given below:
    (i) $1100_2$ (ii) $1101_2$
    (iii) $10011_2$ (iv) $10101_2$
    (v) $000_2$ (vi) $1111_2$
    (vii) $0.101_2$ (viii) $100.01_2$
19. Write the 2's complement of the following binary numbers:
    (i) $1011_2$ (ii) $10111_2$
    (iii) $101.101_2$ (iv) $111.011_2$
    (v) $000_2$ (vi) $111_2$
    (vii) $101.01_2$ (viii) $10.001_2$
20. Fill in the blanks:
    (i) $(94.00625)_{10}$ = (.................................)$_2$
    (ii) $(11011.0101)_2$ = (.................................)$_{10}$ = (.................................)$_8$

## ANSWERS

3. (i) 27 (ii) 154
4. (i) 101100 (ii) 10011011
5. (i) 13.75 (ii) 41.8125
6. (i) 10010.10111 (ii) 1001011.1011
7. (i) 101011100 (ii) 110100111
8. (i) 146 (ii) 275
9. (i) 11010111100 (ii) 100110000111111
10. (i) 5B7 (ii) 34C
11. $(55.55)_8$, $(2D.B4)_{16}$
12. 11
14. (i) 47480, 47479 (ii) 0.6733, 0.6732 (iii) 74.361, 74.360
18. (i) 0101 (ii) 010001 (iii) 010.011
    (iv) 000.101 (v) 000 (vi) 001
    (vii) 010.11 (viii) 01.111.
19. (i) 00111 (ii) –10001 (iii) 0100
    (iv) 0.001
20. (i) $(1011110\,.\,00000\,\overline{0011})_2$ (ii) $(27.3125)_{10} = (33.24)_8$
    (iii) American Standard Code for Information Interchange

Chapter 2

# CODES AND BINARY ARITHMETIC

## 2.1 INTRODUCTION

Digital systems are built using binary devices. Coding is a technique by which a set of objects is represented in a machine by a set of binary numbers called codes. Computers and other digital circuits process data in binary format. To achieve this, a process of coding is required where each alphabet, special character or numeral is coded in a unique combination of 0 s and 1 s using a coding scheme known as *code*. Various binary codes are used to represent data which may be numeric, alphabets or special characters. Codes are also used for error detection and error correction in digital systems. Although, in digital systems in every code used, the information is represented in binary form, but the interpretation of the data is only possible if the code in which the data is being represented is known.

The full form of BCD is 'Binary-Coded Decimal'. Since this is coding scheme relating decimal and binary numbers, hence four bits are required to code each decimal number. For example, $(35)_{10}$ is represented as 0011 0101 using BCD code, rather than $(100011)_2$. From the example it is clear that it requires more number of bits to code a decimal number using BCD code than using the straight binary code. However, inspite of this disadvantage it is convenient to use BCD code for input and output operations in digital systems. For example, the binary number 1000011 represents 67 (decimal) in straight binary, 43 (decimal) in BCD and alphabet C in ASCII code. Hence while interpreting the data one must be very careful regarding the code used.

## 2.2 CODES

Codes can be broadly classified into following five groups:

(*i*) Weighted Binary Codes,

(*ii*) Non-weighted Codes,

(*iii*) Alphanumeric Codes,

(*iv*) Error-detecting Codes and

(*v*) Error-correcting Codes.

The commonly used codes are discussed as follows.

### 2.2.1 Weighted Binary Codes

If each position of a number represents a specific weight then the coding scheme is called weighted binary code. In such coding the bits are multiplied by their corresponding individual weight, and then the sum of these weighted bits gives the equivalent decimal digit.

#### 2.2.1.1 NBCD Code

Natural Binary Coded Decimal (NBCD) code is also known as 8-4-2-1 code. It is because 8, 4, 2 and 1 are the weights of the four bits of the BCD code. The weight of the LSB is $2^0$ or 1, that of the next higher order bit is $2^1$ or 2, that of the next higher order bit is $2^2$ or 4, and that of the MSB is $2^3$ or 8. Therefore, this is a *weighted* code and arithmetic operations can be performed using this code which will be discussed later on. The bit assignment 0101, for example, can be interpreted by the weights to represent the decimal digit 5 because $0 \times 8 + 1 \times 4 + 0 \times 2 + 1 \times 1 = 5$. Since four binary bits are used hence the maximum decimal equivalent that may be coded is $15_{10}$ (*i.e.*, $1111_2$). But the maximum decimal digit available is $9_{10}$. Hence the binary codes 1010, 1011, 1100, 1101, 1110, 1111 representing 10, 11, 12, 13, 14 and 15 in decimal are never being used in BCD code. So these six codes are called forbidden codes and the group of these codes is called forbidden group in BCD code. BCD code for decimal digits 0 to 9 is shown in Table 2.1.

**Table 2.1: Illustration of BCD Code of Decimal Digits**

| *Decimal Digits* | *BCD Representation* |
|---|---|
| 0 | 0000 |
| 1 | 0001 |
| 2 | 0010 |
| 3 | 0011 |
| 4 | 0100 |
| 5 | 0101 |
| 6 | 0110 |
| 7 | 0111 |
| 8 | 1000 |
| 9 | 1001 |

The following examples illustrate the BCD encoding:

**Example 1.** *Give the BCD equivalent for the decimal number 509.*

**Solution.** The decimal number is 5 0 9

BCD code is 0101 0000 1001

Hence, $(509)_{10} = (010100001001)_{BCD}$

**Example 2.** *Give the BCD equivalent for the decimal number 49.27.*

**Solution.** The decimal number 4 9 2 7

BCD code 0100 1001 0010 0111

Hence, $(49.27)_{10} = (01001001.00100111)_{BCD}$

Here, we must distinguish carefully between *encoding* and *conversion*. For example, 14 when converted to binary would be 1 1 1 0. On the other hand, when it is encoded each digit must be represented by a 4-bit code and an encoding is 00010100. As mentioned earlier *encoding requires more bits compared to conversion*. On the average $\log_2 10 = 3.32$ bits are required when decimal numbers are converted to binary; as compared with this 4 bits per digit are needed in encoding. The ratio (4/3.3) = 1.2 is a measure of the extra bits (and consequently extra storage) needed if an *encoding* is used. On the other hand, *conversion of decimal to binary is slower compared to encoding*. It is due to the fact that an algorithm involving successive division is required for conversion whereas encoding is by straightforward table look-up. The slowness of conversion is not a major problem in computations having small volume of input/output. In business computers, where input/output dominates, it is necessary to examine BCD representation. In smaller digital system such as desk calculators, digital clocks, etc., it is uneconomical to incorporate complex electronic circuits to convert decimal to binary and vice versa. Thus BCD representation should be preferred.

### 2.2.1.2 $84\bar{2}\bar{1}$ Code

It is also possible to assign negative weights to decimal code, as shown by the $84\bar{2}\bar{1}$ code. In this case the bit combination 0101 is interpreted as the decimal digit 3, as obtained from $0 \times 8 + 1 \times 4 + 0 \times (-2) + 1 \times (-1) = 3$. This is a self-complementary code, that is, the 9's complement of the decimal number is obtained just by changing the 1's to 0's and 0's to 1's, or in effect by getting the 1's complement of the corresponding number. For example, if we change the 1's to 0's and 0's to 1's in the previous example we have 1010 which is interpreted as decimal 6, as obtained from $1 \times 8 + 0 \times 4 + 1 \times (-2) + 0 \times (-1) = 6$. And 6 is the 9's complement of 3. This property is useful when arithmetic operations are done internally with decimal numbers (in a binary code) and subtraction is calculated by means of 9's complement.

**Table 2.2: Binary Codes for Decimal Digits**

| *Decimal Digit* | *(NBCD) 8421* | *$84\bar{2}\bar{1}$* | *2421* | *Excess-3* |
|---|---|---|---|---|
| 0 | 0000 | 0000 | 0000 | 0011 |
| 1 | 0001 | 0111 | 0001 | 0100 |
| 2 | 0010 | 0110 | 0010 | 0101 |
| 3 | 0011 | 0101 | 0011 | 0110 |
| 4 | 0100 | 0100 | 0100 | 0111 |
| 5 | 0101 | 1011 | 1011 | 1000 |
| 6 | 0110 | 1010 | 1100 | 1001 |
| 7 | 0111 | 1001 | 1101 | 1010 |
| 8 | 1000 | 1000 | 1110 | 1011 |
| 9 | 1001 | 1111 | 1111 | 1100 |

#### 2.2.1.3 2421 Code

Another weighted code is 2421 code. The weights assigned to the four digits are 2, 4, 2 and 1. The 2421 code is same as that in BCD from 0 to 4; however it varies from 5 to 9. For example, in this case the bit combination 0100 represents decimal 4; whereas the bit combination 1101 is interpreted as the decimal 7, as obtained from $2 \times 1 + 1 \times 4 + 0 \times 2 + 1 \times 1 = 7$. This is also a *self-complementary code,* that is, the 9's complement of the decimal number is obtained by changing the 1's to 0's and 0's to 1's. The 2421 codes for decimal number 0 through 9 are shown in Table 2.2.

### 2.2.2 Non-Weighted Binary Codes

These codes are not positionally weighted. It basically means that each position of the binary number is not assigned a fixed value. Excess-3 codes and Gray codes are such non-weighted codes.

#### 2.2.2.1 Excess-3 Code

A decimal code that has been used in some old computers is excess-3 code. This is an unweighted code. This code assignment is obtained from the corresponding value of 4 bit binary code after adding 3 to the given decimal digit. Here the maximum value may be $1100_2$ since the maximum decimal digit is 9 hence we have to add 3 to 9 and then get the BCD equivalent. Like 84-2-1 and 2421 codes excess-3 is also a self-complementary code, that is, the 9's complement of the decimal number is obtained by changing the 1's to 0's and 0's to 1's. This self-complementary property of the code helps considerably in performing subtraction operation in digital systems.

The following examples illustrate the Excess-3 code encoding:

**Example 1.** *Convert $(359)_{10}$ into its Excess-3 code.*

**Solution.**

| | | | |
|---|---|---|---|
| The decimal number is | 3 | 5 | 9 |
| Add 3 to each bit | +3 | +3 | +3 |
| Sum | 6 | 8 | 12 |

Converting the above each sum into 4 bit binary equivalent, we have

| | | | |
|---|---|---|---|
| 4 bit binary equivalent | 0110 | 1000 | 1100 |

Hence, the Excess-3 code for $(359)_{10}$ = 0110 1000 1100

**Example 2.** *Convert $(58.43)_{10}$ into its Excess-3 code.*

**Solution.**

| | | | | |
|---|---|---|---|---|
| The decimal number is | 5 | 8 | 4 | 3 |
| Add 3 to each bit | +3 | +3 | +3 | +3 |
| Sum | 8 | 11 | 7 | 6 |

Converting the above each sum into 4 bit binary equivalent, we have

| | | | | |
|---|---|---|---|---|
| 4 bit binary equivalent | 1000 | 1011 | 0111 | 0110 |

Hence, the Excess-3 code for $(58.43)_{10}$ = 10001011.01110110

### 2.2.2.2 *Gray Code*

Gray code (or Cyclic Code or Reflected Code) belongs to a class of code known as minimum change code, in which a number changes by only one bit as it proceeds from one number to the next. Hence this code is not useful for arithmetic operations. This code finds extensive use for shaft encoders, in some types of analog-to-digital converters etc. Gray code is **reflected code** and is shown in Table 2.3. The Gray code may contain any number of bits. Here we take the example of four bit Gray Code. The code shown in Table 2.3 is only one of many possible such codes. To obtain a different reflected code, one can start with any bit combination and proceed to obtain the next bit combination by changing only one bit from 0 to 1 or 1 to 0 in any desired random fashion, as long as two numbers do not have identical code assignments. The Gray code is not a weighted code.

**Table 2.3: Four-bit Reflected Code**

| *Reflected Code* | *Decimal Equivalent* |
|---|---|
| m4 0000 | 0 |
| m3 0001 | 1 |
| 0011 | 2 |
| m2 0010 | 3 |
| 0110 | 4 |
| 0111 | 5 |
| 0101 | 6 |
| m1 0100 | 7 |
| 1100 | 8 |
| 1101 | 9 |
| 1111 | 10 |
| m5 1110 | 11 |
| 1010 | 12 |
| m6 1011 | 13 |
| m7 1001 | 14 |
| 1000 | 15 |

Now we try to analyze the name **"Reflected Code"**. If we look at Table 2.3, we can consider seven virtual mirrors m1, m2, m3, m4, m5, m6 and m7 placed. Now for mirror m1 if we consider the MSB as the refractive index of the input and output medium then leaving out the MSB we can see that all of the eight combinations of three bits each, have its corresponding reflected counterparts. Similarly for mirrors m2 and m5 if we now leave the actual MSB we can consider the combination of three bits where now we consider the third bit as the new MSB. And similar arguments follow as for mirror m1. Similarly we may analyze the cases for mirrors m3, m4, m6 and m7.

**Table 2.4: Binary and Gray Codes**

| *Decimal Numbers* | *Binary Code* | *Gray Code* |
|---|---|---|
| 0 | 0000 | 0000 |
| 1 | 0001 | 0001 |
| 2 | 0010 | 0011 |
| 3 | 0011 | 0010 |
| 4 | 0100 | 0110 |
| 5 | 0101 | 0111 |
| 6 | 0110 | 0101 |
| 7 | 0111 | 0100 |
| 8 | 1000 | 1100 |
| 9 | 1001 | 1101 |
| 10 | 1010 | 1111 |
| 11 | 1011 | 1110 |
| 12 | 1100 | 1010 |
| 13 | 1101 | 1011 |
| 14 | 1110 | 1001 |
| 15 | 1111 | 1000 |

The *Hamming distance* (named after its inventor R.W. Hamming) between two equal length binary numbers is the number of positions in which they differ. For example, if A = 0111 and B = 1011, the Hamming distance between A and B is two as they differ in their first and second positions counting from left. The Hamming distance between two successive code groups in a cyclic code is unity, *i.e.*, each code group is adjacent to the next in sequence. Following map (See Figure 2.1) is coded to ensure that each square is at a unit distance from its adjacent square and each square in this map has four neighbours (adjacent squares).

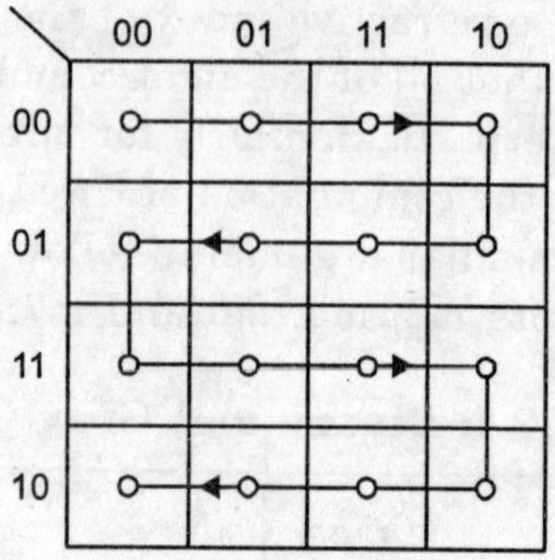


**Fig. 2.1:** A chart depicting a cyclic code.

The map shown in Figure 2.1 is called *Karnaugh map* and can be used to construct a large number of cyclic codes. One such code is shown in Table 2.4. Start assigning the code and proceed as shown by the arrow and the mark 'o' in Figure 2.1. More about Karnaugh map has been discussed in Chapter 3.

### *Conversion of a Binary Number into Gray Code*

Any binary number can be converted into equivalent Gray code by following the steps:

(*i*) The MSB of the Gray code is same as the MSB of the binary number;

(*ii*) The second bit next to MSB of the Gray code equals the Ex-OR of the MSB and second bit of the binary number; it will be 0 if there are same binary bits or it will be 1 for different binary bits;

(*iii*) The third bit for Gray code equals the exclusive-OR of the second and third bits of the binary number, and similarly all the next lower order bits follow the same mechanism.

The following examples illustrate the conversion of binary numbers to Gray code:

**Example 1.** *Convert* $(101011)_2$ *into Gray code.*

**Solution.** **Step 1.** The MSB of the Gray code is same as the MSB of the binary number.

$$\begin{array}{ccccccl} 1 & 0 & 1 & 0 & 1 & 1 & \text{Binary} \\ & \downarrow & & & & & \\ & 1 & & & & & \text{Gray} \end{array}$$

**Step 2.** Perform the Ex-OR between the MSB and the second bits of the binary. The result is 1 which is the second bit of the Gray code.

$$\begin{array}{ccccccl} 1 \oplus & 0 & 1 & 0 & 1 & 1 & \text{Binary} \\ & \downarrow & & & & & \\ 1 & 1 & & & & & \text{Gray} \end{array}$$

**Step 3.** Perform the Ex-OR between the second and the third bits of the binary. The result is 1 which is the third bit of the Gray code.

1 0 ⊕ 1 0 1 1 Binary

↓

1 1 1 Gray

**Step 4.** Perform the Ex-OR between the third and the fourth bits of the binary. The result is 1 which is the fourth bit of the Gray code.

1 0 1 ⊕ 0 1 1 Binary

↓

1 1 1 1 Gray

**Step 5.** Perform the Ex-OR between the fourth and the fifth bits of the binary. The result is 1 which is the fifth bit of the Gray code.

1 0 1 0 ⊕ 1 1 Binary

↓

1 1 1 1 1 Gray

**Step 6.** Perform the Ex-OR between the fifth and the sixth bits of the binary. The result is 0 which is the last bit of the Gray code.

1 0 1 0 1 ⊕ 1 Binary

↓

1 1 1 1 1 0 Gray

After completing the conversion the Gray code of binary 101011 is 111110.

**Example 2.** *Convert* $(564)_{10}$ *into Gray code.*

**Solution. Step 1.** Convert the decimal 564 into equivalent binary.

Decimal number 564

Binary number 1000110100

**Step 2.** Convert the binary number into equivalent Gray code

1 ⊕ 0 ⊕ 0 ⊕ 0 ⊕ 1 ⊕ 1 ⊕ 0 ⊕ 1 ⊕ 0 ⊕ 0 Binary

↓ → ↓ → ↓ → ↓ → ↓ → ↓ → ↓ → ↓ → ↓ → ↓

1 1 0 0 1 0 1 1 1 0 Gray

### *Conversion of Gray Code into a Binary Number*

Any Gray code can be converted into equivalent Binary number by following the steps:

*(i)* The MSB of the binary number is same as the MSB of the Gray code;

*(ii)* The second bit next to MSB of the binary number equals the Ex-OR of the MSB of the binary number and second bit of the Gray code; it will be 0 if there are same binary bits or it will be 1 for different binary bits;

*(iii)* The third bit for binary number equals the exclusive-OR of the second bit of the binary number and third bit of the Gray code, and similarly all the next lower order bits follow the same mechanism.

Following example illustrate the conversion of Gray code into binary number:

**Example.** *Convert the Gray code 101101 into a binary number.*

**Solution. Step 1.** The MSB of the binary number is same as the MSB of the Gray code.

1 0 1 1 0 1 Gray
↓
1 Binary

**Step 2.** Perform the Ex-OR between the MSB of the binary number and the second bit of the Gray code. The result is 1 which is the second bit of the binary number.

1 0 1 1 0 1 Gray
↓
1 → 1 Binary

**Step 3.** Perform the Ex-OR between the second bit of the binary number and the third bit of the Gray code. The result is 0 which is the third bit of the binary number.

1 0 1 1 0 1 Gray
↓
1 1 → 0 Binary

**Step 4.** Perform the Ex-OR between the third bit of the binary number and the fourth bit of the Gray code. The result is 1 which is the fourth bit of the binary number.

1 0 1 1 0 1 Gray
↓
1 1 0 → 1 Binary

**Step 5.** Perform the Ex-OR between the fourth bit of the binary number and the fifth bit of the Gray code. The result is 1 which is the fifth bit of the binary number.

1 0 1 1 0 1 Gray
↓
1 1 0 1 → 1 Binary

**Step 6.** Perform the Ex-OR between the fifth bit of the binary number and the sixth bit of the Gray code. The result is 0 which is the last bit of the binary number.

1 0 1 1 0 1 Gray
↓
1 1 0 1 1 → 0 Binary

After completing the conversion the binary number of the Gray code 101101 is 110110.

## 2.2.3 Alphanumeric Codes

Many applications of computer require not only of handling numbers, but also of letters. To represent alphabet it is necessary to have a binary code for the alphabet. In addition the same binary code must represent the decimal numbers and some other special characters. An alphanumeric code is a binary code of a group of elements consisting of ten decimal digits, the 26 letters of the alphabet (both in upper-case and lower-case), and a certain number of special symbols such as #, /, &, %, etc. The total number of elements in an alphanumeric code is greater than 36. Therefore it must be coded with a minimum number of 6 bits ($2^6 = 64$, but $2^5 = 32$ is insufficient). One possible six bit alphanumeric code is given in Table 2.5. It is used in many computers to represent alphanumeric characters and symbols internally and therefore can be called *"internal code"*. Frequently there is a need to represent more than 64 characters including the lower case letters and special control characters. For this reason the following two codes are normally used.

### 2.2.3.1 ASCII

The full form of ASCII (pronounced "as-kee") is "American Standard Code for Information Interchange", used in most microcomputers. It is actually a seven bit code, where a character is represented with seven bits. The character is stored as one byte with one bit remaining unused. But often the extra bit is used to extend the ASCII to represent an additional 128 characters. Some of the codes are shown in Table 2.5.

Now let us represent the word CODES in ASCII-7 code:

| 1000011 | 1001111 | 1000100 | 1000101 | 1010011 |
|---|---|---|---|---|
| C | O | D | E | S |

The same word CODES in ASCII-8 code can be represented as given below:

| 10100011 | 10101111 | 10100100 | 10100101 | 10110011 |
|---|---|---|---|---|
| C | O | D | E | S |

### 2.2.3.2 EBCDIC

It is pronounced as "ebb-see-dick". It is a 8 bit code and can represent 256 different characters. All of the 256 bit combinations are not meaningful, so the code can still add new characters if required.

The full form of EBCDIC is "Extended Binary Coded Decimal Interchange Code". It is also an alphanumeric code generally used in IBM equipments and in large computers for communicating alphanumeric data. For the different alphanumeric characters the code grouping in this code is different from the ASCII code. It is actually an eight bit code and a ninth bit is added as the parity bit. Out of the 8 bits, the first 4 bits are known as zero bits and the remainder 4 bits represent digit values.

Now let us represent the word CODES in EBCDIC Code:

| 11000011 | 11010110 | 11000100 | 11000101 | 11100010 |
|---|---|---|---|---|
| C | O | D | E | S |

**Table 2.5: Partial List of Alphanumeric Codes**

| *Character* | *6-bit Internal Code* | *7-bit ASCII Code* | *8-bit EBCDIC Code* | *12-bit Hollerith Code* |
|---|---|---|---|---|
| A | 010001 | 1000001 | 11000001 | 12,1 |
| B | 010010 | 1000010 | 11000010 | 12,2 |
| C | 010011 | 1000011 | 11000011 | 12,3 |
| D | 010100 | 1000100 | 11000100 | 12,4 |
| E | 010101 | 1000101 | 11000101 | 12,5 |
| F | 010110 | 1000110 | 11000110 | 12,6 |
| G | 010111 | 1000111 | 11000111 | 12,7 |
| H | 011000 | 1001000 | 11001000 | 12,8 |
| I | 011001 | 1001001 | 11001001 | 12,9 |
| J | 100001 | 1001010 | 11010001 | 11,1 |
| K | 100010 | 1001011 | 11010010 | 11,2 |
| L | 100011 | 1001100 | 11010011 | 11,3 |
| M | 100100 | 1001101 | 11010100 | 11,4 |
| N | 100101 | 1001110 | 11010101 | 11,5 |
| O | 100110 | 1001111 | 11010110 | 11,6 |
| P | 100111 | 1010000 | 11010111 | 11,7 |
| Q | 101000 | 1010001 | 11011000 | 11,8 |
| R | 101001 | 1010010 | 11011001 | 11,9 |
| S | 110010 | 1010011 | 11100010 | 0,2 |
| T | 110011 | 1010100 | 11100011 | 0,3 |
| U | 110100 | 1010101 | 11100100 | 0,4 |
| V | 110101 | 1010110 | 11100101 | 0,5 |
| W | 110110 | 1010111 | 11100110 | 0,6 |
| X | 110111 | 1011000 | 11100111 | 0,7 |
| Y | 111000 | 1011001 | 11101000 | 0,8 |
| Z | 111001 | 1011010 | 11101001 | 0,9 |

| | | | | |
|---|---|---|---|---|
| 0 | 000000 | 0110000 | 11110000 | 0 |
| 1 | 000001 | 0110001 | 11110001 | 1 |
| 2 | 000010 | 0110010 | 11110010 | 2 |
| 3 | 000011 | 0110011 | 11110011 | 3 |
| 4 | 000100 | 0110100 | 11110100 | 4 |
| 5 | 000101 | 0110101 | 11110101 | 5 |
| 6 | 000110 | 0110110 | 11110110 | 6 |
| 7 | 000111 | 0110111 | 11110111 | 7 |
| 8 | 001000 | 0111000 | 11111000 | 8 |
| 9 | 001001 | 0111001 | 11111001 | 9 |
| Blank | 110000 | 0100000 | 01000000 | No punch |
| | 011011 | 0101110 | 01001011 | 12,3,8 |
| ( | 111100 | 0101000 | 01001101 | 12,5,8 |
| + | 010000 | 0101011 | 01001110 | 12,6,8 |
| * | 101100 | 0101010 | 01011100 | 11,4,8 |
| $ | 101011 | 0100100 | 01011011 | 11,3,8 |
| ) | 011100 | 0101001 | 01011101 | 11,5,8 |
| / | 110001 | 0101111 | 01100001 | 0,1 |
| , | 111011 | 0111100 | 01101011 | 0,3,8 |
| = | 001011 | 0111101 | 01111110 | 6,8 |
| – | 100000 | 0101101 | 01100000 | 11 |

### *2.2.3.3 Hollerith Code*

Generally this code is used in punched cards. A punched card consists of 12 rows and 80 columns. An alphanumeric character is represented by each column of 12 bits each by punching holes in the appropriate rows. The presence of a hole represents a 1 and its absence indicates 0. The 12 rows are marked starting from the top, as 12, 11, 0, 1, 2, 3, 4, 5, 6, 7, 8, and 9. The first three rows are called the zone punch and the last nine are called the numeric punch. The code used here is called the Hollerith code. The alphabets are represented as two holes in a column, one in zone punch and the other in numeric punch; decimal digits are represented as a single hole in a numeric punch. Special characters are represented as one, two, or three holes in a column; while the zone is always used, the other two holes, if used, are in a numeric punch with the 8-th punch being commonly used. The Hollerith code is BCD and hence the transmission from EBCDIC is simple. The Hollerith code is used in the card readers and punches of large computers, while EBCDIC may be used within the computer.

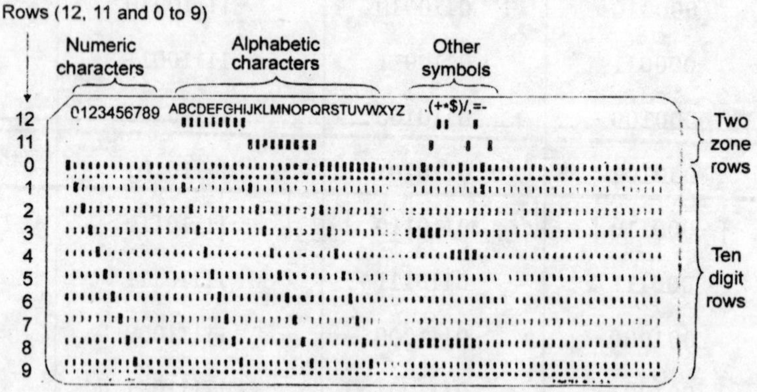


**Fig. 2.2** A modern Hollerith card can handle a maximum of 80 alphanumeric characters. As this sample shown, numbers are coded by making a single punch in the appropriate card column; letters and special characters are coded by using double or triple punches. Note that the upper left-hand corner is missing from the card. This helps the machine operators make sure all the cards are turned the same way and that the deck itself has the proper orientation.

### *2.2.3.4 ISCII*

ISCII stands for *Indian Standard Code for Information Interchange*. There are 18 scheduled languages in India as of today. These are in approximate order of usage: Hindi, Bengali, Telugu, Marathi, Tamil, Urdu, Gujarati, Kannada, Malayalam, Oriya, Punjabi, Assamese, Kashmiri, Sindhi, Konkani, Nepali, Manipuri and Sanskrit.

With the advent of computerization considerable work has been undertaken to facilitate the use of Indian languages on computers. These activities were generally limited to specific languages and were independent exercises of various organizations. Thus making data-interchange impossible. In such a scenario, it was important to have a common standard for coding Indian scripts. GIST (**G**raphics and **I**ntelligence based **S**cript **T**echnology) has played an important role in establishment of Indian standards.

In 1991, the Bureau of Indian Standards (BIS) adopted the Indian Standard Code for Information Interchange (ISCII), the ISCII standard that was evolved by a standardization committee, of which C-DAC was a member, under Department of Electronics during 1986–88. It is an 8 bit code which allows English and Indian Script alphabets to be used simultaneously. It retains the standard ASCII code for English. A common code for all Indian languages is feasible as all Indian scripts have a common origin from the Brahmi script. All GIST products are based on ISCII. Other than this, it has been used by IBM for PC-DOS, Apple for ILK, and several companies are developing products and solutions based on this representation. This has been made mandatory for the data being collected by organizations like the Election Commission, and for projects as Land Records Project etc.

Characters coded in ISCII need 8 bits for each character. This standard does not only apply to the Devnagri script, but also to Gujarati, Bengali, Gurumukhi, Assamese, Telugu, Kannada, Tamil and Malayalam script. Any software which allows ISCII codes, can be used in any Indian script, enhancing its commercial viability. Table 2.6 provides ISCII versions of Devnagri script:

**Table 2.6: Devnagri ISCII Script**

| | 0 | 1 | 2 | 3 | 4 | 5 | 6 | 7 | 10 | 11 | 12 | 13 | 14 | 15 | 16 | 17 |
|---|---|---|---|---|---|---|---|---|---|---|---|---|---|---|---|---|
| 240 | | ँ | ं | ः | अ | आ | इ | ई | उ | ऊ | ऋ | | ए | ऐ | ऍ | |
| 260 | ओ | औ | ऑ | क | ख | ग | घ | ङ | च | छ | ज | झ | ञ | ट | ठ | ड |
| 300 | ढ | ण | त | भ | द | ध | न | | प | फ | ब | भ | म | य | | ऱ |
| 320 | र | ल | ळ | | व | श | ष | स | ह | INV | ा | ि | ी | ु | ू | ृ |
| 340 | | े | ै | ॅ | | ो | ौ | ॉ | ् | ़ | । | | | | | ATR |
| 360 | EXT | ० | १ | २ | ३ | ४ | ५ | ६ | ७ | ८ | ९ | | | | | |

### 2.2.3.5 *UNICODE*

The UNICODE is the new universal coding standard being adopted by all newer platforms. The **Unicode Consortium** is a non-profit organization to develop, extend and promote use of the Unicode Standard, which specifies the representation of text in modern software products and standards. Formally,

**Unicode provides a unique number for every character,**

**no matter what the platform,**

**no matter what the program,**

**no matter what the language.**

Every computer works with numbers. The letters and other characters are stored by assigning a number for each one. Before Unicode was invented, there were hundreds of different encoding systems for assigning these numbers. No single encoding could contain enough characters, for example, the European Union alone requires several encodings to cover all its languages. Even for a single language like English no single encoding was adequate for all the letters, punctuation, and technical symbols in the common use.

These encoding systems also conflict with one another, that is, two encoding can use the same number for two different characters, or use different numbers for the same character. Any system (especially servers) needs to support many different encodings; yet whenever data is passed between different encodings or platforms, that data may be corrupted.

### *Utility of UNICODE*

The Unicode Standard has been adopted by leading computer companies like Apple, IBM, Microsoft, Oracle and many others. Unicode is required by modern standards like such as JAVA, CORBA 3.0 etc. and is the official way to implement ISO. It is supported in many operating systems, all modern browsers and many other products. The emergence of the Unicode Standard, and the availability of tools supporting it, are among the most significant recent global software technology trends.

Unicode's significance is quite clear from the following points:

(*i*) Incorporating Unicode into client-server or multi-tiered applications and websites offers significant cost savings over the use of legacy character sets.

(*ii*) Unicode enables a single software product or a single website to be targeted across multiple platforms, languages and countries without re-engineering.

(*iii*) It allows data to be transported through many different systems without corruption.

The first version of the Unicode Standard, that is, Unicode 1.0.0 was released in October, 1991. Version numbers for the Unicode Standard consist of three fields: the major version, the minor version and the update version. For historical reasons the numbering within each of these fields is not necessarily consecutive. The latest Unicode Version is Unicode 4.0.0 which is in use from April, 2003. Unicode Version 3.2 represented 95,221 characters, whereas Unicode Version 4.0.0 has added many more characters.

## 2.2.4 Error Detecting Codes

Binary information may be transmitted through some form of communication medium such as wires or radio waves or fiber optic cables etc. Any external noise introduced into a physical communication medium changes bit values from 0 to 1 or vice versa. *An error detection code can be used to detect errors during transmission. The detected error cannot be corrected, but its presence may be indicated.*

### *2.2.4.1 Parity Bit Coding Technique*

A parity bit is an extra bit included with a message to make the total number of 1's either odd or even. A message of four bits and a parity bit, P, are shown in Table 2.7. In (*a*), P is chosen so that the sum of all 1's is odd (including the parity bit). In (*b*), P is chosen so that the sum of all 1's is even (including the parity bit). In the sending end, the message (in this case the first four bits) is applied to a "parity generation" circuit where the required P bit is generated. The message, including the parity bit, is transferred to its destination. In the receiving end, all the incoming bits (in this case five) are applied to a "parity check" circuit to check the proper parity adopted. An error is detected if the checked parity does not correspond to the adopted one. The parity method detects the presence of one, three, five, or any odd combination of errors. An even combination of errors is undetectable since even number of errors will not change the parity of the bits. The parity bit may be included with the message bits either on the MSB or on the LSB side. Hence in such cases some other coding scheme is to be adopted. Such a coding technique is Check Sums, which is discussed in next section.

**Table 2.7: Parity Bit**

| (a) Message | P (Odd) | (b) Message | P (Even) |
|---|---|---|---|
| 0000 | 1 | 0000 | 0 |
| 0001 | 0 | 0001 | 1 |
| 0010 | 0 | 0010 | 1 |
| 0011 | 1 | 0011 | 0 |
| 0100 | 0 | 0100 | 1 |
| 0101 | 1 | 0101 | 0 |
| 0110 | 1 | 0110 | 0 |
| 0111 | 0 | 0111 | 1 |
| 1000 | 0 | 1000 | 1 |
| 1001 | 1 | 1001 | 0 |
| 1010 | 1 | 1010 | 0 |
| 1011 | 0 | 1011 | 1 |
| 1100 | 1 | 1100 | 0 |
| 1101 | 0 | 1101 | 1 |
| 1110 | 0 | 1110 | 1 |
| 1111 | 1 | 1111 | 0 |

#### 2.2.4.2 *Check Sums Technique*

As we have discussed above the parity bit technique fails for double error, hence we use the Check Sums method in such case. Initially any word A 10010011 is transmitted; next another word B 01110110 is transmitted. The binary digits in the two words are added and the sum obtained is retained in the transmitter. Then any other word C is transmitted and added to the previous sum retained in the transmitter and the new sum is now retained. In the similar manner, each word is added to the previous sum already been retained; after transmitting all the words, the final sum which is called the Check Sum is also transmitted. The same operation is done at the receiving end and the final sum which has been obtained here is being checked against the transmitted Check Sum. There is no error, if the two sums are equal.

### 2.2.5 Error Correcting Codes

We have already discussed two coding techniques, which may be used in data transmission to detect errors. But unfortunately the above discussed techniques are not capable of correcting the errors. For correction of errors now we will discuss a code called Hamming code.

### *Hamming Code*

This coding had been developed by R. W. Hamming where one or more parity bits are added to a data character methodically in order to detect and correct errors. The number of bits changed from one code word to another is known as *Hamming distance*.

Let us consider $A_i$ and $A_j$ to be any two code words in any particular block code. Now the Hamming distance $d_{ij}$ between the two vectors $A_i$ and $A_j$ is defined by the number of components in which they differ. Assuming that $d_{ij}$ is determined for each pair of code words, the minimum value of $d_{ij}$ is called the minimum Hamming distance, $d_{min}$.

For example,

| | | | | | | | |
|---|---|---|---|---|---|---|---|
| $A_i$ | 1 | 0 | 0 | 1 | 0 | 1 | 1 |
| | ↓ | | ↓ | | | ↓ | |
| $A_j$ | 0 | 0 | 1 | 1 | 0 | 0 | 1 |

Here, these code words differ in the MSB and in the third and sixth bit positions from the left. Hence, $d_{ij}$ is 3.

From Hamming's analysis of code distances, some important properties have been derived:

(*i*) For detection of single error $d_{min}$ should be at least two.

(*ii*) For single error correction, $d_{min}$ should be at least three, since the number of errors, $E \le [(d_{min} - 1)/2]$.

(*iii*) Greater values of $d_{min}$ will provide detection and/or correction of more number of errors.

The 7-bit Hamming (7, 4) code word $h_1\, h_2\, h_3\, h_4\, h_5\, h_6\, h_7$ associated with a 4-bit binary number $b_3\, b_2\, b_1\, b_0$ is:

$$h_1 = b_3 \oplus b_2 \oplus b_0$$
$$h_2 = b_3 \oplus b_1 \oplus b_0$$
$$h_4 = b_2 \oplus b_1 \oplus b_0$$
$$h_3 = b_3$$
$$h_5 = b_2$$
$$h_6 = b_1$$
$$h_7 = b_0$$

Bits $h_1$, $h_2$ and $h_4$ produce even parity bits for the bit fields $b_3\, b_2\, b_0$, $b_3\, b_1\, b_0$ and $b_2\, b_1\, b_0$ respectively. Generally the parity bits ($h_1$, $h_2$, $h_4$, $h_8$, $h_{16}$...) are located in the positions corresponding to ascending powers of two (*i.e.*, $2^0$, $2^1$, $2^2$, $2^3$, $2^4$... = 1, 2, 4, 8, 16...).

The $h_1$ parity bit has a 1 in the LSB position of its binary representation. Therefore it can check all the bit positions, including it, which have 1's in the LSB position in the binary representation (*i.e.*, $h_1$, $h_3$, $h_5$ and $h_7$). The binary representation of $h_2$ has a 1 in the middle bit position. Therefore it can check all the bit positions, including it, which have 1's in the middle bit position in the binary representation (*i.e.*, $h_2$, $h_3$, $h_6$ and $h_7$). The

$h_4$ parity bit has a 1 in the MSB position of its binary representation. Therefore it can check all the bit positions, including it, which have 1's in the MSB position in the binary representation (*i.e.*, $h_4$, $h_5$, $h_6$ and $h_7$).

To decode a Hamming code, checking is to be done for odd parity over the bit fields in which even parity were previously established. For example, a single bit error is indicated by a non-zero parity word $a_4\ a_2\ a_1$, where

$$a_1 = h_1 \oplus h_3 \oplus h_5 \oplus h_7$$
$$a_2 = h_2 \oplus h_3 \oplus h_6 \oplus h_7$$
$$a_4 = h_4 \oplus h_5 \oplus h_6 \oplus h_7$$

If $a_4\ a_2\ a_1 = 000$, we conclude there is no error in Hamming code. On the other hand, if it has a non-zero value, it indicates the bit position in error. For example, if $a_4\ a_2\ a_1 = 110$, then bit 6 is in error. To correct this error, bit 6 has to be complemented.

**Example 1.** *Encode data bits 0110 into a 7-bit even parity Hamming code.*

**Solution.** Given $b_3\ b_2\ b_1\ b_0 = 0\ 1\ 1\ 0$

Therefore,

$$h_1 = b_3 \oplus b_2 \oplus b_0 = 0 \oplus 1 \oplus 0 = 1$$
$$h_2 = b_3 \oplus b_1 \oplus b_0 = 0 \oplus 1 \oplus 0 = 1$$
$$h_4 = b_2 \oplus b_1 \oplus b_0 = 1 \oplus 1 \oplus 0 = 0$$
$$h_3 = b_3 = 0$$
$$h_5 = b_2 = 1$$
$$h_6 = b_1 = 1$$
$$h_7 = b_0 = 0$$

| $h_1$ | $h_2$ | $h_3$ | $h_4$ | $h_5$ | $h_6$ | $h_7$ |
|---|---|---|---|---|---|---|
| 1 | 1 | 0 | 0 | 1 | 1 | 0 |

**Example 2.** *A 7-bit Hamming code is received as 0110110. What is its correct code?*

**Solution.**

| $h_1$ | $h_2$ | $h_3$ | $h_4$ | $h_5$ | $h_6$ | $h_7$ |
|---|---|---|---|---|---|---|
| 0 | 1 | 1 | 0 | 1 | 1 | 0 |

Now, to find the error,

$$a_1 = h_1 \oplus h_3 \oplus h_5 \oplus h_7 = 0 \oplus 1 \oplus 1 \oplus 0 = 0$$
$$a_2 = h_2 \oplus h_3 \oplus h_6 \oplus h_7 = 1 \oplus 1 \oplus 1 \oplus 0 = 1$$
$$a_4 = h_4 \oplus h_5 \oplus h_6 \oplus h_7 = 0 \oplus 1 \oplus 1 \oplus 0 = 0$$

Thus, $a_4\ a_2\ a_1 = 010$. Therefore, bit 2 is in error and the corrected code can be obtained by complementing the second bit in the received as 00 10110.

## 2.3 ARITHMETIC OPERATIONS

You are very well familiar with the decimal number system and with the various operations such as addition, subtraction, multiplication and division on these decimal numbers. The decimal number system is also known as **International Number System.** However, this decimal number system does not fulfil the needs of computers and as such is unsuitable for computers. The computers need a number system consisting of two symbols only, to represent the logical state of various components (ON—1, OFF—0) used by them. Such a number system having two symbols only is known as **Binary Number System** and comprises of bits 0 and 1 only, sometimes written as '0' and '1' to distinguish these from decimal numbers 0 and 1 respectively. Since, the digits 0 and 1 are common in decimal as well as binary number systems, these must be understood clearly in the context.

The conversion of decimal numbers to binary and *vice versa* has been discussed earlier. It was noticed that a decimal number was represented as a long string of 0's and 1's which caused a lot of difficulty in writing binary equivalents of decimal numbers. To overcome this difficulty, other number systems such as **Octal** number system and **Hexadecimal** number system were developed, which have, bases 8 and 16 respectively. At present hexadecimal system of numbers is most popular for use with computers but it is only a matter of convenience in writing that the hexadecimal number system is used, the inner working of computer still remains in binary system. The binary number system has played a very significant role in the design and development of digital computers.

Let us study the fundamental arithmetic operations of addition, subtraction, multiplication and division on binary, octal and hexadecimal numbers. Even out of these four basic operations, the addition operation is the most important as far as the computer is concerned because a computer can perform addition only. The subtraction operation is reduced to addition by complement methods. The multiplication and division operations are nothing else except repetitive additions and subtractions.

### 2.3.1 Addition of Binary Numbers

Addition in binary system is very simple. There are only four possible combination of digits to be added. These are given in Table 2.8.

**Table 2.8: Binary Addition Table**

| *Augend* | *Addend* | *Sum* | *Carry* | *Result* |
|---|---|---|---|---|
| 0 | 0 | 0 | 0 | 0 |
| 0 | 1 | 1 | 0 | 1 |
| 1 | 0 | 1 | 0 | 1 |
| 1 | 1 | 0 | 1 | 10 |

In binary addition, like the decimal addition, it is frequently necessary to shift a carry 1 to next place.

Let us add $110_2$ to $11_2$. We write these numbers in columns $C_1$, $C_2$, $C_3$, $C_4$, $C_5$ etc. and add them as per rules given in Table 2.8.

| | | | | |
|---|---|---|---|---|
| $C_4$ | $C_3$ | $C_2$ | $C_1$ | |
| ① | ① | | | Carry overs |
| | 1 | 1 | 0 | First binary number |
| | | 1 | 1 | Second binary number |
| 1 | 0 | 0 | 1 | Result of binary addition |

**Explanation.** To find the sum, add the numbers in the column $C_1$ (addition begins from the rightmost column $C_1$, then to $C_2$, $C_3$ and $C_4$ and so on). Now, 0 + 1 = 1 by the binary addition table, so write 1 in the column $C_1$. Then move to column $C_2$, here 1 + 1 = 10, so write 0 in column $C_2$ and carry over 1 to column $C_3$. The carryover is shown circled at the top of column $C_3$. In column $C_3$, we get 1 + 1 = 10, so write 0 in column $C_3$ and carry over 1 to column $C_4$. Since, there is no element to be added to 1, it is written as it is in column $C_4$. Hence, the final result is $1001_2$. It is important to note that the carry 1 written on the top of the next left column.

The resultant of 1 + 1 + 1 gives 1 + 10 = $11_2$. The following examples illustrate this concept:

**Example 1.** *Add $111_2$ to $1101_2$.*

**Solution.**

| | | | | | |
|---|---|---|---|---|---|
| $C_5$ | $C_4$ | $C_3$ | $C_2$ | $C_1$ | |
| ① | ① | ① | ① | | Carry overs |
| | | 1 | 1 | 1 | First binary number |
| | 1 | 1 | 0 | 1 | Second binary number |
| 1 | 0 | 1 | 0 | 0 | Result of binary addition |

So, the result of addition is $10100_2$.

**Example 2.** *Add $11111_2$ to $1101_2$.*

**Solution.**

| | | | | | | |
|---|---|---|---|---|---|---|
| $C_6$ | $C_5$ | $C_4$ | $C_3$ | $C_2$ | $C_1$ | |
| ① | ① | ① | ① | ① | | Carry overs |
| | 1 | 1 | 1 | 1 | 1 | First binary number |
| | | 1 | 1 | 0 | 1 | Second binary number |
| 1 | 0 | 1 | 1 | 0 | 0 | Result of binary addition |

So, the result of addition is $101100_2$.

**Example 3.** *Add the binary numbers 1101.1011 and 11001.01.*

**Solution.** In case of binary numbers with binary points the same procedure (as with decimal numbers) is repeated. Number of places after the binary point should be made equal by placing zeros, as shown below:

| $C_{11}$ | $C_{10}$ | $C_9$ | $C_8$ | $C_7$ | $C_6$ | $C_5$ | $C_4$ | $C_3$ | $C_2$ | $C_1$ | |
|---|---|---|---|---|---|---|---|---|---|---|---|
| | (1) | | | (1) | | | | | | | Carry overs |
| | | 1 | 1 | 0 | 1 | . | 1 | 0 | 1 | 1 | First binary number |
| | 1 | 1 | 0 | 0 | 1 | . | 0 | 1 | 0 | 0 | Second binary number |
| 1 | 0 | 0 | 1 | 1 | 0 | . | 1 | 1 | 1 | 1 | Result of binary addition |

So, the result of addition is $100110.1111_2$.

### 2.3.2 Binary Subtraction

The binary subtraction like the decimal subtraction is performed by using the technique of borrowing. Following are the four rules of binary subtraction given in Table 2.9.

**Table 2.9: Binary Subtraction Table**

| *Minuend* | *Subtrahend* | *Difference* | *Borrow* |
|---|---|---|---|
| 0 | 0 | 0 | 0 |
| 0 | 1 | 1 | 1 |
| 1 | 0 | 1 | 0 |
| 1 | 1 | 0 | 0 |

In binary subtraction, like the decimal subtraction, it is frequently necessary to borrow a 1 from the next higher binary bit (as shown in the second row of Table 2.9).

Actually, the subtraction between two numbers can be performed in the following three ways:

- The direct method,
- The *r*'s complement method and
- The $(r - 1)$'s complement method.

#### *2.3.2.1 Using Direct method*

The following examples illustrate the procedure of subtraction:

**Example 1.** *Subtract $11_2$ from $11100_2$.*

**Solution.**

| $C_5$ | $C_4$ | $C_3$ | $C_2$ | $C_1$ | |
|---|---|---|---|---|---|
| | | (0) | (1) | (10) | Borrowings |
| 1 | 1 | 1 | 0 | 0 | Minuend |
| | | | 1 | 1 | Subtrahend |
| 1 | 1 | 0 | 0 | 1 | Result of binary subtraction |

So, the result of subtracting $11_2$ from $11100_2$ is $111001_2$.

**Explanation:**

**Step 1.** In the first column $C_1$, it is not possible to subtract 1 from 0 so 1 is borrowed from the column $C_2$ by the rule (*d*), so 0 becomes 10 and 10 – 1 = 1. The numbers obtained after borrowing are circled.

**Step 2.** 1 is borrowed by the column $C_1$ from the column $C_2$, thereby, the 0 of the column $C_2$ is replaced to 1 and 1 of the column $C_3$ by 0. Now, in column $C_2$, we get 1 – 1 = 0.

**Step 3.** In column $C_3$, 0 – 0 = 0.

**Step 4.** There is no borrowing for the column $C_3$ from column $C_4$, so in column $C_4$, 1 – 0 = 1.

**Step 5.** There is no borrowing for the column $C_4$ from column $C_5$, so in column $C_5$, 1 – 0 = 1.

Hence, the result of subtraction is $11001_2$.

**Example 2.** *Subtract $1_2$ from $1000_2$.*

**Solution.**

| $C_4$ | $C_3$ | $C_2$ | $C_1$ | |
|---|---|---|---|---|
| | (1) | (1) | (10) | Borrowings |
| 1 | 0 | 0 | 0 | Minuend |
| | | | 1 | Subtrahend |
| 0 | 1 | 1 | 1 | Result of binary subtraction |

So, the result of subtracting $1_2$ from $1000_2$ is $111_2$.

**Explanation:**

**Step 1.** In the column $C_1$, 1 is borrowed from the column $C_2$ so 10 – 1 = 1.

**Step 2.** Since 1 is borrowed from the column $C_2$ and there are 0's in the columns $C_2$, $C_3$ so they are replaced by 1, 1 and the 1 of column $C_4$ is replaced by 0.

**Step 3.** For column $C_2$, 1 – 0 = 1

For column $C_3$, 1 – 0 = 1

For column $C_4$, 0 – 0 = 0

Hence, the result on subtraction is $0111_2$.

The rest of the two binary subtraction methods, *i.e.*, the r's complement and the ($r$–1)'s complement method for base or radix 2, *i.e.*, subtraction by 2's complement method and 1's complement method are discussed below.

#### *2.3.2.2 Using 1's Complement Method*

The computer performs the binary subtraction by using the technique called **complementing.** The binary complement of a number is written simply by writing 0 in place of 1 and 1 in place of 0. Table 2.10 gives some binary number and their complements.

**Table 2.10: Illustration of Some Binary Numbers and their Complements**

| *Binary Number* | *Binary Complement* |
|---|---|
| 10010 | 01101 |
| 1100110 | 0011001 |
| 1111111 | 0000000 |
| 1 | 0 |
| 0101 | 1010 |

It is important to note that the complement in the binary system is actually the difference between each of the bits in a binary number and 1 as 1 – 0 = 1 and 1 – 1 = 0. In effect, the 1's complement of a binary number is obtained by changing 1 to 0 and 0 to 1.

***2's Complement:*** The 2's complement of a binary number is obtained by adding 1 to its 1's complement.

**Example.** *Store $37_{10}$ in a 16 bit binary register. Hence, find its 2's complement.*

**Solution.**

16 Bit Register

| | | | | | | | | | | | | | | | |
|---|---|---|---|---|---|---|---|---|---|---|---|---|---|---|---|
| 0 | 0 | 0 | 0 | 0 | 0 | 0 | 0 | 0 | 1 | 0 | 0 | 1 | 0 | 1 | $37_{10}$ as an 16 bit number |
| 1 | 1 | 1 | 1 | 1 | 1 | 1 | 1 | 1 | 0 | 1 | 1 | 0 | 1 | 0 | 1's complement obtained by changing '0' to '1' and '1' to '0' |
| | | | | | | | | | | | | | | 1 | Add 1 |
| 1 | 1 | 1 | 1 | 1 | 1 | 1 | 1 | 1 | 0 | 1 | 1 | 0 | 1 | 1 | Result of addition gives 2's complement |

The reverse of complementation can be derived by using the same rules as that for obtaining complement of a number. So, the complement of a number has the number as the complement. Complements are used:

(*i*) To represent negative numbers.

(*ii*) To subtract numbers.

### *Rules For Subtraction Using I's Complement Method*

The rules of subtraction by this method are given below:

(*i*) Write the 1's complement of the binary number to be subtracted.

(*ii*) Add this to the other number which is called the minuend.

(*iii*) It there is a carry over then add the carry over to the result. The result so obtained is the final answer.

(*iv*) If there is no carry over then the result is recomplemented and a negative sign is attached to it to obtain the final result.

The following examples illustrate the rules given above.

**Example 1.** *Subtract $1001_2$ from $1101_2$, by the 1's complement method.*

**Solution.** The 1's complement of 1001 is 0110. Adding 0110 to 1101

| | | | | | | |
|---|---|---|---|---|---|---|
| | | 1 | 1 | 0 | 1 | Minuend |
| | | 0 | 1 | 1 | 0 | 1's complement of subtrahend |
| Carry over | 1 | 0 | 0 | 1 | 1 | Result of binary addition |
| | | | | | +1 | Add the carry over |
| | | 0 | 1 | 0 | 0 | The result of binary subtraction |

So, the result is $0100_2$.

**Example 2.** *Subtract $1010_2$ from $0011_2$.*

**Solution.** The 1's complement of 1010 is 0101. Adding 0011 and 0101

| | | | | | |
|---|---|---|---|---|---|
| | 0 | 0 | 1 | 1 | Minuend |
| + | 0 | 1 | 0 | 1 | 1's complement of subtrahend |
| | 1 | 0 | 0 | 0 | Result of addition |

Since, there is no carry over, so the result of addition is to be recomplemented, 1's complement of 1000 is 0111. For obtaining the final result, a negative sign is attached before it.

So, the result is $-0111_2$.

### 2.3.2.3 Using 2's Complement Method

The rules of subtraction by this method are given below:

(*i*) Write the 2's complement of the number to be subtracted.

(*ii*) Add this 2's complement to the minuend.

(*iii*) Drop the final carry over.

(*iv*) If the carry over is 1, the answer is positive.

(*v*) If there is no carry over, subtract 1 from the answer and then recomplement it and attach the negative sign to get the final result.

The following examples illustrate this method.

**Example 1.** *Using 2's complement method, subtract $1001_2$ from $1110_2$.*

**Solution.** The 1's complement of $1001_2 = 0110_2$

The 2's complement of $1001_2 = 0110_2 + 1_2 = 0111_2$

Now adding 2's complement $0111_2$ to the minuend $1110_2$.

| | | | | | |
|---|---|---|---|---|---|
| | 1 | 1 | 1 | 0 | Minuend |
| + | 0 | 1 | 1 | 1 | 2's complement of subtrahend |
| Carry over [1] | 0 | 1 | 0 | 1 | Result of binary addition |

After dropping the carry over, the result of subtraction by the 2's complement method is $0101_2$ or $101_2$.

**Example 2.** *Use 2's complement method to subtract $1110_2$ from $1001_2$.*

**Solution.** The 1's complement of $1110_2 = 0001_2$

The 2's complement of $1110_2 = 0001_2$

$$\begin{array}{r} 0001_2 \\ +\ 1_2 \\ \hline 0010_2 \end{array}$$

Now adding 2's complement $0010_2$ to $1001_2$

| | |
|---|---|
| 1 0 0 1 | Minuend |
| + 0 0 1 0 | 2's complement of subtrahend |
| 1 0 1 1 | Result of binary addition |
| – 1 | Subtracting 1 as there is no carry over |
| 1 0 1 0 | Result after subtracting 1 |

Now 1's complement of $1010_2$ is $0101_2$. On attaching the negative sign, we get the final result as $-0101_2$.

### 2.3.3 Binary Multiplication

Binary Multiplication like, the binary addition and binary subtraction, is performed the same way as the decimal multiplication. A binary multiplication table is given below:

**Table 2.11: Binary Multiplication Table**

| *Multiplicand* | *Multiplier* | *Result* |
|---|---|---|
| 0 | 0 | 0 |
| 0 | 1 | 0 |
| 1 | 0 | 0 |
| 1 | 1 | 1 |

It is important to note that any binary number multiplied by zero gives the result as zero and if the binary number is multiplied by 1 then it equals the same number. Making use of this, some simple results are given below:

(*i*) $1 \times 0 = 0$

(*ii*) $1 \times 1 = 1$

(*iii*) $1101 \times 0 = 0$

(*iv*) $11010 \times 1 = 11010$

(*v*) $1 \times 100 = 100$

(*vi*) $0 \times 1101 = 0$.

### Important Points to Remember in Binary Multiplication

1. In binary multiplication, like the decimal multiplication, the partial products are shifted over to the left.
2. To get the results, the partial products are added.
3. Multiplication by zero adds one zero to the right of the binary number, multiplication by two zeros adds two zeros to the right and so on. For example,

   (*i*) 11 × 10 = 110

   (*ii*) 1101 × 100 = 110100

   (*iii*) 101 × 1000 = 101000

   (*iv*) 1011 × 10000 = 10110000

See some more examples to explain the binary multiplication process:

**Example 1.** *Multiply* $1101_2$ *by* $10_2$.

**Solution.**

| | | | | | |
|---|---|---|---|---|---|
| | 1 | 1 | 0 | 1 | |
| × | | | 1 | 0 | |
| | 0 | 0 | 0 | 0 | 1st partial product |
| + 1 | 1 | 0 | 1 | – | 2nd partial product |
| 1 | 1 | 0 | 1 | 0 | Sum of the partial products |

So, the result of multiplication is $11010_2$.

**Explanation:**

**Step 1.** The 1st partial product is obtained by multiplying the number 1101 by 0. Since, multiplication by 0 results in 0, so 0000 is the result of multiplication.

**Step 2.** The 2nd partial product is obtained by multiplying the number 1101 by 1, the result 1101 is shifted by one column to the left.

**Step 3.** Addition of the two partial products gives the required result as 11010.

**Example 2.** *Multiply* $111_2$ *by* $101_2$.

**Solution. 1st Method:**

| | | | | | | |
|---|---|---|---|---|---|---|
| | | | 1 | 1 | 1 | |
| | | × | 1 | 0 | 1 | |
| | | | 1 | 1 | 1 | 1st partial product |
| | | 0 | 0 | 0 | – | 2nd partial product |
| | 1 | 1 | 1 | – | – | 3rd partial product |
| 1 | 0 | 0 | 0 | 1 | 1 | Sum of the partial products |

So, the result of multiplication is $100011_2$.

**Explanation:**

**Step 1.** When 111 is multiplied by 1, the result is the 1st partial product.

**Step 2.** When 111 multiplied by 0, the 2nd partial product 000 is written by shifting it one place to the left. The first blank space is represented by '–'.

**Step 3.** The 3rd partial product is 111 and is written by shifting it two places to the left. The two blank space are represented by '–' and '–'.

**Step 4.** The three partial products are added to obtain the result of multiplication as 100011.

**Second Method:**

| | | | | | | |
|---|---|---|---|---|---|---|
| | | | 1 | 1 | 1 | |
| | | × | 1 | 0 | 1 | |
| | | | 1 | 1 | 1 | 1st partial product |
| | 1 | 1 | 1 | 0 | – | 2nd partial product |
| 1 | 0 | 0 | 0 | 1 | 1 | Sum of two partial products |

**Explanation:**

**Step 1.** The 1st partial product is the same as in the method 1.

**Step 2.** The 2nd partial product is the result of multiplying 111 by 10 which is 1110. The result is shifted one place to the left and the first blank is represented by '–'.

**Step 3.** The 1st and 2nd partial sums are added to obtain the desired result as 100011.

**Example 3.** *Multiply* $1001_2$ *by* $1111_2$.

**Solution.**

| | | | | | | | | |
|---|---|---|---|---|---|---|---|---|
| | | | | 1 | 0 | 0 | 1 | |
| | | | × | 1 | 1 | 1 | 1 | |
| | | | | 1 | 0 | 0 | 1 | 1st partial product |
| | | | 1 | 0 | 0 | 1 | – | 2nd partial product |
| | | 1 | 0 | 0 | 1 | – | – | 3rd partial product |
| | 1 | 0 | 0 | 1 | – | – | – | 4th partial product |
| 1 | 0 | 0 | 0 | 0 | 1 | 1 | 1 | Sum of four partial products |
| $C_8$ | $C_7$ | $C_6$ | $C_5$ | $C_4$ | $C_3$ | $C_2$ | $C_1$ | |

So, the result of multiplication is $10000111_2$.

**Explanation.** When $1001_2$ is multiplied by 1, 1, 1 and 1 the 1st, 2nd, 3rd and 4th partial products are obtained. When all the four partial products are added, the result is $10000111_2$. If $C_1$, $C_2$, $C_3$, $C_4$, $C_5$, $C_6$, $C_7$, $C_8$ are the columns from right to left side then the addition of the partial sums are given below:

| *Column Number* | *Sum* | *Carry Over to the Next Column* | *Bit to be Written* |
|---|---|---|---|
| $C_1$ | 1 | X | 1 |
| $C_2$ | 0 + 1 | X | 1 |
| $C_3$ | 0 + 0 + 1 | X | 1 |
| $C_4$ | 1 + 0 + 0 + 1 = 10 | 1 | 0 |
| $C_5$ | 1 + 1 + 0 + 0 = 10 | 1 | 0 |
| $C_6$ | 1 + 1 + 0 = 10 | 1 | 0 |
| $C_7$ | 1 + 1 = 10 | 1 | 0 |
| $C_8$ | 1 | X | 1 |

When large numbers are to be multiplied, then the addition of so many partial products becomes difficult. It becomes simpler if the two partial sums are added at a time. Computer multiplies the number by adding two partial products at a time. The following examples illustrate the method.

**Example 4.** *Multiply $10111_2$ by $11101_2$.*

**Solution.**

| | | | | | | | | | | |
|---|---|---|---|---|---|---|---|---|---|---|
| | | | | | 1 | 0 | 1 | 1 | 1 | |
| | | | | | 1 | 1 | 1 | 0 | 1 | |
| | | | | | 1 | 0 | 1 | 1 | 1 | 1st partial product |
| | | | 1 | 0 | 1 | 1 | 1 | 0 | – | 2nd partial product (one zero for the zero product) |
| | | | 1 | 1 | 1 | 0 | 0 | 1 | 1 | 1st partial sum |
| | | 1 | 0 | 1 | 1 | 1 | – | – | – | 3rd partial product (on shifting three places to the left) |
| | 1 | 0 | 0 | 1 | 0 | 1 | 0 | 1 | 1 | 2nd partial sum |
| | 1 | 0 | 1 | 1 | 1 | – | – | – | – | 4th partial product (on shifting four places to the left) |
| 1 | 0 | 1 | 0 | 0 | 1 | 1 | 0 | 1 | 1 | 3rd partial sum which is the result |

So, $10111_2 \times 11101_2 = 1010011011_2$

Multiplication of binary numbers with binary points is to be performed in the same way as if the binary points were missing. The rule for placing the binary point is the same as for the decimal numbers. *For example,*

**Example 5.** *Multiply $11.001_2$ by $10.01_2$.*

**Solution.** Multiplication of 11001 by 1001 gives

| | | | | | | | | |
|---|---|---|---|---|---|---|---|---|
| | | | 1 | 1 | 0 | 0 | 1 | |
| | | | × | 1 | 0 | 0 | 1 | |
| | | | 1 | 1 | 0 | 0 | 1 | 1st partial product |
| 1 | 1 | 0 | 0 | 1 | 0 | 0 | – | 2nd partial product when 11001 is multiplied by 100 |
| 1 | 1 | 1 | 0 | 0 | 0 | 0 | 1 | Sum of the partial products |

So, $11.001_2 \times 10.01_2 = 111.00001_2$

### 2.3.3.1 Additive Method of Multiplication

The multiplication is performed by method of addition only. For example, suppose we want to evaluate 3 × 5. This can be obtained simply by adding the digit 5 three times (5 + 5 + 5). Same concept is used by the computers to perform all multiplication operations in binary. It may look a slow process manually but due to fast speed of computers it is quite simple to perform. This helps in simplification of the internal circuit design to a great extent.

#### 2.3.3.2 Multiplication of Signed Numbers

We have discussed earlier the method of multiplying two binary numbers represented in a sign magnitude notation. If one of the numbers, say the multiplicand is negative and is represented in the 2's complement form then multiplication can be carried out with careful attention to the sign bits. This is illustrated in the following example:

**Example 6.** *Multiply –13 by 6.*

**Solution.**

```
            1 0 0 1 1   (–13) Multiplicand
            0 0 1 1 0   (+6)  Multiplier
            ---------
0 0 0 0 0   0 0 0 0 0
1 1 1 1 1   0 0 1 1 –
1 1 1 1 0   0 1 1 – –
0 0 0 0 0   0 0 – – –
0 0 0 0 0   0 – – – –
---------------------
1 1 1 0 1   1 0 0 1 0   (–78) Answer in 2's complement form
```

Observe that the leading bits of the negative partial products are made 1. This is known as sign bit extension. This is necessary if we remember that the leading zeros of a positive number would become ones when their 2's complement is taken. For example, +5= 00000101 and –5 = 11111011.

If the multiplier is negative and the multiplicand is positive we can interchange them and carry out the same procedure or we can 2's complement the multiplier, carry out the procedure and 2's complement the result. If both are negative then both can be complemented and we can use the procedure used for positive operands.

#### 2.3.3.3 Multiplication Using Booth's Coding

Booth's method of dealing with operands in 2's complement form was proposed by Booth. This methods has two advantages:

- It deals with both positive and negative multipliers uniformly.
- It reduces the number of addition operations in the multiplication in cases where the multiplier has a long sequence of ones.

For example, see the multiplication shown in the following two examples:

**Example 1.** *Multiply 6 by 14.*

**Solution.**

```
      000110  (+6)  Multiplicand
      001110  (+14) Multiplier
------------
000000000000
00000000110–
0000000110––
000000110–––
00000000––––
0000000–––––
------------
000001010100 (+84) Product
```

**Example 2.** *Multiply 6 by 14 using Booth multiplication.*

**Solution.**

| | |
|---|---|
| 0 1 0 0 0 0 | (16) |
| − 0 0 0 0 1 0 | (2) |
| 0 0 1 1 1 0 | (14) |

| | |
|---|---|
| 000110 | (+6) Multiplicand |
| 0 + 100 − 10 | (+14) Multiplier |
| 0000000 000 00 | |
| 1111111101 0– | →(−1 × 00110) |
| 0000000 000– – | |
| 0000000 00– – – | |
| 0000011 0– – – – | →(1 × 000110) |
| 0000000 – – – – – | |
| 0000010 101 00 | (+84) Product |

See that we can express 14 as (16 – 2). As shown in Example 2 the same multiplication operation can be replaced by one 2's complement addition and one addition instead of three additions. Observe that in this example +14 = 001110 is represented by an equivalent coded representation + 100 – 10 which facilitates multiplication. This coding proposed by Booth is called **Booth coding**. The Booth coding for the multiplier is obtained by following the procedure given below:

- Scan the number from right to left.
- Replace the rightmost bit by –1 if it is 1 and by 0 if it is 0.
- Replace $i^{th}$ bit by an appropriate code using Table 2.12.

**Table 2.12 : Booth Coding for the Multiplier**

| *Equivalent Code for $i^{th}$ Bit* | *$i^{th}$ Bit* | *$(i - 1)^{th}$ Bit* |
|---|---|---|
| 0 | 0 | 0 |
| –1 | 1 | 0 |
| +1 | 0 | 1 |
| 0 | 1 | 1 |

Here are some examples of the Booth coding:

| | *Binary Number* | *Decimal Equivalent Number* |
|---|---|---|
| Number: | 0 1 1 0 1 1 1 1 1 0 1 | (893) |
| Booth coded number: | + 10 – 1 + 10000 – 1 + 1 – 1 | (– 1 + 2 – 4 + 128 – 256 + 1024 = 893) |
| Number: | 0 0 0 1 1 1 1 1 0 1 1 0 | (+ 502) |
| Booth coded number: | 00 + 10000 – 1 + 10 – 10 | (– 2 + 8 – 16 + 512 = 502) |

Observe that the coding effectively replaces each occurrence of a sequence of ones by 1 followed by appropriate number of zeros minus 1. (11111 = 100000 – 000001) which has a coded representation 0000 – 1. Thus the multiplication by the coded number will be correct.

The same coding scheme also works for negative numbers represented in the 2's complement notation. Let us take some examples of negative numbers and their Booth coding:

| | *Binary Number* | *Decimal Equivalent Number* |
|---|---|---|
| Two's complement number:<br>Booth code: | 1 1 1 1 0 1 0 1<br>0 0 0 – 1 + 1 – 1 + 1 – 1 | (1 + 4 + 16 + 32 + 64 – 128) = –11<br>(– 1 + 2 – 4 + 8 – 16 = – 11) |
| Two's complement number:<br>Booth code: | 1 0 0 0 0 1 1 0<br>– 1 0 0 0 + 1 0 – 1 0 | (2 + 4 – 128 = – 122)<br>( – 2 + 8 – 128 = – 122) |
| Two's complement number:<br>Booth code: | 1 1 0 1 1 1 1 1<br>0 – 1 + 1 0 0 0 0 – 1 | (1 + 2 + 4 + 8 + 16 + 64 – 128 = –33)<br>( – 1 + 32 – 64 = – 33) |

The fact that Booth coding works correctly for negative numbers may be shown as given below:

*Case 1.* If

$$N = \frac{n \ldots 3210 \leftarrow \text{Bit number}}{1 \ldots 1111} = -2^n + (2^{n-1} + 2^{n-2} + \ldots + 2^0) = -1$$

$$\text{Booth code} = 00 \ldots 00 - 1 = -1$$

*Case 2.* If

$$N = \frac{(k+m) \;\ldots\; k(k-1)\;(k-2)\;(k-3) \ldots 0 \leftarrow \text{Bit number}}{1 \quad 1 \;\ldots\; 1 \quad 0 \quad x_{k-2} \quad x_{k-3} \ldots x_0}$$

where $x_{k-i}$ s are either 0 or 1.

We have seen that for the sequence $(0x_{k-2}\, x_{k-3} \ldots x_0)$ the Booth coding correctly computes the product. Let the partial product computed be $P_0$. The sequence 111...1 to the left of this sequence will, by Booth coding, yield $-2^k$. Thus

$$\text{Product} = P_0 \times (-2^k)$$

By straightforward interpretation the product is given by

$$\text{Product} = P_0 \times (-2^{m+k} + 2^{m+k-1} + \ldots + 2^{k+1} + 2^k)$$

Add $-2^k$ to both terms multiplying $P_0$ given above

$$-2^{m+k} + 2^{m+k-1} + \ldots + 2^{k+1} = -2^{k+1}$$

$$(\because -2^k - 2^k = -2^k(1+1) = -2^k \times 2 = -2^{k+1})$$

Adding $-2^{k+1}$ on both sides we have,

$$-2^{m+k} + 2^{m+k-1} + \ldots + 2^{k+2} = -2^{k+2}$$

Continuing similarly we will finally have

$$-2^{m+k} + 2^{m+k-1} = -2^{m+k-1}$$

Now adding $-2^{m+k-1}$ to both sides we have the identity

$$-2^{m+k} = -2^{m+k}$$

Which proves the equality with which we started. Let us take an example of multiplication of a positive multiplicand by a negative Booth coded multiplier.

**Example.** *Multiply 6 by –14 using Booth multiplication.*

**Solution.**

| | |
|---|---|
| 0 0 0 1 1 0 | (+6) Multiplicand |
| 1 1 0 0 1 0 | (–14) Multiplier |
| 0 – 1 0 +1 –1 0 | (–14) Booth coded |
| 0 0 0 0 0 0 0 0 0 0 0 0 | (0) |
| 1 1 1 1 1 1 1 1 0 1 0 – | (–6 in 2's complement form) |
| 0 0 0 0 0 0 0 1 1 0 – – | (+6) |
| 0 0 0 0 0 0 0 0 0 – – – | (0) |
| 1 1 1 1 1 0 1 0 – – – – | (–6) |
| 0 0 0 0 0 0 0 – – – – – | (0) |
| 1 1 1 1 1 0 1 0 1 1 0 0 | (–84 in 2's complement form) |

## 2.3.4 Binary Division

Like other operations binary division is performed in the same way as in the decimal systems. Here,

(*i*) 0/1 = 0

(*ii*) 1/1 = 1

(*iii*) 0/0 is meaningless

(*iv*) 1/0 is meaningless

We take the following examples which are self explanatory.

**Example 1.** *Divide 101100 by 100.*

**Solution.**

```
100)101100(1011  (Quotient)
    -100
     ----
      110
     -100
     ----
      100
     -100
     ----
      000       (Remainder)
```

The steps are explained below:

**Step 1.** Since 100 contains three digits, so 100 is multiplied by 1 and the result 100 is written below the first three digits 101. The difference so obtained is 1.

**Step 2.** Now 1 is brought down giving 11. Since, it is not divisible by 100 so a '0' is written in the quotient. Again 0 is brought down making the number 110.

Multiplication of 100 by 1 gives 100 which is written below 110. The subtraction gives 10. 1 is written in the third place in the quotient.

**Step 3.** The last 0 is brought down to give 100. Since, 100 × 1 = 100. So, 1 is written in the fourth place of quotient and 100 below 100 giving the difference as 000.

Thus, the result of division = $1011_2$.

(This is equivalent to 44/4 = 11 in the decimal system)

**Example 2.** *Divide $1001110_2$ by $110_2$.*

**Solution.**

```
110 )1001110 ( 1101  (Quotient)
     -110
     ----
      0111
      -110
     -----
      00110
       -110
     ------
        000          (Remainder)
```

Therefore, the result of division = $1101_2$.

(This is equivalent to 78/6 = 13 in the decimal system)

**Example 3.** *Divide $100111_2$ by $110_2$.*

**Solution.**

```
110)100111 (0110  (Quotient)
    110  ←—— Divisor greater than 100, hence, put 0 in quotient
    ----
    1001 ←—— Add digit from dividend to group used above
     110 ←—— Subtraction possible, hence, put 1 in quotient
    ----
     111 ←—— Remainder from subtraction plus digit from dividend
     110 ←—— Subtraction possible, hence, put 1 in quotient
    ----
      11 ←—— Add digit from subtraction plus digit from dividend
    ----     (Subtraction not possible, put a 0 in quotient) Remainder is 11
```

The result may be verified by dividing $39_{10}$ ($100111_2$) by $6_{10}$ ($110_2$), which gives a quotient of $6_{10}$ ($110_2$) and a remainder of $3_{10}$ ($11_2$).

### *Additive Method of Division*

Most of the computers perform the division operation by using the process of addition only. Got surprised !, but this is true. The computers perform the division operation essentially by repeating the complementary subtraction method. For example, 24 ÷ 6 may be thought of as:

$$24 \div 6 = 18$$
$$18 - 6 = 12$$
$$12 - 6 = 6$$
$$6 - 6 = 0$$

Here, the divisor is subtracted repeatedly from the dividend, until the result of subtraction is less than or equal to zero. The number of times the subtraction is performed gives the value of the quotient. If the result of last subtraction is zero, then there is no remainder for the division. In case, it is less than zero, ignore the last subtraction, and take the result of the previous subtraction as the value of the remainder. In this case, the quotient is the number of times the subtraction has taken place (ignoring the last one).

**Example.** *Divide $38_{10}$ by $6_{10}$ using the method of addition.*

**Solution.**

$$38 - 6 = 32$$
$$32 - 6 = 26$$
$$26 - 6 = 20$$
$$20 - 6 = 14$$
$$14 - 6 = 8$$
$$8 - 6 = 2$$
$$2 - 6 = -4$$

Here, the total number of subtractions are 7. On ignoring the last one, remainder is negative here, we get quotient = 7 – 1 = 6. Remainder = 2 (result of previous subtraction). Hence, 38 ÷ 6 = 6 with a remainder 2.

We have assumed here that all the subtraction operations are performed using the complementary subtraction method (additive method). This method of addition is easily performed by computers (*i.e.*, addition and complementation) and helps in designing simple circuits. The high speed of computers implements these large number of individual steps very quickly, which is not a disadvantage at all.

## SUMMARY

- Codes are used to represent information, error detection and error correction.
- Integers can be represented in computer memory using sign and magnitude, 1's complement and 2's complement forms.
- In general, the negative numbers are stored in the computer memory in 2's complement form and positive numbers in sign and magnitude form.
- Arithmetic operations are possible on binary numbers.
- Booths multiplication method deals with operands in 2's complement form.

## REVIEW QUESTIONS AND EXERCISES

1. What are BCD codes?
2. Write a short note on the following:
   (*i*) Character codes
   (*ii*) Error detecting codes
   (*iii*) Error correcting codes

3. Differentiate between ASCII and EBCDIC character codes. Why is EBCDIC code used ?
4. What are the advantages of Grey codes? Discuss their areas of applications.
5. Write a short note on the following:
   (*i*) ISCII (*ii*) UNICODE
6. Write the 4-bit BCD code for the following numbers:
   (*i*) $27_{10}$ (*ii*) $135_{10}$ (*iii*) $86_{10}$ (*iv*) $1034_{10}$
7. Using binary notation, show the BCD coding for the following words:
   (*i*) CODES (*ii*) COMPUTER (*iii*) OLYMPICS (*iv*) PROGRAM
8. Why was BCD code extended to EBCDIC?
   (*i*) EARTH (*ii*) LION (*iii*) FOX (*iv*) PROCESS
   How many bytes are needed for each of these representations?
9. Using binary notation, write the ASCII-7 and ASCII-8 codes coding for the following words:
   (*i*) LONG (*ii*) SHORT (*iii*) MEDAL (*iv*) EXAM
   How many bytes are needed for each of these representations?
10. Perform the following additions using binary number system only.
    (*i*) $1011_2 + 11_2$ (*ii*) $111_2 + 0101_2$
    (*iii*) $1010_2 + 10_2$ (*iv*) $110011_2 + 1100_2$
    (*v*) $11001_2 + 111000_2$ (*vi*) $111111_2 + 110000_2$
    (*vii*) $101.011_2 + 10.110_2$ (*viii*) $1011.1010_2 + 1000.001_2$
    (*ix*) $11001.1011_2 + 10011.0110_2$
11. Evaluate:
    (*i*) $1100_2 - 101_2$ (*ii*) $1101_2 - 1011_2$
    (*iii*) $1010_2 - 111_2$ (*iv*) $11100_2 - 111_2$
    (*v*) $11100_2 - 11011_2$ (*vi*) $1111_2 - 100011_2$
    (*vii*) $101.101_2 - 11.011_2$ (*viii*) $1100.01_2 - 1001.10_2$
    (*ix*) $1001.1_2 - 101.11_2$
12. Find the difference using 1's and 2's complements methods:
    (*i*) $10001_2 - 01010_2$ (*ii*) $10_2 - 10011_2$
    (*iii*) $1101_2 - 1001_2$ (*iv*) $0.11_2 - 0.101_2$
13. Perform the following multiplications:
    (*i*) $1100_2 \times 10_2$ (*ii*) $1110_2 \times 111_2$
    (*iii*) $10101_2 \times 101_2$ (*iv*) $1010.101_2 \times 1.01_2$
    (*v*) $1100.001_2 \times 110.1_2$ (*vi*) $01011_2 \times 1001_2$
    (*vii*) $110111_2 \times 111_2$ (*viii*) $1100_2 \times 1001_2$
14. Divide the following binary numbers:
    (*i*) $1100_2/10_2$ (*ii*) $11000_2/110_2$

(*iii*) $1110011_2/101_2$ (*iv*) $1100010_2/111_2$

(*v*) $11110_2/101_2$ (*vi*) $111011_2/111_2$

15. **Why are subtractions using 2's complements used in modern computers? What are the difficulties with BCD or simple binary subtractions?**
16. **Give the advantages and disadvantages of performing the various arithmetic operations by additive method in the digital computer.**
17. **Explain Booths multiplication with an example.**
18. **Subtract $(1010)_2$ from $(1101)_2$ using the 1's and 2's complement methods.**
19. ASCII stands for .................................. .
20. **Write the Booth coded number for the following binary numbers in 2's complement form:**

(*i*) 11101101 (*ii*) 11000110

## ANSWERS

| | | | |
|---|---|---|---|
| 6. | (*i*) 00100111 | (*ii*) 000100110101 | (*iii*) 10000110 |
| | (*iv*) 0001000000110100 | | |
| 10. | (*i*) 1110 | (*ii*) 1100 | (*iii*) 1100 |
| | (*iv*) 111111 | (*v*) 1010001 | (*vi*) 1101111 |
| | (*vii*) 1000.001 | (*viii*) 10011.1100 | (*ix*) 101101.0001 |
| 11. | (*i*) 111 | (*ii*) 10 | (*iii*) 101 |
| | (*iv*) 10101 | (*v*) 1 | (*vi*) -10100 |
| | (*vii*) 10.010 | (*viii*) 10.11 | (*ix*) 11.11 |
| 12. | (*i*) 00111 | (*ii*) –10001 | (*iii*) 0100 |
| | (*iv*) 0.001 | | |
| 13. | (*i*) 11000 | (*ii*) 1100010 | (*iii*) 1101001 |
| | (*iv*) 1101.01001 | (*v*) 1001110.1101 | (*vi*) 1100011 |
| | (*vii*) 110000001 | (*viii*) 1101100 | |
| 14. | (*i*) 110 | (*ii*) 100 | (*iii*) 10111 |
| | (*iv*) 1110 | (*v*) 110 | (*vi*) Quotient 1000, Remainder 11 |

Chapter 3

# Boolean Algebra and Simplification Techniques

## 3.1 INTRODUCTION

Binary logic deals with variables that have two discrete values—1 for TRUE and 0 for FALSE. A simple switching circuit containing active elements such as diode and transistor can demonstrate the binary logic, which can either be ON (switch closed) or OFF (switch open). Electrical signals such as voltage and current exist the digital system in either one of the two recognized values, except during transition.

The switching functions can be expressed with Boolean equations. Complex Boolean equations can be simplified by a new kind of algebra, which is popularly called as *Switching Algebra* or *Boolean Algebra*, invented by the mathematician *George Boole* in the year of 1854. The Boolean Algebra deals with the rules by which logical operations are carried out.

## 3.2 SWITCHING ALGEBRA

Is there any connection between mathematics and logic? This question remained unanswered for centuries. The missing link was found by *George Boole, an English mathematician*. *Boolean Algebra was developed by George Boole*. In 1854, he published a book titled as "*An Investigation of the Laws of Thought*" in which he discussed **Boolean algebra** also known as the *algebra of logic. Each variable in Boolean algebra has either of two values*: *true or false*. The original purpose of this two-state algebra was to solve logic problems. *Claude E. Shannon* in 1938 came with a paper titled '*A Symbolic Analysis of Relay Switching Circuits*'. He applied the concepts of Boolean algebra to the design of electrical circuits. He let the variables represent closed and open relays.

Any logic problem relates to binary decisions and the Boolean algebra effectively deals with binary values, so it is also known as **'Switching Algebra'.** Perhaps, no one at that time might have thought that this algebra was going to result in the development of modern high speed digital computers, which have changed the entire world today.

## 3.3 BOOLEAN VARIABLE AND BOOLEAN ALGEBRA

Consider the following logic statements:

- Should I meet Sachin Tendulkar or not?
- Should I opt for Computer Science or not?
- Should I prepare for I.I.T. examination or not?
- The only possible answers to the above stated questions are **YES** or **NO.**

A **Binary decision** *always results into either YES (TRUE) or NO (FALSE).* So the above mentioned statements are binary decisions. Binary decision making is also applicable to formal logic. For example,

(*i*) Indian Kabaddi team won a gold medal in the Asian Games 2006 in Doha.

(*ii*) 2 + 2 = 5.

(*iii*) What are your suggestions on removing terrorism?

Here, 1st sentence is TRUE and 2nd is FALSE; 3rd is a question which cannot be TRUE or FALSE. Therefore, sentences 1st and 2nd are known as *logical statements* or *truth functions* and their results TRUE or FALSE are known as *truth values.*

A variable which takes values from the Boolean Algebra is called a *Boolean variable* or *logical variable.*

## 3.4 BOOLEAN CONSTANT AND OPERATORS

Boolean Algebra is based on the binary number system and uses the numeric constants 0 and 1. Just as we have the arithmetic operators such as +, –, × etc. and arithmetic operations using these operators and constants, similarly *Boolean Algebra has what are called* **boolean constants (logical constants)** *and* **operators.**

In Boolean Algebra the truth values are represented by **logical constants** given below:

| | | |
|---|---|---|
| **TRUE** | or | 1 |
| **FALSE** | or | 0 |

*Every logical statement or expression has a definite value which is either of the logical constants TRUE or FALSE but not both.*

*The Boolean variables/logical variables or binary valued variables are required to store one of the two values TRUE (1) or FALSE (0).*

*Boolean Algebra has logical operators which are used to form* **logical expressions** *using the operands, that is, logical variables and logical constants (0 and 1). The logical or Boolean operators are:*

| *Logical / Boolean Operator* | *Symbol* |
|---|---|
| NOT | "–" (bar) or "/" |
| AND | "." or ∧ |
| OR | "+" or ∨ |

Let A, B, C be logical variables. An example of a logical expression would be:

A OR (A AND B) = A

This would be denoted as:

$$A \vee (A \wedge B) = A$$

or as:

$$A + (A \, . \, B) = A$$

We can have logical expressions with three variables also. For example,

A AND B OR (NOT (A AND C)) = ((NOT A) OR B) AND (A OR (NOT C))

This would be denoted as:

$$A \, . \, B + \overline{A \, . \, C} = (\overline{A} + B) \, . \, (A + \overline{C})$$

### 3.4.1 NOT Operator

The *NOT operator is a unary operator (that is, it operates on a single variable) and the operation performed by NOT operator is known as* **complementation** *or* **negation**. *The symbol used for it is* ‾ *(bar)*. For example,

If the statement A is a logical statement, $\overline{A}$ or ~ A (pronounced as not A) means negation of A. Thus if the statement A is *true*, then the statement $\overline{A}$ is *false*. Similarly if the statement A is *false*, then $\overline{A}$ is a *true* statement.

It means that the logical statements A and $\overline{A}$ are logically opposite of each other

So, the complement operation is defined as:

$$\overline{0} = 1$$

$$\overline{1} = 0$$

The NOT operation can be defined using Venn diagram as shown in Figure 3.1

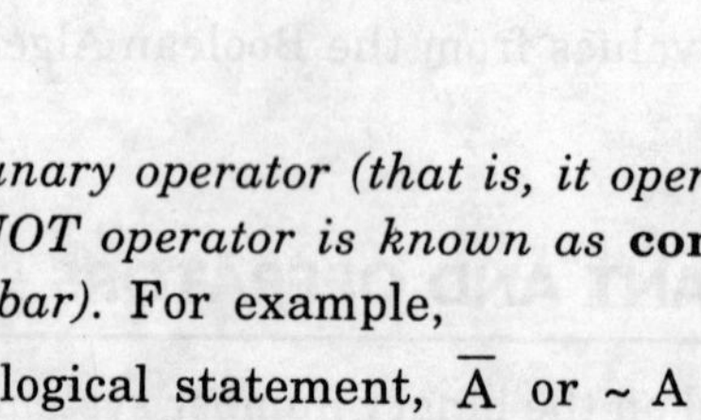


**Fig. 3.1:** Venn diagram of $\overline{A}$.

### 3.4.2 AND Operator

*The AND operator is a binary operator (that is, it operates on two variables) and the operation performed by AND operator is known as* **logical multiplication.** *The symbol used for it is (.) dot.* For example, if A and B are logical statements then A . B means A AND B. The AND operation rules are:

$$0 \cdot 0 = 0$$

$$0 \cdot 1 = 0$$

$$1 \cdot 0 = 0$$

$$1 \cdot 1 = 1$$

The AND operator gives the result TRUE (1) when both the logical statements are TRUE and FALSE (0) otherwise.

The AND operation can be defined using Venn diagram as shown in Figure 3.2.

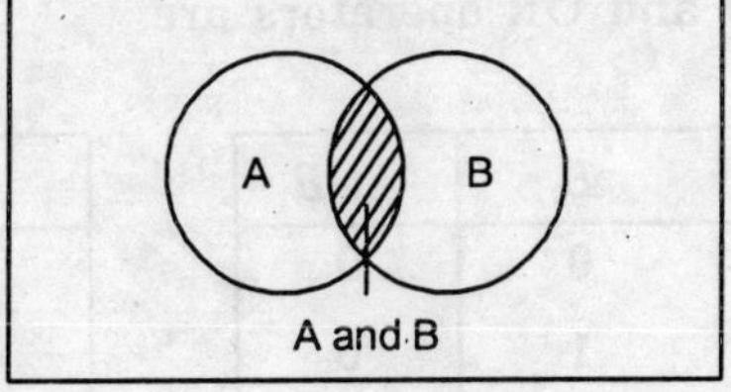


**Fig. 3.2:** Venn diagram of (A . B).

### 3.4.3 OR Operator

*The OR operator is a binary operator (that is, it operates on two variables) and the operation performed by OR operator is known as* **logical addition.** *The symbol used for it is +. The + symbol, therefore, does not have the 'normal' meaning, but it is a logical OR symbol.* For example, If A and B are logical statements then A + B means A OR B. The OR operation rules are:

$$0 + 0 = 0$$

$$0 + 1 = 1$$

$$1 + 0 = 1$$

$$1 + 1 = 1$$

The OR operator gives the result FALSE (0) when both the logical statements are FALSE and TRUE (1) otherwise.

The OR operation can be defined using Venn diagram as shown in Figure 3.3.

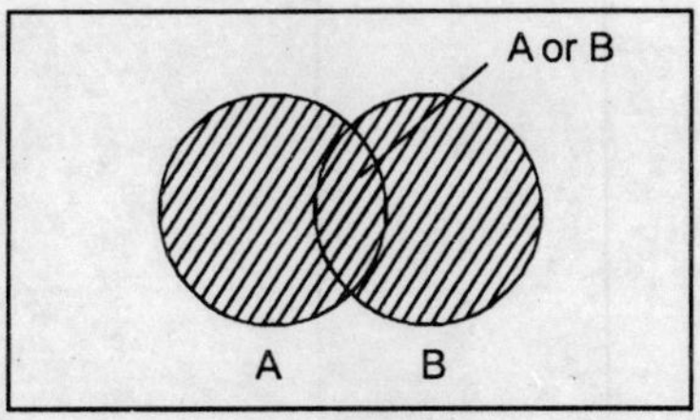


**Fig. 3.3:** Venn diagram of A + B.

## 3.5 BOOLEAN FUNCTIONS AND TRUTH TABLES

Binary variables have two values, either 0 or 1. A *Boolean function is an expression formed with binary variables, the two binary operators AND and OR, one unary operator NOT, parentheses and equal sign.* The value of function may 0 or 1, depending on values of variables present in the Boolean *function* or *expression*. For example, if a Boolean function is expressed algebraically as

$$F = A\bar{B}C$$

Then the value of F will be 1, when A = 1, B = 0 and C = 1. For other values of A, B, C the value of F is 0.

Boolean functions can also be represented by truth tables, which are discussed in next section.

**Truth Table** *is a table that, shows all input and output possibilities for logical variables / statements. The input pattern is / are written in binary progression.* For example, the Truth Tables of NOT, AND and OR operators are:

| $A$ | $\bar{A}$ |
|---|---|
| 0 | 1 |
| 1 | 0 |

Truth Table for NOT operator

| $A$ | $B$ | $A.B$ |
|---|---|---|
| 0 | 0 | 0 |
| 0 | 1 | 0 |
| 1 | 0 | 0 |
| 1 | 1 | 1 |

Truth Table for AND operator for two variables

| $A$ | $B$ | $A+B$ |
|---|---|---|
| 0 | 0 | 0 |
| 0 | 1 | 1 |
| 1 | 0 | 1 |
| 1 | 1 | 1 |

Truth Table for OR operator for two variables

If the result of a logical statement or expression is always TRUE or 1, it is known as **TAUTOLOGY** and if the result is always FALSE or 0 it is known as **FALLACY.**

The truth table for Boolean expressions of two variables contains four rows, three variables contains eight rows and four variables contains sixteen rows. As mentioned earlier the input combinations taking values from {0, 1} are in binary progression.

For an expression having 3 variables, all possible combinations of the variables A, B and C taking values from {0, 1} are:

| *A* | *B* | *C* | *Combination Number* |
|---|---|---|---|
| 0 | 0 | 0 | 0 |
| 0 | 0 | 1 | 1 |
| 0 | 1 | 0 | 2 |
| 0 | 1 | 1 | 3 |
| 1 | 0 | 0 | 4 |
| 1 | 0 | 1 | 5 |
| 1 | 1 | 0 | 6 |
| 1 | 1 | 1 | 7 |

For an expression having 4 variables, all possible combinations of the variables A, B, C and D taking values from {0, 1} are:

| *A* | *B* | *C* | *D* | *Combination Number* |
|---|---|---|---|---|
| 0 | 0 | 0 | 0 | 0 |
| 0 | 0 | 0 | 1 | 1 |
| 0 | 0 | 1 | 0 | 2 |
| 0 | 0 | 1 | 1 | 3 |
| 0 | 1 | 0 | 0 | 4 |
| 0 | 1 | 0 | 1 | 5 |
| 0 | 1 | 1 | 0 | 6 |
| 0 | 1 | 1 | 1 | 7 |
| 1 | 0 | 0 | 0 | 8 |
| 1 | 0 | 0 | 1 | 9 |
| 1 | 0 | 1 | 0 | 10 |
| 1 | 0 | 1 | 1 | 11 |
| 1 | 1 | 0 | 0 | 12 |
| 1 | 1 | 0 | 1 | 13 |
| 1 | 1 | 1 | 0 | 14 |
| 1 | 1 | 1 | 1 | 15 |

Thus, for $n$ variables, the number of possible combinations is $2^n$, which are binary representation of the integers from 0 to $(2^n - 1)$. So a *Boolean expression can be evaluated using a truth table.*

When a Boolean expression is evaluated, a certain hierarchy of precedence order must be followed. The innermost parentheses are evaluated first, then the parentheses next to it and so on using the precedence of logical operators given as follows:

NOT (First precedence)

AND (Second precedence)

OR (Last precedence)

The unnecessary parentheses are eliminated when evaluation of Boolean expression takes place. For example, We can write

$$A + (B \cdot C) \text{ as } A + B \cdot C$$

$$A \cdot \overline{(B + (A \cdot C))} \text{ as } A \cdot \overline{(B + A \cdot C)}$$

Without any ambiguity, we can write BC in place of B . C and A (B + C) in place of A . (B + C).

**Example 1.** *Evaluate* $A + \overline{B}C$ *using the truth table.*

**Solution.** For evaluation of $A + \overline{B}C$. First evaluate $\overline{B}$, followed by evaluation of $\overline{B}C$ and finally $A + \overline{B}C$. The following truth table illustrates it:

| $A$ | $B$ | $C$ | $\overline{B}$ | $\overline{B}C$ | $A + \overline{B}C$ |
|---|---|---|---|---|---|
| 0 | 0 | 0 | 1 | 0 | 0 |
| 0 | 0 | 1 | 1 | 1 | 1 |
| 0 | 1 | 0 | 0 | 0 | 0 |
| 0 | 1 | 1 | 0 | 0 | 0 |
| 1 | 0 | 0 | 1 | 0 | 1 |
| 1 | 0 | 1 | 1 | 1 | 1 |
| 1 | 1 | 0 | 0 | 0 | 1 |
| 1 | 1 | 1 | 0 | 0 | 1 |

Here, the evaluation of each sub-expression is shown in the output and this process is followed until the full expression is evaluated.

**Example 2.** *Draw truth table for the Boolean expression*

$$A \,.\, (B + \overline{C}) + A \,.\, (\overline{B} + C) \,.\, \overline{D}$$

**Solution.**

| $A$ | $B$ | $C$ | $D$ | $\overline{C}$ | $B + \overline{C}$ | $A \,.\, (B + \overline{C})$ | $\overline{B}$ | $\overline{B} + \overline{C}$ | $A \,.\, (\overline{B} + \overline{C})$ | $\overline{D}$ | $A \,.\, (\overline{B} + \overline{C}) \,.\, \overline{D}$ | $A \,.\, (B + \overline{C}) + A \,.\, (\overline{B} + \overline{C}) \,.\, \overline{D}$ |
|---|---|---|---|---|---|---|---|---|---|---|---|---|
| 0 | 0 | 0 | 0 | 1 | 1 | 0 | 1 | 1 | 0 | 1 | 0 | 0 |
| 0 | 0 | 0 | 1 | 1 | 1 | 0 | 1 | 1 | 0 | 0 | 0 | 0 |
| 0 | 0 | 1 | 0 | 0 | 0 | 0 | 1 | 1 | 0 | 1 | 0 | 0 |
| 0 | 0 | 1 | 1 | 0 | 0 | 0 | 1 | 1 | 0 | 0 | 0 | 0 |
| 0 | 1 | 0 | 0 | 1 | 1 | 0 | 0 | 1 | 0 | 1 | 0 | 0 |
| 0 | 1 | 0 | 1 | 1 | 1 | 0 | 0 | 1 | 0 | 0 | 0 | 0 |
| 0 | 1 | 1 | 0 | 0 | 1 | 0 | 0 | 0 | 0 | 1 | 0 | 0 |
| 0 | 1 | 1 | 1 | 0 | 1 | 0 | 0 | 0 | 0 | 0 | 0 | 0 |
| 1 | 0 | 0 | 0 | 1 | 1 | 1 | 1 | 1 | 1 | 1 | 1 | 1 |
| 1 | 0 | 0 | 1 | 1 | 1 | 1 | 1 | 1 | 1 | 0 | 0 | 1 |
| 1 | 0 | 1 | 0 | 0 | 0 | 0 | 1 | 1 | 1 | 1 | 1 | 1 |

| | | | | | | | | | |
|---|---|---|---|---|---|---|---|---|---|
| 1 0 1 1 | 0 | 0 | 0 | 1 | 1 | 1 | 0 | 0 | 0 |
| 1 1 0 0 | 1 | 1 | 1 | 0 | 1 | 1 | 1 | 1 | 1 |
| 1 1 0 1 | 1 | 1 | 1 | 0 | 1 | 1 | 0 | 0 | 1 |
| 1 1 1 0 | 0 | 1 | 1 | 0 | 0 | 0 | 1 | 0 | 1 |
| 1 1 1 1 | 0 | 1 | 1 | 0 | 0 | 0 | 0 | 0 | 1 |

## 3.6 EQUIVALENCE OF BOOLEAN EXPRESSIONS

*In Boolean algebra, two Boolean expressions are said to be* ***equivalent*** *if the Boolean functions corresponding to the expressions are equal, that is, they take identical values for all possible combinations.* The " = " sign is generally used for equivalence relation. For example,

If two Boolean expressions E and F are equivalent, then we write E = F.

We can verify the equivalence of two Boolean expressions in the following ways:

1. *Algebraically.*
2. *Using Truth tables.*

The algebraic method will be discussed after discussing the laws of Boolean Algebra.

### 3.6.1 Truth Table Method for Examining the Validity of Boolean Expressions

It is a straight forward method. The truth tables for each expression is prepared and the final columns are compared. The two expressions are *equivalent* if the values in two final columns of both are similar. The two expressions are *not equivalent* if there is a difference even at one place. The following examples illustrate this concept:

**Example 1.** *Examine the validity of*

$$(x + y) \cdot (y + z) \cdot (z + x) = (\overline{x} + \overline{y}) \cdot (\overline{x} + \overline{z}) \cdot (\overline{y} + \overline{z})$$

**Solution. Truth Table for L.H.S.:**

| $x$ | $y$ | $z$ | $x + y$ | $y + z$ | $z + x$ | L.H.S. |
|---|---|---|---|---|---|---|
| 0 | 0 | 0 | 0 | 0 | 0 | 0 |
| 0 | 0 | 1 | 0 | 1 | 1 | 0 |
| 0 | 1 | 0 | 1 | 1 | 0 | 0 |
| 0 | 1 | 1 | 1 | 1 | 1 | 1 |
| 1 | 0 | 0 | 1 | 0 | 1 | 0 |
| 1 | 0 | 1 | 1 | 1 | 1 | 1 |
| 1 | 1 | 0 | 1 | 1 | 1 | 1 |
| 1 | 1 | 1 | 1 | 1 | 1 | 1 |

**Truth Table for R.H.S.:**

| $x$ | $y$ | $z$ | $\overline{x}$ | $\overline{y}$ | $\overline{z}$ | $\overline{x}+\overline{y}$ | $\overline{x}+\overline{z}$ | $\overline{y}+\overline{z}$ | *R.H.S.* |
|---|---|---|---|---|---|---|---|---|---|
| 0 | 0 | 0 | 1 | 1 | 1 | 1 | 1 | 1 | 1 |
| 0 | 0 | 1 | 1 | 1 | 0 | 1 | 1 | 1 | 1 |
| 0 | 1 | 0 | 1 | 0 | 1 | 1 | 1 | 1 | 1 |
| 0 | 1 | 1 | 1 | 0 | 0 | 1 | 1 | 0 | 0 |
| 1 | 0 | 0 | 0 | 1 | 1 | 1 | 1 | 1 | 1 |
| 1 | 0 | 1 | 0 | 1 | 0 | 1 | 0 | 1 | 0 |
| 1 | 1 | 0 | 0 | 0 | 1 | 0 | 1 | 1 | 0 |
| 1 | 1 | 1 | 0 | 0 | 0 | 0 | 0 | 0 | 0 |

Here the values under L.H.S. (first row) is not identical with the value under R.H.S. (first row) for ($x = 0$, $y = 0$, $z = 0$). Hence the expressions are not equivalent and the equation is invalid.

**Example 2.** *In the Boolean Algebra, verify using truth table that* $(\overline{a} + \overline{b}) . (a + b) = \overline{a} . b + a . \overline{b}$ *for each a, b in {0, 1}.*

**Solution. Truth Table for L.H.S.:**

| $a$ | $b$ | $\overline{a}$ | $\overline{b}$ | $\overline{a}+\overline{b}$ | $a + b$ | *L.H.S.* |
|---|---|---|---|---|---|---|
| 0 | 0 | 1 | 1 | 1 | 0 | 0 |
| 0 | 1 | 1 | 0 | 1 | 1 | 1 |
| 1 | 0 | 0 | 1 | 1 | 1 | 1 |
| 1 | 1 | 0 | 0 | 0 | 1 | 0 |

**Truth Table for R.H.S.:**

| $a$ | $b$ | $\overline{a}$ | $\overline{a} . b$ | $\overline{b}$ | $a . \overline{b}$ | *R.H.S.* |
|---|---|---|---|---|---|---|
| 0 | 0 | 1 | 0 | 1 | 0 | 0 |
| 0 | 1 | 1 | 1 | 0 | 0 | 1 |
| 1 | 0 | 0 | 0 | 1 | 1 | 1 |
| 1 | 1 | 0 | 0 | 0 | 0 | 0 |

Since row-wise every value of L.H.S. equals to every value of R.H.S. (the two columns are identical), hence the equation is verified, that is, valid.

**Note.** *The Truth Table proving method is also known as Perfect Induction Method.*

## 3.7 BOOLEAN POSTULATES

*Boolean algebra has a set of basic postulates which are assumed to be true. These are also known as* **fundamental laws.** The basic theorems of Boolean algebra are based on these postulates. The postulates and theorems are useful in reducing logical expressions to the smallest expression possible so that a simple logical circuit can be designed. The Boolean algebra having two elements B = {0, 1} is primarily used for this purpose.

**Postulate 1:**

A Boolean variable, X, has two possible values, 0 and 1. These values are mutually exclusive, that is,

If $X = 0$ then $X \neq 1$

If $X = 1$ then $X \neq 0$

**Postulate 2:**

The NOT operation "–" is defined as

$$\overline{0} = 1$$

$$\overline{1} = 0$$

**Postulate 3:**

The logical multiplication AND operation is defined as

$$0 . 0 = 0$$
$$0 . 1 = 0$$
$$1 . 0 = 0$$
$$1 . 1 = 1$$

**Postulate 4:**

The logical addition OR operation is defined as

$$0 + 0 = 0$$
$$0 + 1 = 1$$
$$1 + 0 = 1$$
$$1 + 1 = 1$$

## 3.8 BOOLEAN LAWS AND THEOREMS

Using Boolean postulates we can build a set of useful theorems for manipulation and simplification of logical expressions. We shall prove the theorems using truth tables.

### 3.8.1 Closure Property

For all $x, y \in$ B (Boolean Algebra)

(*i*) $x + y \in B$ (*ii*) $x . y \in B$

| $x$ | $y$ | $x + y$ |
|---|---|---|
| 0 | 0 | 0 |
| 0 | 1 | 1 |
| 1 | 0 | 1 |
| 1 | 1 | 1 |

| $x$ | $y$ | $x . y$ |
|---|---|---|
| 0 | 0 | 0 |
| 0 | 1 | 0 |
| 1 | 0 | 0 |
| 1 | 1 | 1 |

Here the result of the two operations, that is, $x + y$ or $x . y$ is either 0 or 1. So the closure property holds good in Boolean algebra.

### 3.8.2 Commutative Law

These laws state that

(*i*) $x + y = y + x$

| $x$ | $y$ | $x + y$ | $y + x$ |
|---|---|---|---|
| 0 | 0 | 0 | 0 |
| 0 | 1 | 1 | 1 |
| 1 | 0 | 1 | 1 |
| 1 | 1 | 1 | 1 |

(*ii*) $x . y = y . x$

| $x$ | $y$ | $x . y$ | $y . x$ |
|---|---|---|---|
| 0 | 0 | 0 | 0 |
| 0 | 1 | 0 | 0 |
| 1 | 0 | 0 | 0 |
| 1 | 1 | 1 | 1 |

The last two columns in both the truth tables are identical, hence the law is verified.

### 3.8.3 Associative Law

These laws state that

(*i*) $x + (y + z) = (x + y) + z$

(*ii*) $x . (y . z) = (x . y) . z$

(*i*) $x + (y + z) = (x + y) + z$

| $x$ | $y$ | $z$ | $y + z$ | $x + (y + z)$ | $x + y$ | $(x + y) + z$ |
|---|---|---|---|---|---|---|
| 0 | 0 | 0 | 0 | 0 | 0 | 0 |
| 0 | 0 | 1 | 1 | 1 | 0 | 1 |
| 0 | 1 | 0 | 1 | 1 | 1 | 1 |
| 0 | 1 | 1 | 1 | 1 | 1 | 1 |
| 1 | 0 | 0 | 0 | 1 | 1 | 1 |
| 1 | 0 | 1 | 1 | 1 | 1 | 1 |
| 1 | 1 | 0 | 1 | 1 | 1 | 1 |
| 1 | 1 | 1 | 1 | 1 | 1 | 1 |

On comparing the columns $x + (y + z)$ and $(x + y) + z$ we see that all the values are identical. Hence the associative law $x + (y + z) = (x + y) + z$ holds good in Boolean algebra.

(*ii*) $x \cdot (y \cdot z) = (x \cdot y) \cdot z$

| $x$ | $y$ | $z$ | $y \cdot z$ | $x \cdot (y \cdot z)$ | $(x \cdot y)$ | $(x \cdot y) \cdot z$ |
|---|---|---|---|---|---|---|
| 0 | 0 | 0 | 0 | 0 | 0 | 0 |
| 0 | 0 | 1 | 0 | 0 | 0 | 0 |
| 0 | 1 | 0 | 0 | 0 | 0 | 0 |
| 0 | 1 | 1 | 1 | 0 | 0 | 0 |
| 1 | 0 | 0 | 0 | 0 | 0 | 0 |
| 1 | 0 | 1 | 0 | 0 | 0 | 0 |
| 1 | 1 | 0 | 0 | 0 | 1 | 0 |
| 1 | 1 | 1 | 1 | 1 | 1 | 1 |

The columns $x \cdot (y \cdot z)$ and $(x \cdot y) \cdot z$ are identical. Hence the law is verified.

### 3.8.4 Identity Law

In Boolean algebra there exist identity elements 0 (known as additive identity) and 1 (known as multiplicative identity) such that

(*i*) $x + 0 = x$ (*ii*) $x \cdot 1 = x$

| $x$ | $x + 0$ |
|---|---|
| 0 | 0 |
| 1 | 1 |

| $x$ | $x \cdot 1$ |
|---|---|
| 0 | 0 |
| 1 | 1 |

### 3.8.5 Inverse Law

There exists an inverse such that

(*i*) $x + \overline{x} = 1$ (*ii*) $x \cdot \overline{x} = 0$

| $x$ | $\overline{x}$ | $x + \overline{x}$ |
|---|---|---|
| 0 | 1 | 1 |
| 1 | 0 | 1 |

| $x$ | $\overline{x}$ | $x \cdot \overline{x}$ |
|---|---|---|
| 0 | 1 | 0 |
| 1 | 0 | 0 |

### 3.8.6 Principle of Duality

Observe carefully the above postulates and theorems, we see that there are two forms for each law. So we have proved both forms everywhere. The duality principle helps a lot in this effort. *It states that*:

If a theorem/property holds good in Boolean algebra, then by

(*i*) *Interchanging 0 and 1*

(*ii*) *Interchanging + and .*

(*iii*) *Keeping the form of variables as such also holds true.* The result obtained by doing so is called **dual** of the theorem/property.

**Example 1.** *Write the dual of the Boolean expression $A + B' . C$.*

**Solution.** Given expression is $A + B' . C$. Using duality principle, changing (+) to (.) and vice versa and by keeping the form of variables as such, the dual of the expression is

$$A . (B' + C)$$

**Example 2.** *Write the dual of the Boolean expression $(B' + C) . A$.*

**Solution.** Given expression is $(B' + C) . A$.

Using duality principle, changing (+) to (.) and vice versa and by keeping the form of variables as such, the dual of the expression is

$$(B' . C) + A$$

**Example 3.** *Write the dual of the Boolean function*

$$\overline{x} . (y + z) + \overline{x} . (\overline{y} + \overline{z})$$

**Solution.** Given expression is $\overline{x} . (y + z) + \overline{x} . (\overline{y} + \overline{z})$

Using duality principle, changing (+) to (.) and vice versa and by keeping the form of variables as such, the dual of the expression is

$$(\overline{x} . (y . z)) . (\overline{x} + (\overline{y} + \overline{z}))$$

### 3.8.7 Idempotent Law

This law states that

(*i*) $x + x = x$ (*ii*) $x . x = x$

| $x$ | $x$ | $x + x$ |
|---|---|---|
| 0 | 0 | 0 |
| 1 | 1 | 1 |

Let us prove the above *Idempotent law algebraically* also

$x + x = (x + x) . 1$ Identity element

$= (x + x) . (x + \overline{x})$ Using law of complementarity

$= x + x . \overline{x}$ Using Distributive law

$= x + 0$ Using law of complementarity

$= x$ Identity element

$\therefore$ $x + x = x$

The (*ii*) Idempotent law holds true by duality principle.

### 3.8.8 Distributive Law

This law states that

(*i*) $x + (y \, . \, z) = (x + y) \, . \, (x + z)$

(*ii*) $x \, . \, (y + z) = x \, . \, y + x \, . \, z$

(*i*) $x + (y \, . \, z) = (x + y). \, (x + z)$ does not hold good in ordinary algebra but it is true in Boolean algebra.

| $x$ | $y$ | $z$ | $y \, . \, z$ | $x + (y \, . \, z)$ | $x + y$ | $x + z$ | $(x + y) \, . \, (x + z)$ |
|---|---|---|---|---|---|---|---|
| 0 | 0 | 0 | 0 | 0 | 0 | 0 | 0 |
| 0 | 0 | 1 | 0 | 0 | 0 | 1 | 0 |
| 0 | 1 | 0 | 0 | 0 | 1 | 0 | 0 |
| 0 | 1 | 1 | 1 | 1 | 1 | 1 | 1 |
| 1 | 0 | 0 | 0 | 1 | 1 | 1 | 1 |
| 1 | 0 | 1 | 0 | 1 | 1 | 1 | 1 |
| 1 | 1 | 0 | 0 | 1 | 1 | 1 | 1 |
| 1 | 1 | 1 | 1 | 1 | 1 | 1 | 1 |

Here the columns for $x + (y \, . \, z)$ and $(x + y) \, . \, (x + z)$ are identical. So the law is valid. The (*ii*) Distributive law holds true by duality principle.

### 3.8.9 Absorption Law

According to this law

(*a*) (*i*) $x + x \, . \, y = x$ (*ii*) $x \, . \, (x + y) = x$

(*b*) (*i*) $x + \overline{x} \, . \, y = x + y$ (*ii*) $x \, . \, (\overline{x} + y) = x \, . \, y$

(*c*) (*i*) $x \, . \, ((x + y) + z) = x$ (*ii*) $x + ((x \, . \, y) \, . \, z) = x$

(*d*) (*i*) $(x + y) \, . \, (\overline{x} + z) \, . \, (y + z) = (x + y) \, . \, (\overline{x} + z)$

(*ii*) $(x \, . \, y) + (\overline{x} \, .. \, z) + (y \, . \, z) = (x \, . \, y) + (\overline{x} \, . \, z)$

(*a*) (*i*) $x + x \, . \, y = x$

| $x$ | $y$ | $x \, . \, y$ | $x + x \, . \, y$ |
|---|---|---|---|
| 0 | 0 | 0 | 0 |
| 0 | 1 | 0 | 0 |
| 1 | 0 | 0 | 1 |
| 1 | 1 | 1 | 1 |

Using the duality principle the second form is

$$x \, . \, (x + y) = x$$

(*b*) (*i*) $x + \overline{x} \cdot y = x + y$

| $x$ | $y$ | $\overline{x}$ | $\overline{x} \cdot y$ | $x + \overline{x} \cdot y$ | $x + y$ |
|---|---|---|---|---|---|
| 0 | 0 | 1 | 0 | 0 | 0 |
| 0 | 1 | 1 | 1 | 1 | 1 |
| 1 | 0 | 0 | 0 | 1 | 1 |
| 1 | 1 | 0 | 0 | 1 | 1 |

From the last two columns (which are identical) the law holds.

Let us prove the above **absorption law algebraically:**

$x + \overline{x}y = (x + \overline{x}) \cdot (x + y)$ Using Distributive law

$= 1 \cdot (x + y)$ Using law of complementarity

$= x + y$ Identity element

Using the duality principle the second form is

$$x \cdot (\overline{x} + y) = x \cdot y$$

(*c*) $x \cdot ((x + y) + z) = x$

| $x$ | $y$ | $z$ | $(x + y)$ | $(x + y) + z$ | $x \cdot ((x + y) + z)$ |
|---|---|---|---|---|---|
| 0 | 0 | 0 | 0 | 0 | 0 |
| 0 | 0 | 1 | 0 | 1 | 0 |
| 0 | 1 | 0 | 1 | 1 | 0 |
| 0 | 1 | 1 | 1 | 1 | 0 |
| 1 | 0 | 0 | 1 | 1 | 1 |
| 1 | 0 | 1 | 1 | 1 | 1 |
| 1 | 1 | 0 | 1 | 1 | 1 |
| 1 | 1 | 1 | 1 | 1 | 1 |

Using the duality principle the second form is

$$x + ((x \cdot y) \cdot z) = x$$

(*d*) (*i*) $(x + y) \cdot (\overline{x} + z) \cdot (y + z) = (x + y) \cdot (\overline{x} + z)$

| $x$ | $y$ | $z$ | $(x + y)$ | $\overline{x}$ | $(\overline{x} + z)$ | $(x + y) \cdot (\overline{x} + z)$ | $(y + z)$ | $(x + y)(\overline{x} + z) \cdot (y + z)$ |
|---|---|---|---|---|---|---|---|---|
| 0 | 0 | 0 | 0 | 1 | 1 | 0 | 0 | 0 |
| 0 | 0 | 1 | 0 | 1 | 1 | 0 | 1 | 0 |
| 0 | 1 | 0 | 1 | 1 | 1 | 1 | 1 | 1 |

| | | | | | | | | |
|---|---|---|---|---|---|---|---|---|
| 0 | 1 | 1 | 1 | 1 | 1 | 1 | 1 | 1 |
| 1 | 0 | 0 | 1 | 0 | 0 | 0 | 0 | 0 |
| 1 | 0 | 1 | 1 | 0 | 1 | 1 | 1 | 1 |
| 1 | 1 | 0 | 1 | 0 | 0 | 0 | 1 | 0 |
| 1 | 1 | 1 | 1 | 0 | 1 | 1 | 1 | 1 |

Columns $(x + y) . (\bar{x} + z) . (y + z)$ and $(x + y) . (\bar{x} + z)$ are identical. So the law holds.

Using the duality principle the second form is

$$(x . y) + (\bar{x} . z) + (y . z) = (x . y) + (\bar{x} . z).$$

### 3.8.10 Involution Law

This law states that $(\bar{\bar{x}}) = x$

| $x$ | $\bar{x}$ | $(\bar{\bar{x}})$ |
|---|---|---|
| 0 | 1 | 0 |
| 1 | 0 | 1 |

Let us prove the Involution law algebraically:

$\bar{\bar{x}} = \bar{\bar{x}} + 0$ Identity element

$= \bar{\bar{x}} + (\bar{x} . x)$ Using law of complementarity

$= (\bar{\bar{x}} + x) . (\bar{\bar{x}} + \bar{x})$ Using Distributive law

$= (\bar{\bar{x}} + x . 1$ Using law of complementarity

$= \bar{\bar{x}} + x$ Identity element

and $\bar{\bar{x}} = \bar{\bar{x}} . 1$ Identity element

$= \bar{\bar{x}} . (x + \bar{x})$ Using law of complementarity

$= (\bar{\bar{x}} . x) + (\bar{\bar{x}} . \bar{x})$ Using Distributive law

$= \bar{\bar{x}} . x + 0$ Using law of complementarity

$= \bar{\bar{x}} . x$ Identity element

Putting $\bar{\bar{x}} = \bar{\bar{x}} . x$ in the right hand side of $\bar{\bar{x}} = \bar{\bar{x}} + x$, we have

$\bar{\bar{x}} = \bar{\bar{x}} . x + x$

$= x + \bar{\bar{x}} . x$ Using Commutative law

$= x + x . \bar{\bar{x}}$ Using Commutative law

$= x$ Using Absorption law ($\because x + x . y = x$)

### 3.8.11 De Morgan's Law

It is a very interesting and important law which is useful in designing logic networks. This law states that:

(*i*) $\overline{(x + y)} = \overline{x} \cdot \overline{y}$ (*ii*) $\overline{(x \cdot y)} = \overline{x} + \overline{y}$

(*i*) $\overline{(x + y)} = \overline{x} \cdot \overline{y}$

| $x$ | $y$ | $x + y$ | $\overline{(x + y)}$ | $\overline{x}$ | $\overline{y}$ | $\overline{x} \cdot \overline{y}$ |
|---|---|---|---|---|---|---|
| 0 | 0 | 0 | 1 | 1 | 1 | 1 |
| 0 | 1 | 1 | 0 | 1 | 0 | 0 |
| 1 | 0 | 1 | 0 | 0 | 1 | 0 |
| 1 | 1 | 1 | 0 | 0 | 0 | 0 |

Columns $(\overline{x + y})$ and $\overline{x} \cdot \overline{y}$ are identical. So the law holds. Using the duality principle the second form is $\overline{(x \cdot y)} = \overline{x} + \overline{y}$.

Let us prove the De Morgan's law algebraically:

We shall show that the complement of $x + y$ is $\overline{x} \cdot \overline{y}$ by showing that

$$(x + y) + (\overline{x} \cdot \overline{y}) = 1 \quad \text{and} \quad (x + y) \cdot (\overline{x} \cdot \overline{y}) = 0$$

$(x + y) + \overline{x} \cdot \overline{y} = ((x + y) + \overline{x}) \cdot ((x + y) + \overline{y})$ Using Distributive law

$= (x + (y + \overline{x})) \cdot (x + (y + \overline{y}))$ Using Associative law

$= (x + (\overline{x} + y)) \cdot (x + (y + \overline{y}))$ Using Commutative law

$= (x + (\overline{x} + y)) \cdot (x + 1)$ Using law of complementarity

$= ((x + \overline{x}) + y) \cdot (x + 1)$ Using Associative law

$= (1 + y) \cdot (x + 1)$ Using law of complementarity

$= (y + 1) \cdot (x + 1)$ Using Commutative law

$= 1 \cdot 1$ Dominance of 1

$= 1$ Identity element

$(x + y) \cdot (\overline{x} \cdot \overline{y}) = (x \cdot (\overline{x} \cdot \overline{y})) + (y \cdot (\overline{x} \cdot \overline{y}))$ Using Distributive law

$= ((x \cdot \overline{x}) \cdot \overline{y}) + ((y \cdot \overline{x}) \cdot \overline{y})$ Using Associative law

$= (0 \cdot \overline{y}) + ((y \cdot \overline{x}) \cdot \overline{y})$ Using law of complementarity

$= (\overline{y} \cdot 0) + ((\overline{x} \cdot y) \cdot \overline{y})$ Using Commutative law

$= 0 + ((\overline{x} \cdot y) \cdot \overline{y})$ Dominance of 0

$= (\overline{x} \cdot y) \cdot \overline{y}$ Identity element and commutative law

$= \overline{x} \cdot (y \cdot \overline{y})$ Using Associative law

$= \overline{x} \cdot 0$ Using law of complementarity

$= 0$ Dominance of 0

The utility of De Morgan's Law will be observed when NAND and NOR gate applications will be studied.

When 3 inputs are involved. De Morgan's Law states that

(*i*) $\overline{(x + y + z)} = \bar{x} . \bar{y} . \bar{z}$ (*ii*) $\overline{(x . y . z)} = \bar{x} + \bar{y} + \bar{z}$

If 4 inputs are used then De Morgan's Law is written as

(*i*) $\overline{(x_1 + x_2 + x_3 + x_4)} = \bar{x}_1 . \bar{x}_2 . \bar{x}_3 . \bar{x}_4$

(*ii*) $\overline{(x_1 . x_2 . x_3 . x_4)} = \bar{x}_1 + \bar{x}_2 + \bar{x}_3 + \bar{x}_4$

From (*i*), we can say that the complement of a sum equals the product of complements.

From (*ii*), we can say that the complement of a product equals the sum of the complements.

So, in general we have

(*i*) $\overline{(x_1 + x_2 + x_3 + .... + x_n)} = \bar{x}_1 . \bar{x}_2 . \bar{x}_3 ...... \bar{x}_n$

(*ii*) $\overline{x_1 . x_2 . x_3 ...... x_n} = \bar{x}_1 + \bar{x}_2 + \bar{x}_3 ...... + \bar{x}_n$.

## 3.9 ALGEBRAIC TECHNIQUE FOR VERIFICATION

The validity of boolean expression can be checked by using laws of Boolean algebra. The following examples illustrate this:

**Example 1.** *Verify* $X . Y' + Y' . Z = X. Y' . Z + X . Y' . Z' + X' . Y' . Z$ *algebraically.*

**Solution.**

$$\text{L.H.S.} = X . Y' + Y' . Z$$
$$= X . Y'. (Z + Z') + (X + X') . Y' . Z \quad [\because Z + Z' = 1, X + X' = 1]$$
$$= X . Y' . Z + X . Y'. Z' + X . Y' . Z + X' . Y' . Z$$
$$= X . Y' . Z + X . Y' . Z' + X' . Y' . Z = \text{R.H.S.} \quad [\because X . Y'. Z + X . Y' . Z = X . Y'. Z]$$

**Example 2.** *Prove* $XY+YZ + YZ' = Y$*, algebraically.*

**Solution.** L.H.S.

$$= XY + YZ + YZ'$$
$$= XY + Y (Z + Z')$$
$$= XY + Y \quad [\because Z + Z' = 1]$$
$$= (X + 1) = Y = \text{R.H.S.} \quad [\because X + 1 = 1]$$

**Example 3.** *Prove* $XY + YZ + Y'Z = XY + Z$*, algebraically.*

**Solution.**

$$\text{L.H.S.} = XY + YZ + Y'Z$$
$$= XY + (Y + Y') Z$$
$$= XY + Z = \text{R.H.S.} \quad [\because Y + Y' = 1]$$

**Example 4.** *Prove algebraically* $X . Y + X' . Z + Y . Z = X . Y + X' . Z$.

**Solution.**

$$\text{L.H.S.} = X . Y + X' . Z + Y . Z$$
$$= X . Y + X' . Z + (X + X') . Y . Z \quad [X + X' = 1]$$

$= X . Y + X' . Z + X . Y . Z + X' . Y . Z$

$= X . Y + X . Y . Z + X' . Z + X' . Y . Z$

$= X . Y (1 + Z) + X' . Z (1 + Y)$

$= X . Y + X' . Z = \text{R.H.S.}$ $[\because 1 + Z = 1, 1 + Y = 1]$

**Example 5.** *Prove algebraically* $x'y'z' + x'y'z + x'yz + x'yz' + xy'z' + xy'z = x' + y'$.

**Solution.** L.H.S. $= x'y'z' + x'y'z + x'yz + x'yz' + xy'z' + xy'z$

$= x'y'(z' + z) + x'y(z + z') + xy'(z' + z)$

$= x'y' + x'y + xy'$ $[\because z' + z = 1]$

$= x'(y' + y) + xy'$ $[\because y' + y = 1]$

$= x' + xy'$

$= x' + y' = \text{R.H.S.}$

$[\because x' + xy' = x' + y'$ (Absorption Law)]

**Example 6.** *Prove by algebraic method* $\bar{x}\bar{y}\bar{z} + \bar{x}\bar{y}z + x\bar{y}z = \bar{y}(\bar{x} + z)$.

**Solution.** L.H.S. $= \bar{x}\bar{y}\bar{z} + \bar{x}\bar{y}z + x\bar{y}z$

$= \bar{x}\bar{y}(\bar{z} + z) + x\bar{y}z + \bar{x}\bar{y} = x\bar{y}z$ $[\because \bar{z} + z = 1]$

$= \bar{y}(\bar{x} + xz)$

$= \bar{y}(\bar{x} + z) = \text{R.H.S.}$ $[\because \bar{x} + xz = \bar{x} + z$

(Absorption Law)]

**Example 7.** *Verify* $x\bar{y} + \bar{x}y = \overline{(xy + \bar{x}\bar{y})}$ *algebraically.*

**Solution.** R.H.S. $= \overline{(xy + \bar{x}\bar{y})}$

$= \overline{xy} . \overline{\bar{x}\bar{y}}$ [De Morgan's Law]

$= (\bar{x} + \bar{y}) . (\bar{\bar{x}} + \bar{\bar{y}}) = (\bar{x} + \bar{y}) . (x + y)$

$= \bar{x}x + \bar{x}y + \bar{y}x + \bar{y}y$

$= \bar{x}y + x\bar{y}$ $[\because x\bar{x} = 0, y\bar{y} = 0]$

$= x\bar{y} + \bar{x}y = \text{R.H.S.}$

**Example 8.** *Verify* $(x + y + z)\,\overline{(xyz)} = x\bar{y} + y\bar{z} + z\bar{x}$ *algebraically.*

**Solution.** L.H.S. $= (x + y + z)\,\overline{(xyz)}$

$= (x + y + z)(\bar{x} + \bar{y} + \bar{z})$ [De Morgan's Law]

$= x\bar{x} + x\bar{y} + x\bar{z} + y\bar{x} + y\bar{y} + y\bar{z} + z\bar{x} + z\bar{y} + z\bar{z}$

$$= x\bar{y} + x\bar{z} + \bar{x}y + y\bar{z} + \bar{x}\bar{z} + \bar{y}z$$

$$[\because x\bar{x} = 0,\ y\bar{y} = 0,\ z\bar{z} = 0]$$

$$= \left(x\bar{y} + x\bar{z} + y\bar{z}\right) + \bar{x}y + \bar{x}\bar{z} + \bar{y}z$$

$$= x\bar{y} + y\bar{z} + \bar{x}y + \bar{x}\bar{z} + \bar{y}z$$

$$[\because x\bar{y} + y\bar{z} + x\bar{z} = x\bar{y} + y\bar{z} \text{ (Absorption Law)}]$$

$$= x\bar{y} + \left(y\bar{z} + \bar{x}y + \bar{x}\bar{z}\right) + \bar{y}z$$

$$= x\bar{y} + y\bar{z} + \bar{x}\bar{z} + \bar{y}z$$

$$[\because y\bar{z} + \bar{x}\bar{z} + \bar{x}y = y\bar{z} + \bar{x}\bar{z} \text{ (Absorption Law)}]$$

$$= \left(x\bar{y} + \bar{x}\bar{z} + \bar{y}z\right) + y\bar{z}$$

$$= x\bar{y} + \bar{x}\bar{z} + y\bar{z} = \text{R.H.S.}$$

$$[\because x\bar{y} + \bar{x}\bar{z} + \bar{y}z = x\bar{y} + \bar{x}\bar{z} \text{ (Absorption Law)}]$$

**Example 9.** *Prove* $x\bar{y} + y\bar{z} + z\bar{x} = \bar{x}y + \bar{y}z + \bar{z}x$, *algebraically.*

**Solution.** L.H.S. $= x\bar{y} + y\bar{z} + z\bar{x}$

$$= x\bar{y}\left(z+\bar{z}\right) + \left(x+\bar{x}\right)y\bar{z} + z\bar{x}\left(y+\bar{y}\right) \quad [\because \bar{z} + z = 1]$$

$$= x\bar{y}z + x\,\bar{y}\,\bar{z} + xy\bar{z} + \bar{x}\,y\,\bar{z} + \bar{x}\,y\,z + \bar{x}\,\bar{y}\,z$$

$$= \bar{x}\,y\,\bar{z} + \bar{x}\,y\,z + \bar{y}\,z\,x + \bar{y}\,z\,\bar{x} + \bar{z}\,x\,\bar{y} + \bar{z}\,x\,y$$

$$= \bar{x}\,y(\bar{z} + z) + \bar{y}\,z(x + \bar{x}) + \bar{z}\,x(\bar{y} + y)$$

$$= \bar{x}y + \bar{y}z + \bar{z}x = \text{R.H.S.}$$

**Example 10.** *Prove* $(\bar{a} + \bar{b}) . (\bar{a} + b) . (a + \bar{b}) = \bar{a} . \bar{b}$.

**Solution.** L.H.S. $= (\bar{a} + \bar{b}) . (\bar{a} + b) . (a + \bar{b})$

$$= (\bar{a} + \bar{b} . b) . (a + \bar{b})$$

$$[\because a + bc = (a + b) . (a + c) \text{ Distributive Law}]$$

$$= (\bar{a} + 0) . (a + \bar{b}) \quad [\because \bar{b} . b = 0]$$

$$= \bar{a} . (a + \bar{b}) = \bar{a} . a + \bar{a} . \bar{b}$$

$$= \bar{a} . \bar{b} = \text{R.H.S.} \quad [\because \bar{a} . a = 0]$$

## 3.10 CANONICAL FORMS OF BOOLEAN EXPRESSIONS

Logical functions are generally expressed in terms of different combinations of logical variables with their true forms as well the complement forms. For binary logic values obtained by the logical functions and logic variables are in binary form. An arbitrary logic function can be expressed in the following forms:

(*i*) Sum of Products (SOP)

(*ii*) Product of Sums (POS)

The *standard form* of the Boolean function is, when it is expressed in sum of products or products of sums fashion. However, Boolean functions are also sometimes expressed in nonstandard forms (*i.e.*, neither a sum of products form nor a product of sums form). These nonstandard forms can be converted to a standard form with the help of various. Boolean properties. Let us understand the above mentioned concepts in detail:

Boolean expressions having a single variable or its complement are called **literals.** For example, A or $\bar{B}$ or X. These literals when evaluated as Boolean expressions take the value 1 on half of the combinations of variables. For example, if $\bar{A}$ is a Boolean expression over A, B and C, then out of 8 combinations, it takes value 1 four times.

**Minterm.** *A Minterm is n variables $x_1, x_2, ..., x_n$ is defined as a product of n literals, where each literal has a different variable from $\{x_1, x_2, ..., x_n\}$, that is, in a minterm, each variable must appear once, either as it is or complemented.* Every minterm has the value 1 for exactly one combination of variables and the value 0 for rest of the combinations.

There are four minterms of two variables A and B as shown in the following table alongwith the numbers 0–3 assigned to them:

| *A* | *B* | *Minterm* | *Number Assigned* | *Shorthand Notation* |
|---|---|---|---|---|
| 0 | 0 | $\bar{A}\bar{B}$ | 0 | $m_0$ |
| 0 | 1 | $\bar{A}B$ | 1 | $m_1$ |
| 1 | 0 | $A\bar{B}$ | 2 | $m_2$ |
| 1 | 1 | AB | 3 | $m_3$ |

The logical products $\bar{A}\bar{B}$, $\bar{A}B$, $A\bar{B}$ and AB are called **fundamental products** because each gives a high output for its corresponding input. For example, $\bar{A}\bar{B}$ is a 1 when A is 0 and B is 0, $\bar{A}B$ is a 1 when A is 0 and B is 1, and so on.

The eight minterms corresponding to three variables A, B and C alongwith the numbers 0–7 assigned to them are shown in the following table:

| *A* | *B* | *C* | *Minterm* | *Number Assigned* | *Shorthand Notation* |
|---|---|---|---|---|---|
| 0 | 0 | 0 | $\bar{A}\bar{B}\bar{C}$ | 0 | $m_0$ |
| 0 | 0 | 1 | $\bar{A}\bar{B}C$ | 1 | $m_1$ |
| 0 | 1 | 0 | $\bar{A}B\bar{C}$ | 2 | $m_2$ |
| 0 | 1 | 1 | $\bar{A}BC$ | 3 | $m_3$ |

| | | | | | |
|---|---|---|---|---|---|
| 1 | 0 | 0 | $A\overline{B}\overline{C}$ | 4 | $m_4$ |
| 1 | 0 | 1 | $A\overline{B}C$ | 5 | $m_5$ |
| 1 | 1 | 0 | $AB\overline{C}$ | 6 | $m_6$ |
| 1 | 1 | 1 | $ABC$ | 7 | $m_7$ |

From the above table it is clear from the values of the variables that the value of variable 0 represents the literal in complemented form, while the other literals are not.

When there are 4 input variables, there are 16 possible input conditions i.e. 0000 to 1111.

The corresponding fundamental products are from $\overline{A}\overline{B}\overline{C}\overline{D}$ through ABCD. The name fundamental product is because each produces a high output for its corresponding input. The 16 minterms of four variables A, B, C and D and with numbers 0–15 assigned to them are illustrated in the following table:

| *A* | *B* | *C* | *D* | *Minterm* | *Number Assigned* | *Shorthand Notation* |
|---|---|---|---|---|---|---|
| 0 | 0 | 0 | 0 | $\overline{A}\overline{B}\overline{C}\overline{D}$ | 0 | $m_0$ |
| 0 | 0 | 0 | 1 | $\overline{A}\overline{B}\overline{C}D$ | 1 | $m_1$ |
| 0 | 0 | 1 | 0 | $\overline{A}\overline{B}C\overline{D}$ | 2 | $m_2$ |
| 0 | 0 | 1 | 1 | $\overline{A}\overline{B}CD$ | 3 | $m_3$ |
| 0 | 1 | 0 | 0 | $\overline{A}B\overline{C}\overline{D}$ | 4 | $m_4$ |
| 0 | 1 | 0 | 1 | $\overline{A}B\overline{C}D$ | 5 | $m_5$ |
| 0 | 1 | 1 | 0 | $\overline{A}BC\overline{D}$ | 6 | $m_6$ |
| 0 | 1 | 1 | 1 | $\overline{A}BCD$ | 7 | $m_7$ |
| 1 | 0 | 0 | 0 | $A\overline{B}\overline{C}\overline{D}$ | 8 | $m_8$ |
| 1 | 0 | 0 | 1 | $A\overline{B}\overline{C}D$ | 9 | $m_9$ |
| 1 | 0 | 1 | 0 | $A\overline{B}C\overline{D}$ | 10 | $m_{10}$ |
| 1 | 0 | 1 | 1 | $A\overline{B}CD$ | 11 | $m_{11}$ |
| 1 | 1 | 0 | 0 | $AB\overline{C}\overline{D}$ | 12 | $m_{12}$ |
| 1 | 1 | 0 | 1 | $AB\overline{C}D$ | 13 | $m_{13}$ |
| 1 | 1 | 1 | 0 | $ABC\overline{D}$ | 14 | $m_{14}$ |
| 1 | 1 | 1 | 1 | $ABCD$ | 15 | $m_{15}$ |

### 3.10.1 Obtaining SOP Form from the Truth Table

Consider a Boolean function $f$ of two Boolean variable A, B such that

$$f(A, B) = 0 \text{ or } 1$$

for each of the $2^2 = 4$ possible combinations of A and B. There are $2^4 = 16$ Boolean functions of two variables. Similarly for 3 variables there are $2^8 = 256$ Boolean functions and for 4 variables we have $2^{16} = 65536$ Boolean functions. Here 4, 8, 16 denote the possible number of outputs for 2, 3 and 4 variables respectively, which in turn can have $2^4$, $2^8$ and $2^{16}$ Boolean functions for the different output combinations.

*For writing the expression from a truth table, the minterms are listed for each high (1) output and by ORing these products we get the Boolean function.* The Boolean expression represented purely as sum of minterms or product terms is known to be in **Canonical Sum-of-Products form.**

**Example 1.** *Write the SOP form of a Boolean Function F, which is represented by the following truth table:*

| *A* | *B* | *C* | *F* |
|---|---|---|---|
| 0 | 0 | 0 | 1 |
| 0 | 0 | 1 | 0 |
| 0 | 1 | 0 | 0 |
| 0 | 1 | 1 | 1 |
| 1 | 0 | 0 | 0 |
| 1 | 0 | 1 | 0 |
| 1 | 1 | 0 | 1 |
| 1 | 1 | 1 | 1 |

**Solution.** The last column of the truth table gives the values of F. For each occurrence of 1 in this column we get a minterm corresponding to that row. Thus, for the expression F, we get 4 minterms for row numbers 1, 4, 7 and 8 giving the minterms canonical form or sum of products form

$$F = \bar{A}\bar{B}\bar{C} + \bar{A}BC + AB\bar{C} + ABC.$$

**Example 2.** *Given the following truth table, write the sum of products form of the function F(x,y,z):*

| *x* | *y* | *z* | *F* |
|---|---|---|---|
| 0 | 0 | 0 | 0 |
| 0 | 0 | 1 | 1 |
| 0 | 1 | 0 | 1 |
| 0 | 1 | 1 | 0 |

| | | | |
|---|---|---|---|
| 1 | 0 | 0 | 1 |
| 1 | 0 | 1 | 0 |
| 1 | 1 | 0 | 0 |
| 1 | 1 | 1 | 1 |

**Solution.** The last column of the truth table gives the values of F. For each occurrence of 1 in this column we get a minterm corresponding to that row. Thus, for the expression F, we get 4 minterms for row numbers 2, 3, 5 and 8 giving the minterms canonical form or sum of products form

$$F = \bar{x}\bar{y}z + \bar{x}y\bar{z} + x\bar{y}\bar{z} + xyz.$$

**Wkat is a Maxterm?**

*A maxterm in n variables $x_1, x_2, ..., x_n$ is defined as a sum of n literals, where each literal has a different variable from $\{x_1, x_2, ..., x_n\}$, that is, in a maxterm each variable must appear once, either as it is or complemented.* If the value of the input variable is 1, its complement is taken otherwise the variable is taken as it is.

For example,

If A = 0, B = 1 then the maxterm is $A + \bar{B}$

For three input variables A, B and C the maxterm can be obtained as follows:

| *A* | *B* | *C* | *Maxterm* | *Number Assigned* | *Notation* |
|---|---|---|---|---|---|
| 0 | 0 | 0 | $A + B + C$ | 0 | $M_0$ |
| 0 | 0 | 1 | $A + B + \bar{C}$ | 1 | $M_1$ |
| 0 | 1 | 0 | $A + \bar{B} + C$ | 2 | $M_2$ |
| 0 | 1 | 1 | $A + \bar{B} + \bar{C}$ | 3 | $M_3$ |
| 1 | 0 | 0 | $\bar{A} + B + C$ | 4 | $M_4$ |
| 1 | 0 | 1 | $\bar{A} + B + \bar{C}$ | 5 | $M_5$ |
| 1 | 1 | 0 | $\bar{A} + \bar{B} + C$ | 6 | $M_6$ |
| 1 | 1 | 1 | $\bar{A} + \bar{B} + \bar{C}$ | 7 | $M_7$ |

Maxterms can also be written as M (capital M) with a subscript which is decimal equivalent of the given input combination as shown in the above table. The number of maxterms for 2 and 4 variables are 4 and 16 respectively.

### 3.10.2 Obtaining POS Form from the Truth Table

*For writing the expression from a truth table, the maxterms are listed for each low (0) output and by ANDing these sums we get the Boolean function.* The Boolean expression represented purely as product of maxterms or sum terms is known to be in **Canonical Product-of-Sum form.**

**Example 1.** *Write the POS form of a Boolean Function F, which is represented by the following truth table:*

| *X* | *Y* | *Z* | *F* |
|---|---|---|---|
| *0* | *0* | *0* | *1* |
| *0* | *0* | *1* | *1* |
| *0* | *1* | *0* | *0* |
| *0* | *1* | *1* | *1* |
| *1* | *0* | *0* | *0* |
| *1* | *0* | *1* | *1* |
| *1* | *1* | *0* | *0* |
| *1* | *1* | *1* | *0* |

**Solution.** The last column of the truth table gives the values of F. For each occurrence of 0 in this column we get a maxterm corresponding to that row. Thus for the expression F, we get 4 maxterms for row numbers 3, 5, 7 and 8 giving the product of sums form

$$F = (X + \bar{Y} + Z) . (\bar{X} + Y + Z) . (\bar{X} + \bar{Y} + Z) . (\bar{X} + \bar{Y} + \bar{Z}).$$

**Example 2.** *Write the POS form of a Boolean Function F (U, V, W), which is represented in a truth table as follows:*

| *U* | *V* | *W* | *F* |
|---|---|---|---|
| *0* | *0* | *0* | *0* |
| *0* | *0* | *1* | *0* |
| *0* | *1* | *0* | *1* |
| *0* | *1* | *1* | *0* |
| *1* | *0* | *0* | *1* |
| *1* | *0* | *1* | *0* |
| *1* | *1* | *0* | *1* |
| *1* | *1* | *1* | *1* |

**Solution.** The last column of the truth table gives the values of F. For each occurrence of 0 in this column we get a maxterm corresponding to that row. Thus for the expression F, we get 4 maxterms for row numbers 1, 2, 4 and 6 giving the product of sums form

$$F = (U + V + W) . (U + V + \bar{W}) . (U + \bar{V} + \bar{W}) . (\bar{U} + V + \bar{W}).$$

### 3.10.3 Sum Term and Product Term

*Sum term does not necessarily mean that all the variables must be present whereas in a* **maxterm** *all variables must be present.* For example, For a 3 variables function F(A, B, C): $A + \overline{B}, A + C, \overline{B} + \overline{C}$ etc. are sum terms whereas $A + B + C, A + B + \overline{C}, \overline{A} + \overline{B} + \overline{C}$ etc. are maxterms. *Product term does not necessarily mean that all the variables must be present whereas in a* **minterm** *all variables must be present.* For example, F or a 3 variables function F(*x, y, z*): $\overline{x}\,\overline{y}\,\overline{z}, \overline{x}\,\overline{y}z$, $xyz$ etc. are minterms whereas $x\overline{y}, \overline{x}\,\overline{y}, \overline{x}z$ etc. are product terms only.

Similarly, *a* **Canonical** *SOP or POS expression must have all the minterms or maxterms whereas a simple SOP or POS expression can just have product terms or sum terms.*

## 3.11 DON'T CARE CONDITIONS

In certain digital systems, some input combinations never occur during the process of a normal operation because those input conditions are guaranteed never to occur. Such input combinations are called *Don't Care Conditions.* The function output may be either 1 or 0 and these functions are called incompletely specified functions. These input combinations can be plotted on the Karnaugh map for further simplification of the function. The *Don't Care Conditions* are represented by *d* or X or $\phi$.

When an incompletely specified function, *i.e.*, a function with don't care conditions is simplified to obtain minimal SOP expression, the value 1 can be assigned to the selected don't care conditions. This is done to form the groups like pair, quad, octet etc., for further simplification. In each case, choice depends only on need to achieve simplification. Similarly, selected don't care conditions may be assumed as 0's to form groups of 0's for obtaining the POS expression.

## 3.12 SIMPLIFICATION TECHNIQUES OF BOOLEAN FUNCTIONS

*The Boolean expressions or functions are used in the design of switching circuits, so it is desirable to use an expression that requires the minimum circuitary.* For this we can obtain a minimal expression for representing a given expression. The term **minimal** is understood to mean minimal only with respect to a particular form of expression. We may obtain an expression simpler than the earlier one if we write it in other form. For example,

$$E = AB + A\overline{C}$$

which is in minimal SOP form. However,

$$E = A(B + \overline{C})$$

is simpler, but it is not in the SOP form.

There are three techniques for simplification of Boolean expression, which are as follows:

(*i*) Algebraic Simplification Technique

(*ii*) Karnaugh-Map (K-Map) Simplification Technique

(*iii*) Quine-McCluskey Tabular Simplification Technique.

### 3.12.1 Algebraic Simplification Technique

The Algebraic simplification technique helps in minimization of expressions. The Boolean postulates and other laws are very useful in the process of simplification.

**Example 1.** *Simplify* $F = \bar{x}\bar{y}\bar{z} + \bar{x}y\bar{z} + x\bar{y}\bar{z} + xy\bar{z}$.

**Solution.**

$$\begin{aligned} F &= \bar{x}\bar{y}\bar{z} + \bar{x}y\bar{z} + x\bar{y}\bar{z} + xy\bar{z} \\ &= \bar{x}\bar{z}(\bar{y} + y) + x\bar{z}(\bar{y} + y) \\ &= \bar{x}\bar{z} + x\bar{z} && [\because\ y + \bar{y} = 1] \\ &= \bar{z}(\bar{x} + x) \\ &= \bar{z} && [\because\ x + \bar{x} = 1] \end{aligned}$$

**Example 2.** *Simplify* $F = \bar{x}y\bar{z} + \bar{x}yz + xy\bar{z}$.

**Solution.**

$$\begin{aligned} F &= \bar{x}y\bar{z} + \bar{x}yz + xy\bar{z} \\ &= \bar{x}y(\bar{z} + z) + xy\bar{z} \\ &= \bar{x}y + xy\bar{z} && [\because\ \bar{z} + z = 1] \\ &= y(\bar{x} + x\bar{z}) \\ &= y(\bar{x} + \bar{z}) && [\because\ \bar{x} + x\bar{z} = \bar{x} + \bar{z}] \end{aligned}$$

**Example 3.** *Simplify* $F = \bar{x}\bar{y}\bar{z} + \bar{x}yz + xyz + x\bar{y}\bar{z} + x\bar{y}z$.

**Solution.**

$$\begin{aligned} F &= \bar{x}\bar{y}\bar{z} + \bar{x}yz + xyz + x\bar{y}\bar{z} + x\bar{y}z \\ &= \bar{x}\bar{y}\bar{z} + (\bar{x} + x)yz + x\bar{y}(\bar{z} + z) \\ &= \bar{x}\bar{y}\bar{z} + yz + x\bar{y} && [\because\ \bar{x} + x = 1, \bar{z} + z = 1] \\ &= x\bar{y} + \bar{x}\bar{y}\bar{z} + yz \\ &= \bar{y}(x + \bar{x}\bar{z}) + yz \\ &= \bar{y}(x + \bar{z}) + yz && [\because\ x + \bar{x}\bar{z} = x + \bar{z}] \\ &= x\bar{y} + \bar{y}\bar{z} + yz. \end{aligned}$$

**Example 4.** *Minimize the following Boolean function:*

$$Q = (x + y + z) \cdot (x + y + \bar{z}) \cdot (\bar{x} + y + z) \cdot (\bar{x} + y + \bar{z}) \cdot (\bar{x} + \bar{y} + \bar{z}).$$

**Solution.** $Q = (x + y + z) \cdot (x + y + \bar{z}) \cdot (\bar{x} + y + z) \cdot (\bar{x} + y + \bar{z}) \cdot (\bar{x} + \bar{y} + \bar{z})$

Let $x + y = A$ and $\bar{x} + y = B$

$$\begin{aligned} \therefore\quad Q &= (A + z) \cdot (A + \bar{z}) \cdot (B + z) \cdot (B + \bar{z}) \cdot (\bar{x} + \bar{y} + \bar{z}) \\ &= (A + z\bar{z}) \cdot (B + z\bar{z}) \cdot (\bar{x} + \bar{y} + \bar{z}) && [\because (A + z) \cdot (A + \bar{z}) = A + z \cdot \bar{z}] \\ &= (A + 0) \cdot (B + 0) \cdot (\bar{x} + \bar{y} + \bar{z}) && [\because z\bar{z} = 0] \\ &= A \cdot B \cdot (\bar{x} + \bar{y} + \bar{z}) \\ &= (x + y) \cdot (\bar{x} + y) \cdot (\bar{x} + \bar{y} + \bar{z}) \end{aligned}$$

$= (y + x\overline{x}) \cdot (\overline{x} + \overline{y} + \overline{z})$ $\quad [\because (y + x) \cdot (y + \overline{x}) = y + x\overline{x}]$

$= (y + 0) \cdot (\overline{x} + \overline{y} + \overline{z})$

$= y\overline{x} + \overline{y}y + y\overline{z} = \overline{x}y + y\overline{z}$ $\quad [\because y\overline{y} = 0]$

Though Boolean Expressions can be simplified usin Algebraic simplification technique but it can't always gurantee its simplification in the minimal form.

### 3.12.2 Karnaugh Map (K-map) Simplification Technique

Many engineers and technicians do not simplify equations with Boolean algebra. Instead, they use a method based on **Karnaugh maps.** *Maurice Karnaugh developed Karnaugh maps which are used for minimizing Boolean expressions of few variables. These maps are also known as* **Veitch diagrams.**

**Karnaugh Map:** *It is a graphical representation of the truth table of the given expression.*

It consists of a rectangle having squares inside, where each square denotes a particular combination of all the variables either as it is or complemented, *i.e.*, each square corresponds to a minterm or maxterm. K-Maps for 1, 2, 3 and 4 variables have 2, 4, 8 and 16 squares respectively. We put values 1 or 0 of the expression in the square corresponding to a particular term.

*In a K-Map the contigeous squares differ in the values of exactly one variable which may change from 0 to 1 or from 1 to 0. Also the squares on the opposite edges are considered contigeous and the four corner squares are considered contiguous.* Figure 3.4 shows the K-Maps for one, two, three and four variables representing minterms:

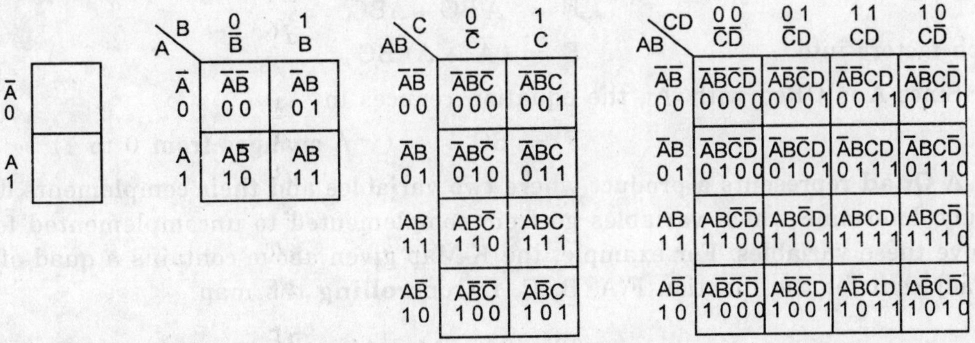


**Fig. 3.4:** K-Map for One, Two, Three and Four variables representing minterms.

*The numbers written on the top (horizontally) and left side (vertically) of the 4 variable K-map differ only at one place while moving from left to right or top to bottom, that is, 00, 01, 11, 10. This coding scheme is known as Gray coding. In this binary code successive numbers differ only at one place.*

The following terms must be clearly understood for K-Map simplification in SOP form:

**Pair.** A group of two adjacent 1s on a K-Map. These 1s may be horizontally or vertically aligned.

**Quad.** A group of four adjacent 1s on a K-Map.

**Octet.** A group of eight adjacent 1s on a K-Map.

**Redundant block.** A block all of whose 1s are embedded into other blocks or groups.

**Isolated 1.** A 1 which cannot be included in any block or group.

**Overlapping blocks.** Overlapping means same 1 can be encircled more than once. It leads to simpler expressions.

**Map Rolling.** It means roll the K-Map, that is, consider the K-Map as its opposite edges horizontally and vertically are touching each other.

A **pair** represents a product where a variable and its complement drop out, that is, remove the variable which changes from 0 to 1 or 1 to 0. A pair always removes one variable. For example, the following K-Map contains a pair of 1s that are adjacent for the function F(A, B, C).

| AB \ C | 0 $\bar{C}$ | 1 $C$ |
|---|---|---|
| $\bar{A}\bar{B}$ 00 | 0 | 0 |
| $\bar{A}B$ 01 | 0 | 1 |
| $AB$ 11 | 0 | 1 |
| $A\bar{B}$ 10 | 0 | 0 |

The sum-of-products equation corresponding to above K-Map is

$$F = \bar{A}BC + ABC$$

which factors into

$$F = (\bar{A} + A)BC$$

Since A is ORed with $\bar{A}$, the equation reduces to

$$F = BC \qquad (\because \text{A changes from 0 to 1})$$

A **Quad** represents a product where two variables and their complements drop out. Merely determine which variables go from complemented to uncomplemented form and remove these variables. For example, the K-Map given above contains a quad of 1s that are adjacent for the function F(A, B, C, D), on **rolling** the map.

| AB \ CD | 00 $\bar{C}\bar{D}$ | 01 $\bar{C}D$ | 11 $CD$ | 10 $C\bar{D}$ |
|---|---|---|---|---|
| $\bar{A}\bar{B}$ 00 | 1 | 0 | 0 | 1 |
| $\bar{A}B$ 01 | 0 | 0 | 0 | 0 |
| $AB$ 11 | 0 | 0 | 0 | 0 |
| $A\bar{B}$ 10 | 1 | 0 | 0 | 1 |

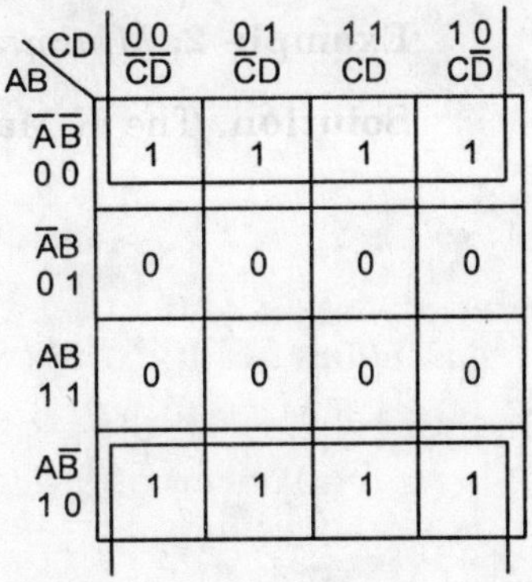


As mentioned earlier the four corner squares are adjacent. The equation corresponding to the above shown quad in simplified form is

$$F = \overline{B}\overline{D} \quad (\because \text{ A and C change from 0 to 1})$$

An **Octet** represents a product where three variables and their complements drop out. Just step through the 1's of the octet and determine which three variables change form and remove these variables. For example, the adjacent K-Map contains an octet of 1s that are adjacent for the function F(A, B, C, D), on **rolling** the map.

The equation corresponding to the above shown octet in simplified form is

$$F = \overline{B} \qquad (\because \text{ A, C and D change from 0 to 1})$$

### 3.12.2.1 K-Map Simplification for SOP Forms

The use of K-Map for minimisation of Boolean expressions is described as follows:

(*i*) *Enter 1s for minterms on K-Map and Os in the remaining squares.*

(*ii*) *Keeping in view the contiguity of opposite edges and four corner squares, encircle all blocks, consisting of the octets first, the quads second, and the pairs last. Also encircle any 1s which are not covered under any block.*

(*iii*) *Select a block satisfying following conditions:*

(*a*) *There are a minimum number of blocks.*

(*b*) *Each block should be maximally sized.*

(*c*) *Avoid redundant blocks.*

(*iv*) *Write the reduced expressions for all the blocks and OR (+) these.*

Using the above method we get a minimal sum-of-products form. However, there are choices in step (*iii*) which are sometimes difficult to resolve.

> **Note.** *K-Map simplification is not always unique. It depends upon grouping.*

**Example 1.** *Obtain the simplified form of the boolean expression using Karnaugh Map.*

$$F(x, y, z) = \Sigma(2, 3, 6, 7).$$

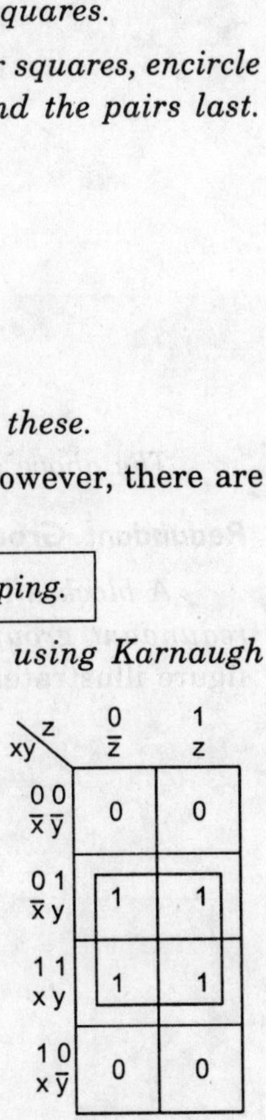


**Solution.** The boolean expression F(*x*, *y*, *z*) = Σ(2, 3, 6, 7) can be written as

$$F(x, y, z) = \overline{x}y\overline{z} + \overline{x}yz + xy\overline{z} + xyz.$$

The K-Map for the above expression is shown below:

The 1s on the K-Map are corresponding to 4 minterms and these form a quad as shown in a block.

So, the simplified form of the boolean expression is

$$F(x, y, z) = y \qquad (\because x \text{ and } z \text{ change values from 0 to 1})$$

**Example 2.** *Minimize* $F(x, y, z) = \bar{x}\,\bar{y}\,\bar{z} + \bar{x}yz + xyz + x\bar{y}\,\bar{z} + x\bar{y}z$ *using K-Map.*

**Solution.** The K-Map for the boolean expression F(*x*, *y*, *z*) is shown as follows:

| xy \ z | 0 ($\bar{z}$) | 1 (z) |
|---|---|---|
| 0 0 ($\bar{x}\,\bar{y}$) | 1 | 0 |
| 0 1 ($\bar{x}$ y) | 0 | 1 |
| 1 1 (x y) | 0 | 1 |
| 1 0 (x $\bar{y}$) | 1 | 1 |

Now the above shown K-Map can be simplified in two ways using overlapping.

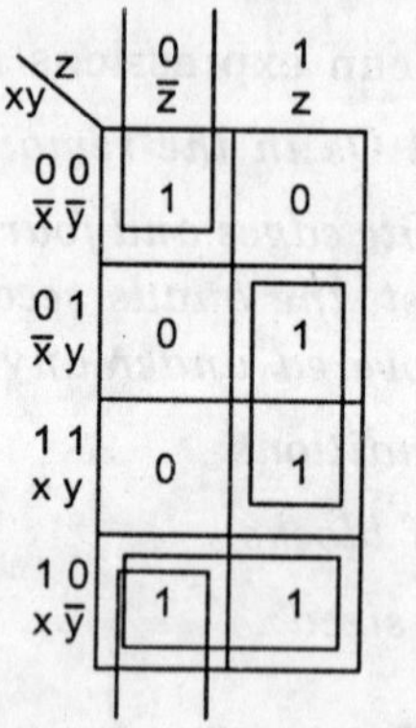

$F(x, y, z) = \bar{y}\,\bar{z} + y\,z + x\,\bar{y}$

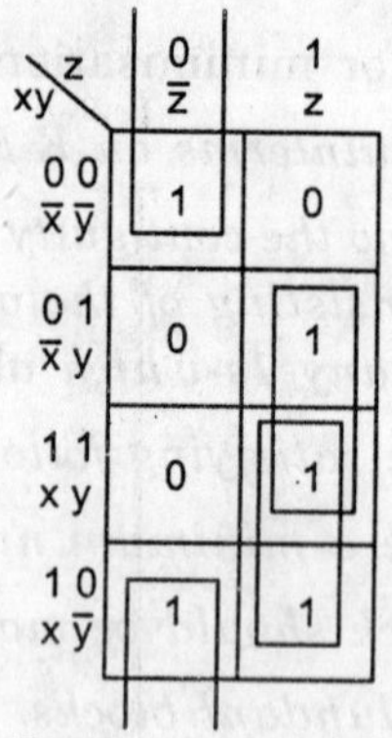

$F(x, y, z) = \bar{y}\,\bar{z} + y\,z + x\,z$

*The above example shows that the K-Map simplification is not always unique.*

## Redundant Group or Block

*A block all of whose 1s are embedded (overlapped) into other blocks is known as a redundant group. It must be eliminated for getting minimal expression.* The following figure illustrates a redundant group and eliminated form.

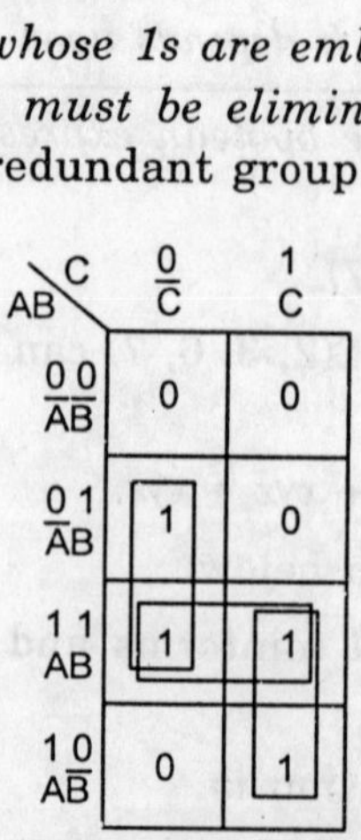

Redundant group
**(Incorrect way of grouping)**

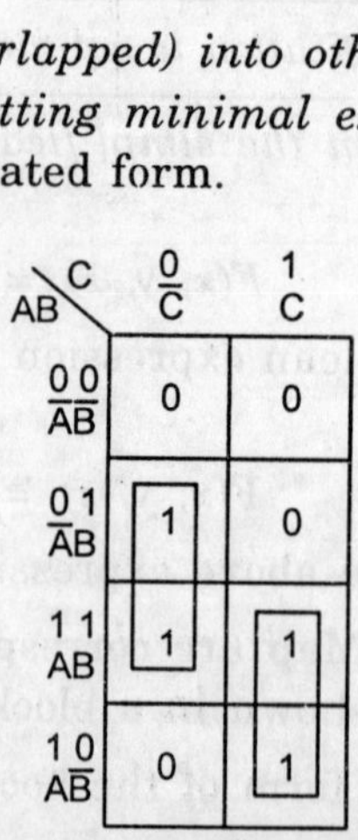

Redundant group eliminated
**(correct way of grouping)**

**Example 1.** *Reduce the following Boolean expression using K-Map:*

$$F(A, B, C, D) = \Sigma(0, 1, 2, 3, 4, 5, 10, 11, 15).$$

**Solution.** Given F(A, B, C, D) = Σ(0, 1, 2, 3, 4, 5, 10, 11, 15)

$$= m_0 + m_1 + m_2 + m_3 + m_4 + m_5 + m_{10} + m_{11} + m_{15}$$

$$m_0 = 0000 = \bar{A}\bar{B}\bar{C}\bar{D}$$

$$m_1 = 0001 = \bar{A}\bar{B}\bar{C}D$$

$$m_2 = 0010 = \bar{A}\bar{B}C\bar{D}$$

$$m_3 = 0011 = \bar{A}\bar{B}CD$$

$$m_4 = 0100 = \bar{A}B\bar{C}\bar{D}$$

$$m_5 = 0101 = \bar{A}B\bar{C}D$$

$$m_{10} = 1010 = A\bar{B}C\bar{D}$$

$$m_{11} = 1011 = A\bar{B}CD$$

$$m_{15} = 1111 = ABCD$$

Mapping the given function F in a K-map we have

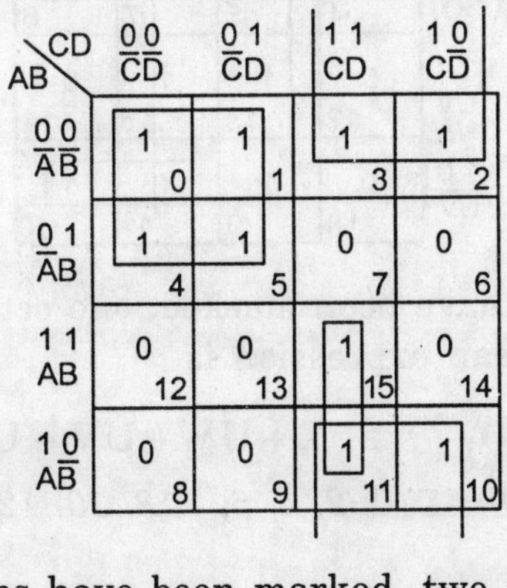


In the K-Map three groups have been marked, two quads and one pair.

So the simplified form of the Boolean expression is

$$F(A, B, C, D) = \bar{A}\bar{C} + \bar{B}C + ACD.$$

**Example 2.** *Obtain a simplified form for a Boolean expression*

*F(U, V, W, Z) = Σ(0, 1, 3, 4, 5, 6, 7, 9, 10, 11, 13, 15) using Karnaugh Map.*

**Solution.** Given F(U, V, W, Z) = Σ(0, 1, 3, 4, 5, 6, 7, 9, 10, 11, 13, 15)

$$= m_0 + m_1 + m_3 + m_4 + m_5 + m_6 + m_7 + m_9 + m_{10} + m_{11} + m_{13} + m_{15}$$

$$m_0 = 0000 = \bar{U}\,\bar{V}\,\bar{W}\,\bar{Z}$$

$$m_1 = 0001 = \bar{U}\,\bar{V}\,\bar{W}\,Z$$

$$m_3 = 0011 = \bar{U}\,\bar{V}\,W\,Z$$

$$m_4 = 0100 = \overline{U}\,V\,\overline{W}\,\overline{Z}$$
$$m_5 = 0101 = \overline{U}\,V\,\overline{W}\,Z$$
$$m_6 = 0110 = \overline{U}\,V\,W\,\overline{Z}$$
$$m_7 = 0111 = \overline{U}\,V\,W\,Z$$
$$m_9 = 1001 = U\,\overline{V}\,\overline{W}\,Z$$
$$m_{10} = 1010 = U\,\overline{V}\,W\,\overline{Z}$$
$$m_{11} = 1011 = U\overline{V}WZ$$
$$m_{13} = 1101 = UV\overline{W}Z$$
$$m_{15} = 1111 = UVWZ$$

Mapping the given function F in a K-Map we have

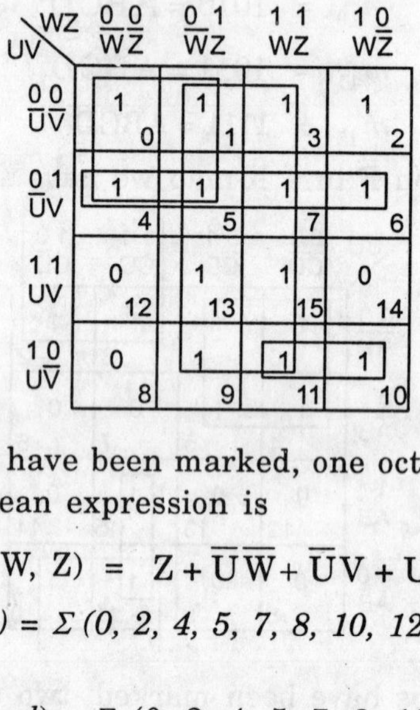


In the K-Map four groups have been marked, one octet, two quads and one pair. So the simplified form of the boolean expression is

$$F\,(U, V, W, Z) = Z + \overline{U}\,\overline{W} + \overline{U}\,V + U\overline{V}\,W.$$

**Example 3.** *If F(a, b, c, d) = Σ (0, 2, 4, 5, 7, 8, 10, 12, 13, 15), obtain the simplified form using K-Map.*

**Solution.** Given F(*a*, *b*, *c*, *d*) = Σ (0, 2, 4, 5, 7, 8, 10, 12, 13, 15)

$$= m_0 + m_2 + m_4 + m_5 + m_7 + m_8 + m_{10} + m_{12} + m_{13} + m_{15}$$

$$m_0 = 0000 = \bar{a}\,\bar{b}\,\bar{c}\,\bar{d}$$
$$m_2 = 0010 = \bar{a}\,\bar{b}\,c\,\bar{d}$$
$$m_4 = 0100 = \bar{a}\,b\,\bar{c}\,\bar{d}$$
$$m_5 = 0101 = \bar{a}\,b\,\bar{c}\,d$$
$$m_7 = 0111 = \bar{a}\,b\,c\,d$$
$$m_8 = 1000 = a\,\bar{b}\,\bar{c}\,\bar{d}$$
$$m_{10} = 1010 = a\,\bar{b}\,c\,\bar{d}$$

$$m_{12} = 1100 = a\,b\,\bar{c}\,\bar{d}$$

$$m_{13} = 1101 = a\,b\,\bar{c}\,d$$

$$m_{15} = 1111 = a\,b\,c\,d$$

Mapping the given function F in a K-Map we have

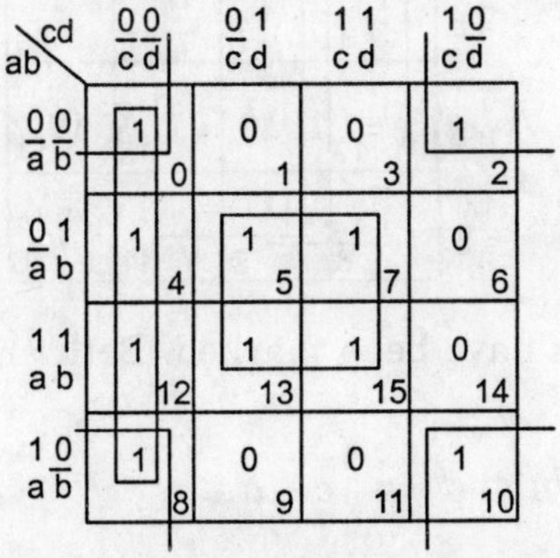


In the K-Map three groups have been marked. All are quads (the four corner squares having 1s always form a quad).

So the simplified form of the boolean expression is

$$F(a, b, c, d) = \bar{b}\,\bar{d} + \bar{c}\,\bar{d} + bd.$$

**Example 4.** *If F(a, b, c, d) = Σ (0, 1, 3, 4, 5, 7, 8, 9, 11, 12, 13, 15), obtain the simplified form using K-Map.*

**Solution.** Given F(*a*, *b*, *c*, *d*) = Σ (0, 1, 3, 4, 5, 7, 8, 9, 11, 12, 13, 15)

$$= m_0 + m_1 + m_3 + m_4 + m_5 + m_7 + m_8 + m_9 + m_{11} + m_{12} + m_{13} + m_{15}$$

$$m_0 = 0000 = \bar{a}\,\bar{b}\,\bar{c}\,\bar{d}$$

$$m_1 = 0001 = \bar{a}\,\bar{b}\,\bar{c}\,d$$

$$m_3 = 0011 = \bar{a}\,\bar{b}\,c\,d$$

$$m_4 = 0100 = \bar{a}\,b\,\bar{c}\,\bar{d}$$

$$m_5 = 0101 = \bar{a}\,b\,\bar{c}\,d$$

$$m_7 = 0111 = \bar{a}\,b\,c\,d$$

$$m_8 = 1000 = a\,\bar{b}\,\bar{c}\,\bar{d}$$

$$m_9 = 1001 = a\,\bar{b}\,\bar{c}\,d$$

$$m_{11} = 1011 = a\,\bar{b}\,c\,d$$

$$m_{12} = 1100 = a\,b\,\bar{c}\,\bar{d}$$

$$m_{13} = 1101 = a\,b\,\bar{c}\,d$$

$$m_{15} = 1111 = a\,b\,c\,d$$

Mapping the given function F in a K-Map we have

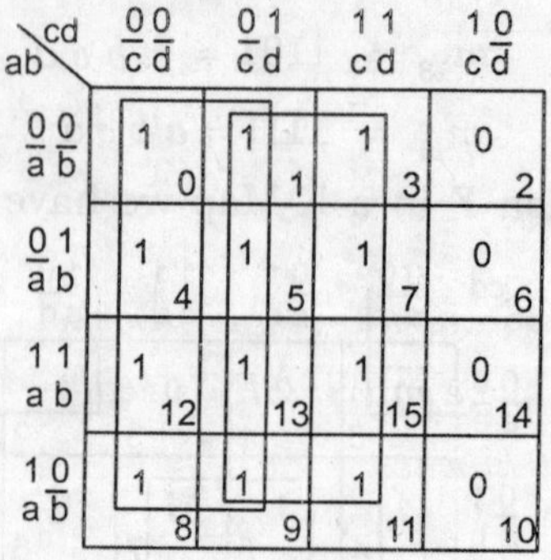


In the K-Map two groups have been marked. Both are octets. So the simplified form of the boolean expression is

$$F(a, b, c, d) = \bar{c} + d.$$

### 3.12.2.2 K-Map Simplification for POS Forms

*In POS form the boolean expression represented in a K-Map consists of maxterms. As stated earlier in a K-Map the contiguous squares differ in values of exactly one variable which may change from 0 to 1 or from 1 to 0. Also the squares on the opposite edges are considered contiguous and the four corner squares are considered contiguous.* Figure 3.5 shows the K-Maps for one, two, three and four variables representing maxterms:

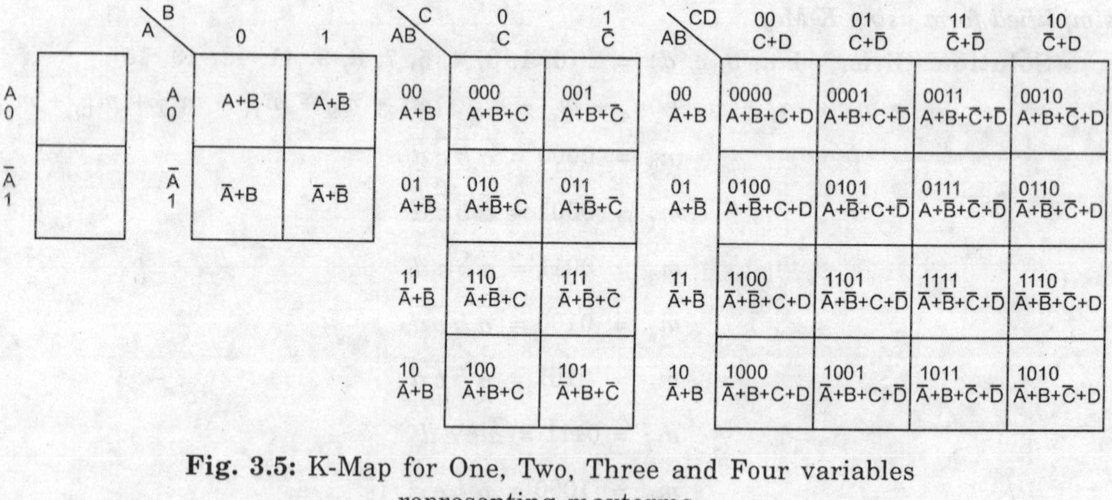


**Fig. 3.5:** K-Map for One, Two, Three and Four variables representing maxterms.

The numbers represented on the K-Map are same in both POS and SOP forms. Also the numbers shown on the top (horizontally) and to the left side (vertically) represent the **Gray code** *i.e.*, 00, 01, 11, 10. In this code the binary numbers in succession differ only at one place.

The use of K-Map for minimization of Boolean expressions in Product of Sums (POS) form is described as follows:

(i) *Enter 0s for maxterms on K-Map and 1s in the remaining squares.*

(ii) *Keeping in view the contiguity of opposite edges and four corner squares, encircle all blocks, consisting of the octets first (having all 0s), the quads second (having all 0s), and the pairs last (having all 0s). Also encircle any 0s which are not covered under any group or block.*

(iii) *Select a block satisfying the following conditions:*

(a) *There are a minimum number of blocks.*

(b) *Each block should be maximally sized.*

(c) *Avoid redundant blocks.*

(iv) *Write the reduced expressions for all the blocks and AND (.) these. Using the above method we get a minimal product-of-sums form. However, there are choices in step (iii) which are sometimes difficult to resolve.*

**Note.** *K-Map simplification is not always unique. It depends upon grouping.*

**Example 1.** *Obtain the simplified form of the boolean expression using Karnaugh Map.*

$$F(a, b, c) = \pi\ (3, 4, 5, 6, 7).$$

**Solution.** The boolean expression $F(a, b, c) = \pi\ (3, 4, 5, 6, 7)$ can be written as

$$F(a, b, c) = M_3 \,.\, M_4 \,.\, M_5 \,.\, M_6 \,.\, M_7$$

$$M_3 = 011 = a + \overline{b} + \overline{c}$$

$$M_4 = 100 = \overline{a} + b + c$$

$$M_5 = 101 = \overline{a} + b + \overline{c}$$

$$M_6 = 110 = \overline{a} + \overline{b} + c$$

$$M_7 = 111 = \overline{a} + \overline{b} + \overline{c}$$

Mapping the given function F in a K-Map we have

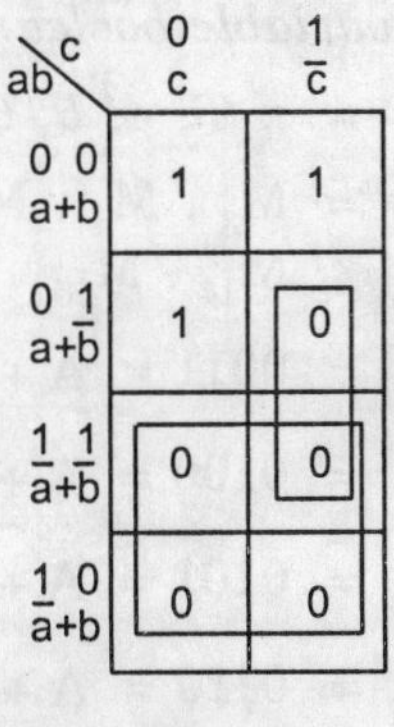


The 0s on the K-Map are corresponding to 5 maxterms. In the K-Map two groups have been marked, one quad and one pair.

So the simplified form of the boolean expression is

$$F(a, b, c) = \overline{a} \,.\, (\overline{b} + \overline{c}).$$

**Example 2.** *Minimize the following logic function in POS form using Karnaugh map*

$$F(A, B, C, D) = \Sigma\,(0, 1, 2, 3, 5, 7, 8, 9, 11, 14).$$

**Solution.** The given equation can be expressed in standard POS form as

$$F(A, B, C, D) = \pi\,(4, 6, 10, 12, 13, 15)$$
$$= M_4 \cdot M_6\, M_{10} \cdot M_{12} \cdot M_{13} \cdot M_{15}$$
$$M_4 = 0100 = A + \overline{B} + C + D$$
$$M_6 = 0110 = A + \overline{B} + \overline{C} + D$$
$$M_{10} = 1010 = \overline{A} + B + \overline{C} + D$$
$$M_{12} = 1100 = \overline{A} + \overline{B} + C + D$$
$$M_{13} = 1101 = \overline{A} + \overline{B} + C + \overline{D}$$
$$M_{15} = 1111 = \overline{A} + \overline{B} + \overline{C} + \overline{D}$$

Now the K-Map simplification can be done in any one of the two ways shown below:

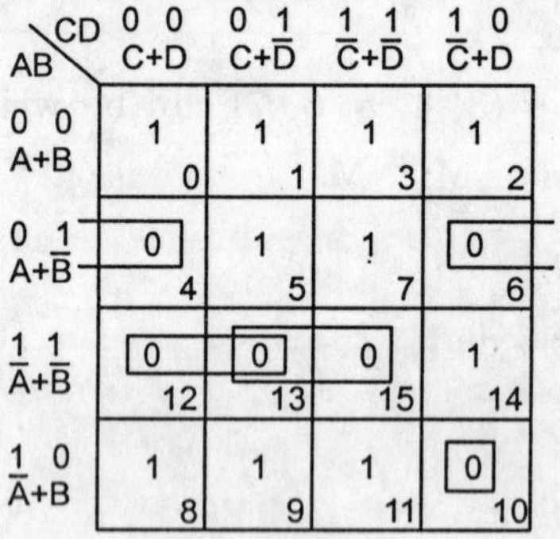


$F = (A+\overline{B}+D) \cdot (\overline{A}+\overline{B}+C) \cdot (\overline{A}+\overline{B}+\overline{D}) \cdot (\overline{A}+B+\overline{C}+D)$

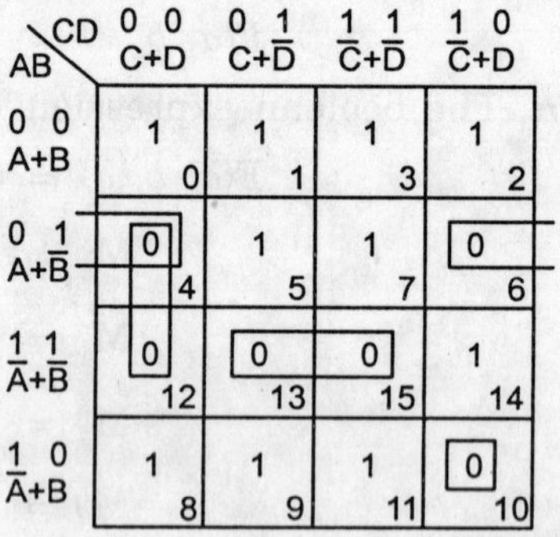


$F = (A+\overline{B}+D) \cdot (\overline{B}+C+D) \cdot (\overline{A}+\overline{B}+\overline{D}) \cdot (\overline{A}+B+\overline{C}+D)$

*The above simplification shows that K-Map minimization in not always unique.*

**Example 3.** *Minimize the four variable boolean function*

$$F(A, B, C, D) = \pi\,(3, 4, 5, 6, 7, 9, 11, 12, 13, 14, 15).$$

**Solution.**
$$F(A, B, C, D) = M_3 \cdot M_4 \cdot M_5 \cdot M_6 \cdot M_7 \cdot M_9 \cdot M_{11} \cdot M_{12} \cdot M_{13} \cdot M_{14} \cdot M_{15}$$
$$M_3 = 0011 = A + B + \overline{C} + \overline{D}$$
$$M_4 = 0100 = A + \overline{B} + C + D$$
$$M_5 = 0101 = A + \overline{B} + C + \overline{D}$$
$$M_6 = 0110 = A + \overline{B} + \overline{C} + D$$
$$M_7 = 0111 = A + \overline{B} + \overline{C} + \overline{D}$$
$$M_9 = 1001 = \overline{A} + B + C + \overline{D}$$
$$M_{11} = 1011 = \overline{A} + B + \overline{C} + \overline{D}$$

$$M_{12} = 1100 = \overline{A} + \overline{B} + C + D$$
$$M_{13} = 1101 = \overline{A} + \overline{B} + C + \overline{D}$$
$$M_{14} = 1110 = \overline{A} + \overline{B} + \overline{C} + D$$
$$M_{15} = 1111 = \overline{A} + \overline{B} + \overline{C} + \overline{D}$$

Mapping the given function F in a K-Map, we have

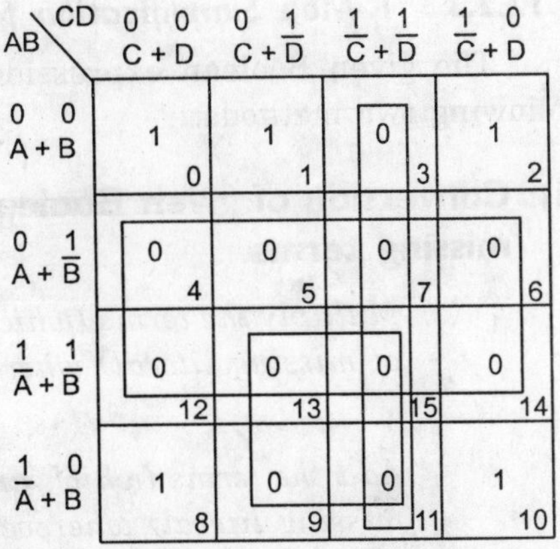

The 0s on the K-Map are corresponding to 11 maxterms. In the K-Map three groups have been marked, one octet and two quads.

So the simplified form of the boolean expression is

$$F(A, B, C, D) = \overline{B} . (\overline{C} + \overline{D}) . (\overline{A} + \overline{D}).$$

**Example 4.** *Reduce the following Boolean expression using K-Map:*

*F(A, B, C, D) = π (0, 1, 2, 3, 4, 5, 10, 11, 15).*

**Solution.** $F(A, B, C, D) = M_0 . M_1 . M_2 . M_3 . M_4 . M_5 . M_{10} . M_{11} . M_{15}$

$$M_0 = 0000 = A + B + C + D$$
$$M_1 = 0001 = A + B + C + \overline{D}$$
$$M_2 = 0010 = A + B + \overline{C} + D$$
$$M_3 = 0011 = A + B + \overline{C} + \overline{D}$$
$$M_4 = 0100 = A + \overline{B} + C + D$$
$$M_5 = 0101 = A + \overline{B} + C + \overline{D}$$
$$M_{10} = 1010 = \overline{A} + B + \overline{C} + D$$
$$M_{11} = 1011 = \overline{A} + B + \overline{C} + \overline{D}$$
$$M_{15} = 1111 = \overline{A} + \overline{B} + \overline{C} + \overline{D}$$

Mapping the given function F in a K-Map we have

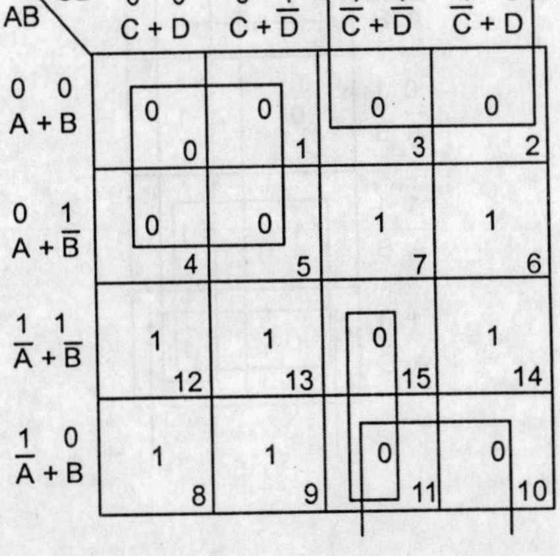

The 0s on the K-Map are corresponding to 9 maxterms. In the K-Map three groups have been marked, two quads and one pair.

So the simplified form of the Boolean expression is

$$F(A, B, C, D) = (A + C) . (B + \overline{C}) . (\overline{A} + \overline{C} + \overline{D}).$$

### 3.12.2.3 K-Map Simplification for Forms other than SOP

The given Boolean expression can be converted into standard forms by using the following two methods:

**(i) Conversion of given Boolean expression to standard form by supplying the missing terms**

(a) *Multiply the terms (which are not minterms) with (missing literal + complement of missing literal) wherever a literal is missing for SOP form of expression.*

*Or*

*Add the terms (which are not maxterms) with (missing literal . complement of missing literal) wherever a literal is missing for POS form of expression.*

(b) *Avoid duplicate term(s) if any*

(c) *Now prepare K-Map and simplify it, that is, minimize it.*

**Example.** *Minimize* $F(A, B, C) = \overline{A}BC + A\overline{B}\overline{C} + A\overline{B}C + AB + \overline{A}\overline{B}$ *using Karnaugh map.*

**Solution.** $F(A, B, C) = \overline{A}BC + A\overline{B}\overline{C} + A\overline{B}C + AB + \overline{A}\overline{B}$ is converted to standard or canonical SOP form as follows:

$$F(A, B, C) = \overline{A}BC + A\overline{B}\overline{C} + A\overline{B}C + AB(C + \overline{C}) + \overline{A}\overline{B}(C + \overline{C})$$

$$= \overline{A}BC + A\overline{B}\overline{C} + A\overline{B}C + ABC + AB\overline{C} + \overline{A}\overline{B}C + \overline{A}\overline{B}\overline{C}$$

Now the above Boolean expression has no duplicate terms and all the terms are minterms. Mapping the function F in a K-Map we have

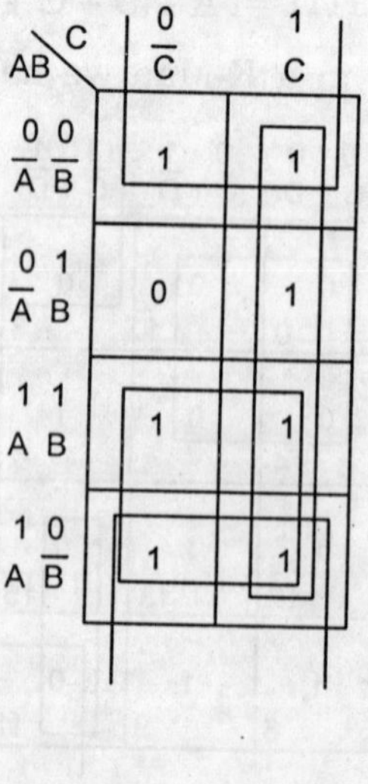

In the K-Map three groups have been marked, all three are quads. So the simplified form of the boolean expression is

$$F(A, B, C) = \overline{B} + C + A.$$

### (ii) Direct Method

Prepare K-Map as given below:

(a) *Enter 1s/0s for minterms/maxterms.*

(b) *Enter a pair of 1s/0s for each of the terms with one variable less than the total number of variables.*

(c) *Enter four adjacent 1s/0s for terms having two variables less than the total number of variables.*

(d) *Repeat for other terms in similar way.*

*Once the K-Map is prepared, minimize it.*

**Example.** *Minimize the 4 variable boolean function*

$$F(A, B, C, D) = AB\overline{C}D + \overline{A}BCD + \overline{A}\overline{B}C + \overline{A}\overline{B}\overline{D} + A\overline{C} + A\overline{B}C + \overline{B}.$$

**Solution.** Prepare K-Map as given below:

Enter 1s for two minterms $AB\overline{C}D$ and $\overline{A}BCD$.

Enter a pair of 1s for terms $\overline{A}\overline{B}\overline{C}$, $\overline{A}\overline{B}\overline{D}$ and $A\overline{B}\overline{C}$ (after looking at the numbers on the top and left side of the K-Map) keeping already existing 1s as such. Enter a quad of 1s for the term $A\overline{C}$ (keeping already existing 1s as such).

Enter an octet of 1s for the term $\overline{B}$ in same way.

The given function after mapping looks as:

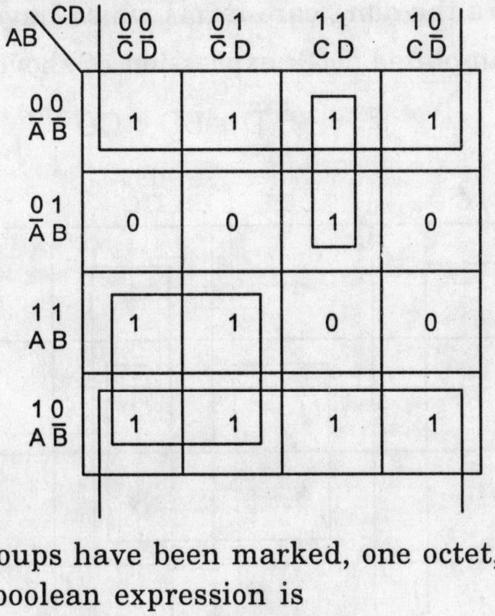


In the K-Map three groups have been marked, one octet, one quad and one pair. So the simplified form of the boolean expression is

$$F(A, B, C, D) = B + A\overline{C} + \overline{A}CD.$$

#### 3.12.2.4 K-Map Simplification for Boolean Functions With Don't Care Conditions

**Example 1.** *Obtain the minimal sum of the products for the function*

$$F(A, B, C, D) = \Sigma(1, 3, 7, 11, 15) + \phi(0, 2, 5)$$

**Solution.** The Karnaugh map for the given function is shown below:

In the Karnaugh map shown below, the minterm $m_0$ and $m_2$ *i.e.*, $\overline{A}\overline{B}\overline{C}\overline{D}$ and $\overline{A}\overline{B}C\overline{D}$ are the don't care terms which have been assumed as 1's, while making a quad. So the simplified SOP expression of above function can be written as

$$F = \overline{A}\overline{B} + CD$$

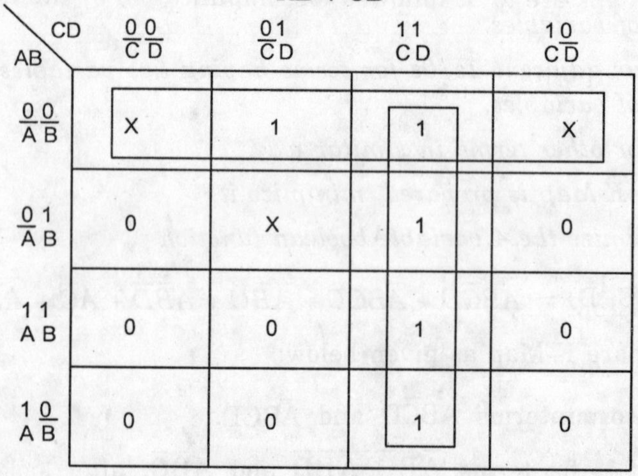


**Example 2.** *Obtain the minimal sum of products for the function*

$$F(A, B, C, D) = \Sigma(0, 3, 4, 5, 7) + \phi(8, 9, 10, 11, 12, 13, 14, 15)$$

**Solution.** The Karnaugh map for the given function is shown below:

In the K-Map shown above the minterms $m_8$, $m_{11}$, $m_{12}$, $m_{13}$, and $m_{15}$ *i.e.*, $A\overline{B}\overline{C}\overline{D}$, $A\overline{B}CD$, $AB\overline{C}\overline{D}$, $AB\overline{C}D$ and $ABCD$ are the don't care terms which have been assumed as 1's while making the quads. So the simplified. SOP expression of above function can be written as

$$F = \overline{C}\,\overline{D} + BD + CD$$

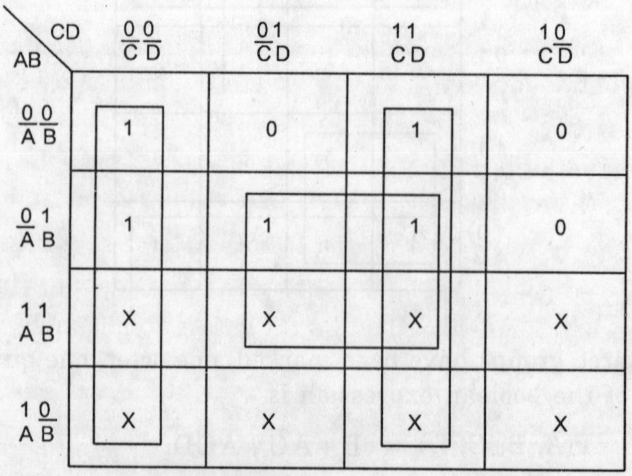

### 3.12.3 Quine-McCluskey Tabular Simplification Technique

The Karnaugh map method is very useful and convenient tool for simplification of Boolean functions as long as the number of variables does not exceed four (at the most six). But if the number of variables increases, the visualization and selection of patterns of adjacent cells in the Karnaugh map becomes complicated and difficult. The tabular method, also known as *Quine-McCluskey method*, overcomes this difficulty. It is a specific step by step procedure to achieve guaranteed simplified standard form of expression for a function.

The following steps are to be followed for simplification by tabular method or Quine-McCluskey method.

1. An exhaustive search is to be done to find the terms which may be included in the simplified functions. These terms are called *prime implicants.*
2. Form the set of prime implicants, essential prime implicants are to be determined by preparing a prime implicants chart.
3. The minterms that are not covered by the essential prime implicants, are to be taken into consideration by selecting some more prime implications to obtain an optimized Boolean expression.

#### *Determination of Prime Implicants*

The prime implicants are obtained by the following procedure:

1. Each minterm of the function is to be expressed by its binary representation.
2. The minterms are to be arranged according to increasing index (index is defined as the number of 1's in a minterm). Each set of minterms possessing same index are separated by lines.
3. Now each of the minterms is to be compared with the minterms of higher index. For each pair of terms that can combine, the new terms are formed. If two minterms are differed by only one variable, that variable is replaced by a '-' (dash) to form the new term with one less number of literals. A line is drawn when all the minterms of one set is compared with all the minterms of higher index.
4. The same process is repeated for all the groups of minterms. A new list of terms is obtained after the first stage of elimination is completed.
5. At the next stage of elimination two terms from the new list with the '-' of same position differing by only one variable are compared and again another new term is formed with further less number of literals.
6. The process is to be continued till no new match is possible.
7. All the terms which remain unchecked *i.e.*, where no match is found during the process are considered to be the prime implicants.

#### *Prime Implicant Chart*

1. After obtaining the prime implicants, a chart or table is to be prepared where

rows are represented by the prime implicants and the columns are represented by the minterms of the function.

2. Crosses are to be placed in each row to show the composition of the minterms that makes the prime implicants.
3. A completed prime implicant table is to be inspected for the columns containing only a single cross. Prime implicants that cover the minterms with a single cross are called the essential prime implicants.

The above process to find the prime implicants and preparation of the chart can be illustrated by the following examples.

**Example 1.** *Obtain the minimal sum of the products for the function*

$$F(A, B, C, D) = \Sigma (1, 4, 6, 7, 8, 9, 10, 11, 15)$$

**Solution.** The table in the following figure shows the step by step procedure Quine-McCluskey method to obtain the simplified expression of the above function.

Column I consists of the decimal equivalent of the function or the minterms and column II is the corresponding binary representation. They are grouped according to their index *i.e.*, number of 1's in the binary equivalents. In column III, two minterms are grouped if they are differed by only single variable and equivalent terms are written with a '-' in the place where the variable changes its logic value. As example minterms 1 (0001) and 9 (1001) are grouped and written as 1,9 (– 001) and so the others. Also the terms of column II, which are considered to form the group in column III, are marked with '√'.

| *I* | *II* | | | | | *III* | | | *IV* | |
|---|---|---|---|---|---|---|---|---|---|---|
| *Decimal equivalent* | *Binary equivalent* A | B | C | D | | | ABCD | | | ABCD |
| 1 | 0 | 0 | 0 | 1 | √ | 1,9 | –001 | | 8,9,10,11 | 10– – |
| 4 | 0 | 1 | 0 | 0 | √ | 4,6 | 01–0 | | 8,10,9,11 | 10– – |
| 8 | 1 | 0 | 0 | 0 | √ | 8,9 | 100– | √ | | |
| | | | | | | 8,10 | 10–0 | √ | | |
| 6 | 0 | 1 | 1 | 0 | √ | 6,7 | 011– | | | |
| 9 | 1 | 0 | 0 | 1 | √ | 9,11 | 10–1 | √ | | |
| 10 | 1 | 0 | 1 | 0 | √ | 10,11 | 101– | √ | | |
| 7 | 0 | 1 | 1 | 1 | √ | 7,15 | –111 | | | |
| 11 | 1 | 0 | 1 | 1 | √ | 11,15 | 1–11 | | | |
| 15 | 1 | 1 | 1 | 1 | √ | | | | | |

The terms which are not marked with '√' are the Prime implicants. To express the prime implicants algebraically, variables are to be considered as true form in place of 1's, as complemented form in place of 0's and no variable if '-' appears. Here the prime implicants are B′C′D, A′BD′, A′BC, BCD, ACD (from column III) and AB′ (from column IV). So Boolean expression of the given function can be written as

$$F = AB' + B'C'D + A'BD' + A'BC + BCD + ACD$$

But the above expression may not be of minimized form, as all the prime implicants may not be necessary. To find out the essential prime implicants, following steps are to be carried out. A table or chart consisting of prime implicants and decimal equivalent of minterms as given in the expression, like the following figure is to be prepared.

| *Prime Implicants* | *1* | *4* | *6* | *7* | *8* | *9* | *10* | *11* | *15* |
|---|---|---|---|---|---|---|---|---|---|
| √ AB′ | | | | | X | X | X | X | |
| √ B′C′D | X | | | | | X | | | |
| √ A′BD′ | | X | X | | | | | | |
| A′BC | | | X | X | | | | | |
| BCD | | | | X | | | | | X |
| ACD | | | | | | | | X | X |
| | √ | √ | √ | | √ | √ | √ | √ | |

In the table, the prime implicants are listed at 1st column and 'X's are placed against the corresponding minterms. The completed prime implicant table is now to be inspected for the columns containing only a single 'X'. As in above figure, the minterm 1 is represented by only single prime implicant B′C′D, and only a single 'X' in that column, it should be marked as well as the corresponding column is to be marked. Similarly, the prime implicants AB′ and AB′D′ are marked. These are the essential prime implicants as they are absolutely necessary to form the minimized Boolean expression. Now all the others minterms corresponding to these prime implicants are marked at the end of the columns *i.e.*, the minterms 1, 4, 6, 8, 9, 10, 11 are marked. Note that the terms A′BC, BCD and ACD are not marked. So they are not the essential prime implicants. However the minterms 7 and 15 are still unmarked and both of them are covered by the term BCD and is to be included in the Boolean expression. Therefore, the simplified Boolean expression of the given function can be written as

$$F = AB' + B'C'D + A'BD' + BCD$$

The simplified expressions derived in the preceeding example are in the Sum of Products form. The Quine-McClusky method can also be adopted to derive the simplified expression in Product of Sums form. In the Karnaugh map method the complement of the function was considered by taking 0's from the initial list of the minterms. Similarly the tabulation method or Quine-McClusky method may be carried out by considering the 0's of the function to derive the Sum of Products form. Finally by making the complement again, we obtain the simplified expression in the form of Product of Sums.

A function with don't-care conditions can simplified by the tabulation method with slight modification. The don't-care conditions are to be included in the list of minterms while determining the prime implicants. This allows the derivation of prime implicants with least number of literals. But the don't-care conditions are excluded in the list of minterms when prime implicants table is prepared, because these terms do not have to be covered by the selected prime implicants.

**Example 2.** *Obtain the minimal Sum of the Products for the function F (A,B,C,D) = Σ (1, 2, 3, 7, 8, 9, 10, 11, 14, 15) by Quine-McClusky method.*

**Solution.** The first step is to find out the prime implicants as described by the table in the following figure.

| *I* | *II* | | | | | *III* | | | *IV* | |
|---|---|---|---|---|---|---|---|---|---|---|
| *Decimal equivalent* | *Binary equivalent* *A* | *B* | *C* | *D* | | | *ABCD* | | | *ABCD* |
| 1 | 0 | 0 | 0 | 1 | √ | 1,3 | 00–1 | √ | 1,3,9,11 | –0–1 |
| 2 | 0 | 0 | 1 | 0 | √ | 1,9 | –001 | √ | 2,3,10,11 | –01– |
| 8 | 1 | 0 | 0 | 0 | √ | 2,3 | 001– | √ | 8,9,10,11 | 10– – |
| | | | | | | 2,10 | –010 | √ | 3,7,11,15 | – –11 |
| | | | | | | 8,9 | 100– | √ | 10,11,14,15 | 1–1– |
| | | | | | | 8,10 | 10–0 | √ | | |
| 3 | 0 | 0 | 1 | 1 | √ | 3,7 | 0–11 | √ | | |
| 9 | 1 | 0 | 0 | 1 | √ | 3,11 | –011 | √ | | |
| 10 | 1 | 0 | 1 | 0 | √ | 9,11 | 10–1 | √ | | |
| | | | | | | 10,11 | 101– | √ | | |
| | | | | | | 10,14 | 1–10 | √ | | |
| 7 | 0 | 1 | 1 | 1 | √ | 7,15 | –111 | √ | | |
| 11 | 1 | 0 | 1 | 1 | √ | 11,15 | 1–11 | √ | | |
| 14 | 1 | 1 | 1 | 0 | √ | 14,15 | 111– | √ | | |
| 15 | 1 | 1 | 1 | 1 | √ | | | | | |

The prime implications are B'D, B'C, AB', CD and AC. The prime implicant table is prepared as in the following figure.

| *Prime Implicants* | *1* | *2* | *3* | *7* | *8* | *9* | *10* | *11* | *14* | *15* |
|---|---|---|---|---|---|---|---|---|---|---|
| √ B′D | X | | X | | | X | | X | | |
| √ B′C | | X | X | | | | X | X | | |
| √ AB′ | | | | | X | X | X | X | | |
| √ CD | | | X | X | | | | X | | X |
| √ AC | | | | | | | X | X | X | X |
| | √ | √ | √ | √ | √ | √ | √ | √ | √ | √ |

All the prime implicants are essential. So the simplified Boolean expression of the given function is

$$F = B'D + B'C + AB' + CD + AC$$

**Example 3.** *Using Quine-McClusky method obtain the minimal sum of the products expression for the function F(A, B, C, D) = Σ (1, 3, 4, 5, 9, 10, 11) + Φ (6, 8).*

**Solution.** The prime implicants are obtained from the table in the following figure.

| *I* | *II* | | | | | *III* | | | *IV* | |
|---|---|---|---|---|---|---|---|---|---|---|
| *Decimal equivalent* | *Binary equivalent* *A* | *B* | *C* | *D* | | | *ABCD* | | | *ABCD* |
| 1 | 0 | 0 | 0 | 1 | √ | 1,3 | 00–1 | √ | 1,3,9,11 | –0 –1 |
| 4 | 0 | 1 | 0 | 0 | √ | 1,5 | 0–01 | | 8,9,10,11 | 10– – |
| 8 | 1 | 0 | 0 | 0 | √ | 1,9 | –001 | √ | | |
| | | | | | | 4,5 | 010– | | | |
| | | | | | | 4,6 | 01–0 | | | |
| | | | | | | 8,9 | 100– | √ | | |
| | | | | | | 8,10 | 10–0 | √ | | |
| 3 | 0 | 0 | 1 | 1 | √ | 3,11 | –011 | √ | | |
| 5 | 0 | 1 | 0 | 1 | √ | 9,11 | 10–1 | √ | | |
| 6 | 0 | 1 | 1 | 0 | √ | 10,11 | 101– | √ | | |
| 9 | 1 | 0 | 0 | 1 | √ | | | | | |
| 10 | 1 | 0 | 1 | 0 | √ | | | | | |
| 11 | 1 | 0 | 1 | 1 | √ | | | | | |

The prime implicants are A′C′D, A′BC′, A′BD′, B′D and AB′. The prime implicant table is prepared as in the following figure.

| *Prime Implicants* | *1* | *3* | *4* | *5* | *9* | *10* | *11* |
|---|---|---|---|---|---|---|---|
| A′C′D | X | | | X | | | |
| A′BC′ | | | X | X | | | |
| A′BD′ | | | X | | | | |
| √ B′D | X | X | | | X | | X |
| √ AB′ | | | | | X | X | X |
| | √ | √ | | | √ | √ | √ |

From the table, we obtain the essential prime implicants B′D and AB′. The minterms 4 and 5 are not marked in the table. The term A′BC′ is to be considered which covers both the minterms 4 and 5. So the simplified Boolean expression for the given function is

F = A′BC′ + B′D + AB′.

**Example 4.** *Using Quine-McClusky method obtain the minimal sum of the products expression for the function*

*F(A,B,C,D,E) = Σ (0, 2, 3, 5, 7, 9, 11, 13, 14, 16, 18, 24, 26, 28, 30)*

**Solution.** The prime implicants are obtained from the table in the following figure.

| *I* | *II* | | | | | | *III* | | | *IV* | |
|---|---|---|---|---|---|---|---|---|---|---|---|
| *Decimal equivalent* | *Binary equivalent* | | | | | | | | | | |
| | *A* | *B* | *C* | *D* | *E* | | | *ABCDE* | | | *ABCDE* |
| 0 | 0 | 0 | 0 | 0 | 0 | √ | 0,2 | 000–0 | √ | 0,2,16,18 | –00–0 |
| 2 | 0 | 0 | 0 | 1 | 0 | √ | 0,16 | –0000 | √ | 16,18,24,26 | 1–0–0 |
| 16 | 1 | 0 | 0 | 0 | 0 | √ | | | | 24,26,28,30 | 11– –0 |
| 3 | 0 | 0 | 0 | 1 | 1 | √ | 2,3 | 0001– | | | |
| 5 | 0 | 0 | 1 | 0 | 1 | √ | 2,18 | –0010 | √ | | |
| 9 | 0 | 1 | 0 | 0 | 1 | √ | 16,18 | 100–0 | √ | | |
| 18 | 1 | 0 | 0 | 1 | 0 | √ | 16,24 | 1–000 | √ | | |
| 24 | 1 | 1 | 0 | 0 | 0 | √ | | | | | |
| 7 | 0 | 0 | 1 | 1 | 1 | √ | 3,7 | 00–11 | | | |
| 11 | 0 | 1 | 0 | 1 | 1 | √ | 3,11 | 0–011 | | | |
| 13 | 0 | 1 | 1 | 0 | 1 | √ | 5,7 | 001–1 | | | |

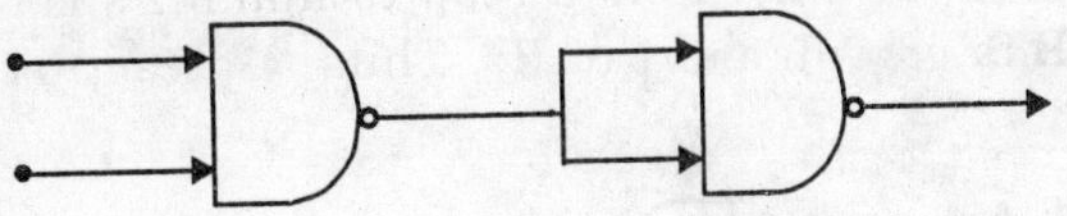

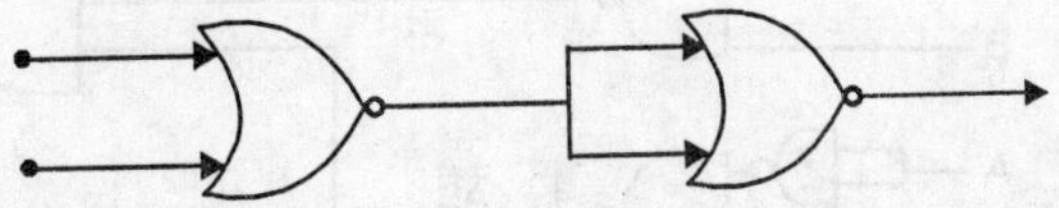

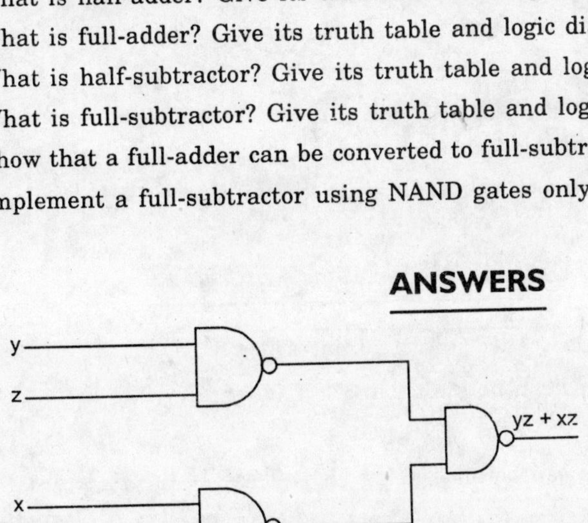

NAND gate can be used for the design of switching circuit which is expressed in sum of products (S – O – P) form. Suppose a Boolean expression E is in the sum of products form, that is,

$$E = P_1 + P_2 + \dots P_k$$

where each $P_i$ $(1 \le i \le k)$ is a product. Than

$$\bar{E} = \overline{P_1 + P_2 + \dots + P_k}$$

$$= \bar{P}_1 . \bar{P}_2 \dots \bar{P}_k$$

$$\therefore \quad E = \text{NAND}(\bar{P}_1, \bar{P}_2, \dots, \bar{P}_k)$$

Since each $P_i$ is itself a product, $\bar{P}_i$ can be easily implemented using a NAND gate. For example, let

$$E = XY + YZ + XZ$$

Then

$$\bar{E} = \overline{XY + YZ + XZ}$$

$$= \overline{(XY)} . \overline{(YZ)} . \overline{(XZ)}$$

$$\therefore \quad E = \text{NAND}(\overline{XY}, \overline{YZ}, \overline{XZ})$$

The sum of products form of E is realized by a 2-stage AND-OR circuit as shown in figure.

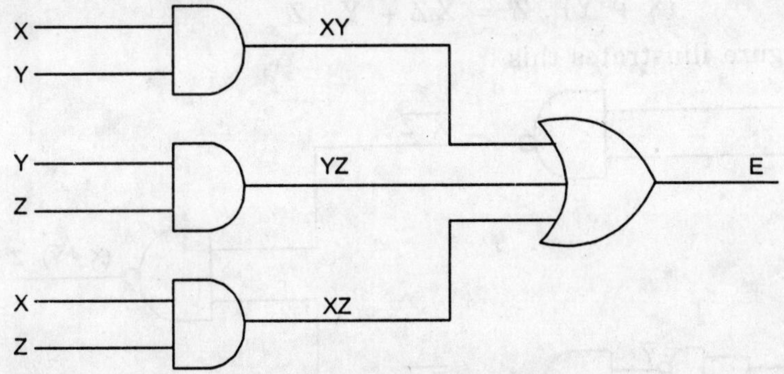


In the figure shown above if we simply replace all the AND gates and one OR gate by NAND gates, we get the circuit corresponding to the equivalent NAND expression for E as shown in the following figure.

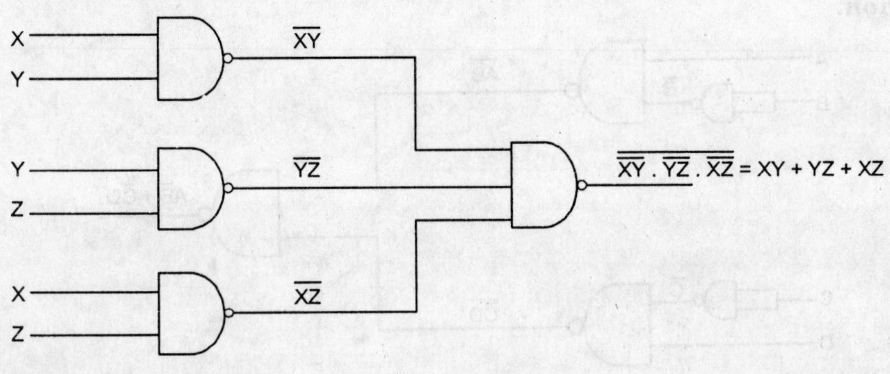


Therefore, the NAND gate and sum of products form are very useful in design of practical application.

**Example 1.** *Represent the Boolean expression $x\overline{y} + y\overline{z}$ with the help of NAND gates only.*

**Solution.** The Boolean expression $x\overline{y} + y\overline{z}$ can be implemented as given below:

$$x\overline{y} + y\overline{z} = \overline{\overline{x\overline{y} + y\overline{z}}} = \overline{\overline{x\overline{y}} \cdot \overline{y\overline{z}}}$$

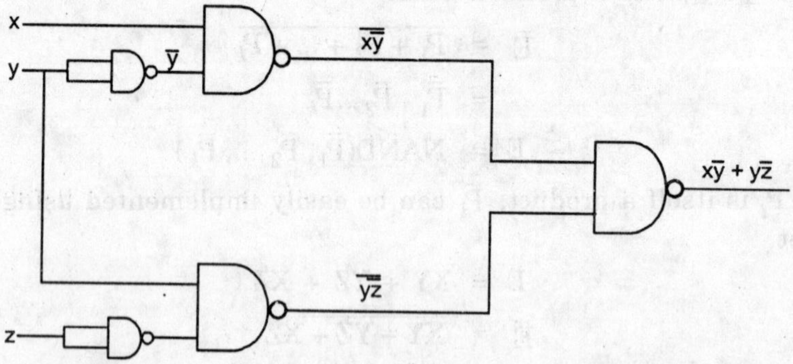


**Example 2.** *Represent the Boolean expression $(X + \overline{Y}). Z$ with the help of NAND gates only.*

**Solution.** The Boolean expression $(X + \overline{Y}). Z$ can be implemented as:

$$(X + \overline{Y}) . Z = X.Z + \overline{Y} . Z$$

Following figure illustrates this

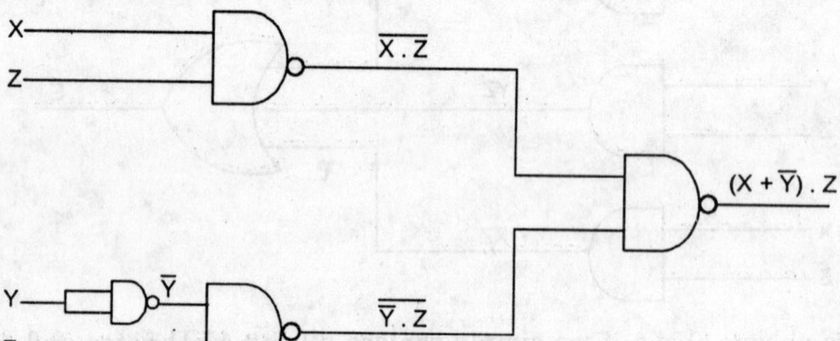


**Example 3.** *Design $A\overline{B} + \overline{C}D$ using NAND gate only.*

**Solution.**

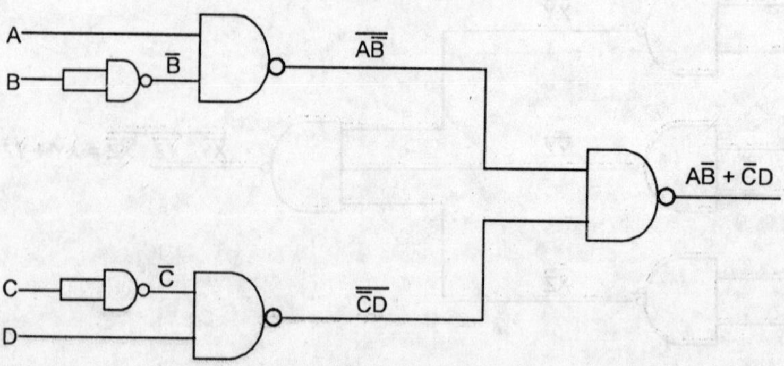

**Example 4.** *Design (A + B) . (C + D) using NAND gate only.*

**Solution.** $(A + B) . (C + D) = \overline{\overline{(A + B) . (C + D)}} = \overline{\overline{(A + B)} + \overline{(C + D)}}$

$= \overline{(\overline{A} . \overline{B}) + (\overline{C} . \overline{D})} = \overline{(\overline{A} . \overline{B})} . \overline{(\overline{C} . \overline{D})}$

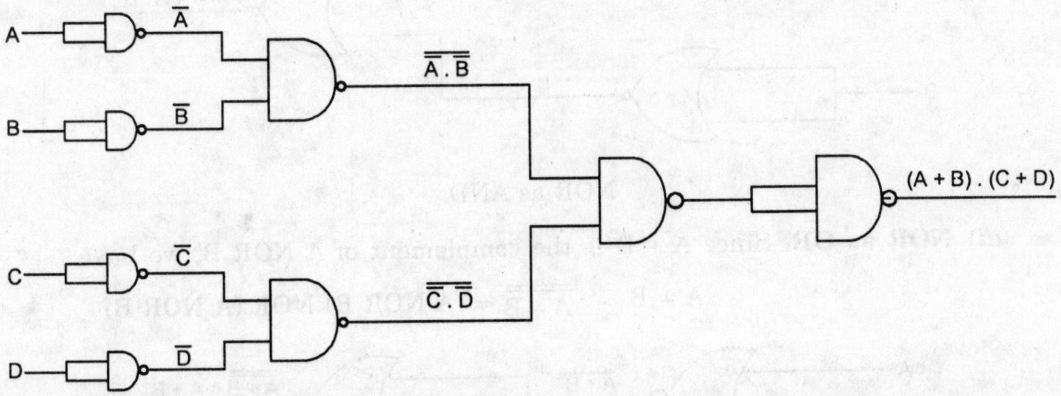


## 4.4.2 NOR Gate and its Usefulness

As stated earlier, all Boolean functions can be expressed using the gates NOT, AND and OR. Here we realize these three gates NOT, AND and OR in terms of NOR only. This is why, NOR is known as a **universal** gate.

(*i*) **NOR as NOT** (or NOT in terms of NOR)

$$A \text{ NOR } A$$

$$= \overline{A + A}$$

$$= \overline{A}$$

It shown that A is the complement of A NOR A. This is shown in the following figure.

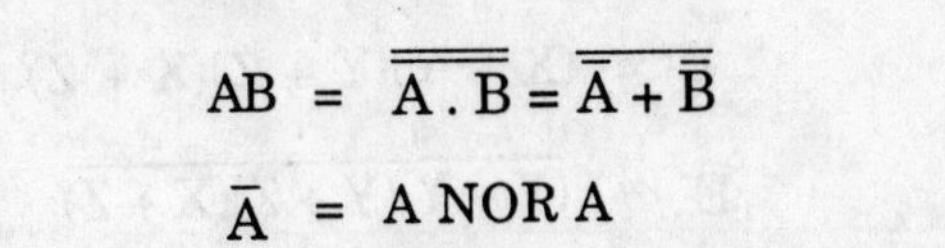


NOR as NOT.

(*ii*) **NOR as AND.** We know that

$$AB = \overline{\overline{A . B}} = \overline{\overline{A} + \overline{B}}$$

and $\overline{A} = A \text{ NOR } A$

So $AB = (A \text{ NOR } A) \text{ NOR } (B \text{ NOR } B)$

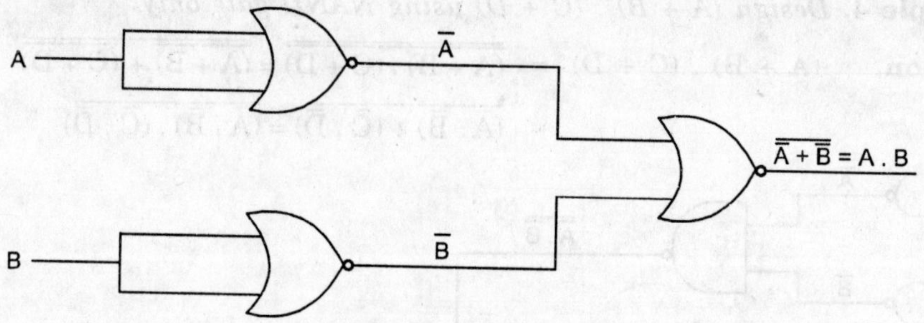


NOR as AND.

(*iii*) **NOR as OR.** Since A + B is the complement of A NOR B, we have

$$A + B = \overline{\overline{A+B}} = \text{(A NOR B) NOR (A NOR B)}$$

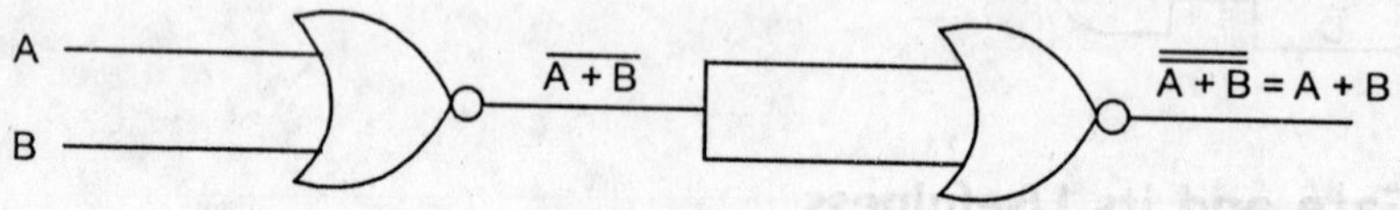


NOR as OR.

So, it is clear from the above discussion that all Boolean functions can be realized using only NOR gates.

NOR gate can be used for the design of switching circuit which is expressed in product of sums (P – O – S) form. Suppose a Boolean expression E is in the product of sums form, that is,

$$E = S_1 \cdot S_2 \ldots S_k$$

where each $S_i$ $(1 \le i \le k)$ is a sum. Then

$$\overline{E} = \overline{S_1 . S_2 \ldots S_k}$$

$$= \overline{S}_1 + \overline{S}_2 + \ldots + \overline{S}_k$$

$\therefore$

$$E = \text{NOR}\,(\overline{S}_1, \overline{S}_2, \ldots, \overline{S}_k)$$

Since each $S_i$ is itself a sum, $\overline{S}_i$ can be easily implemented using a NOR gate. For example, let

$$E = (X + Y)(Y + Z)(X + Z)$$

Then

$$\overline{E} = \overline{(X+Y)(Y+Z)(X+Z)}$$

$$= \overline{(X+Y)} + \overline{(Y+Z)} + \overline{(X+Z)}$$

$\therefore$

$$E = \text{NOR}\,(\overline{(X+Y)}, \overline{(Y+Z)}, \overline{(X+Z)})$$

The product of sums form of E is realized by a 2-stage OR-AND circuit as shown in the following figure.

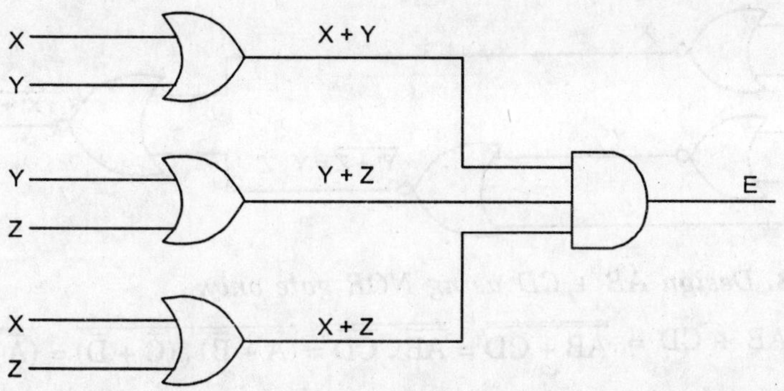


In the figure shown above if we simply replace all the OR gates and one AND gate by NOR gates, we get the circuit corresponding to the equivalent NOR expression for E as shown in the following figure.

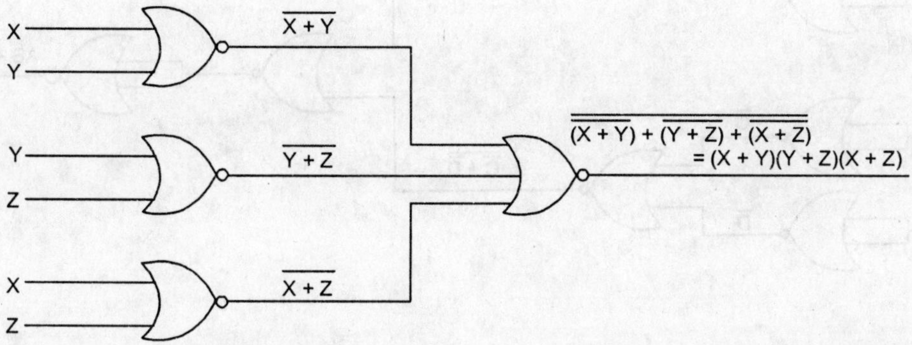


Therefore, the NOR gate and product of sums form are very useful in design of practical application.

**Example 1.** *Represent the Boolean expression X . Y′ + Z with the help of NOR gates only.*

**Solution.** The Boolean expression X . Y′ + Z can be implemented using the following steps:

$$X . Y' = \overline{\overline{X . Y'}} = \overline{X' + Y}, \text{ where } X' = X \text{ NOR } X$$

and $$(X . Y') + Z = (X . Y' \text{ NOR } Z) \text{ NOR } (X . Y' \text{ NOR } Z)$$

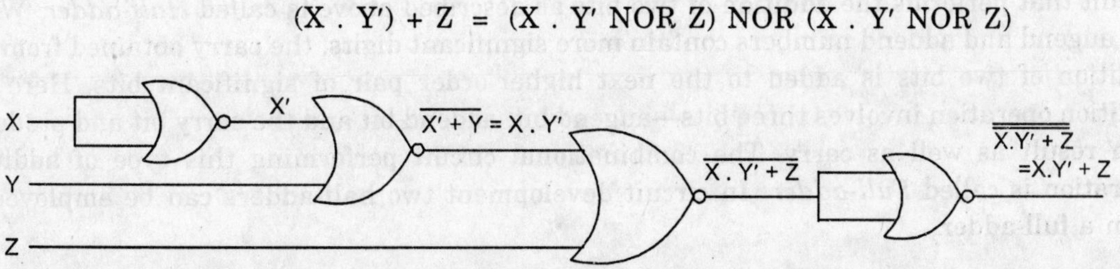


**Example 2.** *Design X (Y′ + Z) with the help of NOR gate only.*

**Solution.** $$X . (Y' + Z) = \overline{\overline{X . (Y' + Z)}} = \overline{X' + Y . Z'}$$

$$= Y . Z' = \overline{\overline{Y . Z'}} = \overline{Y' + Z}$$

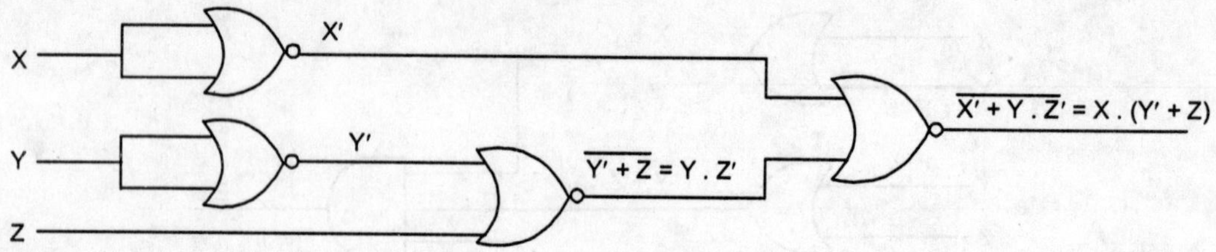


**Example 3.** *Design AB + CD using NOR gate only.*

**Solution.** $AB + CD = \overline{\overline{AB + CD}} = \overline{\overline{AB} \,.\, \overline{CD}} = \overline{(\bar{A} + \bar{B}) \,.\, (\bar{C} + \bar{D})} = \overline{\overline{(\bar{A} + \bar{B})} + \overline{(\bar{C} + \bar{D})}}$

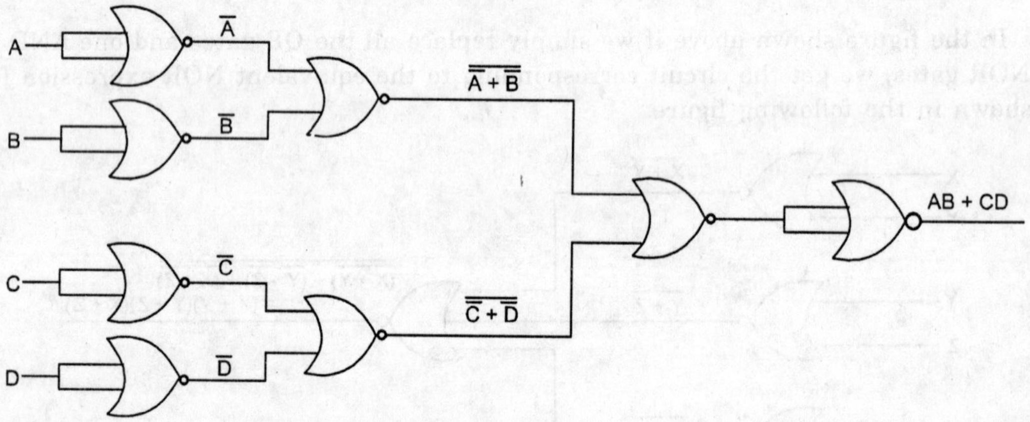


## 4.5 ADDERS

Various information-processing jobs are carried out by the digital computers. Arithmetic operations are among the basic functions of a digital computer. Addition of two binary digits is most basic arithmetic operation. The simple addition consists of four possible elementary operations, which are 0 + 0 = 0, 0 + 1 = 1, 1 + 0 = 1 and 1 + 1 = 10. The first three operations produce a sum of one digit, but at fourth operation produces sum consists of two digits. The higher significant bit of this result is called *carry*. A combinational circuit that performs the addition of two bits as described above is called *Half-adder*. When the augend and addend numbers contain more significant digits, the carry obtained from the addition of two bits is added to the next higher-order pair of significant bits. Here the addition operation involves three bits—augend bit, addend bit and the carry bit and produces sum result as well as carry. The combinational circuit performing this type of addition operation is called *Full-adder*. In circuit development two half-adders can be employed to form a full-adder.

### 4.5.1 Half-adder

As described above, a half-adder has two inputs and two outputs. Let the input variables augend and addend are designated as X and Y, and output functions are designated as S for sum and C for carry.

**Block Diagram.** The block diagram of half-adder is given below:

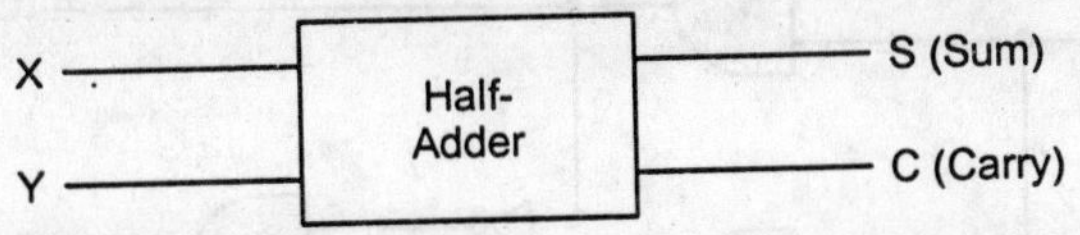


**Fig. 4.1:** Block diagram of Half-adder.

**Truth Table.** The truth table of the functions is given below:

| *Input Variables* | | *Output Variables* | |
|---|---|---|---|
| *X* | *Y* | *S* | *C* |
| 0 | 0 | 0 | 0 |
| 0 | 1 | 1 | 0 |
| 1 | 0 | 1 | 0 |
| 1 | 1 | 0 | 1 |

**Fig. 4.2:** Truth table of Half-adder.

From the truth table of Figure 4.2, it can be seen that the outputs S and C functions are similar to Exclusive-OR and AND functions respectively. The Boolean expressions are

$$S = \overline{X}Y + X\overline{Y} = X \oplus Y$$

and

$$C = XY$$

Figures 4.3(*a*), 4.3(*b*) and 4.3(*c*) show the logic diagrams to implement the half-adder circuit.

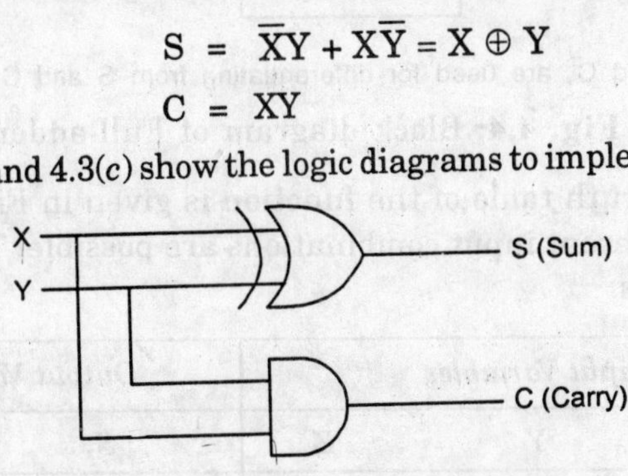


**Fig. 4.3(*a*):** Half-adder circuit.

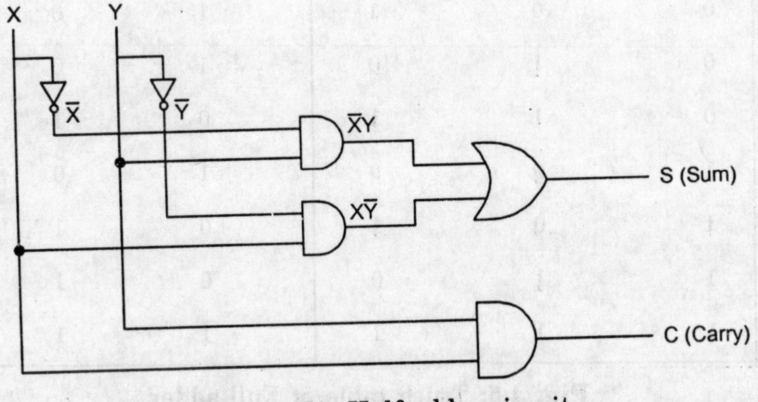


**Fig. 4.3(*b*):** Half-adder circuit.

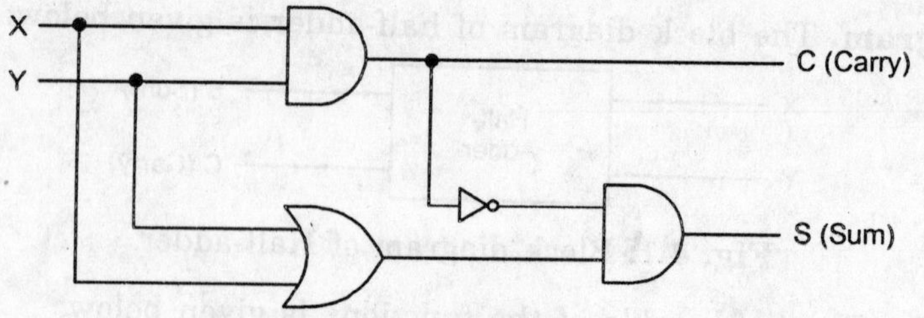


**Fig. 4.3(*c*):** Half-adder circuit.

### 4.5.2 Full-adder

A combinational circuit of full-adder performs the operation of addition of three bits—augend, addend and previous carry, and produces the outputs sum and carry. Let us designate the input variables augend as X, addend as Y and previous carry as Z, and outputs sum as $S_1$ and carry as $C_1$.

**Block Diagram.** The block diagram of full-adder is given below:

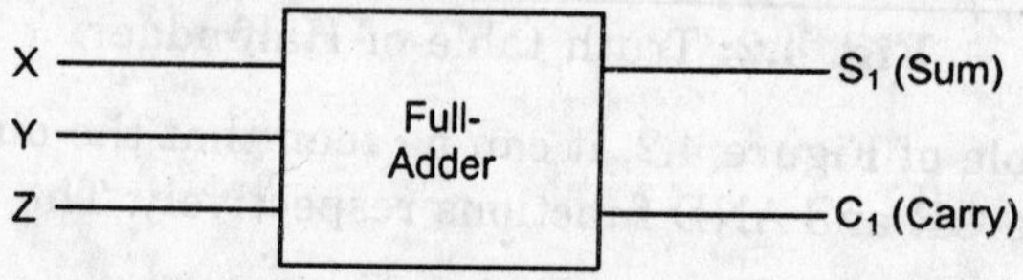


Here, $S_1$ and $C_1$ are used for differentiating from S and C of half-adder

**Fig. 4.4:** Block diagram of Full-adder.

**Truth Table.** The truth table of the function is given in Figure 4.5. As there is three input variables, eight different input combinations are possible. The truth table is prepared according to its functions.

| *Input Variables* | | | *Output Variables* | |
|---|---|---|---|---|
| *X* | *Y* | *Z* | $S_1$ | $C_1$ |
| 0 | 0 | 0 | 0 | 0 |
| 0 | 0 | 1 | 1 | 0 |
| 0 | 1 | 0 | 1 | 0 |
| 0 | 1 | 1 | 0 | 1 |
| 1 | 0 | 0 | 1 | 0 |
| 1 | 0 | 1 | 0 | 1 |
| 1 | 1 | 0 | 0 | 1 |
| 1 | 1 | 1 | 1 | 1 |

**Fig. 4.5:** Truth table of Full-adder.

To derive the simplified Boolean expression from the truth table, Karnaugh map method is adopted as in Figures 4.6(*a*) and 4.6(*b*).

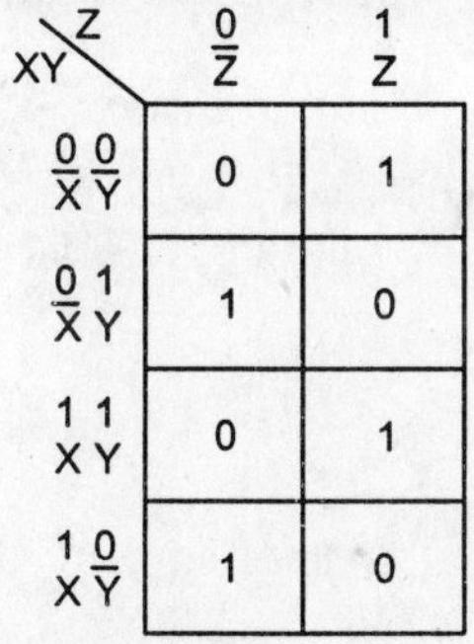


**Fig. 4.6(*a*):** K-Map for function $S_1$.

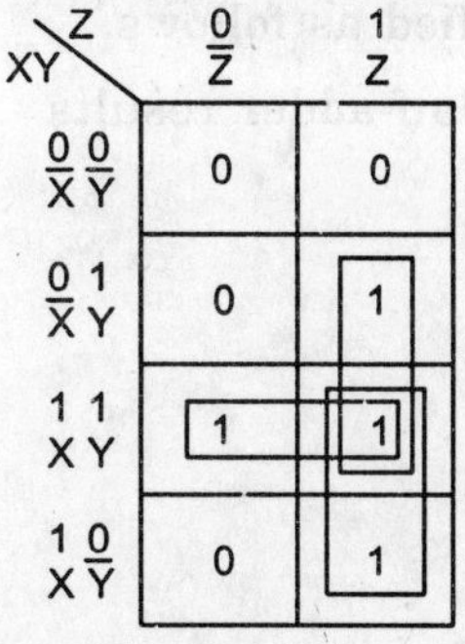


**Fig. 4.6(*b*):** K-Map for function $C_1$.

The simplified Boolean expressions of the outputs are

$$S_1 = \overline{X}\,\overline{Y}Z + \overline{X}Y\overline{Z} + X\overline{Y}\,\overline{Z} + XYZ$$

and $$C_1 = XY + YZ + XZ$$

The logic diagram for above functions is shown in Figure 4.7(*a*).

Note that one type of configuration of the combinational circuit diagram for full-adder is realized in Figure 4.7(*a*), with three Not gates, two-input and three-input AND

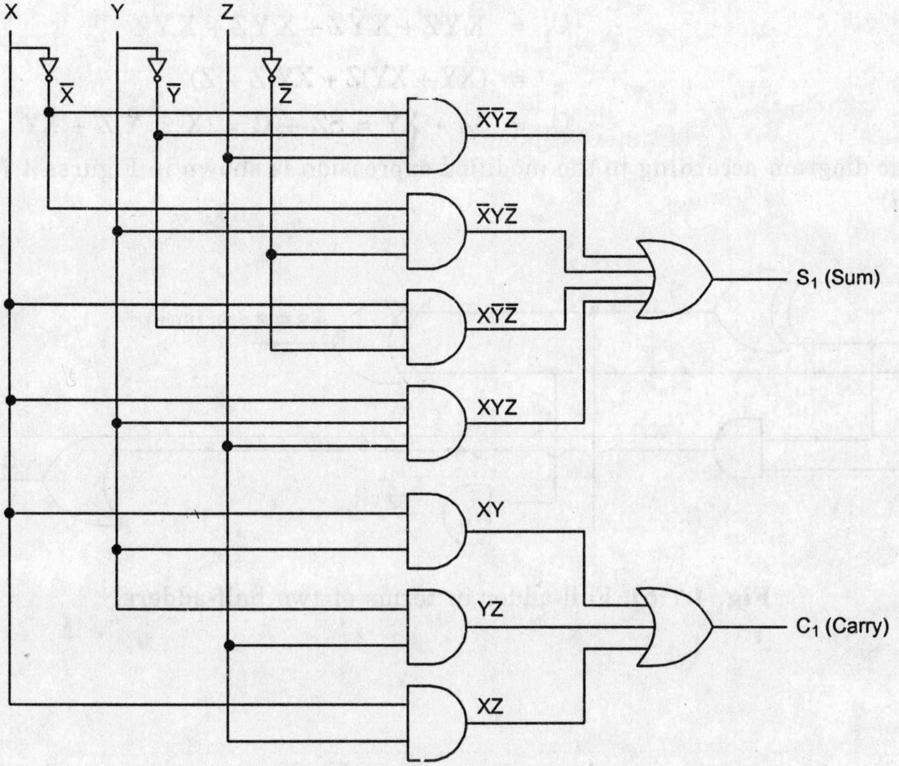


**Fig. 4.7(*a*):** Full-adder circuit.

gates, and three input and four-input OR gates. Other configurations can also be developed where number and type of gates are reduced. For this, the Boolean expressions of $S_1$ and $C_1$ are modified as follows.

From Half-adder results

$$S = \bar{X}Y + X\bar{Y} = X \oplus Y$$

$$C = XY$$

$$\bar{S} = \overline{\bar{X}Y + X\bar{Y}}$$

$$= \overline{\bar{X}Y} \cdot \overline{X\bar{Y}}$$

$$= (X + \bar{Y}) \cdot (\bar{X} + Y)$$

$$= X\bar{X} + XY + \bar{X}\bar{Y} + Y\bar{Y}$$

$$\therefore \quad \bar{S} = XY + \bar{X}\bar{Y}$$

Now $$S_1 = \bar{X}\bar{Y}Z + \bar{X}Y\bar{Z} + X\bar{Y}\bar{Z} + XYZ$$

$$= \bar{X}\bar{Y}Z + XYZ + \bar{X}Y\bar{Z} + X\bar{Y}\bar{Z}$$

$$= (\bar{X}\bar{Y} + XY)Z + (\bar{X}Y + X\bar{Y})\bar{Z}$$

$$= \bar{S}Z + S\bar{Z}$$

$$\therefore \quad S_1 = S \oplus Z = X \oplus Y \oplus Z$$

$$C_1 = \bar{X}YZ + X\bar{Y}Z + XY\bar{Z} + XYZ$$

$$= (\bar{X}Y + X\bar{Y})Z + XY(\bar{Z} + Z)$$

$$\therefore \quad C_1 = SZ + XY = SZ + C = (X \oplus Y)Z + XY$$

Logic diagram according to the modified expression is shown in Figures 4.7(*b*), 4.7(*c*) and 4.7(*d*).

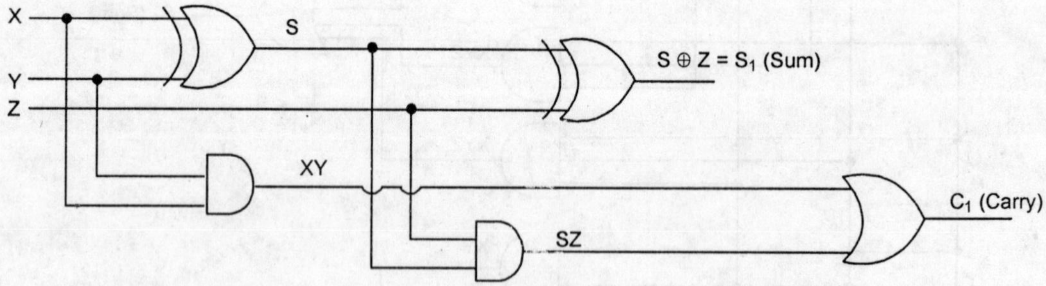


**Fig. 4.7(*b*): Full-adder in terms of two half-adders.**

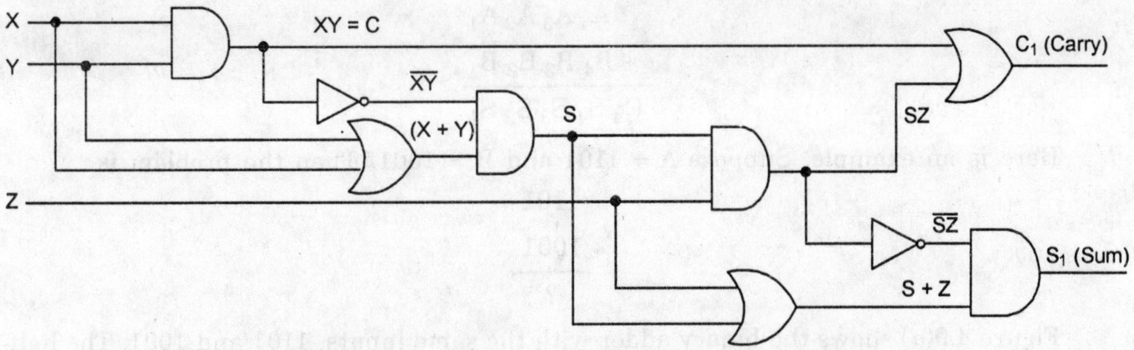


**Fig. 4.7(*c*):** Full-adder in terms of two half-adders.

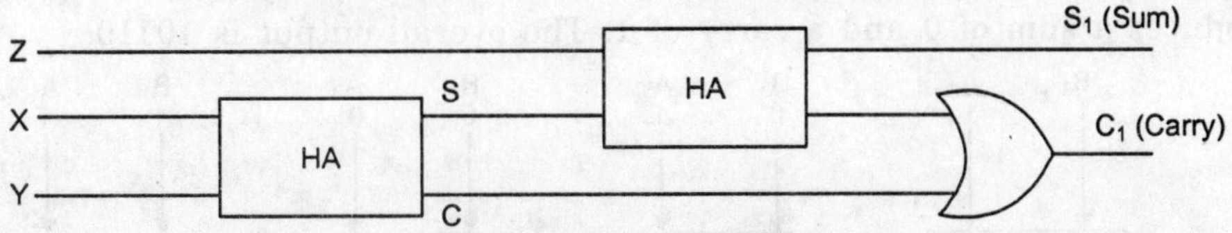


**Fig. 4.7(*d*):** Full-adder.

It may be noticed that the full-adder developed at Figure 4.7(*b*) consists of two two-input AND gates, two two-input XOR (Exclusive-OR) gates and one two-input OR gate. This contains reduced number of gates as well as type of gates as compared to Figure 4.7(*a*). Also if compared with half-adder circuit, the full-adder circuit can be formed with two half-adders and one OR gate, as shown in Figure 4.7(*d*).

## 4.6 APPLICATION OF BINARY ADDERS

Figure 4.8 shows a *binary adder*, a logic circuit that can add two binary numbers. The block on the right (labelled HA) represents a half-adder. (We can take the block on the right as a full-adder also; the inputs in that case will be $A_1$, $B_1$ and $C_0 = 0$). The inputs are $A_1$ and $B_1$; the outputs are $S_1$ (SUM) and $C_1$ (CARRY). All other blocks are full adders (abbreviated FA). Each of these adders has three inputs ($A_n$, $B_n$ and $C_n$) and two outputs.

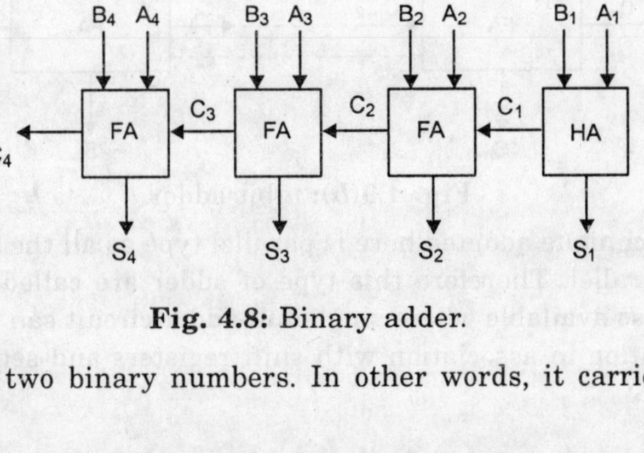


**Fig. 4.8:** Binary adder.

The circuit adds two binary numbers. In other words, it carries out the following addition:

$$\begin{array}{r} A_4\,A_3\,A_2\,A_1 \\ +\,B_4\,B_3\,B_2\,B_1 \\ \hline C_4\,S_4\,S_3\,S_2\,S_1 \end{array}$$

Here is an example. Suppose A = 1101 and B = 1001. Then the problem is

$$\begin{array}{r} 1101 \\ +\,1001 \\ \hline ? \end{array}$$

Figure 4.9(*a*) shows the binary adder with the same inputs, 1101 and 1001. The half-adder produces a sum of 0 and carry of 1, the first full-adder produces a sum of 1 and a carry of 0, the second full-adder produces a sum of 1 and a carry of 0, and the third full-adder produces a sum of 0 and a carry of 1. The overall output is 10110.

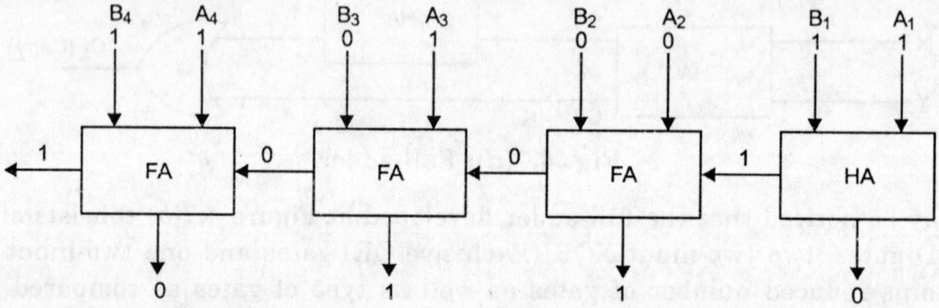


**Fig. 4.9(*a*):** Adding 13 to 9 to get 22.

In practical situation it is required to add two data each containing more than one bit. Two binary numbers each of *n* bits can be added by means of full-adder circuit.

For addition of two *n* bits data, *n* numbers of full-adders can be cascaded as demonstrated in Figure 4.9(*b*). It can be constructed with four-bit, two-bit and one-bit full-adder IC (Integrated Circuit) packages. The carry output of one package must be connected to the carry input of the next higher order bits IC package of higher order bits.

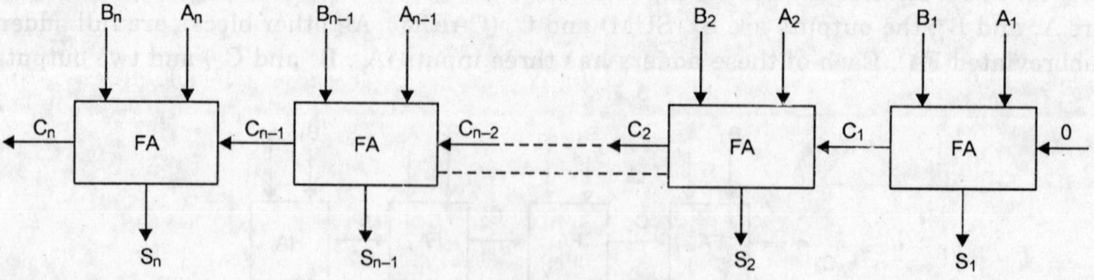


**Fig. 4.9(*b*):** *n*-bit adder.

The addition technique adopted here is parallel type as all the bit addition operations are performed in parallel. Therefore this type of adder are called *parallel adder.* Serial type of adders are also available where single full-adder circuit can perform any *n* number of bit addition operation in association with shift registers and sequential logic network.

## 4.7 SUBTRACTORS

Subtraction is the other basic function of arithmetic operations of information-processing tasks of digital computer. Similar to addition function, subtraction of two binary digits consists of four possible elementary operations, which are 0 – 0 = 0, 0 – 1 = 1 with borrow of 1, 1 – 0 = 1 and 1 – 1 = 0. The first, third and fourth operations produce a subtraction of one digit, but second operation produces a difference bit as well as a *borrow* bit. The borrow bit is used for subtraction of next higher significant bit. A combinational circuit that performs the subtraction of two bits as described above is called *Half-subtractor*. The digit from which other digit is subtracted is called minuend and the digit which is to be subtracted is called *subtrahend*. When the minuend and subtrahend numbers contain more significant digits, the borrow obtained from the subtraction of two bits is subtracted from the next higher-order pair of significant bits. Here the subtraction operation involves three bits—minuend bit, subtrahend bit and the borrow bit, and produces difference result as well as borrow. The combinational circuit which performs this type of addition operation is called *Full-subtractor*. Similar to adder circuit, a full-subtractor combinational circuit can be developed by using two half-subtractors.

### 4.7.1 Half-subtractor

A half-subtractor has two inputs and two outputs. Let the input variables minuend and subtrahend are designated as X and Y respectively and output functions are designated as D for difference and B for borrow.

**Block Diagram:** The block diagram of half-subtractor is given below:

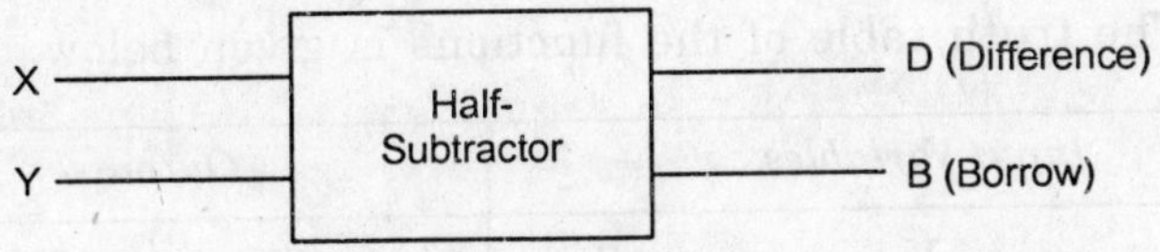


**Fig. 4.10:** Block diagram of Half-subtractor.

**Truth Table.** The truth table of the functions is given below:

| *Input Variables* | | *Output Variables* | |
|---|---|---|---|
| *X* | *Y* | *D* | *B* |
| 0 | 0 | 0 | 0 |
| 0 | 1 | 1 | 1 |
| 1 | 0 | 1 | 0 |
| 1 | 1 | 0 | 0 |

**Fig. 4.11:** Truth table of Half-subtractor.

By considering the minterms of the truth table of Figure 4.11, the Boolean expressions of the outputs D and B functions can be written as

$$D = \bar{X}Y + X\bar{Y}$$

and

$$B = \bar{X}Y$$

Figure 4.12 shows the logic diagram to realize the half-subtractor circuit.

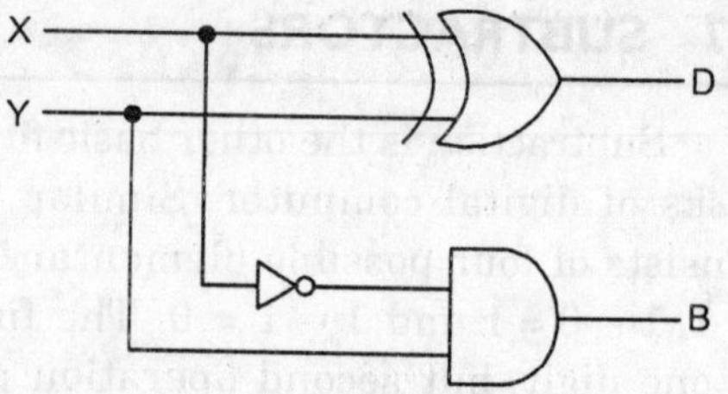


**Fig. 4.12:** Half-subtractor circuit.

### 4.7.2 Full-subtractor

A combinational circuit of full-subtractor performs the operation of subtraction of three bits—minuend, subtrahend and borrow generated from the subtraction operation of previous significant digits and produces the outputs difference and borrow. Let us designate the input variables minuend as X, subtrahend as Y and previous borrow as Z, and outputs difference as D and borrow as B. Eight different input combinations are possible for three input variables.

**Block Diagram.** The block diagram of full-subtractor is given below:

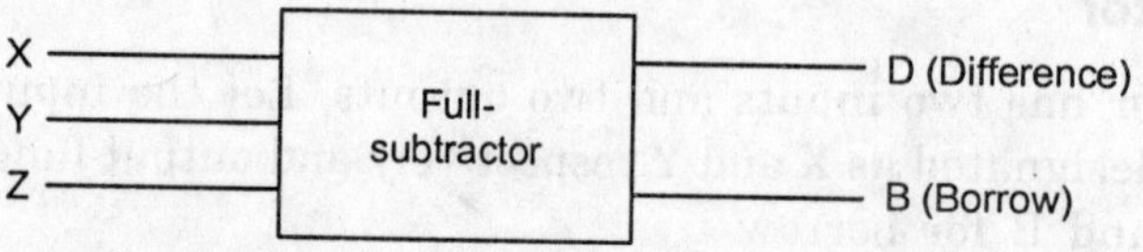


**Fig. 4.13:** Block diagram of Full-subtractor.

**Truth Table.** The truth table of the functions is given below:

| *Input Variables* | | | *Outputs* | |
|---|---|---|---|---|
| *X* | *Y* | *Z* | *D* | *B* |
| 0 | 0 | 0 | 0 | 0 |
| 0 | 0 | 1 | 1 | 1 |
| 0 | 1 | 0 | 1 | 1 |
| 0 | 1 | 1 | 0 | 1 |
| 1 | 0 | 0 | 1 | 0 |
| 1 | 0 | 1 | 0 | 0 |
| 1 | 1 | 0 | 0 | 0 |
| 1 | 1 | 1 | 1 | 1 |

**Fig. 4.14(*a*):** Truth table of Full-subtractor.

To derive the simplified Boolean expression from the truth table, Karnaugh map method is adopted as shown in Figures 4.14(*b*) and 4.14(*c*).

| XY \ Z | 0 ($\bar{Z}$) | 1 (Z) |
|---|---|---|
| 0 0 ($\bar{X}\bar{Y}$) | 0 | 1 |
| 0 1 ($\bar{X}Y$) | 1 | 0 |
| 1 1 (XY) | 0 | 1 |
| 1 0 ($X\bar{Y}$) | 1 | 0 |

**Fig. 4.14(*b*):** K-Map for function D.

| XY \ Z | 0 ($\bar{Z}$) | 1 (Z) |
|---|---|---|
| 0 0 ($\bar{X}\bar{Y}$) | 0 | 1 |
| 0 1 ($\bar{X}Y$) | 1 | 1 |
| 1 1 (XY) | 0 | 1 |
| 1 0 ($X\bar{Y}$) | 0 | 0 |

**Fig. 4.14(*c*):** K-Map for function B.

The simplified Boolean expressions of the output are

$$D = \bar{X}\bar{Y}Z + \bar{X}Y\bar{Z} + X\bar{Y}\bar{Z} + XYZ$$

and

$$B = \bar{X}Z + \bar{X}Y + YZ$$

The logic diagram for above functions is shown in Figure 4.15(*a*).

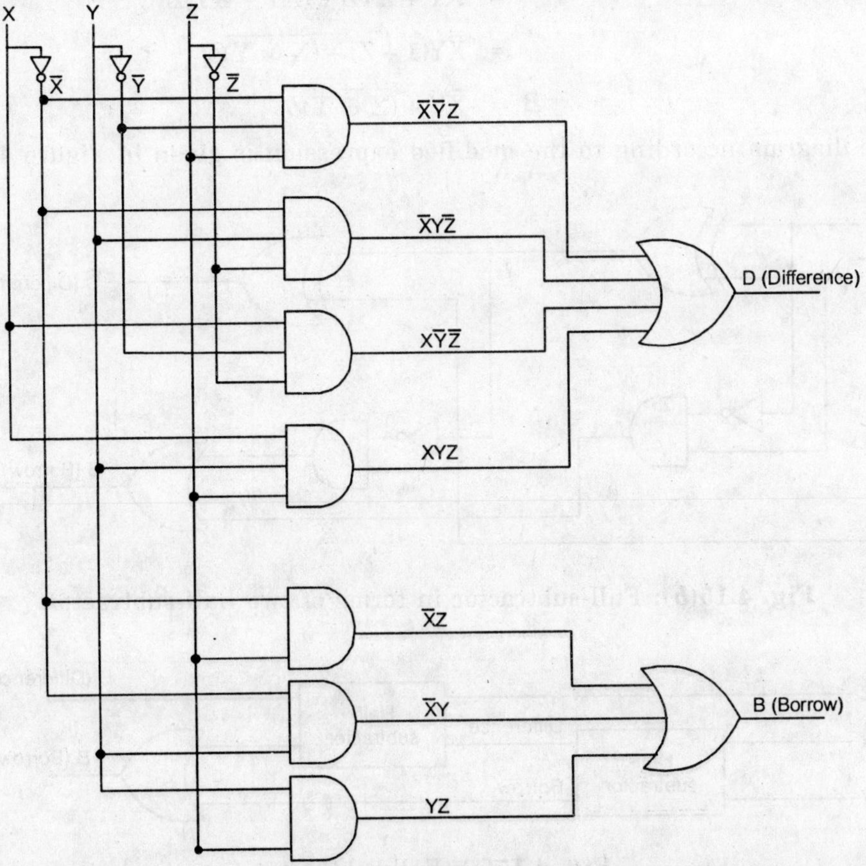


**Fig. 4.15(*a*):** Full-subtractor circuit.

Similar to full-adder circuit, it should be noticed that the configuration of the combinational circuit diagram for full-subtractor as realized in Figure 4.15($a$) contains three NOT gates, two-input and three-input AND gates, and three input and four-input OR gates. Other configurations can also be developed where number and type of gates are reduced. For this, the Boolean expressions of D and B are modified as follows.

$$D = \bar{X}\bar{Y}Z + \bar{X}Y\bar{Z} + X\bar{Y}\bar{Z} + XYZ$$

$$= \bar{X}(\bar{Y}Z + Y\bar{Z}) + X(\bar{Y}\bar{Z} + YZ)$$

$$= \bar{X}(Y \oplus Z) + X(\overline{Y \oplus Z})$$

$$\therefore \quad D = X \oplus Y \oplus Z$$

$$B = \bar{X}Z + \bar{X}Y + YZ$$

$$= \bar{X}Y + \bar{X}Z + YZ$$

$$= \bar{X}Y + (\bar{X} + Y)Z$$

$$= \bar{X}Y + (\bar{X}(Y + \bar{Y}) + (\bar{X} + X)Y)Z$$

$$= \bar{X}Y + (\bar{X}Y + \bar{X}\bar{Y} + \bar{X}Y + XY)Z$$

$$= \bar{X}Y + (\bar{X}Y + \bar{X}\bar{Y} + XY)Z$$

$$= \bar{X}Y + \bar{X}YZ + (\bar{X}\bar{Y} + XY)Z$$

$$= \bar{X}Y(1 + Z) + (\overline{X \oplus Y})Z$$

$$\therefore \quad B = \bar{X}Y + (\overline{X \oplus Y})Z$$

Logic diagram according to the modified expression is given in Figure 4.15($b$):

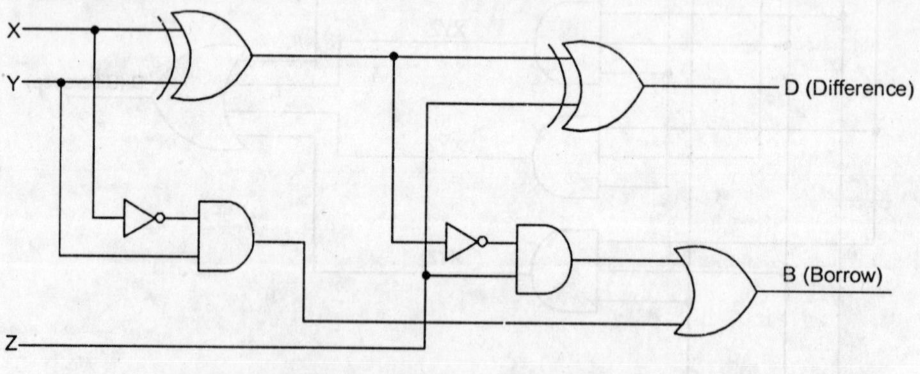


**Fig. 4.15(*b*):** Full-subtractor in terms of two half-subtractor.

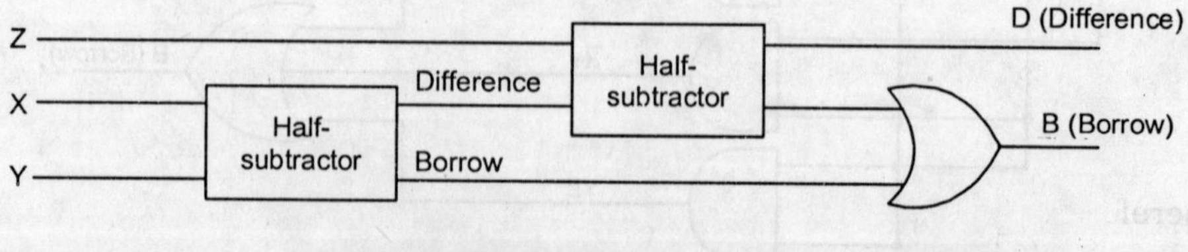


**Fig. 4.15(*c*):** Full-subtractor.

Note that the full-subtractor developed in Figure 4.15(*b*) consists of two two-input AND gates, two two-input XOR (Exclusive-OR) gates, two INVERTER gates and one two-input OR gate. This contains reduced number of gates as well as type of gates as compared to Figure 4.15(*a*). Also it may be observed, if compared with half-subtractor circuit, the full-subtractor circuit can be developed with two half-subtractors and one OR gate as shown in Figure 4.15(*c*).

## 4.8 ADDER-SUBTRACTOR

In a computer the same circuit performs addition as well as subtraction. The subtraction is performed using 2's complement. An adder-subtractor circuit consists of a controlled inverter and *n* number of full-adders. A controlled inverter is shown in Figure 4.16(*a*).

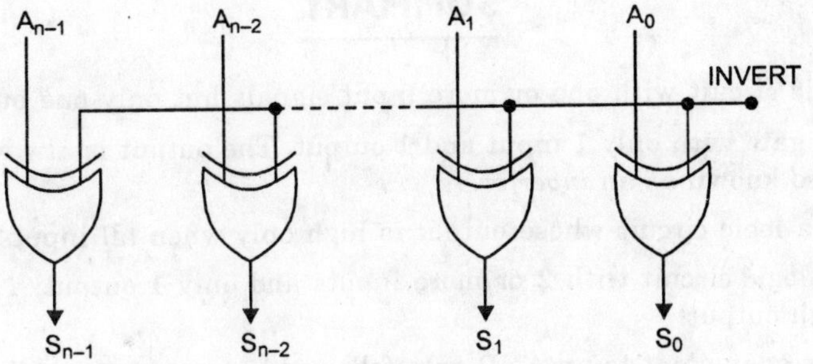


**Fig. 4.16(*a*):** Controlled inverter.

When INVERT terminal is low, *i.e.*, 0, the controlled inverter transmits the *n*-bit input to the output. When INVERT signal is high, it transmits the 1's complement of the input. To get 2's complement 1 is added to 1's complement.

An adder-subtractor is shown in Figure 4.16(*b*). It includes controlled inverter and *n* number of full adders. For addition $A_0$ and $B_0$ are added to give $S_0$, $A_1$ and $B_1$ are added

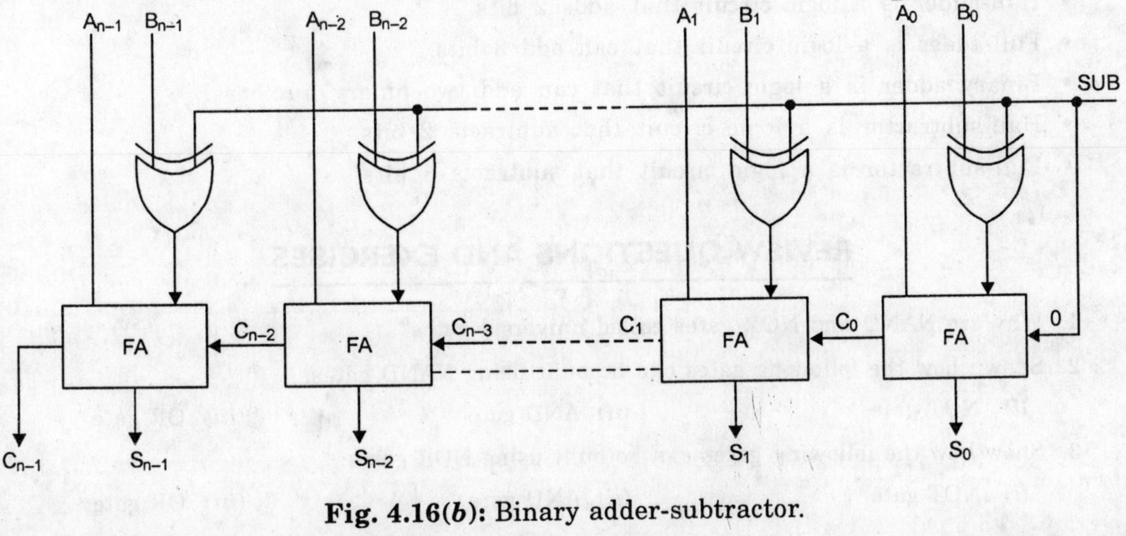


**Fig. 4.16(*b*):** Binary adder-subtractor.

to give $S_1$ and so on. So $B_0$, $B_1$, ... $B_{n-1}$ should be applied to full-adders. For this, INVERT signal of the controlled inverter portion of the circuit has to be low. In Figure 4.16(*b*), this is marked as SUB. This low signal is also applied to the carry-in terminal of the full-adder of the LSB stage. The full-adders perform addition of $A_n$ and $B_n$. Thus addition is performed when SUB is low.

To perform subtraction SUB signal is made high. So the controlled inverter portion of the circuit inverts $B_n$. So 1's complement of $B_n$ is obtained. The SUB signal is also applied to the carry-in terminal of the full-adder of the LSB stage. As SUB is high, 1 is added to the sum of $A_0$ and $B_0$. It is a step to make 2's complement of $B_n$. The full-adder add $A_n$ and the 2's complement of $B_n$. Thus subtraction is performed when SUB is high.

## SUMMARY

- Gate is a logic circuit with one or more input signals but only one output signal.
- Not gate is a gate with only 1 input and 1 output. The output is always the complement of the input. Also known as an *inverter*.
- AND gate is a logic circuit whose output is high only when all inputs are high.
- OR gate is a logic circuit with 2 or more inputs and only 1 output; 1 or more high inputs produce a high output.
- NAND gate is equivalent to an AND gate followed by an inverter. All inputs must be high to get a low output.
- NOR gate is equivalent to an OR gate followed by an inverter. All inputs must be low to get a high output.
- XOR gate is an EXCLUSIVE-OR gate. It has a high output only when the number of 1s input is odd.
- XNOR gate is equivalent to an EXCLUSIVE-OR gate followed by an invertor. It has a high output only when the number of 1s input is even.
- Half-adder is a logic circuit that adds 2 bits.
- Full-adder is a logic circuit that can add 3 bits.
- Binary adder is a logic circuit that can add two binary numbers.
- Half-subtractor is a logic circuit that subtracts 2 bits.
- Full-subtractor is a logic circuit that subtracts 3 bits.

## REVIEW QUESTIONS AND EXERCISES

1. Why are NAND and NOR gates called universal gates?
2. Shown how the following gates can be built using NAND gates:
   (*i*) NOT gate (*ii*) AND gate (*iii*) OR gate
3. Show how the following gates can be built using NOR gates:
   (*i*) NOT gate (*ii*) AND gate (*iii*) OR gate

4. Draw the circuit diagram for the Boolean function F(X, Y, Z) = (X′ + Y) (Y′ + Z) using NOR gates only.
5. Represent the Boolean expression $(x+\overline{y})(y+\overline{z})(z+\overline{x})$ with the help of NOR gates only.
6. Represent the Boolean expression $yz + xz$ with the help of NAND gates only.
7. Represent the Boolean expression X + Y . Z′ with the help of NOR gates only.
8. Represent the Boolean expression X + Y . Z′ with the help of NAND gates only.
9. Given the following circuit:

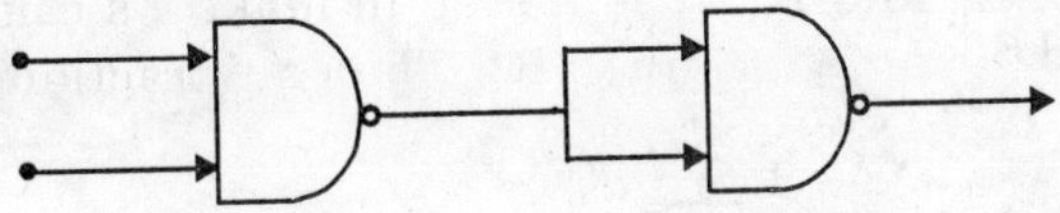

What is the output if (*i*) both inputs are FALSE (*ii*) one is FALSE and the other is TRUE?

10. Given the following circuit:

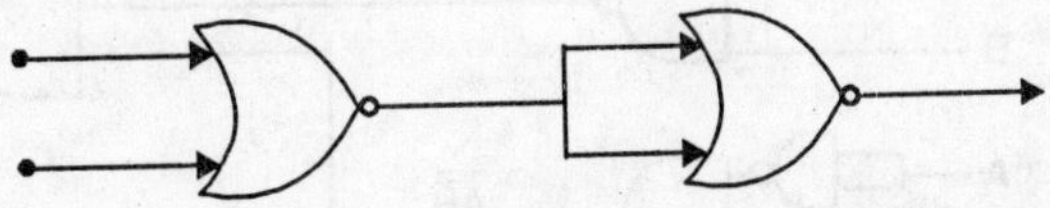

What is the input if (*i*) both inputs are FALSE (*ii*) one is FALSE and the other is TRUE?

11. Draw the simplified logic diagram using NAND gates to implement the three input function F denoted by the expression:

$$F = \Sigma(0, 1, 2, 5)$$

12. Represent the Boolean expression $\overline{X}Y + \overline{Y}Z$ with the help of NAND gates only.
13. Prove algebraically $x+\overline{x}y = x+y$.
14. Draw the logic circuit diagram using NAND gates only for the following expression : $AB + \ddot{A}B + \overline{A}\overline{B}$
15. What is half-adder? Give its truth table and logic diagram.
16. What is full-adder? Give its truth table and logic diagram.
17. What is half-subtractor? Give its truth table and logic diagram.
18. What is full-subtractor? Give its truth table and logic diagram.
19. Show that a full-adder can be converted to full-subtractor with the addition of INVERTER.
20. Implement a full-subtractor using NAND gates only.

## ANSWERS

6.

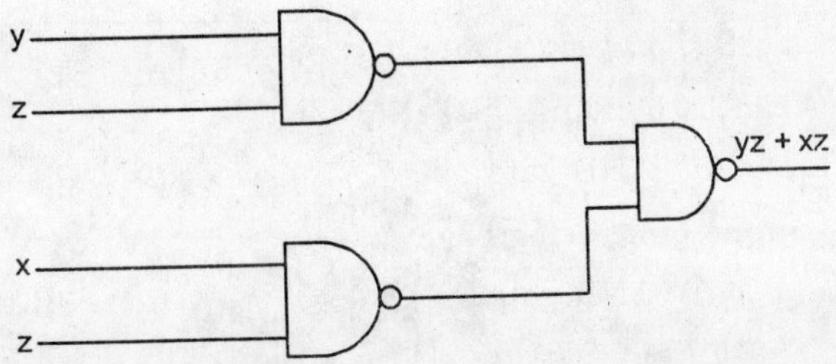

13. L.H.S. $= x + \bar{x}y$

$= x \,.\, 1 + \bar{x}y$ $(\because x \,.\, 1 = x)$

$= x \,.\, (1 + y) + \bar{x}y$ $(\because 1 + y = 1)$

$= x + xy + \bar{x}y$ Using Distributive law

$= x + (x + \bar{x})y$ Using Distributive law

$= x + 1 \,.\, y$ Using law of complementarity

$= x + y$ $(\because 1 \,.\, y = y)$

= R.H.S.

14.

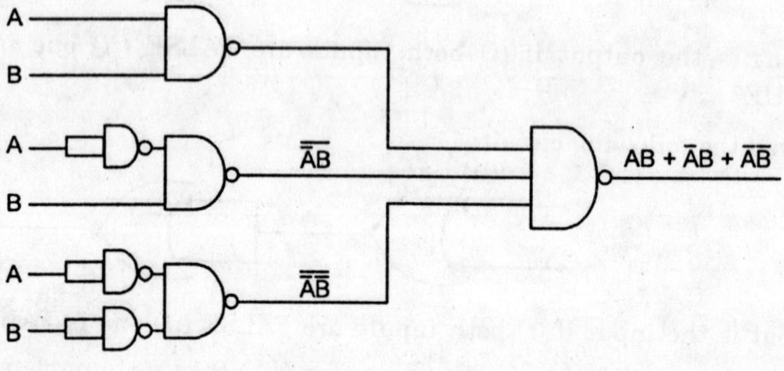

Chapter 5

# COMBINATIONAL CIRCUITS

## 5.1 INTRODUCTION

Combinational circuits are the circuits in which the output at any point of time depends upon the combination of the input signals present at that time only, and does not depend upon any past conditions. The digital systems consist two types of circuits, namely,

(i) Combinational circuits and

(ii) Sequential circuits

A combinational circuit consists of logic gates, where outputs are at any instant are determined only by the present combination of inputs without regard of previous inputs or previous state of outputs. A combinational circuit performs a specific information-processing operation assigned logically by a set of Boolean functions. Sequential circuits contain logic gates as well as memory cells. Their outputs depends on the present inputs and also on the states of memory elements. Since the outputs of sequential circuits depend not only on the present inputs but also on past inputs, the circuit behavior must be specified by a time sequences of inputs and memory states. The sequential circuits will be discussed in next Chapter.

In the previous Chapters, we have already discussed on binary numbers, codes, Boolean algebra, simplification of Boolean function, logic gates, economical gate implementation and binary arithmetic circuitry. Binary numbers and codes bear discrete quantities of information and the binary variables are the representation of electric voltages or some other signals. In this Chapter, we will discuss various types of combinational circuits.

## 5.2 COMBINATIONAL CIRCUIT AND ITS TYPES

A combinational circuit consists of input variables, logic gates, and output variables. The logic gates accepts signals from inputs and output signals are generated according to the logic circuits employed in it. Binary information from the given data transforms to desired output data in this process. Both input and output are obviously the binary signals, *i.e.*, both the input and output signals are of two possible states, logic 1 and logic 0. Figure 5.1 shows a block diagram of combinational logic circuit. There are $n$ number of input variables coming from electric source and $m$ number of output signals go to external destination. The source and/or destination may consist of memory elements or sequential logic circuit or shift registers, located either in the vicinity of the combinational logic circuit or in remote external location. But external circuit does not interfere in the behavior of the combinational circuit.

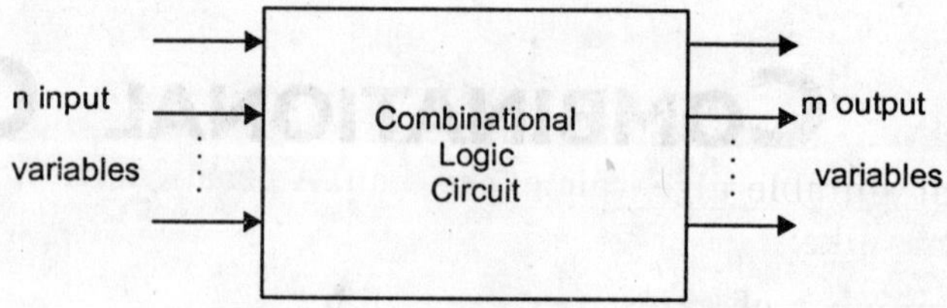


**Fig. 5.1**

For $n$ number of input variables to a combinational circuit, $2^n$ possible combinations of binary input states are possible. For each possible combination, there is one and only one possible output combination. A combinational logic circuit can be described by $m$ Boolean functions and each output can be expressed in terms of $n$ input variables.

The following are most important types of combinational circuits that are readily available in IC packages:

- Encoders
- Decoders
- Adders
- Subtractors
- Code converters
- Multiplexers
- De-multiplexers
- Comparators
- Parity genertors/checkers

## 5.3 DESIGN PROCEDURE FOR COMBINATIONAL CIRCUITS

Any combinational circuit can be designed by the following steps of design procedure.

1. The problem is stated.
2. Identify the input variables and output functions.
3. The input and output variables are assigned letter symbols.
4. The truth table is prepared that completely defines relationship between the input variables and output functions.
5. The simplified Boolean expression is obtained by any method of minimization—algebraic method or Karnaugh map method.
6. Logic diagram is to be realized from the simplified expression using logic gates.

It is very important that the design problem or the verbal specifications should be interpreted correctly to prepare the truth table. Sometimes the designer must use his intuition and experience to arrive at the correct interpretation. Word specification are very seldom exact and complete. Any wrong interpretation results in incorrect truth table and combinational circuit.

Varieties of simplification methods are available to derive the output Boolean functions from the truth table, such as algebraic method, the Karnaugh map. However, one must consider different aspects, limitations, restrictions and criteria for a particular design application to arrive at suitable algebraic expression. A practical design approach should consider the constraints like:

1. Minimum number of gates,
2. Minimum number of outputs,
3. Minimum propagation time of the signal through circuit,
4. Minimum number of interconnections, and
5. Limitations of the driving capabilities of each logic gates.

Since the importance of each constraint is dictated by the particular application, it is difficult to make all these criteria satisfied simultaneously, and also difficult to make a general statement on the process of achieving an acceptable simplification. However, in most cases, first the simplified Boolean expression at standard form is derived and then other constraints are taken care of as far as possible for a particular application.

## 5.4 ENCODERS

The process of assigning a code to every possible object is called encoding, *e.g.*, binary coding for decimal digits, ASCII code, etc. An encoder performs this function electronically. It's typical application is an electronic keyboard which incorporates an encoder, which converts each key's signal into a short, precise binary string, which is unique to each key.

A typical encoder has N-bit wide input port and a K-bit wide output port, where N is in the vicinity of $2^K$. One and only one input line can take a value 1 at a time and the encoder generates the same pre-assigned binary code on K-output lines.

**Block diagram** of a typical encoder is given below:

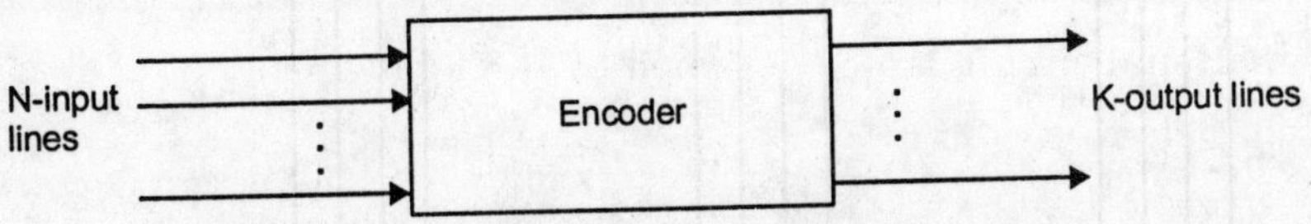


**Fig. 5.2(*a*):** Block diagram of an encoder.

**Block diagram** of 8 by 3 encoder is given below:

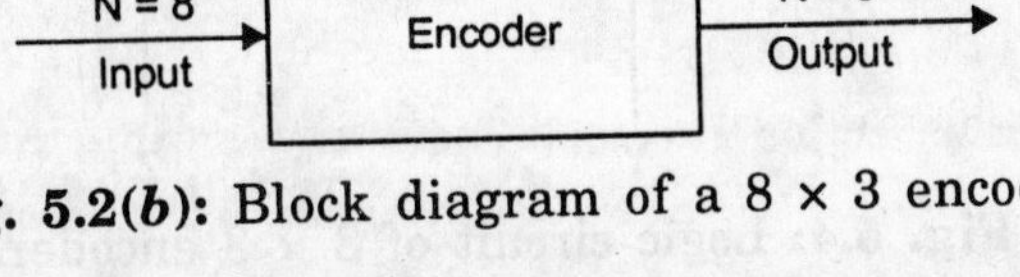


**Fig. 5.2(*b*):** Block diagram of a 8 × 3 encoder.

**Truth Table:** Truth Table for 8 by 3 encoder is given below:

| *Inputs* | | | | | | | | *Outputs* | | |
|---|---|---|---|---|---|---|---|---|---|---|
| $D_0$ | $D_1$ | $D_2$ | $D_3$ | $D_4$ | $D_5$ | $D_6$ | $D_7$ | $X$ | $Y$ | $Z$ |
| 1 | 0 | 0 | 0 | 0 | 0 | 0 | 0 | 0 | 0 | 0 |
| 0 | 1 | 0 | 0 | 0 | 0 | 0 | 0 | 0 | 0 | 1 |
| 0 | 0 | 1 | 0 | 0 | 0 | 0 | 0 | 0 | 1 | 0 |
| 0 | 0 | 0 | 1 | 0 | 0 | 0 | 0 | 0 | 1 | 1 |
| 0 | 0 | 0 | 0 | 1 | 0 | 0 | 0 | 1 | 0 | 0 |
| 0 | 0 | 0 | 0 | 0 | 1 | 0 | 0 | 1 | 0 | 1 |
| 0 | 0 | 0 | 0 | 0 | 0 | 1 | 0 | 1 | 1 | 0 |
| 0 | 0 | 0 | 0 | 0 | 0 | 0 | 1 | 1 | 1 | 1 |

**Fig. 5.3:** Truth Table of 8 × 3 encoder.

Output functions for X, Y, Z can be read directly from table as follows:

$$X = D_4 + D_5 + D_6 + D_7$$
$$Y = D_2 + D_3 + D_6 + D_7$$
$$Z = D_1 + D_3 + D_5 + D_7$$

**Logic diagram** for 8-to-3 line encoder is shown in Figure 5.4.

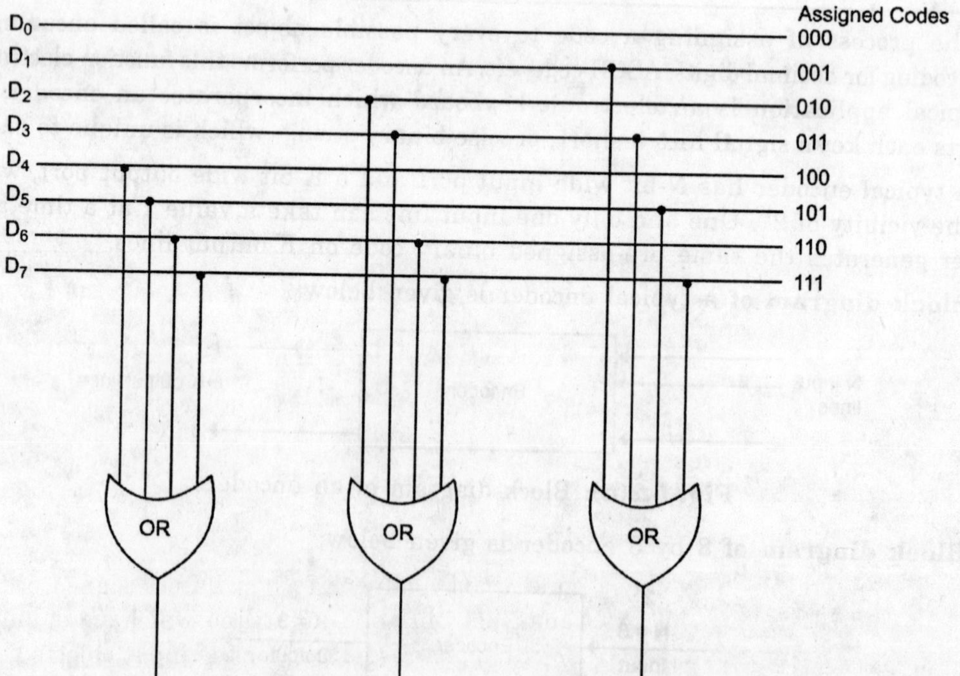


**Fig. 5.4:** Logic circuit of 8 × 3 encoder.

Note that $D_0$ is not connected to any OR gate as we must have X = Y = Z = 0 when $D_0$ = 1.

Each OR gate has only those input lines coming into it, whose assigned code have value 1 in their respective bit position. Since only one input line will have value 1 at a time, the proper assigned code will appear as output for the input objects.

### 5.4.1 Decimal-to-Binary Encoder

A decimal-to-binary *encoder* is a circuit that converts decimal-to-binary. Its truth table is given in Figure 5.5(*a*) and logic circuit in Figure 5.5(*b*).

**Truth Table of Decimal-to-Binary Encoder**

| *Inputs* | | | | | | | | | | *Outputs* | | | |
|---|---|---|---|---|---|---|---|---|---|---|---|---|---|
| $D_0$ | $D_1$ | $D_2$ | $D_3$ | $D_4$ | $D_5$ | $D_6$ | $D_7$ | $D_8$ | $D_9$ | $Y_3$ | $Y_2$ | $Y_1$ | $Y_0$ |
| 1 | 0 | 0 | 0 | 0 | 0 | 0 | 0 | 0 | 0 | 0 | 0 | 0 | 0 |
| 0 | 1 | 0 | 0 | 0 | 0 | 0 | 0 | 0 | 0 | 0 | 0 | 0 | 1 |
| 0 | 0 | 1 | 0 | 0 | 0 | 0 | 0 | 0 | 0 | 0 | 0 | 1 | 0 |
| 0 | 0 | 0 | 1 | 0 | 0 | 0 | 0 | 0 | 0 | 0 | 0 | 1 | 1 |
| 0 | 0 | 0 | 0 | 1 | 0 | 0 | 0 | 0 | 0 | 0 | 1 | 0 | 0 |
| 0 | 0 | 0 | 0 | 0 | 1 | 0 | 0 | 0 | 0 | 0 | 1 | 0 | 1 |
| 0 | 0 | 0 | 0 | 0 | 0 | 1 | 0 | 0 | 0 | 0 | 1 | 1 | 0 |
| 0 | 0 | 0 | 0 | 0 | 0 | 0 | 1 | 0 | 0 | 0 | 1 | 1 | 1 |
| 0 | 0 | 0 | 0 | 0 | 0 | 0 | 0 | 1 | 0 | 1 | 0 | 0 | 0 |
| 0 | 0 | 0 | 0 | 0 | 0 | 0 | 0 | 0 | 1 | 1 | 0 | 0 | 1 |

Output functions for $Y_3$, $Y_2$, $Y_1$, $Y_0$ can be read directly from table as follows:

$$Y_3 = D_8 + D_9$$

$$Y_2 = D_4 + D_5 + D_6 + D_7$$

$$Y_1 = D_2 + D_3 + D_6 + D_7$$

$$Y_0 = D_1 + D_3 + D_5 + D_7 + D_9$$

Note that $D_0$ is not connected to any OR gate as we must have

$Y_3 = Y_2 = Y_1 = Y_0 = 0$ when $D_0 = 1$.

Each OR gate has only those input lines coming into it, whose assigned code have value 1 in their respective bit position. Since only one input line will have value 1 at a time, the proper assigned code (0 to 9) will appear as output for the input objects $D_0$ to $D_9$.

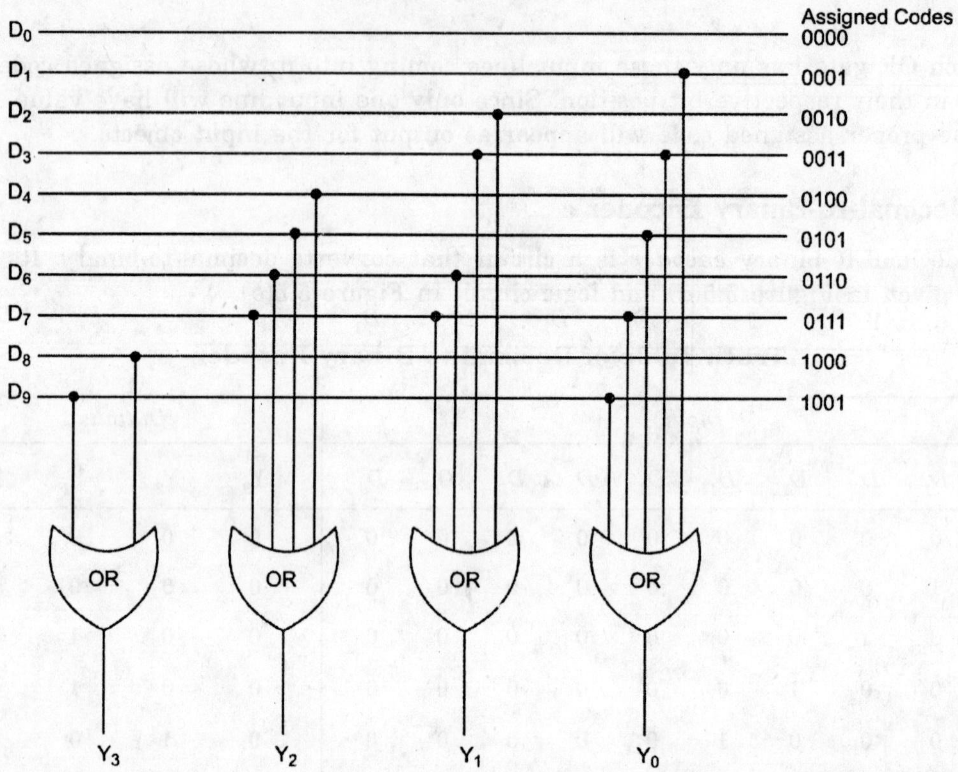


**Fig. 5.5:** Decimal-to-binary encoder.

## 5.5 DECODERS

A decoder is a combinational circuit whose function is to convert binary strings from one coded form to another coded form. Decoders are used to address memories, to display digits in a seven segment display and in multiplexers/demultiplexers. An N-input decoder can be used to select any one of the $2^N$ options, depending on the input pattern. Such a decoder is called N-to-$2^N$ line decoder.

**Block diagram** of a N by $2^N$ decoder is given below:

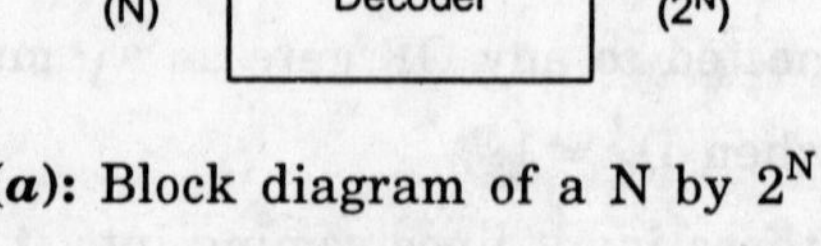


**Fig. 5.6(*a*):** Block diagram of a N by $2^N$ decoder.

### 5.5.1 3 x 8 Decoder

**Block diagram** of a 3 by 8 decoder is shown in Figure 5.6(*b*).

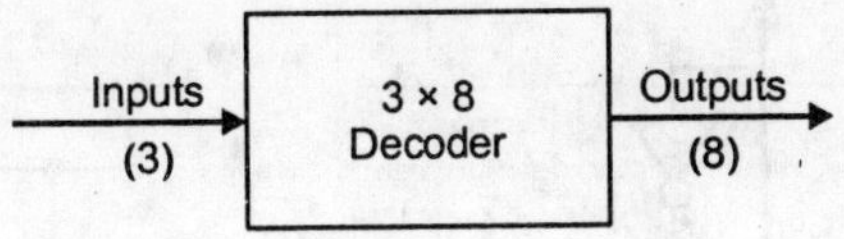


**Fig. 5.6(*b*):** Block diagram of a 3 by 8 decoder.

**Truth Table** for a 3 × 8 decoder is given below:

| *Input* | | | *Output* | | | | | | | |
|---|---|---|---|---|---|---|---|---|---|---|
| *X* | *Y* | *Z* | $D_0$ | $D_1$ | $D_2$ | $D_3$ | $D_4$ | $D_5$ | $D_6$ | $D_7$ |
| 0 | 0 | 0 | 1 | 0 | 0 | 0 | 0 | 0 | 0 | 0 |
| 0 | 0 | 1 | 0 | 1 | 0 | 0 | 0 | 0 | 0 | 0 |
| 0 | 1 | 0 | 0 | 0 | 1 | 0 | 0 | 0 | 0 | 0 |
| 0 | 1 | 1 | 0 | 0 | 0 | 1 | 0 | 0 | 0 | 0 |
| 1 | 0 | 0 | 0 | 0 | 0 | 0 | 1 | 0 | 0 | 0 |
| 1 | 0 | 1 | 0 | 0 | 0 | 0 | 0 | 1 | 0 | 0 |
| 1 | 1 | 0 | 0 | 0 | 0 | 0 | 0 | 0 | 1 | 0 |
| 1 | 1 | 1 | 0 | 0 | 0 | 0 | 0 | 0 | 0 | 1 |

**Fig. 5.7:** Truth table for a 3 × 8 decoder.

The combinational circuit for 3 × 8 decoder consists of eight AND gates and three NOT gates. Each of the eight AND gates corresponds to one of the eight minterms of the three input variables X, Y, Z and the NOT gates are used to generate $\overline{X}, \overline{Y}, \overline{Z}$ required for minterms. The complete logic circuit of a 3 by 8 decoder is shown in Figure 5.8.

Output values are mutually exclusive and only one output variable can be equal to 1 at any given time.

Sometimes, an *enable input* is used in a decoder to control circuit operations. In this case, the circuit functions only when enable input is 1. Whenever enable input is 0, all outputs remain at 0 and when enable input is 1, the outputs of the decoder take their values as usual. This is achieved by simply inputting the enable input to all the AND gates of the decoder circuit. The 3 by 8 decoder with an enable input is shown in Figure 5.9 and the logic diagram in Figure 5.10.

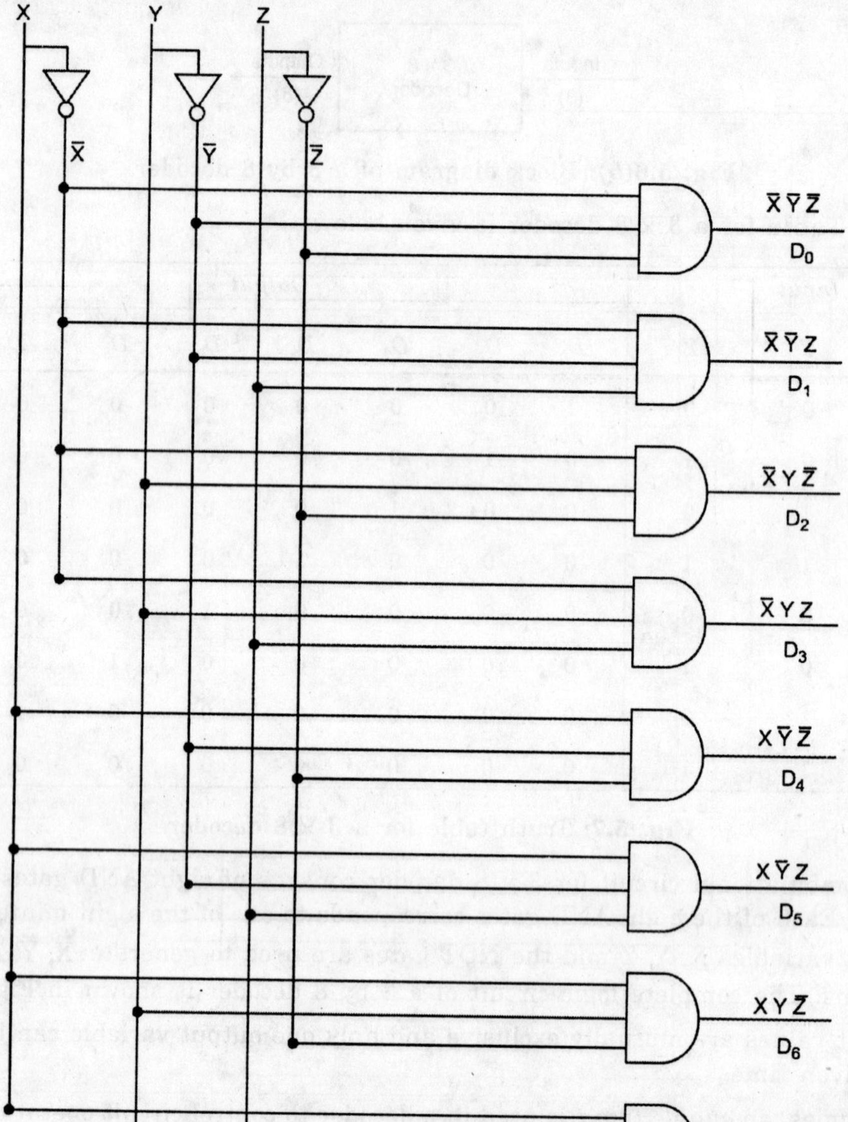


**Fig. 5.8:** Logic circuit of a 3 by 8 decoder.

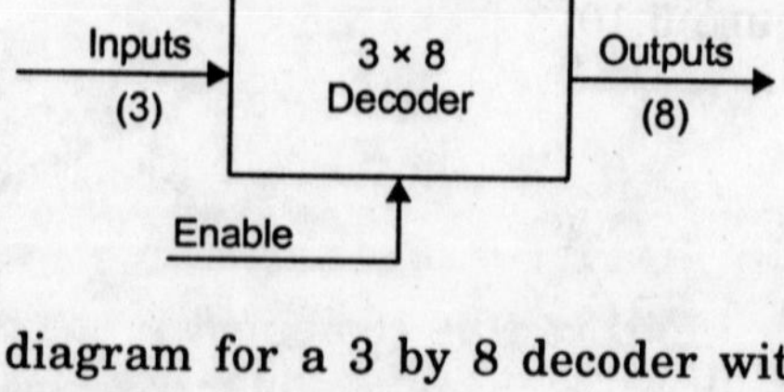


**Fig. 5.9:** Block diagram for a 3 by 8 decoder with enable input.

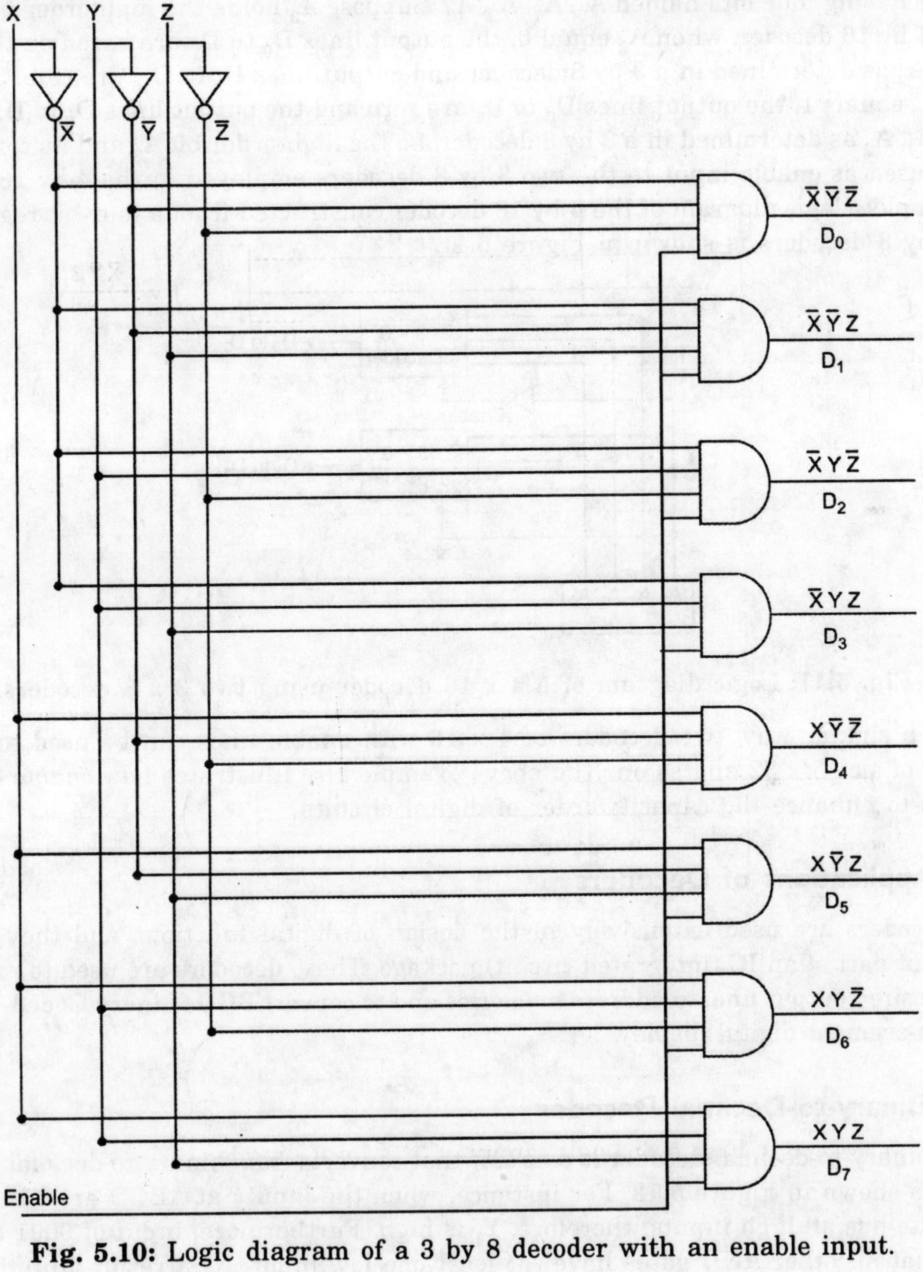


**Fig. 5.10: Logic diagram of a 3 by 8 decoder with an enable input.**

### 5.5.2 4 x 16 Decoder

Decoders with an enable input can be combined to make decoders of higher order. For example, two 3 by 8 decoders with an enable input can be combined to make a decoder of 4 by 16. The binary information held in a four-bit register (a group of memory elements that stores a word) can be decoded with a 4 by 16 decoder. We shall illustrate this application by using two 3 by 8 decoders with enable inputs and connect them to the register having four bits named $A_0$, $A_1$, $A_2$, $A_3$. Suppose $A_3$ holds the high-order bit so that in the 4 by 16 decoder, when $A_3$ equal 0, the output lines $D_0$ to $D_7$ are based on the inputs $A_0$, $A_1$, $A_2$ as determined in a 3 by 8 decoder and output lines $D_8$ to $D_{15}$ are zero. Similarly, when $A_3$ equals 1, the output lines $D_0$ to $D_7$ are zero and the output lines $D_8$ to $D_{15}$ depend on $A_0$, $A_1$, $A_2$ as determined in a 3 by 8 decoder. So the high-order bit $A_3$ and its compliment $A_3$ are used as enable input to the two 3 by 8 decoders employed in the 4 by 16 decoder. The complete logic diagram of the 4 by 16 decoder constructed from a four-bit register and two 3 by 8 decoders is shown in Figure 5.11.

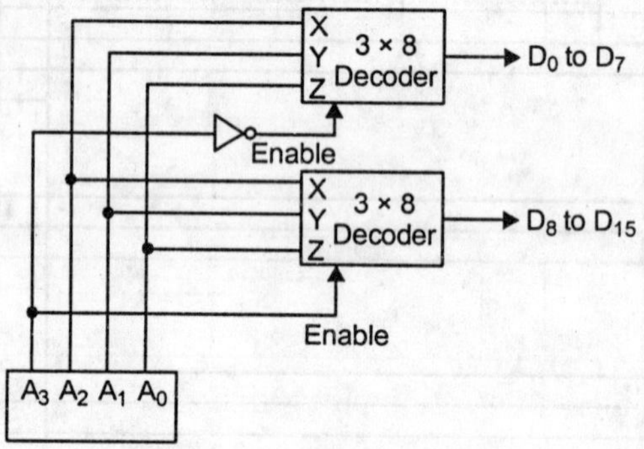


**Fig. 5.11:** Logic diagram of a 4 x 16 decoder using two 3 x 8 decoders.

In a similar way, two decoders of 4 × 16 with enable lines can be used to make a decoder of size 5 × 32 and so on. The above example also illustrates how *enable* lines can be used to enhance the capacity/order of digital circuits.

### 5.5.3 Applications of Decoders

Decoders are used extensively in the design of digital functions and they form an important part of an IC (integrated circuit) package. These decoders are used to route data to the desired output line, to address memories and to convert BCD (Binary-Coded-Decimal) to seven-segment digital display.

### 5.5.4 Binary-to-Decimal Decoder

A binary-to-decimal decoder is a circuit that converts from binary to decimal. Its logic circuit is shown in Figure 5.12. For instance, when the inputs at ABCD are 0001, the $Y_1$ AND gate has all high inputs; therefore, $Y_1$ is high. Furthermore, input of 0001 at ABCD mean that all other AND gates have at least one low input. As a result, all other AND gates have low outputs.

If the input ABCD change to 0000, only the $Y_0$ AND gate has all high inputs; therefore, only $Y_0$ is high. If the input ABCD change to 0111, $Y_7$ is the only high output.

In general, the subscript of the high output equals the decimal equivalent of the binary number inputted at ABCD. This is why the circuit is called a *binary-to-decimal* decoder.

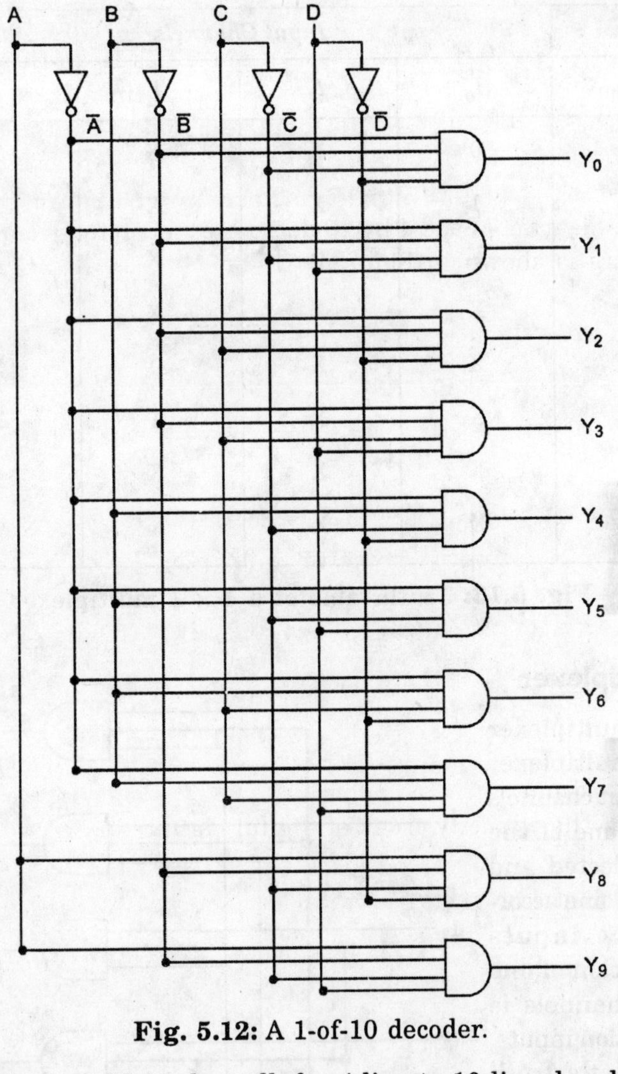


**Fig. 5.12:** A 1-of-10 decoder.

The circuit in Figure 5.12 is also called a 4-line-to-10-line decoder because there are 4 input lines are 10 output lines. Another name for it is a 1-of-10 decoder because only 1 of 10 output lines has a high voltage.

## 5.6 MULTIPLEXERS

Multiplexer is one of important combinational circuits and has wide range of applications. The term multiplex means *"many into one"*. Multiplexer transmits large numbers of information channels to a smaller numbers of channels. A *digital multiplexer* is a combinational circuit that selects binary information from one of the many input channels and transmits to a single output line. That is why the multiplexers are also called as ***Data Selectors.*** The selection of the particular input channel is controlled by a set of select inputs. A digital multiplexer of $2^n$ input channels can be controlled by $n$ numbers of select lines and input line is selected according to the bit combinations of select lines.

| *Selection Inputs* | | *Input Channels* | | | | *Output* |
|---|---|---|---|---|---|---|
| $S_1$ | $S_0$ | $I_0$ | $I_1$ | $I_2$ | $I_3$ | $Y$ |
| 0 | 0 | 0 | X | X | X | 0 |
| 0 | 0 | 1 | X | X | X | 1 |
| 0 | 1 | X | 0 | X | X | 0 |
| 0 | 1 | X | 1 | X | X | 1 |
| 1 | 0 | X | X | 0 | X | 0 |
| 1 | 0 | X | X | 1 | X | 1 |
| 1 | 1 | X | X | X | 0 | 0 |
| 1 | 1 | X | X | X | 1 | 1 |

**Fig. 5.13:** Truth table of a 4 × 1 multiplexer.

### 5.6.1 4 x 1 Multiplexer

A 4 to 1 line multiplexer is defined as the multiplexer consisting of four input channels and information of one of the channels can be selected and transmitted to output line according to the select inputs combinations. Selection of one of the four input channels is possible by two selection inputs. Figure 5.13 illustrates the truth table. Inputs channels $I_0$, $I_1$, $I_2$ and $I_3$ are selected by the combinations of select inputs $S_1$ and $S_0$. The circuit diagram is shown in Figure 5.14. To demonstrate the operation, let us consider that select input combination $S_1S_0$ is 01. The AND gate associated with $I_1$ will have two of inputs equal to logic 1 and third input is connected to $I_1$. Therefore output of this AND gate is according to the information provided by channel $I_1$. The other three AND gates have logic 0 to at least one of their inputs which makes their outputs to logic 0. Hence OR output (Y) is equal to the data provided by the channel $I_1$. Thus information

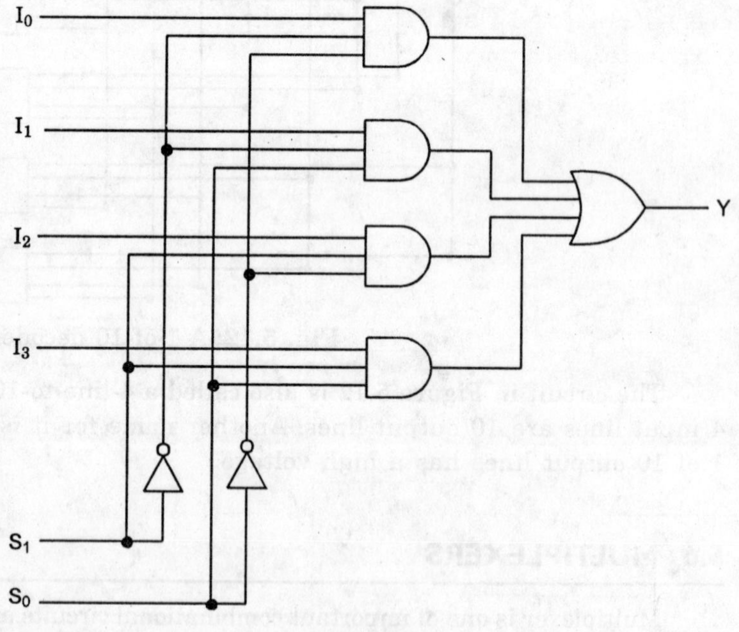


Fig. 5.14

from $I_1$ is available at Y. Normally a multiplexer has an ENABLE input also to control its operation. The ENABLE input (also called as STROBE) is useful to expand two or more multiplexer ICs to a digital multiplexer with a larger number of inputs which will be demonstrated at later part of this section. A multiplexer is often abbreviated as MUX. Its block diagram is shown in Figure 5.15.

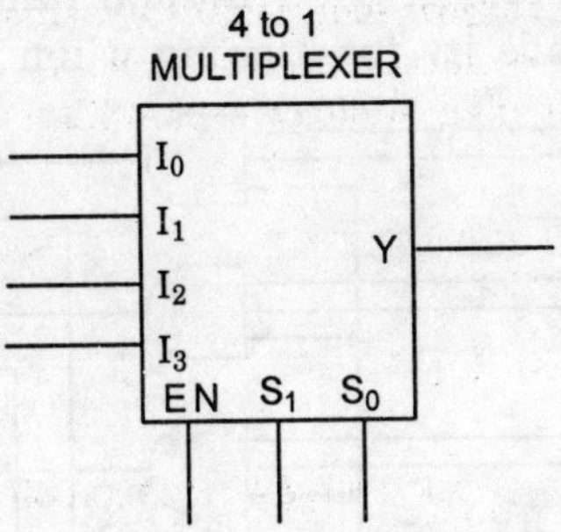


**Fig. 5.15**

## 5.6.2 Using Decoder to Form Multiplexer

If the multiplexer circuit is inspected critically, it may be observed that multiplexer circuit resembles with decoder circuit and indeed the $n$ select lines are decoded to $2^n$ lines which are ANDed with the channel inputs. Figure 5.16 demonstrates how decoder is employed to form a 4 to 1 multiplexer.

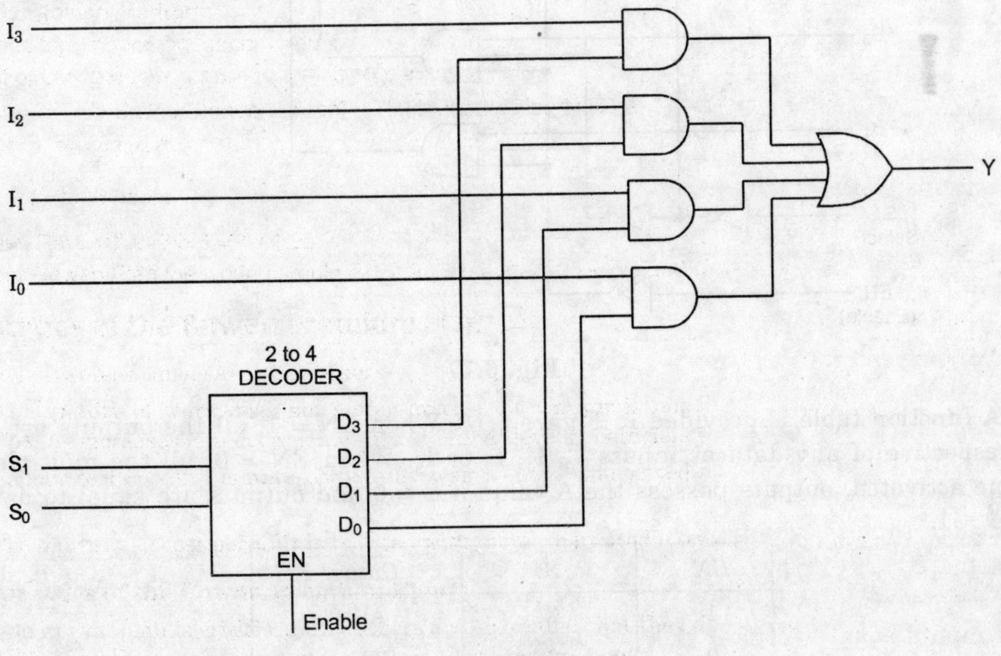


**Fig. 5.16**

In some cases two or more multiplexers are accommodated within one IC package. The selection and ENABLE inputs in multiple-unit ICs may be common to all multiplexers.

The internal circuit diagram of a quadruple 2 to 1 multiplexer IC is illustrated in Figure 5.17. It has four multiplexers, each capable of selecting one of two input lines. Either of the inputs $A_1$ or $B_1$ may be selected to provide output at $Y_1$. Similarly $Y_2$ may have the value of $A_2$ or $B_2$ and so on. One input selection line S is sufficient to perform the selection operation of one of the two input lines in all four multiplexers. The control input EN enables the multiplexers for their normal function when it is at logic 0 state, and all the multiplexers suspends its functioning when EN is logic 1.

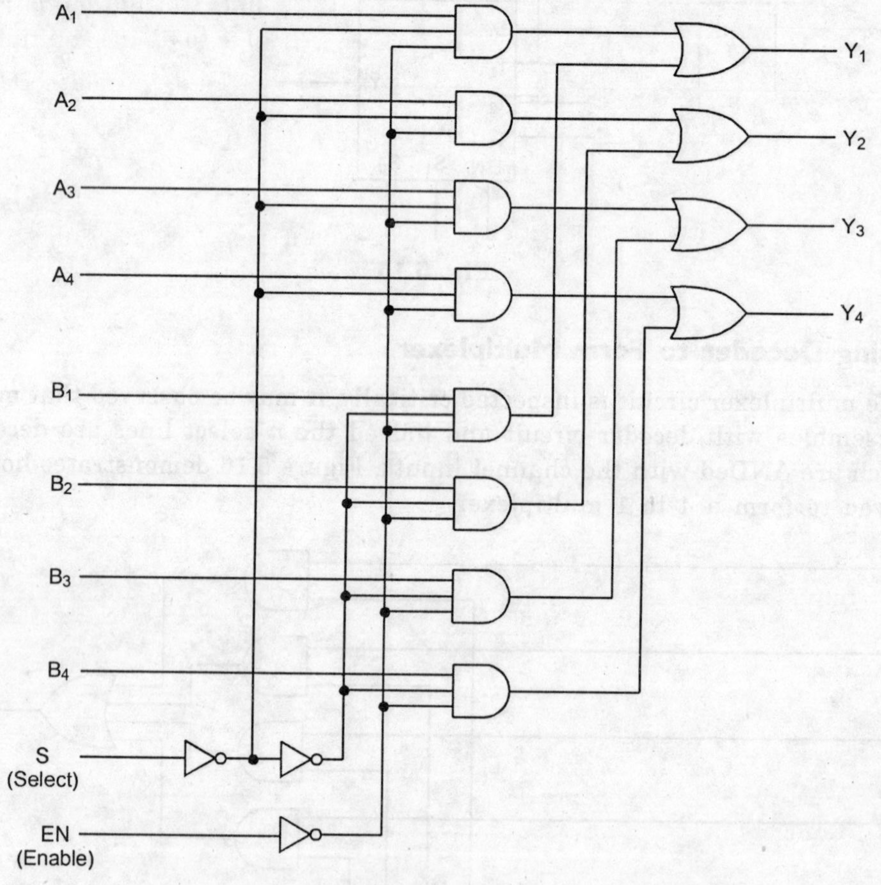


**Fig. 5.17**

A function table is provided in Figure 5.18. When EN = 1, all the outputs are logic 0, irrespective of any data at inputs $I_0$, $I_1$, $I_2$ or $I_3$. When EN = 0, all the multiplexers become activated, outputs possess the A value if S = 0 and outputs are equal to data at B if S = 1.

| *EN* | *S* | *Output Y* |
|---|---|---|
| 1 | X | All 0's |
| 0 | 0 | Select A |
| 0 | 1 | Select B |

**Fig. 5.18**

### 5.6.3 Cascading of Multiplexers

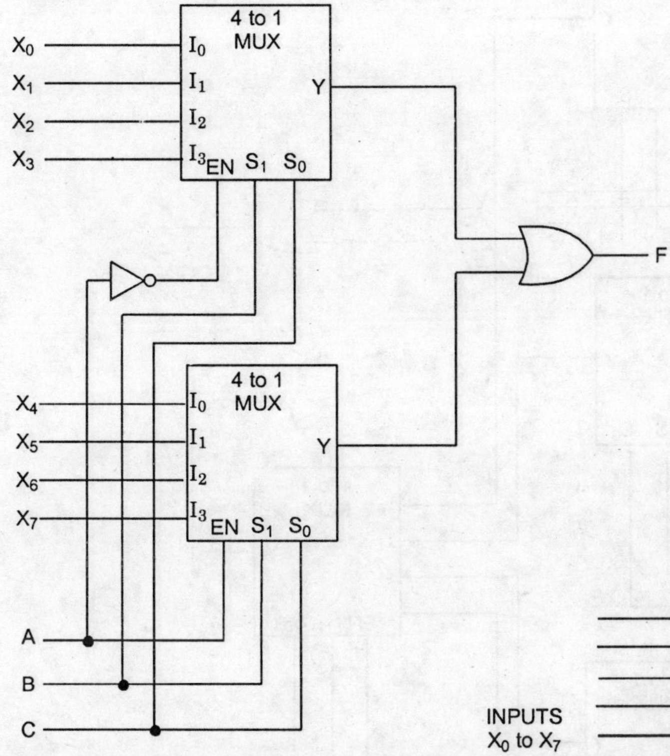


**Fig. 5.19:** Implementing a 8 × 1 MUX using two 4 × 1 MUXs.

As stated earlier multiplexers of larger number of inputs can be implemented by the multiplexers of smaller number of input lines. Figure 5.19 illustrates that a 8 to 1 line multiplexer is realized by two 4 to 1 line multiplexers.

Here variables B and C are applied to select inputs $S_1$ and $S_0$ of both the multiplexer whereas ENABLE input of upper multiplexer is connected to $\overline{A}$ and lower multiplexer is connected to A. So for A = 0, upper multiplexer is selected and input lines $X_0$ to $X_3$ are selected according to select inputs and data is transmitted to output through OR gate. When A = 1, lower multiplexer is activated and input lines $X_4$ to $X_7$ are selected according to select inputs.

Similarly 16 to 1 multiplexer may be developed by two 8 to 1 multiplexers as shown in Figure 5.20. Alternatively a 16 to 1 multiplxer can be realized with five 4 to 1 multiplexers as shown in Figure 5.21.

The multiplexer is very useful MSI function and has various ranges of applications in data communication. Signal routing and data communication are the important applications of multiplexer. It is used for connecting two or more sources to guide to a single destination among computer units and it is useful for constructing a common bus system.

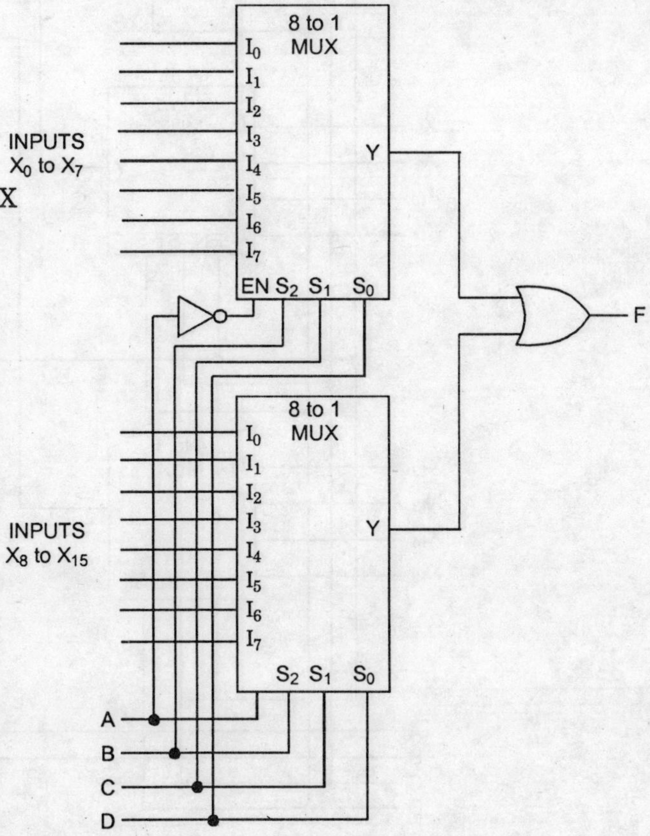


**Fig. 5.20:** Implementing a 16 × 1 MUX using two 8 × 1 MUXs.

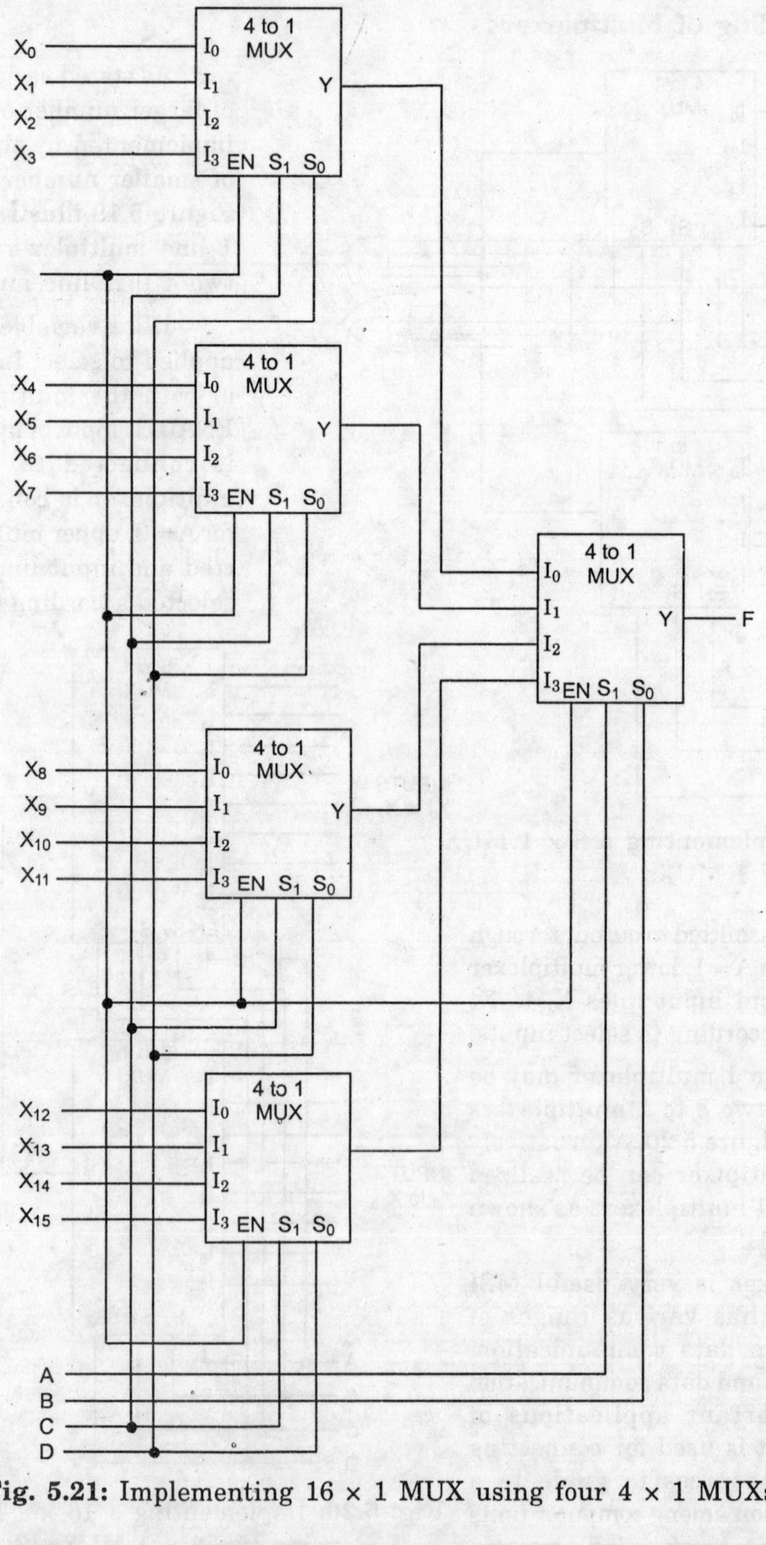


**Fig. 5.21:** Implementing 16 × 1 MUX using four 4 × 1 MUXs.

A 16-to-1 multiplexer can also be implemented as shown in Figure 5.22.

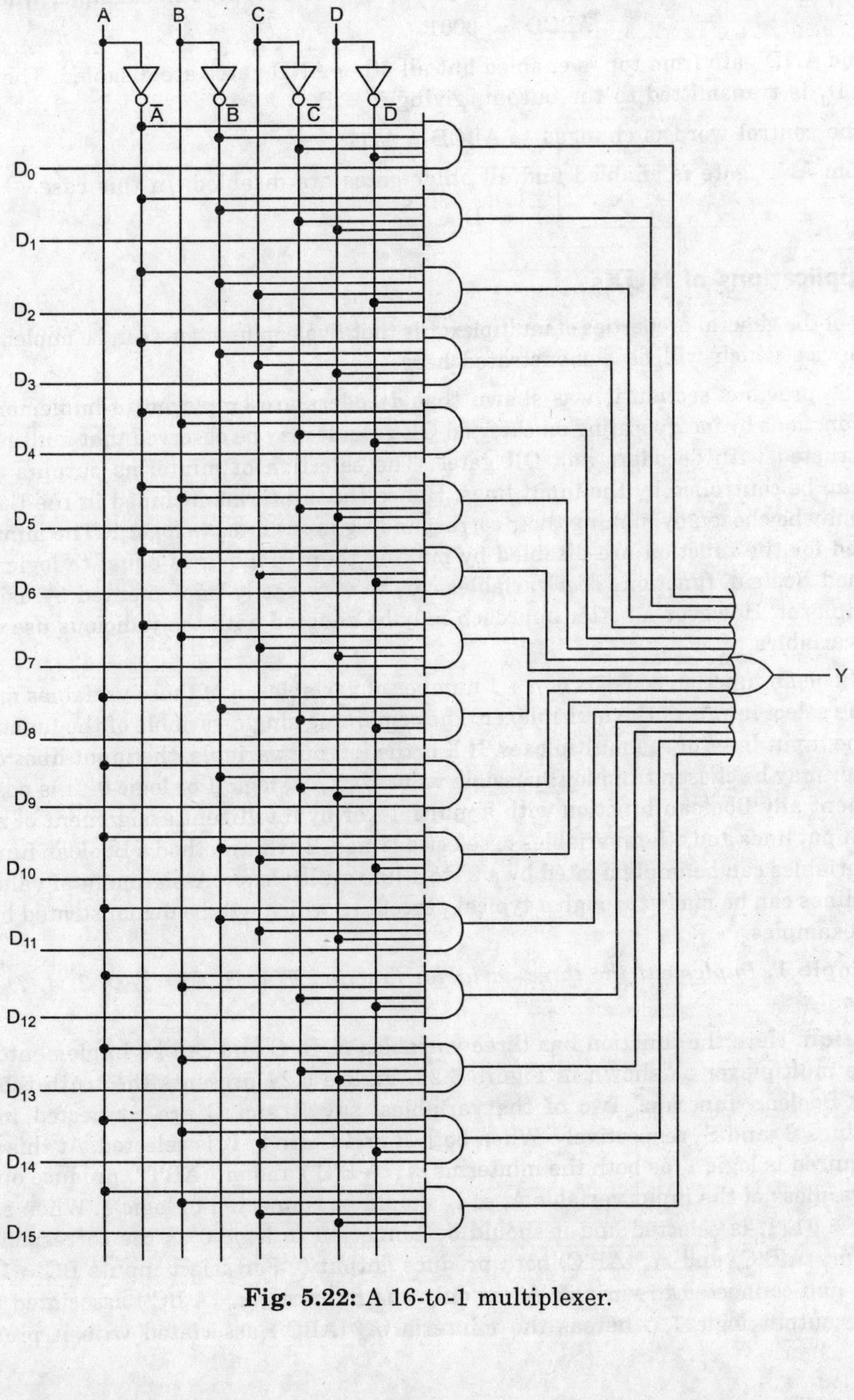


**Fig. 5.22:** A 16-to-1 multiplexer.

The input bits are $D_0$ to $D_{15}$. Only one of these is transmitted to the output. Control word ABCD determines which data bit is passed to the output. For example, when

$$ABCD = 0001$$

the second AND gate from top is enabled but all other AND gates are disabled. Therefore, data bit $D_1$ is transmitted to the output, giving $Y = D_1$.

If the control word is changed to ABCD = 1111

the bottom AND gate is enabled and all other gates are disabled. In this case,

$$Y = D_{15}.$$

### 5.6.4 Applications of MUXs

One of the general properties of multiplexer is that Boolean functions can be implemented by this device which will be demonstrated here.

In the previous section it was shown that decoders are employed to implement the Boolean functions by incorporating an external OR gate. It may be observed that multiplexers are constructed with decoders and OR gates. The selection of minterms outputs of the decoder can be controlled by the input lines. Hence the minterms included in the Boolean function may be chosen by making their corresponding input lines to logic 1. The minterms not needed for the function are disabled by making their input lines equal to logic 0. By this method Boolean functions of $n$ variables can be very easily implemented by using $2^n$ to 1 multiplexer. However a better approach may be adopted with the judicious use of the function variables.

If a Boolean function consists of $n + 1$ number of variables, $n$ of these variables may be used as the select inputs of the multiplexer. The remaining single variable of the function is used as the input lines of the multiplexer. If X is the left out variable, the input lines of the multiplexer may be chosen from four possible values, - X, X′, logic 1 or logic 0. It is possible to implement any Boolean function with a multiplexer by intelligent assignment of above values to input lines and other variables to selection lines. By this method a Boolean function of $n + 1$ variables can be implemented by a $2^n$ to 1 line multiplexer. Assignment of values to the input lines can be made through a typical procedure which will be demonstrated by the following examples.

**Example 1.** *Implement the three variables function* $F(A, B, C) = \Sigma\,(0, 2, 4, 7)$ *with multiplexer.*

**Solution.** Here the function has three variables A, B, C and can be implemented by 4 to 1 line multiplexer as shown in Figure 5.23. Figure 5.24 presents the truth table of the above Boolean function. Two of the variables, say B and C are connected to the selection lines $S_1$ and $S_0$ respectively. When both B and C are 0, $I_0$ is selected. At this time output required is logic 1, as both the minterms $m_0$ (A′B′C′) and $m_4$ (AB′C′) produce output logic 1 regardless of the input variable A, so $I_0$ should be connected to logic 1. When select inputs BC = 01, $I_1$ is selected and it should be connected to logic 0 as the corresponding minterms $m_1$ (A′B′C) and $m_5$ (AB′C) both produce output 0. For select inputs BC = 10, $I_2$ is selected and connected to variable A′, as only one minterm $m_2$ (A′BC′) associated with A′ produce output logic 1, whereas the minterm $m_6$ (ABC′) associated with A produce output 0. And finally $I_3$ is selected and connected to variable A, when select inputs BC = 11, because only the minterm $m7$ (ABC) produce output 1, whereas output is 0 for the minterm $m_3$ (A′BC). Multiplexer must be at enabled mode to be at its working condition. Hence EN input is connected to logic 1.

| *Minterms* | *A* | *B* | *C* | *F* |
|---|---|---|---|---|
| 0 | 0 | 0 | 0 | 1 |
| 1 | 0 | 0 | 1 | 0 |
| 2 | 0 | 1 | 0 | 1 |
| 3 | 0 | 1 | 1 | 0 |
| 4 | 1 | 0 | 0 | 1 |
| 5 | 1 | 0 | 1 | 0 |
| 6 | 1 | 1 | 0 | 0 |
| 7 | 1 | 1 | 1 | 1 |

**Fig. 5.23**

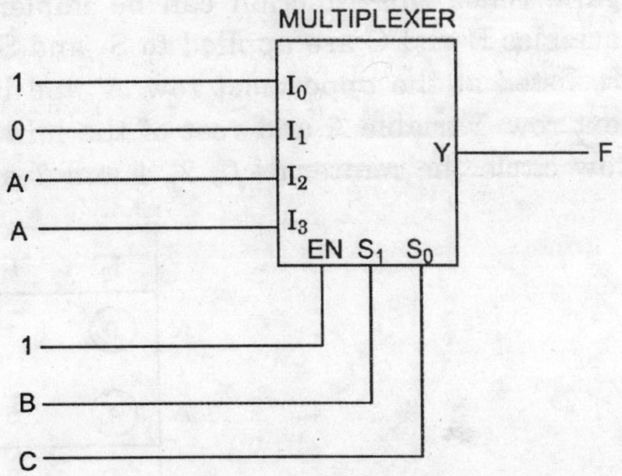


**Fig. 5.24**

The above analysis describes how a Boolean function can be implemented with the help of multiplexers. However there is a general procedure for implementation of Boolean function of $n$ variables with a $2^{n-1}$ to 1 multiplexer.

First, the function is to be expressed in its sum of the minterms form. Assume that most significant variable will be used at input lines and other $n$–1 variables will be connected to selection lines of the multiplexer in ordered sequence. This means lowest significant variable is connected to $S_0$ input, next higher significant variable is connected to $S_1$, next higher variable to $S_2$ and so on. Now consider the single variable A. Since this variable represents the highest order position in the sequence of variables, it will be at complemented form in the minterms 0 to $2^{n-1}$ which comparises of the first half in the list of minterms. The variable A is at uncomplemented form in the second half of list of the minterms. For a three variables function like example 1, among the possible eight minterms, A is complemented for the minterms 0 to 3 and at uncomplemented form for the minterms 4 to 7.

An implementation table is now formed, where the input designations of the multiplexer is listed in the first row. Under them the minterms where A is at complemented form in row-wise. At the next row other minterms of A at uncomplemented form are listed. Circle those minterms which produce output to logic 1.

If two elements or minterms of a column are not circled, write 0 under that column.

If both the two elements or minterms of a column are circled, write 1 under that column.

If upper element or minterm of a column is circled but not the bottom, write A′ under that column.

If lower element or minterm of a column is circled but not the upper one, write A under that column.

The lower most row now indicates input behavior of the corresponding input lines of the multiplexer as marked at the top of the column.

The above procedure can be more clearly understood if we consider the example 1 again. Since this function can be implemented by a multiplexer, the lower significant variables B and C are applied to $S_1$ and $S_0$ respectively. The inputs of multiplexer $I_0$ to $I_3$ are listed at the uppermost row. A′ and its corresponding minterms 0 to 3 are placed at next row. Variable A and rest of the minterms 4 to 7 are placed next as in Figure 5.25. Now circle the minterms 0, 2, 4 and 7 as these minterms produce logic 1 output.

| | $I_0$ | $I_1$ | $I_2$ | $I_3$ |
|---|---|---|---|---|
| A′ | (0) | 1 | (2) | 3 |
| A | (4) | 5 | 6 | (7) |
| | 1 | 0 | A′ | A |

**Fig. 5.25**

From Figure 5.25, it can seen that both the elements of the first column 0 and 4 are circled. Therefore '1' is placed at the bottom of that column. At the second column no elements are circled and so '0' is placed at the bottom of the column. At third column only '2' is circled. Its corresponding variable is A′ and so A′ is written at the bottom of this column. And finally, at fourth column only '7' is circled and A is marked at the bottom of the column. Muxltiplexer inputs are now decided as $I_0$ =1, $I_1$ =0, $I_2$ = A′ and $I_3$ = A.

It may be noted that it is not necessary to reserve the most significant variable for the use at multiplexer inputs. The example 1 may also be implemented if variable C is used at multiplexer inputs and, A and B are applied to selection inputs $S_1$ and $S_0$ respectively. In this case the function table is to be modified as Figure 5.26 and circuit implementation is shown at Figure 5.27. Note that the places of minterms are changed in the implementation table in Figure 5.26 due to change in assignment of selection inputs.

| | $I_0$ | $I_1$ | $I_2$ | $I_3$ |
|---|---|---|---|---|
| C′ | (0) | (2) | (4) | 6 |
| C | 1 | 3 | 5 | (7) |
| | C′ | C′ | C′ | C |

**Fig. 5.26**

It is also to be noted that it is not always necessary to assign the most significant variable or the least significant variable out of *n* variables to the multiplexer inputs and rest are applied to selection inputs. It is also not necessary that the selection inputs are connected in order. However these types of connections will increase the complexities at preparation of implementation table as well as circuit implementation.

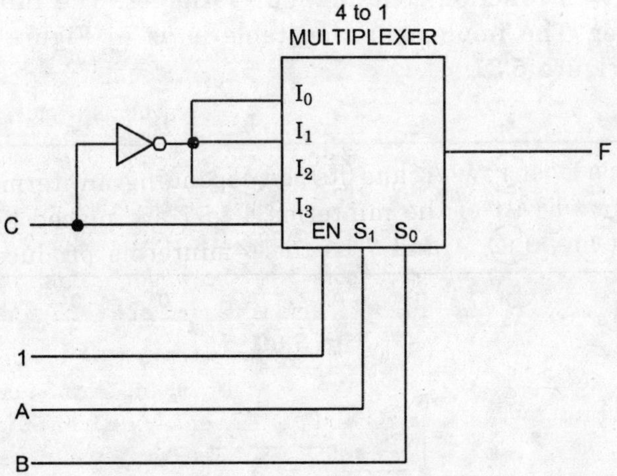


**Fig. 5.27**

Multiplexers are employed at numerous applications in digital systems. They are immensely used in the field of data communication, data selection, data routing, operation sequencing, parallel to serial conversion, waveform generation, logic function implementation.

**Example 2.** *Implement the following function using multiplexer.*

$$F(A, B, C) = \Sigma\ (1, 3, 5, 6)$$

**Solution.** The given function contains three variables. The function can be realized by one 4:1 multiplexer. The implementation table is as in Figure 5.28 and the circuit diagram is given in Figure 5.29.

| | $I_0$ | $I_1$ | $I_2$ | $I_3$ |
|---|---|---|---|---|
| A' | 0 | ① | 2 | ③ |
| A | 4 | ⑤ | ⑥ | 7 |
| | 0 | 1 | A | A' |

**Fig. 5.28**

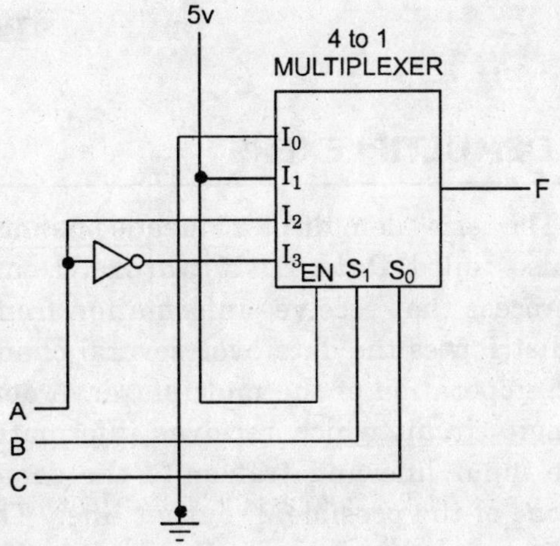


**Fig. 5.29**

**Example 3.** *Implement the following function with a multiplexer.*

$$F\ (A, B, C, D) = \Sigma\ (0, 1, 3, 4, 8, 9, 15)$$

**Solution.** The given function contains four variables. The function can be realized by one 8:1 multiplexer. The implementation table is as in Figure 5.30 and the circuit diagram is given in Figure 5.31.

| | $I_0$ | $I_1$ | $I_2$ | $I_3$ | $I_4$ | $I_5$ | $I_6$ | $I_7$ |
|---|---|---|---|---|---|---|---|---|
| A′ | (0) | (1) | 2 | (3) | (4) | 5 | 6 | 7 |
| A | (8) | (9) | 10 | 11 | 12 | 13 | 14 | (15) |
| | 1 | 1 | 0 | A′ | A′ | 0 | 0 | A |

**Fig. 5.30**

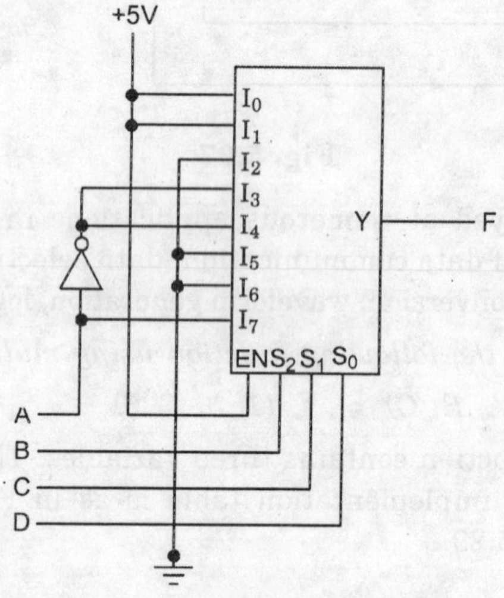


**Fig. 5.31**

## 5.7 DEMULTIPLEXERS

The term "demultiplex" means one into many. These are also called **Data Distributors.** Demultiplexing is the process that receives information from one channel and distributes the data over several channels. It is the reverse operation of the multiplexer. A demultiplexer is the logic circuit which receives information through a single input line and transmits the same information over one of the possible $2^n$ output lines. The selection of specific output line is controlled by the bit combinations of selection lines.

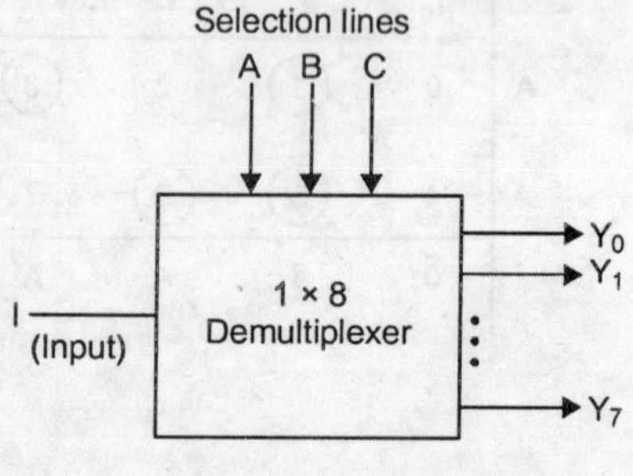


**Fig. 5.32:** Block diagram of a 1 × 8 demultiplexer.

### 5.7.1 1 x 8 Demultiplexer

**Block diagram** of a 1 × 8 demultiplexer is given in Figure 5.32.

**Truth Table** for 1 × 8 demultiplexer is given below:

| *Selection Inputs* | | | *Outputs* | | | | | | | |
|---|---|---|---|---|---|---|---|---|---|---|
| *A* | *B* | *C* | $Y_0$ | $Y_1$ | $Y_2$ | $Y_3$ | $Y_4$ | $Y_5$ | $Y_6$ | $Y_7$ |
| 0 | 0 | 0 | $Y_0$ = I | 0 | 0 | 0 | 0 | 0 | 0 | 0 |
| 0 | 0 | 1 | 0 | $Y_1$ = I | 0 | 0 | 0 | 0 | 0 | 0 |
| 0 | 1 | 0 | 0 | 0 | $Y_2$ = I | 0 | 0 | 0 | 0 | 0 |
| 0 | 1 | 1 | 0 | 0 | 0 | $Y_3$ = I | 0 | 0 | 0 | 0 |
| 1 | 0 | 0 | 0 | 0 | 0 | 0 | $Y_4$ = I | 0 | 0 | 0 |
| 1 | 0 | 1 | 0 | 0 | 0 | 0 | 0 | $Y_5$ = I | 0 | 0 |
| 1 | 1 | 0 | 0 | 0 | 0 | 0 | 0 | 0 | $Y_6$ = I | 0 |
| 1 | 1 | 1 | 0 | 0 | 0 | 0 | 0 | 0 | 0 | $Y_7$ = I |

**Fig. 5.33:** Truth table of 1 × 8 demultiplexer.

A 1 to 8 demultiplexer circuit is demonstrated in Figure 5.34. The selection input lines A, B and C activate an AND gate according to its bit combination. The input line

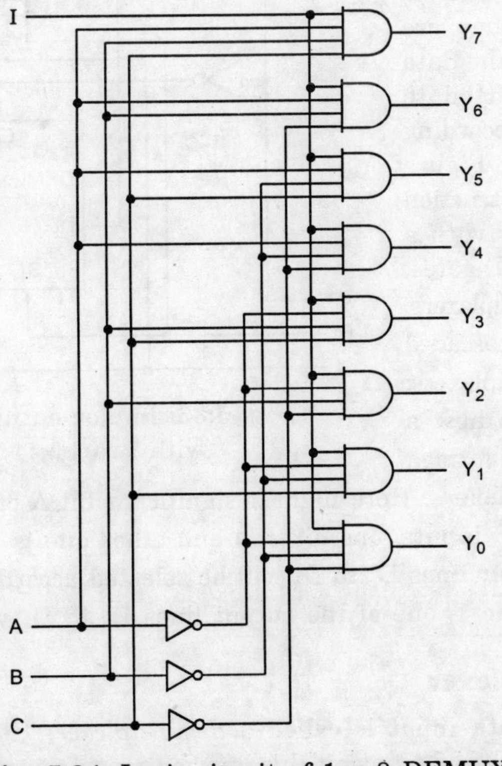


**Fig. 5.34:** Logic circuit of 1 × 8 DEMUX.

I is common to one of the inputs of all the AND gates. So information of I is passed to the output line as activated by the particular AND gate. As example, for selection input combination 000, input I is transmitted to $Y_0$. A truth table is prepared in Figure 5.33 to illustrate relation of selection inputs and output lines.

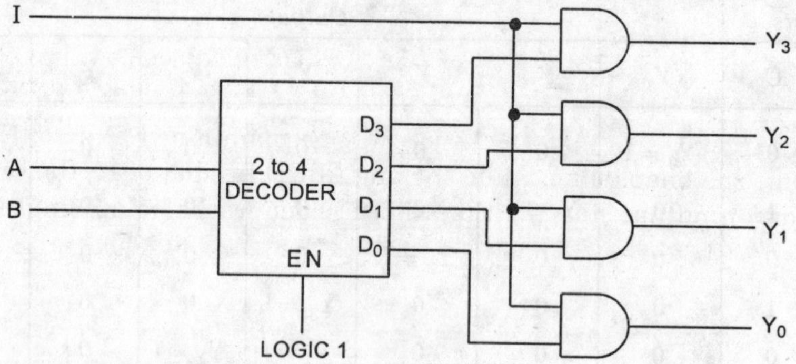


**Fig. 5.35**

It may be noticed that demulti-plexers circuit may be derived from decoder with the use of AND gates. As we have already seen that decoder outputs are equivalent to the minterms, these minterms can be used as the selection of output lines and when they are ANDed with input line I, the data form input I is transmitted to output lines as activated according to the enabled minterms. Figure 5.35 demonstrates the construction of a 1 to 4 demulti-plexer with a 2 to 4 decoder and four AND gates.

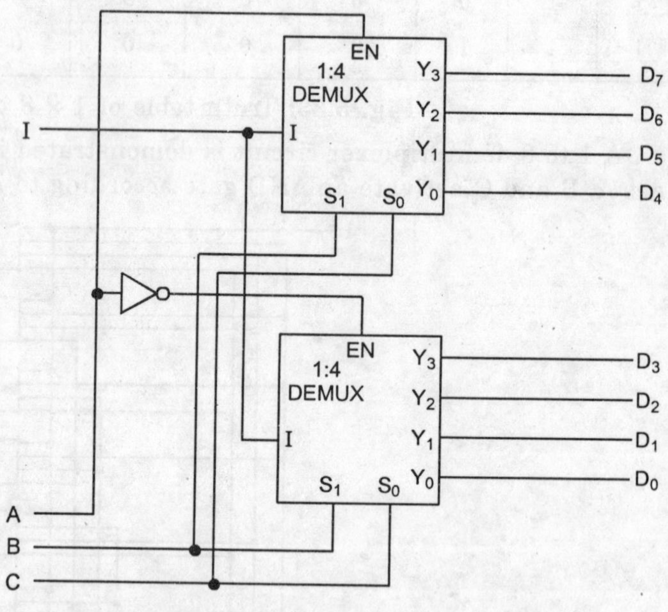


**Fig. 5.36:** Implementing 1 × 8 DEMUX with two 1 × 4 DEMUXs.

Like decoders and multiplexers, demulti-plexers can also be cascaded to form higher order demultiplexers. Figure 5.36 demonstrates how a 1 to 8 demultiplexer can be formed with two 1 to 4 demultiplexers. Here highest significant bit A of the selection inputs is connected to the ENABLE inputs, one directly and other one is complemented. When A is logic 0, one of the output lines $D_0$ to $D_3$ will be selected according to the select inputs B and C, and for A is logic 1, one of the output lines $D_4$ to $D_7$ will be selected.

## 5.7.2 1 x 16 Demultiplexer

A decoder with a data input is called a *demultiplexer*. Its function is to receive information on a single line and transmit this information to any one of $2^n$ possible output lines. The particular output line is selected by the *n*-bit input address. The enable line is used as the data input. We can demonstrate the use of a 4 × 16 decoder as a 1-to-16 demultiplexer as follows. The first 4 input lines ABCD specify the 4-bit destination address for the data and the last input $D_{in}$ (enable line) is for the data. This data input variable (enable line) has a path to all the 16 output lines, but the data input/information is directed to only one of the output lines as specified by the 4 input address lines. For example, if the 4-bit destination address ABCD equals 0011, then output will come on line $D_3$ and all other lines $D_0$, $D_1$, $D_2$, $D_4$ ...., $D_{15}$ will be maintained at zero. Now as the data information comes on enable line, while keeping ABCD fixed at 0011, the same information gets transmitted on output line $D_3$, thus the decoder works as a demultiplexer.

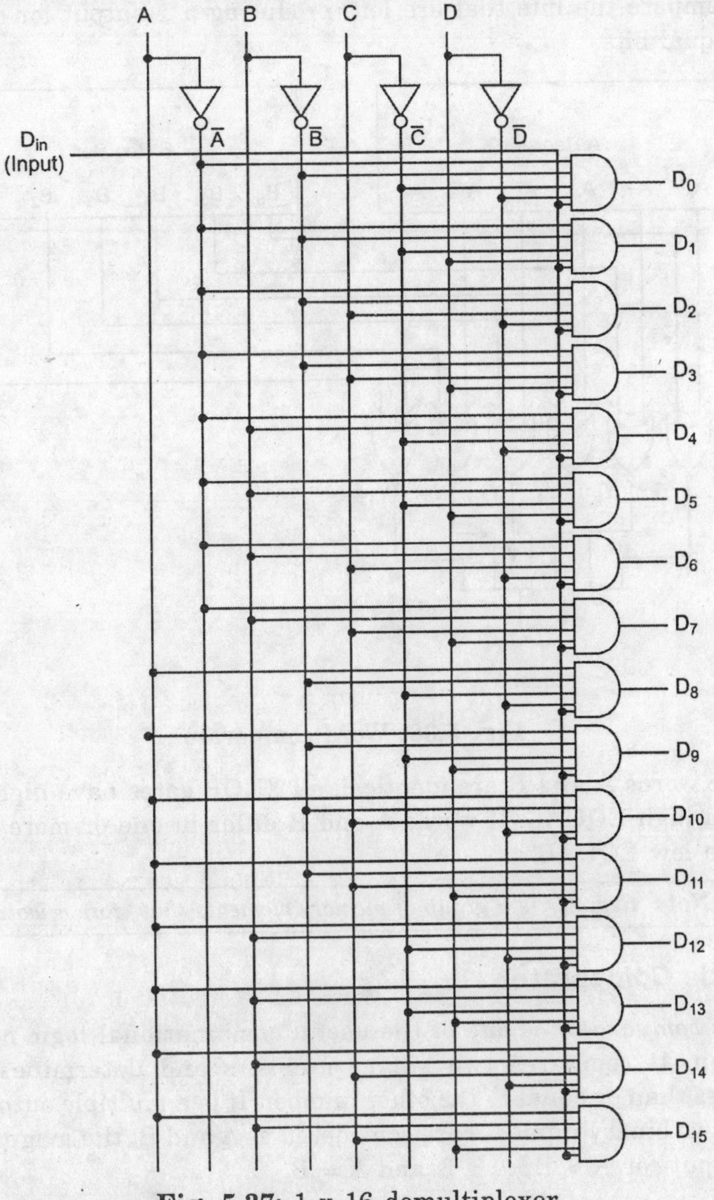


**Fig. 5.37:** 1 x 16 demultiplexer.

## 5.8 COMPARATORS

Comparators are used to compare two binary numbers. These are explained below.

### 5.8.1 Word Comparator

A word comparator is a combinational circuit which recognizes two identical words. Figure 5.38 shows a **word comparator** for six bit words.

The left most XNOR gate compares $A_6$ and $B_6$; if they are same, $Y_6$ is a 1. The second XNOR gate compares $A_5$ and $B_5$; if they are the same, $Y_5$ is a 1. Similarly, the remaining XNOR gates compare the bits that are left, producing a 1 output for equal bits and a 0 output for unequal bits.

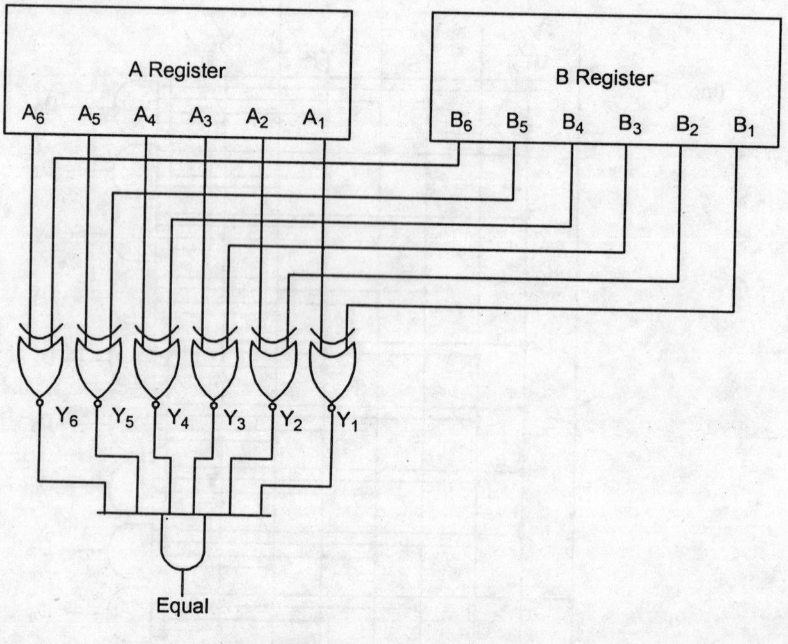


**Fig. 5.38:** Word comparator.

In case the words **A** and **B** are identical, all XNOR gates have high outputs and the AND gate has a high EQUAL. If words **A** and **B** differ in one or more bit positions, the AND gate has a low EQUAL.

> **Note.** *Register is a group of memory elements that store a word.*

### 5.8.2 Magnitude Comparator

*Magnitude comparator* is one of the useful combinational logic networks and has wide application. It compares two binary numbers and determines one number is greater than, less than or equal to the other number. It is a multiple output combinational logic circuit. If two binary numbers are considered as A and B, the magnitude comparator gives three output for A > B, A < B and A = B.

For comparison of two $n$ bit numbers, the classical method to achieve the Boolean expressions requires truth table of $2^{2n}$ entries and becomes too lengthy and cumbersome. It is also desired to have a digital circuit possessing a certain amount of regularity, so that similar circuit can be applied for the comparison of any number of bits. Digital functions which follow an inherent well-defined regularity can be usually developed by means of algorithmic procedure if it exists. An *algorithm* is a process which follows a finite set of steps to arrive at the solution to a problem. A method is illustrated here by deriving an algorithm to design a four bit magnitude comparator.

The algorithm is the direct application of the procedure to compare the relative magnitudes of two binary numbers. Let us consider the two binary numbers A and B are expanded in terms of bits in descending order as

$$A = A_4A_3A_2A_1$$
$$B = B_4B_3B_2B_1$$

Where each subscripted letter represents one of the digits in the number. It is observed from the bit contents of the two numbers that A = B when $A_4 = B_4$, $A_3 = B_3$, $A_2 = B_2$ and $A_1 = B_1$. As the numbers are binary they possess the value of either 1 or 0, the equality relation of each pair can be expressed logically by the equivalence function as

$$X_i = A_i B_i + \overline{A}_i\overline{B}_i \qquad \text{for} \quad i = 1, 2, 3, 4$$

$$\text{Or,} \quad X_i = \overline{(A \oplus B)} \qquad \text{Or,} \quad \overline{X}_i = A \oplus B$$

$$\text{Or,} \quad X_i = \overline{(A_i\overline{B}_i + \overline{A}_iB_i)}$$

$X_i$ is logic 1 when both $A_i$ and $B_i$ are equal *i.e.*, either 1 or 0 at the same instant. To satisfy the equality condition of two numbers A and B, it is necessary that all $X_i$ must be equal to logic 1. This dictates AND operation of all $X_i$ variables. In other words we can write the Boolean expression for two equal four bits numbers

$$F(A = B) = X_4X_3X_2X_1$$

To determine the relative magnitude of two numbers A and B, the relative magnitudes of pairs of significant bits are to be inspected from the most significant position. If the two digits of most significant position are equal, next significant pair of digits are to be compared. The comparison process is to be continued until a pair of unequal digits is found. It may be concluded that A>B, if the corresponding digit of A is 1 and B is 0. On the other hand A<B if the corresponding digit of A is 0 and B is 1. Therefore we can derive the logical expression of such sequential comparison by the following two Boolean functions,

$$F(A>B) = A_4\overline{B}_4 + X_4A_3\overline{B}_3 + X_4X_3A_2\overline{B}_2 + X_4X_3X_2A_1\overline{B}_1$$

and

$$F(A<B) = \overline{A}_4B_4 + X_4\overline{A}_3B_3 + X_4X_3\overline{A}_2B_2 + X_4X_3X_2\overline{A}_1B_1$$

The logic gates implementation for the above expressions are not too complex as they contains many sub-expressions of repetitive nature and can be used at different places. The complete logic diagram of a four bit magnitude comparator is shown in Figure 5.39. This is a multilevel implementation and it may be noticed that the circuit maintains a regular pattern. Therefore expansion of binary magnitude comparator of higher bits can be easily obtained. This combinational circuit is also applicable to the comparison of BCD numbers.

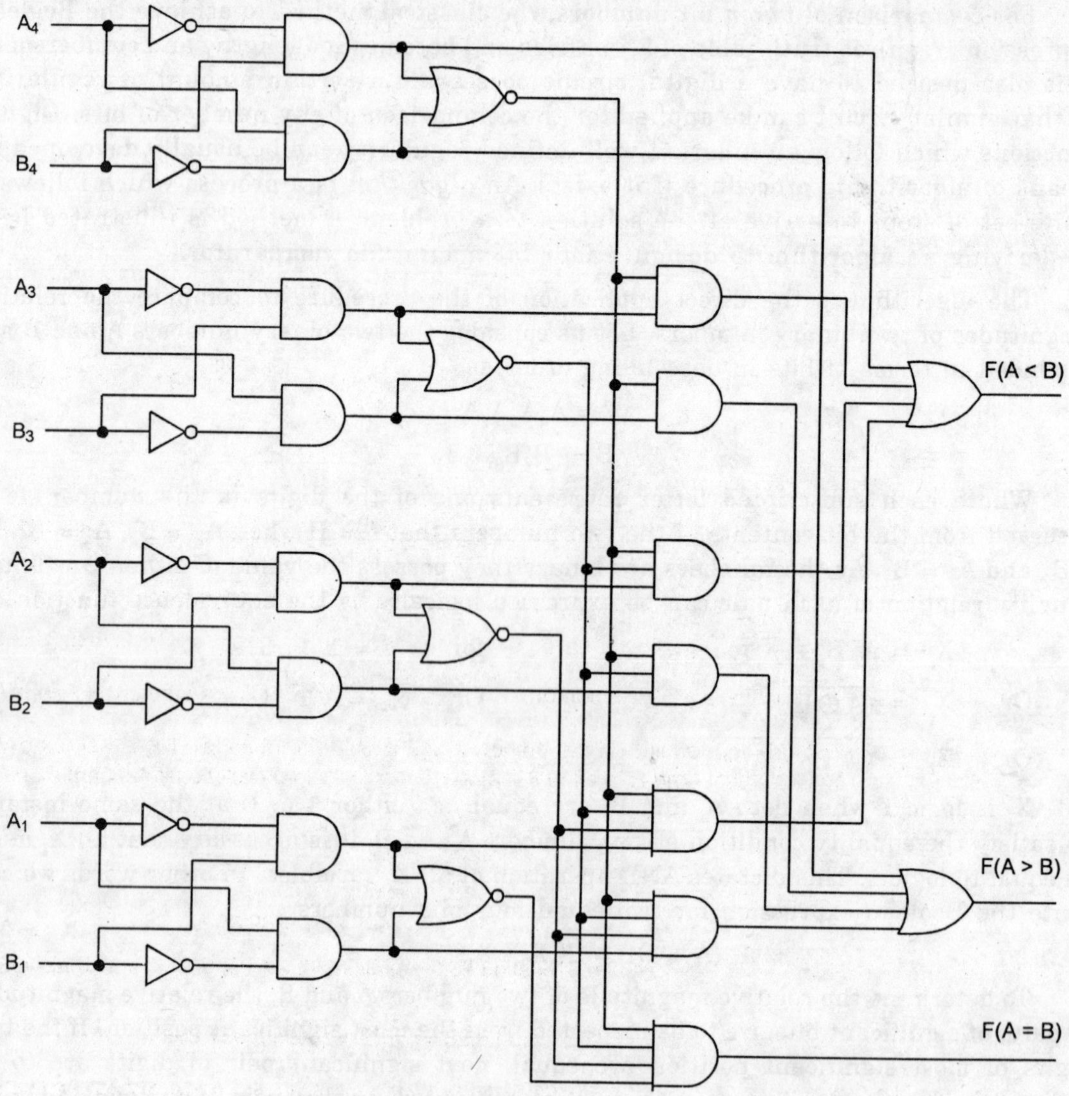


**Fig. 5.39:** Magnitude comparator.

## SUMMARY

- Connected arrangement of logic gates having input and output are called combinational circuits.
- An encoder is a logic circuit that converts from one form to a particular code.
- In a decoder, the binary code of $n$ bits represent up to $2^n$ distinct elements of the coded information.
- Multiplexer is a combinational circuit that receives binary information from multiple lines and sends it into one output line.
- Demultiplexer is the logic circuit which receives information through a single input line and transmits the same information over one of the possible $2^n$ output lines.

- Magnitude comparator is a combinational logic network that compares two binary numbers. It is a multiple output combinational logic circuit.

## REVIEW QUESTIONS AND EXERCISES

1. What is a combinational circuit? How is it different from sequential circuit? Explain.
2. Explain the design procedure of combinational circuit. What are its constraints?
3. What is an encoder? Give the truth table and draw a logic circuit for an encoder which converts a decimal number into binary.
4. Draw a circuit for a hexadecimal encoder.
5. What is a decoder? Give the truth table and draw a logic circuit for a decoder which converts a binary number into decimal number.
6. Explain the 3 to 8 decoder with logic diagram.
7. What is a multiplexer? How are the multiplexers useful to develop combinational circuit?
8. Design a 8 × 1 MUX by using 2 × 1 Multiplexers. Use block diagram only.
9. Implement the following function by using a 4 × 1 multiplexer:

$$F(A, B, C) = \Sigma(1, 2, 3, 5, 7).$$

10. What is a demultiplexer? Design a 1 to 8 demultiplexer using two 1 to 4 demultiplexers.
11. What are comparators? Explain the magnitude comparator.
12. What is the difference between a full-adder and full-subtractor?
13. Draw truth table for full-subtractor, derive expressions for outputs and draw logic diagram using NOR gates.
14. What is the function of enable input(s) for a decoder?
15. What are the major application of multiplexers?
16. A certain multiplexer can switch one of 32 data inputs to output. How many different inputs does this MUX have?
17. State True or False:
    (*i*) The simpler the expression, the simpler the circuit needed for it.
    (*ii*) The keyboard encoder translates binary data into decimal data.
    (*iii*) Encoder is a part of output device in a computer system.
    (*iv*) A decoder is many to one digital device.
18. Fill in the blanks:
    (*i*) The digital circuit used for encoding is known as ............... .
    (*ii*) A ............... is a digital circuit that takes ............... input lines and select exactly one of the possible ............... output lines.

## ANSWERS

17. State True or False:
    (*i*) True (*ii*) False (*iii*) False (*iv*) True
18. Fill in the blanks:
    (*i*) encoder (*ii*) decoder, $n$, $2^n$.

Chapter 6

# FLIP FLOPS

## 6.1 INTRODUCTION

So far all logic circuits we have studied were basically based on the analysis and design of combinational digital circuits. Though these type of circuits are very important, but these constitute only a part of digital systems. The other major aspect of digital system is the analysis and design of sequential digital circuits. However, sequential circuit design depends, greatly, on the combinational circuit design.

The logic circuits whose outputs at any instant of time depend only on the input signals present at that time are known as combinational circuits. The output in combinational circuits does not depend upon any past inputs or outputs. Moreover, in a combinational circuit, the output appears immediately for a change in input, except for the propagation delay through circuit gates.

On the other hand, the logic circuits whose outputs at any instant of time depend on the present inputs as well as on the past outputs are called sequential circuits. In sequential circuits, the output signals are fed back to the input side. A block diagram of a sequential circuit is shown in Figure 6.1.

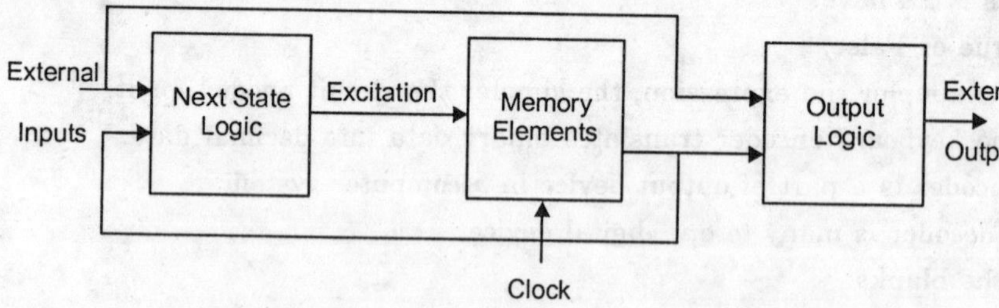


**Fig. 6.1:** Block diagram of a sequential circuit.

From Figure 6.1, we find that it consists of combinational circuits which accept digital signals from external inputs and from outputs of memory elements and generates signals for external outputs and for inputs to memory element referred to as excitation.

A memory element is a medium in which one bit of information (0 or 1) can be stored or retained until necessary, and thereafter its contents can be replaced by a new value. The contents of memory elements can be changed by the outputs of combinational circuits which are connected to its input.

Combinational circuits are often faster than sequential circuits since the combinational circuits do not require memory elements whereas the sequential circuit needs memory elements to perform their operations in sequence.

Sequential circuits are broadly classified in two main categories, known as synchronous or clocked and asynchronous or unclocked sequential circuits depending on the timing of their signals.

A sequential circuit whose behavior can be defined from the knowledge of its signal at discrete instants of time is referred to as a synchronous sequential circuit. In these systems, the memory elements are affected only at discrete instants of time. The synchronization is achieved by a timing device known as system clock which generates a periodic train of clock pulses as shown in Figure 6.2. The outputs are affected only with the application of a clock pulses. The rate at which the master clock generates pulses must be slow enough to permit the slowest circuit to respond. This limits the speed of all circuits. Synchronous circuits have gained considerable domination and wide popularity.

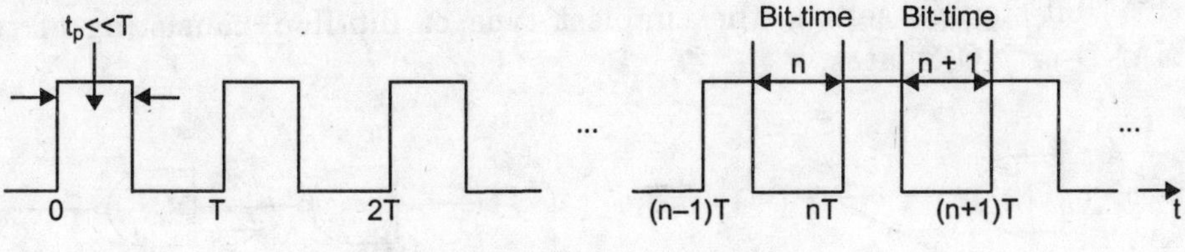


**Fig. 6.2:** Train of pulses.

A sequential circuit whose behavior depends upon the sequence in which the input signals change is referred to as an asynchronous sequential circuit. The output will be affected whenever the input changes. The commonly used memory elements in these circuits are time delay devices. There is no need to wait for a clock pulse. Therefore, in general, asynchronous circuits are faster than synchronous sequential circuits. However, in an asynchronous circuit, events are allowed to occur without any synchronization. And in such a case, the system becomes unstable. Since the designs of asynchronous circuits are more tedious and difficult, therefore their uses are rather limited. The memory elements used in sequential circuits are flip-flops which are capable of storing binary information.

## 6.2 FLIP-FLOPS

The basic one bit digital memory circuit is known as *flip-flop*. It can have only two states, either the 1 state or the 0 state. A flip-flop is also known as *bistable multivibrator*. Flip-flop can be obtained by using NAND or NOR gates. The general block diagram representation of a flip-flop is shown in Figure 6.3. It has one or more inputs and two outputs. The two outputs are complementary to each other. If Q is 1 *i.e.*, Set, then $\overline{Q}$ is 0; if Q is 0 *i.e.*, Reset, then $\overline{Q}$ is 1. That means Q and $\overline{Q}$ cannot be at the same state simultaneously. If it happens by any chance, it violates the definition of flip-flop and hence is called *undefined* condition. Normally the state of Q is called the *state* of flip-flop, whereas the state of $\overline{Q}$ is called the *complementary state* of the flip-flop. When the output Q is either 1 or 0, it remains in that state unless one or more inputs are excited to effect a change in the output. Since the output of the flip-flop remains in the same state until the trigger pulse is applied to change the state, it can be regarded as a memory device to store one binary bit.

As mentioned earlier, a flip-flop is also known as a *bistable multivibrator* whose trigger inputs are named as Set and Reset.

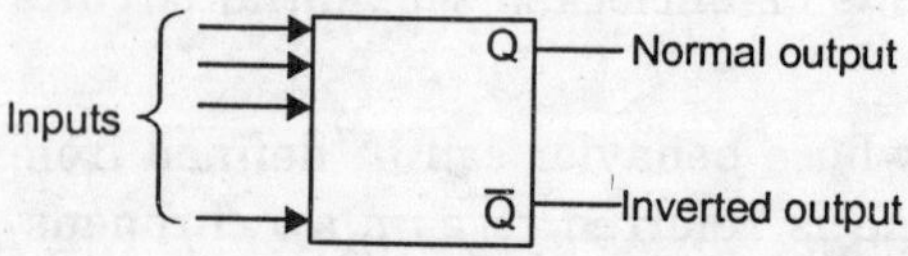


**Fig. 6.3:** Block diagram of a flip-flop.

So, *a flip-flop is a two state circuit that can remain in either state (1 state or 0 state). An external trigger can change the output state.*

### 6.2.1 Latch

Latch (1-bit-storage cell) is the simplest type of flip-flop, consisting of two cross-coupled NAND or NOR gates.

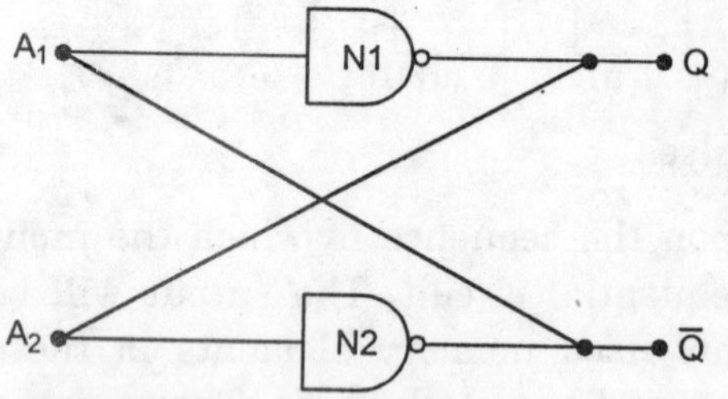


**Fig. 6.4(*a*):** A 1-bit memory or latch.

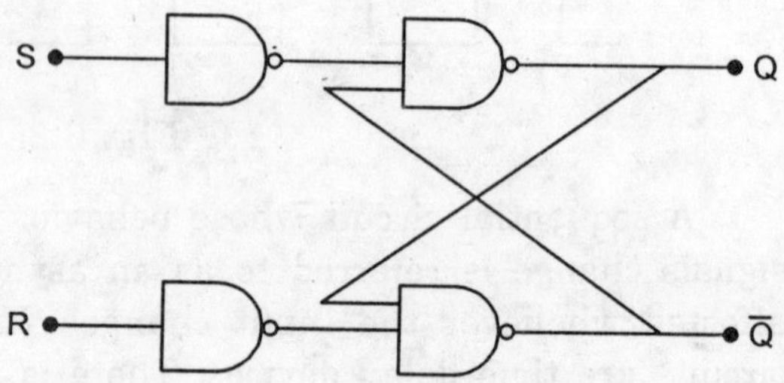


**Fig. 6.4(*b*):** The flip-flop provided with means for presetting or for clearing the state of the cell.

The basic digital memory circuit is obtained by cross-coupling two NOT circuits N1 and N2 (signal input NAND gates) in the manner in Figure 6.4(*a*). The output of each gate is connected to the input of the other, and this feedback combination is called a *flip-flop*. The most important property of the flip-flop is that it can exist in one of two stable states, either Q = 1 ($\overline{Q}$ = 0), called the 1 state or Q = 0 ($\overline{Q}$ = 1) referred to as the 0 state.

It is readily verified that the situation in which both outputs are in the same state (both 1 or both 0) is not consistent with the inter connection. Since the flip-flop has two stable states, it is also called a *binary*, or bistable, MULTI. Since it may store one bit of information (either Q = 1 or Q = 0), it is called a 1-bit memory unit, or a 1-bit storage cell. Since this information is locked or latched in place, this flip-flop is also known as **latch.**

Suppose we want to store a specific state Q = 1 or Q = 0 in the latch. We may do so by arrangement as in Figure 6.4(*b*).

If S = 1, R = 0 then Q = 1, so the input S is called **set** or **preset,** input.

If S = 0, R = 1 then Q = 0, so R is referred to as **reset** or **clear,** input.

The input combination S = R = 0 leads to an undetermined state (Q could be either 1 or 0). Also S = R = 1 is not allowed.

## 6.3 TYPES OF FLIP-FLOPS

There are different types of flip-flops depending on how their inputs and clock pulses cause the transition between two states. We will discuss the following types of flip-flops in this UNIT:

*S-R flip-flop, J-K flip-flop, Master slave flip-flop, D type flip-flop and T type flip-flop.*

### 6.3.1 Clocked S-R Flip-Flop

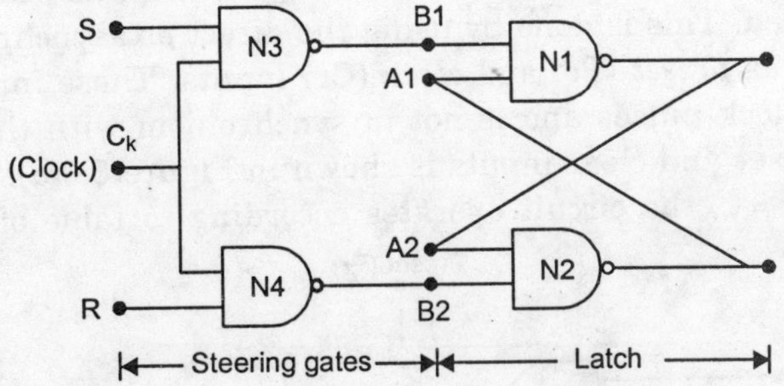


**Fig. 6.5(*a*):** An S-R clocked flip-flop.

| *Inputs* | | *Output* |
|---|---|---|
| $S_n$ | $R_n$ | $Q_{n+1}$ |
| 0 | 0 | $Q_n$ |
| 1 | 0 | 1 |
| 0 | 1 | 0 |
| 1 | 1 | ? |

**Fig. 6.5(*b*):** Truth table.

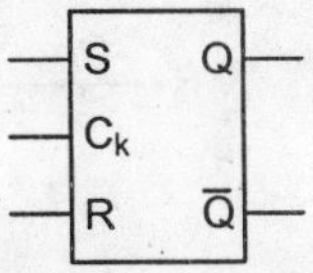


**Fig. 6.5(*c*):** The logic symbol.

In a sequential system it is required to **set** or **reset** a flip-flop in synchronism (operate at the same time, speed etc.) with clock pulses. This is shown in Figure 6.5(*a*) [*i.e.*, a triggered set-reset (abbreviated S-R or R-S) flip-flop]. The gates N1 and N2 form a latch, whereas N3 and N4 are the *control* or *steering*, gates which program the state of the flip-flop after the pulse appears. Note that *between clock pulses* ($C_k$ = 0), the output of N3 and N4 are 1 independentaly of the values of R or S. Hence the circuit works as a latch. If Q = 1, it remains 1, whereas if Q = 0, it remains 0. In other words, the flip-flop doesn't change state between the clock pulses; it is invarient within a bit time.

Now consider the time $t = n$T(+) when a clock pulse is present ($C_k$ = 1). If S = 0 and R = 0 then the outputs of N3 and N4 are 1 and by the above argument the state $Q_n$ of the flip-flop does not change.

If $C_k$ = 1, $S_n$ = 1 and $R_n$ = 0 as shown in second row of truth table we find $Q_{n+1}$ = 1.

If R and S are interchanged and if Q is interchanged with $\overline{Q}$ then 3rd row follows from 2nd row.

If $C_k = 1$, $S_n = 1$, $R_n = 1$ then outputs of NAND gates N3 and N4 are both 0. Hence the inputs B1 of N1 and B2 of N2 are 0 so that outputs of both N1 and N2 must be 1. This condition is logically inconsistent with the labelling of two outputs Q and $\overline{Q}$.

This state is indeterminate, ambiguous or undefined, and it must be prevented from taking place.

### *Preset and Clear*

In the flip-flops shown in Figure 6.5(*a*) when the power is switched on, the state of the circuit is uncertain. It may come to reset (Q = 0) or set (Q = 1) state. But in many applications it is required to initially set or reset the flip-flop, *i.e.*, the initial state of the flip-flop is to be assigned. This is done by using the direct or asynchronous inputs. These inputs are referred to as *preset* (Pr) and *clear* (Cr) inputs. These inputs may be applied at any time between clock pulses and is not in synchronism with the clock. Such a S-R flip-flop containing preset and clear inputs is shown in Figure 6.6(*a*). From Figure 6.6(*a*), we see that if Pr = Cr = 1, the circuit operates according to table of Figure 6.5(*b*).

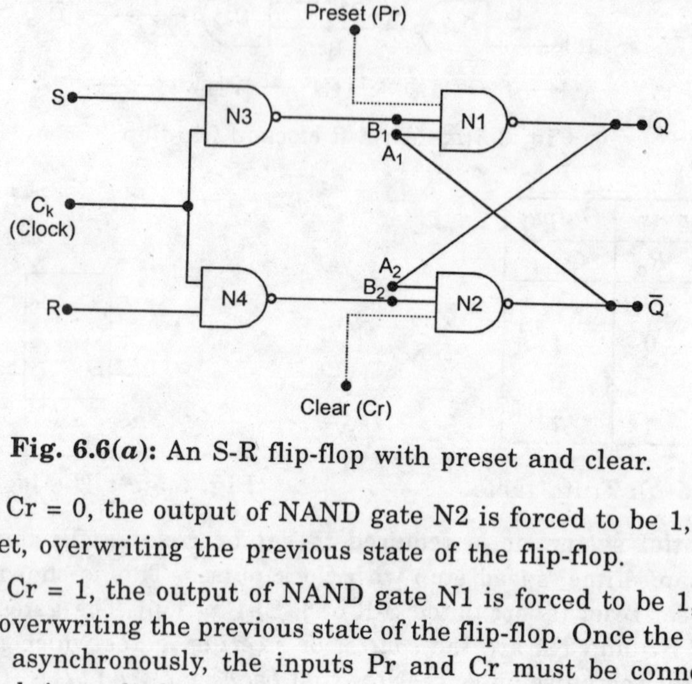


**Fig. 6.6(*a*):** An S-R flip-flop with preset and clear.

If Pr = 1 and Cr = 0, the output of NAND gate N2 is forced to be 1, *i.e.*, $\overline{Q}$ = 1 and the flip-flop is reset, overwriting the previous state of the flip-flop.

If Pr = 0 and Cr = 1, the output of NAND gate N1 is forced to be 1, *i.e.*, Q = 1 and the flip-flop is set, overwriting the previous state of the flip-flop. Once the state of the flip-flop is established asynchronously, the inputs Pr and Cr must be connected to logic 1 before the next clock is applied.

The condition Pr = Cr = 0 must not be applied, since this leads to an uncertain state.

The logic symbol of S-R flip-flop with Pr and Cr inputs is shown in Figure 6.6(*b*). Here bubbles are used for Pr and Cr inputs, which indicate these are active low inputs, which means that the intended function is performed if the signal applied to Pr and Cr is LOW. The operation of Figure 6.6(*b*) is shown in table given in Figure 6.6(*c*). The circuit can be designed such that the asynchronous inputs override the clock, *i.e.*, the circuit can be set or reset even in the presence of the clock pulse.

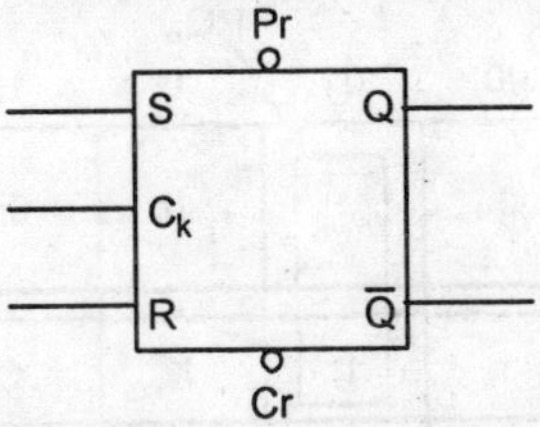


**Fig. 6.6(*b*):** Logic symbol of S-R flip-flop with preset and clear.

| *Inputs* | | | *Output Q* | *Operation Performed* |
|---|---|---|---|---|
| $C_k$ | *Cr* | *Pr* | | |
| 1 | 1 | 1 | $Q_{n+1}$ (Figure 6.3) | Normal flip-flop |
| 0 | 1 | 0 | 1 | Preset |
| 0 | 0 | 1 | 0 | Clear |
| 0 | 0 | 0 | – | Uncertain |

**Fig. 6.6(*c*)**

**Note.** *A bubble at an input means an active low state: the input has to go low to produce an effect. When no bubble is present, the input has to go high to have an effect.*

### *Characteristic Table of S-R Flip-Flop*

From the name itself it is very clear that *characteristic table* of a flip-flop actually gives us an idea about the character, *i.e.*, the working of the flip-flop. Now from all our above discussions, we know that the next state flip-flop output ($Q_{n+1}$) depends on the present inputs as well as the present output ($Q_n$). So in order to know the next state output of a flip-flop, we have to consider the present state output also. The characteristic table of S-R flip-flop is given in table in Figure 6.7(*a*). From the characteristic table we have to find out the characteristic equation of the S-R flip-flop.

| *Flip-flop Inputs* | | *Present Output* | *Next Output* |
|---|---|---|---|
| *S* | *R* | $Q_n$ | $Q_{n+1}$ |
| 0 | 0 | 0 | 0 |
| 0 | 0 | 1 | 1 |
| 0 | 1 | 0 | 0 |
| 0 | 1 | 1 | 0 |
| 1 | 0 | 0 | 1 |
| 1 | 0 | 1 | 1 |
| 1 | 1 | 0 | X |
| 1 | 1 | 1 | X |

**Fig. 6.7(*a*):** Characteristic table of S-R flip-flop.

Now we will find out the characteristic equation of the S-R flip-flop from the characteristic table with the help of Karnaugh map shown in Figure 6.7(*b*).

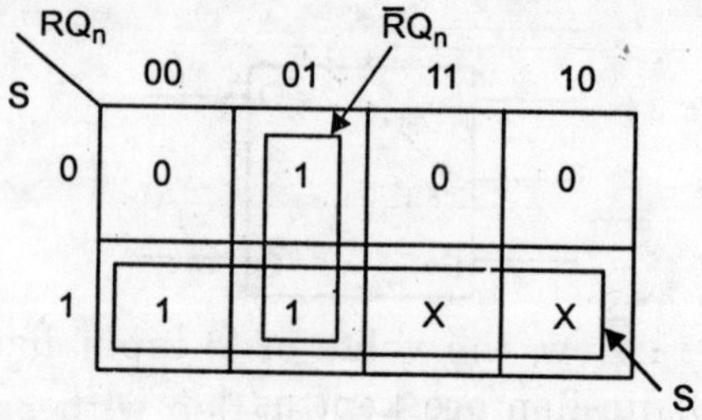


**Fig. 6.7(*b*)**

From the Karnaugh map given in Figure 6.7(*b*) we find the expression for $Q_{n+1}$ as

$$Q_{n+1} = S + \overline{R}Q_n \qquad ...(1)$$

Along with the above equation we have to consider the fact that S and R cannot be simultaneously 0. In order to take that fact into account we have to incorporate another equation for S-R flip-flop. The equation is given below.

$$SR = 0 \qquad ...(2)$$

Hence the characteristic equations of S-R flip-flop are

$$Q_{n+1} = S + \overline{R}Q_n$$

$$SR = 0$$

### 6.3.2 Clocked D Flip-Flop

The D flip-flop has only one input referred as D input or data input and two outputs as usual Q and $\overline{Q}$. It transfers the data at the input after the delay of one clock pulse at the output Q. So in some cases the input is referred to as delay input and the flip-flop gets the name *delay* (D) flip-flop. It can be easily constructed from S-R flip-flop by simply incorporating an inverter between S and R such that the input of the inverter is at the S end and the output of the inverter is at the R end. We can get rid of the undefined condition, *i.e.*, S = R = 1 condition, of the S-R flip-flop in the D flip-flop. The D flip-flop is either used as a delay device or as a latch to store 1-bit of binary information. The truth table of D flip-flop is given in table in Figure 6.8(*b*). The structure of D flip-flop is shown in Figure 6.8(*a*), which is being constructed using NAND gates. The same structure can be constructed using only NOR gates.

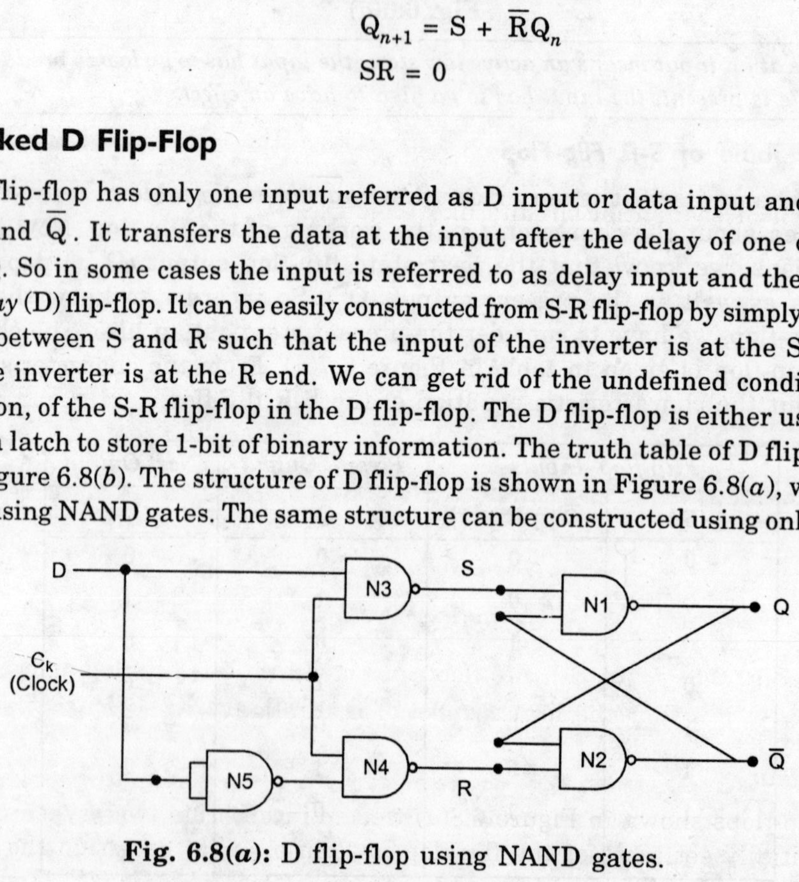


**Fig. 6.8(*a*):** D flip-flop using NAND gates.

| *Input* $D_n$ | *Output* $Q_{n+1}$ |
|---|---|
| 0 | 0 |
| 1 | 1 |

**Fig. 6.8(*b*)**

**Case 1.** If the $C_k$ input is low, the value of D input has no effect, since the S and R inputs of the basic NAND flip-flop are kept as 1.

**Case 2.** If the $C_k$ = 1, and D = 1, the NAND gate N5 produces 0, which forces the output of NAND gate N4 as 1. On the other hand both the inputs of NAND gate N3 are 1, which gives the output of gate N3 as 0. Hence the output of NAND gate N1 is forced to be 1, *i.e.*, Q = 1, whereas both the inputs of gate N2 are 1 and the output is 0, *i.e.*, $\overline{Q}$ = 0. Hence, we observe that when D = 1, after one clock pulse passes Q = 1, which means the output follows D.

**Case 3.** If the $C_k$ = 1, and D = 0, the NAND gate N5 produces 1. Hence both the inputs of NAND gate N4 are 1, which gives the output of gate N4 as 0. On the other hand, D = 0 forces the output of NAND gate N3 to be 1. Hence the output of NAND gate N2 is forced to be 1, *i.e.*, $\overline{Q}$ = 1, whereas both the inputs of gate N1 are 1 and the output is 0, *i.e.*, Q = 0. Hence, we find that when D = 0, after one clock pulse passes Q = 0, which means the output again follows D.

A simple way to construct a D flip-flop using S-R flip-flop is shown in Figure 6.9(*a*). The logic symbol of D flip-flop is shown in Figure 6.9(*b*). D flip-flop is most often used in the construction of sequential circuits like registers.

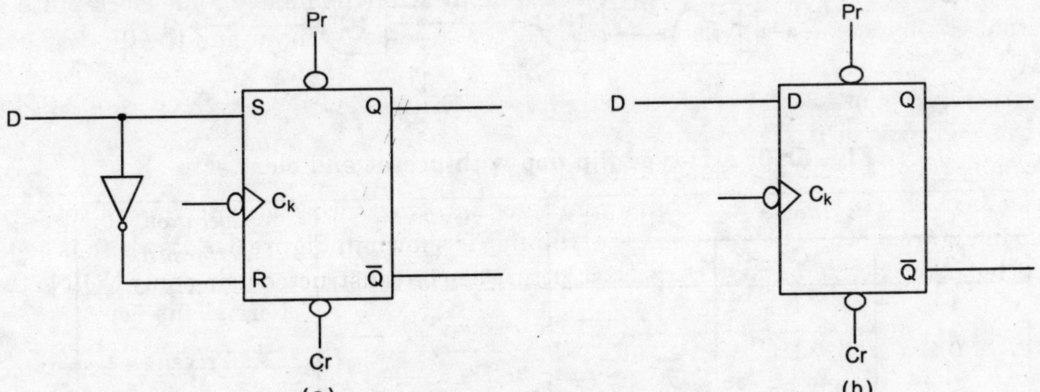


**Fig. 6.9:** (*a*) A S-R flip-flop converted into a D flip-flop and (*b*) the logic symbol of D flip-flop.

## *Preset and Clear*

In the flip-flops shown in Figure 6.8(*a*) we can incorporate two asynchronous inputs in order to initially set or reset the flip-flop., *i.e.*, in order to be assign the initial state of the flip-flop. These inputs are referred to as *preset* (Pr) and *clear* (Cr) inputs as we did in case of S-R flip-flop. These inputs may be applied at any time between clock pulses and is not in synchronism with the clock. Such a D flip-flop containing preset and clear inputs is shown in Figure 6.10. From Figure 6.10, we see that if Pr = Cr=1, the circuit operates according to table of Figure 6.8(*b*).

If Pr = 1 and Cr = 0, the output of NAND gate N2 is forced to be 1, *i.e.*, $\overline{Q}$ = 1 and the flip-flop is reset, overwriting the previous state of the flip-flop.

If Pr = 0 and Cr = 1, the output of NAND gate N1 is forced to be 1, *i.e.*, Q = 1 and the flip-flop is set, overwriting the previous state of the flip-flop. Once the state of the flip-flop is established asynchronously, the inputs Pr and Cr must be connected to logic 1 before the next clock is applied.

The condition Pr = Cr = 0 must not be applied, since this leads to an uncertain state.

The logic symbol of D flip-flop with Pr and Cr inputs is shown in Figure 6.9(*b*). Here bubbles are used for Pr and Cr inputs, which indicate these are active low inputs, which means that the intended function is performed if the signal applied to Pr and Cr is LOW. The operation of Figure 6.10 is shown in table at Figure 6.11. The circuit can be designed such that the asynchronous inputs override the clock, *i.e.*, the circuit can be set or reset even in the presence of the clock pulse.

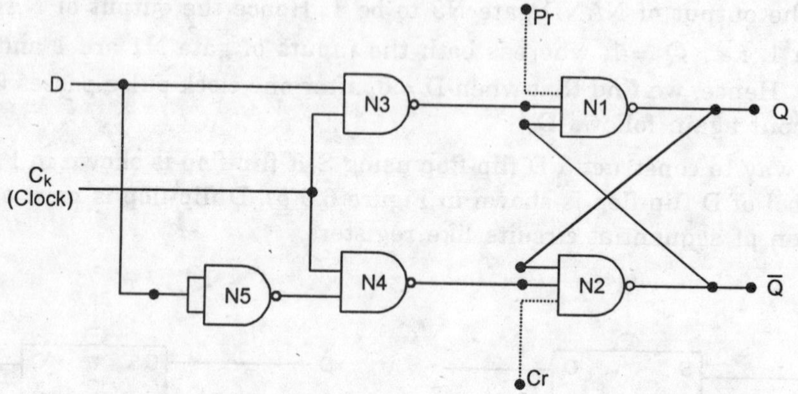


**Fig. 6.10:** A D-type flip-flop with preset and clear.

| *Inputs* | | | *Output* | *Operation* |
|---|---|---|---|---|
| $C_k$ | *Cr* | *Pr* | Q | *Performed* |
| 1 | 1 | 1 | $Q_{n+1}$ | Normal flip-flop |
| 0 | 1 | 0 | 1 | Preset |
| 0 | 0 | 1 | 0 | Clear |
| 0 | 0 | 0 | – | Uncertain |

**Fig. 6.11**

### *Characteristic Table of D Flip-Flop*

As we have already discussed about the characteristic equation of S-R flip-flop, we can similarly find out the characteristic equation of D flip-flop. The characteristic table of

D flip-flop is given in table of Figure 6.12. From the characteristic table we have to find out the characteristic equation of the D flip-flop.

| *Flip-flop Input* | *Present Output* | *Next Output* |
|---|---|---|
| $D$ | $Q_n$ | $Q_{n+1}$ |
| 0 | 0 | 0 |
| 0 | 1 | 0 |
| 1 | 0 | 1 |
| 1 | 1 | 1 |

**Fig. 6.12**

Now we will find out the characteristic equation of the D flip-flop from the characteristic table with the help of Karnaugh map given in Figure 6.13.

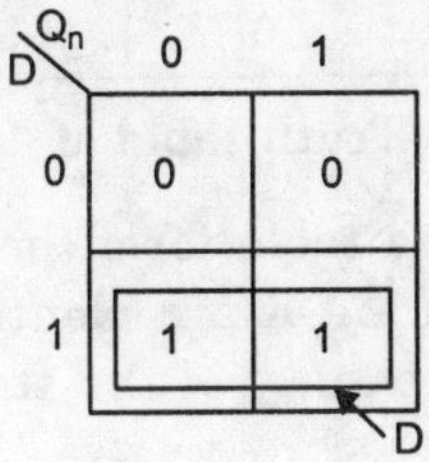


**Fig. 6.13**

From the map, we obtain $Q_{n+1} = D$

Hence the characteristic equations of D flip-flop is

$$Q_{n+1} = D$$

### 6.3.3 J-K Flip-Flop

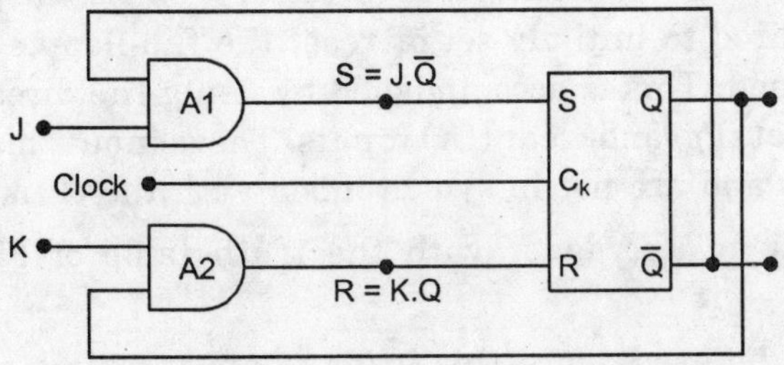


**Fig. 6.14:** An S-R flip-flop is converted into a J-K flip-flop.

| *Inputs* | | *Output* |
|---|---|---|
| $J_n$ | $K_n$ | $Q_{n+1}$ |
| 0 | 0 | $Q_n$ |
| 1 | 0 | 1 |
| 0 | 1 | 0 |
| 1 | 1 | $\overline{Q}_n$ |

**Fig. 6.15(*a*):** The truth table.

The uncertainty in the state of an S-R flip-flop when $S_n = R_n = 1$ can be eliminated by converting it into a J-K flip-flop. The data inputs are J and K which are ANDed with $\overline{Q}$ and Q respectively to obtain S and R inputs *i.e.*, $S = J.\overline{Q}$, $R = K.Q$.

The logic can be verified by the following table:

| *Column* | *1* | *2* | *3* | *4* | *5* | *6* | *7* | *8* |
|---|---|---|---|---|---|---|---|---|
| *Row* | $J_n$ | $K_n$ | $Q_n$ | $\overline{Q}_n$ | $S_n$ | $R_n$ | $Q_{n+1}$ | |
| 1 | 0 | 0 | 0 | 1 | 0 | 0 | $Q_n$ | $Q_n$ |
| 2 | 0 | 0 | 1 | 0 | 0 | 0 | $Q_n$ | |
| 3 | 1 | 0 | 0 | 1 | 1 | 0 | 1 | 1 |
| 4 | 1 | 0 | 1 | 0 | 0 | 0 | $Q_n$ | |
| 5 | 0 | 1 | 0 | 1 | 0 | 0 | $Q_n$ | 0 |
| 6 | 0 | 1 | 1 | 0 | 0 | 1 | 0 | |
| 7 | 1 | 1 | 0 | 1 | 1 | 0 | 1 | $\overline{Q}_n$ |
| 8 | 1 | 1 | 1 | 0 | 0 | 1 | 0 | |

**Fig. 6.15(*b*):** Truth table of J-K flip-flop.

Columns 1, 2 and 8 of the above table form the J-K flip-flop truth table of Figure 6.15(*a*). Note that first three rows of a J-K are identical with the corresponding rows of an S-R truth table. However the ambiguity of the state $S_n = 1 = R_n$ is now replaced by $Q_{n+1} = \overline{Q}_n$ for $J_n = 1 = K_n$.

*If the two data inputs in the J-K flip-flop are high, the output will be complemented by the clock pulse. i.e.*, the flip-flop is said to be in *toggle state.* It is not really necessary to use the AND gates A1 and A2 of Figure 6.14 since the same function can be performed by adding an extra input terminal to each NAND gates N3 and N4 as shown in Figure 6.16(*a*) ignoring the dashed inputs Pr and Cr (assume both 1).

### Preset and Clear

The state of the circuit shown in Figure 6.16(*a*) is uncertain (arbitrary) before the pulse is applied. In many applications it is desired to initially set or reset the flip-flop *i.e.*, the initial state of the flip-flop is to be assigned. This is accomplished by using the direct, or asynchronous—inputs, referred to as preset (Pr) and clear (Cr) inputs. These inputs may be applied at any time between clock pulses and are not in synchronism with the clock.

If Pr = Cr = 1 the circuit operates in accordance with the truth table of Figure 6.16(*d*).

The condition Pr = Cr = 0 must not be used, since this leads to an uncertain state.

For example, it may be allowed to clear the latch *i.e.*, to specify that Q = 0 when $C_k = 0$.

*The Clear operation* may be accomplished by programming the clear input to 0 and 1 input at preset, *i.e., Cr = 0, Pr = 1,* $C_k = 0$.

Similarly, if it is required to preset (set) the latch into the 1 state, it is necessary to choose Pr = 0, Cr = 1, $C_k = 0$.

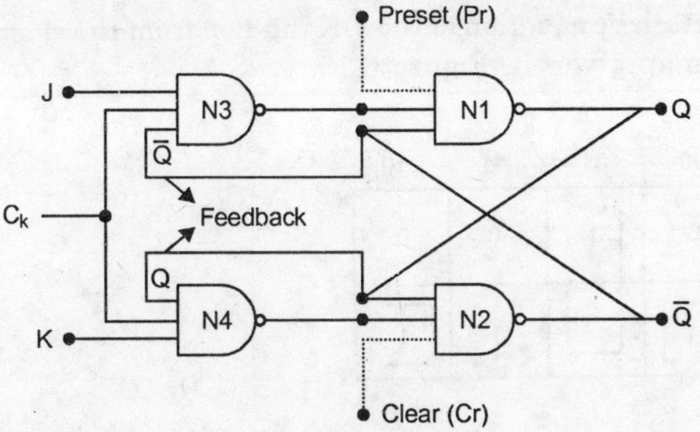


(a) A J-K flip-flop

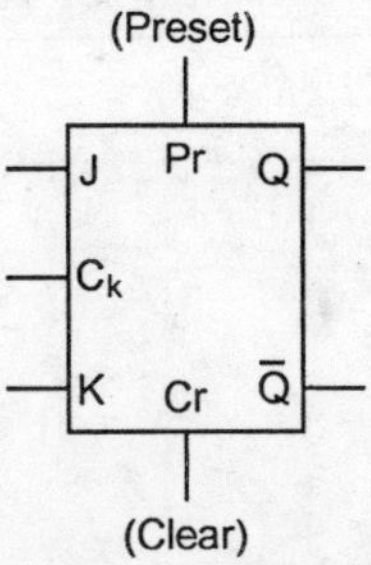


(b) Logic symbol

| | $C_k$ | Cr | Pr | Q |
|---|---|---|---|---|
| Enable | 1 | 1 | 1 | Table 6.15(b) |
| Reset or Clear | 0 | 0 | 1 | 0 |
| Set or Preset | 0 | 1 | 0 | 1 |

Necessary conditions for
- Synchronous operation (Row 1)
- Asynchronous operation (Row 2)
- Presetting operation (Row 3)

(c)

| Inputs | | Output |
|---|---|---|
| $J_n$ | $K_n$ | $Q_{n+1}$ |
| 0 | 0 | $Q_n$ |
| 1 | 0 | 1 |
| 0 | 1 | 0 |
| 1 | 1 | $\overline{Q}_n$ |

(d)

**Fig. 6.16**

### *Characteristic Table of J-K Flip-Flop*

As we have already discussed about the characteristic equation of S-R flip-flop, we can similarly find out the characteristic equation of J-K flip-flop. The characteristic table of J-K flip-flop is given in table shown in Figure 6.17 (See Figure 6.15(*b*)). From the characteristic table we have to find out the characteristic equation of the J-K flip-flop.

| *Flip-flop Inputs* | | *Present Output* | *Next Output* |
|---|---|---|---|
| *J* | *K* | $Q_n$ | $Q_{n+1}$ |
| 0 | 0 | 0 | 0 |
| 0 | 0 | 1 | 1 |
| 1 | 0 | 0 | 1 |
| 1 | 0 | 1 | 1 |
| 0 | 1 | 0 | 0 |
| 0 | 1 | 1 | 0 |
| 1 | 1 | 0 | 1 |
| 1 | 1 | 1 | 0 |

**Fig. 6.17**

Now we will find out the characteristic equation of the J-K flip-flop from the characteristic table with the help of Karnaugh map given in Figure 6.18.

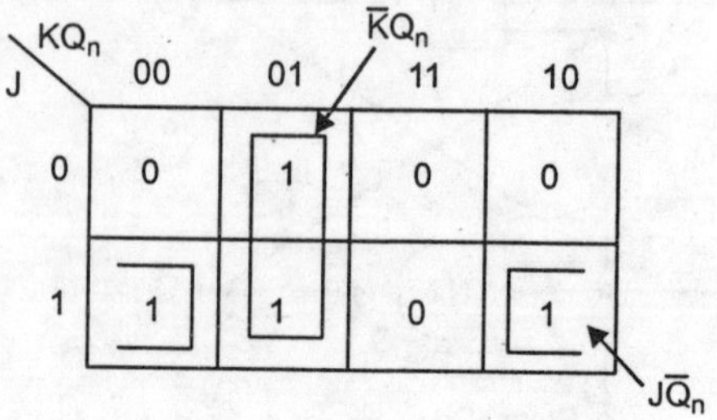


**Fig. 6.18**

From the Karnaugh map, we obtain

$$Q_{n+1} = J\overline{Q}_n + \overline{K}Q_n$$

Hence the characteristic equations of J-K flip-flop is

$$Q_{n+1} = J\overline{Q}_n + \overline{K}Q_n$$

### The Race-around Condition of J-K Flip-Flop

There is a possible physical difficulty with the J-K flip-flop constructed in Figure 6.14. Truth table of Figure 6.15(*b*) is based upon *combinational logic*, which assumes that the inputs are independent of the outputs.

However *because of the feedback connection* Q at input to K (and $\overline{Q}$ at input to J), the input will change during the clock-pulse ($C_k$ = 1) if the output changes state. For example, when the inputs to Figure 6.14 are J = 1, K = 1 and Q = 0 then after applying pulse output becomes Q = 1. Now J = 1, K = 1, Q = 1 from row 8 of Figure 6.15(*b*) we find that input changes back to Q = 0. So the output oscillates back and forth between 0 and 1. It is called *race-around condition.*

The race-around condition can be avoided if $t_p < \Delta t < T$.

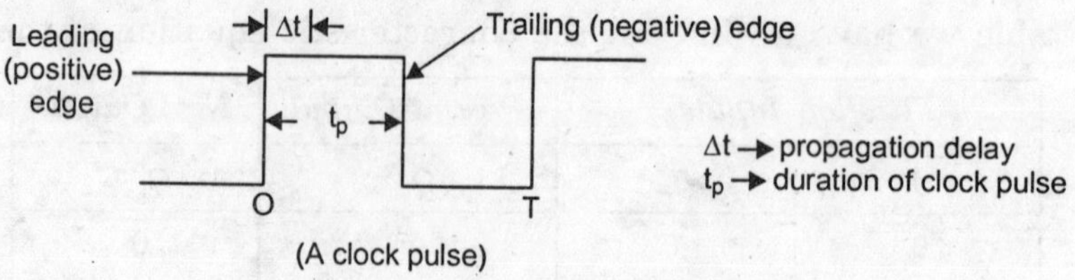


**Fig. 6.19**

It is very difficult to satisfy this inequality because of very small propagation delays in ICs (Integrated chips). This can be avoided using Master-slave configuration.

### 6.3.4 Master-Slave J-K Flip-Flop

Figure 6.20(*a*) is a cascade of two S-R flip-flops with feedback from the output of the second (called the *slave*) to the input of the first (called the master).

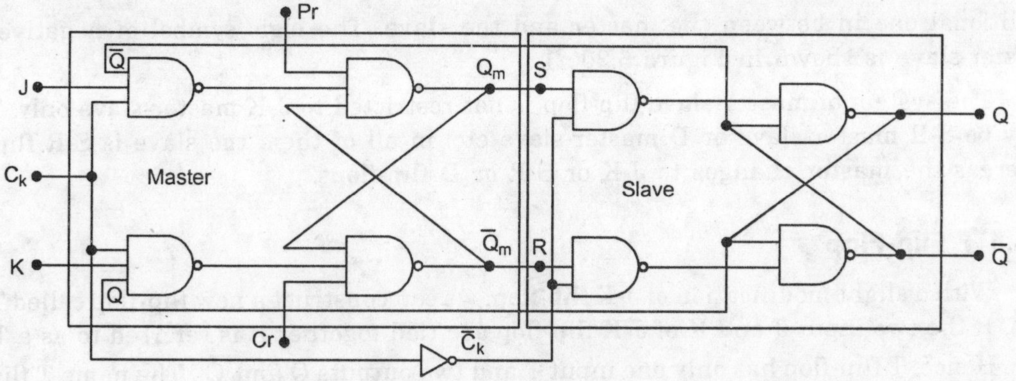


**Fig. 6.20(*a*):** Master-slave flip-flop.

| $J_n$ | $K_n$ | $Q_{n+1}$ |
|---|---|---|
| 0 | 0 | $Q_n$ |
| 1 | 0 | 1 |
| 0 | 1 | 0 |
| 1 | 1 | $\overline{Q}_n$ |

**Fig. 6.20(*b*)**

| $S_n$ | $R_n$ | $Q_{n+1}$ |
|---|---|---|
| 0 | 0 | $Q_n$ |
| 1 | 0 | 1 |
| 0 | 1 | 0 |
| 1 | 1 | ? |

**Fig. 6.20(*c*)**

*Positive clock pulses are applied to the master, and these are inverted before* used to **excite** the slave. For Pr = 1, Cr = 1 and $C_k$ = 1, the master is enabled and its operation follows the truth table of Figure 6.20(*b*). Since $\overline{C}_k = 0$, the slave S-R flip-flop is inhibited (**can't change** state) so that $Q_n$ is invarient for the pulse duration $t_p$. Clearly, *the race around difficulty is circumvented with the master slave topology.* After the pulse passes, $C_k$ = 0 so that the master is inhibited and $\overline{C}_k = 1$, which causes the slave to be **enabled.** The slave is an S-R flip-flop which follows the logic of Figure 6.20(*c*).

If S = $Q_m$ = 1 and R = $\overline{Q}_m$ = 0 then Q = 1 and $\overline{Q}$ = 0. Similarly if S = $Q_m$ = 0 and R = $\overline{Q}_m$ = 1 then Q = 0 and $\overline{Q}$ = 1. In other words, in the interval between clock pulses, the value of $Q_m$ is transferred to the output Q. In summary, during a clock pulse the output Q does not change but $Q_m$ follows J-K logic; at the end of the pulse, the value of $Q_m$ is transferred to Q. It should be emphasized that the data J and K must remain constant for the pulse duration or an erroneous output may result.

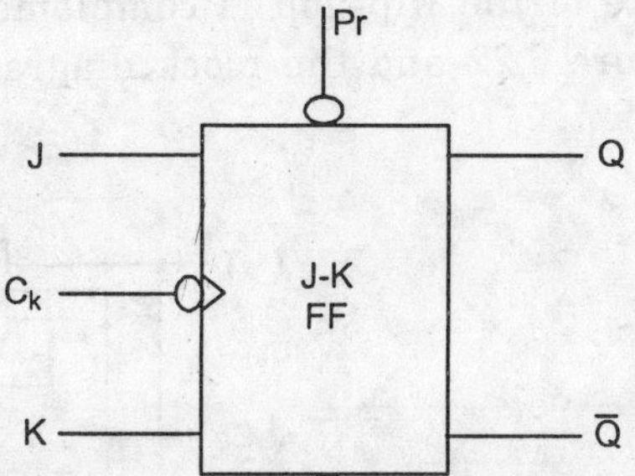


**Fig. 6.20(*d*):** A negative edge-transition Master-Slave J-K flip-flop.

The state of the master-slave flip-flop, shown in Figure 6.20(*a*), changes at the negative transition (trailing edge) of the clock pulse. Hence it becomes negative triggering master-slave flip-flop. This can be changed to positive edge triggering flip-flop by adding two inverters to the system—one before the clock pulse is applied to the master and an additional one in between the master and the slave. The logic symbol of negative edge master-slave is shown in Figure 6.20(*d*).

The system of master-slave flip-flop is not restricted to J-K master-slave only. There may be S-R master-slave or D master-slave etc. in all of them the slave is S-R flip-flop, whereas the master changes to J-K or S-R or D flip-flops.

### 6.3.5 T Flip-Flop

With a slight modification of J-K flip-flop, we can construct a new flip-flop called T flip-flop. If the two input J and K of J-K flip-flop are tied together it is referred to as a T flip-flop. Hence, T flip-flop has only one input T and two outputs Q and $\overline{Q}$. The name T flip-flop actually indicates the fact that the flip-flop has the ability to toggle. It has actually only two states *toggle state* and *memory state*. Since there are only two states, T flip-flop is a very good option to use in counter design and in sequential circuits design where switching operation is required. The truth table of T flip-flop is given in Figure 6.21.

| $T$ | $Q_n$ | $Q_{n+1}$ |
|---|---|---|
| 0 | 0 | 0 |
| 0 | 1 | 1 |
| 1 | 0 | 1 |
| 1 | 1 | 0 |

**Fig. 6.21:** Truth table of T flip-flop.

If the T input is in 0 state (*i.e.*, J = K = 0) prior to a clock pulse, the Q output will not change with the clock pulse. On the other hand if the T input is in 1 state (*i.e.*, J = K = 1) prior to a clock pulse, the Q output will change to $\overline{Q}$ with the clock pulse. In other words we may say that, if T = 1 and the device is clocked then the output toggles its state.

The truth table shows that when T = 0, then $Q_{n+1} = Q_n$, *i.e.*, the next state is the same as the present state and no change occurs. When T = 1, then $Q_{n+1} = \overline{Q}_n$, *i.e.*, the state of the flip-flop is complemented. The circuit diagram of a T flip-flop is shown in Figure 6.22 and the block diagram of the flip-flop is shown in Figure 6.23.

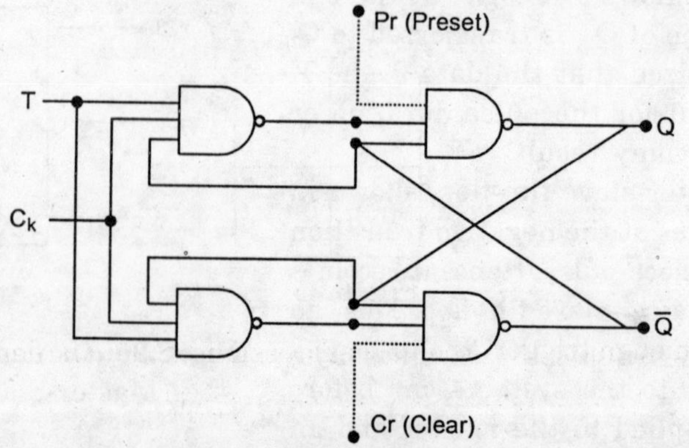


**Fig. 6.22:** T flip-flop.

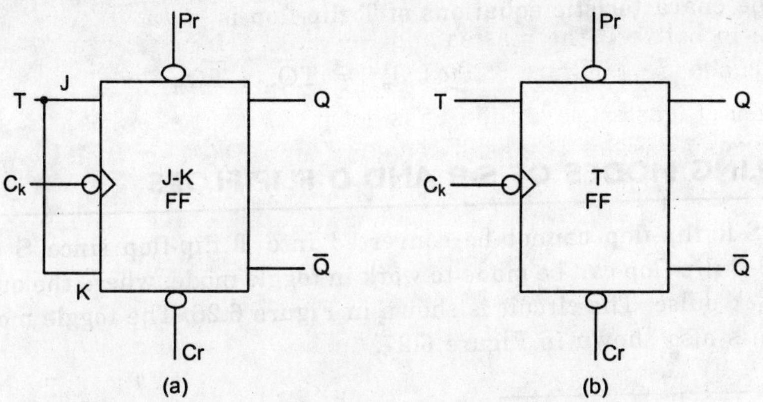


**Fig. 6.23:** (*a*) A J-K flip-flop converted into a T flip-flop
(*b*) the logic symbol of T flip-flop.

### *Characteristic Table of T Flip-Flop*

As we have already discussed about the characteristic equation of J-K flip-flop, we can similarly find out the characteristic equation of T flip-flop. The characteristic table of T flip-flop is given in Figure 6.24. From the characteristic table we have to find out the characteristic equation of the T flip-flop.

| *Flip-flop Input* | *Present Output* | *Next Output* |
|---|---|---|
| $T$ | $Q_n$ | $Q_{n+1}$ |
| 0 | 0 | 0 |
| 0 | 1 | 1 |
| 1 | 0 | 1 |
| 1 | 1 | 0 |

**Fig. 6.24**

Now we will find out the characteristic equation of the T flip-flop from the characteristic table with the help of Karnaugh map of Figure 6.25.

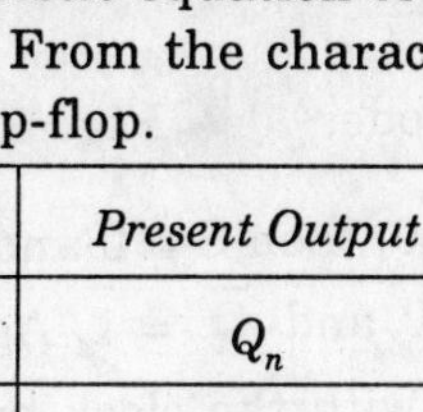


**Fig. 6.25**

From the Karnaugh map, the Boolean expression of $Q_{n+1}$ is derived as

$$Q_{n+1} = T\overline{Q}_n + \overline{T}Q_n$$

Hence the characteristic equations of T flip-flop is

$$Q_{n+1} = T\overline{Q}_n + \overline{T}Q_n$$

## 6.4 TOGGLING MODES OF S-R AND D FLIP-FLOPS

Though S-R flip-flop cannot be converted into T flip-flop since S = R = 1 is not allowed, but S-R flip-flop can be made to work in toggle mode, where the output Q changes with every clock pulse. The circuit is shown in Figure 6.26. The toggle mode of operation for D flip-flop is also shown in Figure 6.27.

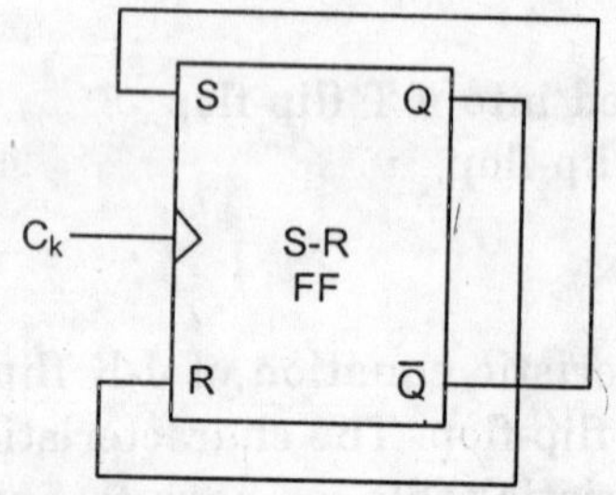


**Fig. 6.26:** S-R flip-flop in toggle mode.

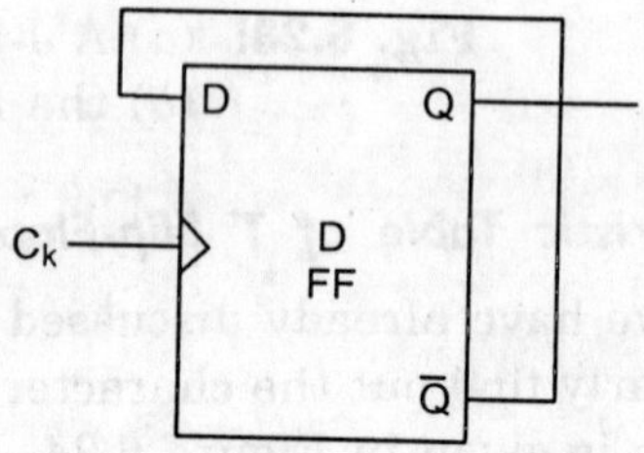


**Fig. 6.27:** D flip-flop in toggle mode.

If at any instant, Q = 1 and $\overline{Q}$ = 0, then S = 0 and R = 1. Hence with the clock pulse the S-R flip-flop gets reset, *i.e.*, Q = 0 and $\overline{Q}$ = 1. Again, if at any instant, Q = 0 and $\overline{Q}$ = 1, then S = 1 and R = 0. Hence with the clock pulse the S-R flip-flop gets set, *i.e.*, Q = 1 and $\overline{Q}$ = 0. Hence the flip-flop acts like a toggle flip-flop where the output is changing with each clock pulse.

Similarly for D flip-flop, if at any instant, Q = 1 and $\overline{Q}$ = 0, then D = 0. Hence with the clock pulse the D flip-flop gets reset, *i.e.*, Q = 0 and $\overline{Q}$ = 1. Again, if at any instant, Q = 0 and $\overline{Q}$ = 1, then D = 1. Hence with the clock pulse the D flip-flop gets set, *i.e.*, Q = 1 and $\overline{Q}$ = 0. Hence the flip-flop acts like a toggle flip-flop where the output is changing with each clock pulse.

## 6.5 TRIGGERING OF FLIP-FLOPS

Flip-flops are synchronous sequential circuits. This type of circuits work with the application of a synchronization mechanism, which is termed as a *clock*. Based on the specific interval or point in the clock during or at which triggering of the flip-flop takes place, it can be classified into two different types—*level triggering* and *edge triggering*.

A clock pulse starts from an initial value of 0 goes momentarily to 1, and after a short interval, returns to the initial value.

### 6.5.1 Level Triggering of Flip-Flops

If a flip-flop gets enabled when a clock pulse goes HIGH and remains enabled throughout the duration of the clock pulse remaining HIGH, the flip-flop is said to be *level triggered flip-flop*. If the flip-flop changes its state when the clock pulse is positive, it is termed as *positive level triggered flip-flop*. On the other hand if a NOT gate is introduced in the clock input terminal of the flip-flop, then the flip-flop changes its state when the clock pulse is negative, it is termed as *negative level triggered flip-flop*.

The main drawback of level triggering is that, as long as the clock pulse is active, the flip-flop changes its state more than once or many times for the change in inputs. If the inputs do not change during one clock pulse, then the output remains stable. On the other hand, if the frequency of the input change is higher than the input clock frequency, the output of the flip-flop undergoes multiple changes as long as the clock remains active. This can be overcome by using either master-slave flip-flops or the edge-triggered flip-flop.

### 6.5.2 Edge Triggering of Flip-Flops

A clock pulse goes from 0 to 1 and then returns from 1 to 0. Figure 6.28 shows the two transitions and they are defined as the *positive edge* (0 to 1 transition) and the *negative edge* (1 to 0 transition). The term *edge-triggered* means that the flip-flop changes its state only at either the positive or negative edge of the clock pulse.

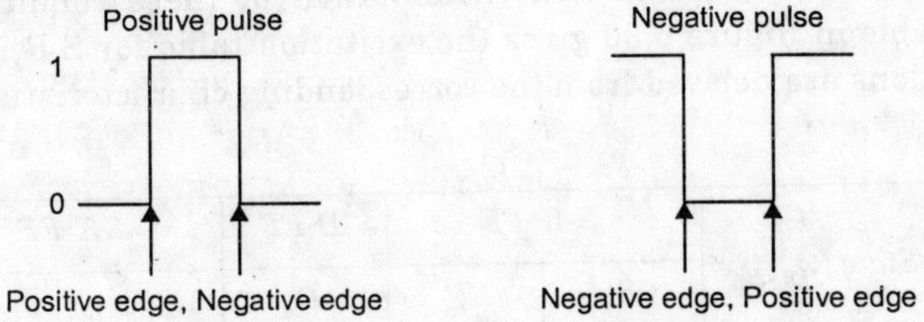


**Fig. 6.28:** Clock pulse transition.

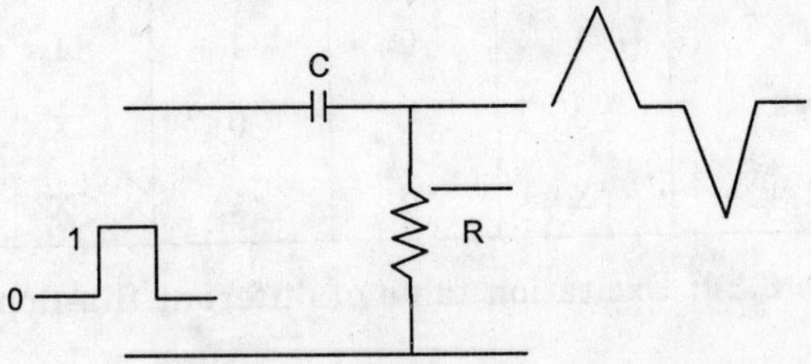


**Fig. 6.29:** RC differentiator circuit for edge triggering.

One way to make the flip-flop respond to only the edge of the clock pulse is to use capacitive coupling. An R-C circuit is shown in Figure 6.29, which is to be inserted in the clock input of the flip-flop. By deliberate design, the RC time constant is made much smaller than the clock pulse width. The capacitor can charge fully when the clock goes HIGH. This exponential charging produces a narrow positive spike across the resistor. Later, the trailing edge of the pulse results in a narrow negative spike. The circuit is so designed that one of the spikes (either the positive or negative) is neglected and the edge triggering occurs due to the other spike.

## 6.6 EXCITATION TABLE OF FLIP-FLOP

The truth table of a flip-flop is also referred to as characteristic table of flip-flop, since this table refers to the operational characteristic of the flip-flop. But in designing sequential circuits, we often face situations where the present state and the next state of the flip-flop is specified, and we have to find out the input conditions that must prevail for the desired output condition. By present and next states we mean to say the conditions before and after the clock pulse respectively. For example, the output of an S-R flip-flop before the clock pulse is $Q_n = 1$ and it is desired that the output does not change when the clock pulse is applied.

Now from the characteristic table of S-R flip-flop (Figure 6.7(*a*)), we obtain the following conditions:

1. S = R = 0 (second row)
2. S = 1, R = 0 (sixth row)

We come to the conclusion from the above conditions that the R input must be 0, whereas the S input may be 0 or 1 (*i.e.*, don't care). Similarly, for all possible situations the input conditions can be found out. A tabulation of these conditions is known as *excitation table*. Table in Figure 6.30 gives the excitation table for S-R, D, J-K and T flip-flops. These conditions are derived from the corresponding characteristic tables of the flip-flops.

| *Present State* ($Q_n$) | *Next State* ($Q_{n+1}$) | *S-R FF* | | *D-FF* | *J-K FF* | | *T-FF* |
|---|---|---|---|---|---|---|---|
| | | $S_n$ | $R_n$ | $D_n$ | $J_n$ | $K_n$ | $T_n$ |
| 0 | 0 | 0 | X | 0 | 0 | X | 0 |
| 0 | 1 | 1 | 0 | 1 | 1 | X | 1 |
| 1 | 0 | 0 | 1 | 0 | X | 1 | 1 |
| 1 | 1 | X | 0 | 1 | X | 0 | 0 |

**Fig. 6.30:** Excitation table of different flip-flops.

## 6.7 INTERCONVERSION OF FLIP-FLOPS

In many applications, we are being given a type of flip-flop, whereas we may require some other type. In such cases we may have to convert the given flip-flop to our required flip-flop. Now we may follow a general model for such conversion of flip-flops. This model is illustrated in Figure 6.31.

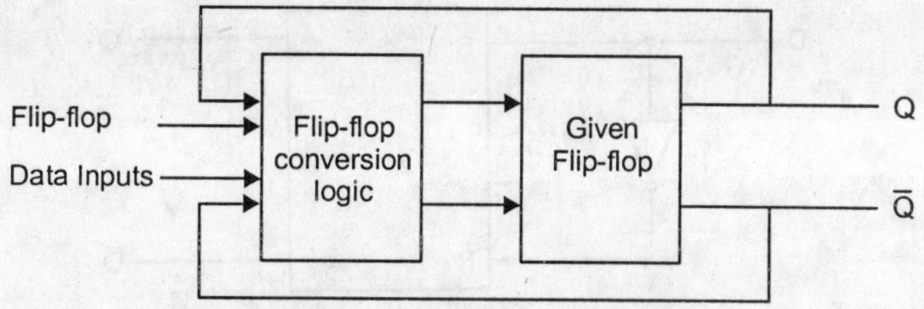


**Fig. 6.31:** General model for conversion of one type of flip-flop to another type.

From the model we see that it is required to design the conversion logic for converting new input definitions into input codes which will cause the given flip-flop to work like the desired flip-flop. To design the conversion logic we need to combine the excitation table for both flip-flops and to make a truth table with data input(s) and Q as the inputs and the input(s) of the given flip-flop as output(s).

### 6.7.1 S-R Flip-Flop to D Flip-Flop

The excitation tables of S-R and D flip-flops are given in table of Figure 6.30 from which we make the truth table given in Figure 6.32.

| *FF Data Inputs* | *Output* | *S-R FF Inputs* | |
|---|---|---|---|
| *D* | *Q* | *S* | *R* |
| 0 | 0 | 0 | X |
| 1 | 0 | 1 | 0 |
| 0 | 1 | 0 | 1 |
| 1 | 1 | X | 0 |

**Fig. 6.32**

From the table of Figure 6.32, we make the Karnaugh maps for inputs S and R as shown in Figure 6.33(*a*) and Figure 6.33(*b*).

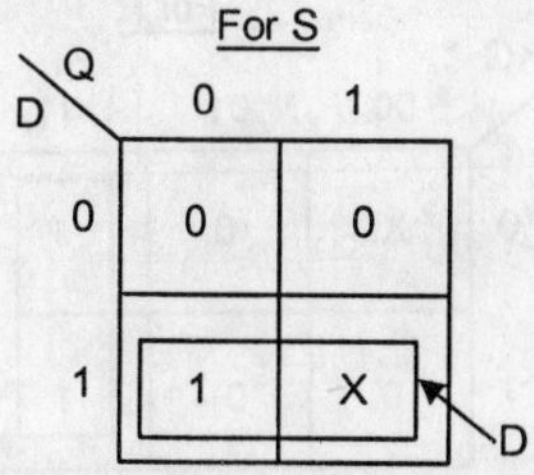


**Fig. 6.33(*a*)**

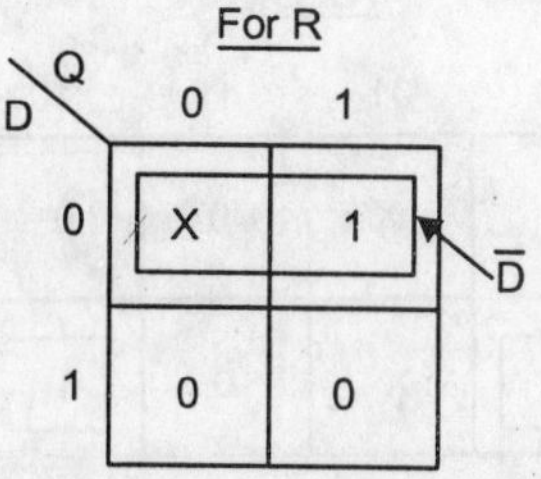


**Fig. 6.33(*b*)**

Simplifying with the help of the Karnaugh maps, we obtain S = D and R = $\overline{D}$. Hence the circuit may be designed as shown in Figure 6.34.

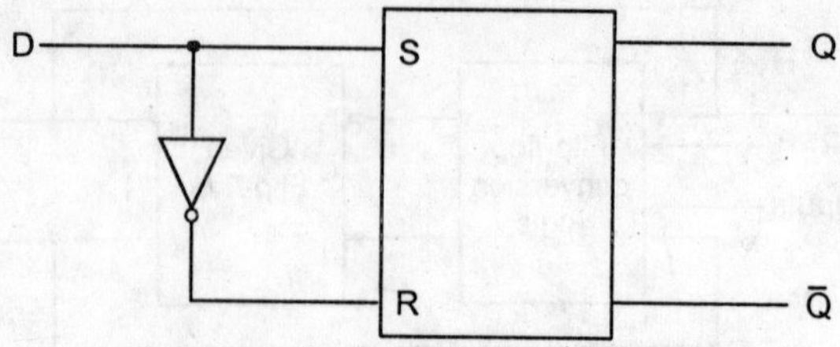


**Fig. 6.34:** D flip-flop using S-R flip-flop.

## 6.7.2 S-R Flip-Flop to J-K Flip-Flop

The excitation tables of S-R and J-K flip-flops are given in table of Figure 6.30 from which we make the truth table given in Figure 6.35.

| *FF Data Inputs* | | *Output* | *S-R FF Inputs* | |
|---|---|---|---|---|
| *J* | *K* | *Q* | *S* | *R* |
| 0 | 0 | 0 | 0 | X |
| 0 | 1 | 0 | 0 | X |
| 1 | 0 | 0 | 1 | 0 |
| 1 | 1 | 0 | 1 | 0 |
| 0 | 1 | 1 | 0 | 1 |
| 1 | 1 | 1 | 0 | 1 |
| 0 | 0 | 1 | X | 0 |
| 1 | 0 | 1 | X | 0 |

**Fig. 6.35**

From the truth table in Figure 6.35, the Karnaugh map is prepared as shown in Figure 6.36(*a*) and Figure 6.36(*b*).

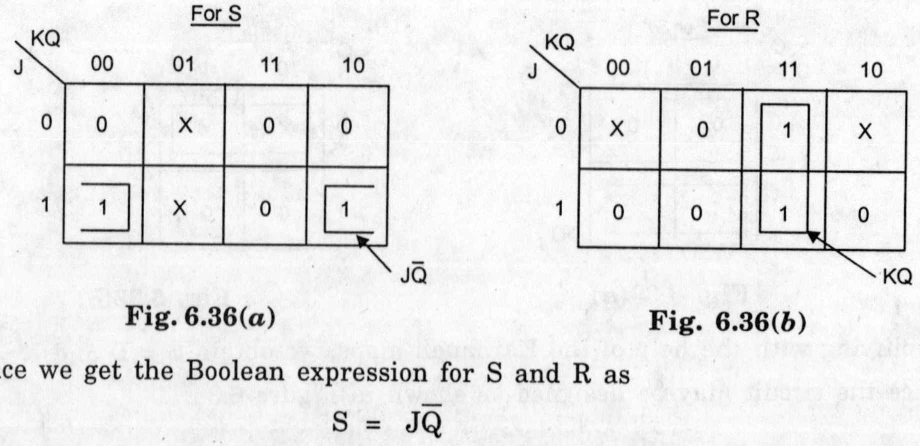


**Fig. 6.36(*a*)** **Fig. 6.36(*b*)**

Hence we get the Boolean expression for S and R as

$$S = J\overline{Q}$$

and $R = KQ$

Hence the circuit may be realized as shown in Figure 6.37.

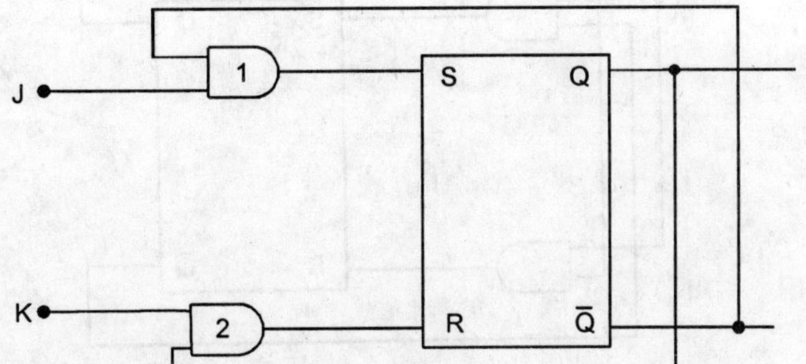


**Fig. 6.37:** J-K flip-flop using S-R flip-flop.

### 6.7.3 S-R Flip-Flop to T Flip-Flop

The excitation tables of S-R and T flip-flops are given in table of Figure 6.30 from which we make the truth table given in Figure 6.38.

| *FF Data Inputs* | *Output* | *S-R FF Inputs* | |
|---|---|---|---|
| *T* | *Q* | *S* | *R* |
| 0 | 0 | 0 | X |
| 1 | 0 | 1 | 0 |
| 1 | 1 | 0 | 1 |
| 0 | 1 | X | 0 |

**Fig. 6.38**

From the table of Figure 6.38, we prepare the Karnaugh maps as shown in Figure 6.39(*a*) and Figure 6.39(*b*).

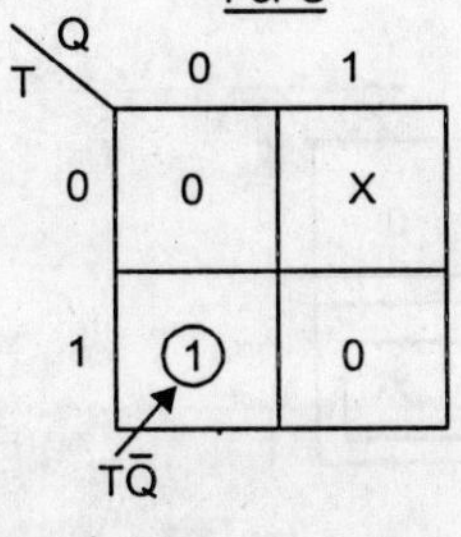


**Fig. 6.39(*a*)**

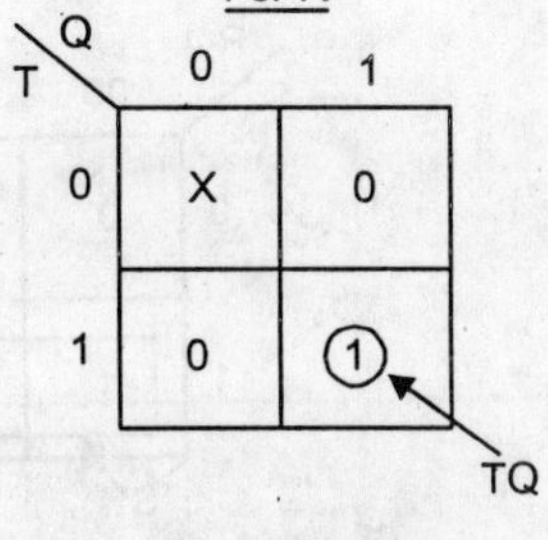


**Fig. 6.39(*b*)**

Hence we get, $S = T\overline{Q}$

and $R = TQ$

Hence the circuit may be designed as shown in Figure 6.40.

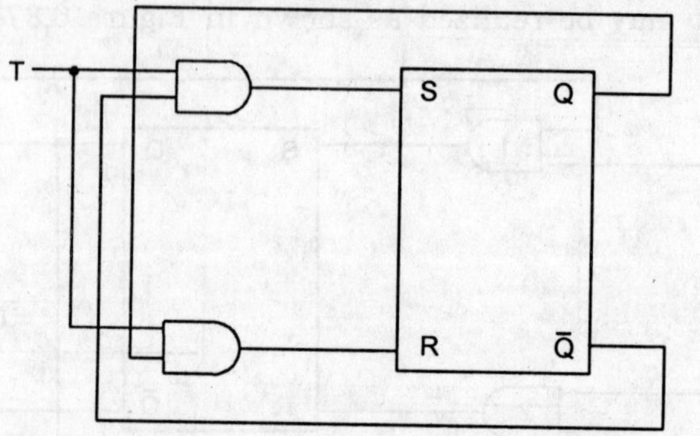


**Fig. 6.40:** T flip-flop using S-R flip-flop.

### 6.7.4 D Flip-Flop to S-R Flip-Flop

The excitation tables of S-R and D flip-flops are given in table of Figure 6.30 from which we derive the truth table as shown in Figure 6.41.

| *FF Data Inputs* | | *Output* | *D FF Inputs* |
|---|---|---|---|
| *S* | *R* | *Q* | *D* |
| 0 | 0 | 0 | 0 |
| 0 | 1 | 0 | 0 |
| 1 | 0 | 0 | 1 |
| 0 | 1 | 1 | 0 |
| 0 | 0 | 1 | 1 |
| 1 | 0 | 1 | 1 |

**Fig. 6.41**

The Karnaugh map is prepared in Figure 6.42 according to the truth table of Figure 6.41.

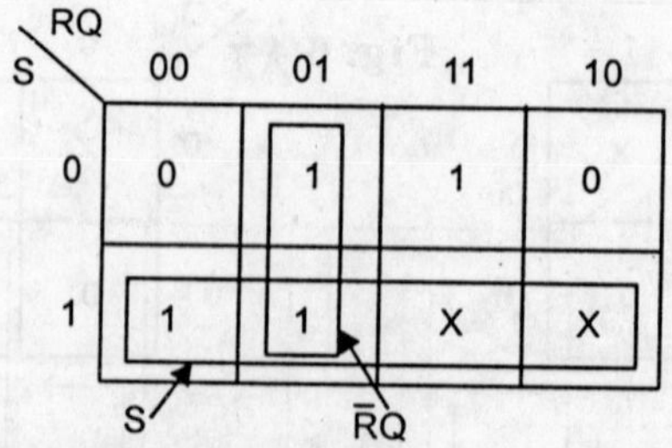


**Fig. 6.42**

Hence we get

$$D = S + \overline{R}Q$$

Hence the circuit may be realized as shown in Figure 6.43.

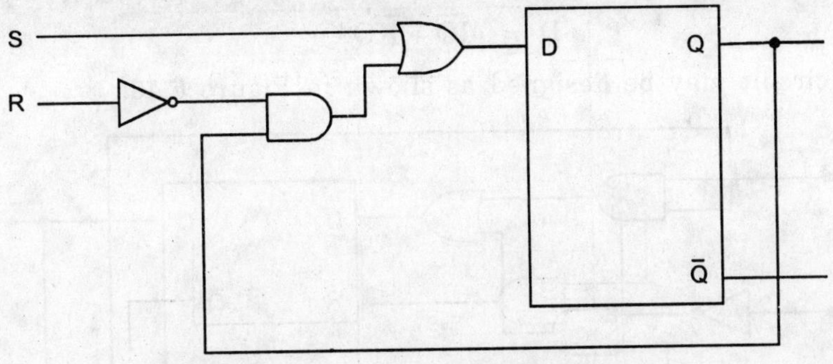


**Fig. 6.43:** S-R flip-flop using D flip-flop.

### 6.7.5 D Flip-Flop to J-K Flip-Flop

The excitation tables of J-K and D flip-flops are given in table of Figure 6.30 from which we make the truth table given in Figure 6.44.

From the truth table of Figure 6.44, Karnaugh map is drawn as shown in Figure 6.45.

| *FF Data Inputs* | | *Output* | *D FF Inputs* |
|---|---|---|---|
| *J* | *K* | *Q* | *D* |
| 0 | 0 | 0 | 0 |
| 0 | 1 | 0 | 0 |
| 1 | 0 | 0 | 1 |
| 1 | 1 | 0 | 1 |
| 0 | 1 | 1 | 0 |
| 1 | 1 | 1 | 0 |
| 0 | 0 | 1 | 1 |
| 1 | 0 | 1 | 1 |

**Fig. 6.44**

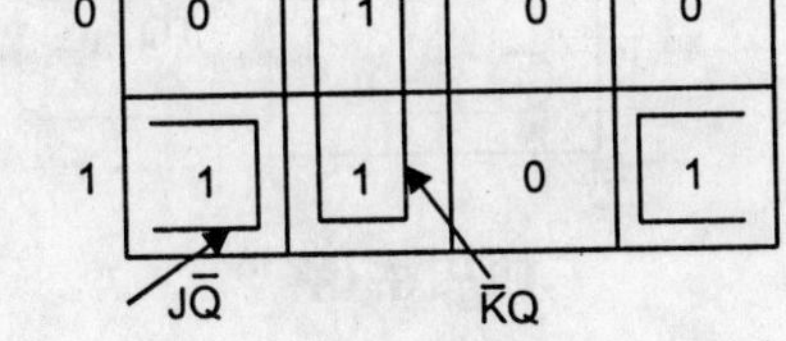


**Fig. 6.45**

From the Karnaugh map given in Figure 6.45. The Boolean expression for D is derived as

$$D = J\overline{Q} + \overline{K}Q$$

Hence the circuit may be designed as shown in Figure 6.46.

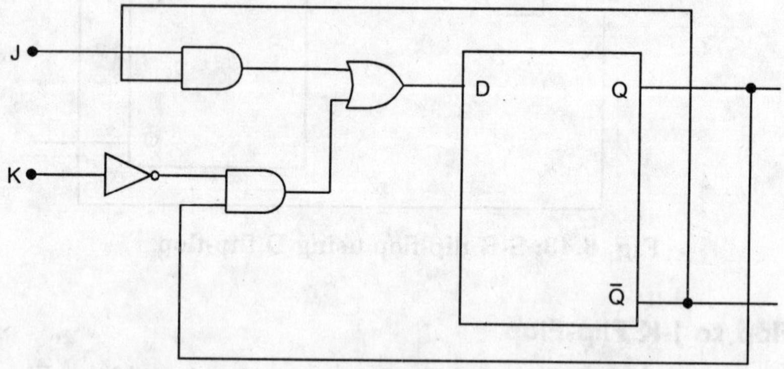


**Fig 6.46:** J-K flip-flop using D flip-flop.

### 6.7.6 D Flip-Flop to T Flip-Flop

The excitation tables of D and T flip-flops are given in table of Figure 6.30 from which we derive the required truth table as given in Figure 6.47.

From the truth table of Figure 6.47, we make the Karnaugh map as shown in Figure 6.48.

| *FF Data Inputs* | *Output* | *D FF Inputs* |
|---|---|---|
| *T* | *Q* | *D* |
| 0 | 0 | 0 |
| 1 | 0 | 1 |
| 1 | 1 | 0 |
| 0 | 1 | 1 |

**Fig. 6.47**

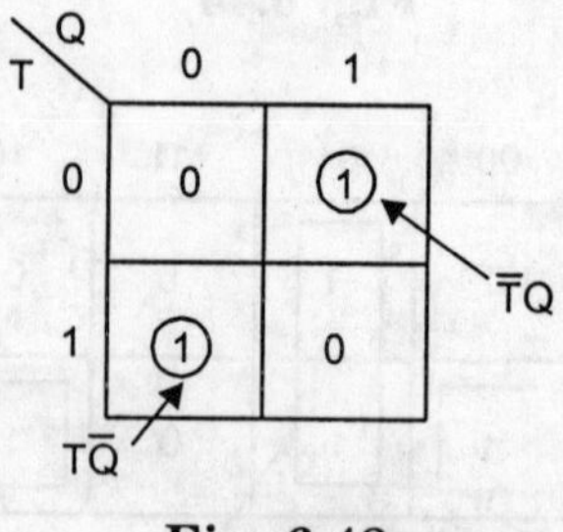


**Fig. 6.48**

Hence we get $D = T\overline{Q} + \overline{T}Q$

Hence the circuit may be designed as shown in Figure 6.49.

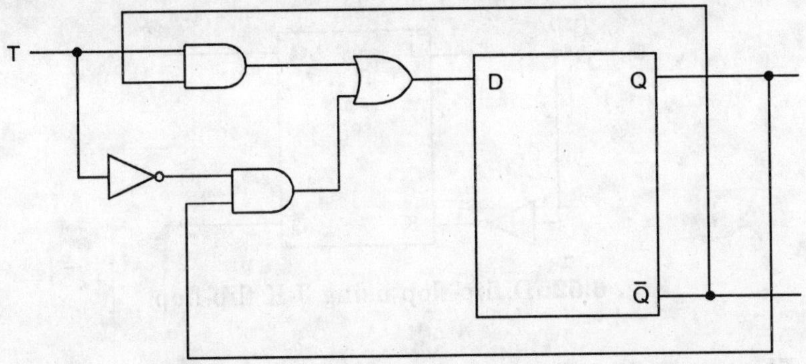


**Fig. 6.49:** T flip-flop using D flip-flop

### 6.7.7 J-K Flip-Flop to D Flip-Flop

The excitation tables of J-K and D flip-flops are given in Figure 6.30 from which we make the truth table as shown in Figure 6.50.

| *FF Data Inputs* | *Output* | *J-K FF Inputs* | |
|---|---|---|---|
| *D* | *Q* | *J* | *K* |
| 0 | 0 | 0 | X |
| 1 | 0 | 1 | X |
| 0. | 1 | X | 1 |
| 1 | 1 | X | 0 |

**Fig. 6.50**

The Karnaugh maps are prepared for J and K as shown in Figure 6.51(*a*) and Figure 6.51(*b*).

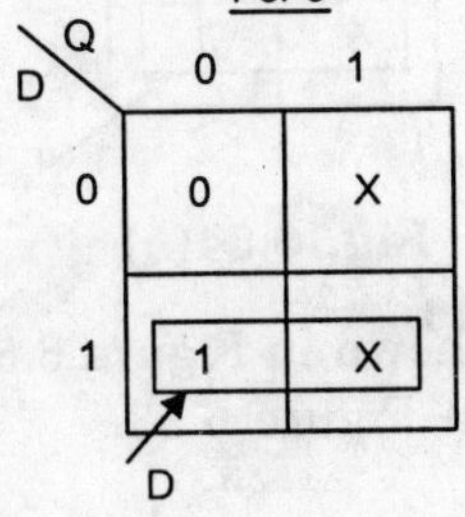


**Fig. 6.51(*a*)**

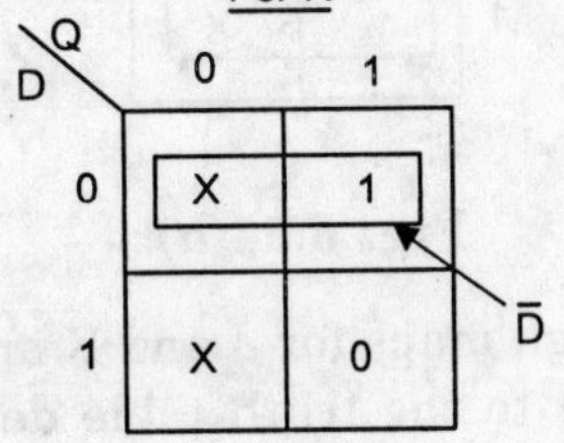


**Fig. 6.51(*b*)**

The Boolean expression for J and K are obtained as,

$$J = D$$

and
$$K = \overline{D}$$

Hence the circuit may be designed as shown in Figure 6.52.

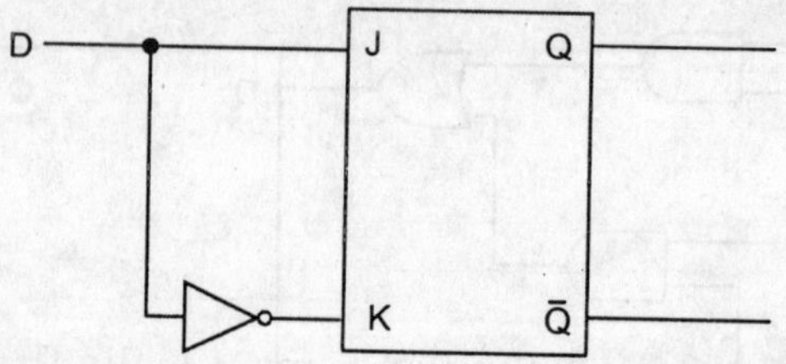


**Fig. 6.52:** D flip-flop using J-K flip-flop.

### 6.7.8 J-K Flip-Flop to T Flip-Flop

The excitation tables of J-K and T flip-flops are given in Figure 6.30 from which the required truth table is derived as shown in Figure 6.53.

| *FF Data Inputs* | *Output* | *J-K FF Inputs* | |
|---|---|---|---|
| *T* | *Q* | *J* | *K* |
| 0 | 0 | 0 | X |
| 1 | 0 | 1 | X |
| 1 | 1 | X | 1 |
| 0 | 1 | X | 0 |

**Fig. 6.53**

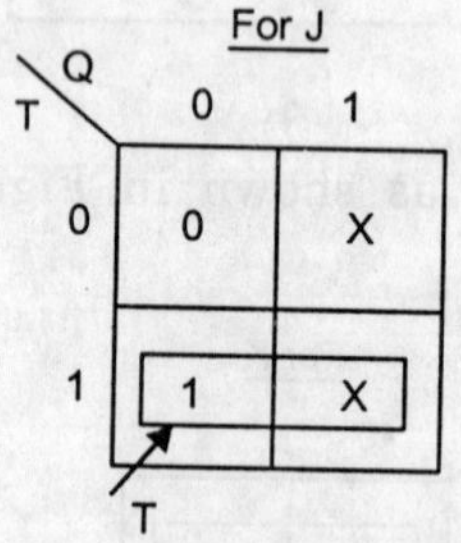


**Fig. 6.54(*a*)**

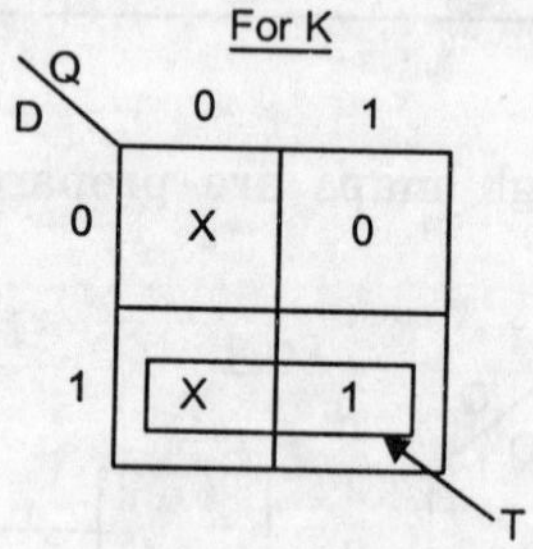


**Fig. 6.54(*b*)**

The Karnaugh maps for J and K are prepared as shown in Figure 6.54(*a*) and Figure 6.54(*b*), according to the truth table described above in Figure 6.53.

Hence we get,

$$J = T$$

and

$$K = T$$

The circuit may be realized as shown in Figure 6.55.

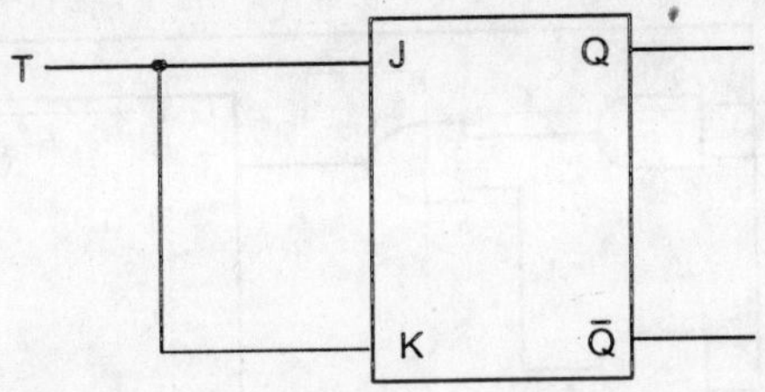


**Fig. 6.55:** T flip-flop using J-K flip-flop.

### 6.7.9 T Flip-Flop to S-R Flip-Flop

The truth table for the relation between S-R and T flip-flops is derived as shown in Figure 6.56, from the excitation table as mentioned in Figure 6.30.

| *FF Data Inputs* | | *Output* | *D FF Inputs* |
|---|---|---|---|
| *S* | *R* | *Q* | *T* |
| 0 | 0 | 0 | 0 |
| 0 | 1 | 0 | 0 |
| 1 | 0 | 0 | 1 |
| 0 | 1 | 1 | 1 |
| 0 | 0 | 1 | 0 |
| 1 | 0 | 1 | 0 |

**Fig. 6.56**

From the truth table of Figure 6.56, we make the Karnaugh map as shown in Figure 6.57.

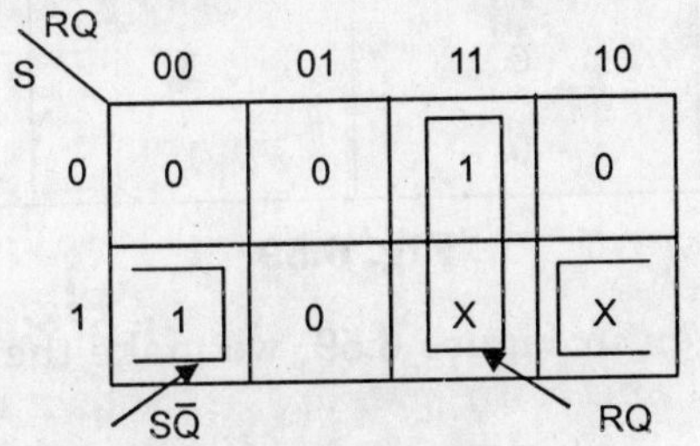


**Fig. 6.57**

We obtain the Boolean expression,

$$T = S\bar{Q} + RQ$$

Hence the circuit may be designed as shown in Figure 6.58.

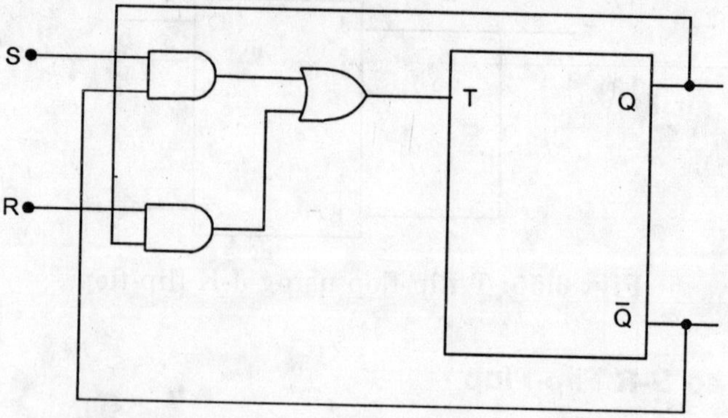


**Fig. 6.58:** S-R flip-flop using T flip-flop.

### 6.7.10 T Flip-Flop to J-K Flip-Flop

The excitation tables of J-K and T flip-flops are given in Figure 6.30, from which we make the truth table given in Figure 6.59.

| *FF Data Inputs* | | *Output* | *D FF Inputs* |
|---|---|---|---|
| *J* | *K* | *Q* | *T* |
| 0 | 0 | 0 | 0 |
| 0 | 1 | 0 | 0 |
| 1 | 0 | 0 | 1 |
| 1 | 1 | 0 | 1 |
| 0 | 1 | 1 | 1 |
| 1 | 1 | 1 | 1 |
| 0 | 0 | 1 | 0 |
| 1 | 0 | 1 | 0 |

**Fig. 6.59**

From the truth table given in Figure 6.59, we make the Karnaugh map as shown in Figure 6.60.

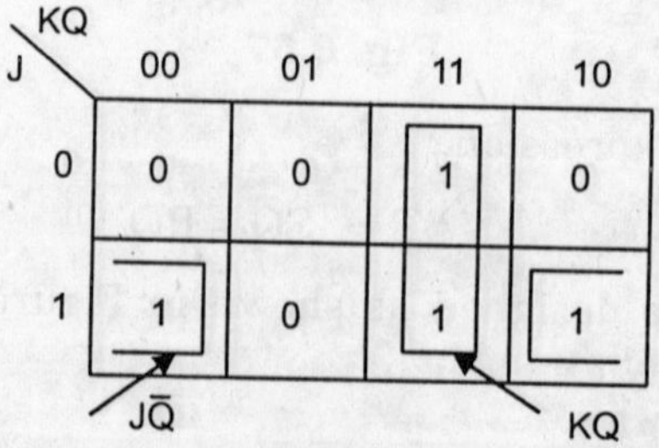


**Fig. 6.60**

We get,

$$T = J\bar{Q} + KQ$$

Hence the circuit may be designed as shown in Figure 6.61,

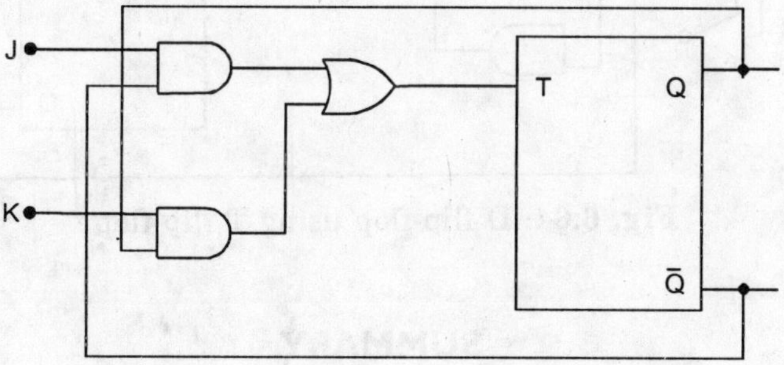


**Fig. 6.61:** J-K flip-flop using T flip-flop.

### 6.7.11 T Flip-Flop to D Flip-Flop

The excitation tables of D and T flip-flops are given in Figure 6.30 from which we make the truth table given in Figure 6.62.

| *FF Data Inputs* | *Output* | *T FF Inputs* |
|---|---|---|
| *D* | *Q* | *T* |
| 0 | 0 | 0 |
| 1 | 0 | 1 |
| 0 | 1 | 1 |
| 1 | 1 | 0 |

**Fig. 6.62**

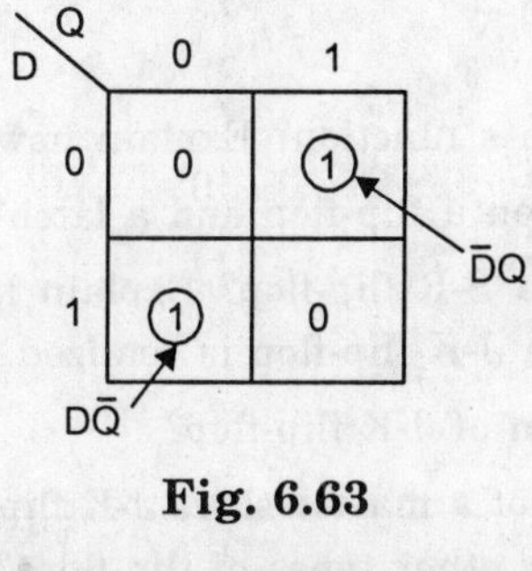


**Fig. 6.63**

The Karnaugh map is given in Figure 6.63 and the Boolean expression is derived as

$$T = \bar{D}Q + D\bar{Q}$$

Hence the circuit may be designed as shown in Figure 6.64.

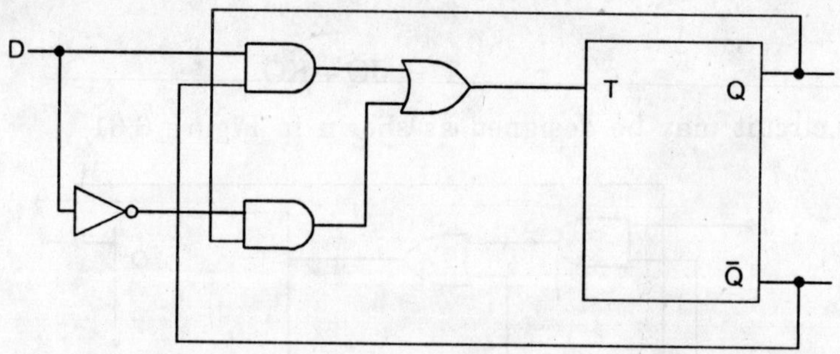


**Fig. 6.64:** D flip-flop using T flip-flop.

## SUMMARY

- Latch is the simplest type of flip-flop, having two cross-coupled NAND or NOR gates.
- A flip-flop is a two-state circuit that can remain in either state indefinitely. Also called a multivibrator. An external trigger can change the output state.
- The different types of flip-flops depend on how their inputs and clock pulses cause transition between two states. The types are S-R, D, J-K, Master Slave and T.
- Toggle means the change of the output to the opposite state is a J-K flip-flop.
- Race around condition is an undesirable condition which may exist in a system when two or more inputs change together. If the final output depends on which input changes first, a race around condition exists.
- Preset and clear inputs are often called **direct set** and **direct reset.** The word "direct" means unclocked.

## REVIEW QUESTIONS AND EXERCISES

1. What is a latch?
2. What is a flip-flop? What is its function? Explain how an S-R flip-flop is realized.
3. What is the difference between a flip-flop and a latch?
4. What is the shortcoming of a S-R flip-flop? Explain how this shortcoming is removed in J-K flip-flops. Describe how a J-K flip-flop is realized. Describe its operating principle.
5. What is race around condition of J-K flip-flop?
6. Draw the schematic diagram of a master-slave J-K flip-flop? Discuss its working principle. What are its advantages over other types of flip-flops?
7. What is a D flip-flop? What is its advantage over S-R flip-flop?
8. What is a T flip-flop? Explain.
9. What is triggering of flip-flops? Discuss different types of triggering with examples.

Chapter 7

# Registers and Counters

## 7.1 INTRODUCTION

In the previous chapter, we have described one of the basic elements of digital design *i.e.,* flip-flops. We have demonstrated several types of flip-flops, which may be further used to design complex digital subsystems that further enable us to design a computer system. In this chapter, we have discussed two types of digital subsystems, namely, registers and counters.

## 7.2 REGISTERS

A *register* is a group of binary storage cells capable of holding binary information. A group of flip-flops constitutes a register, since each flip-flop can work as a binary cell. A $n$-bit register, has hence $n$ flip-flops and is capable of holding $n$-bit of information. In addition to flip-flops a register can have a combinational part that performs data processing tasks.

Various types of registers are available in MSI (Medium Scale Integration) circuits. The simplest possible register is one that contains no external gates, and is constructed of only flip-flops. Figure 7.1 shows such a type of register constructed of four S-R flip-flops, with a common clock pulse input. The clock pulse enables all the flip-flops at the same instant so that the information available at the four inputs can be transferred into the 4-bit register. All the flip-flops in a register should respond to the clock pulse transition. Hence they should be either of the edge-triggered type or the master-slave type. A group of flip-flops sensitive to the pulse duration is commonly called a *gated latch*. Latches are

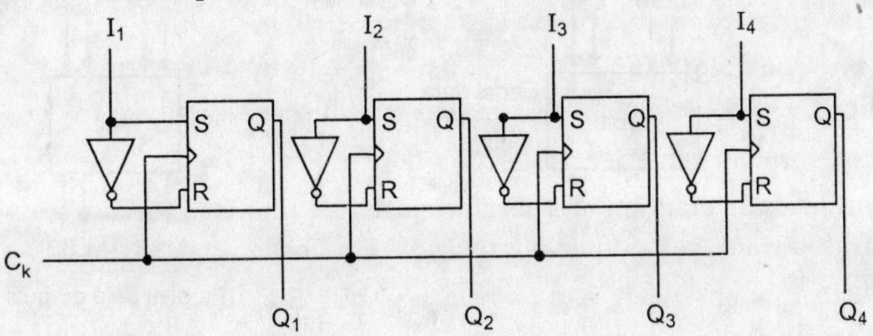


**Fig. 7.1:** A 4-bit register.

suitable to temporarily store binary information that is to be transferred to an external destination. They should not be used in the design of sequential circuits that have feedback connections.

## 7.3 SHIFT REGISTERS AND ITS TYPES

A register capable of shifting its binary contents either to the left or to the right is called a *shift register*. The shift register permits the stored data to move from a particular location to some other location within the register. Registers can be designed using discrete flip-flops (S-R, J-K and D-type).

The data in a shift register can be shifted in two possible ways: (*a*) serial shifting and (*b*) parallel shifting. The serial shifting method shifts one bit at a time for each clock pulse in a serial manner, beginning with either LSB or MSB. On the other hand, in parallel shifting operation, all the data (input or output) gets shifted simultaneously during a single clock pulse. Hence we may say that parallel shifting operation is much faster than serial shifting operation.

There are two ways to shift data into a register (serial or parallel) and similarly two ways to shift the data out of the register. This leads to the construction of four basic types of register as shown in Figures 7.2(*a*) to 7.2(*d*). These are given below:

- Serial-in Serial-out (SISO)
- Parallel-in Serial-out (PISO)
- Serial-in Parallel-out (SIPO)
- Parallel-in Parallel-out (PIPO)

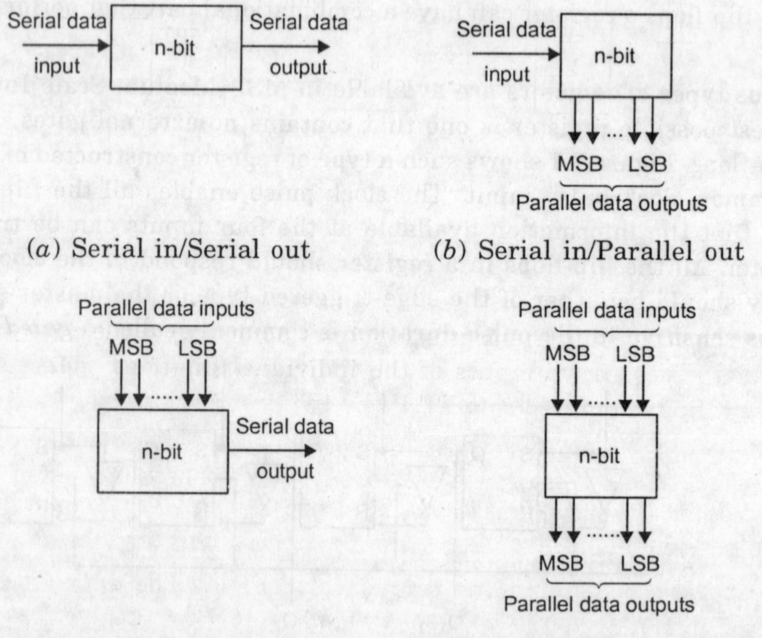


(*a*) Serial in/Serial out (*b*) Serial in/Parallel out

(*c*) Parallel in/Serial out (*d*) Parallel in/Parallel out

**Fig. 7.2:** Four types of shift registers.

## 7.4 SERIAL IN-SERIAL OUT SHIFT REGISTER

From the name itself it is obvious that this type of register accepts data serially, *i.e.*, one bit at a time at the single input line. The output is also obtained on a single output line in a serial fashion. The data within the register may be shifted from left to right using *shift-left* register, or may be shifted from right to left using *shift-right* register.

### 7.4.1 Shift-Right Register

A shift-right register can be constructed with either J-K or D flip-flop as shown in Figure 7.3. A J-K flip-flop based shift register requires connection of both J and K inputs. Input data are connected to the J and K inputs of the left most (lowest order) flip-flop. To input a 0, one should apply a 0 at the J input, *i.e.*, J = 0 and K = 1 and vice versa. With the application of a clock pulse the data will be shifted by one bit to the right.

In the shift register using D flip-flop D input of the left most flip-flop is used as a serial input line. To input 0, one should apply 0 at the D input and vice versa.

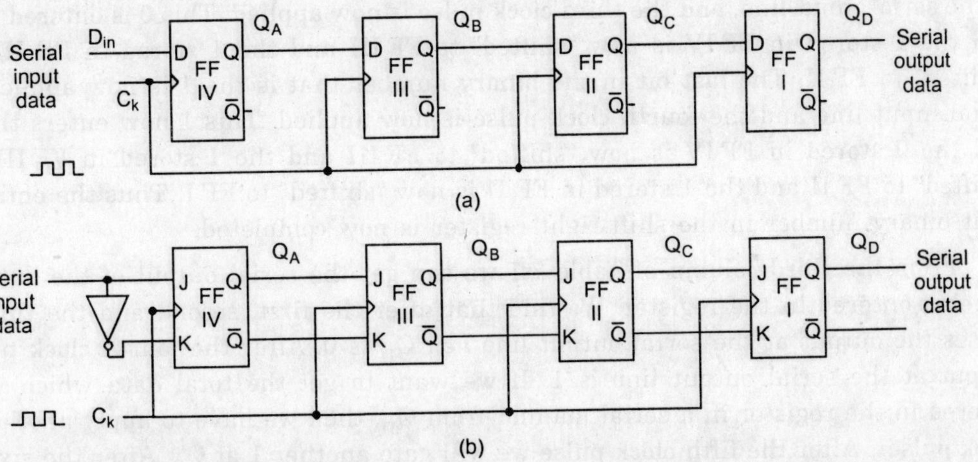


**Fig. 7.3:** Shift-right register (*a*) using D flip-flop, (*b*) using J-K flip-flop.

The clock pulse is applied to all the flip-flops simultaneously. When the clock pulse is applied, each flip-flop is either set or reset according to the data available at that point of time at the respective inputs of the individual flip-flops. Hence the input data bit at serial input line is entered into FF IV by the first clock pulse. At the same time the data of $Q_A$ is shifted into $Q_B$ and so on to the following flip-flops. For each clock pulse, data stored in the register is shifted to the right by one flip-flop. New data in entered into FF IV, whereas the data present in FF I are shifted out (to the right).

For example, consider that all the flip-flops are reset and a logical input 1011 is applied at the serial input line connected to FF IV. The data after four clock pulses is shown in Table 7.1.

Let us now illustrate the entry of the 4-bit number 1011 into the register, beginning with the right most bit. A 1 is applied at the serial input line, making $D_{in}$ = 1. As the first clock pulse is applied, FF IV is SET, thus storing the 1. Next a 1 is applied to the serial input, making D = 1 for FF IV and D = 1 for FF III also, because the input of FF III is connected to the $Q_A$ output.

**Table 7.1: Operation of the Shift-Right Register**

| *Timing Pulse* | $Q_A$ | $Q_B$ | $Q_C$ | $Q_D$ | *Serial Output at* $Q_D$ |
|---|---|---|---|---|---|
| Initial value | 0 | 0 | 0 | 0 | 0 |
| After 1st clock pulse | 1 | 0 | 0 | 0 | 0 |
| After 2nd clock pulse | 1 | 1 | 0 | 0 | 0 |
| After 3rd clock pulse | 0 | 1 | 1 | 0 | 0 |
| After 4th clock pulse | 1 | 0 | 1 | 1 | 1 |

When the second clock pulse occurs, the 1 on the data input is "shifted" to the FF IV and the 1 in the FF IV is "shifted" to FF III. The 0 in the binary number is now applied at the serial input line, and the third clock pulse is now applied. This 0 is entered in FF IV and the 1 stored in FF IV is now "shifted" to FF III and the 1 stored in FF III is now "shifted" to FF II. The last bit in the binary number that is the 1 is now applied at the serial input line and the fourth clock pulse is now applied. This 1 now enters the FF IV and the 0 stored in FF IV is now "shifted" to FF III and the 1 stored in FF III is now "shifted" to FF II and the 1 stored in FF II is now "shifted" to FF I. Thus the entry of the 4-bit binary number in the shift-right register is now completed.

From the third column of Table 7.1 we can get the serial output of the data which is being entered in the register. We find that after the first, second and the third clock pulses the output at the serial output line *i.e.*, $Q_D$ is 0. After the fourth clock pulse the output at the serial output line is 1. If we want to get the total data which we have entered in the register in a serial manner from $Q_D$, then we have to apply another three clock pulses. After the fifth clock pulse we will gate another 1 at $Q_D$. After the sixth clock pulse the output at $Q_D$ will be 0 and after the seventh clock pulse the output at $Q_D$ will be 1. In this process of the fifth, sixth and the seventh clock pulses if the no data is being supplied at the serial input line then the FF IV, FF III and FF II flip-flops will again be RESET with output 0.

The waveforms shown in Figure 7.4 illustrate the entry of a 4-bit number 1011. For a J-K flip-flop, the data bit to be shifted into the flip-flop must be present at the J and K inputs when the clock transitions from low to high occur. Since the data bit is either 1 or 0, there can be two different cases:

1. To shift a 1 into the flip-flop, J = 1 and K = 0,
2. To shift a 0 into the flip-flop, J = 0 and K = 1.

**At time $t_1$:** All the flip-flops are reset. At the serial data input line a 1 is given and with the first clock pulse this 1 is shifted at $Q_A$ making $Q_A = 1$. At the same time the 0 in $Q_A$ is shifted to $Q_B$, and the 0 in $Q_B$ is shifted to $Q_C$ and the 0 in $Q_C$ is shifted to $Q_D$. Hence the flip-flop outputs just after time $t_1$ are $Q_AQ_BQ_CQ_D = 1000$.

**At time $t_2$:** The flip-flop A contains 1, and all other flip-flop contains 0. Now again 1 is given at the serial data input line. With the second clock pulse this 1 is shifted to $Q_A$. The 1 in $Q_A$ is shifted to $Q_B$ and the 0 in $Q_B$ is shifted to $Q_C$ and the 0 in $Q_C$ is shifted to $Q_D$. Hence the flip-flop outputs just after time $t_2$ are $Q_AQ_BQ_CQ_D$ = 1100.

**At time $t_3$:** The flip-flop A and flip-flop B contain 1, and all other flip-flops contain 0. Now a 0 is given at the serial data input line. With the third clock pulse this 0 is shifted to $Q_A$. The 1 in $Q_A$ is shifted to $Q_B$ and the 1 in $Q_B$ is shifted to $Q_C$ and the 0 in $Q_C$ is shifted to $Q_D$. Hence the flip-flop outputs just after time $t_3$ are $Q_AQ_BQ_CQ_D$ = 0110.

**At time $t_4$:** The flip-flop B and flip-flop C contain 1, and all other flip-flops contain 0. Now another 1 is given at the serial data input line. With the fourth clock pulse this 1 is shifted to $Q_A$. The 0 in $Q_A$ is shifted to $Q_B$ and the 1 in $Q_B$ is shifted to $Q_C$ and the 1 in $Q_C$ is shifted to $Q_D$. Hence the flip-flop outputs just after time $t_4$ are $Q_AQ_BQ_CQ_D$ = 1011.

To summarize, we have shifted 4 data bits in a serial manner into four flip-flops. These 4 data bits could represent a 4-bit binary number 1011, assuming that we began shifting with the LSB first. Notice that the LSB is in $Q_D$ and the MSB is in $Q_A$. These four flip-flops could be defined as a 4-bit shift register.

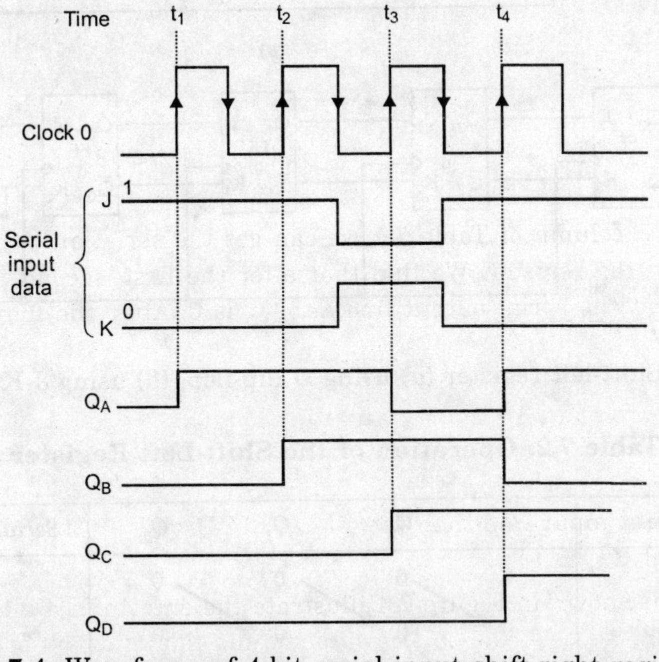


**Fig. 7.4:** Waveforms of 4-bit serial input shift-right register.

## 7.4.2 Shift-Left Register

A shift-left register can also be constructed with either J-K or D flip-flop as shown in Figure 7.5. Let us now illustrate the entry of the 4-bit number 0111 into the register, beginning with the MSB (most significant bit). A 0 is applied at the serial input line, making $D_{in}$ = 0. As the first clock pulse is applied, the right most FF I is RESET, thus storing the 0. Next a 1 is applied to the serial input, making $D_0$ = 1 for FF I and $D_1$ = 0 for FF II, because the input of FF II is connected to the $Q_0$ output.

When the second clock pulse occurs, the 1 on the data input is "shifted" to the FF I and the 0 in the FF I is "shifted" to FF II. The 1 in the binary number is now applied at the serial input line, and the third clock pulse is now applied. This 1 is entered in FF I and the 1 stored in FF I is now "shifted" to FF II and the 0 stored in FF II is now "shifted" to FF III. The last bit (LSB) in the binary number that is the 1 is now applied at the serial input line and the fourth clock pulse is now applied. This 1 now enters the FF I and the 1 stored in FF I is now "shifted" to FF II and the 1 stored in FF II is now "shifted" to FF III and the 0 stored in FF III is now "shifted" to FF IV. Thus the entry of the 4-bit binary number in the shift-right register is now completed as shown in Table 7.2. The waveforms of this data entry are shown in Figure 7.6.

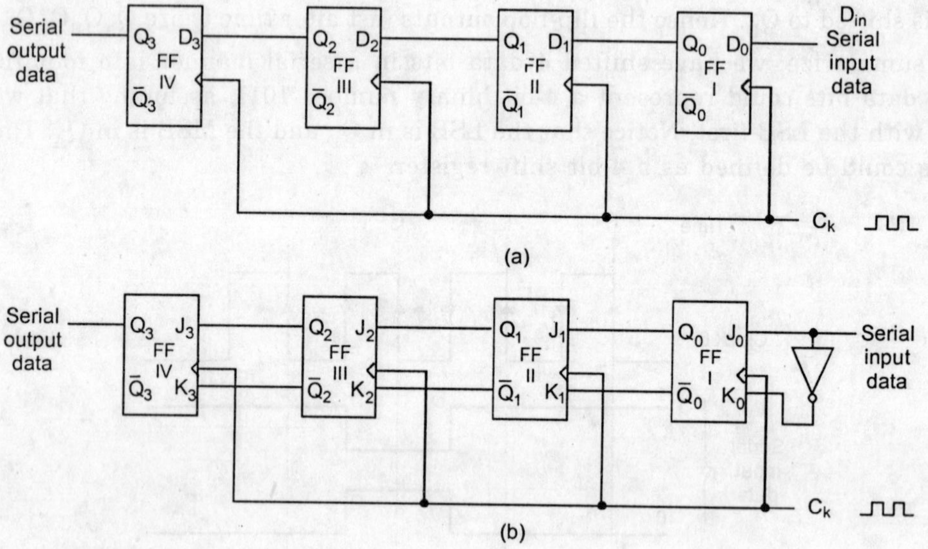


**Fig. 7.5:** Shift-left register (*a*) using D flip-flop, (*b*) using J-K flip-flop.

**Table 7.2: Operation of the Shift-Left Register**

| *Timing Pulse* | $Q_3$ | $Q_2$ | $Q_1$ | $Q_0$ | *Serial Output at* $Q_3$ |
|---|---|---|---|---|---|
| Initial value | 0 | 0 | 0 | 0 | 0 |
| After 1st clock pulse | 0 | 0 | 0 | 0 | 0 |
| After 2nd clock pulse | 0 | 0 | 0 | 1 | 0 |
| After 3rd clock pulse | 0 | 0 | 1 | 1 | 0 |
| After 4th clock pulse | 0 | 1 | 1 | 1 | 0 |

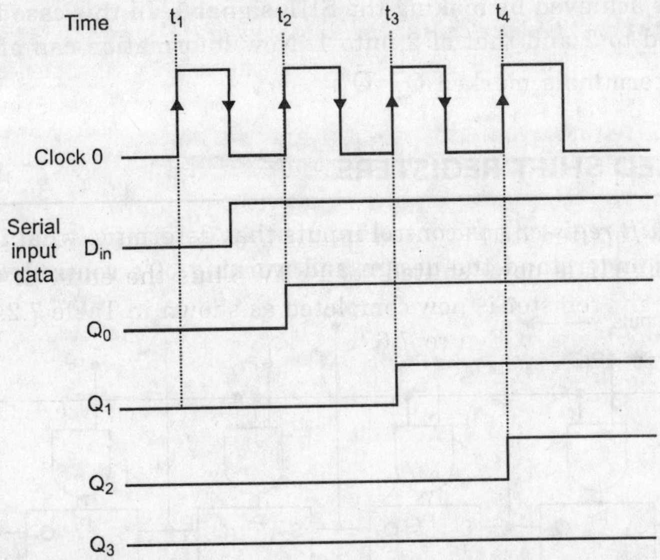


**Fig. 7.6:** Waveforms of 4-bit serial input shift-left register.

### 7.4.3 Left-Right Shift Register

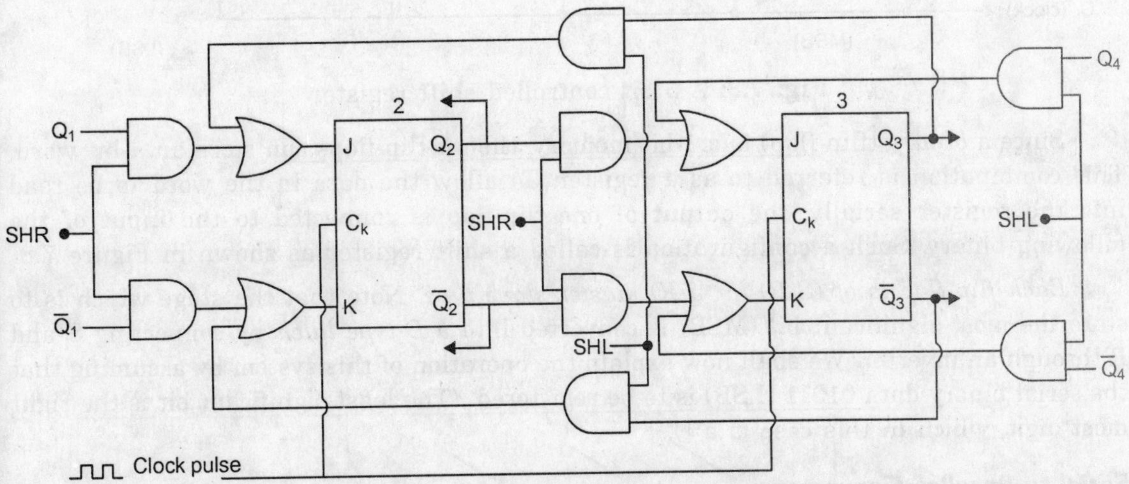


**Fig. 7.7:** Left-right shift register.

For shifting the contents of the register left or right, the arrangement as shown in Figure 7.7 can be used. When SHR signal is '1' information is transferred from flip-flop 1 to 2, 2 to 3 etc. *As the triggering of each flip-flop takes place at the trailing edge of the clock pulse, there is no ambiguity in the transfer of information.* In other words we can simultaneously write fresh information in a flip-flop and read its previous content. This becomes possible since the new information does not get into the flip-flop till the trailing edge of the clock pulse arrives and the old content is safely transferred to the next flip-flop.

Shifting left is achieved by making the SHL signal 1. In this case the content of flip-flop 3 is transferred to 2 and that of 2, into 1. New information can also be entered into flip-flop 3 via the terminals marked $Q_4$, $\overline{Q}_4$.

## 7.5 CONTROLLED SHIFT REGISTERS

A *controlled shift register* has control inputs that determine what it does on the next clock pulse. Let us understand the design and working of a controlled shift register.

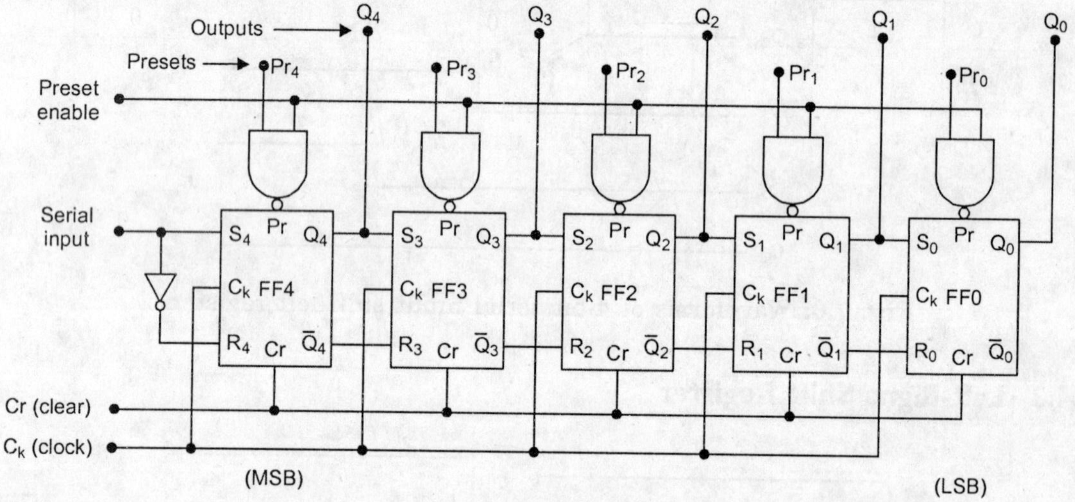


**Fig. 7.8:** A 5 bit controlled shift register.

Since a *binary* (flip-flop) is a 1-bit memory, then *n* flip-flops can store an *n*-bit word. This combination is referred to as a register. To allow the data in the word to be read into the register serially, the output of one flip-flop is connected to the input of the following binary. Such a configuration is called a shift register as shown in Figure 7.8.

*Each flip-flop is of (S-R) (or J-K) master slave type.* Note that the stage which is to store the most significant bit (MSB) is converted into a *D-type latch* by connecting S and R through an inverter. We shall now explain the operation of this system by assuming that the serial binary data 01011 (LSB) is to be registered. (The least significant bit is the right most digit, which in this case is a 1).

### *Serial-to-Parallel Converter*

The flip-flops are cleared by applying a 0 to the *clear* input so that every output $Q_0$, $Q_1$, ... $Q_4$ is 0. *Then Cr is set to 1* and *Pr is held constant at 1* (by keeping the preset enable at 0). The serial data train and the synchronous clock are now applied. The LSB is entered into FF4 when $C_k$ changes from a 0 to a 1 by action of a D-type flip-flop. After the clock pulse $Q_4$ = 1, while all other outputs remain at 0.

At the second clock pulse the state of $Q_4$ is transferred to a master latch of FF3 by the action of an S-R flip-flop. Simultaneously, the next bit (a 1 in 01011) enters the master of FF4. After the second clock pulse the bit in each master transfers to its slave and $Q_4$ = 1, $Q_3$ = 1, and the other outputs remain 0. *Of course, the clock pulses must stop a' the moment the word is registered.* Each output is available on a separate line and they may be read simultaneously.

Since the data entered the system serially and came out in parallel this shift register is a *serial-to-parallel converter.*

**Table 7.3: Reading of Shift Register after each Clock Pulse**

| *Clock Pulse* | *Word Bit* | $Q_4$ | $Q_3$ | $Q_2$ | $Q_1$ | $Q_0$ |
|---|---|---|---|---|---|---|
| 1 | 1 | 1 | 0 | 0 | 0 | 0 |
| 2 | 1 | 1 | 1 | 0 | 0 | 0 |
| 3 | 0 | 0 | 1 | 1 | 0 | 0 |
| 4 | 1 | 1 | 0 | 1 | 1 | 0 |
| 5 | 0 | 0 | 1 | 0 | 1 | 1 |

***Parallel to Serial Converter***

Consider the situation where the word bit are available in parallel. It is desired to present this code say 01011 is serial form.

The LSB is applied to $Pr_0$ the $2^1$ bit to $Pr_1$, ..... so that $Pr_0 = 1$, $Pr_1 = 1$, $Pr_2 = 0$, $Pr_3 = 1$ and $Pr_4 = 0$. *The register is first cleared by Cr = 0 and then Cr = 1 is maintained.* A 1 given at the *preset enable* input activates all *k*th input NAND gates for which $Pr_k = 1$. The preset of the corresponding *k*th flip-flop is Pr = 0 and this stage is therefore present to 1. In the present illustration FF0, FF1 and FF3 are preset and the input word 01011 is written into the register, all bits in parallel, by preset enable pulse. This kind of entry is called *parallel* or *broad side loading.* Now the stored word may be read serially at $Q_0$ by applying five clock pulses. This is a *parallel to serial converter.*

By adding more flip-flops we can build a controlled shift register of any length.

## 7.6 PARALLEL IN-PARALLEL OUT REGISTER

There is a fourth type of register already mentioned which is designed such that data can be shifted into or out of the register in parallel. The parallel input of data has already been discussed in the preceding section of parallel-in serial-out shift register. Also in this type of register there is no inter connection between the flip-flops since no serial shifting is required. Hence the moment the parallel entry of the data is accomplished the data will be available at the parallel outputs of the register. A simple parallel-in parallel-out shift register is shown in Figure 7.9.

Here the parallel inputs to be applied at A, B, C and D inputs are directly connected to the D inputs of the respective flip-flops. On applying the clock transitions, these inputs are entered into the register and are immediately available at the outputs $Q_A$, $Q_B$, $Q_C$, and $Q_D$.

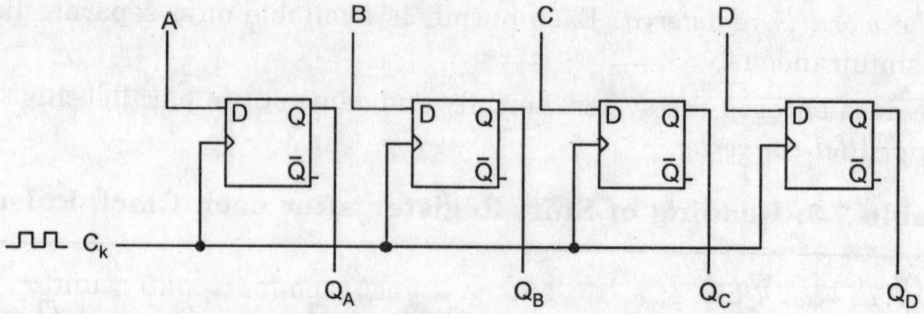


**Fig. 7.9:** A 4-bit parallel-in parallel-out shift register.

## 7.7 COUNTERS AND ITS TYPES

As the name suggests, the counter has the ability to count and is a very important and useful subsystem of a digital system. A flip flop can store one binary information. Thus to store more binary information, a group of cascaded flip flops called registers, are required. **A counter is a register, which is capable of counting the number of clock pulses, which have arrived at its clock input.** Thus the counter has to actually remember the number of clock pulses applied at the input. The counters are used for counting pulses in large variety of counting applications such as control systems, computers, electronic and scientific instruments, etc. The wide range of applications of counters include counting the occurence of events, frequency division, time-sequence of operation of equipments and digital systems.

Counters can be broadly classified into following two types:

(1) Asynchronous or ripple counter

(2) Synchronous counter.

A ripple counter is also called an asynchronous counter, because it is an asynchronous sequential circuit. Whereas a synchronous counter is a synchronous sequential circuit. All the flip-flops in a synchronous counter are under the control of same clock pulse, which is synchronously applied to all the flip-flops. An asynchronous counter is not under the control of same clock pulse.

## 7.8 ASYNCHRONOUS OR RIPPLE COUNTER

An $n$-bit binary ripple counter can count up to maximum of $2^n$ states. A ripple counter is a basic and simple counter, which is most commonly used, but has limitation on speed of operation. Let us take few examples of ripple counters.

**Example 1.** *Draw a 4-bit binary ripple counter. Explain its working.*

**Solution.** A 4 bit-binary ripple counter can count up to a maximum of $2^4$ states, *i.e.*, 16 states, that is why it is also known by other names like **four stage or modulo-16 (Mod-16)** or **divide by 16** ripple counter. It uses four, negative edge triggered type J-K flip-flops. Initially all the four flip-flops A, B, C and D are in logic '0' state. That is Q output of A, B, C and D flip-flops are all in logic '0' state as illustrated in Figures 7.10 (*a*) and (*b*).

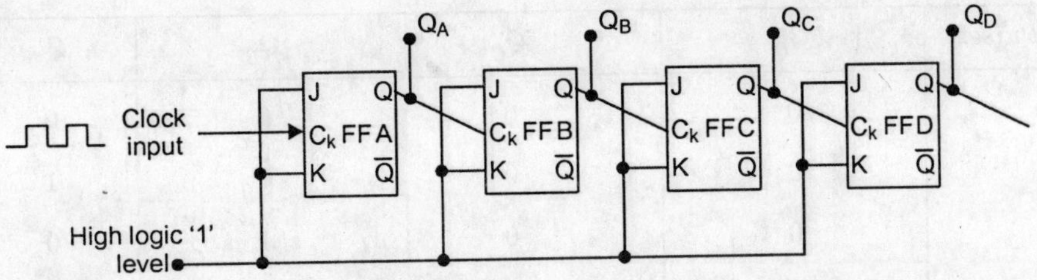


**Fig. 7.10 (*a*):** 4-bit (Mod-16) binary asynchronous (ripple) counter.

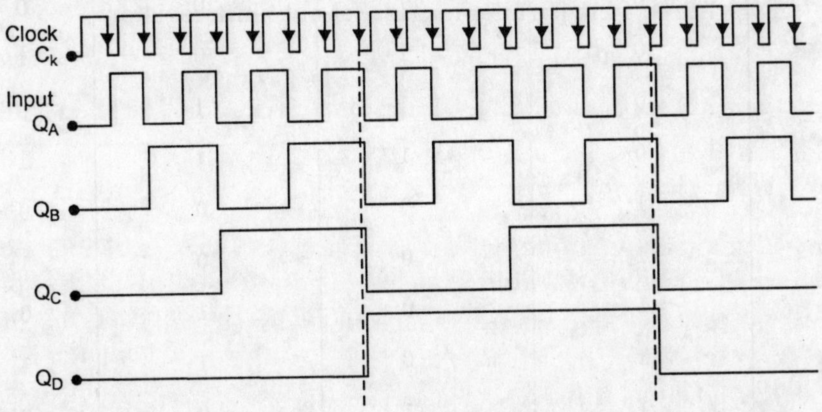


**Fig. 7.10 (*b*):** Modulo-16 (Mod-16) ripple counter's timing diagram.

A clock pulse is applied to the clock input of flip-flop A only, which makes output $Q_A$ of flip-flop A to change from logic 0 to logic 1 state. At this instant, flip-flops B, C and D do not change their state and thus remain in logic '0' state, so after application of the first clock pulse to the clock input, the counter reads,

$$Q = Q_D\, Q_C\, Q_B\, Q_A = 0\ 0\ 0\ 1$$

Now when second clock pulse is applied to flip-flop A, output $Q_A$ changes state from '1' to '0'. Due to this change of slate of Q going from '1' to '0', a negative going pulse is created at $Q_A$, which is connected to clock input of flip-flop B. Thus this negative going pulse triggers the flip-flop B, changing the state of Q from its previous or original state '0' to '1'. At this instant the outputs $Q_C$ and $Q_D$ of flip-flops C and D respectively continue to remain in their logic '0' state, and thus the counter reads.

$$Q = Q_D\, Q_C\, Q_B\, Q_A = 0\ 0\ 1\ 0$$

The counter will continue to count the input clock pulses in the binary form as explained above up to state till $Q_D$, $Q_C$, $Q_B$ and $Q_A$ all become high, *i.e.*, logic level '1', and counter will read $Q = Q_D\, Q_C\, Q_B\, Q_A = 1\ 1\ 1\ 1$, which in decimal form means that it will count upto 15 clock pulses. On arrival of the 16th clock pulse, all the four flip-flops A, B, C and D will go to '0' and the counter will once again repeat its counting from 0000 to 1111 *i.e.*, from 0 to 15 (see Figure 7.11). Thus in this ripple counter, it is seen that output of the first flip-flop is driving the clock of the second flip-flop and output of the second flip-flop drives the clock of the third flip-flop and so on.

| *Clock Pulses* | $Q_D$ | $Q_C$ | $Q_B$ | $Q_A$ |
|---|---|---|---|---|
| 0 | 0 | 0 | 0 | 0 |
| 1 | 0 | 0 | 0 | 1 |
| 2 | 0 | 0 | 1 | 0 |
| 3 | 0 | 0 | 1 | 1 |
| 4 | 0 | 1 | 0 | 0 |
| 5 | 0 | 1 | 0 | 1 |
| 6 | 0 | 1 | 1 | 0 |
| 7 | 0 | 1 | 1 | 1 |
| 8 | 1 | 0 | 0 | 0 |
| 9 | 1 | 0 | 0 | 1 |
| 10 | 1 | 0 | 1 | 0 |
| 11 | 1 | 0 | 1 | 1 |
| 12 | 1 | 1 | 0 | 0 |
| 13 | 1 | 1 | 0 | 1 |
| 14 | 1 | 1 | 1 | 0 |
| 15 | 1 | 1 | 1 | 1 |
| 16 | 0 | 0 | 0 | 0 |

**Fig. 7.11:** Truth table of a 4-bit binary ripple counter or modulo-16 ripple counter.

There will be a small delay between the clock input and the output of the first flip-flop. The output of the first flip-flop ripples through the other flip-flops in tandem. For instance when the count is to change form 0111 to 1000, the trailing edge of the pulse from flip-flop A triggers flip-flop B. This is turn, triggers C and the output of flip-flop C then triggers D. Thus, the last flip-flop changes state only after a cumulative delay of 4 flip-flops (see Figure 7.10(*b*)). This counter is called **ripple carry counter.**

**Example 2.** *Explain the general technique to design a divide by N ripple counter, assuming J-K flip-flops with Preset are available.*

**Solution.** The general technique involves, the steps given below to be followed in sequence.

(*i*) Calculate the number, $n$ of J-K flip-flops, which are required to be used, by using the formula

$$n = \log_2 N$$

where symbol $\log_2$ N indicates the rounded off smallest integer, which is greater then or equal to $\log_2$ N.

(*ii*) Connect these N J-K flip-flops as ripple counter.

(*iii*) Obtain the binary equivalent of the number N–1.

(*iv*) All these flip-flop outputs, which are high or '1' at the count N–1 are connected as inputs to NAND gate. The clock pulse should also be fed to the NAND gate.

(*v*) The output of the NAND gate should be connected to the Preset (Pr) inputs of all those J-K flip-flops for which the output Q was equal to '0' at the count N–1 in binary representation.

On the arrival of the positive going edge of the $N^{th}$ clock pulses, all flip-flops will be preset to '1' or high state. On the arrival of the trailing edge of the same clock pulse, all flip-flops will count to the '0' state and thus the counter will be RESET or will recycle its counting once again.

**Example 3.** *Based on the general technique to design a divide by–N ripple counter, design a decade (Modulo-10 or divide by 10) ripple counter, using J-K flip-flops.*

**Solution.** For Mod-10 or divide by 10 ripple counter, value of N = 10

$$\therefore \quad n = \log_2 N = \log_2 10 = 3.322$$

This 3.322 is rounded off to 4, which is the smallest integer equal to or greater than 3.322. Therefore we require four J-K, negative edge triggered flip-flops, which are to be connected as ripple counter, as shown in Figure 7.12. Binary equivalent of number N–1 (=10 – 1 = 9) is 1001.

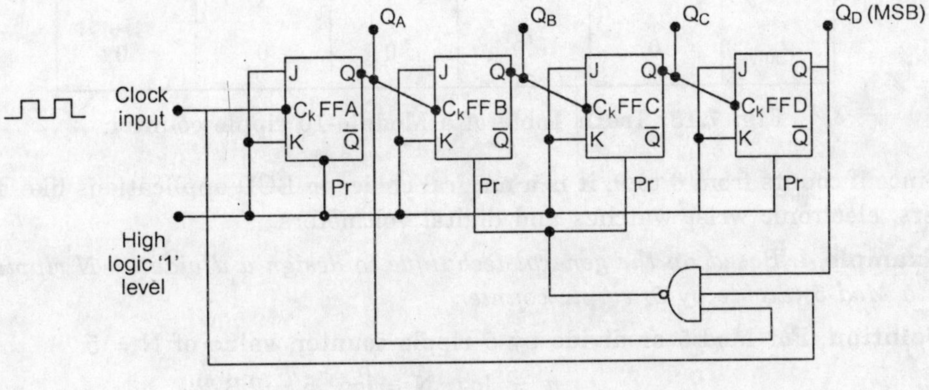


**Fig. 7.12:** Decade (Mod-10) ripple counter.

Thus $$Q = Q_D\, Q_C\, Q_B\, Q_A = 1001$$

Which means $Q_D$ = 1 and $Q_A$ = 1. Therefore outputs $Q_D$ and $Q_A$, which are high or '1' are connected as inputs to the NAND gate as illustrated in Figure 7.12. The clock pulse input is also fed as input to this NAND gate. The output of the NAND gate is connected to the Preset inputs Pr of the J-K flip-flops B and C, for which; the outputs $Q_B$ and $Q_C$ were equal to '0' at the count N–1 (=1001).

The J-K inputs of all the four flip-flops are connected to logic level '1' (high), so as to work as a ripple counter.

On the arrival of the positive going edge of the $10^{th}$ clock pulse, all flip-flops will be preset to '1' and on the arrival of the trailing (negative) edge of the same $10^{th}$ clock pulse, all flip-flops will count to the '0' state. Thus the counter will be reset and will recycle its counting once again as illustrated in Figure 7.13.

| *Time* | *Count* | $Q_D$ | $Q_C$ | $Q_B$ | $Q_A$ |
|---|---|---|---|---|---|
| $t_0$ | 0 | 0 | 0 | 0 | 0 |
| $t_1$ | 1 | 0 | 0 | 0 | 1 |
| $t_2$ | 2 | 0 | 0 | 1 | 0 |
| $t_3$ | 3 | 0 | 0 | 1 | 1 |
| $t_4$ | 4 | 0 | 1 | 0 | 0 |
| $t_5$ | 5 | 0 | 1 | 0 | 1 |
| $t_6$ | 6 | 0 | 1 | 1 | 0 |
| $t_7$ | 7 | 0 | 1 | 1 | 1 |
| $t_8$ | 8 | 1 | 0 | 0 | 0 |
| $t_9$ | 9 | 1 | 0 | 0 | 1 |
| $t_{10}$ | 0 | 0 | 0 | 0 | 0 |

**Fig. 7.13:** Truth Table of a Modulo-10 ripple counter.

Since if counts from 0 to 9, it is a natural choice in BCD applications like, frequency counters, electronic wrist watches and digital voltmeters.

**Example 4.** *Based on the general technique to design a divide by–N ripple counter, design a Mod-5 (divide by 5) ripple counter.*

**Solution.** For Mod-5 or divide by 5 ripple counter, value of N = 5.

$$\therefore \quad n = \log_2 N = \log_2 5 = 2.322$$

Now 2.322 is rounded off to 3, which is the smallest integer equal to or greater than 2.322. Therefore we need three J-K, negative edge triggered flip-flops, which are to be connected as ripple counter as is shown in Figure 7.14.

The binary equivalent of number N–1 (= 5 – 1 = 4) is 100

Thus $$Q = Q_C\, Q_B\, Q_A = 100$$

which means only $Q_C$ is high or at logic level '1'. Therefore output $Q_C$ which is high at the count N–1, is connected as input to the NAND gate, as shown in Figure 7.14. The clock pulse input is also fed as input to this NAND gate. The output of the NAND gate is connected to the preset inputs Pr of the J-K flip-flops A and B, for which the outputs ($Q_A = 0$, $Q_B = 0$) were equal to '0' at the count N–1 (= 100). The J-K inputs of all the three flip-flops are connected to logic level '1', so as to work as a ripple counter. The circuit will have five states 0, 1, 2, 3 and 4. Nothing unusual happens when the circuit is counting from 0 to 4. On arrival of the positive going edge of $5^{th}$ clock pulse, all the flip-flops will be preset to '1' and on arrival of the trailing or negative edge of the same clock pulse, all flip-flops will count to '0' state. Thus the counter will reset and will be ready to start over or recycle again as shown in Figure 7.15.

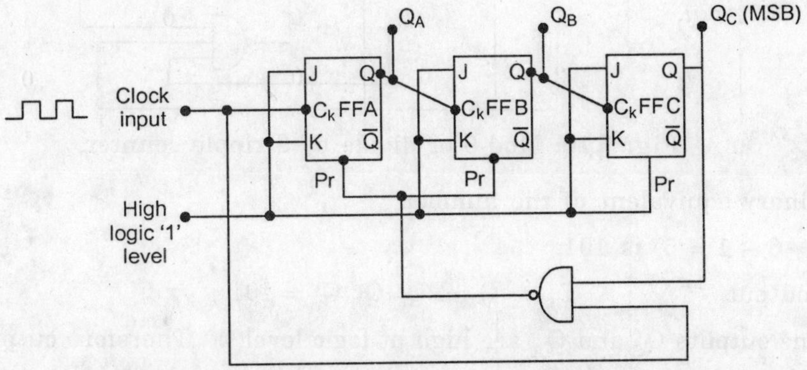


**Fig. 7.14:** Mod-5 or divide by 5 ripple counter.

| *Time* | *Count* | $Q_C$ | $Q_B$ | $Q_A$ |
|---|---|---|---|---|
| $t_0$ | 0 | 0 | 0 | 0 |
| $t_1$ | 1 | 0 | 0 | 1 |
| $t_2$ | 2 | 0 | 1 | 0 |
| $t_3$ | 3 | 0 | 1 | 1 |
| $t_4$ | 4 | 1 | 0 | 0 |
| $t_5$ | 0 | 0 | 0 | 0 |

**Fig. 7.15:** Truth Table of a Modulo-5 ripple counter.

Since it takes 5 clock pulses to reset the counter, the output frequency of the flip-flop C is one fifth of the clock frequency. Therefore a Mod-5 counter is also known as a divide by 5 ripple counter.

**Example 5.** *Based on the general technique to design a divide by N ripple counter, design a Mod-6 (divide by 6) ripple counter.*

**Solution.** For Mod-6 or divide by 6 ripple counter, value of N = 6.

$$n = \log_2 N = \log_2 6 = 2.585$$

which is rounded off to 3, which is the smallest integer equal to or greater than 2.585. Therefore we need three J-K, negative edge triggered flip-flops, which are connected as ripple counter as illustrated in Figure 7.16.

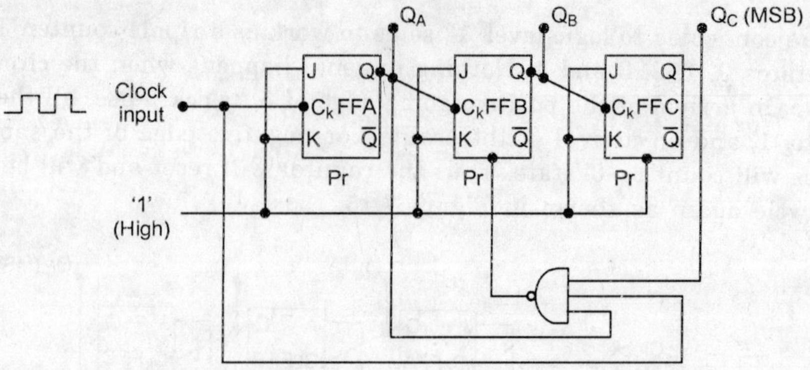


**Fig. 7.16:** Mod-6 or divide by 6 ripple counter.

The binary equivalent of the number

N–1 (= 6 – 1 = 5) is 101.

Thus output $Q = Q_C\, Q_B\, Q_A = 101$

which means outputs $Q_C$ and $Q_A$ are high at logic level '1'. Therefore outputs $Q_C$ and $Q_A$ which are '1' at the count N–l, are connected as input to the NAND gate as shown in Figure 7.16. The clock pulse input is also fed as input to this NAND gate. The output of the NAND gate is connected to the preset input Pr of J-K flip-flop B, for which the output ($Q_B = 0$) was equal to '0', at the count N–l (= 101). The J-K inputs of all the three flip-flops are connected to level '1', so as to work as a ripple counter. The circuit will have six states 0, 1, 2, 3, 4 and 5. The circuit counts from 0 to 5 in the usual manner. On arrival of the positive going edge of the $6^{th}$ clock pulse, all the flip-flops will be preset to '1' and on arrival of trailing or negative edge of the same clock pulse, all flip-flops will count to '0' state. Then the counter will reset and will be ready to start over a recycle again.

| *Time* | *Count* | $Q_C$ | $Q_B$ | $Q_A$ |
|---|---|---|---|---|
| $t_0$ | 0 | 0 | 0 | 0 |
| $t_1$ | 1 | 0 | 0 | 1 |
| $t_2$ | 2 | 0 | 1 | 0 |
| $t_3$ | 3 | 0 | 1 | 1 |
| $t_4$ | 4 | 1 | 0 | 0 |
| $t_5$ | 5 | 1 | 0 | 1 |
| $t_6$ | 0 | 0 | 0 | 0 |

**Fig. 7.17:** Truth Table of Modulo-6 ripple counter.

Since it takes 6 clock pulses to reset the counter, the output frequency of flip-flop C is one sixth of the clock frequency. Therefore a Mod-6 counter is also known as divide by 6 ripple counter. Figure 7.17 shows the truth table of the counter.

**Example 6.** *Based on general the technique to design a divide by N ripple counter, design a Mod-12 (divide by 12) ripple counter using J-K flip-flop. Also draw its truth table.*

**Solution.** For Mod-12 or Modulo 12 counter, value of N = 12

$$n = \log_2 N = \log_2 12 = 3.478$$

which when rounded off to the smallest interger equal to or greater than 3.478 becomes 4. Therefore we need four J-K flip-flops available with preset, with negative edge triggering. The binary equivalent of number N–1( = 12 – 1 = 11) is 1011.

Thus output $$Q = Q_D\, Q_C\, Q_B\, Q_A = 1011$$

which means that outputs $Q_D$, $Q_B$ and $Q_A$ of flip-flops D, B and A respectively are high at level '1'. Therefore these outputs, which are '1' at the count N–1, are connected as inputs to the NAND gate. The clock pulse is also fed as input to this NAND gate as illustrated in Figure 7.18.

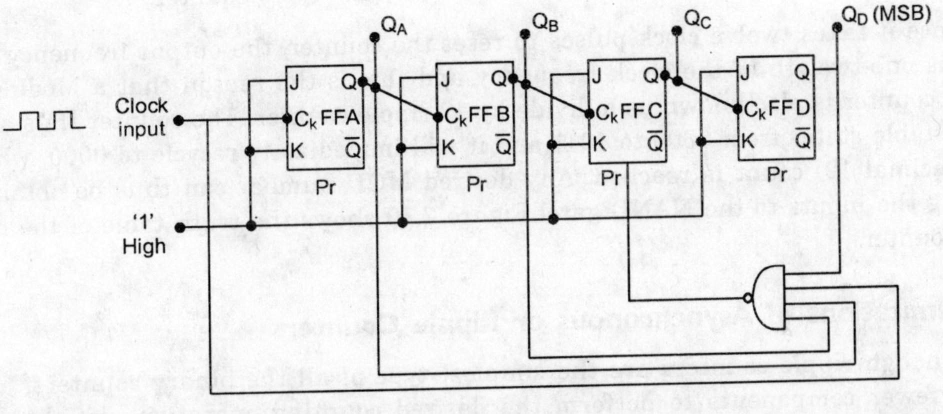


**Fig. 7.18:** Divide by 12 ripple counter.

The output of NAND gate is connected to the preset input Pr of J-K flip-flop C, for which the output ($Q_C$ = 0) was equal to '0' at the count N–1 (= 1011). The J-K inputs of all the four flip-flops are connected to logic level '1' (High), so that the circuit works as a ripple counter. The circuit will have twelve states from 0 to 11. It counts from 0 to 11 successively in the usual manner. On arrival of positive going edge of the 12th clock pulse, all the four flip-flops will be preset to '1' and on arrival of the trailing or negative edge of the same clock pulse, all flip-flops will count to '0' state. The counter will thus reset itself and will be ready to start over counting once again.

| *Time* | *Count* | $Q_D$ | $Q_C$ | $Q_B$ | $Q_A$ |
|---|---|---|---|---|---|
| $t_0$ | 0 | 0 | 0 | 0 | 0 |
| $t_1$ | 1 | 0 | 0 | 0 | 1 |
| $t_2$ | 2 | 0 | 0 | 1 | 0 |
| $t_3$ | 3 | 0 | 0 | 1 | 1 |

| | | | | | |
|---|---|---|---|---|---|
| $t_4$ | 4 | 0 | 1 | 0 | 0 |
| $t_5$ | 5 | 0 | 1 | 0 | 1 |
| $t_6$ | 6 | 0 | 1 | 1 | 0 |
| $t_7$ | 7 | 0 | 1 | 1 | 1 |
| $t_8$ | 8 | 1 | 0 | 0 | 0 |
| $t_9$ | 9 | 1 | 0 | 0 | 1 |
| $t_{10}$ | 10 | 1 | 0 | 1 | 0 |
| $t_{11}$ | 11 | 1 | 0 | 1 | 1 |
| $t_{12}$ | 12 | 0 | 0 | 0 | 0 |

**Fig. 7.19:** Truth table of modulo-12 ripple counter.

Since it takes twelve clock pulses to reset the counter, the output frequency of flip-flop D is one-twelvth of the clock frequency and this is the reason that a Modulo-12 or Mod-12 counter is also known as a divide by 12 ripple counter. The counter thus actually has 12 stable states from 0000 to 1011 and it will immediately recycle to 0000, when the 1100 (decimal 12) count is reached. Any desired MOD number can thus be obtained by changing the inputs to the NAND gate. Figure 7.19 shows the truth table of the Mod-12 ripple counter.

### 7.8.1 Limitations of Asynchronous or Ripple Counters

Although ripple counters are the simplest type of all the binary counters, as they require fewer components to perform the desired counting operation, yet they suffer from a serious limitation or drawback of being too slow for carrying out the counting, when the number of flip-flops increases. Since each flip-flop is triggered by the transition taking place at the output of previous flip-flop, the overall propagation delay time becames $n$ times $t_p$ *i.e.*, $n.t_p$, where $n$ is the number of flip-flops used and $t_p$ is the inherent propagation delay time of each flip-flop. Due to the inevitable delays introduced, while the carry ripples through, these types of ripple counters, usually became unacceptable for large-capacity counters involving output decoding or for counting operation at high speeds. Therefore, it became necessary to design counters in which all the flip-flops receive the trigger pulse at the same time or synchronously and are known as synchronous counters.

## 7.9 SYNCHRONOUS COUNTERS

Synchronous counters are used to eliminate the cumulative flip-flop delays encountered in asynchronous counters. There are two methods of controlling the flip-flops in synchronous counters, one with ripple carry and the other with parallel carry. The second method of controlling the flip-flops with parallel carry is the faster method. In the synchronous counter all the flip-flops change their state simultaneously and thus are capable of operating at higher frequencies and speed. But synchronous counters are more complicated and require more components. Both the methods of 4-bit synchronous counters are described as follows:

### (i) Four-bit synchronous counter with serial or ripple carry

Figure 7.20 illustrates an arrangement for a 4-bit synchronous counter using positive edge triggered J-K flip-flops, with serial or ripple carry. It requires two input logic gates and the speed of operation is limited. On arrival of the clock input pulse, which is connected to all the flip-flops simultaneously, all the flip-flops change their state simultaneously.

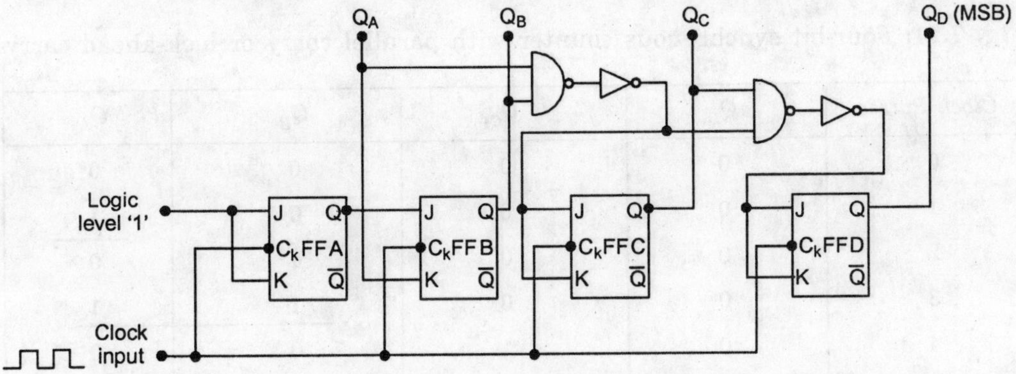


**Fig. 7.20:** Four-bit synchronous counter with serial or ripple carry.

Here J-K flip-flops have been converted into T flip-flops by ensuring that J-K inputs of each flip-flops are tied together separately. Inputs to different flip-flops are as follows:

$$J_A = K_A = 1,\ J_B = K_B = Q_A,\ J_C = K_C = Q_A.Q_B,\ J_D = K_D = Q_A.Q_B.Q_C$$

The circuit has primarily been realized using NAND gates along with inverter, but it could have been realized using AND gate in place of the NAND gate-Inverter Combination.

### (ii) Four-bit synchronous Counter with parallel carry or look-ahead carry

Figure 7.21 illustrates an arrangement for a 4-bit synchronous counter using positive edge triggered J-K flip-flops with parallel carry or look-ahead carry.

Here the state of each flip-flop is fed in parallel to all succeeding flip-flops. The LSB flip-flop A has its J-K inputs tied together to a high voltage level '1', as such it responds to each positive clock edge. The remaining flip-flops will respond to the next positive clock edge only if all the lower bits are '1's. Here the input clock pulses drive all the flip-flops in parallel. Due to the simultaneous clocking, the counter counts the correct binary word at output after one propagation delay time only, as compared to four propagation delay time, in the case of asynchronous or ripple counters. In this case the inputs to the flip-flops A, B, C, D are as given below:

$$J_A = K_A = 1,\ J_B = K_B = Q_A,\ J_C = K_C = Q_A.Q_B,\ J_D = K_D = Q_A.Q_B.Q_C$$

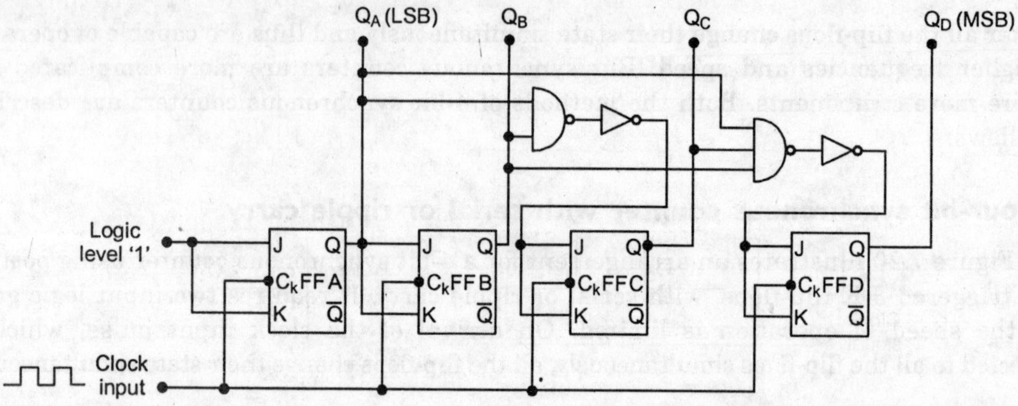


**Fig. 7.21:** Four-bit synchronous counter with parallel carry or look-ahead carry.

| *Clock Pulses* | $Q_D$ | $Q_C$ | $Q_B$ | $Q_A$ |
|---|---|---|---|---|
| 0 | 0 | 0 | 0 | 0 |
| 1 | 0 | 0 | 0 | 1 |
| 2 | 0 | 0 | 1 | 0 |
| 3 | 0 | 0 | 1 | 1 |
| 4 | 0 | 1 | 0 | 0 |
| 5 | 0 | 1 | 0 | 1 |
| 6 | 0 | 1 | 1 | 0 |
| 7 | 0 | 1 | 1 | 1 |
| 8 | 1 | 0 | 0 | 0 |
| 9 | 1 | 0 | 0 | 1 |
| 10 | 1 | 0 | 1 | 0 |
| 11 | 1 | 0 | 1 | 1 |
| 12 | 1 | 1 | 0 | 0 |
| 13 | 1 | 1 | 0 | 1 |
| 14 | 1 | 1 | 1 | 0 |
| 15 | 1 | 1 | 1 | 1 |
| 16 | 0 | 0 | 0 | 0 |

**Fig. 7.22:** Truth table of a synchronous binary counter (natural binary counting sequence).

## 7.10 RING COUNTER

Ring counter is the simplest form of shift register counters. It is basically a circulating shift register, connected in such a manner that the last flip-flop shifts or circulates its value into the first flip-flop. Figure 7.23 illustrates a **circulating shift register** or **ring counter** using D flip-flops. The flip-flops are connected in such a fashion that the information shifts from left to right and circulates around from $Q_3$ to $Q_0$. Usually there is only a single '1' in the register, which is circulated around the register, as in a ring, so long as the clock pulses are applied. That is why it is called a **circulating register** or a **ring counter.**

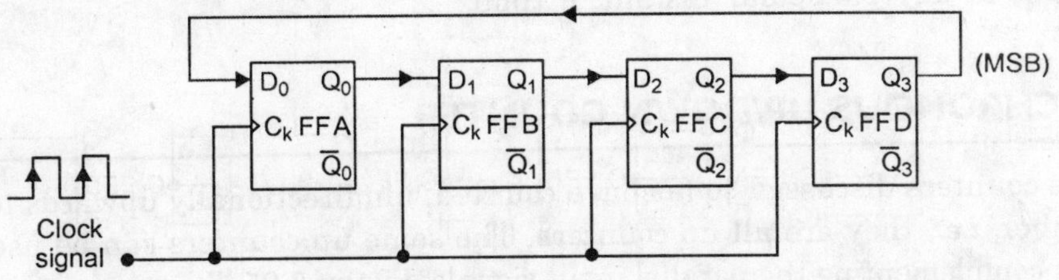


**Fig. 7.23:** Four-bit ring counter.

Here the output $Q = Q_3\ Q_2\ Q_1\ Q_0$.

Assuming a starting state of $Q_0 = 1$, the initial output word is $Q = 0001$, since $Q_3 = Q_2 = Q_1 = 0$. After the arrival of first positive clock edge, the MSB shifts into the LSB position of the output. The remaining bits in the output shift left by one position and the output word becomes $Q = 0010$, which means that '1' has shifted from $Q_0$ to $Q_1$. The second positive clock edge produces $Q = 0100$ and the third positive clock edge produces $Q = 1000$. On arrival of the fourth positive clock edge, the 1 from $Q_3$ is transferred to $Q_0$, resulting in $Q = 0001$, which is of course the initial starting state again. Thus it is seen that **the stored '1' bit follows a circular path like a ring, until the final flip-flop sends this '1' back to the first flip-flop and that is why it is called a ring counter.**

Circulating shift registers or ring counters can also be connected using J-K flip-flops as illustrated in Figure 7.24. Here a single '1' is entered in the shift register, with all the remaining flip-flops in the opposite state '0'. The position of '1' will shift and move through the flip-flop outputs on arrival of successive clock pulses to give four different states. The four different states for the circuit of Figure 7.24 will be 0001, 0010, 0100 and 1000. On arrival of the input the fourth clock pulse, the states will return to the initial starting state *i.e.*, $Q = 0001$.

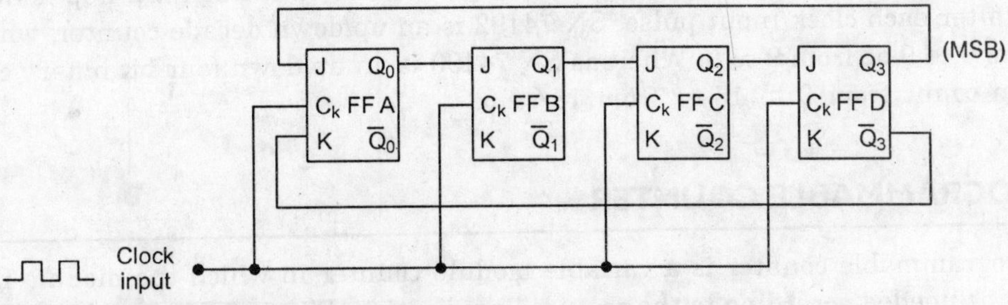


**Fig. 7.24:** Four-bit ring counter using J-K flip-flops.

Ring counters can be designed for any required modulo number. A mod–N ring counter will use N flip-flops connected as shown in Figures 7.23 and 7.24. Thus a ring counter will require more flip-flops than the ripple counter for the same mod-number. A

Mod-16 ring counter requires sixteen flip-flops, whereas a Mod-16 ripple counter requires only four flip-flops as described earlier.

Although a ring counter has the disadvantage of being inefficient because of requiring one flip-flop for each bit, but it is still useful as it can be decoded without using decoding gates. A ring counter works as a counter as well as a decoder, because only one flip-flop has '1' output at any particular instant of time.

## 7.11 SYNCHRONOUS UP/DOWN COUNTER

All the counters discussed so far have counted, unidirectionally upwards towards the higher number, *i.e.*, they are all up counters. The same up counters can be used as down counters, by complementing the parallel input signals. Figure 7.25 illustrates an arrangement to build an up/down counter, realized by using J-K flip-flops and NAND gates. It is a four-bit counter, which can count both up and down and is useful in many industrial applications. A binary counter with reverse count is called a down counter. In a down counter, the binary count is decremented by 1 every time with every input count pulse. When up input control is '1', the circuit counts up and when the down input control is '1', the circuit

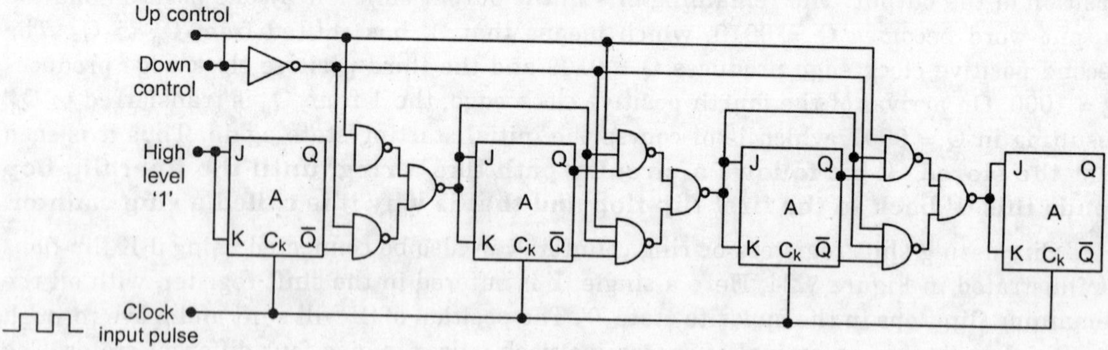


**Fig. 7.25:** Four-bit up/down counter.

counts down. Some easily available MSI/TTL Counters chips are SN 74192 and SN 74193, both of which can be reset, preset and can count up and down. Each flip-flop is designed to toggle after each clock input pulse. SN 74192 is an up/down decade counter, which can count from 0 to 9 or from 9 to 0. Whereas SN 74193 is an up/down four-bit binary counter, which can count from 0 to 15 or from 15 to 0.

## 7.12 PROGRAMMABLE COUNTER

A programmable counter is a variable modulo counter in which the modulo number can be set as needed according to the required application. Figure 7.26(*a*) and 7.26(*b*) show 4-bit programmable counter schemes. Four-bit programmable counters are realized here by two methods. In the first method as shown in Figure 7.26(*a*), a divide by 16 binary counter 74193 is being used in the UP mode. This 74193 is a synchronous binary counter, which counts from 0 to 15 and automatically resets to 0 after it counts 15, in its normal working. But by activating the reset input to active high, the counter can be reset to 0 at any desired count. For resetting a four-bit binary word magnitude comparator, 7485 available in chip form is being used, here. This chip 7485 can compare straight binary and straight BCD ($842\overline{1}$) codes. The programming input, which is the 4-bit binary number N by which we desire to count, is fed as input to one set of the inputs of the magnitude comparator:

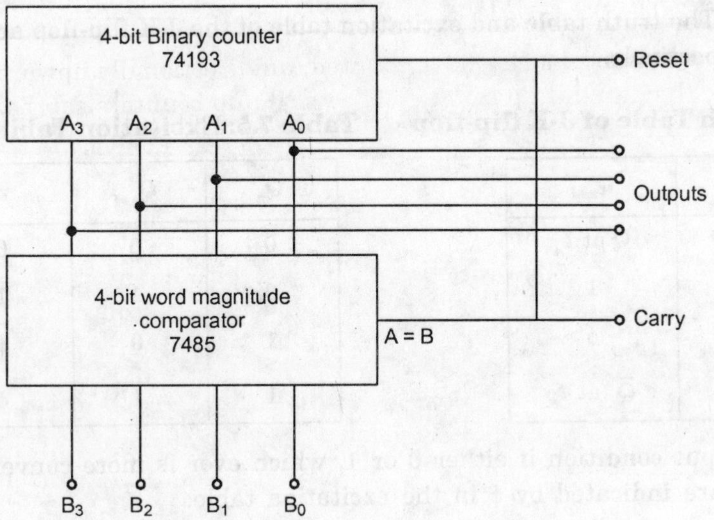


**Fig. 7.26(*a*):** Four-bit programmable counter.

The output of the binary-counter is fed to the other set of inputs of the magnitude comparator. When these two binary numbers *i.e.*, $B = B_3\ B_2\ B_1\ B_0$ and $A = A_3\ A_2\ A_1\ A_0$ are both equal (B = A), the output is available at (A = B), output terminals. This is fed to the reset input of the binary counter. When ever the output of the binary counter is equal to the program input, a reset pulse is obtained and the counter is reset to Zero. Thus we get a divide by N programmable counter.

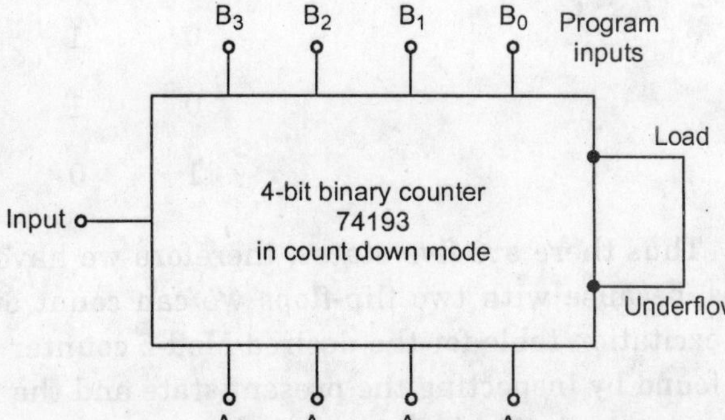


**7.26(*b*):** Four-bit programmable counter.

In the second method, to obtain a programmable counter, an up/down synchronous 4-bit binary counter 74193 is used in the count down mode as illustrated in Figure 7.26(*b*).

When the counter output is zero, the parallel entry is enabled and the program inputs are fed to the counter. The counter now counts down and as soon as it counts down to zero, it again resets to the desired count value N. Thus by this method a programmable counter can be realized by using one IC only. However, here it should be kept in mind that the binary counting is taking place in a downward direction and not in a upward direction as is the case in normal up counters.

**Example 1.** *Design a synchronous Mod-5 counter with M/s J/K flip-flops to run through the states 000, 001, 010, 011 and 100 only. For designing use the excitation table of J-K flip-flops and obtain the minimal digital hardware using Karnaugh Map's method of minimization.*

**Solution.** The truth table and excitation table of the J-K flip-flop are given in Tables 7.4 and 7.5 respectively.

**Table 7.4: Truth Table of J-K flip-flop**

| $J$ | $K$ | $Q_{n+1}$ |
|---|---|---|
| 0 | 0 | Q at $t_n$ |
| 1 | 0 | 1 |
| 0 | 1 | $\phi$ |
| 1 | 1 | $\bar{Q}$ at $t_n$ |

**Table 7.5: Excitation Table of J-K flip-flop**

| $Q_n$ | $Q_{n+1}$ | $J$ | $K$ |
|---|---|---|---|
| 0 | 0 | 0 | $\phi$ |
| 0 | 1 | 1 | $\phi$ |
| 1 | 0 | $\phi$ | 1 |
| 1 | 1 | $\phi$ | 0 |

The J-K input condition if either 0 or 1, which ever is more convenient, are called don't care and are indicated by $\phi$ in the excitation table.

The synchronous Mod-5 counter has to run through the states given below:

| | | |
|---|---|---|
| 0 | 0 | 0 |
| 0 | 0 | 1 |
| 0 | 1 | 0 |
| 0 | 1 | 1 |
| 1 | 0 | 0 |

Thus there are five states, therefore we have to use minimum of three M/s, J/K flip-flops, because with two flip-flops we can count only up to ($2^n = 2^2$) 4. Now constructing the excitation table for the desired Mod-5 counter design, keeping in mind that J-K inputs are found by inspecting the present state and the next state of the output. $Q_A$, $Q_B$ and $Q_C$. Thus we obtain Table 7.6.

It is seen from Table 7.5 that whenever Q output changes from 0 in one state to 0 in the next state then J = 0 and K = $\phi$. When it changes from 0 to 1 then J = 1 and K = $\phi$. When it changes from 1 to 0, then J = $\phi$ and K = 1, and when the output changes from 1 to 1, then J = $\phi$ and K = 0. Taking these points into consideration Table 7.6 is preapred.

**Table 7.6: Excitation Table of Mod-5 Counter Design**

| *Time* | $Q_A$ | $Q_B$ | $Q_C$ | $J_A$ | $K_A$ | $J_B$ | $K_B$ | $J_C$ | $K_C$ |
|---|---|---|---|---|---|---|---|---|---|
| $t_0$ | 0 | 0 | 0 | 0 | $\phi$ | 0 | $\phi$ | 1 | $\phi$ |
| $t_1$ | 0 | 0 | 1 | 0 | $\phi$ | 1 | $\phi$ | $\phi$ | 1 |
| $t_2$ | 0 | 1 | 0 | 0 | $\phi$ | $\phi$ | 0 | 1 | $\phi$ |
| $t_3$ | 0 | 1 | 1 | 1 | $\phi$ | $\phi$ | 1 | $\phi$ | 1 |
| $t_4$ | 1 | 0 | 0 | $\phi$ | 1 | 0 | $\phi$ | 0 | $\phi$ |
| $t_5$ | 0 | 0 | 0 | | | | | | |

Now we have to draw the Karnaugh maps for $J_A$, $K_A$, $J_B$, $K_B$, $J_C$ and $K_C$. Since there are three variables A, B, and C thus 3-variable maps are drawn. In a 3 variable map there are $2^3 = 8$ spaces, and we have only 5 entries for $J_A$, $K_A$, $J_B$, $K_B$ and $J_C$, $K_C$. In all the Karnaugh maps, the spaces for a decimal value 5, 6 and 7 will be empty. These empty spaces on Karnaugh maps are for the forbidden BCD inputs, which are not shown in the truth table. Since forbidden BCD inputs do not occur under normal operating conditions, the empty spaces can be treated as 0's or 1's, whichever is more convenient. These empty spaces are also filled by $\phi$, which means don't care conditions.

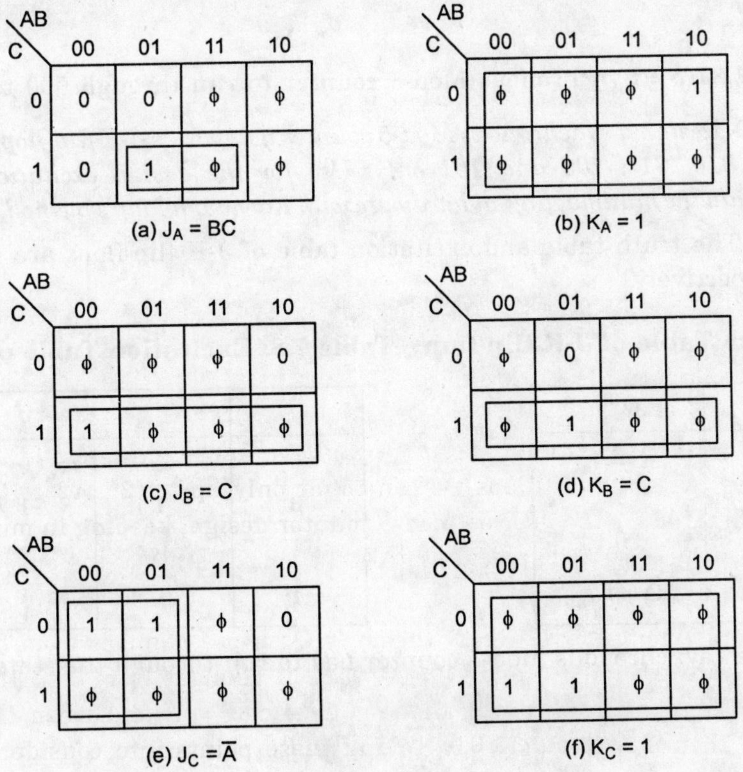


(a) $J_A = BC$ (b) $K_A = 1$

(c) $J_B = C$ (d) $K_B = C$

(e) $J_C = \overline{A}$ (f) $K_C = 1$

**Fig. 7.27(*a*)**

Using Karnaugh maps method of minimization, the following values are obtained for different inputs of the flip-flops.

$$J_A = BC \qquad K_A = 1$$
$$J_B = C \qquad K_B = C$$
$$J_C = \overline{A} \qquad K_C = 1$$

Figure 7.27(*b*) illustrates the diagram of the Mod-5 synchronous counter to run through the states 000 to 100, using the minimal digital hardware obtained with Master-slave J-K flip-flops.

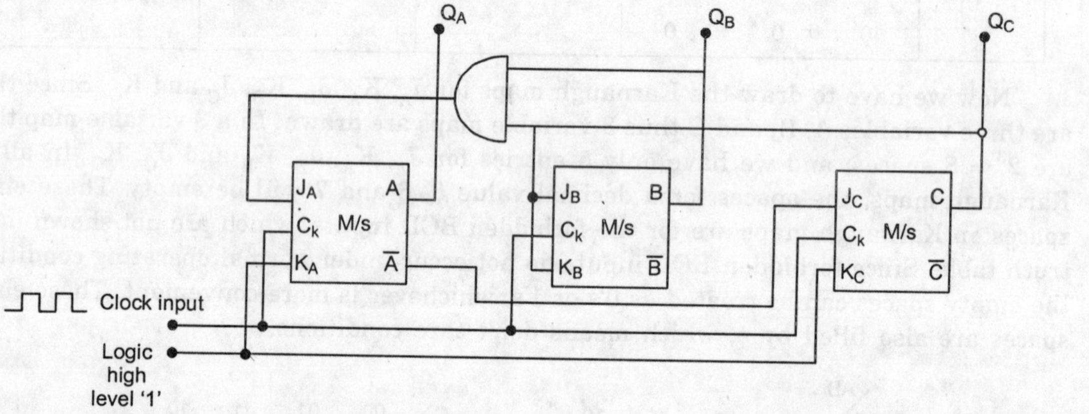


**Fig. 7.27(*b*):** Synchronous Mod-5 counter to run through 000 to 100.

**Example 2.** *Design a synchronous Mod-5 counter using M/s J-K flip-flops to run through the states 001, 010, 011, 100 and 101 only. Use for the design excitation table of J-K flip-flops and obtain the minimal digital hardware with Karnaugh Map's method of minimization.*

**Solution.** The truth table and excitation table of J-K flip-flops are given in Tables 7.7 and 7.8 respectively.

**Table 7.7: Truth Table of J-K flip-flop**

| $J$ | $K$ | $Q_{n+1}$ |
|---|---|---|
| 0 | 0 | Q at $t_n$ |
| 1 | 0 | 1 |
| 0 | 1 | 0 |
| 1 | 1 | $\overline{Q}$ at $t_n$ |

**Table 7.8: Excitation Table of J-K flip-flop**

| $Q_n$ | $Q_{n+1}$ | $J$ | $K$ |
|---|---|---|---|
| 0 | 0 | 0 | $\phi$ |
| 0 | 1 | 1 | $\phi$ |
| 1 | 0 | $\phi$ | 1 |
| 1 | 1 | $\phi$ | 0 |

The required synchronous Mod-5 counter has to run through the states given below:

| | | |
|---|---|---|
| 0 | 0 | 1 |
| 0 | 1 | 0 |
| 0 | 1 | 1 |
| 1 | 0 | 0 |
| 1 | 0 | 1 |

Thus there are five states and so we have to use a minimum of three M/s J-K flip-flops. It is seen from Table 7.8 that whenever Q output changes from 0 in one state to 0 in the next state, then J = 0, K = ϕ when it changes from 0 to 1, then J = 1 and K = ϕ. When it changes from 1 to 0, then J = ϕ, K = 1 and when the output changes from 1 to 1, then J = ϕ, K = 0. Taking these inputs into consideration, Table 7.9 is constructed, which is the excitation table for Mod-5 counter design for the given states.

**Table 7.9: Excitation Table of Mod-5 Counter Design**

| *Time* | $Q_A$ | $Q_B$ | $Q_C$ | $J_A$ | $K_A$ | $J_B$ | $K_B$ | $J_C$ | $K_C$ |
|---|---|---|---|---|---|---|---|---|---|
| $t_0$ | 0 | 0 | 1 | 0 | ϕ | 1 | ϕ | ϕ | 1 |
| $t_1$ | 0 | 1 | 0 | 0 | ϕ | ϕ | 0 | 1 | ϕ |
| $t_2$ | 0 | 1 | 1 | 1 | ϕ | ϕ | 1 | ϕ | 1 |
| $t_3$ | 1 | 0 | 0 | ϕ | 0 | 0 | ϕ | 1 | ϕ |
| $t_4$ | 1 | 0 | 1 | ϕ | 1 | 0 | ϕ | ϕ | 0 |
| $t_5$ | 0 | 0 | 1 | | | | | | |

Using Karnaugh maps method of minimization, the following values are obtained for the different inputs of Master-slave J-K flip-flops.

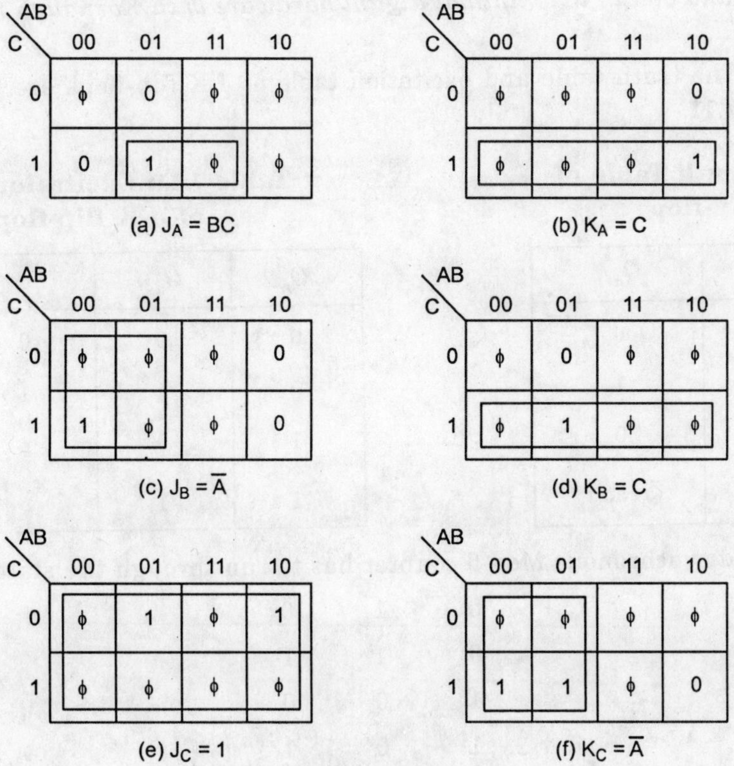


**Fig. 7.28(*a*)**

$$J_A = BC \qquad K_A = C$$
$$J_B = \bar{A} \qquad K_B = C$$
$$J_C = 1 \qquad K_C = \bar{A}$$

Figure 7.28(*b*) illustrates diagram of the Mod-5 synchronous counter to run through the states 001 to 101, using the minimal digital hardware, with master slave J-K flip-flops.

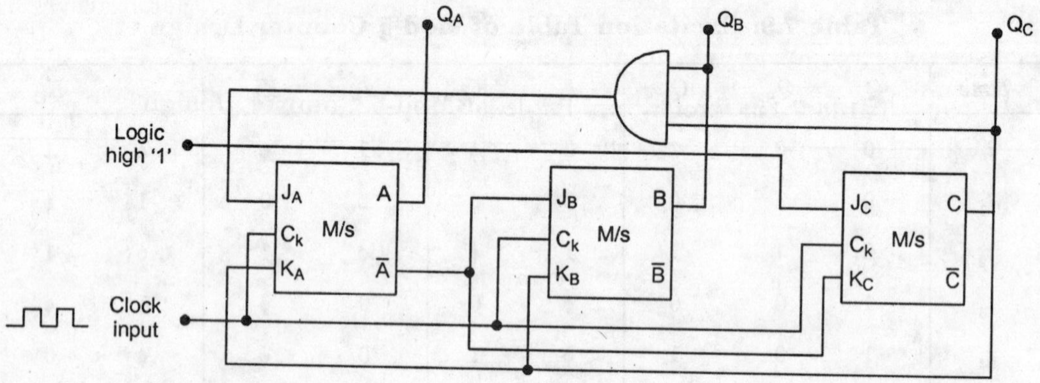


**Fig. 7.28(*b*):** Design of required synchronous Mod-5 counter.

**Example 3.** *Design a synchronous Mod-5 counter using M/s J-K flip-flops to run through the states 010,011,100,101 and 110 only. Use for the design, the excitation table of J-K flip-flops and obtain the minimal digital hardware with Karnaugh maps method of minimization.*

**Solution.** The truth table and excitation table of J-K flip-flops are given in Table 7.10 and Table 7.11.

**Table 7.10: Truth Table of J-K flip-flop**

| $J$ | $K$ | $Q_{n+1}$ |
|---|---|---|
| 0 | 0 | Q at $t_n$ |
| 1 | 0 | 1 |
| 0 | 1 | 0 |
| 1 | 1 | $\bar{Q}$ at $t_n$ |

**Table 7.11: Excitation Table of J-K flip-flop**

| $Q_n$ | $Q_{n+1}$ | $J$ | $K$ |
|---|---|---|---|
| 0 | 0 | 0 | $\phi$ |
| 0 | 1 | 1 | $\phi$ |
| 1 | 0 | $\phi$ | 1 |
| 1 | 1 | $\phi$ | 0 |

The required synchronous Mod-5 counter has to run through the states given below:

| | | |
|---|---|---|
| 0 | 1 | 0 |
| 0 | 1 | 1 |
| 1 | 0 | 0 |
| 1 | 0 | 1 |
| 1 | 1 | 0 |

Since there are five states, so we have to use minimum of three M/s J-K flip-flops. It is seen from Table 7.11 that whenever Q output changes from 0 in one state to 0 in the next state, then J = 0, K = ϕ. When it changes from 0 to 1, then J = 1, K = ϕ. When it changes from 1 to 0, then J = ϕ, K = 1 and when output changes from 1 in one state to 1 in the next state, then J = ϕ, K = 0. Taking all these inputs into consideration, Table 7.12 is obtained, which is the excitation table for the design of the Mod-5 synchronous counter to run through the given states.

**Table 7.12: Excitation Table of Mod-5 Counter Design**

| *Time* | $Q_A$ | $Q_B$ | $Q_C$ | $J_A$ | $K_A$ | $J_B$ | $K_B$ | $J_C$ | $K_C$ |
|---|---|---|---|---|---|---|---|---|---|
| $t_0$ | 0 | 1 | 0 | 0 | ϕ | ϕ | 0 | 1 | ϕ |
| $t_1$ | 0 | 1 | 1 | 1 | ϕ | ϕ | 1 | ϕ | 1 |
| $t_2$ | 1 | 0 | 0 | ϕ | 0 | 0 | ϕ | 1 | ϕ |
| $t_3$ | 1 | 0 | 1 | ϕ | 0 | 1 | ϕ | ϕ | 1 |
| $t_4$ | 1 | 1 | 0 | ϕ | 1 | ϕ | 0 | 0 | ϕ |
| $t_5$ | 0 | 1 | 0 | | | | | | |

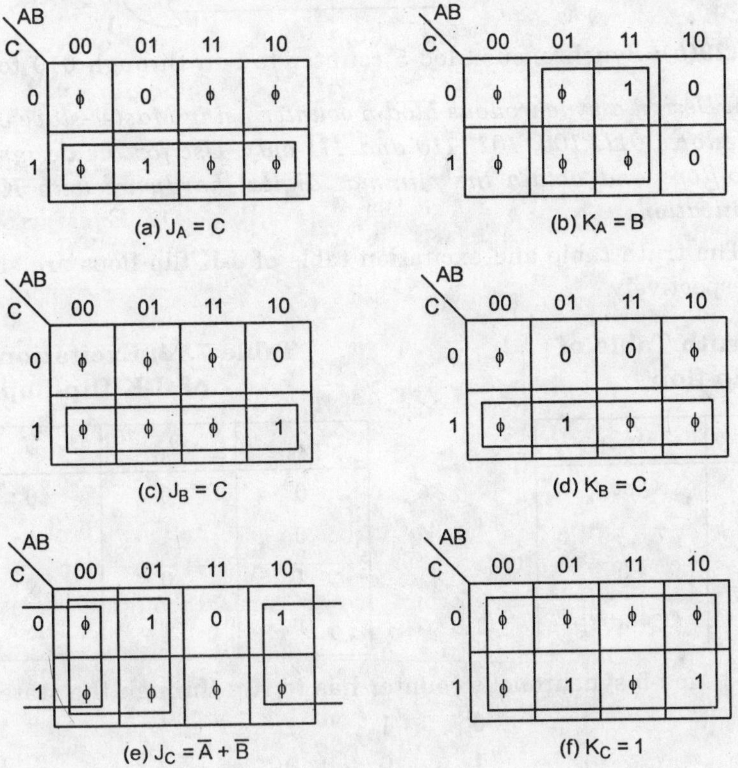


**Fig. 7.29(*a*)**

Using Karnaugh maps method of minimization, following values are obtained for the different inputs of Master-Slave J-K flip-flops, as shown.

$$J_A = C \qquad K_A = B$$
$$J_B = C \qquad K_B = C$$
$$J_C = \bar{A} + \bar{B} \qquad K_C = 1$$

Figure 7.29(*b*) illustrates the diagram of the Mod-5 synchronous counter to run through the states 010 to 110, using the minimal digital hardware, with Master-Slave J-K flip-flops.

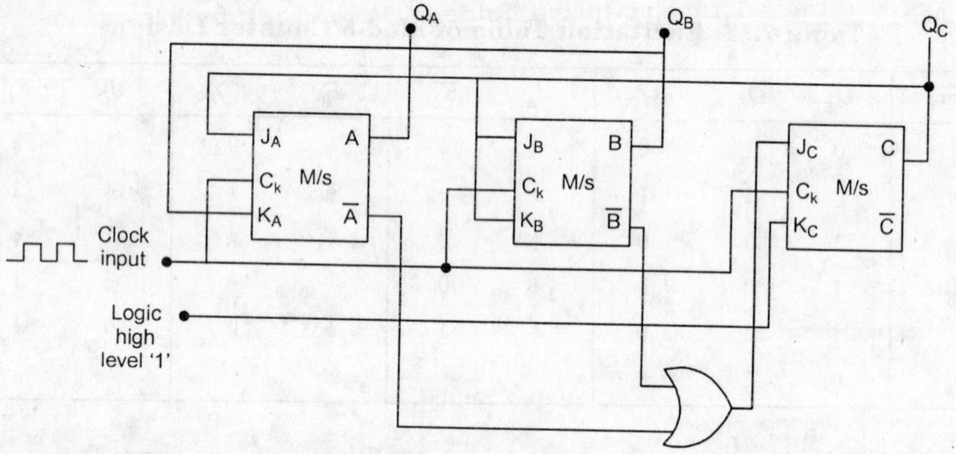


**Fig. 7.29(*b*):** Synchronous Mod-5 counter to run through 010 to 110.

**Example 4.** *Design a synchronous Mod-5 counter using Master-slave J-K flip-flops to run through the states 011, 100, 101, 110 and 111 only. Use for the design the excitation table of J-K flip-flops and obtain the minimal digital hardware with Karnaugh maps method of minimization.*

**Solution.** The truth table and excitation table of J-K flip-flops are shown in Tables 7.13 and 7.14 respectively.

**Table 7.13: Truth Table of J-K flip-flop**

| *J* | *K* | $Q_{n+1}$ |
|---|---|---|
| 0 | 0 | Q at $t_n$ |
| 1 | 0 | 1 |
| 0 | 1 | 0 |
| 1 | 1 | $\bar{Q}$ at $t_n$ |

**Table 7.14: Excitation Table of J-K flip-flop**

| $Q_n$ | $Q_{n+1}$ | *J* | *K* |
|---|---|---|---|
| 0 | 0 | 0 | ϕ |
| 0 | 1 | 1 | ϕ |
| 1 | 0 | ϕ | 1 |
| 1 | 1 | ϕ | 0 |

The required Mod-5 synchronous counter has to run through the states given below:

| | | |
|---|---|---|
| 0 | 1 | 1 |
| 1 | 0 | 0 |
| 1 | 0 | 1 |
| 1 | 1 | 0 |
| 1 | 1 | 1 |

Since there are five states, therefore we have to use atleast three Master-Slave J-K flip-flops, it is seen from Table 7.14 that whenever Q output changes from 0 in one state to 0 in the next state, then J = 0, K = ϕ. When it changes from 0 to 1, then J = 1, K = ϕ. When it changes from 1 to 0, then J=ϕ, K = 1 and when output changes from 1 in one state to 1 in the next state, then J = ϕ, K = 0. Taking all these inputs into consideration, Table 7.15 is obtained, which is the excitation table for the design of Mod-5 synchronous counter to run through the states 011 to 111.

**Table 7.15: Excitation Table of Mod-5 Counter Design**

| *Time* | $Q_A$ | $Q_B$ | $Q_C$ | $J_A$ | $K_A$ | $J_B$ | $K_B$ | $J_C$ | $K_C$ |
|---|---|---|---|---|---|---|---|---|---|
| $t_0$ | 0 | 1 | 1 | 1 | ϕ | ϕ | 1 | ϕ | 1 |
| $t_1$ | 1 | 0 | 0 | ϕ | 0 | 0 | ϕ | 1 | ϕ |
| $t_2$ | 1 | 0 | 1 | ϕ | 0 | 1 | ϕ | ϕ | 1 |
| $t_3$ | 1 | 1 | 0 | ϕ | 0 | ϕ | 0 | 1 | ϕ |
| $t_4$ | 1 | 1 | 1 | ϕ | 1 | ϕ | 0 | ϕ | 0 |
| $t_5$ | 0 | 1 | 1 | | | | | | |

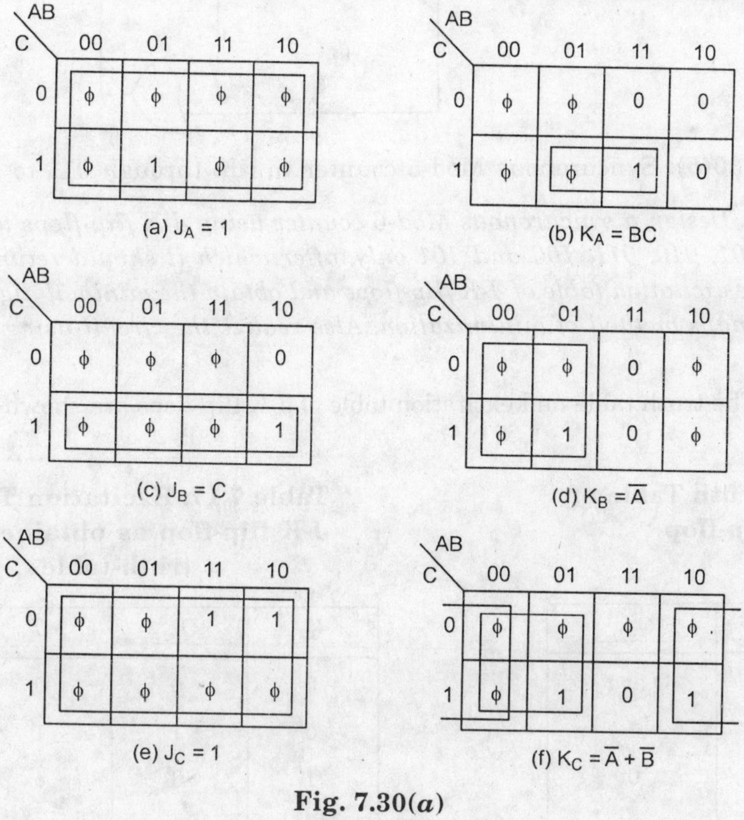


**Fig. 7.30(*a*)**

Using Karnaugh maps method of minimization, the following values are obtained for the different inputs of Master-Slave J-K flip-flops as shown:

$$J_A = 1 \qquad K_A = BC$$
$$J_B = C \qquad K_B = \bar{A}$$
$$J_C = 1 \qquad K_C = \bar{A} + \bar{B}$$

Figure 7.30(*b*) illustrates the diagram of the Mod-5 synchronous counter to run through the states 011 to 111, using the minimal digital hardware, with Master-Slave J-K flip-flops.

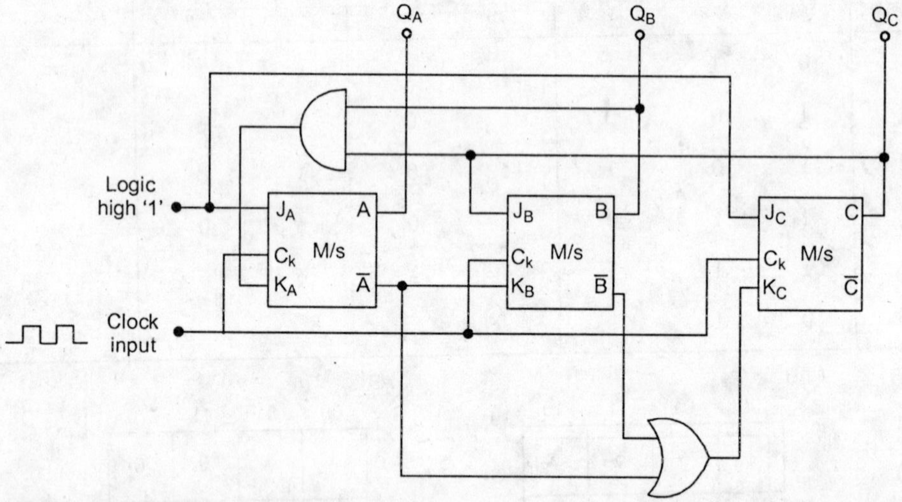


**Fig. 7.30(*b*):** Synchronous Mod-5 counter to run through 011 to 111.

**Example 5.** *Design a synchronous Mod-6 counter using J-K flip-flops to run through the states 000, 001, 010, 011, 100 and 101 only, after which it should return to 000. Use for the design, the excitation table of J-K flip-flops and obtain the minimal digital hardware with Karnaugh maps method of minimization. Also realize the circuit using J-K flip-flops and basic gates.*

**Solution.** The truth table and excitation table of J-K flip-flops are shown in Tables 7.16 and 7.17.

**Table 7.16: Truth Table of J-K flip-flop**

| *J* | *K* | $Q_{n+1}$ |
|---|---|---|
| 0 | 0 | Q at $t_n$ |
| 1 | 0 | 1 |
| 0 | 1 | 0 |
| 1 | 1 | $\bar{Q}$ at $t_n$ |

**Table 7.17: Excitation Table of J-K flip-flop as obtained from truth-table**

| $Q_n$ | $Q_{n+1}$ | *J* | *K* |
|---|---|---|---|
| 0 | 0 | 0 | $\phi$ |
| 0 | 1 | 1 | $\phi$ |
| 1 | 0 | $\phi$ | 1 |
| 1 | 1 | $\phi$ | 0 |

The entries in excitation Table, 7.17 are obtained from truth Table 7.16. When output ($Q_n$ = 0) goes to ($Q_{n+1}$ = 0) in the next state, then as is clear from the truth table that J-K inputs are either 00 or 01 which means J is 0 and K can be either 0 or 1 *i.e.*, don't care ($\phi$). Similarly when output $Q_n$ = 0 changes to $Q_{n+1}$ = 1 in the next state, then J = 1 but K can be either 0 or 1 as is evident from the second and last entries of the truth table, thus J = 1 and K = $\phi$. When output $Q_n$ = 1 changes to $Q_{n+1}$ = 0, then J can be either 0 or 1 *i.e.*, don't care ($\phi$) and K = 1 as is evident from third and last entries in the truth table. Similarly when output 1 goes to 1 in the next state, then J can be either 0 or 1 *i.e.*, don't care ($\phi$) and K = 0 as is evident from first and second entries of the truth table. Now the required Mod-6 synchronous counter has to run through the states given below:

0 0 0

0 0 1

0 1 0

0 1 1

1 0 0

1 0 1 and back to 000.

Thus there are six states only, as such we have to use 3 J-K flip-flops, which can count upto $2^3$ = 8 states. Taking into consideration excitation table, (Table 7.16) and corresponding J-K inputs. Table 7.18 is obtained, which is the excitation table for the design of Mod-6 synchronous counter to run through the states 000 to 101.

**Table 7.18: Excitation Table for the required Mod-6 Counter Design**

| *Time* | $Q_A$ | $Q_B$ | $Q_C$ | $J_A$ | $K_A$ | $J_B$ | $K_B$ | $J_C$ | $K_C$ |
|---|---|---|---|---|---|---|---|---|---|
| $t_0$ | 0 | 0 | 0 | 0 | $\phi$ | 0 | $\phi$ | 1 | $\phi$ |
| $t_1$ | 0 | 0 | 1 | 0 | $\phi$ | 1 | $\phi$ | $\phi$ | 1 |
| $t_2$ | 0 | 1 | 0 | 0 | $\phi$ | $\phi$ | 0 | 1 | $\phi$ |
| $t_3$ | 0 | 1 | 1 | 1 | $\phi$ | $\phi$ | 1 | $\phi$ | 1 |
| $t_4$ | 1 | 0 | 0 | $\phi$ | 0 | 0 | $\phi$ | 1 | $\phi$ |
| $t_5$ | 1 | 0 | 1 | $\phi$ | 1 | 0 | $\phi$ | $\phi$ | 1 |
| $t_6$ | 0 | 0 | 0 | | | | | | |

From the above excitation table, using the values of $J_A$, $K_A$, $J_B$, $K_B$ etc. Karnaugh maps of $J_A$, $K_A$, $J_B$, $K_B$ and $J_C$, $K_C$ are constructed as given in Figure 7.31(*a*):

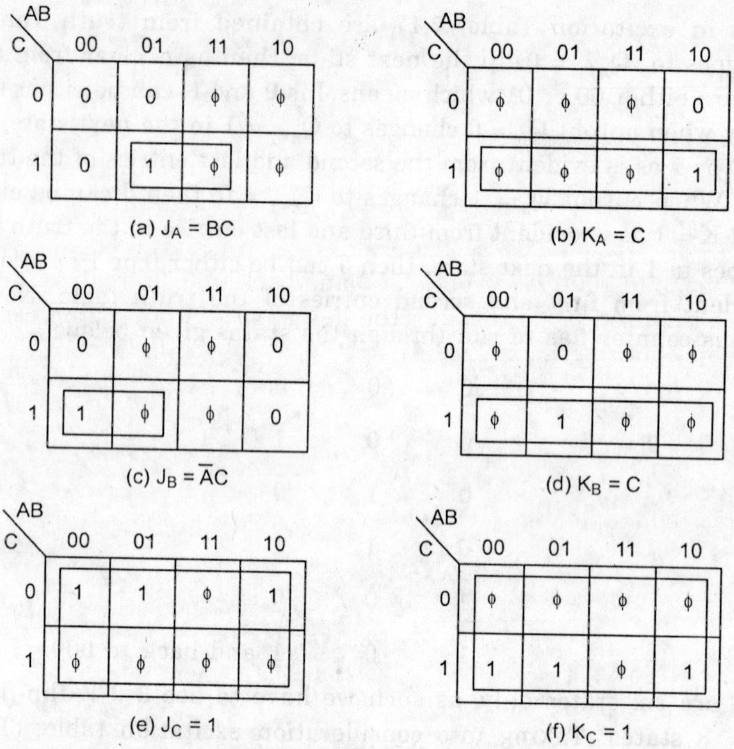


**Fig. 7.31(*a*)**

The flip-flop input functions from the excitation table are simplified and minimized by using Karnaugh maps. The unused states for minterms 6(=110) and 7(=111) are taken as don't care terms and are represented by ϕ. The simplified values for inputs of J-K flip-flops are given below:

$$J_A = BC \qquad K_A = C$$
$$J_B = \overline{A}C \qquad K_B = C$$
$$J_C = 1 \qquad K_C = 1$$

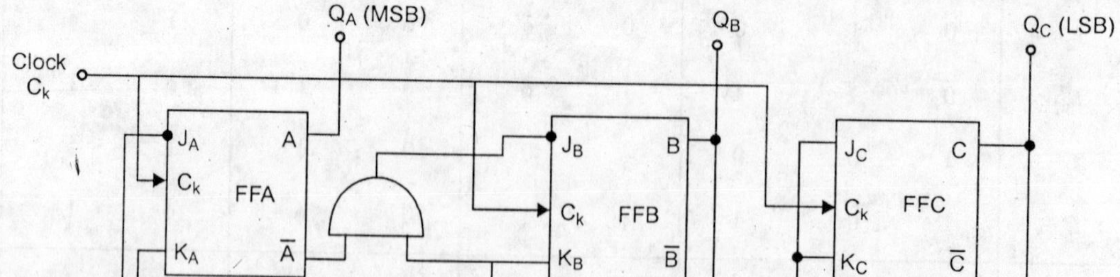


**Fig. 7.31(*b*):** Synchronous Mod-6 counter to run through the states 000 to 101.

Figure 7.31(*b*) illustrates the realization of the circuit using three J-K flip-flops and two AND gates.

**Example 6.** *Design a synchronous BCD (Mod-10) counter using T flip-flops. Use for the design, excitation table of T flip-flops and obtain minimal digital hardware, using Karnaugh maps. Also realize the counter using T flip-flops and basic gates.*

**Solution.** A synchronous BCD counter counts in binary coded decimal form from 0000 to 1001 and back to 0000 *i.e.*, from 0 to 9 and back to 0. To realize the circuit of BCD counter, it is first required to go through the design procedure, using excitation table of T-flip-flop and then obtain the minimal digital hardware using Karnaugh map.

**Table 7.19**

| $J$ | $K$ | $Q_{n+1}$ |
|---|---|---|
| 0 | $Q_n$ | $\bar{Q}_n$ |
| 1 | $\bar{Q}_n$ | $Q_n$ |

**Table 7.20**

| $Q_n$ | $Q_{n+1}$ | $T$ |
|---|---|---|
| 0 | 0 | 0 |
| 0 | 1 | 1 |
| 1 | 0 | 1 |
| 1 | 1 | 0 |

Table 7.19 shows truth table of flip-flop. The entries in the excitation Table 7.20 are obtained from the truth Table 7.19. When output '0' goes to '0' in the next state, then T input is 0. When output '0' changes to '1' then T input is 1. Similarly when output '1' changes to '0' in the next state, then T input is 1, when output '1' goes to '1' in the next state then T input is 0. Thus the excitation table (Table 7.20) is derived from truth table, (Table 7.19) of the T flip-flop. The required BCD counter has to run through ten states from 0000 to 1001 and then back to 0000. Thus we have to use 4-T flip-flops, which can count up to $2^4 = 16$ states. The count sequence and excitation table (Table 7.21) of the BCD counter is obtained from the excitation table (Table 7.20) of the T flip-flop.

**Table 7.21**

| | *Count Sequence in BCD form* | | | | *Inputs of T flip-flops* | | | |
|---|---|---|---|---|---|---|---|---|
| *Count* | $Q_A$ | $Q_B$ | $Q_C$ | $Q_D$ | $T_A$ | $T_B$ | $T_C$ | $T_D$ |
| 0 | 0 | 0 | 0 | 0 | 0 | 0 | 0 | 1 |
| 1 | 0 | 0 | 0 | 1 | 0 | 0 | 1 | 1 |
| 2 | 0 | 0 | 1 | 0 | 0 | 0 | 0 | 1 |
| 3 | 0 | 0 | 1 | 1 | 0 | 1 | 1 | 1 |
| 4 | 0 | 1 | 0 | 0 | 0 | 0 | 1 | 1 |
| 5 | 0 | 1 | 0 | 1 | 0 | 0 | 1 | 1 |

| | | | | | | | | |
|---|---|---|---|---|---|---|---|---|
| 6 | 0 | 1 | 1 | 0 | 0 | 0 | 0 | 1 |
| 7 | 0 | 1 | 1 | 1 | 1 | 1 | 1 | 1 |
| 8 | 1 | 0 | 0 | 0 | 0 | 0 | 0 | 1 |
| 9 | 1 | 0 | 0 | 1 | 1 | 0 | 0 | 1 |
| 10 | 0 | 0 | 0 | 0 | | | | |

The flip-flop input values for various T inputs can be simplified and minimized using Karnaugh maps. While constructing Karnaugh maps for $T_A$, $T_B$, $T_C$ and $T_D$, the unused states for miniterms 10 to 15 *i.e.*, 1010, 1011, 1100, 1101, 1110 and 1111 are all taken as don't care terms and are represented and designated by ϕ in the maps as shown below:

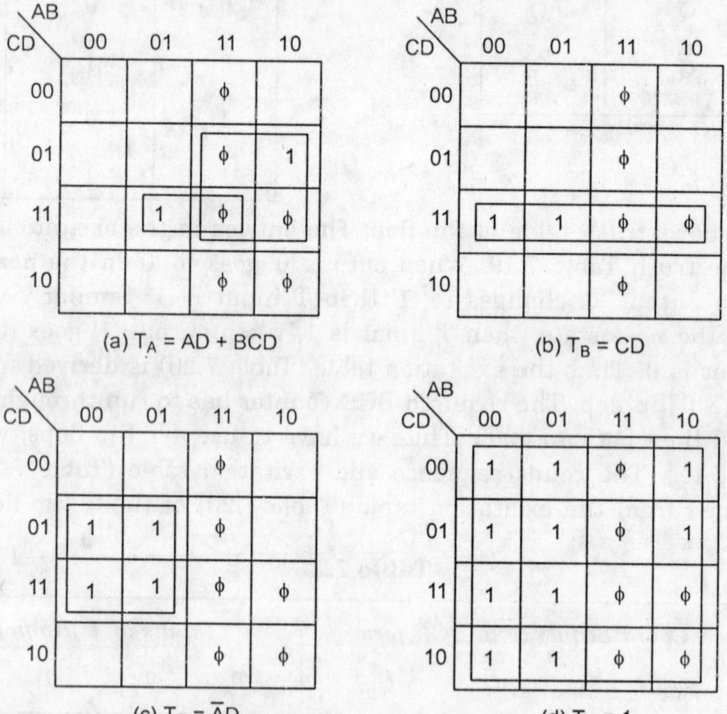

(a) $T_A = AD + BCD$ (b) $T_B = CD$ (c) $T_C = \bar{A}D$ (d) $T_D = 1$

**Fig. 7.32(*a*)**

Using K-maps the simplified and minimized values for the inputs of the four T flip-flops are obtained as shown below:

$$T_A = AD + BCD$$
$$T_B = CD$$
$$T_C = \bar{A}D$$
$$T_D = 1$$

Figure 7.32(*b*) illustrates the realization of BCD counter using four T flip-flops, four AND gates and one OR gate.

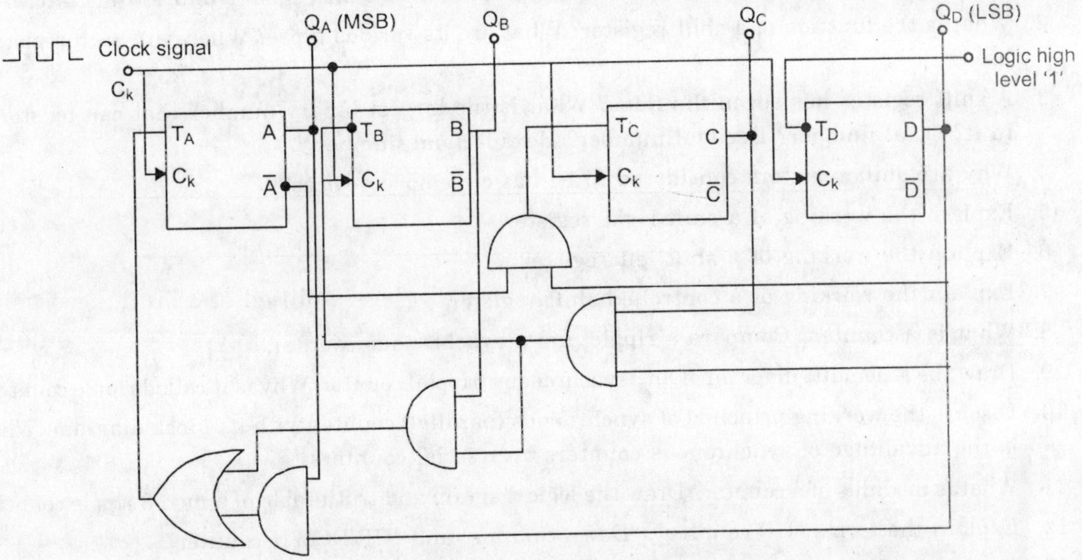


**Fig. 7.32(*b*):** Synchronous BCD counter.

## SUMMARY

- **Register** is a group of memory elements that store a word.
- Buffer register temporarily stores a word during data processing.
- A **shift register** moves the stored bits left or right. This bit shifting is essential for certain arithmetic and logic operations used in microcomputers.
- A **controlled shift register** has control inputs that determine what it does on the next clock pulse.
- A parallel-in-parallel out register is designed such that data can be shifted into or out of the register in parallel.
- A **counter** is a register capable of counting the number of clock pulses that have arrived at its clock input.
- The **modulus** of a counter is the number of output states it has.
- A **ripple counter** has cascaded flip-flops. It means that the carry has to propagate in series through the flip-flops.
- In a **synchronous counter** the clock drives each flip-flop to eliminate the delay.
- A **ring counter** uses words that have only a single high bit.
- Ring counters are invaluable when it's necessary to control a sequence of operations.
- **Presettable counter** allows you to preset a number from which the count begins. It is also called a programmable counter.

## REVIEW QUESTIONS AND EXERCISES

1. What are registers? What is the difference between a $n$-bit register and a $n$-bit latch?
2. What is the function of a shift register? What are its various types? Where are such registers used?
3. A shift register has seven flip-flops? What is the largest binary number that can be stored in it? Octal number? Decimal number? Hexadecimal number?
4. Why are shift registers considered to be basic memory devices?
5. Explain the working of a shift right register.
6. Explain the working of a shift left register.
7. Explain the working of a controlled shift register.
8. What is a counter? Compare a ripple and a synchronous counter.
9. Draw the schematic diagram of an asynchronous (ripple) counter. Why is it called ripple counter?
10. Discuss the working principle of synchronous (parallel) counter with its block diagram. What is the advantage of synchronous counters over serial counters.
11. What is modulus of a counter? Draw the logic diagram and truth table of a mod-8 ripple counter.
12. Explain the terms "UP counter", "Down counter" and "UP/DOWN counter".
13. Draw the schematic block diagram of a ring counter. Describe its working principle. Mention its applications.
14. Write a short note on programmable counter.
15. Explain the operation of the following circuit:

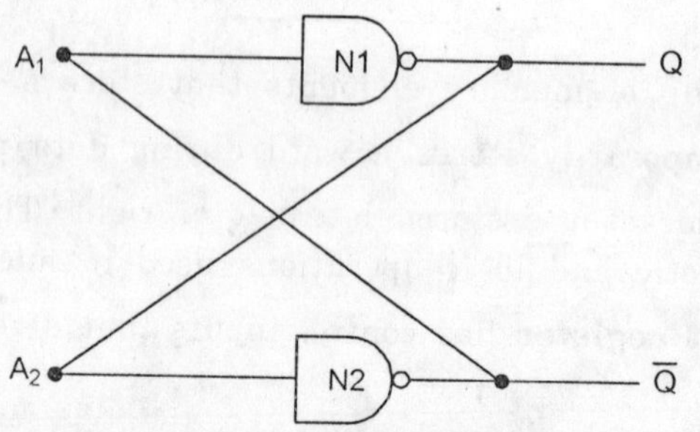


16. Explain a general method for the design of flip-flops.
17. How will you SET/CLEAR a flip-flop asynchronously?
18. Differentiate between S-R and J-K flip-flops.
19. Draw the logic diagram of a mod-20 counter.
20. Give the differences between combinational circuit and sequential circuit.
21. State True or False:
    (*i*) A flip-flop is a device with three stable states.
    (*ii*) A timing diagram shows how the input signals interact to produce the output signal.
    (*iii*) Positive clocking makes a latch wait until the clock signal is high before the output can change.
    (*iv*) The master-slave flip-flop is susceptible to a race around condition.
    (*v*) A register is a group of binary storage cells capable of holding binary information.

(*vi*) A shift register cannot shift its binary contents to the left.

(*vii*) The clock pulse can be applied to all flip-flops simultaneously in a shift register.

(*viii*) There is no inter connection between the flip-flops in a parallel in-parallel out register.

(*ix*) The function of counters is to count electrical pulses.

(*x*) Asynchronous counter is also called *parallel counter*.

(*xi*) Synchronous counter is also called *serial counter*.

(*xii*) A ring counter uses a binary word which has only a single high bit.

22. Fill in the blanks:

(*i*) A flip-flop is a ............... element that stores a binary digit as a low or high voltage.

(*ii*) Changing the output state of a flip-flop on the rising or falling edge of a lock pulse is called ............... .

(*iii*) ............... means change of the output to the opposite state in a J-K flip-flop.

(*iv*) The ............... is the time it takes for the output of a gate or flip-flop to change after the inputs have changed.

(*v*) ............... is a group of memory elements that stores a word.

(*vi*) A register that can shift the stored bits one position to the left or right is called a ............... .

(*vii*) Parallel entry means loading all bits of a word in parallel during one clock pulse. It is also called ............... .

(*viii*) A shift register in which data can be shifted into or out of the register in parallel is called a ............... .

(*ix*) A ................... is a special kind of register, designed to count the number of clock pulses arriving at its input.

(*x*) The ................... of a counter is the number of output states it has.

(*xi*) ................... counters cannot complete with ripple and synchronous counters when it comes to ordinary counting, but they are invaluable when it is necessary to control a sequence of operations.

(*xii*) A mod-10 counter is also known as a *divide-by-10 circuit* or ................... .

## ANSWERS

3. $(1111111)_2$, $(177)_8$, $(127)_{10}$, $(7F)_{16}$

11. The **modulus** of a counter is the number of output states it has. The logic diagram and truth table of a mod-8 ripple counter are given as follows:

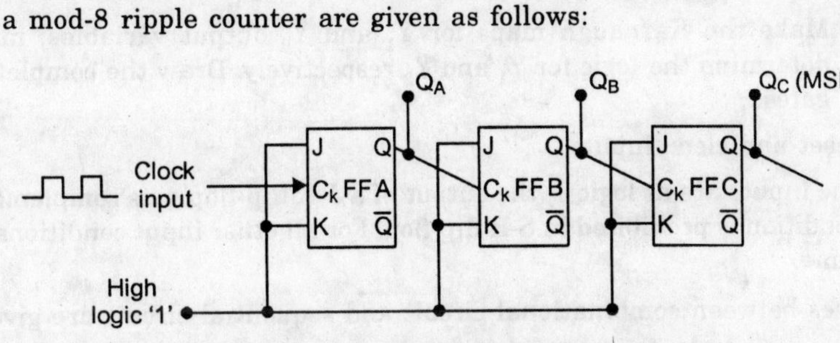


Logic diagram of a mod-8 ripple counter

**Truth Table of Mod-8 ripple Counter**

| *Time* | *Count* | $Q_C$ | $Q_B$ | $Q_A$ |
|---|---|---|---|---|
| $t_0$ | 0 | 0 | 0 | 0 |
| $t_1$ | 1 | 0 | 0 | 1 |
| $t_2$ | 2 | 0 | 1 | 0 |
| $t_3$ | 3 | 0 | 1 | 1 |
| $t_4$ | 4 | 1 | 0 | 0 |
| $t_5$ | 5 | 1 | 0 | 1 |
| $t_6$ | 6 | 1 | 1 | 0 |
| $t_7$ | 7 | 1 | 1 | 1 |
| $t_8$ | 0 | 0 | 0 | 0 |

16. Consider the general model of the flip-flop shown below. Any flip-flop, basically consists of a binary cell coupled with some combinational set/reset decoding logic. The steps for the design are given below:

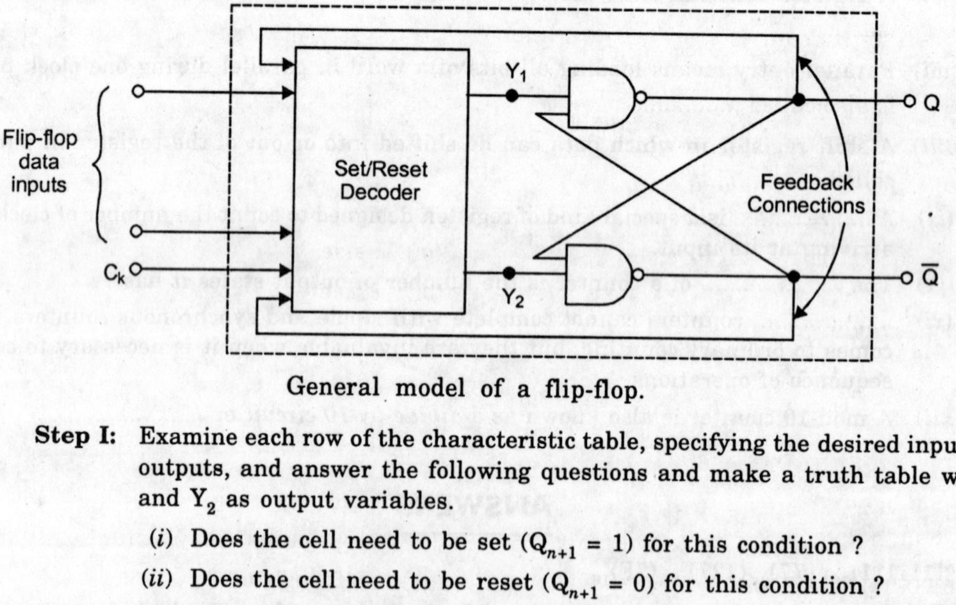


General model of a flip-flop.

**Step I:** Examine each row of the characteristic table, specifying the desired inputs and outputs, and answer the following questions and make a truth table with $Y_1$ and $Y_2$ as output variables.

(*i*) Does the cell need to be set ($Q_{n+1} = 1$) for this condition ?

(*ii*) Does the cell need to be reset ($Q_{n+1} = 0$) for this condition ?

(*iii*) Does the cell need to be left as it is ?

**Step II:** Make the Karnaugh maps for $Y_1$ and $Y_2$ output variables, minimize it and determine the logic for $Y_1$ and $Y_2$ respectively. Draw the complete circuit using gates.

17. By using preset and clear inputs.

18. When both the inputs are at logic 1, the output of a J-K flip-flop gets complemented, whereas this inputs condition is prohibited in S-R flip-flop. For all other input conditions the behaviour of both is same.

20. The differences between combinational circuit and sequential circuit are given below:

**Differences between combinational and sequential circuit**

| *S. No.* | *Combinational Circuit* | *Sequential Circuit* |
|---|---|---|
| 1. | It is a digital logical circuit whose output at any time depends solely on the combined set of input applied to it simultaneously at that instant of time. | It is a digital logic circuit whose output depends on the present inputs as well as on the previous history of inputs. |
| 2. | It has no memory elements. | It has at least one memory element. |
| 3. | It can be totally described by the set of output values only. | Its performance is totally described by the set of subsequence state values as well as set of output values. |
| 4. | It is easy to design, due to absence of memory. | It is difficult to design due to presence of memory. |
| 5. | Faster is speed because all primary inputs applied simultaneously. | It is comparatively slower in speed because it has secondary inputs also, which are applied after a delay. |
| 6. | It requires more hardware for its realization. | It requires less hardware for its realization. |
| 7. | It is expensive in cost. | It is cheaper in cost. |

21. State True or False:

(*i*) False (*ii*) True
(*iii*) True (*iv*) False
(*v*) True (*vi*) False
(*vii*) True (*viii*) True
(*ix*) True (*x*) False
(*xi*) False (*xii*) True

22. Fill in the blanks:

(*i*) memory (*ii*) edge triggering
(*iii*) Toggle (*iv*) propagation delay time
(*v*) Register (*vi*) shift register
(*vii*) broadside loading (*viii*) parallel in-parallel out register.
(*ix*) counter (*x*) modulus
(*xi*) Ring (*xii*) decade counter

Chapter 8

# MEMORY ORGANISATION AND SECONDARY STORAGE SYSTEM

## 8.1 INTRODUCTION

For a computer to work, it must contain memory where it can store data and programs until they are needed. Two or three levels of memories such as main memory, secondary memory and cache memory are provided in a digital computer. The *main memory* (or primary memory) is a fast memory. It stores programs along with data, which are to be executed. It also stores necessary programs of system software, which are required to execute the user's program. The *cache memory* is placed in between the CPU and the main memory. It is much faster than the main memory. Secondary memory is permanent storage used to store programs and data that the user is not using at the moment. Computer memory exhibits perhaps the widest range of type, technology, organization, performance, and cost of any feature of a computer.

The memory is equivalent to thousands of registers, each storing a binary word. The latest generation of computers use semiconductor memories as main memories, because they are less expensive and easier to work with than core memories. A typical microcomputer has a semiconductor memory with upto 1,048,576 memory locations, each capable of storing 2 bytes of information.

## 8.2 BINARY STORAGE CELL AND ITS CHARACTERISTICS

A memory unit consists of a large number of binary storage cells and information is stored semi-permanently in it during data processing. Besides the large number of storage cells, a memory has a few registers to facilitate storage and retrieval of information from memory and a set of control signals.

For a physical device to be usable as a binary storage cell in a memory unit, it must have the following desirable characteristics:

(*i*) It must have two stable states.

(*ii*) Power consumption must be small.

(*iii*) It should be possible to switch between the two stable states an infinite number of times.

(*iv*) The information stored in a cell should not decay with the passage of time.

(*v*) The physical size should be as small as possible.

(*vi*) The cost of each cell must be low.

(*vii*) The time taken to read/write information from/to a group of cells must be small.

The currently used popular binary cells are semiconductor ICs, magnetic surfaces on a disk or tape and pits/lands on a laser disk.

## 8.3 MEMORY SYSTEM DESIGN

A set of binary cells are strung together of form a unit known as a word. A word in always treated as an entity and moves in and out of memory as one unit. The movement of words in and out of memory is controlled by signals known as write and read signals. Words to be written and read are first entered in a register known as the *memory buffer register* (MBR). The location in the memory unit where word is to be stored is known as the address of the word. For retrieval of a word from memory, one has to provide its address. The address is entered in a register known as the *memory address register* (MAR). For writing a word into memory, one has to provide its address in the MAR. So, it is clear that a memory unit is organized in such a way that it has a number of addressed locations, each location storing a word. The address generally start at 0 and the highest address equals one less than the number of words that can be stored in the memory and is known as its **"address space".** For example, if a memory has 1,048,576 locations then the address ranges between 0 and 1,048,575. For storing the value of the address, the MAR register, in this case, should have 20 bits. 1,048,576 is usually abbreviated as 1 MB or 1024 KB.

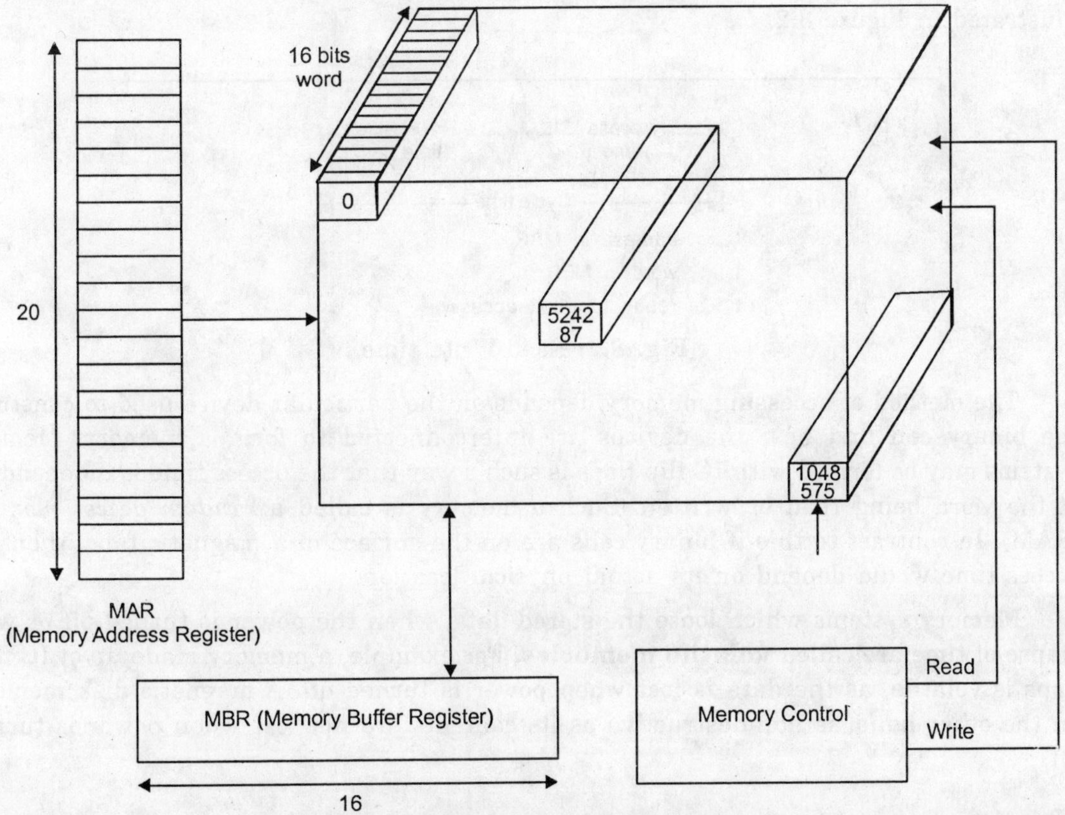


**Fig. 8.1:** Block diagram of a memory.

Figure 8.1 shows the block diagram of a memory system. This memory is assumed to store 1,048,576 words (*i.e.*, 1024K words) with 16 bits per word. If a number 104 is to be stored in location 524287, then this number is placed in MBR. The address where the number is to be stored is entered in MAR. The write signal is then initiated. This signal replaces the current contents of the location 524287 by the contents of MBR.

For reading the contents of some location, its address is entered in MAR. The read signal is initiated by the control unit. The contents of the specified location are copied into MBR and the information lying in the selected location remains unchanged. It is called *non-destructive read out.* Reading information from a memory must be non-destructive for the memory unit to be useful in a data processing system.

The destructive or non-destructive read out depends on the device being used as a memory cell in the memory. For example, flip-flop binary cells are non-destructive. Reading from binary cells made with capacitors is destructive. In this case, whatever was read from the selected memory cell must be written back to retain its contents. The time interval between the initiation of a read signal and the availability of the required word in MBR is called the **access time** of the memory. The time interval between the initiation of a write signal and the storing of the word in the specified address in the memory is known as the **write time.** In case of destructive reading, it is necessary to write the word back in memory. The time required for this combined read and write operations is known as the **memory cycle time.** Even if reading from memory is non-destructive the time that should elapse between two successive references to memory read or write is more than the access time. This time is the cycle time of the memory. These terms are illustrated in Figure 8.2.

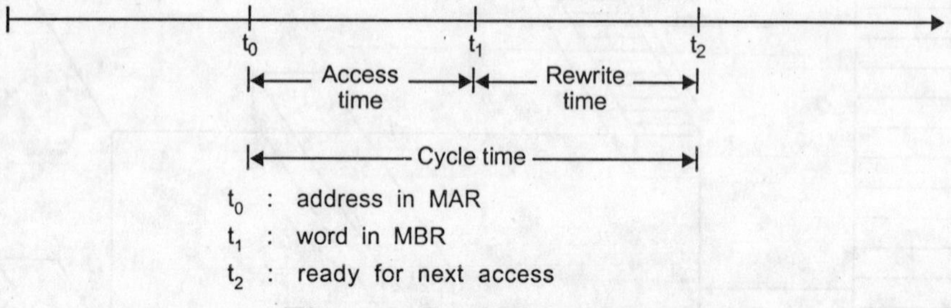


**Fig. 8.2:** Read/Write time.

The method of accessing memory depends on the particular device used to construct the binary cell and how the devices are interconnected to form a memory. Memory systems may be formed with IC flip-flops is such a way that the access time is independent of the word being read or written. Such a memory is called a *random access memory* (RAM). In contrast to this if binary cells are on the surface of a magnetic tape, then the access time would depend on its actual physical location.

Memory systems which loose the stored data, when the power is turned off or with elapse of time are called **volatile memories.** For example, a memory made up of IC flip-flops is volatile, as the data is lost when power is turned off. A magnetic disk memory, on the other hand, is non-destructive as its contents are not lost when power is turned off.

## 8.4 MEMORY HIERARCHY

On the basis of their location inside the computer, the memories can be divided into two categories:

- Internal memory and
- External memory

**Internal Memory.** Internal memory is the part of CPU. Registers, main memory and cache memory all are the examples of internal memory. These memories reside in the computer system and forms the main part of CPU. These memories are adjacent to CPU, so the access time is very less. These memories are very compact in size and too costly as compared to other memories. So, we cannot store large volume of data in the internal memories.

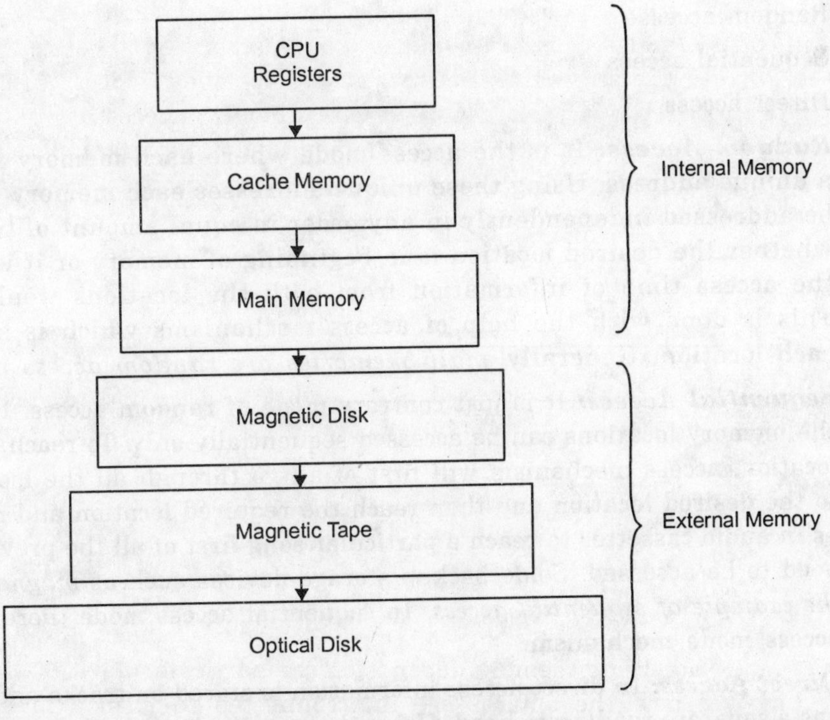


**Fig. 8.3:** Memory Hierarchy.

**External Memory.** It is also called secondary or auxiliary memory. It is not the permanent part of a computer, *i.e.*, availability of these memories is optional in a computer. It is attached to the computer if needed. These are located far from CPU within a computer, so access time is more. These memories are very spacious and can store large volume of data. Also they are cheap as compared to primary memory. All backup storage devices are secondary memory.

## 8.5 MEMORY CHARACTERISTICS

To identify the behaviour of various memories certain characteristics are considered. These are given below:

**Storage Capacity:** It provides the size of memory. The internal memory is measured in terms of words or bytes. External memory is measured in terms of bytes *viz.* Kilobytes, Megabytes, Gigabytes or Terabytes.

**Location:** The memory which is inside the processor is called the *internal memory*. The memory which is external to processor and can be replaced is known as *external memory*.

**Access Method:** Each memory is a collection of various memory locations. Accessing the memory means finding and reaching the desired location and then reading information from that memory location. Information from memory locations can be accessed in the following ways:

(*i*) Random access

(*ii*) Sequential access

(*iii*) Direct access

(*i*) ***Random Access:*** It is the access mode where each memory location has a unique address. Using these unique addresses each memory location can be addressed independently in any order in equal amount of time. That is whether the desired location is in beginning of memory or it is in the end the access time of information from both the locations would be same. This is done with the help of access mechanisms which is separate for each location. Generally, *main memories are random access memories.*

(*ii*) ***Sequential Access:*** It is just contrary mode of random access. In this mode the memory locations can be accessed sequentially only. To reach a particular location, access mechanism will first of all go through all the locations prior to the desired location and then reach the required location and read it. Just as in audio cassettes to reach a particular song first of all the previous portion need to be accessed. Some backup storage devices such as *magnetic tape are the example of sequential access.* In sequential access mode there is only one access mode mechanism.

(*iii*) ***Direct Access:*** In direct access information is stored on tracks and each track has a separate read/write head. Using that read/write head information of that track could be accessed sequentially. This features makes it a semi-random mode which is generally used in *magnetic disks.*

**Access Time:** The access time is the time between the request made for some read/write operation and the availability of data at the desired location. Usually it is for read operation. The access time depends on the access mode and physical characteristics of any memory. For random access mode, it is minimum. For the sequential access mode, it is maximum.

**Life of Storage** This is another characteristics which specifies that how long the information stored in the memory will remain intact. Some memories require constant refreshing of data. This is because as time passes the 1 value tends to become 0. These memories are known as *dynamic memories*. The memories which do not require to be refreshed again and again are known as *static memories*. Some memories need to have constant electric current supply to store the information, otherwise they loose their contents. Such memories are known as *volatile memories*. *Non-volatile memories* do not loose their contents when power is switched off. Their contents remain intact even when the power is switched off. Semiconductor memories are volatile and magnetic memories are non-volatile.

**Physical Characteristics:** Taking into account the *technology* used in manufacturing the memory devices can be divided into four main categories as given below:

- Electronic
- Magnetic
- Mechanical
- Optical

## 8.6 MEMORY CLASSIFICATION

Memory is an integral and an important component of a digital computer. It is required to store data, programs and results. Memory can broadly be classified into 3 categories depending upon the technology and material used for making storage devices:

(*i*) Semiconductor memory

(*ii*) Magnetic memory

(*iii*) Optical memory.

The **semiconductor memory** is static device. It is faster, light-weight and compact. But it is expensive. On the other hand **magnetic** and **optical memory** are slower and cheaper than semiconductor memory. They are not static devices and generally come in the form of a rotating disk or tape.

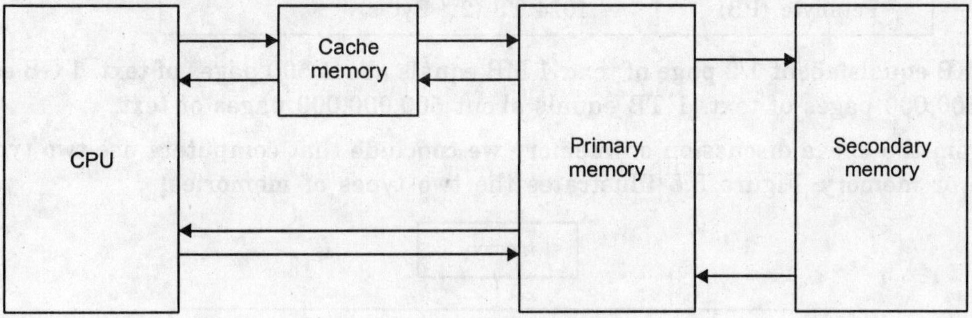


**Fig. 8.4**

A computer uses a combination of above memories for storing relevant data, programs and results. Now CPU is a semiconductor device and it operates at very high speeds. Therefore, the memory should also be fast otherwise there will be a speed mismatch between the two *i.e.*, if the memory is slow, the CPU has to wait for data and instructions.

This leads to the wastage of precious CPU processing time. To overcome this drawback a very fast semiconductor memory called **'Cache Memory'** is placed between the CPU and main memory. Cache memory is much faster than main memory and it stores currently needed data and instructions of the program in execution.

Next to cache memory comes **main memory** or **primary memory.** It is again semiconductor memory which employs dynamic RAMs. It stores data and instructions currently needed by the CPU. It is comparatively cheaper than cache memory. The information which is not being currently processed resides on the **magnetic memory** also called **secondary memory.** The information which is needed by the CPU is transferred from secondary memory to main memory. Secondary memory is much slower than main memory and it is as cheaper. The size of main memory is much smaller than secondary memory because of its high cost. Secondary memory is employed for mass storage. It has much larger capacity than main memory. Storage is permanent in secondary memory until we delete it.

Data and information stored in a computer is often valuable and result be protected from any damage. One way to protect the data is to store a copy of important programs on backup storage media like floppy disks, magnetic tapes and CD-ROM.

Table 8.1 gives units of memory measurement:

**Table 8.1: Units of Memory**

| | |
|---|---|
| Bit | A binary digit (0 to 1) |
| Byte | 8 bits, or 1 character |
| Kilobyte (KB) | 1024 Bytes ($2^{10}$ Bytes) |
| Megabyte (MB) | 1024 KB ($2^{20}$ Bytes) |
| Gigabyte (GB) | 1024 MB ($2^{30}$ Bytes) |
| Terabyte (TB) | 1024 GB ($2^{40}$ Bytes) |
| Petabyte (PB) | 1024 TB ($2^{50}$ Bytes) |

1 KB equals about 1/2 page of text. 1 MB equals about 500 pages of text. 1 GB equals about 500,000 pages of text. 1 TB equals about 500,000,000 pages of text.

From the above discussion on memory we conclude that computers use two types of storage or memory. Figure 8.5 illustrates the two types of memories.

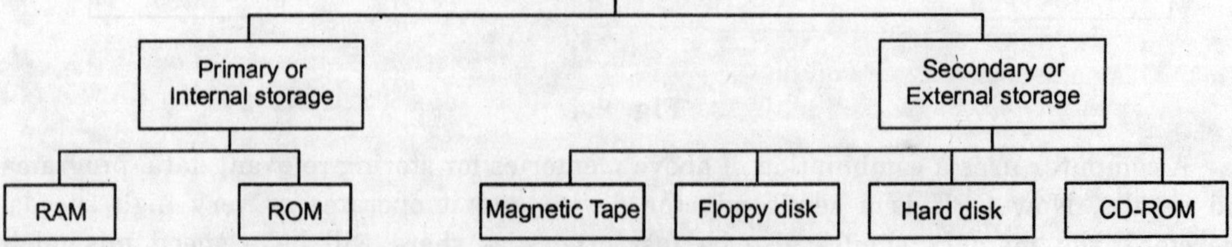


**Fig. 8.5:** Computer memory types.

## 8.7 BUFFER

The programs and data must be brought to main memory before any operation can be performed on these. Sometimes it is sufficient to bring in only one byte or word and use or operate on it by itself but generally a sequence of bytes or words is needed before the data become meaningful. If several bytes or words are required, then it is necessary to transfer them to a set of consecutive locations in memory before they are used. A set of locations used for such purpose is known as a **memory buffer** or **simply buffer.** For example, the characters in a typed line may represent a command to the operating system. Because the command could not be interpreted until the entire line has been input, the sequence of characters being input would need to be stored in a memory buffer until a carriage return/line feed combination is encountered.

Many times, it is necessary to temporarily store input data until it can be converted into a suitable form or any other operation can be performed on it. Some operations may require more than one buffer so that one buffer can be input to while the other buffer is being operated on; then, when the buffer being filled is full, it can be operated on and the input can be directed to the other buffer. This mode of operation is referred to as *double buffering*. Sometimes more than two buffers may be required and the term multiple buffering is used to describe them. The concept of buffering also applies to outputting. Triple buffering is needed when inputting, processing, and outputting must be carried on simultaneously.

Therefore, from the above discussion we conclude that *buffers are a portion of the main memory which the Input/Output devices can access directly*. Buffering reduces the idle time of CPU significantly. Figure 8.6 illustrates multiple buffering:

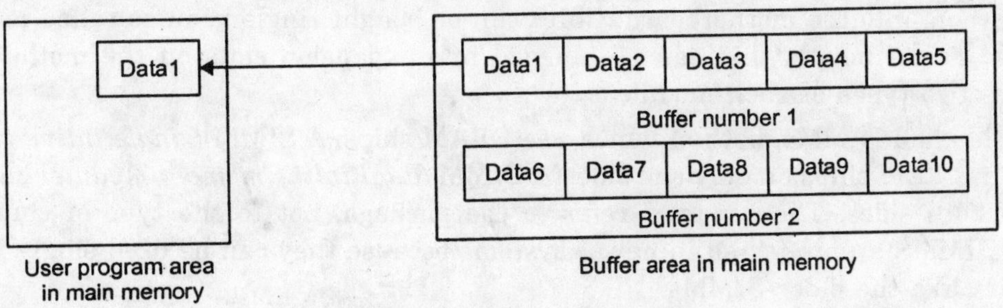


**Fig. 8.6:** Multiple buffering.

## 8.8 SEMICONDUCTOR RAMs AND THEIR CLASSIFICATION

RAM is used as read/write memory of the computer. It is volatile in nature. RAM stands for Random Access Memory. The main memory is usually referred to as RAM. In RAM it is possible to select any memory location randomly to store the information or to retrieve information from a random memory location. The access time is same for every memory location. Since the information can be written into or read from RAMs, or they are used as read/write memory of the computer system.

This memory is volatile because it retains information as long as power supply is on. This is why you should frequently-every 5–10 minutes, say-transfer (save) your work to a secondary-storage medium such as your hard disk, in case the power goes off while you are woking. Thus, the programmer has to reload all the programs each time the power supply is interrupted.

Four types of RAM chips are used in personal computers:

- DRAM
- SDRAM
- SRAM and
- RDRAM

**DRAM:** Pronounced "dee-ram", DRAM (dynamic RAM) must be constantly refreshed by the CPU otherwise it will loose its contents. It is achieved by refreshing and control circuitry.

**SDRAM:** Dynamic RAM used in most PCs today is SDRAM (synchronous dynamic RAM), which is synchronized by the system clock and is much faster than DRAM. Its speed is expressed in **megahertz.**

**SRAM:** Pronounced "ess-ram", SRAM (static RAM) is faster than any DRAM and will retain its contents without having to be refreshed by the CPU. These are costlier and consume more power.

**RDRAM:** Rambus dynamic RAM, or RDRAM, is faster and more expensive than SDRAM and is the type of memory used with Intel's P4 chip.

Microcomputers come with different amounts of RAM, which is usually measured in megabytes. The more RAM you have, the faster the computer operates, and the better your software performs. *Having enough RAM is a critical matter.* Before using a software package, see how much RAM is required. For example, Microsoft Office 2000, required a minimum of 16 megabytes of RAM.

If you are short on memory capacity, you can usually add more RAM chips by plugging them into the motherboard. Chips can be bought single or in so-called **memory modules,** circuit boards that can be plugged into expansion slots on the motherboard. There are two types of such modules:

SIMMs and DIMMs, both of which use DRAM chips. A SIMM *(single inline memory module)* has RAM chips on only one side. A DIMM *(dual inline memory module)* has RAM chips on both sides. These names refer to the package, not to the type of chips they contain. DIMMS are preferred in newer systems because they can be used singly instead of in pairs like the older SIMMs.

For now, RAM is volatile, but researchers have recently developed a nonvolatile form of RAM that may be available in market in near future. It is called M-RAM—the M stands for magnetic. It uses minuscule magnets rather than electric charges to store the 0s and 1s of binary data. M-RAM would use much less power than current RAM, and whatever is in memory when the computer's power is turned off or lost will remain there.

## 8.9 SEMICONDUCTOR MEMORY ORGANISATION

Semiconductor memory may be organised into the following two ways:

- 2 D Organisation
- 2½ D Organisation

### 8.9.1 2 D Organisation

Static memory cells may be organised into a 2D-memory system as shown in Figure 8.7.

Figure 8.7 shows the organisation of a 16 word, 4-bit/word 2D-memory. An address decoder is used to decode the address in a 4-bit MAR (Memory Address Register). The address decoder selects one out of 16 word wires. The voltage applied to a selected wire is V. A number of memory cells equal to the bits/word are connected to each word wire. Here, 4 memory cells are connected to each word wire. The bit wires $B_{0i}$ and $B_{1i}$ of bit $i$ of all the words are connected together as shown in Figure 8.7. The bit wires $B_{0i}$, $B_{1i}$ of bit $i$ are fed to *sense amplifier* $SA_i$. To read the contents of a word, the address of the word is entered in MAR. The address decoder selects the appropriate word wire. The voltage on the word wire is taken to V/2. All the memory cells belonging to this word experience this voltage. Depending on whether a cell had a 0 or 1 stored, the voltage on the corresponding bit wires dip. This is detected by the respective sense amplifiers. If the $B_{0i}$ wires experience a dip in voltage, $SA_i$ will store a 0 in bit $i$ of MBR (Memory Buffer Register). If the voltage dip is in $B_{1i}$ wire then a 1 is detected by the $SA_i$ and a 1 is stored in bit $i$ of MBR.

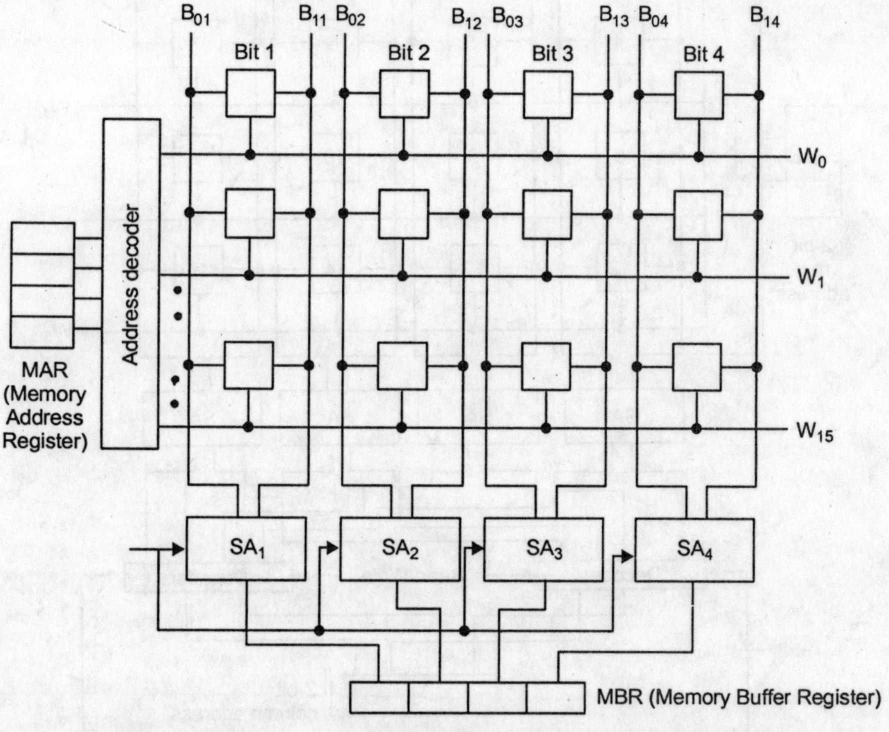


**Fig. 8.7:** A semiconductor 2D memory (16W, 4b/w).

To write, say 1010, in word 2 the following is done. Word address 0010 is stored in MAR. When decoded it selects word $W_2$ and the voltage on line $W_2$ is made V. The data 1010 is stored in MBR. $SA_1$ brings the voltage on $B_{11}$ to 0, $SA_2$ brings voltage on $B_{02}$ to

0, $SA_3$ brings the voltage on $B_{13}$ to 0 and $SA_4$ brings the voltage on $B_{04}$ to 0. Thus cell 1 of word 2 will store a 1, cell 2 of word 2 will store a 0, cell 3 of word 2 will store a 1 and finally cell 4 of word 2 will store a 0.

### 8.9.2 2½D Organisation

In the 2D organisation the number of word lines equals the number of words in the memory. If it is a 16K memory we will require 16K word wires. The address decoder is complex. Another organisation called 2½D organisation uses only $\sqrt{W}$ word wires, allows the use of simpler decoders and it also enables the construction of memories modularly. For instance if a memory of W words with 6-bits/word is required then six such W × 1 memory chips can be put together with ease.

We will illustrate this organisation by examining a 16 words, 1-bit/word memory. Figure 8.8 illustrates the way the cells are arranged in the memory.

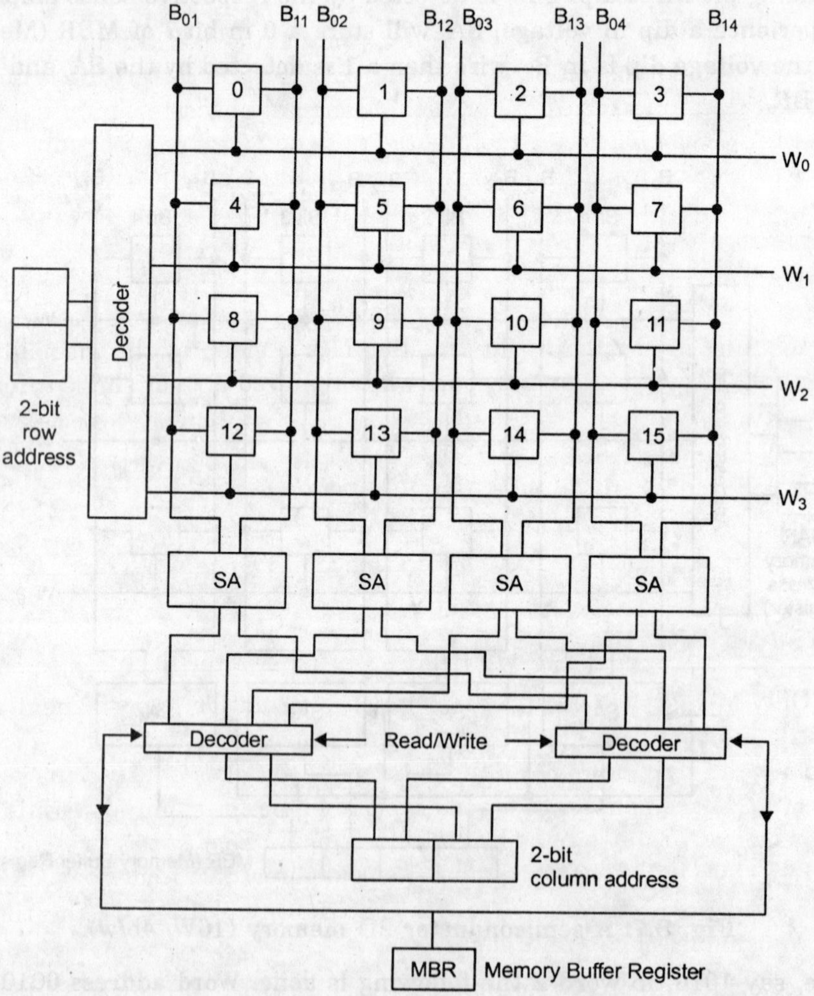


**Fig. 8.8:** A semiconductor 2½D memory (1W, 1 b/w).

The 4-bit word address is split into a 2 bit row address and a 2-bit column address. To read a bit from the memory the most significant bits of the word address are entered in the row register and two least significant bits in the column register. The voltage of the selected row is lowered and all the 4-bit cells in this row are read. The column decoder, however, routes only the bit in the selected column as data output. To write a bit in the given cell the two most significant bits of the address are again entered in the row register and the two least significant bits in the column register. The bit to be written is entered in the MBR. The appropriate row is selected by the decoder. The column decoder selects the appropriate bit wire $B_{1i}$ or $B_{0i}$ and its voltage is lowered writing the required information in the selected cell.

## 8.10 ERROR DETECTION AND CORRECTION IN MEMORIES

Memory is an important part of a computer. It is thus essential to ensure that the data read from a memory do not have errors. Sometimes data read/stored in a memory are corrupted due to noise or hardware faults. When data read has an error it should be detected and if possible corrected. Various error detection/correction techniques have been used in designing memories. Most of the commonly used techniques use Hamming Code (discussed in Unit 1). The technique used is to add $k$ error detecting/correcting bits to $i$ information bits and write $(k + i)$ bits in each addressable word in memory. When a word is read the $(k + i)$ bits stored in it are read. The $k$-bits are used to find out whether there are any errors in the $i$ information bits.

In the simplest case, to detect, a single error in data read, a single parity bit is sufficient. However, if we want to detect and correct a single error then the number of parity bits $k$ required in data with $i$ information bits is given by the inequality $(2^k - 1) \geq i + k$. Thus for a 32-bit word number of parity bits required is 6 for single error correction.

Usually in memory systems one uses a code for Single Error Correction Double Error Detection (Abbreviated SECDED). For this at least 7 parity bits are required with 32 information bits (an overhead of 21.8%). The overhead goes down if the word length is larger. For a 64-bit word the number of parity bits required for SECDED is 8, an overhead of 12.5%.

## 8.11 ROMS AND THEIR CLASSIFICATION

A Read Only Memory (ROM) is one in which information is permanently stored *i.e.*, it is non-volatile memory. It is used to store fixed start-up instructions. The information from the memory can only be read and it is not possible to write fresh information on it. The contents of ROM are not lost or erased even when power supply is terminated, unlike RAM. Such memories are also called *field stores, permanent stores or dead stores*. It is generally used to store initializing programs of a computer, microcodes of a CISC processor, fixed programs in micro-controllers etc. Its contents are written at the time of its IC fabrication. It is simple, cheap and dense.

ROM is a specific case of a Programmable Logic Device (PLD). In ROM the AND array of the PLD is fixed and the OR array is programmable. A 3-bit input, 4-bit output, Read Only Memory (ROM) is shown in Figure 8.9. Note that all the 8 minterms corresponding to the

3-input bits are generated. These can be thought as addressing 8 words in the ROM. The output bits are programmed by blowing fuses selectively in the OR array. The ROM shown in Figure 8.9 has contents shown in Table 8.2.

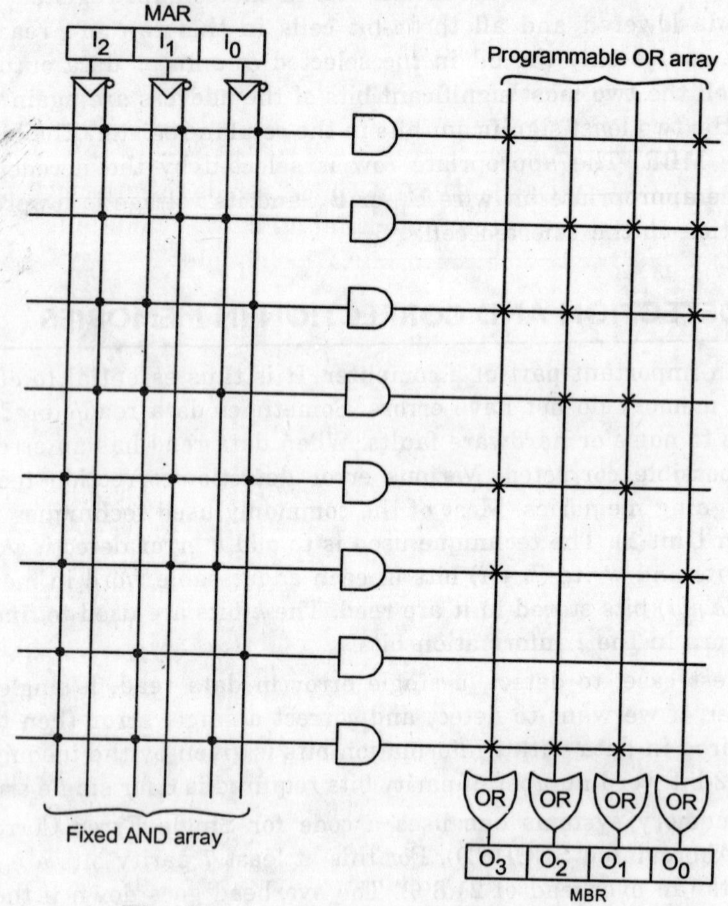


**Fig. 8.9:** A read only memory (ROM).

**Table 8.2: Contents of ROM of Fig. 8.9**

| *MAR* | | | *MBR* | | | |
|---|---|---|---|---|---|---|
| $I_2$ | $I_1$ | $I_0$ | $O_3$ | $O_2$ | $O_1$ | $O_0$ |
| 0 | 0 | 0 | 1 | 0 | 0 | 1 |
| 0 | 0 | 1 | 0 | 1 | 1 | 1 |
| 0 | 1 | 0 | 1 | 1 | 0 | 1 |
| 0 | 1 | 1 | 0 | 1 | 1 | 0 |
| 1 | 0 | 0 | 1 | 0 | 1 | 0 |
| 1 | 0 | 1 | 1 | 0 | 0 | 1 |
| 1 | 1 | 0 | 0 | 0 | 0 | 0 |
| 1 | 1 | 1 | 1 | 1 | 1 | 0 |

The other types of ROMs are given below:

**PROM:** A PROM is a programmable ROM. ROM chips are provided by the computer manufacturers and it is not possible for the user to change the contents of a ROM chip. However, in a PROM the contents are decided by the user. The user can store permanent programs, data or any other kind of information in a PROM. PROMs are programmed to store information using a facility known as PROM programmes. However, once the chip has been programmed the recorded information cannot be changed *i.e.*, PROM becomes a ROM. So PROM is also a permanent storage.

**EPROM:** A variation to PROM is EPROM which stands for erasable PROM. As the name suggests it is possible to erase the contents of a EPROM chip unlike a PROM chip. The stored data in EPROMs is erased by exposing it to high intensity short wave ultraviolet light for about 20 minutes. EPROMs are used to store programs which are permanent but need updating.

**EEPROM:** EEPROM is an electrically erasable PROM. The chip can be erased and reprogrammed on byte by byte basis. Hence selective erasing is possible. Its disadvantage is that it requires different voltages for erasing (21 V), writing (21 V) and reading (5 V) the stored information. It also has high cost and low reliability.

**Table 8.3: Types of ROMs**

| *Type* | *Purpose* |
|---|---|
| ROM | Read Only Memory. Factory written. Cannot be altered at all. |
| PROM | Programmable ROM. Can be programmed at the field. Can be written only once; but not rewritten. |
| EPROM or UVEPROM | Ultraviolet erasable programmable ROM. |
| EAPROM or | Electrically alterable and programmable ROM. Can be erased and rewritten. |
| EEPROM or $E^2$ PROM | Erasing needs special operations; not simple overwriting as in RAM. |

As mentioned earlier, the primary advantage of a ROM is that, unlike a RAM, the information stored in it is not lost when power fails and is applied again. So the computer programs can be safely stored in them. Another advantage is the higher density of packing memory cells in it. The cost per bit of ROM storage is cheaper than RAM storage. 64 K bytes per ROM chip are now commercially available.

## 8.12 APPLICATIONS OF ROMS

ROMs are very useful in designing digital systems and few applications are discussed below:

(*i*) **Code Converter:** This application is the most obvious use of a ROM. For instance, the ROM of Figure 8.9 implements the truth table given in Table 8.2.

ROMs for common code conversions such as Hollerith code to ASCII code are readily available. Other code converters may be made to order. In general a ROM with an $n$-bit MAR and $m$-bit MBR can realize any $n$ input $m$ output combinational circuit.

(*ii*) **Function Generators:** Table for commonly used functions such as sine, cosine, and arctangent may be stored in ROMs. The arguments are entered in MAR and the function values are provided by the output register.

(*iii*) **Character Generators:** Character displays in dot matrix form use ROMs for decoding and activating the display. Consider a 5 × 7 dot matrix shown in Figure 8.10. If each of the dot positions is a lamp, then a letter D, for instance, may be displayed by selecting a set of lamps and turning them ON as shown. If ON lamps represent a 1 an OFF lamps a 0, then a character may be displayed by setting a subset of 35-bits to 1. Generally a 5 × 7 matrix is used for displaying characters from a 64 character set. The 6-bit code for a character is fed as the input to the ROM. The output is a 35-bit number which selects the appropriate dots to be lighted.

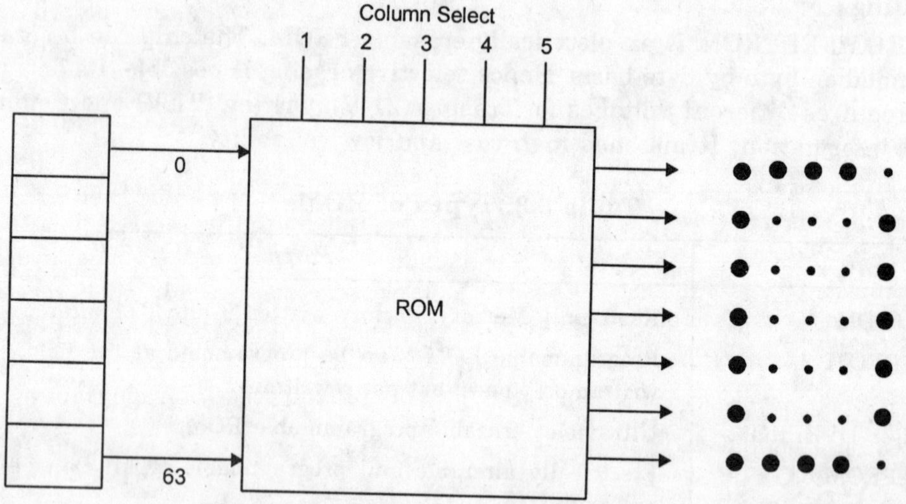


**Fig. 8.10:** A ROM character generator.

The ROM may be simplified if, instead of requiring all 35-bits to be retrieved in parallel, we need only 7-bits belonging to a specified column of the dot matrix be available. The column address in such a case is provided as an additional input to the ROM (see Figure 8.10).

In microcomputers ROMs are used to store programs, particularly those which are for dedicated applications.

In summary, we can say that a number of functions performed by combinational switching circuits may now be delegated to systems which incorporate ROMs.

## 8.13 SECONDARY STORAGE DEVICES

A computer is capable of storing bulk of data and retrieving or accessing the stored data as and when required. A personal computer may store a few thousand of characters whereas a mainframe may store billion of characters. The bulk of data can't be stored in the main memory as this memory is costly and naturally some other cheaper memory devices are required. These cheaper memory devices, called **secondary storage devices** can store bulk of data at very less cost. Data are stored in secondary storage in the same binary codes as in the main storage and are made available to main storage as needed. The commonly used secondary storage devices are Magnetic Tape, Floppy Disk, Hard Disk and CD-ROM.

The choice of a particular secondary storage device for a given application mainly depends upon how the stored information needs to be accessed. Basically there are two methods of accessing information.

(*i*) Sequential or Serial Access

(*ii*) Direct or Random Access

A Sequential Access Device is one in which the data can be retrieved in the same sequence in which it is stored, so that the access time varies according to the location of storage. Sequential processing is quite suitable for applications like preparation of monthly payslips, monthly electrically bills etc. In these applications, each record needs to be processed at scheduled intervals. Magnetic tape and punched paper media are widely used examples of sequential access storage devices.

In many applications we need to retrieve a record directly rather than going through all the records to reach the desired one. For example, in a computerised bank, we might need to check the account status of a particular customer at any instant of time. In such applications, it is inefficient to use a sequential storage device as most of the time is wasted in looking for the particular record. For such online real time processing applications Direct Access Storage Devices are used. These direct access devices are also called Random-Access devices because the information is available randomly. Thus, a Direct Access Storage Device is a device in which the data can be stored randomly and it can be accessed directly. Magnetic Disk and Magnetic Drum are typical examples of Direct-Access Storage Devices.

## 8.14 FLOPPY DISK AND ITS TYPES

A floppy disk is a very popular direct access secondary storage medium for micro and minicomputers.

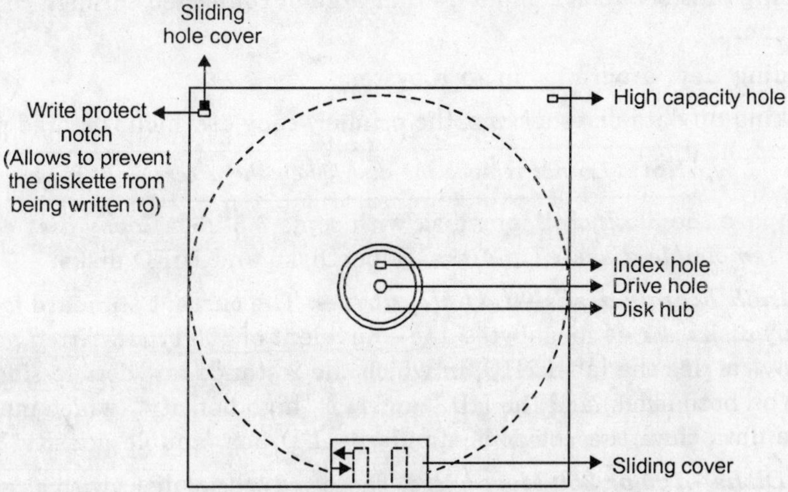


**Fig. 8.11:** 3½ inch floppy disk.

*A floppy disk, often called a diskette or simply a disk, is a removable flat piece of mylar plastic packaged in a 3.5–inch plastic case.* Data and programs are stored on the disk's coating by means of magnetized spots, following standard on/off patterns of data representation (such as ASCII). The plastic case protects the mylar disk from being touched by human hands. Originally, when most disks were larger (5.25 inches), the disks actually were **"floppy",** not rigid; now the plastic disk inside is flexible or floppy.

Floppy disks are inserted into a floppy-disk drive, a device that holds, spins, reads data from, and writes data to a floppy disk. **Read** means taking data from secondary storage (converted to electronic signals) to the computer's memory (RAM). **Write** means copying the electronic information processed by the computer to secondary storage.

On the diskette, data is recorded in concentric circles called **tracks.** On a formatted disk each track is divided into *sectors, invisible wedge-shaped sections used for storage reference purpose.* The *read / write head is used to transfer data between the computer and the disk.* Figure 8.11 illustrates a 3½ inch floppy disk:

The Floppy Drive is of a moving head variety and therefore the floppy can be removed and replaced by another. The head actually contacts the surface during reading/ writing, though in other times it is lifted up from the surface. The hole at the centre is to allow a spindle to lock the floppy so that it can rotate. The Index hole is used to recognize the starting sector of any track. The purpose of *write permit notch is to protect valuable information recorded on the floppy from accidental damage.* If this notch is covered, writing is not allowed on the floppy, only reading is possible. If the notch is not covered reading as well as writing is possible.

A new floppy can't be used without formatting it. Formatting a disk is to create a set of magnetic concentric circles called tracks. Tracks are further divided into sectors. Most high density disks have 80 tracks.

Floppies offer a number of advantages. They are exchangeable. The storage capacity is high as compared to its size and weight. These are portable. Floppies are inexpensive also as compared to hard disks. The most common uses of floppy disks are as follows:

(*i*) Moving files between computers that are not connected through communication channel.

(*ii*) Loading new programs on to a system.

(*iii*) Backing up data or programs, the primary copy of which is stored on hard disk.

**Note.** *Do not remove the disk when the access light is on.*

Let us compare the 3.5 inch floppy disk with some 3.5 inch *floppy-disk cartridges,* or *higher-capacity removable disks*—Zip disks, SuperDisks and HiFD disks:

- ***3.5 Inch Floppy-disks—1.44 Megabytes.*** The current standard for traditional floppy disks is 1.44 megabytes, the equivalent of 400 type-written pages. Today's floppy carries the label 2HD, in which the 2 stands for "double-sided" (it stores data on both sides) and the HD stands for "high density" (which means it stores more data than the previous standard—DD, for "double density").
- ***Zip Disks—100 or 250 Megabytes.*** These are special disks with a capacity of 100 or 250 megabytes, produced by Iomega Corp. At 100–250 megabytes, this is at least

70 times the storage capacity of the standard floppy. These are used to store large spreadsheet files, database files, image files, websites and multimedia representation files. These require their own Zip disk drives, which may come installed on new computers, although external Zip drives are also available in market.

- ***SuperDisks—120 Megabytes.*** These are disks with a capacity of 120 megabytes, produced by Imation. The Super Disk drive can also read standard 1.44 megabyte floppy disks, which Zip drives cannot do.
- ***HiFD Disks—200 Megabytes.*** These are disks with a capacity of 200 megabytes, produced by Sony Corp. The disk drive can also read standard 1.44 megabytes floppies. These have 140 times the capacity of today's standard floppy disks.

## 8.15 HARD DISK AND ITS TYPES

Magnetic disk is the most popular direct access storage medium. A magnetic disk is made of aluminium or other metals or metal alloys instead of plastic. The disk is coated on both sides with magnetic material (iron oxide). Unlike a floppy disk, a hard disk cannot

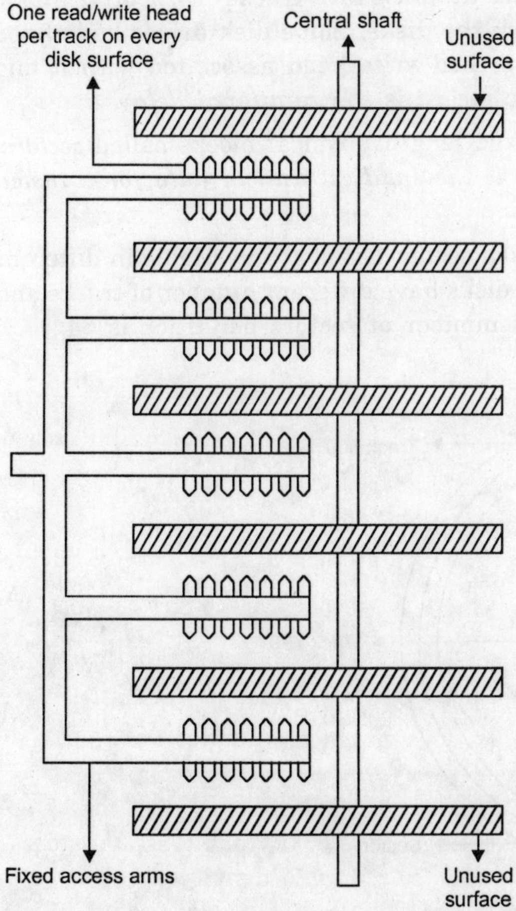


**Fig. 8.12:** A disk drive having fixed head.

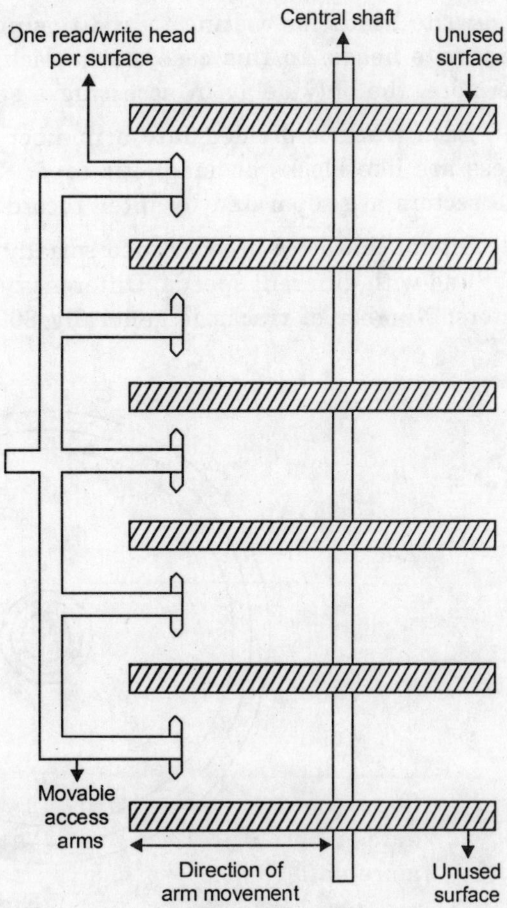


**Fig. 8.13:** A movable head disk.

be inserted or removed from the hard disk drive. A disk drive is a device that writes information on recording platters that resemble gramophone records. Disk drive reads information written on to the disk. In order to increase the storage capacity a large number of disks or platters are grouped together and are mounted on a common drive to form a disk pack. A term cylinder is usually used in case of a disk pack. A disk pack generally contains 6 platters. One platter has two recording surfaces one above and the other below it. No data is recorded on the topmost and the bottommost surfaces.

Hard disks are quite sensitive devices. The read/write head does not actually touch the disk but rather rides on a cushion of air about 0.000001 inch thick. The disk is sealed from impurities within a container, and the whole apparatus is manufactured under sterile conditions. Otherwise, all it would take is a human hair a finger print smudge, a dust particle, or a smoke particle to cause what is called head crash. A *head crash happens when the surface of the read/write head or particles on its surface come into contact with the surface of the hard-disk platter, causing the loss of some or all the data on the disk.* A head crash can also happen when you bump a computer too hard or drop something heavy on the system cabinet. So, always take up backup of data.

Each surface has concentric circles dividing the disk into tracks. Disk drives have read/write heads for writing to and reading from the disks. Some disk drives have fixed read/write heads. In this case, each track has a read/write head associated with it and therefore, the only delay in accessing a specific record is the *rotational delay.*

Each track is divided into a number of fixed length physical blocks called *sectors.* These are like blocks on magnetic tape. *Sector is the smallest unit of data for transfer.* The sectors are separated by inter record gaps.

Bits of character are recorded serially in each sector. Disks are available in different sizes and with different speeds. Different type of disks have different number of tracks and sectors. Number of tracks is generally 800 and number of sectors per track is 64.

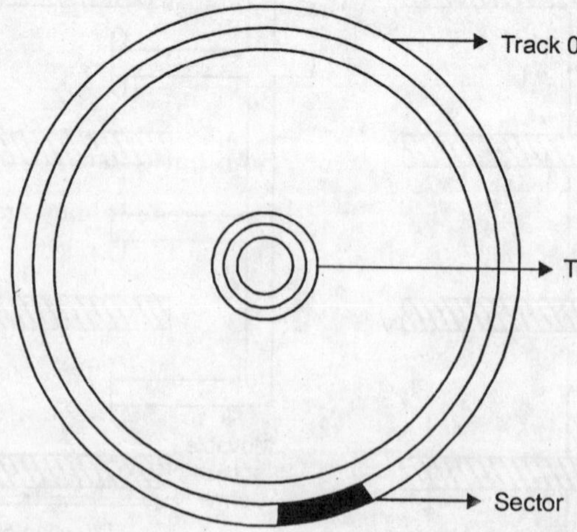


**Fig. 8.14**

Movable head disk drives have single read/write head per recording surface. The arm having read/write head moves on the recording surface so that it can be positioned on any track for reading or writing. All the read/write heads move together and therefore, all the read/write heads are positioned on the tracks on surfaces in the same plane. The same number of the track on each of the surfaces together are said to form a **cylinder.**

Microcomputer hard drives with capacities measured in tens of gigabytes—upto 40 gigabytes, according to current ads—are becoming essential because today's programs are so huge. Microsoft Office alone is 500 megabytes. These allow faster access to data than floppy disks do, because a hard disk spins many times faster. Computer ads frequently specify speeds in revolutions per minute. A floppy disk drive rotates at only 360 rpm; a 7200-rpm hard drive is going about 300 miles per hour.

**Access Time:** The access time of a record on a disk consists of 3 factors viz. Seek Time, Latency Time and Data Transfer Time.

**Seek Time:** It refers to the time taken to position the read/write head at the desired track on the disk.

**Latency Time:** It refers to the time taken to position the read/write head at the desired sector of the track. Latency time depends on the speed of rotation of the disk.

**Data Transfer Time:** It is the actual time required to transfer the data. The data transfer time depends upon density of stored data and rotational speed of the disk.

## 8.16 FLOPPY DISK VS. HARD DISK

The differences between a floppy disk and a hard disk is given in Table 8.4

**Table 8.4: Differences between Floppy Disk and Hard Disk**

| *Floppy Disk* | *Hard Disk* |
|---|---|
| Floppy disks are also known as floppies or microdisks. | Hard disks are also known as fixed disks. |
| The computer takes more time to read from a floppy disk. | The computer takes less time to read from hard disk. |
| More prone to damage by heat, dust and improper handling as it is made of a flexible material. | Less prone to damage as it is within the system unit. |
| Can be used to store 1.44 MB of data. | Can be used to store far more data than floppy disks. They can be used to store data in the range a few GBs. |
| It is cheap. | It is costly. |

### *For Magnetic Disk Numerical Problems*

Storage capacity of one surface = No. of tracks × no. of sectors × bytes per sector

Storage capacity of the disk pace = Storage capacity of one surface × no. of surfaces

Number of cylinders = No. of tracks per surface

Transfer rate = No. of bytes per track × rotational speed

**Example 1.** *A 6 disk pack has 600 tracks per surface. There are 10 sectors per track and 512 bytes per sector.*

(i) *What is the storage capacity of the disk pack?*

(ii) *How many cylinders does the disk pack have?*

(iii) *How many tracks are there per cylinder?*

**Solution.** (i) Storage capacity of one surface

= No. of tracks × No. of sectors × bytes stored per sector

= 600 × 10 × 512

= 3072000 bytes

Storage capacity of the disk pack

= Storage capacity of one surface × no. of surfaces

= (3072000 × 10) bytes

(∵ upper and lower surfaces are not used)

= (30720000) bytes

$$= \frac{30720000}{1024 \times 1024} \text{Mb}$$

= 29.29 Mb ≃ 30 Mb

(ii) No. of cylinders = No. of tracks on each disk

= 600

(iii) No. of tracks per cylinder = No. of usable surfaces on the disk = 10

**Example 2.** *A fixed head disk unit divides each track into 40 sectors. Each sector stores 1024 bytes. There are 20 cylinders with 10 tracks per cylinder. The disk pack rotates at the rate of 1000 revolutions per minute. Calculate:*

(i) *The data transfer rate of the disk unit*

(ii) *The storage capacity of the disk pack.*

**Solution.**

Here, No. of cylinders = 20

No. of tracks per cylinder = 10

No. of sectors per track = 40

No. of bytes per sector = 1024

(i) No. of bytes stored per track = No. of sectors × No. of bytes per sector

= 40 × 1024 bytes

= 40960 bytes

Rotation speed = 1000 revolutions per minute

$$= \frac{1000}{60} \text{ revolutions per second}$$

$$= \frac{50}{3} \text{ revolutions per second}$$

Transfer rate = No. of bytes per track × rotational speed

$$= 40960 \times \frac{50}{3} \text{ bytes per second}$$

$$= \frac{2048000}{3} \text{ bytes per second}$$

$$= \frac{2048000}{3 \times 1024} \text{ kb/second} = 666.66 \text{ kb/second}$$

(*ii*) Total capacity of the disk pack = Number of usable surfaces × number of tracks × number of sectors × number of bytes per sector

= 10 × 20 × 40 × 1024 bytes

= 8192000 bytes ≃ 8 Mb

(∴ Number of usable surfaces = Number of tracks per cylinder and Number of tracks on each disk = Number of cylinders)

## 8.17 OPTICAL DISK AND ITS TYPES

Everyone who has ever played an audio CD is familiar with optical disks. *An optical disk is a removable disk, usually 4.75 inches in diameter and less than one-twentieth of an inch thick, on which data is written and read through the use of laser beams.* An audio CD holds upto 74 minutes of high-fidelity stereo sound. Some optical disks are used strictly for digital data storage, but many are used to distribute multimedia programs that combine text, visuals and sound.

Optical disk storage system consists of a rotating disk which is coated with a thin metal or other material that is highly reflective. Optical storage techniques make use of pinpoint precision which is possible with laser beams. A laser uses a concentrated and narrow beam of light. Hence, a laser beam is used to write information to or read information from an optical disk.

Optical storage devices focus a laser beam on the recording medium, which is a spinning disk. Some areas of the disk reflect the laser light into sensor, whereas others scatter the light. As the disk rotates past the laser and the sensor, a spot that reflects the laser beam into the sensor is interpreted as binary one, and the absence of reflection is interpreted as binary zero.

The storage density of optical disks is enormous, the storage cost is extremely low and the access time is relatively fast. An optical disk can hold over 4.7 gigabytes of data, the equivalent of 1 million typewritten pages. A typical shortcoming of optical storage devices is that they are permanent storage devices. Data once recorded cannot be erased and hence the disk cannot be reused. Extensive research is being carried out to develop erasable optical disks. The types of optical disks are:

(*i*) CD-ROM—Compact Disk Read Only Memory

(*ii*) CD-R (Compact Disk Recordable)

(*iii*) CD-RW (Compact Disk Rewritable)

(*iv*) DVD-ROM (Digital Versatile or Digital Video Disk, with Read Only Memory)

(*i*) **CD-ROM.** For PC users, the best known type of optical disk is the CD-ROM. CD-ROM (Compact Disk Read Only Memory) is an optical-disk format that is used to hold pre-recorded text, graphics and sound. The disk's content is recorded at the time of manufacture and cannot be written on or erased by the user. CD-ROM uses the same technology that is used in music CDs. The disk is made of a resin, such as polycarbonate and is coated with a material that is highly reflective, usually aluminium. Data is recorded by focussing a laser beam on the surface of the disk. The laser beam is turned on and off at a varying rate because of which tiny holes (or pits) are produced on the metal coating. In order to read the stored data, a less powerful laser beam is focussed on the disk surface. This beam is strongly reflected by the coated surface and weakly reflected by the pits, thereby producing patterns of on-off reflections that can be converted into electronic signals.

CD-ROMs do not use concentric circles. Rather they use simple spiral tracks. The capacity of CD-ROM is 650 MB, equal to over 300,000 pages of text.

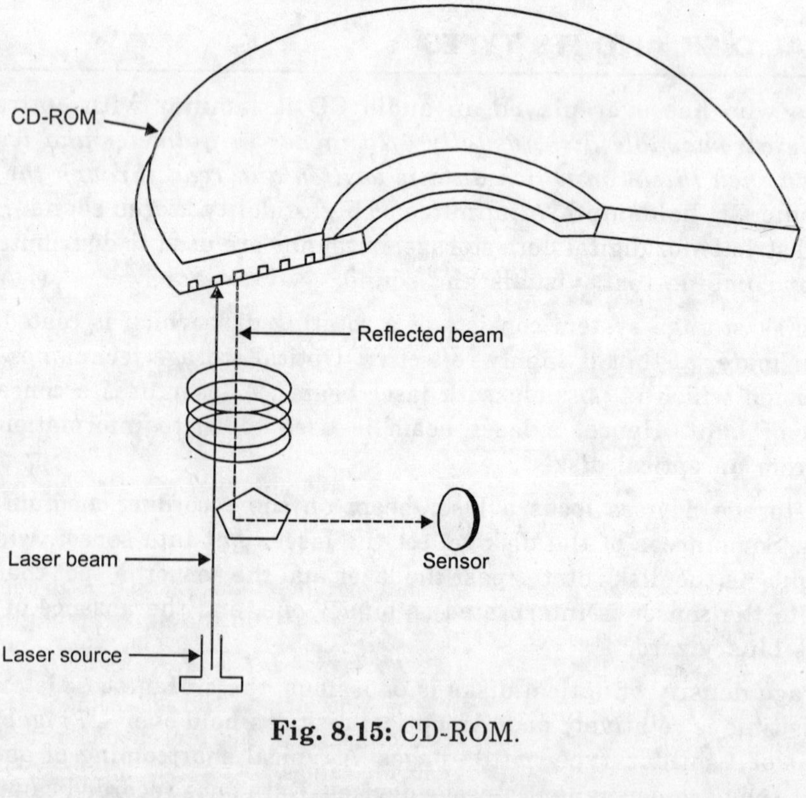


**Fig. 8.15:** CD-ROM.

(*ii*) **CD-R (Compact Disk Recordable).** *CD-R can be written to only once but can be read many times.* This allows users to make their own CD disks, though it is a slow process. (Recording a complete disk takes 20–60 minutes). The information recorded once cannot be erased. CD-R disks are most commonly used for archival applications. Its advantage is high capacity, better reliability and longer life.

(*iii*) **CD-RW (Compact Disk Rewritable).** *A CD-RW disk, also known as an erasable optical disk, allows users to record and erase data, so that the disk can be used over and over again.* Special CD-RW drives and software are needed. CD-RW disks are useful for archiving and backing up large amount of data or work in multimedia production or desktop publishing. CD-RW disks cannot be read by CD-ROM drives.

(*iv*) **DVD-ROM.** A DVD-ROM (**Digital Versatile Disk or Digital Video Disk, with Read Only Memory**) *is a CD-style disk with extremely high capacity, able to store 4.7–17 gigabytes.* The surface of a DVD contains microscopic pits, which represent the 0s and 1s of digital code than can be read by a laser.

The DVD drives can also take standard CD-ROM disks, so a user can watch DVD movies and play CD-ROMs using these. DVDs have enormous potential to replace CDs for archival storage, mass distribution of software and entertainment. DVDs not only store far more data but are different in quality from CDs. The variants of DVDs are:

| | |
|---|---|
| DVD-R | (DVD-Recordable)—Permits one-time recording by the user. |
| DVD-RW | (DVD-Rewritable) |
| DVD – RAM | (DVD – Random Access Memory) |
| DVD + RW | (DVD + Rewritable) |

All of these three types are reusable, that is these can be recorded on and erased many times.

## .18 HARD DISK VS. CD-ROM

The differences between a hard disk and a CD-ROM are given below:

**Table 8.5: Differences between a Hard Disk and a CD-ROM**

| *Hard Disk* | *CD-ROM* |
|---|---|
| Hard disks are also known as fixed disks. | CD-ROMs are also known as optical disks. |
| Data is stored in the form of concentric circles. | Data is stored in the form of a single spiral track. |
| The computer takes less time to read from hard disk. It is in the range of 10 to 30 milliseconds. | The computer takes more time to read from CD-ROM. It is in the range of 100 to 300 milliseconds. |
| Data can be read or written as and when required. These can be reused. | It is a permanent storage medium. Data once recorded, cannot be erased and hence, the CD-ROMs cannot be reused. |

| | |
|---|---|
| Hard disks are not portable. | CD-ROMs are portable. |
| Hard disks require a less complicated drive mechanism. | CD-ROMs require a more complicated drive mechanism. |
| Hard disks have a very large storage capacity (Disk packs have virtually unlimited storage capacity). | It has a storage capacity of about 650 Megabytes. |
| It is costly. | It is cheap. |
| Not a better storage medium for data archiving as compared to CD-ROMs. | CD-ROMs have a data storage life in excess of 30 years. These are a better storage medium for data archiving as compared to Hard disks. |

## 8.19 MAGNETIC TAPE

Magnetic tape is a secondary storage device which can hold large volumes of data on it. The tape is a sequential access media and data on it can be accessed sequentially Large files are stored on them. It is one of the most popular storage media because of lower cost.

The Magnetic tape is made up of thin plastic ribbon coated on one side with ferromagnetic material. It is 1/2 inch in width and over 2500 ft. long. The coated side of the tape is usually divided into nine horizontal rows called tracks. Along the width of the tracks every character is stored with one bit in each track. The eight bits of EBCDIC or ASCII code of the character occupy 8 tracks while the ninth track is used as parity bit.

The density of recording on a tape is the number of characters per inch on the tape Typical tape densities are 800 bpi (bytes per inch), 1600 bpi and 6250 bpi. Records are written one after the other on the tape. The processing program reads one record at a time into the primary memory for the data to be processed. During the time this record is being processed the tape drive stops. It will be moving the tape under the magnetic read/write head when the next record is to be read. So between reading two consecutive records the tape drive stops and starts again. During the time that the drive deaccelerates to stop and accelerates again to a constant speed at which data from the tape is read a certain length of tape is empty. This empty portion of tape which occurs between every two records is called **Inter Record Gap** (IRG).

| | | |
|---|---|---|
| Track 1 | 1 | |
| Track 2 | 1 | |
| Track 3 | 0 | |
| Track 4 | 0 | |
| Track 5 | 1 | |
| Track 6 | 0 | |
| Track 7 | 1 | |
| Track 8 | 0 | |
| Track 9 (Parity Bit) | 0 | |

**Fig. 8.16:** Structure of a nine track tape.

The IRGs are a wastage of storage space of the tape and cause slowing down of the program execution. Hence, a number of records are grouped together into a block and one block is transferred at a time into the buffer area in the computers primary memory. The individual records are read one by one by the program from this buffer memory for processing. The tape drive has to stop and start between reading of blocks. Once again gaps called *Inter Block Gaps* (IBGs) are generated between blocks of data. Since the IBG occur less frequently than the IRGs the empty space in the tape is reduced.

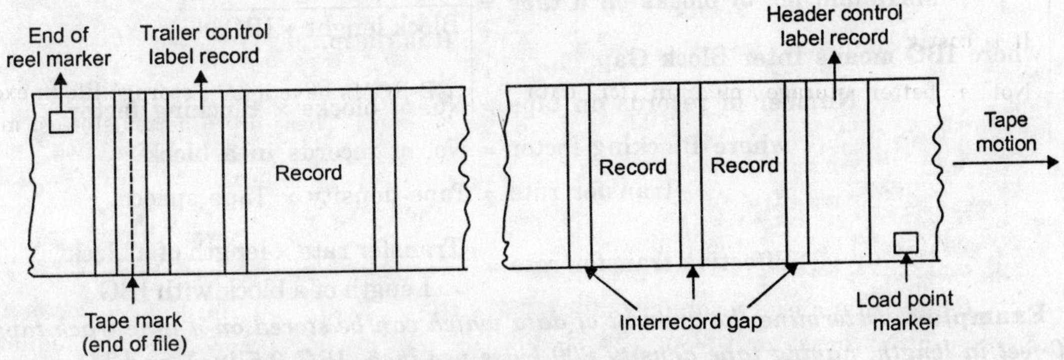


**Fig. 8.17:** Magnetic tape markers and labels.

The initial and final few feet of the magnetic tape are used for winding on a reel and hence can not be used. The beginning and end of the usable part of the tape are marked by markers called "Load Point" and "End of Reel" markers. The first record after load point is known as the Header Control Label. This record gives information about the contents of the tape. Several sequential files may be stored in the tape. Each file has its own header and trailer markers to identify the beginning and end of each file.

The rate at which data is transferred between the tape and the CPU depends on the tape drive speed and the density of recording. The actual rate will, however, be lower than the value due to presence of IBGs and the start/stop time lost.

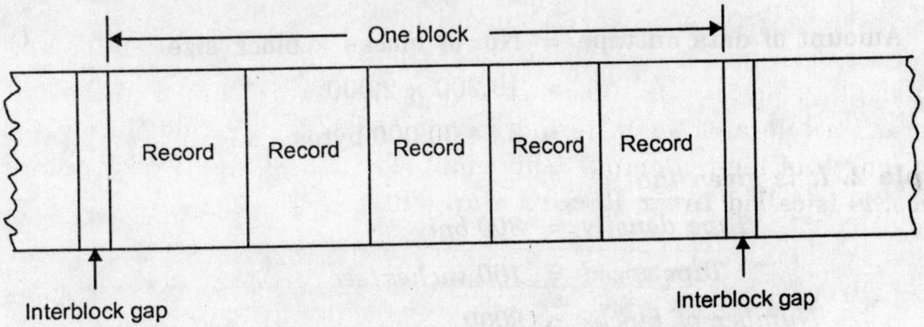


**Fig. 8.18:** Multiple record block.

Today, "map tape" is used mainly for backup and archiving—that is, for maintaining historical records—where there is no need for quick access.

On large computers, tapes are used on magnetic—tape units or reels, and in catridges. On PCs, tape is used in the form of *tape catridges, modules resembling audio cassettes that contain tape in rectangular, plastic housings.* There are three common types of drive tapes—QIC, DAT, and (most expensive) DLT. A tape cassette can hold up to 66 gigabytes, so tape is looking like a better alternative than zip disks.

**For Magnetic Tape Numericals:**

$$\text{Length of a block} = \frac{\text{Block size}}{\text{Tape density}}$$

$$\text{Maximum no. of blocks on a tape} = \frac{\text{Tape length}}{\text{Block lenght + IBG}}$$

where IBG means Inter Block Gap.

$$\text{Number of records on tape} = \text{No. of blocks} \times \text{Blocking factor}$$

$$\text{where Blocking factor} = \text{No. of records in a block}$$

$$\text{Transfer rate} = \text{Tape density} \times \text{Tape speed}$$

$$\text{Effective transfer rate} = \frac{\text{Transfer rate} \times \text{length of a block}}{\text{Length of a block with IBG}}$$

**Example 1.** *Determine the amount of data which can be stored on a nine track tape, 4800 feet in length, having tape density 800 bytes per inch, IBG 0.5 inch and block size-2000 bytes.*

**Solution.** Total length of tape = 4800 × 12 = 57,600 inches (1 ft = 12 inch)

$$\text{Length of a block} = \frac{\text{Block size}}{\text{Tape density}} = \frac{2000}{800} = 2.5 \text{ inch}$$

Actual length of a blocks (Block size + IBG) = 2.5 + 0.5 = 3 inch

$$\text{No. of blocks on the tape} = \frac{\text{Tape length}}{\text{Block length + IBG}}$$

$$= \frac{4800 \times 12}{3} = 19{,}200$$

$$\text{Amount of data on tape} = \text{No. of blocks} \times \text{block size}$$

$$= 19{,}200 \times 2{,}000$$

$$= 3{,}84{,}00{,}000 \text{ bytes}$$

**Example 2.** *It is given that*

*Tape density* = *800 bpi*

*Tape speed* = *100 inches/sec*

*Number of blocks* = *8000*

*Blocking factor* = *5 each of 30 characters*

*Size of an IBG* = *0.5 inch*

*Then calculate the transfer rate, total start/stop time, total time to read all the records and effective transfer rate.*

**Solution.** Transfer rate = Tape density × Tape speed

= 800 × 100 = 80,000 bytes per second

No. of characters in 1 block = Record size × blocking factor

= 30 × 5 = 150 characters

Total no. of characters in 800 blocks = 8000 × 150 = 12,00,000 characters

Number of IBG = No. of blocks = 8,000

$$\text{Time to pass one IBG} = \frac{\text{Size of IBG}}{\text{Tape speed}} = \frac{0.5}{100} = 0.005 \text{ seconds.}$$

Total start/stop time = No. of IBG × time to pass one IBG

= 800 × 0.005 = 40 seconds

$$\text{Total time for reading} = \frac{\text{No. of characters in all blocks}}{\text{Transfer rate}}$$

$$= \frac{120{,}0000}{80{,}000} = 15 \text{ seconds}$$

Total time taken to read all the records

= Time taken to read all blocks + time taken to pass IBG's

= 15 + 40 = 55 seconds

$$\text{Effective transfer rate} = \frac{\text{Tape capacity}}{\text{Total time taken to read all records}}$$

$$= \frac{1200{,}000}{80{,}000} \simeq 21{,}818 \text{ bps}$$

**Example 3.** *A magnetic tape has packing density of 800 bpi and tape transport speed equivalent to 100 inch/sec. If the size of one block is 2400 bytes and length of one IBG = 0.5 inch. Calculate the transfer rate and the effective transfer rate.*

**Solution.** Here, Packing density = 800 bpi

Tape transport speed = 100 inch/sec

Size of one block = 2400 bytes

Length of IBG = 0.5 inch

∴ Transfer rate = Packing density × Tape speed

= 800 × 100 bytes per second

= 80,000 bytes per second

$$= \frac{80{,}000}{1024} = 78.12 \text{ k bytes per second.}$$

$$\text{Length of a block} = \frac{\text{Size of one block}}{\text{Packng density}}$$

$$= \frac{2400}{800} \text{ inch} = 3 \text{ inch}$$

Length of IBG = 0.5 inch

$$\text{Length of one block with IBG} = (3.0 + 0.5) \text{ inch}$$
$$= 3.5 \text{ inch}$$

$$\therefore \quad \text{Effective transfer rate} = \frac{\text{Transfer rate} \times \text{Length of a block}}{\text{Length of a block with IBG}}$$
$$= \frac{78.12 \times 3}{3.5} = 66.96 \text{ k bytes/second}$$

**Example 4.** *A master file is stored on a magnetic tape at a recording density of 1600 bpi. The file contains 1.2 million records of 450 characters each. The blocking factor is 75 and the length of an IBG is 0.5 inch. Calculate the number of reels needed to store the file. What will happen if the recording density is changed to 6250 bpi.*

**Solution.** Here,

$$\text{Packing density} = 1600 \text{ bpi}$$
$$\text{No. of records} = 1.2 \text{ million} = 12{,}00{,}000$$
$$\text{No. of characters per second} = 450$$
$$\text{Length of an IBG} = 0.5 \text{ inch}$$
$$\text{Blocking factor} = 75$$

$$\therefore \quad \text{Total no. blocks in the file} = \frac{\text{Number of records}}{\text{Blocking factor}}$$
$$= \frac{12{,}00{,}000}{75}$$
$$= 16{,}000$$

$$\text{No. of characters in one block} = \text{No. of characters per record} \times \text{blocking factor}$$
$$= 450 \times 75$$

$$\therefore \quad \text{Length of one block} = \frac{\text{No. of characters in one block}}{\text{Packing density}}$$
$$= \frac{450 \times 75}{1600} = \frac{675}{32} \text{ inch}$$

$$\text{Length of an IBG} = 0.5 \text{ inch}$$

$$\therefore \quad \text{Effective lenght of a block with IBG} = \left(\frac{675}{32} + 0.5\right) \text{ inch}$$
$$= \frac{691}{32} \text{ inch}$$

$$\text{Hence the lenght occupied by 16,000 blocks} = \left(\frac{691}{32} \times 16000\right) \text{ inch}$$
$$= 345500 \text{ inch}$$
$$= \frac{345500}{12}$$
$$\simeq 28792 \text{ feet}$$

Also, common length of a reel = 2400 feed

$$\therefore \quad \text{The no. of reels required} = \frac{28792}{2400} \simeq 12$$

Now, when the recording density is changed from 1600 to 6250

$$\text{Length occupied by 16,000 blacks} = \left(\frac{450 \times 75}{6250} + 0.5\right) \times 16{,}000$$

$$= 97{,}404 \text{ inch}$$

$$= \frac{97404}{12} \text{ feet}$$

$$= 8117 \text{ feet}$$

$$\text{Hence, the number of reels required} = \frac{8117}{2400} \simeq 3.4$$

As the reel number cannot be a fractional number, so the actual number of reels required will be 4.

## 8.20 SMART CARDS

Today all over the world, most credit cards are old-fashioned magnetic-strip cards. A magnetic-strip card has a strip of magnetically encoded data on its back. The encoded data might have your name, account number, and PIN (Personal Identification Number). Two other kind of cards, smart cards and optical cards, which hold for more information will soon be popular all over the world.

**Smart Cards:** *A smart card looks like a credit card but contains a microprocessor embedded in the card. Intelligent smart cards* have, in addition to the embedded processor, input, output, and storage capabilities. **Memory cards** have only storage capabilities in addition to the processor. When inserted into a card reader, it transfers data to and from a central computer, and it can store some basic financial records. These cards can be used as telephone debit cards. You insert the card into a slot in the phone, wait for a tone, and dial the number. The duration of your call is automatically calculated on the chip inside the card, and the corresponding charge is deducted from the balance. Many institutions issue student cards as smart cards.

**Optical Cards:** The conventional magnetic-strip credit card holds the equivalent of a half page of data. The smart card with a microprocessor and memory chip holds the equivalent of 250 pages. The optical card presently holds nearly 2000 pages of data. Optical cards use the same type of technology as music compact disks but look like silvery credit cards. *Optical cards are plastic, laser recordable, wallet-type cards used with an optical-card reader.* Because they can cram so much data (6.6 megabytes, as compared to 16 kilobytes for smart cards) into so little space, they may become popular in the future.

## 8.21 FLASH MEMORY

**Flash Memory.** It is used to store flexible programs. Flash memories are RAMs. Also a non-volatile form of memory, *flash memory chips* can be erased an reprogrammed more than once (unlike PROM chips, which can be programmed only once). Flash memory, which does not need a battery and which can range from 1 to 64 megabytes in capacity, is used to store programs not only in personal computers (PCs) but also in pagers, cellphones, MP3 players, Palm organizers, printers, and digital cameras. Flash memory is more expensive than hard disk storage. The capacity is rapidly increasing. The read time of flash memories is tens of nano seconds whereas write time is several micro seconds. They are compact and are made in several shapes such as pens (a few centimeters long) and flat disks (2.5 $cm^2$). Their price per byte is rapidly reducing (a few paise per byte). However, many experts believe that flash memory—a type of **solid state technology**—will eventually replace disk and tape storage and plug into PCs Universal Serial Bus (USB) ports.

## 8.22 FLASH MEMORY CARDS

Disk drives, whether for floppy disks (diskettes), hard disks, or CD-ROMs, all involve moving parts—and moving parts can break. Flash memory cards by contrast, are variations on conventional computer–memory chips, which have no moving parts. *Flash memory cards, or flash RAM cards, consist of circuitry on credit-card-size PC cards that can be inserted into slots connecting to the motherboard.* The Memory Stick from Sony and the Secure Digital (SD) card from Panasonic presently hold upto 64 megabytes and are projected to expand to 1 gigabyte of memory. The Memory stick and SD cards are interoperable between a wide range of computer and electronic devices.

Flash memory cards are not infallible. Their circuits wear out after repeated use, limiting their lifespan. Still, unlike conventional computer memory (RAM or primary storage), flash memory is **nonvolatile.** That is, it retains data even when the power is turned off.

## 8.23 COMPARATIVE CHARACTERISTICS OF SECONDARY MEMORIES

So far we have discussed a number of secondary storage devices to store data in computers. In Table 8.6 we have summarized the average capacity of the devices, the access times of each and the relative cost per byte of storage of each.

**Table 8.6: Comparative Characteristics of Secondary Memories**

| *Memory Types* | *Average Capacity in Bytes* | *Technology Used* | *Average Time to Access a Byte* | *Use in a Computer System* | *Relative Cost per Byte in Units* |
|---|---|---|---|---|---|
| Disk memory (Hard disk) | 100 G | Magnetic surfaces on hard disks | 8 msec | Large data and program files which need fast access | 1 |
| Flash memory EEPROM | 256 M | IC (Integrated Circuit) | 1 μsec | Data entry. As input unit. Data and program files in PCs and laptops | 1/10 |

| | | | | | |
|---|---|---|---|---|---|
| Ultrium (for Magnetic tape) | 200 G | Long ½" tape wound on catridge | NA | Historical files. Back up for disk. Data and program exchange between installations | 1/100 |
| CD-R and CD-RW | 650 M | Laser disk | 500 msec | Store large texts, picture and audio. Software distribution | 1/100 |
| DVDROM | 8 G | Laser disk | 500 msec | Video files | 1/1000 |

## 8.24 CACHE MEMORY AND VIRTUAL MEMORY

Pronounced "cash", *cache temporarility stores instructions and data that the processor is likely to use frequently. Thus, cache speeds up processing*. Cache memory uses special chips, often SRAM (static RAM) chips. On some systems, these chips are four times as fast as regular memory. However, the chips cost six times as much. It's this cost that keeps them from being used for the entire system's memory.

The technique used to access cache memory is very different from that of accessing the main memory. When the CPU accesses main memory, it outputs the data contained at the specified address. On the other hand the cache memory first compares the incoming address to the address stored in the cache. If the address matches, it is said that a **'hit'** has occurred. Then the corresponding data are read. If the address does not match it is said that a **'miss'** has occurred. In this case data is read from the main memory. The data read from main memory is also provided to cache memory so that when this specific address is accessed next time, a **hit** may occur.

Caches are sometimes described by their logical and electrical proximity to the microprocessor's core logic. The closed physically and electrically to the microprocessor's core logic is the *primary cache*, also called a *Level One Cache or L1. A secondary cache (or Level Two Cache i.e., L2)* lies between the primary cache and the main memory. The secondary cache or L2 is generally larger than the primary cache or L1 but it operates at a lower speed (to make its larger mass of memory more affordable).

The currently designed microprocessors have both the primary and secondary caches as part of the microprocessor itself. Earlier designs have the secondary cache in a separate part of a microprocessor module or in external memory.

L1 and L2 caches differ in the way they connect with the core logic of the microprocessor. L1 invariably operates at the full speed of the microprocessor's core logic with the widest possible bit-width connection between the core logic and the cache. L2 often operate at a rate slower than the chip's core logic, although all current chips operate the secondary cache at full core speed.

A major factor that determines how successful the cache will be is how much information it stores. The larger the cache, the more data that is in it and the more likely any required byte will be available there when your system needs it. Obviously, the best cache is one that's as large as, and duplicates, the entirety of system memory. Chip-makers try to design caches as large as possible within the constraints of fabricating microprocessors affordably.

These days primary caches (L1) are of size 64 or 128 KB. Secondary caches (L2) range from 128 to 512 KB for chips, for desktop and mobile applications and upto 2 MB for server-oriented microprocessors.

In addition, most current computer operating systems allow for the use of *virtual memory—that is, some free hard-disk space is used to extend the capacity of RAM.*

Virtual memory reduces the overall cost of the system because it's cheaper to store data on a hard disk drive than it is to add additional memory chips to the computer.

The processor searches for data or program instructions in the following order: first L1, then L2, then RAM, then hard disk (or CD-ROM). In this order, each kind of memory or storage is slower than its predecessor.

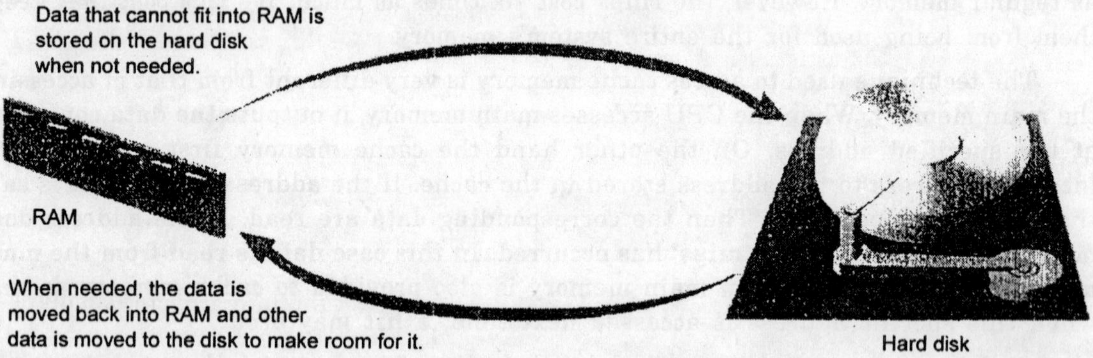


**Fig. 8.19:** Virtual memory.

## SUMMARY

- For a computer to work, it must contain memory where it can store data and programs until they are needed.
- The memory is equivalent to thousands of registers, each storing a binary word.
- The currently used popular binary cells are semiconductor ICs, magnetic surfaces on a disk or tape and bits/lands on a laser disk.
- Reading information from a memory must be non-destructive for the memory unit to be useful in a data processing system.
- RAM (Random Access Memory) temporarily stores program instructions and data. It is volatile as the contents are lost when the power goes off or is turned off.
- Four types of RAM chips used in PCs are DRAM, SDRAM, SRAM and RDRAM.
- ROM (Read Only Memory) stores fixed start-up instructions. It is non-volatile as the contents are not lost when power to the computer is turned off.

- Various types of ROMs are: ROM, PROM, EPROM and EEPROM.
- Storage of data on computer has its own advantages over manual storage.
- Secondary storage hardware devices permanently hold data and information as well as programs.
- The commonly used secondary-storage devices are : floppy disks, hard disks, optical disks, magnetic tape, smart cards and flash memory cards.
- Floppy disk is a small, flexible and easily removable storage device.
- On the diskette (floppy disk) data is recorded in concentric circles called **tracks,** which are further divided into **sectors,** invisible wedge-shaped sections, used for storage reference purposes.
- The read/write head is used to transfer data between the computer and the disk.
- Floppy-disk cartridges or higher-capacity removable disks are Zip disks, SuperDisks, and HiFD disks.
- Hard disks are thin but rigid metal platters covered with a substance that allows data to be held in the form of magnetized spots.
- A head crash happens when the surface of the read/write head or particles on its surface come into contact with the surface of the hard-disk platter, causing the loss of some or all of the data on the disk.
- There are two types of hard disks—nonremovalbe and removable.
- A nonremovable hard disk, also known as fixed disk, is housed in a microcomputer system unit and is used to store nearly all programs and most data files.
- Removable hard disks, or hard-disk catridges, consist of one or two platters enclosed with read/write heads in a hard plastic case, which is inserted into a microcomputer's catridge drive.
- An optical disk (CDs and DVDs) is a removable disk, usually 4.75 inches in diameter and less than one–twentieth of on inch thick, on which data is written and read through the use of laser beams.
- CD-ROM (Compact Disk Read Only Memory) is an optical-disk format that is used to hold pre-recorded text, graphics and sound.
- CD-R (Compact Disk-Recordable) disks can be written to only once but can be read many times.
- A CD-RW (Compact Disk-ReWritable) disk, also known as an erasable optical disk, allows users to record and erase data so that the disk can be used over and over again.
- DVD-ROM (Digital Versatile Disk or Digital Video Disk with Read Only Memory) is a CD-style disk with extremely high capacity, able to store 4.7–17 gigabytes.
- DVD-R (DVD-Recordable) disks allow one time recording by the consumer.
- Magnetic tape is thin plastic tape coated with a substance that can be magnetized. Data is represented by magnetized spots (representing 1s) or non-magnetized spots (representing 0s).
- Tape cartridges modules resemble audio cessettes that contain tape in rectangular, plastic housings.
- A smart card looks like a credit card but contains a microprocessor embedded in the card.

- Optical cards are plastic, laser-recordable, wallet-type cards used with an optical-card reader.
- Flash memory cards, consists of circuitry on credit-card-size PC cards that can be inserted into slots connecting to the motherboard.
- Cache temporarily stores instructions and data that the processor is likely to use frequently. Thus, cache speeds up processing. These are two kinds of cache—Level 1 (L1) and Level 2 (L2).
- Virtual memory, *i.e.*, some free hard-disk space is used to extend the capacity of RAM.

## REVIEW QUESTIONS AND EXERCISES

1. What is memory?
2. What are the desirable characteristics in order that a physical device can be used as a binary storage cell in a memory unit?
3. Write a short note on memory parameters.
4. Explain the following:
   (*i*) Non-destructive read out (*ii*) Access time
   (*iii*) Write time (*iv*) Memory cycle time
5. A computer memory has 8 M words with 32 bits per word. How many bits are needed in MAR if all words are to be addressed? How many bits are needed for MBR? How many binary storage cells are needed?
6. Characterize memories on the basis of their location inside the computer.
7. Give the various characteristics of memories.
8. What are different types of memory? Explain.
9. Write short notes on the following:
   (*i*) RAM (*ii*) ROM
   (*iii*) Buffer (*iv*) Cache memory
   (*v*) Flash memory
10. Write short note on 2D organisation and 2½ D organisation of semiconductor memory.
11. What are different types of RAM and ROM? Explain.
12. What is the difference between RAM and ROM?
13. Give some applications of ROMs.
14. What do you understand by external storage devices? Give examples.
15. Compare floppy disk with a hard disk.
16. What are the differences between a hard disk and a CD-ROM?
17. What is the difference between Primary memory and Secondary memory?
18. Briefly explain the features of hard disk with a neat diagram.
19. A tape drive has a transfer rate of 75,000 bytes/sec and a start/stop time at each IBG of 10 ms. How long will it take to read 15,000 records if each record is 50 characters in length and the blocking factor is 10.

20. A file containing 115,000 records will be stored on a magnetic tape at recording density of 6,250 bpi. The size of each fixed length record is 340 bytes. The IBG is 0.3″.
    (*i*) How much space is needed to store the entire file if it is unblocked? What percentage of a 2400 ft. reel of magnetic tape is occupied by the file?
    (*ii*) If the file is stored using a blocking factor of 60, what length of the tape will be needed to store the entire file?
21. Write short notes on the following:
    (*i*) Magnetic tape
    (*ii*) Floppy disk
    (*iii*) Magnetic disk
    (*iv*) Optical disk
    (*v*) Smart cards and optical cards
    (*vi*) Flash memory cards
22. What is virtual memory? Explain.
23. What is the difference between access time and cycle time of a memory? Which is lager?
24. Is DRAM or SRAM more expensive per bit of storage? Justify your answer.
25. What are the features of floppy disks, hard disks, optical disks, magnetic tape, and smart cards?
26. What would you use a zip disk for?
27. How does L1 cache differ from L2 cache?
28. State True or False:
    (*i*) For a computer to work, it must contain memory where it can store data and programs until they are needed.
    (*ii*) The main memory is also known as secondary memory.
    (*iii*) A binary storage cell must have one stable state.
    (*iv*) Words to be written are first entered in a register called the memory buffer register.
    (*v*) Main memory is nonvolatile.
    (*vi*) ROM chips contain fixed start-up instructions.
    (*vii*) RAM is the working memory of the computer.
    (*viii*) ROM chip can be written on or erased by the computer user without special equipment.
    (*ix*) Magnetic tape is the most common secondary storage medium used with microcomputers.
    (*x*) Unlike conventional credit cards, smart cards can hold a fair amount of data and can store some basic financial records.
    (*xi*) Secondary storage devices temporarily store data and information as well as programs.
    (*xii*) Because head crashes are always a possibility, users should always back up data from their hard disks on another storage medium, such as floppy disks.
29. Fill in the blanks:
    (*i*) Besides the large number of storage cells, a memory has a .................. number of registers to facilitate storage and retrieval of data from memory and a set of control signals.
    (*ii*) The data stored in a cell should not .................. with the passage of time.

(*iii*) MAR stands for .................. .

(*iv*) The time required for the combined read and write operations is known as the ...............

(*v*) Memory can be broadly classified into two categories namely semiconductor memory and .................. memory, depending upon the technology and material used for making storage devices.

(*vi*) .................. is used to hold data and instructions that will be used shortly by the CPU.

(*vii*) .................. are a portion of the main memory which the Input/Output devices can access directly.

(*viii*) The most obvious use of ROM is as .................. converter.

(*ix*) The process of retrieving data from a storage device is referred to as .................. ; the process of copying data to a storage device is called .................. .

(*x*) To avoid losing data, users should always .................. their files.

(*xi*) Formatted diskettes have .................. and .................. that the system software uses to reference data locations.

(*xii*) Part of the disk drive mechanism, the .................., transfers data between the computer and the disk.

## ANSWERS

5. 23, 32, $2^{28}$

19. 25 sec

20. (*i*) 21.72% (*ii*) 569.25 ft

28. State True or False:

| | |
|---|---|
| (*i*) True | (*ii*) False |
| (*iii*) False | (*iv*) True |
| (*v*) False | (*vi*) True |
| (*vii*) True | (*viii*) False |
| (*ix*) False | (*x*) True |
| (*xi*) False | (*xii*) True |

29. Fill in the blanks:

| | |
|---|---|
| (*i*) small | (*ii*) decay |
| (*iii*) memory address register | (*iv*) memory cycle time |
| (*v*) magnetic | (*vi*) RAM |
| (*vii*) Buffers | (*viii*) code |
| (*ix*) read, write | (*x*) backup |
| (*xi*) tracks, sectors | (*xii*) read/write head |

Chapter 9

# MICROPROCESSOR AND CPU DESIGN

## 9.1 INTRODUCTION

The microprocessor has presented us with gifts that we may only barely appreciate—*portability* and *mobility* in electronic devices. Let us start with some important developments during the last century and few basic concepts about CPU, Control memory and Microprogram sequencer:

**Vacuum Tubes:** Old-time radios used vacuum tubes—small light bulb—size electronic tubes with glowing filaments. The ENIAC used 18,000 of them, occupying 1,500 square feet and weighing 30 tons.

**Transistor:** A transistor is essentially a tiny electrically operated switch, or gate, that can alternate between "on" and "off" many millions of times per second. The first transistors were one-hundredth the size of a vacuum tube, needed no warmup time, consumed less energy and were faster and more reliable. Moreover, they marked the beginning of a process of miniaturization that has not ended yet. Today more than 3 million transistors can be squeezed into a half centimetre.

**Integrated Circuit:** It is an entire electronic circuit, including wires, formed on a single "chip" or piece of special material, usually silicon. An integrated circuit embodies what is known *solid-state technology*. Solid state means that the electrons are travelling through solid material—in this case, silicon. Silicon is an element that is widely found in clay and sand. It is cheaper and also a semiconductor.

**Semiconductor:** It is a material whose electrical properties are intermediate between a good conductor of electricity and a non-conductor of electricity. An example of good conductor of electricity is copper in household wiring; an example of a non-conductor is the plastic sheath around that wiring.

**Chip:** A chip or microchip, is a tiny piece of silicon that contains millions of micro-miniature electronic components, mainly transistors.

**Microprocessor (μP):** Also known as "microscopic processor" or "processor on a chip" is the miniaturized circuitry of a computer processor—the part that processes or manipulates, data into information. When modified for use in machines other than computers, microprocessors are called *microcontrollers* or *embedded computers*.

## 9.2 CENTRAL PROCESSING UNIT

The Central Processing Unit (CPU) is the *brain* of a computer. Its primary function is to execute programs. The program which is to be executed is stored in the main memory. A program is a sequence of **instructions** to perform a specified task. The program to be executed must be fetched from the memory. The CPU **fetches** one instruction of the program from the memory at a time, decodes it and then **executes** it. After decoding the instruction the CPU comes to know what operation is to be performed. It also comes to know whether the data to be processed is in the memory or in a register of the CPU. If the data is in the register, it executes the instruction immediately. If the data is in the memory, the CPU reads the data from the memory. Then it executes the instruction. After executing one instruction it fetches the next instruction for its execution. This process is continued until all the instructions of the program are fetched and executed. The result is placed in the memory or sent to an output device according to the instruction given in the program.

Besides executing programs, the CPU also controls input devices, output devices and other components of the computer. It controls input and output devices to receive and send data. Under its control programs and data are stored in the memory and displayed on the CRT screen.

The CPU of a small computer is a microprocessor. The CPU of a large computer contains a number of microprocessors. Each microprocessor in a large central processing unit performs a specified task within the CPU.

**Control Memory:** A memory that is part of a control unit is called a **control memory.** It holds a fixed **microprogram** that cannot be altered by the occasional user. The **microprogram** consists of micro-instructions that specify various internal control signals for execution of register micro-instructions. Each machine instruction initiates a series of micro-instructions in control memory.

**Microprogram Sequencer:** The basic components of a microprogrammed control unit are the control memory and the circuits that select the next address. The address selection part is known as **microprogram sequencer.** A microprogram sequencer can be constructed with digital functions to suit a particular application. It's purpose is to present an address to the control memory so that a micro-instruction may be read and executed.

## 9.3 MICROPROCESSOR AND CPU ORGANISATION

An innovation that has significantly affected the design and implementation of CPUs came in the mid-1970s with the microprocessor. Since the introduction of the first microprocessor (the Intel 4004) in 1969-70 and the first widely-used microprocessor (the Intel 8080) in 1974, this class of CPUs has almost completely overtaken all other implementations. While the previous generation of CPUs was integrated as discrete components on one or more circuit boards, microprocessors are manufactured onto compact Integrated Circuits (ICs), often a single chip. The smaller transistor sizes mean faster switching time due to decreased gate capacitance. This has allowed synchronous microprocessors to utilize clock rates ranging from tens of megahertz to several gigahertz. Additionally, as the ability to construct exceedingly small transistors on an IC has increased, the complexity of and number of transistors in a single CPU has increased dramatically. This trend has been observed by many and is often described by Moore's law, which has proven to be a fairly accurate model of the growth of CPU (and other IC) complexity to date. *Moore's law—describes the prediction that the processing power of computer chip will double approximately every 18 months.*

While the complexity, size, construction, and general form of CPUs has changed drastically over the past sixty years, it is notable that the basic design and function has not changed much at all. Almost all common CPUs today can be very accurately described as Von Neumann stored program machines.

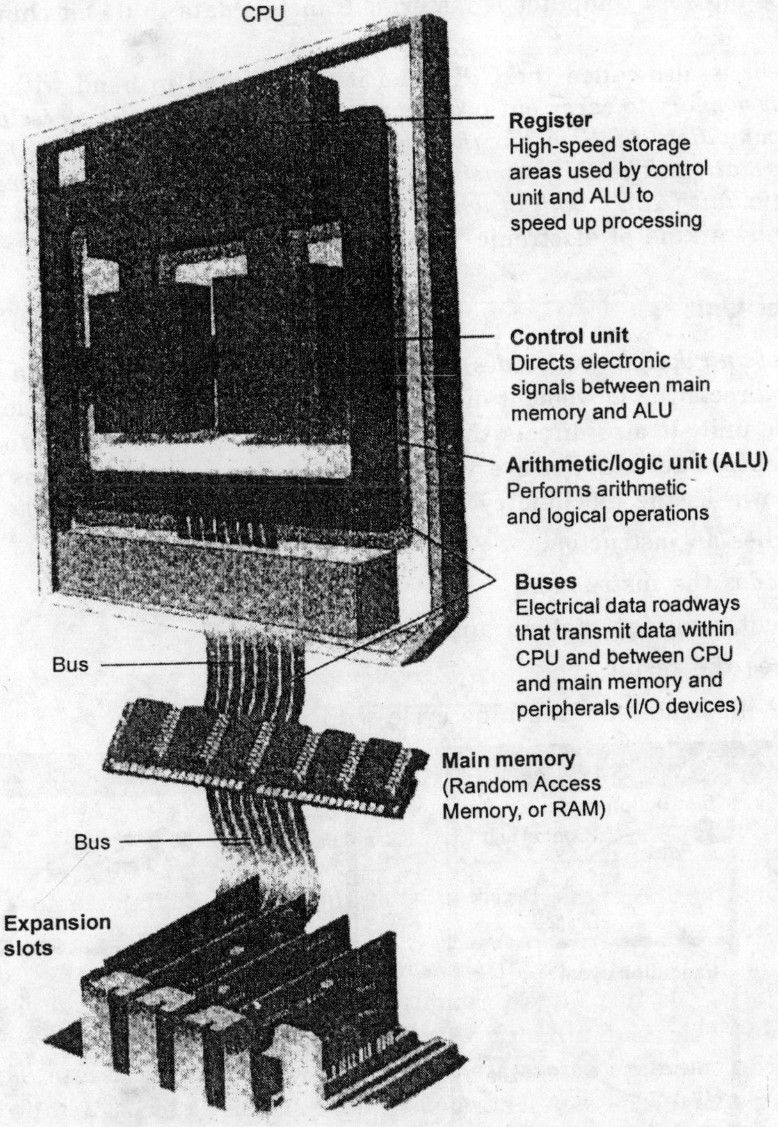


**Fig. 9.1:** CPU (Central Processing Unit).

As the aforementioned Moore's law continues to hold true, concerns about the limits of integrated circuit transistor technology have become much more prevalent. Extreme miniaturization of electronic gates is causing the effects of phenomena like electromigration and subthreshold leakage to become much more significant. These newer concerns are among the many factors causing researchers to investigate new methods of computing such as the quantum computer as well as expand the usage of parallelism and other methods that extend the usefulness of the classical Von Neumann model.

Today, computers are based on microprocessors, less than 1 centimetre square. It may be difficult to visualize components so tiny. *Word size is the number of bits that the processor may process at any one time.* The more bits in a word, the faster the computer. A 32-bit computer—that is, one with a 32-bit-word processor will transfer data within each microprocessor chip in 32-bit chunks or 4 bytes at a time. (We know that there are 8-bits in a byte). A 64-bit-word computer is faster; it transfers data in 64-bit chunks or 8-bytes at a time.

A processor is also called the CPU, and it works hand in hand with other circuits known as *main memory* to carry out processing. *The CPU (Central Processing Unit) is the "brain" of the computer; it follows the instructions of the software (program) to manipulate data into information. The CPU consists of two parts—(1) the control unit and (2) the arithmetic/logic unit (ALU), both of which contain registers, or high-speed storage areas.* All are linked by a kind of electronic "roadway" known as a bus.

### 9.3.1 Control Unit

*The control unit deciphers (decodes) each instruction stored in it and then carries out the instruction.* It directs the movement of electronic signals between main memory and the arithmetic/logic unit. It also directs these electronic signals between main memory and the input and output devices. For every instruction, the control unit carries out four basic operations, known as the machine cycle. In the machine cycle, the CPU

(*i*) fetches an instruction,

(*ii*) decodes the instruction,

(*iii*) executes the instruction, and

(*iv*) stores the result.

Figure 9.2 illustrates the machine cycle with an example.

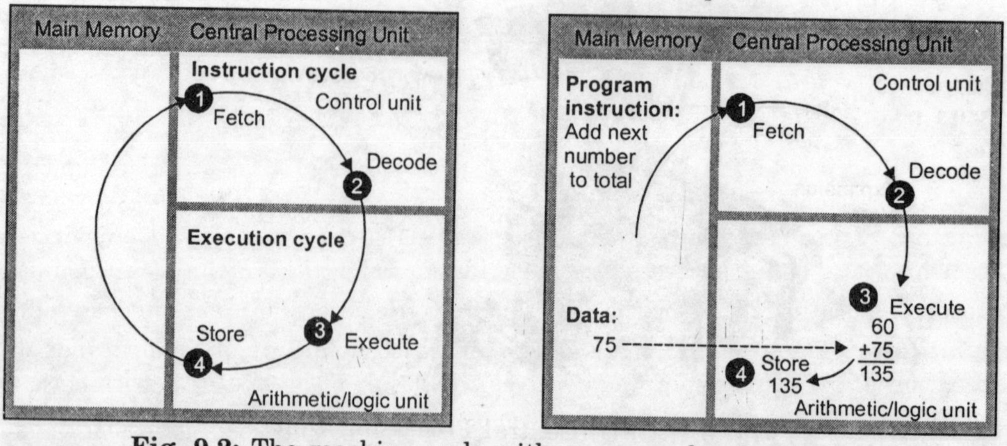


**Fig. 9.2:** The machine cycle with an example of addition.

### 9.3.2 Arithmetic and Logic Unit (ALU)

*It performs arithmetic operations and logical operations and controls the speed of those operations.*

Usually an ALU performs the following arithmetic and logic operations:

(*i*) Addition
(*ii*) Subtraction
(*iii*) Multiplication
(*iv*) Division
(*v*) Logical AND
(*vi*) Logical OR
(*vii*) Logical EXCLUSIVE-OR
(*viii*) Complement (logical NOT)
(*ix*) Increment (*i.e.*, addition of 1)
(*x*) Decrement (*i.e.*, subtraction of 1)
(*xi*) Left or right shift (the content of the accumulator can be shifted left or right by one bit)
(*xii*) Clear (the content of the accumulator or carry flag can be made zero).

As given above *arithmetic operations* are the fundamental math operations: *addition*, *subtraction, multiplication* and *division* etc.

*Logical operations* are comparisons. That is, the ALU compares two pieces of data to see whether one is equal to (=), greater than (>), or less than (<) the other. (The comparisons can also be combined, as in "greater than or equal to" and "less than or equal to.")

Other mathematical operations such as exponential, logarithmic, trigonometric and floating-point operations are not performed by ALU. These operations are performed by special purpose math processor called floating-point unit (FPU). Modern microprocessors contain an FPU on the microprocessor chip itself (*i.e.*, an on-chip FPU). Some cheaper microprocessors which are used for simple automatic control applications may not contain on-chip FPU. Such processors use either software for above mentioned mathematical operation or employ a math processor IC (or math coprocessor) in the microprocessor-based system. The use of software for such mathematical operations makes execution slower. Math processors speed up program execution and reduce programming complexity. The choice depends on actual requirement and cost involved in a particular application.

### 9.3.3 CPU Registers

The control unit and the ALU also use registers, special areas that enhance the computer's performance. *Registers are high-speed storage areas that temporarily store data during processing*. They may store a program instruction while it is being decoded, store data while it is being processed by the ALU, or store the results of a calculation.

Some processors have more registers, someless. Registers are classified as follows:

***Accumulator:*** The accumulator is a register which holds one of the operands prior to the execution of an instruction, and receives the result of most of the arithmetic and logical operations. So an accumulator is the most frequently used register. Some CPUs have a single accumulator; some have several accumulators.

***General Purpose Registers:*** These registers store data and intermediate results during the execution of a program. They are accessible to users through instructions if the users are working in assembly language.

***Special Purpose Registers:*** A CPU contains a number of special purpose registers for different purposes. These are given below:

(*i*) Program Counter (PC)

(*ii*) Stack Pointer (SP)

(*iii*) Status Register

(*iv*) Instruction Register (IR)

(*v*) Index Register

(*vi*) Memory Address Register (MAR)

(*vii*) Memory Buffer Register (MBR) or Data Register (DR)

All CPUs do not contain all of these special registers. A powerful CPU contains most of them. The brief description of these registers is given below:

***Program Counter (PC):*** The Program counter keeps track of the address of the instruction which is to be executed next. So it holds the address of the memory location which contains the next instruction to be fetched from the memory. Its content is automatically incremented after an instruction has been fetched assuming that instructions are normally executed sequentially. In case of a jump instruction its contents are modified, and program jumps to the memory location which contains the desired instruction to be executed next.

***Stack Pointer (SP):*** The stack is a sequence of memory locations defined by the user. It is used to save the contents of a register if it is required during the execution of a program. The stack pointer holds the address of the last occupied memory location of the stack. Thus it indicates upto what memory locations the stack is already filled up. In other words it indicates from which memory location onward the stack is vacant for further storage.

***Status Register:*** The status register is also called **condition code** or **flag register.** It holds 1-bit flags to indicate certain conditions that arise during arithmetic and logical operations. The important indications shown by computer are:

Carry – it indicates whether there is overflow or not

Zero – it indicates whether the result is zero or nonzero

Sign – it indicates whether the result is plus or minus

Parity – it indicates whether the result contains odd number of 1s or even number of 1s.

Auxiliary carry or Half Carry is also indicated.

***Instruction Register:*** It holds an instruction until it is decoded. Some computers have two instruction, registers, and so they can fetch and save the next instruction while the execution of the previous instruction is going on.

***Index Register:*** Index registers are used for addressing. One or more registers are designated as index registers. The address of an operand is the sum of the contents of the index register and a constant. Instructions involving index register contain constant. This constant is added to the contents of index register to form the effective address, *i.e.*, the address of the operand. Usually special instructions are provided to increment or decrement an index register so as to access the entries of a table in a successive manner. Alternatively, some computers have the facility of auto-indexing by which the index register is automatically incremented or decremented.

***Memory Address Register (MAR):*** It holds the address of the instruction or data to be fetched from the memory. The CPU transfers the address of the next instruction form the program counter (PC) to the memory address register. From MAR it is sent to the memory through the address bus. Sometimes it is called simply address register (AR).

***Memory Buffer Register (MBR) or Data Register (DR):*** It holds the instruction code or data received from or sent to the memory. It is connected to data bus. The data which are written into the memory are held in this register until the write operation is completed. It is also called data register (DR). Thus the flow of data from the CPU to the memory or from the memory of CPU is always trough MBR. It is within the CPU.

### 9.3.4 Buses and Its Types

*Buses, or bus lines, are electrical data roadways through which bits are transmitted within the CPU and between the CPU and other components of the motherboard.* A bus resembles a multilane highway: The more lanes it has, the faster the bits can be transferred. The old-fashioned 8 bit-word bus of early microprocessors had only eight pathways. Data is transmitted four times faster in a computer with a 32-bit bus, which has 32 pathways, than in a computer with an 8-bit bus. Intel's Pentium chip is a 64-bit processor.

The components inside a computer talk to each other in various different ways. There are only two ways to connect all the components:

(*i*) Either run wires between each component in the system or

(*ii*) Connect them all to a common set of wires—a bus.

Most of the internal system components, including the processor, cache, memory, expansion cards and storage devices, talk to each other over one or more 'buses'.

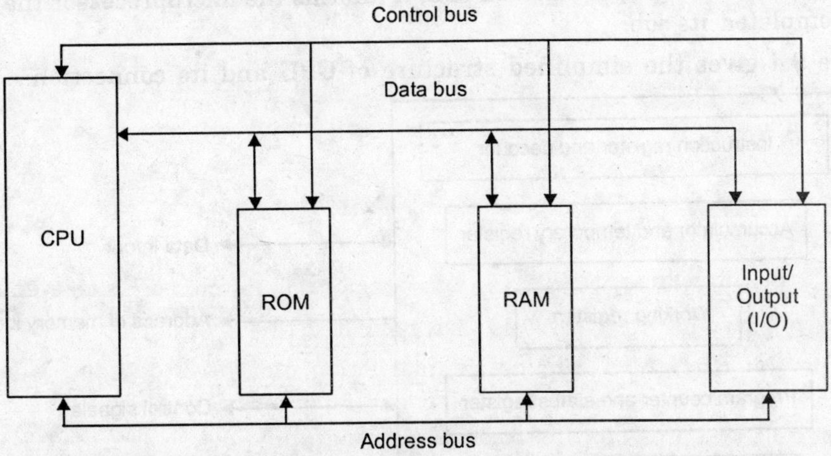


**Fig. 9.3:** Illustration of various buses within a computer.

*A bus, in computer terms, is simply a channel over which information flows between two or more devices (technically, a bus with only two devices on it is considered by some a 'port' instead of a bus).* The bus simplifies the design, reduces the number of required circuits and lowers the cost. A bus normally has access points, or places into which a device can tap to become part of the bus, and devices on the bus can send to, and receive information from, other devices.

The system bus is simply a set of connections that connect the CPU to other devices in the computer.

### Address Bus

Address bus is unidirectional, that is, data/information can flow in one direction only, that is, from the microprocessing unit to the peripheral devices. The first job that the microprocessing unit performs is to identify the peripheral devices by using the address bus. The address of a peripheral is identified by a binary number. This is as like as to identify the address of a house.

### Data Bus

Data buses are bidirectional, that is, they can carry data in both directions between microprocessing unit, memory and peripheral devices. The number of data lines determines the width of the bus. Think of the data bus as a set of parallel wires, each of which can send one bit at a time. The more wires in the bus, the more bits that can be sent. Data buses of different capacities are used in different systems *e.g.*, 8085 uses 8-bit data bus, that is, it can manipulate 256($2^8$) numbers ranging from 00 to FF, that is why 8085 is known as 8-bit μP. The number has increased over the years from 8 to 16 and now 32 to keep up with the performance of the microprocessors. Some high-end systems are already using the next step bus, one that carries 64-bits. Macintosh G4 microcomputers contain buses that are 128-bits, as do some supercomputers.

### Control Bus

The control bus supervises the reading or writing of data. It transmits the signals to all the devices at the proper time. In fact, it informs the microprocessor that a particular unit has completed its job.

Figure 9.4 gives the simplified structure of CPU and its connection:

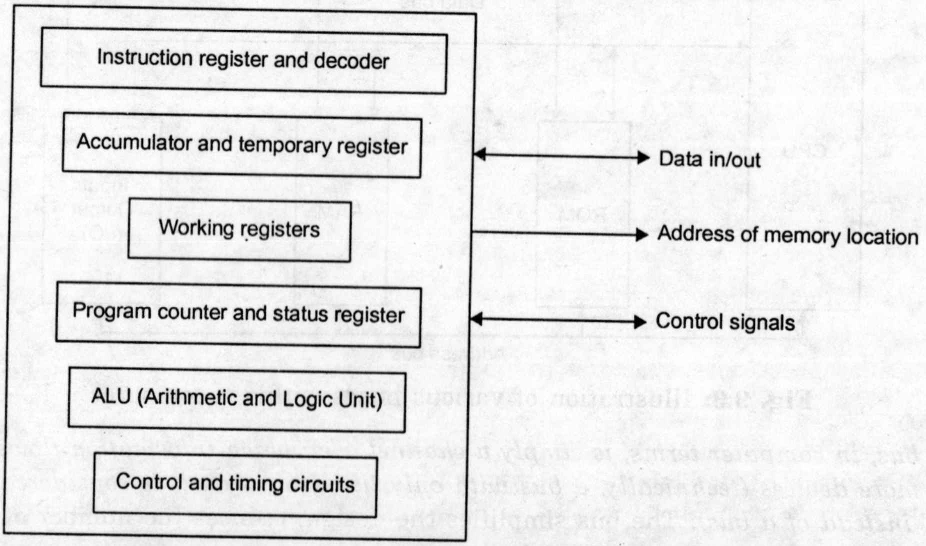


**Fig. 9.4:** The internal structure of a microprocessor.

## 9.4 CLOCK AND ITS SPEED

Every microprocessor contains a *system clock, which controls how fast all the operations within a computer take place.*

In a computer, clock speed refers to the number of pulses or "ticks" per second generated by an **oscillator** that sets the tempo for the **processor.** These ticks are called *cycles*. Clock speed is usually measured in **MHz** (megahertz, or millions of pulses per second) or **GHz** (gigahertz, or billions of pulses per second). Today's personal computers run at a clock speed in the hundreds of megahertz and some exceed one gigahertz. The clock speed is determined by a quartz-crystal circuit, similar to those used in radio communications equipment.

Computer clock speed has been roughly doubling every year. The Intel 8088, common in computers around the year 1990, ran at 4.77 MHz. The 1 GHz mark was passed in the year 2000.

Clock speed is one measure of computer 'power', but it is not always directly proportional to the performance level. If you double the speed of the clock, leaving all other hardware unchanged, you will not necessarily double the processing speed. The type of microprocessor, the **bus** architecture, and the nature of the instruction set all make a difference. In some applications, the Random access memory **(RAM)** is important, too.

Some processors execute only one **instruction** per clock pulse. More advanced processors can perform more than one per clock pulse. The latter type of processor will work faster at a given clock speed than the former type. Similarly, a 32-bit bus will work faster at a given clock speed than a computer with a 16-bit bus. For these reasons, their simplistic, universal relation among clock speed, 'bus speed', and millions of instructions per second (MIPS).

Modern computer technology does allow for some asynchronous operation. Some motherboards now have separate clock for the expansion bus, system bus, video, etc. Although these devices run asynchronously, their individual clocks will still run at multiples or submultiples of each other which allows for the optimization of transfer rates and data exchange.

## 9.5 PROCESSOR AND ITS TYPES

A computer system which contains one CPU is called **uniprocessor system.** Because the computer's microprocessor performs many function, it often causes slowdowns at key points in the computer operation. To relieve part of its burden, some computers have additional microprocessors, called **co-processors**, that are dedicated to specific, time-consuming tasks. These co-processors operate under the control of the CPU. For example, co-processors can be used to accelerate the display on the screen or improve the processing of audio and video. Figure 9.5(*a*) illustrates co-processors:

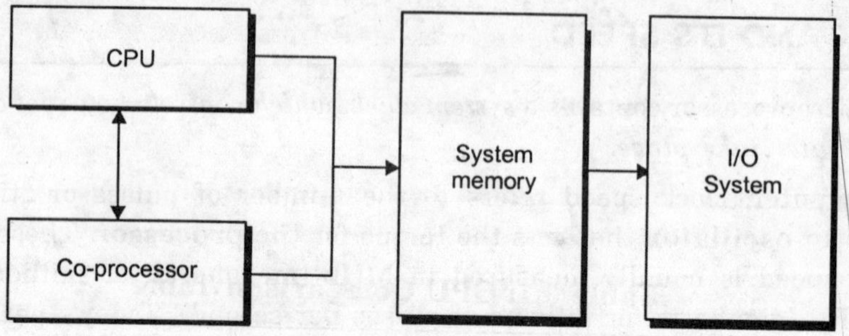


**Fig. 9.5(*a*):** Co-processors.

A co-processor is a special case of a parallel processor. A computer system that contains two or more CPUs is called a **multiprocessor system.** Some large computers and powerful minicomputers contain two or more CPUs. These CPUs operate in parallel under the integrated control of an operating system to handle one task or job.

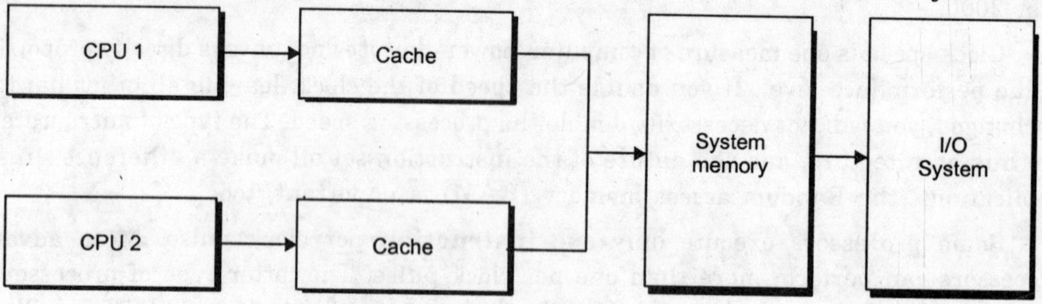


**Fig. 9.5(*b*):** Multiprocessors.

## 9.6 PARALLEL PROCESSING AND PARALLEL COMPUTERS

When several computations are performed concurrently in a computer, it is known as *parallel processing*. A multiprocessor system performs several computations concurrently. Parallel processing is also achieved in a uniprocessor system using pipelining. A computer employing parallel processing is also called parallel computer. There are three types of parallel computers based on their architectural configuration:

(*i*) Pipelined computers

(*ii*) Array processors

(*iii*) Multiprocessor system.

In a pipelined computer, while one instruction is being fetched, the second is being decoded, the operand is being fetched for the third and the fourth is being executed. The instruction fetching unit, the instruction decoding unit, operand fetching unit and the execution unit all operate simultaneously.

An array processor contains several processing elements (PEs) which operate in parallel under the control of a single control unit (CU). A processing element is an arithmetic and logic unit (ALU) with attached registers and local memory. A multiprocessor system is a single computer that contains multiple processors. Processors of multiprocessor computer communicate and cooperate at different levels in solving a given problem. The communication may occur by sending messages from one processor to the other or by sharing a common memory.

## 9.7 COMMONLY USED CPUS AND CPU RELATED TERMINOLOGIES

Table 9.1 gives an overview of various CPUs used over the years:

**Table 9.1: CPU Comparison Table**

| *CPU* | *Generation* | *Process Technology* | *Number of Transistors* | *Data / Address Bus width (bits)* | *GP Register width (bits)* | *Memory Bus Speed* | *Internal Clock Speed* |
|---|---|---|---|---|---|---|---|
| Intel 8080 | 1st | 6.0 microns | 6 000 | 8/16 | 8 | 2 MHz | 2 MHz |
| Intel 8088 | 1st | 3.0 microns | 29 000 | 8/20 | 16 | 4.77-8 MHz | 4.77-8 MHz |
| Intel 8086 | 1st | 3.0 microns | 29 000 | 16/20 | 16 | 4.77-8 MHz | 4.77-8 MHz |
| Intel 80286 | 2nd | 1.5 microns | 134 000 | 16/24 | 16 | 6-20 MHz | 6-20 MHz |
| Intel 80388 DX | 3rd | 1.5/1.0 microns | 275 000 | 32/32 | 32 | 16-33 MHz | 16-33 MHz |
| Intel 80386 SX | 3rd | 1.5/1.0 microns | 275 000 | 16/32 | 32 | 16-33 MHz | 16-33 MHz |
| Intel 80486 DX | 4th | 1.0 microns | 1.2 million | 32/32 | 32 | 25-50 MHz | 25-50 MHz |
| Intel 80486 DX2 | 4th | 0.8 microns | 1.2 million | 32/32 | 32 | 25-40 MHz | 50-80 MHz |
| AMD 5x86 | 4th | 0.35 microns | 1.2 million | 32/32 | 32 | 33 MHz | 133 MHz |
| Intel Pentium (P5/P54C) | 5th | 0.8-0.35 microns | 3.1 million | 64/32 | 32 | 60-66 MHz | 60-200 MHz |
| Cyrix 6x86 (M1) | 5th | 0.6 microns | 3.0 million | 64/32 | 32 | 50-75 MHz | 100-150 MHz (P120-200) |
| AMD K5 | 5th | 0.35 microns | 4.3 million | 64/32 | 32 | 50-66 MHz | 75-116 MHz (P75-166) |
| Intel Pentium MMX (P55C) | 5th | 0.35 microns | 5.5 million | 64/32 | 32 | 66 MHz | 166-233 MHz |

| | | | | | | | |
|---|---|---|---|---|---|---|---|
| Intel Pentium Pro | 6th | 0.6/0.35 microns | 5.5 million (+ IL2C) | 64/32 | 32 | 60-66 MHz | 150-200 MHz |
| AMD K6 (NX686) | 6th | 0.35/0.25 microns | 8.8 million | 64/32 | 32 | 66 MHz | 166-266 MHz |
| Intel Pentium II | 6th | 0.35/0.25 microns | 7.5 million | 64/36 | 32 | 66-100 MHz | 233-450 MHz |
| Intel Pentium III | 6th | 0.18 microns | 28 million | 64/36 | 32 | 100-133 MHz | 450-1200 MHz |
| AMD Athlon | 7th | 0.18/0.13 microns | 37-54 million | 64/36 | 32 | 200-333 MHz | 500-2250 MHz (XP3000+) |
| Intel Pentium 4 | 7th | 0.18/0.13 microns | 42 million | 64/36 | 32 | 400-533 MHz | 1.4-3.3 MHz |
| Intel IA-64 Itanium | 8th | 0.18 microns | 25 million (+ IC) | 64/44 | 64 | 400 MHz | 733-1000 MHz |
| AMDX86-64 (K8-Hammer) | 8th | 0.13/0.09 microns | 110 million | 64/36 | 64 | N/A | >2000 MHz (>XP3400+) |

## SUMMARY

- **Word size** is the number of bits that the processor may process at any one time.
- The CPU consists of Control Unit, Arithmetic Logic Unit, Registers, Buses and Clock.
- The CPU is the "brain" of the computer.
- According to **Moore's low,** the number of transistors that can be packed onto a chip doubles about every 18 months.
- The control unit is for directing electronic signals.
- The arithmetic logic unit (ALU) is for arithmetic and logical operations.
- Registers are high-speed storage areas that temporarily store data during processing.
- Buses are data roadways.
- An instruction code is a group of bits that instruct the computer to perform a specific operation.
- A program residing in the memory unit of the computer consists of a sequence of instructions.
- Accumulator is the register where answers to arithmetic and logic operations are accumulated.
- Instruction register is the register that receives the instruction from the memory.

- Program counter stores the address of the next instruction to be fetched from the memory.
- Instruction register receives the instruction from the memory and holds it until it is decoded.
- Op-code (operation code) is that part of the instruction which tells the computer what operation to perform.

## REVIEW QUESTIONS AND EXERCISES

1. What is a microprocessor? Give its various units.
2. Discuss the function of a CPU. What are the main sections of a CPU? Discuss the function of each section.
3. What operations are performed by an ALU?
4. What is the purpose of providing registers in a CPU? Discuss various registers which are usually provided in a microprocessor.
5. Discuss the function of an index register, memory address register (MAR) and memory buffer register (MBR).
6. What is clock speed? What are its units?
7. Explain the concept of system buses, address bus and data bus.
8. What are single, dual and multiple processors?
9. Write a short note on machine instructions.
10. Describe the instruction cycle.

Chapter 10

# BASIC COMPUTER DESIGN

## 10.1 INTRODUCTION

The basic function of any system is to process data presented to it by the external world. The basic objective is true regardless of whether the actual processing done is digital or analog in nature. Digital processing tends to be more indirect than its analog counterparts. This chapter presents basic issues such as instruction types, instruction cycle, instruction formats and addressing modes that play important role in the basic design of a digital computer system.

## 10.2 MACHINE INSTRUCTIONS AND ITS TYPES

An instruction is a command given to the computer to perform a specified operation on given data. The number of instructions available in a computer and their efficiency in solving the problem at hand are a good indication of the intended application of the machine. Medium-to large-scale computing systems may have hundreds of instructions, while most small computers limit the list to less than 100. *The instructions must be chosen carefully to provide sufficient capabilities to the system for solving a wide range of data processing problems. The minimum requirements of such a list should include a capability for storing and loading words from memory, a sufficient set of arithmetic and logic operations, some address-modification capabilities, unconditional branching and branching under test conditions, register manipulation capabilities, and I/O instructions.* The instruction list chosen for our machine is believed to be close to the absolute minimum required for a restricted but practical data processor.

For better understanding of the machine instruction look at the block diagram of digital computer shown in Figure 10.1. Each block represents a register, except for the memory unit, the master-clock generator, and the control logic. A list of the registers and a brief description of their functions is given in Table 10.1.

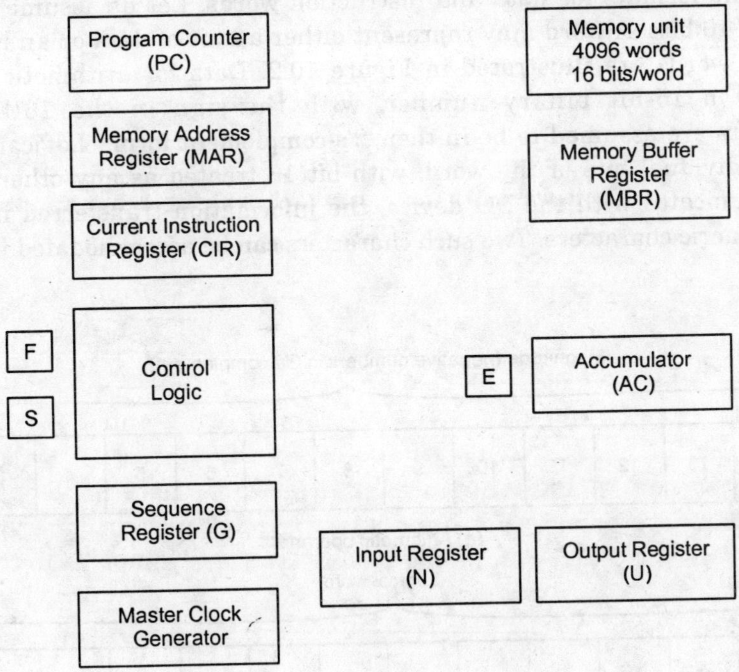


**Fig. 10.1:** Block diagram of digital computer.

**Table 10.1: List of Registers for Computer**

| *Symbolic Designation* | *Name* | *Number of Bits* | *Function* |
|---|---|---|---|
| AC | Accumulator Register | 16 | Processor register |
| MBR | Memory Buffer Register | 16 | Holds contents of memory word |
| PC | Program Counter | 12 | Holds address of next instruction |
| MAR | Memory Address Register | 12 | Holds address of memory word |
| CIR | Current Instruction Register | 4 | Holds current operation code |
| E | Extension flip-flop | 1 | Accumulator extension |
| F | Fetch flip-flop | 1 | Controls fetch and execute cycles |
| S | Start-stop flip-flop | 1 | Starts and stops computer |
| G | Sequence register | 2 | Provides timing signals |
| N | Input register | 9 | Holds information from input device |
| U | Output register | 9 | Holds information for output device |

The formulation of a set of instructions for the computer goes hand in hand with the formulation of the formats for data and instruction words. Let us assume that a memory word consists of 16 bits. A word may represent either a unit of data or an instruction. The formats of data words are illustrated in Figure 10.2. Data for arithmetic operations are represented by a 15-bit binary number, with the sign in the 16th bit position. Negative numbers are assumed to be in their 2's-complement form. Logical operations are performed on individual bits of the word, with bit 16 treated as any other bit. When the computer communicates with the I/O device, the information transferred is considered to be 8-bit alphanumeric characters. Two such characters can be accommodated in one computer word.

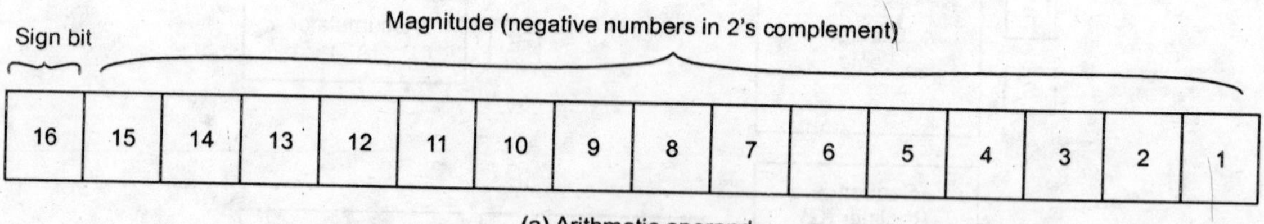


(a) Arithmetic operand

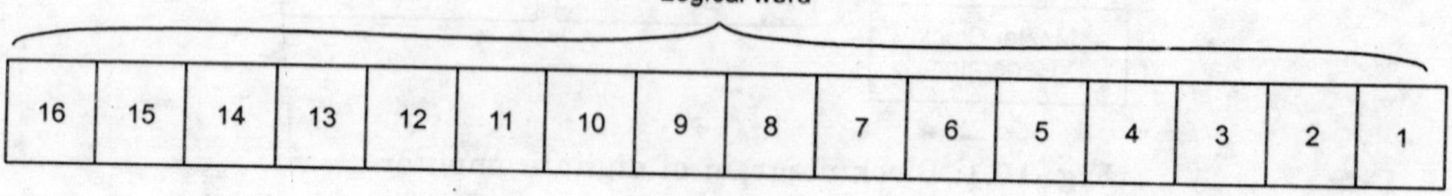


(b) Logical operand

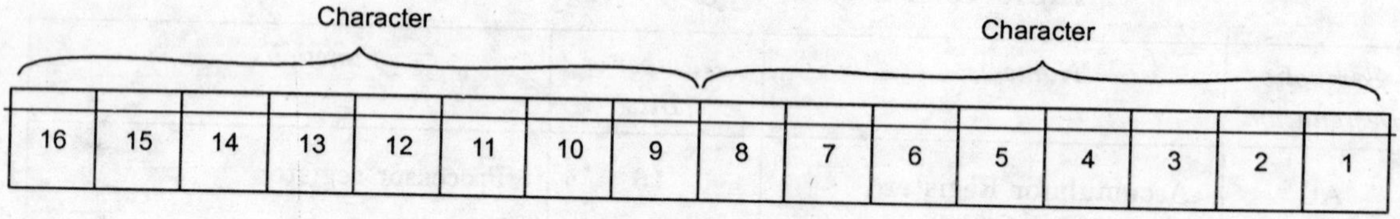


(c) Input/output data

**Fig. 10.2:** Data Formats.

The formats of instruction words are shown in Figure 10.3. The operation part of the instruction has four bits; the meaning of the remaining 12 bits depends on the operation-code encountered. A *memory-reference* instruction uses the remaining 12 bits to specify an address. A *register-reference* instruction implies an operation on, or a test of, the AC or E register. An operand from memory is not required; therefore, the 12 least significant bits are used to specify the operation or test to be executed. A register-reference instruction is recognized by the code 0110 in the operation part. Similarly, an *input-output* instruction does not require a reference to memory and is recognized by the operation code 0111. The remaining 12 bits are used to specify the particular device and the type of operation or test performed.

Only four bits of the instruction are available for the operation code. It would appear then, that the computer is restricted to a maximum of 16 distinct operations. However, since register-reference and input-output instructions use the remaining 12 bits as part of the operation-code, the total number of instructions can exceed 16. In fact, the total number of instructions chosen for the computer is 22.

Of the 16 distinct operations that can be formulated with four bits, only eight have been utilized by the computer because the left most bit of all instructions (bit 16) is always a 0. This leaves open the possibility of adding new instructions and extending the computer capabilities if required.

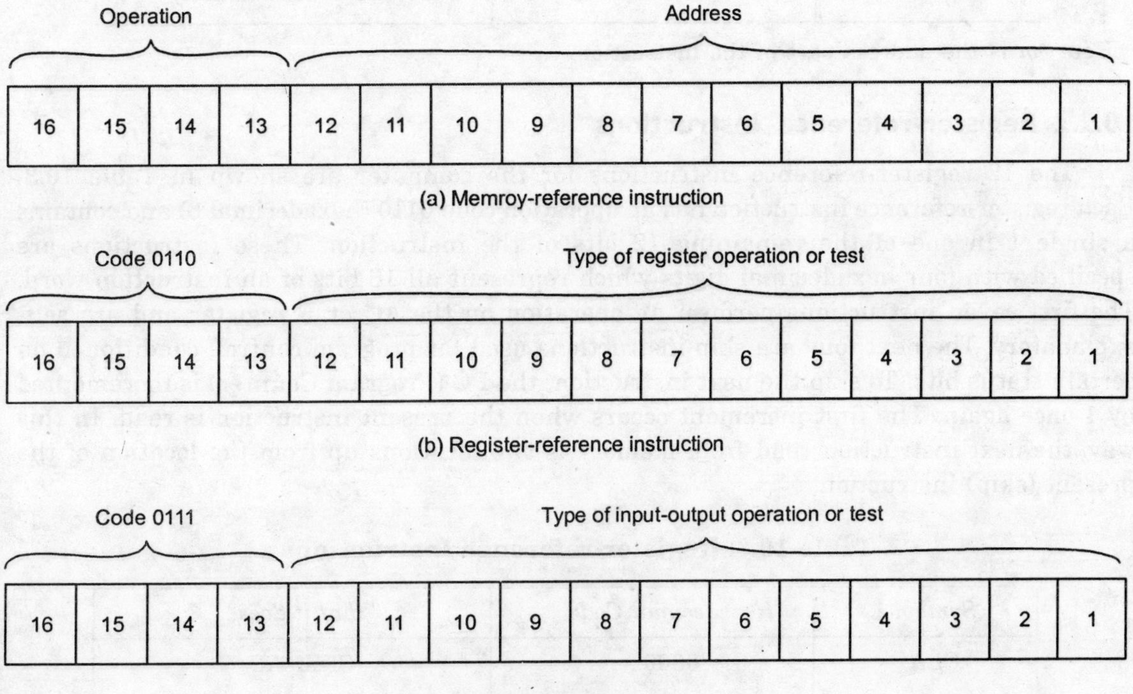

(a) Memroy-reference instruction

(b) Register-reference instruction

(c) Input/output instruction

**Fig. 10.3:** Instruction formats.

## 10.2.1 Memory-reference Instructions

The six memory-reference instructions for the computer are shown in Table 10.2. The symbolic designation is a three-letter word and represents an abbreviation intended for use by programmers and users when writing symbolic programs for the computer. The hexadecimal code listed is an equivalent hexadecimal number of the binary code adopted for the operation-code *i.e.*, op-code. A memory-reference instruction uses one hexadecimal digit (4 bits) for the operation-code; the remaining three hexadecimal digits (12 bits) of the instruction represent an address designated by the letter *m*. A further clarification of each instruction is given below, together with an explanation of its use.

**Table 10.2: Memory-reference Instructions**

| *Symbol* | *Hexadecimal Code* | *What it does ?* |
|---|---|---|
| AND | 0 *m** | AND to AC |
| ADD | 1 *m* | Add to AC |
| STO | 2 *m* | Store in AC |
| ISZ | 3 *m* | Increment and skip if zero |
| BSB | 4 *m* | Branch to subroutine |
| BUN | 5 *m* | Branch unconditionally |

Here **m* is the address part of the instruction.

### 10.2.2 Register-reference Instructions

The 12 register-reference instructions for the computer are shown in Table 10.3. Each register-reference instruction has an operation code 0110 (hexadecimal 6) and contains a single 1 in one of the remaining 12 bits of the instruction. These instructions are specified with four hexadecimal digits which represent all 16 bits of an instruction word. The first seven instructions perform an operation on the AC or E register and are self-explanatory. The next four are skip instructions used for program control, conditioned on certain status bits. To skip the next instruction, the PC (Program Counter) is incremented by 1 once again. The first increment occurs when the present instruction is read. In this way, the next instruction read from memory is two locations up from the location of the present (skip) instruction.

**Table 10.3: Register-reference Instructions**

| *Symbol* | *Hexadecimal Code* | *What it does?* |
|---|---|---|
| CLA | 6800 | Clear AC |
| CLE | 6400 | Clear E |
| CMA | 6200 | Complement AC |
| CME | 6100 | Complement E |
| SHR | 6080 | Shift-right AC and E |
| SHL | 6040 | Shift-left AC and E |
| INC | 6020 | Increment AC |
| SPA | 6010 | Skip on positive AC |
| SNA | 6008 | Skip on negative AC |
| SZA | 6004 | Skip on zero AC |
| SZE | 6002 | Skip on zero E |
| HLT | 6001 | Halt computer |

The status bits for the skip instructions are the sign bit in AC, which is in flip-flop $AC_{16}$, and a zero condition for AC or E. If the designated status condition is present, the next instruction in sequence is skipped; otherwise, the computer continues from the next instruction in sequence because PC is not incremented.

The halt instruction is generally placed at the end of a program if one wishes to stop the computer. Its execution clears the start-stop flip-flop, which prevents further operations to take place.

### 10.2.3 Input-Output Instructions

The computer has four input-output instructions and they are shown in Table 10.4. These instructions have an operation code 0111(hexadecimal 7), and each contains a 1 in only one of the remaining 12 bits of the instruction word. The input-output instructions are specified with four hexadecimal digits starting with 7.

The INP instruction transfers the input character from N to AC and also clears the input flag in $N_9$. The OUT instruction transfers an 8-bit character code from AC into the output register and also clears the output flag in $U_9$. The two skip instructions check the corresponding status flags and cause a skip of the next instruction if the flag bit is 1. The instruction that is skipped is normally a BUN instruction. The BUN instruction is not skipped if the flag bit is 0; this causes a branch back to the skip instruction to check the flag again. If the flag bit is 1, the BUN instruction is skipped and an input or output operation is executed. Thus, the computer stays in a two-instruction loop (skip on flag and branch back to previous instruction) until the flag bit is set by the external device. The next instruction in sequence must be an input or output instruction.

**Table 10.4: Input-output Instructions**

| *Symbol* | *Hexadecimal Code* | *What it does?* |
|---|---|---|
| SKI | 7800 | Skip on input flag |
| INP | 7400 | Input to AC |
| SKO | 7200 | Skip on output flag |
| OUT | 7100 | Output from AC |

## 10.3 INSTRUCTION CYCLE

The CPU executes instructions stored in the main memory of the computer. The size of a computer instruction depends upon the type of computer being used. However, an instruction usually consists of two parts: **Op-code** and **operands.** The *op-code* or *operation code* specifies what is to be done (add, multiply, compare etc). The *operands* specify the main memory addresses of the data or general purpose register or the type of devices to be utilized. The CPU clock or internal clock controls the timing of each basic CPU operation. The length of time required to go through one machine operation is called a *machine cycle*. The number of machine cycles required to execute one program instruction depend on the kind of instruction. Efficient programs, naturally, use as small a number as possible.

To do a particular task, a programmer writes the required instructions in the form of a program. The program is loaded into the main memory of the computer. The CPU fetches the first instruction of the program from the memory and executes it. It fetches the next instruction and executes it. This process is repeated till it encounters the *HLT* instruction (see Figure 10.4).

Thus, the instruction cycle comprises of two parts **fetch** and **execute** cycles.

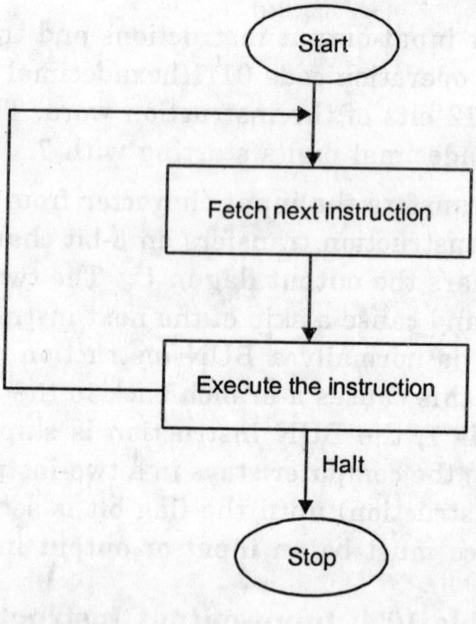


**Fig. 10.4:** Instruction cycle.

### 10.3.1 Fetch Cycle

When a program is executed, the program counter (PC) in the CPU is set to the address of the first instruction in the program. This address is then transferred to memory address register (MAR).

The instruction from the memory is fetched and its op-code part is loaded into the instruction register (IR). *The operand is placed in MAR.* The op-code is then decoded by the instruction decoder to determine as to *'what is to be done'*. The CU initiates the required signals for the ALU and the registers to carry out the required operation.

The contents of the PC are automatically incremented to point to the next instruction. Depending upon a branch instruction, the contents of PC can be reset to point to an instruction in another part of the program.

Thus, the following steps are involved in the fetch cycle:

1. The next instruction address is loaded from PC to MAR.
2. MAR places this address on address bus.
3. Control unit sends a *read* signal to memory.

4. Memory places the data in MDR (Memory Data Register) or MBR (Memory Buffer Register).
5. Program counter is incremented.
6. The instruction is transferred to IR (instruction register).

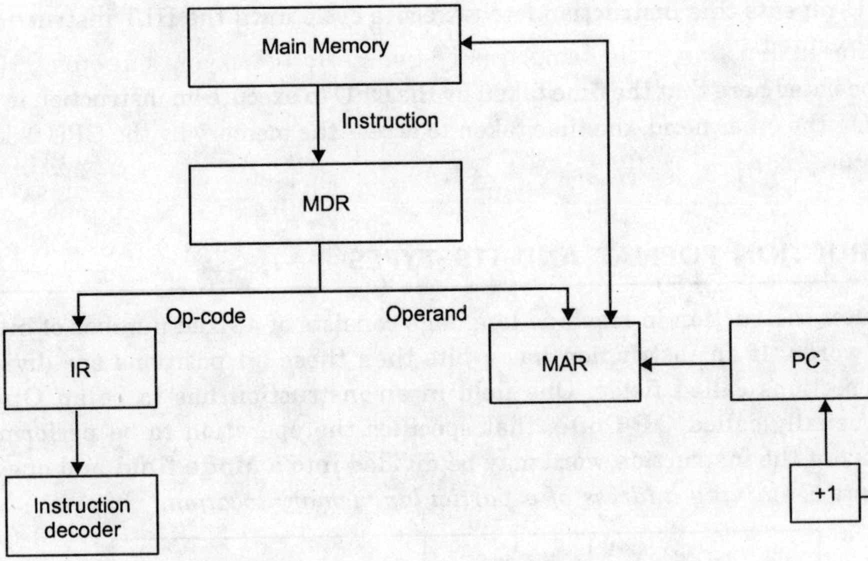


**Fig. 10.5:** Instruction fetch cycle.

## 10.3.2 Execution Cycle

Once an instruction has been fetched and decoded, the instruction execution cycle begins by transferring the required data from the address indicated by MAR. The operation specified by the op-code is then performed on this data in the ALU.

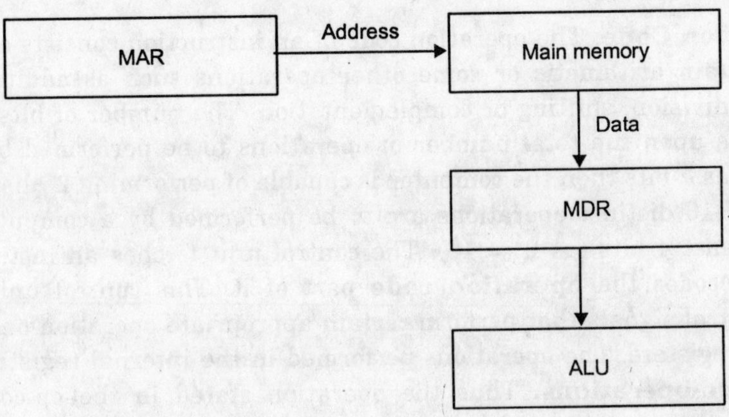


**Fig. 10.6:** Instruction execution cycle.

Thus, the following steps are involved in the execute cycle:

1. Transfer the operand part of IR to MAR.
2. The data is fetched into ALU from the memory location pointed by MAR.
3. The operation specified by the decoded op-code is performed on the data in the ALU.

The CPU repeats this instruction fetch-execute cycle until the HLT instruction of the program is executed.

It may be noted here that the time taken by the CPU to execute an instruction is called as **CPU cycle.** On the other hand, the time taken to access the memory by the CPU is known as **memory cycle.**

## 10.4 INSTRUCTION FORMAT AND ITS TYPES

A computer instruction in machine language consists of a fixed number of bits stored in computer words. If an instruction has $n$-bits then these bit positions are divided into two or more sections called fields. One field in an instruction has to be an **Operation Code field**, usually called **OP-Code**, that specifies the operation to be performed. The remaining part of the instruction word may be divided into a **Mode field** and one or more parts each part *containing address of a particular memory location.*

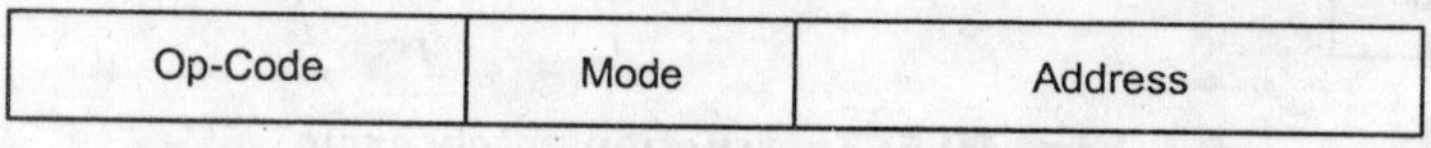


**Fig. 10.7:** Instruction format with mode field.

Thus an instruction in machine language consists of the following parts,

(*i*) Operation code or Op-Code

(*ii*) Address or Addresses of one or more memory locations or a processor register.

(*iii*) A mode field that specifies the way the operand or the effective address is determined.

(*i*) **Operation Code:** The operation code of an instruction consists of a group of bits that define certain arithmetic or some other operations such as addition, subtraction, multiplication, division, shifting or complementation. The number of bits required for an op-code depends upon the total number of operations to be performed by the computer. If the op-code has $k$-bits then the computer is capable of performing $2^k$ distinct operations. For example, if 16 distinct operations are to be performed by a computer then op-code must have at least 4 bits (as $2^4 = 16$). The control unit fetches an instruction from the memory and decodes the **operation code** part of it. This control unit then issues a sequence of control signals that perform certain appropriate operation on the data stored in its internal registers. The operations performed in the internal register of a computer are called **micro-operations.** Thus the operation stated in the op-code is a **micro-operation** and the operations that result in achieving the macro-operation are called micro-operations. For every macro-operation the control unit issues a sequence of control signals to perform the micro-operations.

(*ii*) **Address:** The op-code of an instruction specifies the operation to be performed. Since the operation is to be performed on data or on a set of data, the instruction must also tell where the data is stored. The data may be stored in a register or in a memory location. The data on which the operation is to be performed is called an **operand.** Thus, an instruction must specify the operation to be performed along with the address or addresses of the operand or registers where the result of an operation is to be stored. Moreover, as a computer program consists of a set of instructions, the computer instruction must also tell explicitly or implicitly the memory location, where the next instruction is stored.

(*iii*) **Mode:** The bits that define the mode field of an instruction code specify a variety of alternatives for choosing the operands from the given address. The various addressing modes are given in next Section.

Thus a computer instruction contains the following information:

(*a*) Operation to be performed.

(*b*) Mode field.

(*c*) Address or addresses of memory locations containing the operand or operands.

(*d*) Address of the register or memory location which is to store the result.

(*e*) Address of the memory location containing the instruction to be executed next.

**Type of Instructions.** There are various **instruction formats** depending upon the architecture of the computer. The types of commonly used instructions are:

1. Three address instruction
2. Two address instruction
3. One address instruction
4. Zero address instruction (Stack instruction)

## 10.4.1 Three-Address Instruction Format

In a computer memory the program is stored in the form of instructions and these instructions are stored sequentially. A register called *Program Counter* (PC) is used to compute the address of next instruction. When an instruction is fetched from the memory, the address of this location is copied into program counter. As this instruction is being executed by the ALU, the program counter is incremented by 1 which is the address of the next instruction. However, if the current instruction is a **JUMP** instruction, the PC is updated with the memory address to which the jump has taken place.

The general form of a *three address instruction* is:

| | | | |
|---|---|---|---|
| OP-Code | Address 1 | Address 2 | Address of Destination |

**Fig. 10.8:** Three address instruction.

This three address instruction has the following parts.

(*i*) Operation code

(*ii*) Address of two operands called Address 1 and Address 2

(*iii*) Address of the memory location where the result of the operation is to be stored *i.e.*, address of the destination.

For example let us evaluate the arithmetic statement given in assembly language, X = (A + B) × (C + D) using three address instruction.

ADD, MUL denote addition and multiplication operations.

| | | | |
|---|---|---|---|
| ADD | R1, A, B | R1 ← | M[A] + M[B] |
| ADD | R2, C, D | R2 ← | M[C] + M[D] |
| MUL | X, R1, R2 | M[X] ← | R1 × R2 |

It is assumed that the computer has two processor registers, R1 and R2. The symbol M[A] denotes the operand at memory address symbolized by A.

The advantage of the three address format is that it results in the short programs when evaluating arithmetic expressions.

The disadvantage is that the binary coded instructions require too many bits to specify three addresses.

### 10.4.2 Two-Address Instruction Format

Two-address instructions are the most common in commercial computers. In this type of instruction, one operand is placed in a specified register such as an accumulator and the address of the next instruction is obtained from another register called *Program Counter* (PC) or *Sequence Control Register* (SCR). This implies that such an instruction should have the following parts:

(*i*) Operation code

(*ii*) Address of one of the operands, say Address 1

(*iii*) Address of the storage location where the result is to be stored. This address is denoted by Address 2

The general form of a *two address instruction* is:

| | | |
|---|---|---|
| OP-Code | Address 1 | Address 2 |

**Fig. 10.9:** Two address instruction.

For example, the program to evaluate X = (A + B) × (C + D) using two address instruction is as follows:

| | | | |
|---|---|---|---|
| MOV | R1, A | R1 ← | M[A] |
| ADD | R1, B | R1 ← | R1 + M[B] |
| MOV | R2, C | R2 ← | M[C] |
| ADD | R2, D | R2 ← | R2 + M[D] |
| MUL | R1, R2 | R1 ← | R1 × R2 |
| MOV | X, R1 | M[X] ← | R1 |

ADD denotes addition and the MUL instruction multiplication. The MOV instruction moves or transfers the operands to and from memory and processor registers. The first symbol listed in the instruction is assumed to be both a source and the destination where the result of the operation is transferred.

### 10.4.3 One-Address Instruction Format

As the name suggests, this instruction has address of one operand only, the other operand is stored in accumulator. The results of operation are left in the accumulator (AC) itself, from where these can be moved to main memory by another instruction. The address of next instruction is obtained from the *program counter* (PC). The general form of a *single address instruction* is:

| OP-Code | Address 1 |
|---|---|

**Fig. 10.10:** One address instruction.

For example, the program to evaluate X = (A + B) × (C + D) using *single address* instruction is as follows:

| | | | | |
|---|---|---|---|---|
| LOAD | A | AC | ← | M[A] |
| ADD | B | AC | ← | AC + M[B] |
| STORE | T | M[T] | ← | AC |
| LOAD | C | AC | ← | M[C] |
| ADD | D | AC | ← | AC + M[D] |
| MUL | T | AC | ← | AC × M[T] |
| STORE | X | M[X] | ← | AC |

All operations are done between the AC (accumulator) register and a memory operand. T is the address of a temporary memory location for storing the intermediate result. Obviously, *one address instructions* provide more exhaustive instruction set and a greater capability to address the memory locations, no doubt a great advantage. However, the number of instructions, required in a program, increases a great deal, making the program quite lengthy.

### 10.4.4 Zero-Address Instruction Format

The zero address instructions consist of OP-CODE only. The addresses of operand and destination are implied. The general form of a zero address instruction is:

| OP-Code |
|---|

**Fig. 10.11:** Zero address instruction.

The PUSH and POP instructions, however, need an address field to specify the operand that communicates with the stack.

For example, the program to evaluate X = (A + B) × (C + D) using *zero address* instruction is as follows: (TOS stands for top of stack)

| | | |
|---|---|---|
| PUSH | A | TOS ← A |
| PUSH | B | TOS ← B |
| ADD | | TOS ← (A + B) |
| PUSH | C | TOS ← C |
| PUSH | D | TOS ← D |
| ADD | | TOS ← (C + D) |
| MUL | | TOS ← (C + D) × (A + B) |
| POP | X | M[X] ← TOS |

To evaluate arithmetic expressions in a stack computer, it is necessary to convert the expression into *reverse Polish notation* (Post fix). The name "zero-address" is given to this type of computer because of the absence of an address field in the computational instructions.

## 10.5 ADDRESSING MODES

The manner in which the memory locations are addressed is called **addressing.** Most of the computers especially the micro and mini computers have to address at least 64 K memory locations *i.e.*, 64 × 1024 = 65,536 locations. If a computer word is 16-bit long, it is insufficient to address these 64 K locations because if 4 bits are occupied by the OP-Code then only 12 bits are left for the address part of the instruction and with 12 bits only $2^{12}$ = 4K memory locations can be addressed. However, ways and means have been developed to address more memory locations with the same word length. This is achieved by modifying the address of the operand in an instruction. The modification of the address of the operand is determined by the hardware of the computer. This modified and final address of the operand is called its **Absolute Address** or **Effective Address** and this absolute address is determined by the hardware of the computer.

The techniques of specifying the address of the data are known as **addressing modes.** The important addressing modes are as follows:

(*i*) Direct (or absolute) addressing
(*ii*) Register addressing
(*iii*) Register indirect addressing
(*iv*) Immediate addressing
(*v*) Implicit addressing
(*vi*) Indexed addressing
(*vii*) Based addressing
(*viii*) Based indexed addressing
(*ix*) Relative addressing
(*x*) Relative indexed addressing

(*xi*) Page addressing

(*xii*) Stack addressing

Intel 8085 uses addressing modes only from (*i*) to (*v*). In addition to (*i*) to (*v*) addressing modes other addressing modes are also used by other microprocessors.

Let us describe some of the important addressing modes:

## 10.5.1 Direct Addressing

This is simplest of all the modes.

The **effective address** is contained in the address part of the instruction. Let us consider an instruction.

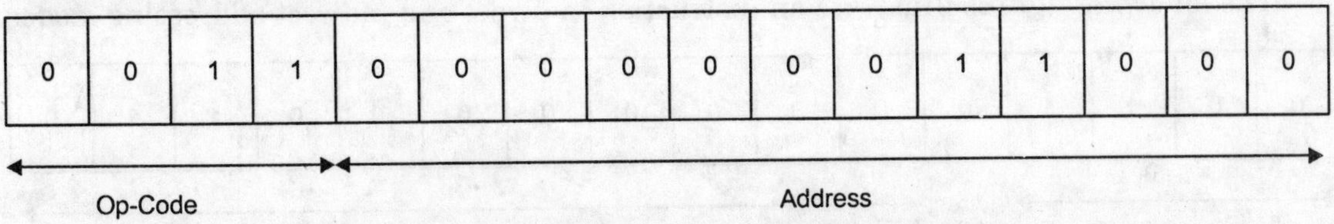


**Fig. 10.12:** Direct addressing mode.

Here the address 000000011000 (decimal equivalent 24) is the direct address of the operand. If the op-code 0011 stands for LOAD Accumulator then this instruction when executed will load the accumulator with the data stored in memory location 24, erasing out the previous contents of the accumulator. This data will reach the accumulator through MDR (Memory Data Register). In a branch-type instruction the address field specifies the actual branch address.

### *Advantages of Direct Addressing*

Direct addressing is the simplest, fast and very effective. In this case only one address of the operand is required.

### *Disadvantages of Direct Addressing Mode*

The direct addressing mode is inconvenient for the computers having large memories. Consider the 16-bit instruction word. The first four bits are occupied by the op-code and only 12 bits are left for the address part. Using these 12 bits for the address of the operand in the memory, only $2^{12}$ (= 4096 = 4K) memory locations can be addressed. If a computer has memory of 4K words then this mode of addressing does not pose any problems. On the other hand if memory size is bigger, say 8K, 16K or 32K words, then all the memory locations in these can't be addressed by the 16 bit instruction word using direct address mode. To address all these locations, either the longer computer word is needed, or more than one computer word may be used to specify the address of the memory location so that more bits are available for the address part of the instruction. This method of using more than one word for addressing a memory location is called *Extended Addressing*.

But use of longer computer words is expensive and quite often wasteful, the extended addressing procedure is slow and causes complications in the fetch and execute cycles.

This disadvantage of addressing memory locations can be overcome by using *Indirect Addressing* or *Immediate Addressing*.

## 10.5.2 Indirect Addressing

Effective address = contents of the memory address specified in instruction.

In the normal implementation of this mode one bit is reserved (known as the "indirection bit") in the instruction format to indicate if indirection is in effect or not. In assembly language a * mark is used in front of the symbolic address to denote indirect addressing. If this bit is 1 then it implies the indirect addressing mode and 0 in this bit signifies direct addressing mode.

The following figures illustrate an instruction in direct and indirect addressing modes.

| | | | | | | | | | | | | | | | |
|---|---|---|---|---|---|---|---|---|---|---|---|---|---|---|---|
| 0 | 0 | 1 | 1 | 0 | 0 | 0 | 0 | 0 | 0 | 0 | 0 | 0 | 1 | 1 | 0 |

Op-Code | Indirect bit | Address

(*a*) Direct addressing mode

| | | | | | | | | | | | | | | | |
|---|---|---|---|---|---|---|---|---|---|---|---|---|---|---|---|
| 0 | 0 | 1 | 1 | 1 | 0 | 0 | 0 | 0 | 0 | 0 | 0 | 0 | 1 | 1 | 0 |

Op-Code | Indirect bit | Address

(*b*) Indirect addressing mode

**Fig. 10.13:** Direct/indirect addressing mode.

Now if 0011 is the op-code for addition, then the instruction in Figure 10.13(*a*) means "Add the contents of the memory location 6 (decimal equivalent of 0000000110) to the contents of the accumulator and leave the result in the accumulator".

On the other hand the instruction in Figure 10.13(*b*) means "ADD the contents of the memory location specified by memory location 6 to the contents of the accumulator and leave the result in the accumulator". Thus the memory location 6 does not contain the operand but address of another memory location which contains the operand.

If contents of memory location 6 are as given in Figure 10.14,

| | | | | | | | | | | | | | | | |
|---|---|---|---|---|---|---|---|---|---|---|---|---|---|---|---|
| 0 | 0 | 0 | 0 | 0 | 0 | 0 | 0 | 0 | 0 | 0 | 0 | 1 | 0 | 1 | 1 |

**Fig. 10.14**

then it means that operand is stored in memory location 11. Now all the bits of memory location 6 are available for specifying the address of the operand because this location is to contain only an address and no bits for op-code.

So $2^{16}$ = 65,536 or 64K locations can be addressed and in direct addressing mode only $2^{12}$ = 4K memory locations, with the same word length.

### *Disadvantages of Indirect Addressing*

The indirect addressing mode although provides a facility to address a large number of memory locations, its suffers from the following draw-backs:

(*i*) This mode of addressing puts severe restrictions on the number of addressible memory locations. Since one bit of address part is reserved for specifying mode of addressing, only 11 bits are left for addressing memory locations which allows only $2^{11}$ = 2048 memory locations to be addressed.

(*ii*) In this mode of addressing for each operand two addresses are required which makes the fetch-execute cycle quite long, resulting is slow speed of computation.

## 10.5.3 Indexed Addressing

Effective Address = address field contents + contents of the specified-index register.

In this mode of addressing an attempt is made to avoid the use of two addresses for an operand. However the addition of the contents of the index register to memory address register makes the execution procedure quite slow. Moreover, one more bit of the address part of the instruction is reserved for indicating the mode as *Indexed Addressing*. This bit is called Index bit. If this bit is set to 1 then control unit interprets it to be an indexed addressing and if this is set to 0, it means that this is not the case of indexed addressing. The indexed addressing may be direct or indirect depending upon whether the indirect bit is 0 or 1. The following instruction is an example of direct indexed addressing:

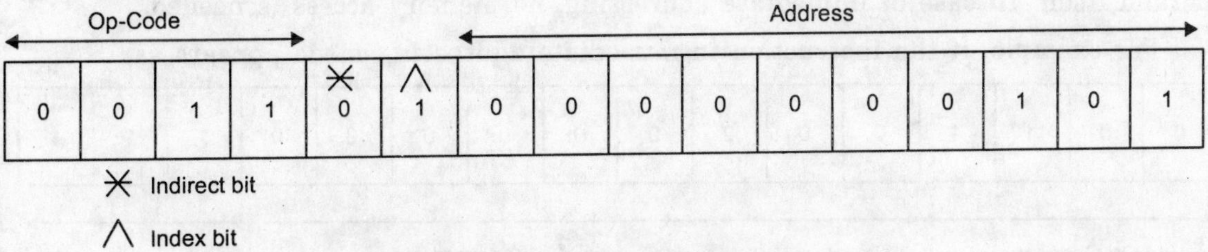


**Fig. 10.15:** Direct indexed addressing mode.

The indirect bit being 0 indicates that it is direct addressing and index bit being 1 signifies indexed addressing.

Let the contents of the index register be 8, which is stored as

| | | | | | | | | | | | | | | | |
|---|---|---|---|---|---|---|---|---|---|---|---|---|---|---|---|
| 0 | 0 | 0 | 0 | 0 | 0 | 0 | 0 | 0 | 0 | 0 | 0 | 1 | 0 | 0 | 0 |

**Fig. 10.16:** Contents of index register.

The decoder gives the absolute (effective) address of the operand which is sum of 5 and 8 to give 13. The effective address is transmitted to MAR. The address obtained by MAR contains the operand which is passed to ALU via MDR.

However, if indirect bit is 1, then it is the case of indirect addressing. In this case the memory location 13 contains the memory address of another location which contains the operand.

***Advantages of indexed addressing***

(*i*) In indexed addressing mode the operand can be loaded in accumulator in one step if it is case of direct indexed addressing.

(*ii*) The addition of the contents of the index register to the address part of the instruction makes it possible to obtain larger addresses, consequently more memory locations can be addressed.

***Disadvantages of indexed addressing***

(*i*) The process of addition of the contents of the index register to the address in the instruction makes the process of the execution of an instruction slower.

(*ii*) The number of address bits in an instruction becomes less. In the above case only 10-bits are left in the address part of the instruction. The range of address specified in the instruction is further reduced.

**Note.** *The index register can be fed with the data in a number of ways. We assume that index register can be loaded through the accumulator by using appropriate instructions.*

## 10.5.4 Immediate Addressing

In case data to be loaded in the accumulator forms part of the instruction then it is called *Immediate Addressing*. Thus, the address part of the instruction is replaced by the operand itself. In case of immediate addressing, no memory access is needed.

For example, if the instruction in immediate addressing mode appears as,

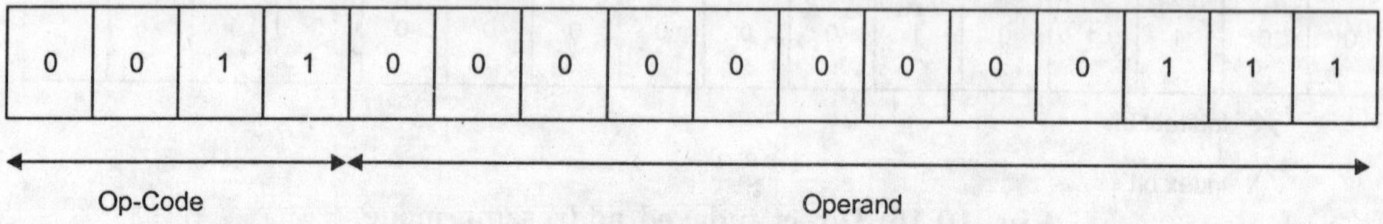


**Fig. 10.17:** Immediate addressing mode.

then, this instruction implies "ADD the number 7, decimal equivalent of 111, to the contents of the accumulator and leave the contents in the accumulator", where 0011 is OP-Code for addition.

This method of addressing is quite simple, efficient and quick. However, it suffers from the drawback that it can deal with small data values.

In this case, only 12 bits are left for the operand, and the largest value of operand can be $2^{12} = 4096$. If a number greater than this is to be used as an operand, this method is unsuitable.

## 10.5.5 Relative Addressing

Effective Address = Contents of the program counter + contents of address field.

This mode of addressing should be called PC-relative addressing.

In this mode the content of the program counter is added to the address part of the instruction to obtain the effective address. The address part of the instruction is usually a signed number (in 2's complement representation) which can be either positive or negative. When this number is added to the contents of the program counter (PC), the result produces an effective address whose position in memory is relative to the address of the next instruction.

This mode of addressing is often used in branch type instructions to set up a short program loop. If 8 bits were available for this purpose in the address field, as in PDP – 11, the range of accessible addresses would be from (PC) – 128 to (PC) + 127, where (PC) stands for the contents of the program counter.

### 10.5.6 Implied Mode

In this mode the operands are specified implicitly in the definition of the instruction. For example, the instruction "complement accumulator" is an implied-mode instruction because the operand in the accumulator register is implied in the definition of the instruction. In fact, all register reference instructions that use an accumulator are implied-mode instructions.

Zero-address instructions in a stack-organized computer are implied-mode instructions since the operands are implied to be on top of the stack.

### 10.5.7 Register Mode

In this mode the operands are in registers that reside within the CPU. The particular register is selected from a register field in the instruction. A $k$-bit field can specify any one of $2^k$ registers.

### 10.5.8 Register Indirect Addressing

In this mode the instruction specifies a register in the CPU whose contents give the address of the operand in memory. In other words, the selected register contains the address of the operand rather than the operand itself. Before using a register indirect mode instruction, the programmer must ensure that the memory address of the operand is placed in the processor register with a previous instruction. A reference to the register is then equivalent to specifying a memory address. The advantage of a register indirect mode instruction is that the address field of the instruction uses fewer bits to select a register than would have been required to specify a memory address directly.

### 10.5.9 Autoincrement/Autodecrement Addressing

This is similar to the register indirect mode except that the register is incremented or decremented after (or before) its value is used to access memory. When the address stored in the register refers to a table of data in memory, it is necessary to increment or decrement the register after every access to the table. This can be achieved by using the increment or decrement instruction. However, because it is such a common requirement, some computers incorporate a special mode that automatically increments or decrements the content of the register after data access.

The address field of an instruction is used by the control unit in the CPU to obtain the operand from memory. Sometimes the value given in the address field is the address of the operand, but sometimes it is just an address from which the address of the operand is calculated. To differentiate among the various addressing modes it is necessary to distinguish between the address part of the instruction and the effective address used by the control when executing the instruction. The **effective address** is defined to be the memory address obtained from the computation dictated by the given addressing mode. The effective address is the address of the operand in a computational-type instruction. It is the address where control branches in response to a branch-type instruction.

### 10.5.10 Base Addressing

In this mode the content of a base register is added to the address part of the instruction to obtain the effective address. This is similar to the indexed addressing mode except that the register is now called a base register instead of an index register. The difference between the two modes is in the way they are used rather than in the way that they are computed. An index register is assumed to hold an index number that is relative to the address part of the instruction. A base register is assumed to hold a base address and the address field of the instruction gives a displacement relative to this base address. The base register addressing mode is used in computers to facilitate the relocation of programs in memory. When programs and data are moved from one segment of memory to another, as required in multiprogramming systems, the address values of instructions must reflect this change of position. With a base register, the displacement values of instructions do not have to change. Only the value of the base register requires updating to reflect the beginning of a new memory segment.

## 10.6 EXAMPLE OF ADDRESSING MODES

To show the differences between the various modes, we will show the effect of the addressing modes on the instruction defined in Figure 10.18.

The two word instruction at address 200 and 201 is a **"load to AC"** instruction with an address field equal to 500. The first word of the instruction specifies the operation code and mode, and the second word specifies the address part. PC (Program Counter) has the value 200 for fetching this instruction. The content of processor register R1 is 400, and the content of an index register IR is 100. AC (Accumulator) receives the operand after the instruction is executed. Figure 10.18 lists a few pertinent addresses and shows the memory content at each of these addresses.

The mode field of the instruction can specify any one of a number of modes. For each possible mode we calculate the **effective address** and the operand that must be loaded into AC.

In the *direct address mode* the effective address is the address part of the instruction 500 and the operand to be loaded into AC is 800.

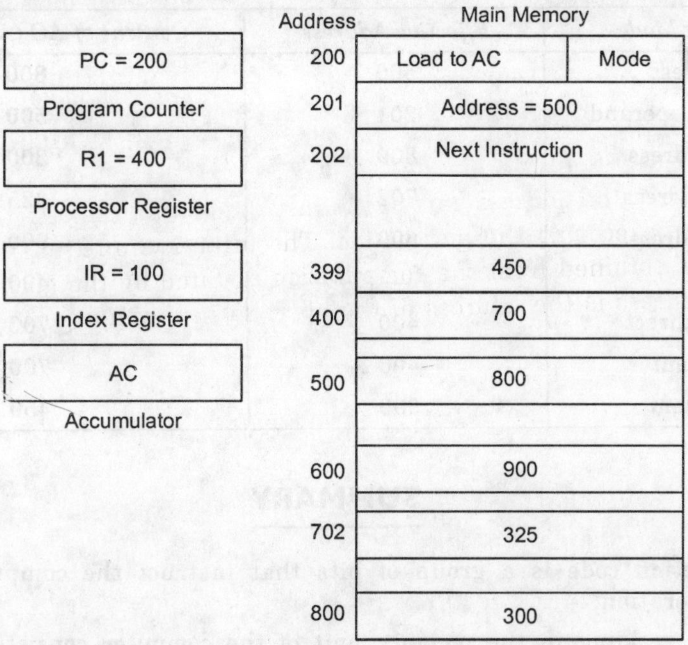


**Fig. 10.18:** Example for addressing modes.

In the *immediate mode* the second word of the instruction is taken as the operand rather than an address, so 500 is loaded into AC. (The effective address in this case is 201).

In the *indirect mode* the effective address is stored in memory at address 500. Therefore, the effective address is 800 and the operand is 300.

In the *relative mode* the effective address is 500 + 202 = 702 and the operand is 325. (Note that the value in PC after the fetch phase and during the execute phase is 202.)

In the *index mode* the effective address is IR + 500 = 100 + 500 = 600 and the operand is 900.

In the *register mode* the operand is in R1 and 400 is loaded into AC. (There is no effective address in this case.)

In the *register indirect mode* the effective address is 400, equal to the content of R1 and the operand loaded into AC is 700.

The *autoincrement mode* is the same as the register indirect mode except that R1 is incremented to 401 after the execution of the instruction.

The *autodecrement mode* decrements R1 to 399 prior to the execution of the instruction. The operand loaded into AC is now 450.

Table 10.5 lists the values of the effective address and the operand loaded into AC for some of the addressing modes.

**Table 10.5: Tabular List of Numerical Example**

| *Addressing Mode* | *Effective Address* | *Content of AC (Accumulator)* |
|---|---|---|
| Direct address | 500 | 800 |
| Immediate operand | 201 | 500 |
| Indirect address | 800 | 300 |
| Relative address | 702 | 325 |
| Indexed address | 600 | 900 |
| Register | — | 400 |
| Register indirect | 400 | 700 |
| Autoincrement | 400 | 700 |
| Autodecrement | 399 | 450 |

## SUMMARY

- An instruction code is a group of bits that instruct the computer to perform a specific operation.
- A program residing in the memory unit of the computer consists of a sequence of instructions.
- Accumulator is the register where answers to arithmetic and logic operations are accumulated.
- Instruction register is the register that receives the instruction from the memory.
- Program counter stores the address of the next instruction to be fetched from the memory.
- **MAR (Memory Address Register)** receives the address of the data to be accessed in memory. It supplies this address to the memory.
- **MBR (Memory Buffer Register)** or **Data Register (DR)** holds the instruction code or data received from or sent to the memory.
- Instruction register receives the instruction from the memory and holds it until it is decoded.
- Op-code (operation code) is that part of the instruction which tells the computer what operation to perform.
- Instruction cycle means all the states needed to fetch and execute an instruction.
- **Instruction format** means way of specifying opcode and data or address.
- The techniques of specifying the address of the data are known as **addressing modes.**

## REVIEW QUESTIONS AND EXERCISES

1. Explain instruction format. What are the various types of instruction formats? Discuss them with suitable examples.

2. Discuss the various types of addressing modes which are usually provided in a microprocessor. Give suitable examples.
3. Write a short note on microprogramming concepts.
4. Describe the microprogram organisation for controlling the processor unit.
5. Describe the microprogram sequencer for a control memory.
6. Write a short note on microprogrammed CPU organisation.
7. Describe the CISC and RISC machines.
8. Compare various CPU's features.
9. What is the purpose of using address mode techniques by a computer ? Summarize the various addressing modes?
10. State True or False:
    (*i*) The CPU is the "leg" of the computer.
    (*ii*) The CPU consists of two parts—the control unit and the arithmetic/logic unit, both of which contain registers.
    (*iii*) Buses are electrical data roadways that transmit data within CPU and between CPU and main memory and peripherals.
    (*iv*) The machine cycle executes instructions one at a time during the instruction cycle and the execution cycle.
    (*v*) The instructions for microprocessor are assigned by the computer manufacturer and tend to be different in different computers.
    (*vi*) The *push* and *pop* instructions transfer data among processor registers and a memory stack.
    (*vii*) The way the operands are determined during program execution is determined from the *addressing mode* of the instruction.
    (*viii*) The address of the operand or the address where control branches in response to a jump, branch, or call instruction is called the *home address*.
11. Fill in the blanks:
    (*i*) The ..................... is often referred to as the "brain" of a computer.
    (*ii*) The ..................... is the part of the microprocessor that tells the rest of the computer how to carry out a program's instructions.
    (*iii*) ..................... is used to measure processing speed in microcomputers.
    (*iv*) The ..................... set of a computer determines its power.
    (*v*) In .................. mode the operand is specified implicitly in the definition of the instruction.
    (*vi*) ..................instructions are used to test status conditions in registers and, depending on results, cause a change in program sequence.
    (*vii*) A ..................sequences the microinstructions in control memory.
    (*viii*) To solve the problem of complexity and comparatively slow speed of CISC machines computer industry is now producing simple and fast .................. machines.

## ANSWERS

9. We know that the addressing modes specify a rule for interpreting or modifying the address field of the instruction before the operand is actually referred. The purpose of using address mode techniques by the computer is to accommodate one or both of the following provisions.

(*i*) To give programming versatility to the user by providing such facilities as pointers to memory, counters for loop control, indexing of data, and program relocation.

(*ii*) To reduce the number of bits in the address field of the instruction.

| Op-code | Mode | Address |
|---|---|---|

Instruction format with mode field.

The various types of addressing modes are summarized below:

- ***Implied Mode.*** In this mode the operand is specified implicitly in the definition of the instruction. Instructions of this type are 1-byte instructions. For example, the instruction "complement accumulator" is an implied-mode instruction because the operand in the accumulator register is implied in the definition of the instruction.
- ***Register Mode.*** In this mode the operands are available in registers which reside within the CPU. Register-mode instructions are 1-byte instructions and can be executed within the CPU without the need to reference memory for operands.
- ***Register-indirect Mode.*** In this mode the instruction specifies a register or a pair of registers in the processor whose contents provide the address of the operand in memory. This mode uses 1-byte instructions even though the operand is in memory. Before using a register-indirect-mode instruction, the programmer must ensure that the address of the operand is placed in the processor register with a previous transfer-type instruction. A reference to the register is then equivalent to specifying a memory address.
- ***Immediate Mode.*** This mode specifies the operand in the instruction itself. In an 8-bit microprocessor, the operand is placed in memory immediately after the operation-code byte. An immediate-mode instruction having an 8-bit operand is a 2-byte instruction. One with a 16-bit operand is a 3-byte instruction.
- ***Direct-addressing Mode.*** In this mode the operand resides in memory and its address is provided directly in the address part of the instruction. In 8-bit microprocessors with 16-bit addresses, a direct instruction consists of 3 bytes. In computers with wider memory words, the address part is combined with the operation and mode code bits to combine the entire instruction in one memory word. Most direct-mode instructions assume that the other operands reside in processor registers. If more than one operand resides in memory, the instruction must include additional addresses to specify their locations.
- ***Zero-page Addressing.*** This addressing mode is similar to the direct-addressing mode except that the address part of the instruction contains only 1 byte. This is a 2-byte instruction, with the second byte specifying the 8 low-order bits of a memory address. The 8 high-order bits of the address are assumed to be all 0's. This restricts the range of addresses to the lowest 256 bytes of memory (0–255) which is defined to be page 0.
- ***Present-page Addressing.*** This mode assumes that the operand resides in memory within the same memory page as the instruction that uses it. Since the program counter always holds the address of the next instruction, its 8 high-order bits also contain the present page number. This mode of addressing uses 2-byte instructions, with an 8-bit address part. The address of the operand is obtained from the page number catenated with the address part of the instruction.

- ***Relative Addressing.*** This mode is similar to the present-page addressing mode except that it is not sensitive to page boundaries. A relative-mode instruction is a 2-byte instruction, with the second byte specifying a signed number in the range between –128 and +127. This is accomplished by representing the number in sign-2's-complement form. The 16-bit address of the operand is computed by adding the 16-bit content presently available in the program counter to the 8-bit signed address in the instruction.

**Effective Address = Address part of instruction + content of CPU register**

where, CPU register may be Program Counter, Index Register or a Base Register. The computation of some of the **effective addresses** is given in the following table.

**Table : Computation of Effective Address for Various Addressing Modes**

| *Address Mode* | *Effective Address* | *Comments* |
|---|---|---|
| Direct | AD16 | 16-bit address part of instruction |
| Zero page | AD8 | 8-bit address part of instruction |
| Present page | PC(H) + AD8 | 8 highest-order bits of PC catenated with AD8 |
| Relative | PC + AD8 | Contents of PC plus signed AD8 |
| Indexed | XR + AD16 | Contents of XR plus AD16 |
| Base register | XR + AD8 | Contents of XR plus AD8 |
| Indirect | M[AD16] | Address stored in location given by AD16 |
| Indexed-indirect | M[XR + AD8] | Address stored in location (XR + AD8) |
| Indirect-indexed | M[AD8] + XR | Address stored in location AD8 plus contents of XR |

Here, PC is the program counter, XR is an index register, AD16 and AD8 denote 2-byte and 1-byte address.

- ***Indexed Addressing.*** Instructions in this mode have 3 bytes, with the last two giving a 16-bit address. The address part of the instruction is added to the value presently stored in the index register to calculate the **effective address.** The index register is often incremented or decremented to facilitate the execution of program loops and to access tables of data stored in memory.
- ***Base-register Addressing.*** It is similar to the indexed-addressing mode, except that the address part of the instruction consists of a number of bits that is less than the number of bits required for a full address. The **effective address** is obtained by adding the contents of the index register to the partial address in the instruction. The register used in this mode is sometimes called a **base register** instead of an index register. The base register holds a base address, and the truncated address in the instruction specifies a displacement with respect to the base address.
- ***Indirect Addressing.*** In this mode the address part of the instruction contains the address where the **effective address** is stored. Control reads the address part of the instruction and uses it to address memory again to read the effective address. Memory

must be accessed again to read the operand if the instruction is of the operation type. In a control-type instruction, the effective address is the branch address which is transferred to PC.

- ***Indexed-indirect Addressing.*** It is an indirect-addressing mode, except that the address part of the instruction is added to the contents of the index register to obtain the address where the **effective address** is stored in memory.
- ***Indirect-indexed Addressing.*** In this mode the value stored in the memory location specified by the address part of the instruction is added to the contents of the index register to get the **effective address.**

10. State True or False:

| | |
|---|---|
| *(i)* False | *(ii)* True |
| *(iii)* True | *(iv)* True |
| *(v)* True | *(vi)* True |
| *(vii)* True | *(viii)* False |

11. Fill in the blanks:

| | |
|---|---|
| *(i)* CPU | *(ii)* control unit |
| *(iii)* Megahertz (MHz) | *(iv)* instruction |
| *(v)* implied | *(vi)* Control |
| *(vii)* microprogram sequencer | *(vii)* RISC |

Chapter 11

# MICROPROGRAMMED DESIGN

## 11.1 INTRODUCTION

The purpose of the control unit is to initiate a series of sequential steps of microoperations. During any given time, certain operations are to be initiated while all others remain idle. Thus, the control variables at any given time can be represented by a string of 1's and 0's known as a **control word.** As such, control words can be programmed to initiate the various components in the system in an organized manner. A control unit whose control variables are stored in a memory is known as a **microprogrammed control unit.**

## 11.2 CONCEPT OF MICROPROGRAMMING

Each control word of memory is known as a **microinstruction,** and a sequence of microinstructions is known as a **microprogram.** Since alteration of the microprogram is seldom needed, the control memory can be a ROM. The use of a microprogram involves placing all control variables in words of the ROM for use by the control unit through successive read operations. The content of the word in the ROM at a given address specifies the microoperations for the system.

A more advanced development known as **dynamic** microprogramming permits a microprogram to be loaded initially from the computer console or from an auxiliary memory such as a magnetic disk. Control units that use dynamic microprogramming employ a **writable control memory** (WCM). This type of memory can be used for writing (to change the microprogram) but is used mostly for reading. A ROM, PLA (Programmable Logic Array—It is an LSI (Large Scale Integration) device that can implement any complex combinational circuit), or WCM, when used in a control unit, is referred to as a **control memory.**

Figure 11.1 shows the general configuration of the microprogram control unit. The control memory is assumed to be a ROM, within which all control information is permanently stored. The control memory address register specifies the control word read from control memory. *It must be realized that a ROM operates as a combinational circuit, with the address value as the input and the corresponding word as the output.* The content of the specified word remains on the output wires as long as the address value remains in the address register. No read signal is needed as in a random-access memory. The word out of the ROM should be transferred to a buffer register if the address register changes while the ROM word is still in use. If the change is address and ROM word can occur simultaneously, no buffer register is needed.

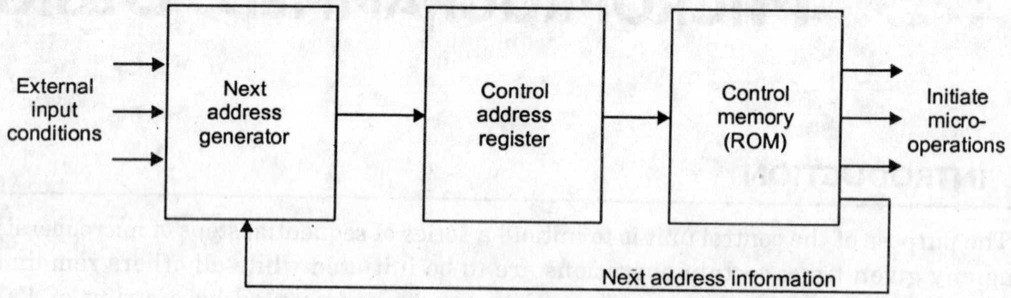


**Fig. 11.1:** Microprogram control logic.

The word read from control memory specifies a microinstruction. The microinstruction represents one or more microoperations for the components of the system. Once these operations are executed, the control unit must determine its next address. The location of the next microinstruction may be the next one in sequence, or it may be located somewhere else in the control memory. For this reason, it is necessary to use some bits of the microinstruction to control the generation of the address for the next microinstruction. The next address may also be a function of external input conditions. While the microoperations are being executed, the next address is computed in the next-address generator circuit and then transferred (with the next clock pulse) into the control address register to read the next microinstruction. The detailed construction of the next address generator depends on the particular application.

## 11.3 MICROPROGRAM CONTROL LOGIC

In a microprogram control, the control variables that initiate microoperations are stored in memory. The control memory is usually a ROM, since the control sequence is permanent and requires no alteration. The control variables stored in memory are read one at a time to initiate the sequence of microoperations for the system.

The words stored in a control memory are microinstructions, and each microinstruction specifies one or more microoperations for the components in the system. Once these microoperations are executed, the control unit must determine its next address. Therefore, a few bits of the microinstruction are used to control the generation of the address for the next microinstruction. Thus, *a microinstruction contains bits for initiating microoperations and bits that determine the next address for the control memory itself.*

In addition to the control memory, a microprogram control unit must include special circuits for selecting the next address as specified by the microinstruction. These circuits and the configuration of the microinstruction bits stored in memory vary from one unit to another. Instead of dwelling on (writing at length about) all the possibilities encountered in different situations, we choose here to introduce the microprogram concept by means of a simple example.

The control logic to be designed is for the sign-magnitude adder-subtracter. A microprogram control will be designed subsequently. Realize, however, that the digital system considered here is too small for a microprogram controller and in practice, a hard-wired control would be more efficient. *The microprogram control organisation is more efficient in large, complicated systems.*

A state in control memory is represented by the address of a microinstruction. An address for control memory specifies a control word within a microinstruction, just as a state in a sequential circuit specifies a microoperation. The control we wish to design is given in Figure 11.2. Since there are eight states in the control, we choose a control memory with eight words having addresses 0 through 7. The address of the control memory corresponds to the subscript number under the T's in the state diagram.

Inspection of the state diagram reveals that the address sequencing in the microprogram control must have the following capabilities.

(*i*) Provision for loading an external address as a result of the occurrence of external signals $q_a$ and $q_s$.

(*ii*) Provision for sequencing consecutive addresses.

(*iii*) Provision for choosing between two addresses as a function of present values of the status variables S and E.

Each microinstruction must have a number of bits to specify the way that the next address is to be selected.

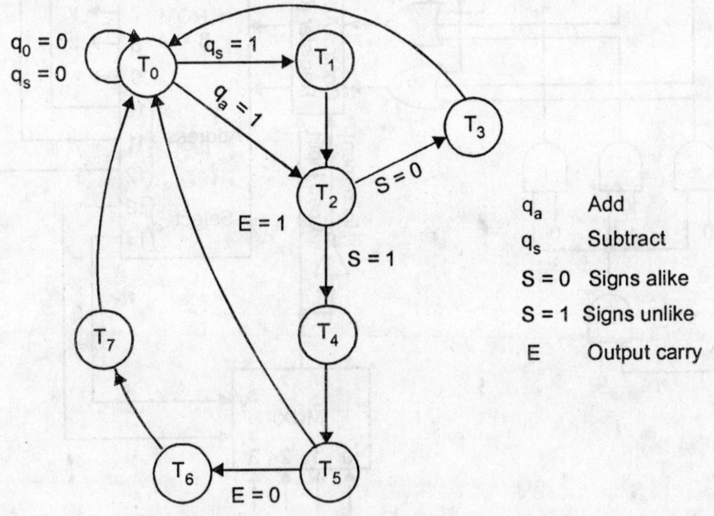


(*a*) State diagram

| | Control Outputs | | | | | | | | |
|---|---|---|---|---|---|---|---|---|---|
| | x | $s_2$ | $s_1$ | $s_0$ | $C_{in}$ | L | y | z | w |
| $T_0$ : Initial state x = 1 | 1 | 0 | 0 | 0 | 0 | 0 | 0 | 0 | 0 |
| $T_1 : B_s \leftarrow \bar{B}_s$ | 0 | 0 | 0 | 0 | 0 | 0 | 1 | 0 | 0 |
| $T_2$ : nothing | 0 | 0 | 0 | 0 | 0 | 0 | 0 | 0 | 0 |
| $T_3 : A \leftarrow A + B, E \leftarrow C_{out}$ | 0 | 0 | 0 | 1 | 0 | 1 | 0 | 0 | 0 |
| $T_4 : A \leftarrow A + \bar{B} + 1, E \leftarrow C_{out}$ | 0 | 0 | 1 | 0 | 1 | 1 | 0 | 0 | 0 |
| $T_5 : E \leftarrow 0$ | 0 | 0 | 0 | 0 | 0 | 0 | 0 | 0 | 1 |
| $T_6 : A \leftarrow \bar{A}$ | 0 | 1 | 1 | 1 | 0 | 1 | 0 | 0 | 0 |
| $T_7 : A \leftarrow A + 1, A_s \leftarrow \bar{A}_s$ | 0 | 0 | 0 | 0 | 1 | 1 | 0 | 1 | 0 |

(*b*) **Sequence of register transfers**

**Fig. 11.2: Control state diagram and sequence of microoperations.**

***Hardware Configuration***

The organisation of the microprogram control unit is shown in Figure 11.3. The control memory is an 8-word by 14-bit ROM. The first nine bits of a microinstruction word

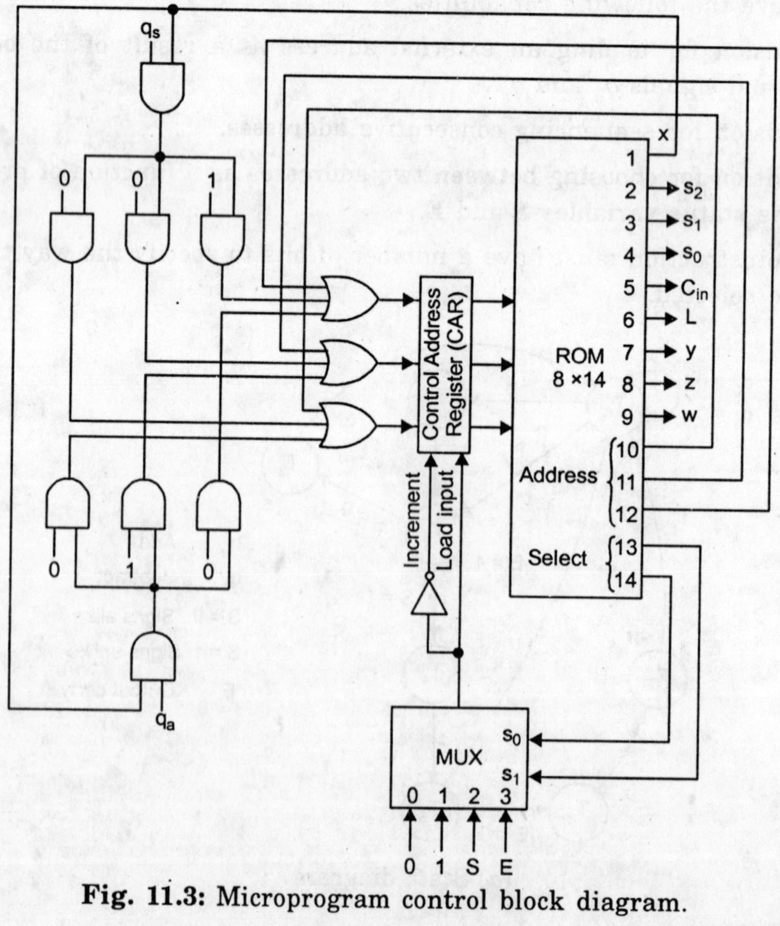


**Fig. 11.3:** Microprogram control block diagram.

contain the control variables that initiate the microoperations. The last five bits provide information for selecting the next address. The control address register (CAR) holds the address for the control memory. This register receives an input value when its load control is enabled; otherwise, it is incremented by 1. CAR is essentially a counter with parallel-load capability.

Bits 10, 11 and 12 of a microinstruction contain an address for CAR. Bits 13 and 14 select an input for a multiplexer. Bit 1 provides the initial state condition denoted by variable $x$ and also enables an external address when $q_s$ or $q_a$ is equal to 1. We stipulate that when $x = 1$, the address field of the microinstruction must be 000. Then if $q_s = 1$, address 001 is available at the inputs of CAR, but if $q_a = 1$, address 010 is applied to CAR. If both $q_s$ and $q_a$ are 0's, the zero address from bits 10, 11, and 12 are applied to the inputs of CAR. In this way, the control memory stays at address zero until an external variable is enabled.

The multiplexer (MUX) has four inputs that are selected with bits 13 and 14 of the microinstruction. The functions of the multiplexer select bits are given in Table 11.1. If bits 13 and 14 are 00, a multiplexer input that is equal to 0 is selected. The output of the multiplexer is 0, and the increment input to CAR is enabled. This configuration increments CAR to choose the next address in sequence. An input of 1 is selected by the multiplexer when bits 13 and 14 are equal to 01. The output of the multiplexer is 1 and the external input is loaded into CAR. Status variable S is selected when bits 13 and 14 are equal to 10. If S = 1, the output of the multiplexer is 1 and the address bits of the microinstruction are loaded into CAR (provided $x = 0$). If S = 0, the output of the multiplexer is 0 and CAR is incremented. With bits 13 and 14 equal to 11, status variable E is selected and the address field is loaded into CAR if E = 1, but CAR is incremented if E = 0. Thus, the multiplexer permits the control to choose between two addresses, depending on the value of the status bit selected.

**Table 11.1: Functions of the Multiplexer Select Bits**

| *ROM* 13 | *Bits* 14 | *MUX Select Function* |
|---|---|---|
| 0 | 0 | Increment CAR |
| 0 | 1 | Load input to CAR |
| 1 | 0 | Load input to CAR if S = 1, increment CAR if S = 0 |
| 1 | 1 | Load inputs to CAR if E = 1, increment CAR if E = 0 |

### Microprogram

Once the configuration of a microprogram control unit is established, the designer's task is to generate the microcode for the control memory. This code generation is called *microprogramming* and is a *process that determines the bit configuration for each and all words in control memory.* To appreciate this process, we will derive the microprogram for the adder-subtractor example. The control memory has eight words and each word contains 14 bits. To microprogram the control memory, we must determine the bit values of each of the eight words.

The register-transfer method can be adopted for developing a microprogram. The microoperation sequence can be specified with register-transfer statements. There is no need for listing control functions with Boolean variables since, in this case, the control variables are the control words stored in control memory. Instead of a control function, we specify an address with each register-transfer statement. The address associated with each symbolic statement corresponds to the address where the microinstruction is to be stored in memory. The sequencing from one address to the next can be indicated by means of conditional control statements. This type of statement can specify the address to which control goes, depending on status conditions. Thus, instead of thinking in terms of the 1's and 0's that must be inserted for each microinstruction, it is more convenient to think in terms of symbols in the register-transfer method. Once the symbolic microprogram is established, it is possible to translate the register-transfer statements to their equivalent binary form.

The microprogram in symbolic form is given in Table 11.2. The eight address of the ROM are given in the first column. In the second column, the microinstruction that must be stored at each address is given in symbolic form.

**Table 11.2: Symbolic Microprogram for Control Memory**

| *ROM Address* | *Microinstruction* | *What it means ?* |
|---|---|---|
| 0 | $x$ = 1, if ($q_s$ = 1) then (go to 1), if ($q_a$ = 1) then (go to 2), if ($q_s \wedge q_a$ = 0) then (go to 0) | Load 0 or external address |
| 1 | $B_s \leftarrow \overline{B}_s$ | $q_s$ = 1, start subtraction |
| 2 | If (S = 1) then (go to 4) | $q_a$ = 1, start addition |
| 3 | $A \leftarrow A + B$, $E \leftarrow C_{out}$, go to 0 | Add magnitudes and return |
| 4 | $A \leftarrow A + \overline{B} + 1$, $E \leftarrow C_{out}$, | Subtract magnitudes |
| 5 | If (E = 1) then (go to 0), $E \leftarrow 0$ | Operation terminated if E = 1 |
| 6 | $A \leftarrow \overline{A}$ | E = 0, complement A |
| 7 | $A \leftarrow A + 1$, $A_s \leftarrow \overline{A}_s$, go to 0 | Done, return to address 0 |

Address 0 is equivalent to the initial state and gives an output $x$ = 1. The next address depends on the values of external variables $q_s$ and $q_a$. The three conditional control statements in this microinstruction use a **go to** statement after the word **then.** It means that if the condition is satisfied, control goes to the address written after the words **go to.** Thus, if both $q_s$ and $q_a$ are 0, control stays in address 0 to repeat the microinstruction. If $q_s$ or $q_a$ is 1, control goes to address 1 or 2, respectively.

The conditional control statements in the other microinstructions use the status variables S and E. The **go to** statement without a condition attached specifies an unconditional branch to the indicated address. For example, go to 0 means that control goes to address 0 after the present microinstruction is executed. It there is no **go to** statement in the microinstruction, it means that the next microinstruction is taken from the next address in sequence. Also, if the condition after an **if** statement is not satisfied, control goes to the next address in sequence.

The microinstructions associated with the eight addresses are derived directly form the control specifications of Figure 11.2. The microoperations listed are identical to the ones listed in Figure 11.2(*b*). The conditional control statement specifies the address sequence as given by the state diagram of Figure 11.2(*a*). Note that each address number is the same as the subscript number under the T's in the state diagram. This should be obvious that the conditional control statements provide a different way to specify a state diagram. It shows that the register-transfer method can be used to specify a sequential circuit.

The microprogram in Table 11.2 can be derived directly from the flowchart of Figure 11.4.

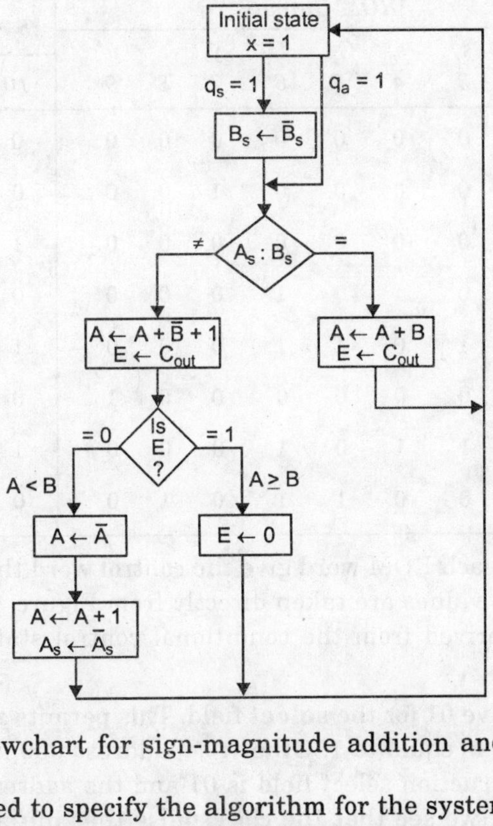


**Fig. 11.4:** Flowchart for sign-magnitude addition and subtraction.

This flowchart is used to specify the algorithm for the system that we are attempting to design. Although the microprogram developed here seems to require many intermediate steps, it must be realized that this is done for explanatory purposes. Once the microprogram concept is understood, there is no reason we could not specify the algorithm directly as a symbolic microprogram without the need for a state diagram. Once the equipment configuration for the data processor and the microprogram control is established, the algorithm can be developed by means of a microprogram.

The symbolic designation is a convenient method for developing the microprogram in a way that people can read and understand. But this is not the way that the microprogram is stored in control memory. The symbolic microprogram must be translated to binary because this is the form that goes into memory. The translation is done by dividing the bits of each microinstruction into their functional parts called **fields.** Here we have three functional parts. Bits 1 through 9 specify the control word for initiating the microoperations. Bits 10 through 12 specify an address field, and bits 13 and 14 select a multiplexer input. For each microinstruction listed in symbolic form, we most choose the appropriate bits in the corresponding microinstruction fields.

The equivalent binary form of the microprogram is given in Table 11.3. The addresses for the ROM control memory are given in binary. The content of each word of ROM is also listed in binary. This table constitutes the truth table required for programming the ROM.

**Table 11.3: Binary Microprogram for Control Memory**

| *ROM Address* | | | *ROM Outputs* | | | | | | | | | *Address* | | | *Select* | |
|---|---|---|---|---|---|---|---|---|---|---|---|---|---|---|---|---|
| | | | $x$ | $s_2$ | $s_1$ | $s_0$ | $C_{in}$ | $L$ | $y$ | $z$ | $w$ | | | | | |
| | | | *1* | *2* | *3* | *4* | *5* | *6* | *7* | *8* | *9* | *10* | *11* | *12* | *13* | *14* |
| 0 | 0 | 0 | 1 | 0 | 0 | 0 | 0 | 0 | 0 | 0 | 0 | 0 | 0 | 0 | 0 | 1 |
| 0 | 0 | 1 | 0 | 0 | 0 | 0 | 0 | 0 | 1 | 0 | 0 | 0 | 1 | 0 | 0 | 1 |
| 0 | 1 | 0 | 0 | 0 | 0 | 0 | 0 | 0 | 0 | 0 | 0 | 1 | 0 | 0 | 1 | 0 |
| 0 | 1 | 1 | 0 | 0 | 0 | 1 | 0 | 1 | 0 | 0 | 0 | 0 | 0 | 0 | 0 | 1 |
| 1 | 0 | 0 | 0 | 0 | 1 | 0 | 1 | 1 | 0 | 0 | 0 | 1 | 0 | 1 | 0 | 1 |
| 1 | 0 | 1 | 0 | 0 | 0 | 0 | 0 | 0 | 0 | 0 | 1 | 0 | 0 | 0 | 1 | 1 |
| 1 | 1 | 0 | 0 | 1 | 1 | 1 | 0 | 1 | 0 | 0 | 0 | 1 | 1 | 1 | 0 | 1 |
| 1 | 1 | 1 | 0 | 0 | 0 | 0 | 1 | 1 | 0 | 1 | 0 | 0 | 0 | 0 | 0 | 1 |

The first nine bits in each ROM word give the control word that initiates the specified microoperations. These bit values are taken directly from Figure 11.2(*b*). The last five bits in each ROM word are derived from the conditional control statements in the symbolic program.

At address 000, we have 01 for the **select** field. This permits an external address to be loaded into CAR if $q_s$ or $q_a$ is equal to 1. Otherwise, address 000 is transferred to CAR. In address 001, the microinstruction select field is 01 and the address field is 010. From the Table 11.1 for Figure 11.3, we see that the clock pulse that initiates the microoperations $B_s \leftarrow \overline{B}_s$ (because $y = 1$) also transfers the address field into CAR. The next microinstruction out of ROM will be the one stored in address 010. The select field at address 001 could have been chosen to be 00. This would have caused CAR to increment and go to address 010.

Looking at the select field in bits 13 and 14, we see that when these two bits are equal to 01, the address field is the next address. When these two bits are 10, status variable S is selected, and when they are 11, status variable E is selected. In the last two cases, the next address is the one provided in the address field if the selected status bit is equal to 1. If the selected status bit is equal to 0, the next address is the one next in sequence because CAR is incremented.

## 11.4 MICROPROGRAMMED CONTROL UNIT

The hardware configuration of the microprogram control unit discussed in section 11.3 is suitable for the particular example considered. *In a practical situation, the hardware organisation of a microprogram control unit must have a general-purpose configuration to suit a wide variety of situations. A general-purpose microprogram control unit must have a control memory large enough to store many microinstructions.* Provisions must be made to include all possible control variables in the system—not only for controlling an ALU. The multiplexer and select bits must include all other possible status bits that one may want to check in the system. A provision must be available to accept an external address to initiate many operations rather than just two operations such as add and subtract.

*The main advantage of the microprogram control is the fact that, once the hardware configuration is established, there should be no need for further hardware or wiring changes. If we want to establish a different control sequence for the system, all we need to do is specify a different set of microinstructions for the control memory. The hardware configuration should not change for different operations; the only change should be in the microprogram residing in control memory.*

To show the general property of the microprogram organisation, we will expand the hardware configuration to include the control of an entire processor unit. A general-purpose processor unit is shown in Figure 11.5.

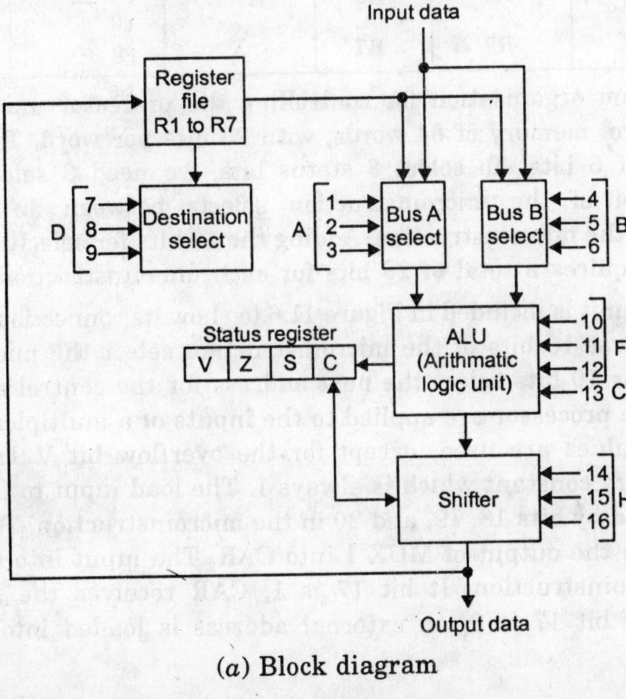


(*a*) Block diagram

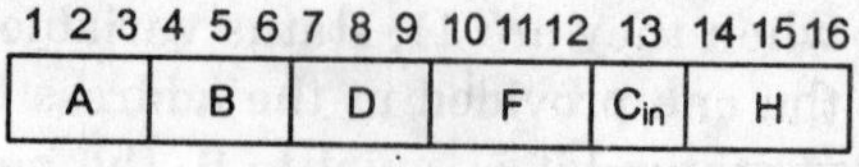


(*b*) Control word

**Fig. 11.5:** Processor unit with control variables.

We note that the processor unit has seven registers an ALU, a shifter, and a status register. A microoperation is selected with a control word of 16 bits. The bits for a given control word can be formulated from the binary code listed in Table 11.4 given as:

**Table 11.4: Functions of Control Variables for the Processor of Fig. 11.5**

| *Binary Code* | *Function of the Selection Variables* | | | | | |
|---|---|---|---|---|---|---|
| | *A* | *B* | *D* | *F with* $C_{in} = 0$ | *F with* $C_{in} = 1$ | *H* |
| 0 0 0 | Input data | Input data | None | A, C ← 0 | A + 1 | No shift |
| 0 0 1 | R1 | R1 | R1 | A + B | A + B + 1 | Shift-right, $I_R = 0$ |
| 0 1 0 | R2 | R2 | R2 | A – B – 1 | A – B | Shift-left, $I_L = 0$ |
| 0 1 1 | R3 | R3 | R3 | A – 1 | A, C ← 1 | 0's to output bus |
| 1 0 0 | R4 | R4 | R4 | A ∨ B | — | — |
| 1 0 1 | R5 | R5 | R5 | A ⊕ B | — | Circulate-right with C |
| 1 1 0 | R6 | R6 | R6 | A ∧ B | — | Circulate-left with C |
| 1 1 1 | R7 | R7 | R7 | $\bar{A}$ | — | — |

A microprogram organisation for controlling the processor unit is shown in Figure 11.6. It has a control memory of 64 words, with 26 bits per word. To select 64 words, we need an address of 6 bits. To select 8 status bits, we need 3 selection lines for the multiplexer. One bit of the microinstruction selects between an external address and the address field of the microinstruction. Adding the 16 bits for selecting the microoperation in the processor requires a total of 26 bits for each microinstruction.

The processor unit is included in Figure 11.6 to show its connection to the microprogram control unit. The first 16 bits of the microinstruction select the microoperations for the processor. The other 10 bits select the next address for the control address register. The status bits from the processor are applied to the inputs of a multiplexer. Both the normal and complement values are used, except for the overflow bit V. Input 0 of MUX 2 is connected to a binary constant which is always 1. The load input to CAR is enabled when this input is selected by bits 18, 19, and 20 in the microinstruction. This causes a transfer of information from the output of MUX 1 into CAR. The input into CAR is a function of bit 17 in the microinstruction. It bit 17 is 1, CAR receives the address field of the microinstruction. If bit 17 is 0, an external address is loaded into CAR. The external address is for the purpose of initiating a new sequence of microinstructions which can be specified by the external environment. The status bit (or its complement) selected by bits 18, 19 and 20 of the microinstruction may be equal to 1 or 0. The input address is loaded into CAR if the selected bit is 1, but CAR is incremented if the selected bit is 0.

For constructing correct microprograms, it is necessary to specify exactly how the status bits are affected by each microoperation in the processor. The S (sign) and Z (zero) bits are affected by all operations. The C (carry) and V (overflow) bits *do not change* after the following ALU operations:

(*i*) The four logic operations OR, AND, XOR, and complement.

(*ii*) The increment and decrement operations.

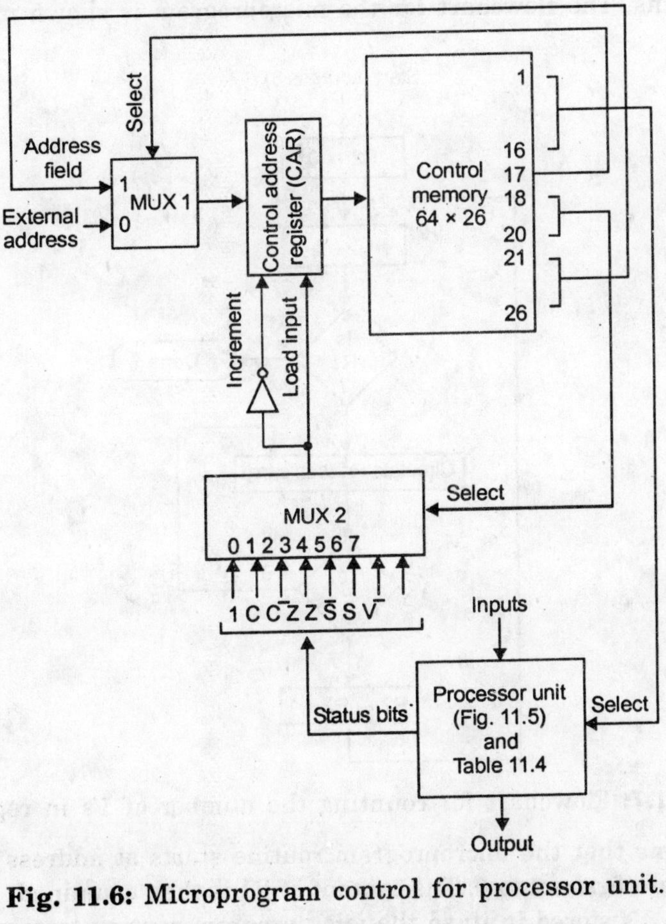


**Fig. 11.6:** Microprogram control for processor unit.

For all other operations, the output carry from the ALU goes into the C bit of the status register. The C bit is also affected after a circular shift with carry operation.

## 11.5 MICROPROGRAM EXAMPLE

Let us demonstrate by taking an example how a microprogram is written to implement a given macrooperation. A macrooperation initiates a sequence of microinstructions in control memory. This sequence constitutes a microprogram **routine** for executing the specified macrooperation. A macrooperation is initiated by an external address that supplies the first address in control memory for the microinstruction routine. The routine is terminated with a microinstruction that loads a new external address to start executing the next macrooperation.

The macrooperation we wish to implement counts the number of 1's presently stored in processor register R1 and sets processor register R2 to that number. For example, if R1 = 00110101, the microprogram routine counts the four 1's stored in the register and sets register R2 to the binary number 100.

Although the microprogram can be derived directly from the statement of the problem, it may be convenient to first construct a flowchart that shows the sequence of microoperations and decision paths. The flowchart for the microprogram is shown in Figure 11.7.

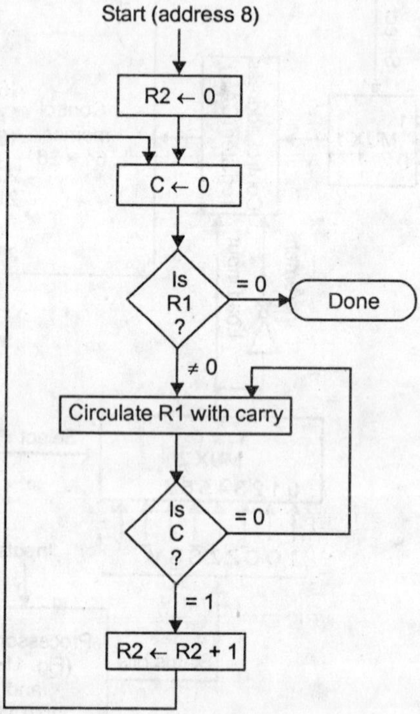


**Fig. 11.7:** Flowchart for counting the number of 1's in register R1

Let us assume that the microprogram routine starts at address 8. Register R2 and the C (carry) bit are first set to 0. The content of R1 is then examined. If it is 0, it signifies that there are no 1's stored in it; so the microprogram routine terminates with R2 equal to 0. If the content of R1 is not 0, it indicates that there are some 1's stored in it. Register R1, together with the carry, is shifted in a circular manner as many times as necessary until a 1 is transferred into C. For every 1 detected in C, there is an increment in register R2 and then control go back to check if R1 is equal to 0. This loop is repeated until all the 1's in R1 are counted. Note that the value of C is always 0 when it is circulated with the content of R1.

The microprogram routine in symbolic form is given in Table 11.5. The routine starts at address 8 by clearing register R2. The microinstruction in address 9 clears the C bit and sets the Z bit if R1 contains all 0's. This is done by transferring the content of R1 into itself through the ALU. The microinstruction in address 10 checks the value of the Z bit. If it is 1, it indicates that R 1 contains all 0's, and the routine is terminated by accepting a new external address to start executing another macrooperation. It Z is not equal to 1, control continues with address 11. The circular right-shift with carry (crc) places the least significant bit of R1 into C. Next we check the value of C. If it is 0, control goes back to address 11 to circulate again until C becomes a 1. When C = 1, control goes to address 13 to increment R2 and then returns to address 9 to check the content of R1 for an all 0's state.

**Table 11.5: Symbolic Microprogram to Count the Number of 1's in R1**

| *ROM Address* | *Microinstruction* | *What it means ?* |
|---|---|---|
| 8 | R2 ← 0 | Clear R2 counter |
| 9 | R1 ← R1, C ← 0 | Clear C, set status bits |
| 10 | If (Z = 1) then (go to external address) | Done if R1 = 0 |
| 11 | R1 ← crc R1 | Circulate R1 right with carry |
| 12 | If (C = 0) then (go to 11) | Circulate again if C = 0 |
| 13 | R2 ← R2 + 1, go to 9 | Carry = 1, increment R2 |

**Table 11.6: Binary Microprogram to Count the Number of 1's in R1**

| *ROM Address* | *ROM Content* | | | | | | | | | | | | | | |
|---|---|---|---|---|---|---|---|---|---|---|---|---|---|---|---|
| | *Microoperation Select* | | | | | *MUX Select* | | | | *Address Field* | | | | | |
| | *A* | *B* | *D* | *F* | *H* | | | | | | | | | | |
| | *1* | | | | *16* | *17* | | | *20* | *21* | | | | | *26* |
| 001000 | 000 | 000 | 010 | 0000 | 011 | 1 | 0 | 0 | 0 | 0 | 0 | 1 | 0 | 0 | 1 |
| 001001 | 001 | 000 | 001 | 0000 | 000 | 1 | 0 | 0 | 0 | 0 | 0 | 1 | 0 | 1 | 0 |
| 001010 | 001 | 001 | 000 | 1000 | 000 | 0 | 0 | 1 | 1 | 0 | 0 | 0 | 0 | 0 | 0 |
| 001011 | 001 | 001 | 001 | 1000 | 101 | 1 | 0 | 0 | 0 | 0 | 0 | 1 | 1 | 0 | 0 |
| 001100 | 001 | 001 | 000 | 1000 | 000 | 1 | 0 | 1 | 0 | 0 | 0 | 1 | 0 | 1 | 1 |
| 001101 | 010 | 000 | 010 | 0001 | 000 | 1 | 0 | 0 | 0 | 0 | 0 | 1 | 0 | 0 | 1 |

The binary microprogram is given in Table 11.6. The 16 bits for the control word that selects the processor microoperations are derived from Table 11.4. In fact, most of the control words listed are explained in conjunction with Table 11.7.

**Table 11.7: Examples of Microoperations for Processor**

| Microoperation | Control Word | | | | | | Function |
|---|---|---|---|---|---|---|---|
| | A | B | D | F | $C_{in}$ | H | |
| R1 ← R1 – R2 | 001 | 010 | 001 | 010 | 1 | 000 | Subtract R2 from R1 |
| R3 – R4 | 011 | 100 | 000 | 010 | 1 | 000 | Compare R3 and R4 |
| R5 ← R4 | 100 | 000 | 101 | 000 | 0 | 000 | Transfer R4 to R5 |
| R6 ← Input | 000 | 000 | 110 | 000 | 0 | 000 | Input data to R6 |
| Output ← R7 | 111 | 000 | 000 | 000 | 0 | 000 | Output data from R7 |
| R1 ← R1, C ← 0 | 001 | 000 | 001 | 000 | 0 | 000 | Clear carry bit C |
| R3 ← shl R3 | 011 | 011 | 011 | 100 | 0 | 010 | Shift-left R3 with $I_L = 0$ |
| R1 ← crc R1 | 001 | 001 | 001 | 100 | 0 | 101 | Circulate-right R1 with carry |
| R2 ← 0 | 000 | 000 | 010 | 000 | 0 | 011 | Clear R2 |

The multiplexer select bits select the inputs to the two multiplexers. Bit 17 is 0 in address 10 for selecting an external address. In all other cases, it is 1 to select the address field of the microinstruction. When bits 18, 19 and 20 are 000, the next address is determined directly from the address field. When these bits are 011, they select the Z bit for MUX 2. If Z = 1, an external address is transferred to CAR. If Z = 0, CAR is incremented and the next address is the next one in sequence. The microinstruction at address 12 selects the complement of the carry bit or $\overline{C}$. If C = 0, then $\overline{C}$ = 1 and the address field (binary 1011) is transferred into CAR. If C = 1, then $\overline{C}$ = 0 and CAR is incremented to give 13 for the next address.

If you are familiar with machine or assembly-language programming for a computer then you will realize that writing microprograms is very similar to writing machine-language programs for a computer. Thus, ***the microprogram concept is a systematic procedure for designing the control unit of a digital system.*** Once the microinstruction format is established the design is done by writing a microprogram, which is similar to writing a program for a computer. For this reason, the microprogram method is sometimes referred to as **firmware** to distinguish it from the hardware method (which we called a ***hard-wired control***) and the software concept which constitutes a programming method.

## 11.6 MICROPROGRAM SEQUENCER

A microprogram control unit should be considered as having two parts:

(i) ***Control memory*** that stores the microinstructions and

**(ii)** ***Associated circuits*** that control the generation of the next address. The address-generation part is sometimes known as **microprogram sequencer**, since it sequences the microinstructions in control memory. A microprogram sequencer can be designed with MSI (Medium Scale Integration) circuits to suit a particular application. However, just as general-purpose processor units are available in IC packages, so are general-purpose sequencers suited for the construction of microprogram control units. To guarantee a wide range of acceptability, an IC sequencer must provide an internal organization that can be adapted to a wide range of applications.

A microprogram sequencer attached to a control memory checks certain bits of the microinstruction, from which it determines the next address for control memory. A typical sequencer provides the following address-sequencing capabilities:

(*i*) *Increments the present address for control memory.*

(*ii*) *Branches to an address as provided by the address field of the microinstruction.*

(*iii*) *Branches to a given address if a specified status bit equals 1.*

(*iv*) *Transfers control to a new address as specified by an external source.*

(*v*) *Has a facility for subroutine calls and returns.*

Generally the microinstructions are read from control memory in succession. This type of sequencing can be easily accomplished by incrementing the address register of the control memory. In some microinstruction formats, each microinstruction contains an address field even for sequential addresses. It eliminates the need to increment the control memory address register, because the address field available in each microinstruction provides the address of the next microinstruction. In any case, provision must be available for branching to an address out of normal sequence.

Occasionally, control must be transferred to a nonsequential microinstruction; thus, the sequencer must have the capability for branching to any one of two addresses, depending on whether a status bit is 0 or 1. The simplest way to accomplish this is to branch to the address specified by the address field of the microinstruction if the status bit specified is equal to 1, but go to the next address in sequence if the status bit is equal to 0. This configuration requires the capability of incrementing the address register.

The sequencer transfers a new address for control memory to start executing a new **macrooperation.** The external address transfers control to the first **microinstruction** in a **microprogram** routine that executes the specified macrooperation.

**Subroutines** are programs used by other routines to perform a particular task. Subroutines can be called (invoked) from any point within the main body of the microprograms. Frequently, many microprograms contain identical sections of code. Microinstructions can he saved by employing subroutines which use common sections of microcode. Microprograms that use subroutines must have a provision for storing the return address during a subroutine call and restoring the address during a subroutine return. This may be done by placing the return address into a special register and then branching to the beginning of the subroutine. This special register can then become the address source for setting the address register for the return to the main routine. The best way to organize a register file that stores addresses for subroutine calls and returns is to use a last-in, first-out (LIFO) stack.

The block diagram of a microprogram sequencer is shown in Figure 11.8. It has a multiplexer that selects an address from four sources and routes it into a control address register (CAR). The output from CAR provides the address for the control memory. The contents of CAR are incremented and applied to the multiplexer and to the stack register file. The register selected in the stack is determined by the stack pointer. Inputs $I_0$, $I_1$, and $I_2$, specify the operation for the sequencer, and input T is a test point for a status bit. The address register can be cleared to zero to initialize the system and the clock pulses synchronize the loading into the registers.

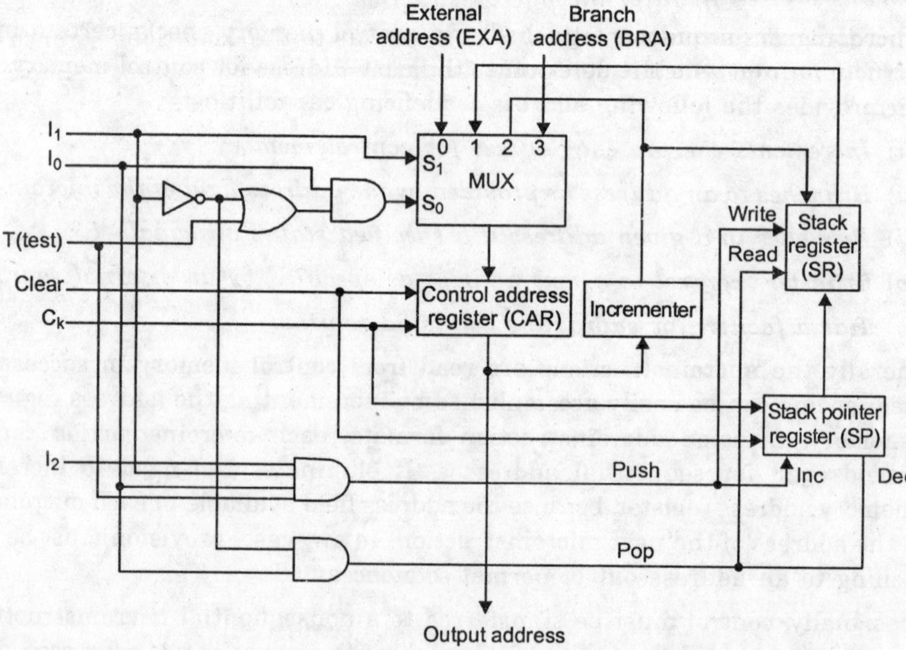


**Fig. 11.8:** Typical microprogram sequencer organisation.

**Table 11.8: Function Table of a Typical Microprogram Sequencer**

| $I_2$ | $I_1$ | $I_0$ | $T$ | $s_1$ | $s_0$ | *Operation* | *What it means ?* |
|---|---|---|---|---|---|---|---|
| X | 0 | 0 | X | 0 | 0 | CAR ← EXA | Transfer external address |
| X | 0 | 1 | X | 0 | 1 | CAR ← SR | Transfer from register stack |
| X | 1 | 0 | X | 1 | 0 | CAR ← CAR + 1 | Increment address |
| 0 | 1 | 1 | 0 | 1 | 0 | CAR ← CAR + 1 | Increment address |
| 0 | 1 | 1 | 1 | 1 | 1 | CAR ← BRA | Transfer branch address |
| 1 | 1 | 1 | 0 | 1 | 0 | CAR ← CAR + 1 | Increment address |
| 1 | 1 | 1 | 1 | 1 | 1 | CAR ← BRA, SR ← CAR + 1 | Branch to subroutine |

The function Table 11.8 specifies the operation of the sequencer. Inputs $I_1$ and I determine the selection variables for the multiplexer. An external address (EXA) is transferre into CAR when $I_1I_0$ = 00. The transfer from the stack register (SR) occurs when $I_1I_0$ = 01, and CAR is incremented when $I_1I_0$ = 10. The T and $I_2$ inputs have no effect during these three operations and they are marked with **don't-care** X entries. When $I_1I_0$ = 11, the sequencer executes a conditional branch operation dependent on the value of the test bit in T. If $I_2$ is also equal to 1, the operation is a conditional call to subroutine. In either case, CAR is incremented if the test bit T is 0. The branch address (BRA) is transferred to CAR if T = 1. Thus, with $I_1I_0$ = 11, the sequencer branches to the BRA if the status bit in T is equal to 1, but increments CAR if the status bit is 0. *The branch address normally comes from the address field of the microinstruction.*

The conditional subroutine call ($I_2$ = 1) is similar to the conditional branch ($I_2$ = 0), except that the former uses the stack and the latter does not. The address stored in the stack during a subroutine call is taken from the incrementer. This is the address next in sequence, and it is called the *return address.* The return address is transferred back into CAR with a subroutine return operation ($I_1I_0$ = 01).

A register (or memory) stack is similar to a memory unit, except that the address for the stack is determined from the value in the stack-pointer register. The access to the stack is in a last-in, first-out (LIFO) sequence and is controlled by incrementing or decrementing the stack pointer. Initially, the stack pointer is cleared and is said to **point** at address 0 in the stack. The **write** or the transfer of information into the stack is called **push.** It consists of writing the input information into the stack at the address specified by the stack pointer and then incrementing the stack-pointer register. In this way, information is transferred into the stack, and the stack pointer points at the next empty location in the stack. The **read** or the transfer of information out of the stack is called **pop.** It consists of first decrementing the stack-pointer register and then reading out the contents of the register (or word) specified by the new value in the stack pointer.

A call to subroutine is executed when $I_2I_1I_0$ = 111 and T = 1. This causes a *push-stack* operation and a branch to the address specified by BRA. This is implemented by first storing the incremented value from CAR into the stack. When clock pulse $C_k$ goes through a positive-edge transition, the BRA address is transferred to CAR and the write input to the stack is inhibited. The stack-pointer register is incremented later when $C_k$ goes through its negative-edge transition. This is shown in Figure 11.9(*a*).

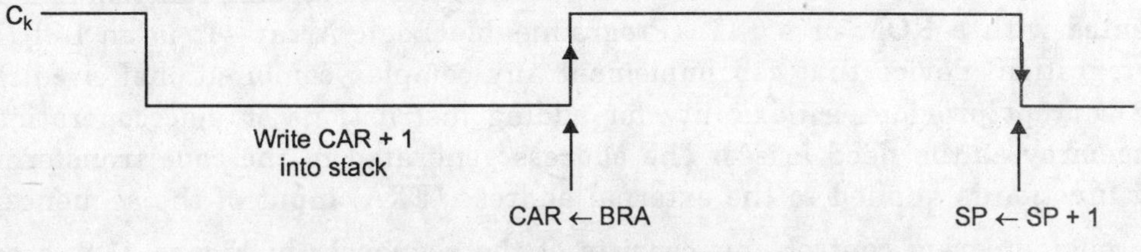


(*a*) Call subroutine (push-stack) $I_2I_1I_0T$ = 1111.

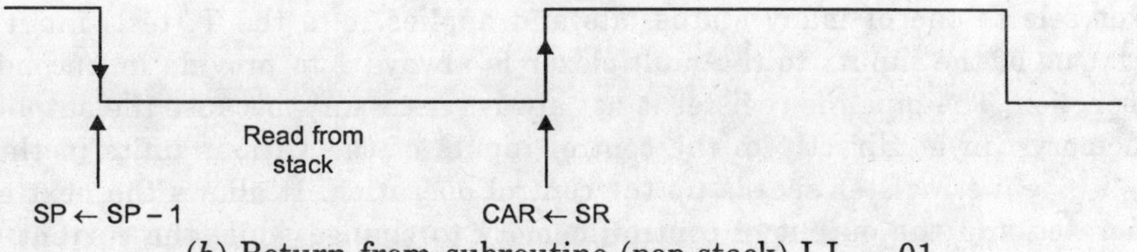


(*b*) Return from subroutine (pop-stack) $I_1I_0$ = 01.

**Fig. 11.9:** Stack operations in microprogram sequencer.

The return from subroutine is executed when $I_1I_0$ = 01. This causes a *pop-stack* operation and a branch to the address stored on top of the stack. This is implemented by first decrementing the stack-pointer register on the negative-edge, transition of $C_k$. The value in the stack, given by the address presently available in the stack pointer, is then read and transferred to CAR on the positive-edge transition of $C_k$. This is shown in Figure 11.9(*b*). Note that CAR is triggered during the positive edge and SP during the negative edge of a clock pulse. The stack-pointer is incremented after the transfer into CAR and decremented prior to the transfer into CAR.

## 11.7 MICROPROGRAMMED CPU ORGANISATION

A digital computer consists of a central processor unit (CPU), a memory unit, and input-output devices. The CPU can be classified into two distinct but interactive functional sections. One section is the processing section and the other is the control section. A processor unit is a useful device for constructing the processor section of a CPU. The microprogram sequencer is a convenient element for constructing a microprogram control for a CPU. Let us develop a computer CPU to show the usefulness of the microprogram sequencer defined earlier in Figure 11.8.

A block diagram of a microprogrammed computer is shown in Figure 11.10. It consists of a memory unit, two processor units, a microprogram sequencer, a control memory, and few other digital functions.

The memory unit stores the instructions and data supplied by the user via an input device. The data processor manipulates the data, and the address processor manipulates the address information received from memory. The two processors can be combined into one unit, but sometimes it is convenient to separate them in order to provide a distinct bus for the memory address. An instruction extracted from memory during the **fetch** cycle goes into the instruction register. The instruction-code bits in the instruction register specify a macrooperation for control memory. A code transformation is sometimes required to convert the operation-code bits of an instruction into a starting address for the control memory. This code transformation constitutes a mapping function and can be implemented with a ROM or a PLA (Programmable Logic Array—It is an LSI (Large Scale Integration) device that can implement any complex combinational circuit). The mapping concept provides a flexibility for adding instructions or macrooperations for control memroy as the need arises. The address generated in the code transformation mapping function is applied to the external address (EXA) input of the sequencer.

The microprogram control unit consists of the sequencer of Figure 11.8, a control memory for storing the microinstructions a multiplexer, and a pipeline register. The multiplexer selects one of many status bits and applies it to the T (test) input of the sequencer. One of the inputs to the multiplexer is always 1 to provide in unconditional branch operation. The pipeline register is not always necessary, because the outputs from control memory can go directly to the control inputs of the various units in the CPU. However, a pipeline register speeds up the control operation. It allows the next address to be generated and the output of control memory to change while the current control word in the pipeline register initiates the microoperations given by the present microinstruction.

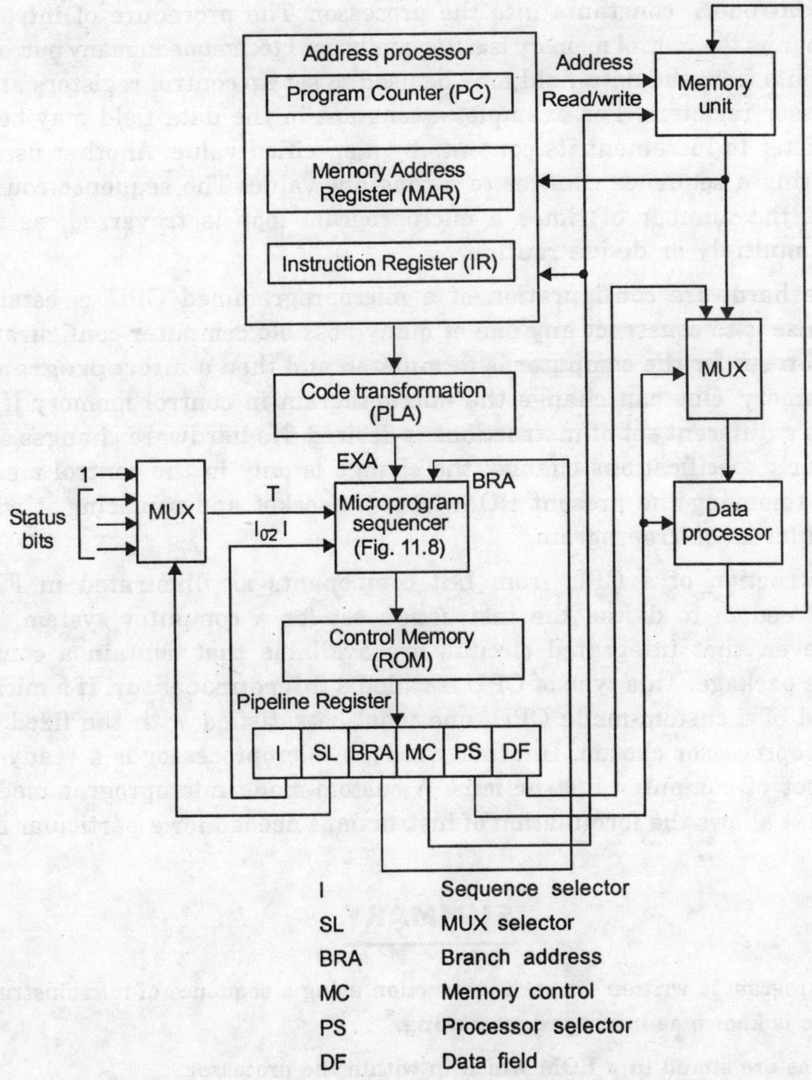


**Fig. 11.10:** Microprogrammed computer organisation.

A possible microinstruction format for the control memory is shown within the pipeline register. The I field consists of three bits and supplies the input information for the sequencer. The SL field selects a status bit for the multiplexer. The BRA field is the address field of the microinstruction and supplies a branch address (BRA) to the sequencer. These three fields of a microinstruction provide information to the sequencer to determine the next address for control memroy. The sequencer generates the next address and the control memory reads the next microinstruction while the present microoperations are being executed in the other units of the CPU.

The remaining three fields in the microinstruction are for controlling the microoperations in the processor and memory units. The memory control (MC) field controls the address processor and the read and write operations in the memory unit. The processor select (PS) field controls the operations in the data processor unit. The last field is a data field

(DF) used to introduce constants into the processor. The procedure of introducing data into the system from the control memory is a frequently used technique in many microprogrammed systems. Outputs from the data field may be used to set up control registers and introduce data in processor registers. For example, a constant in the data field may be added to a processor register to increment its contents by a specified value. Another use of the data field is in setting a sequence counter to a constant value. The sequence counter is then used to count the number of times a microprogram loop is traversed, as is generally required in a multiply or divide routine.

Once the hardware configuration of a microprogrammed CPU is established, the designer can use it to construct any one of many possible computer configurations. First, the **instruction** set for the computer is formulated and then a **microprogram** is written for control memory. One can change the microprogram in control memory if a different computer with a different set of instructions is desired. No hardware changes are required if the computer's specifications change; the change is only in the control memory ROM. This involves removing the present ROM from its socket and replacing it with another unit with a different microprogram.

The construction of a CPU from LSI components as illustrated in Figure 11.10 provides the freedom to define the instruction set for a computer system. It must be realized, however, that integrated circuits are available that contain a complete CPU within a single package. This type of CPU is called a **microprocessor.** If a microprocessor is used instead of a custom-made CPU, one must be satisfied with the fixed instruction set of the microprocessor chosen. In other words, a microprocessor is a ready-made CPU with a fixed set of computer instructions. A custom-made microprogrammed CPU is a flexible unit that allows the formulation of instructions needed for a particular application.

## SUMMARY

- A microprogram is written for each instruction using a sequence of microinstructions. This technique is known as **microprogramming.**
- Microcodes are stored in a ROM which in within the processor.
- Microprogram sequencer sequences the microinstructions in control memory.
- CISC machines are more complex and less efficient.
- The aim of employing RISC design is to increase the computing speed by reducing the execution time of instructions.

## REVIEW QUESTIONS AND EXERCISES

1. Write a short note on microprogramming concepts.
2. Describe the microprogram organisation for controlling the processor unit.
3. Describe the microprogram sequencer for a control memory.
4. Write a short note on microprogrammed CPU organisation.

5. Compare various CPU's features.
6. What is the purpose of using address mode techniques by a computer? Summarize the various addressing modes?
7. What are the advantages of microprogram control?
8. Fill in the blanks:
   (*i*) ..................instructions are used to test status conditions in registers and, depending on results, cause a change in program sequence.
   (*ii*) A ..................sequences the microinstructions in control memory.
   (*iii*) To solve the problem of complexity and comparatively slow speed of CISC machines computer industry is now producing simple and fast .................. machines.

Chapter 12

# INPUT/OUTPUT ORGANISATION

## 12.1 INTRODUCTION

*Input* refers to data entered into a computer for processing—for example, from a keyboard or from a file stored on disk. Input includes program instructions that the CPU receives after commands are issued by the user. *Output* refers to the result of processing—that is, information sent to the screen or the printer or to be stored on disk, or sent to another computer in a network. Some devices combine both input and output functions, examples being not only ATMs but also combination scanner-printer devices. In this unit we focus on the I/O (Input/Output) organisation. Figure 12.1 illustrates the common input and output devices used with a computer.

*Input hardware* consists of devices that translate data into a form the computer can process. The computer readable form consists of binary 0s and 1s, or off and on electrical signals. *Output hardware* consists of devices that translate information processed by the computer into a form that humans can understand. The computer processed information consists of 0s and 1s which need to be translated into words, numbers, and pictures.

We are already familiar with the characteristics and operation of some input devices, output devices and mass storage devices. Mass storage devices are connected to a computer in a manner similar to input and output devices. We will thus describe the principles used in interconnecting input/output devices and mass storage devices with the CPU and Memory in a unified manner.

## 12.2 FUNCTIONS OF I/O DEVICES

There are three main functions which have to be performed by the computer system to handle input/output (I/O) devices. These are given below:

(*i*) Unique addressing of each I/O device (remember many I/O devices are connected to a computer) (See Figure 12.1.)

(*ii*) Specifying the amount of data to be transferred and where it is to be transferred. Data may be transferred from I/O device to the main memory or from main memory to I/O device. We thus have to specify the number of bytes or words to be transferred and the (starting) address in memory where this block of data is to be stored or is to be retrieved.

(*iii*) Synchronizing data transmission between various units. As the speed of information transfer of I/O devices is slow compared to that of a computer's main memory it is necessary to find out methods of synchronizing the information transfer.

In this chapter we will describe various methods which are used to perform the above mentioned three functions.

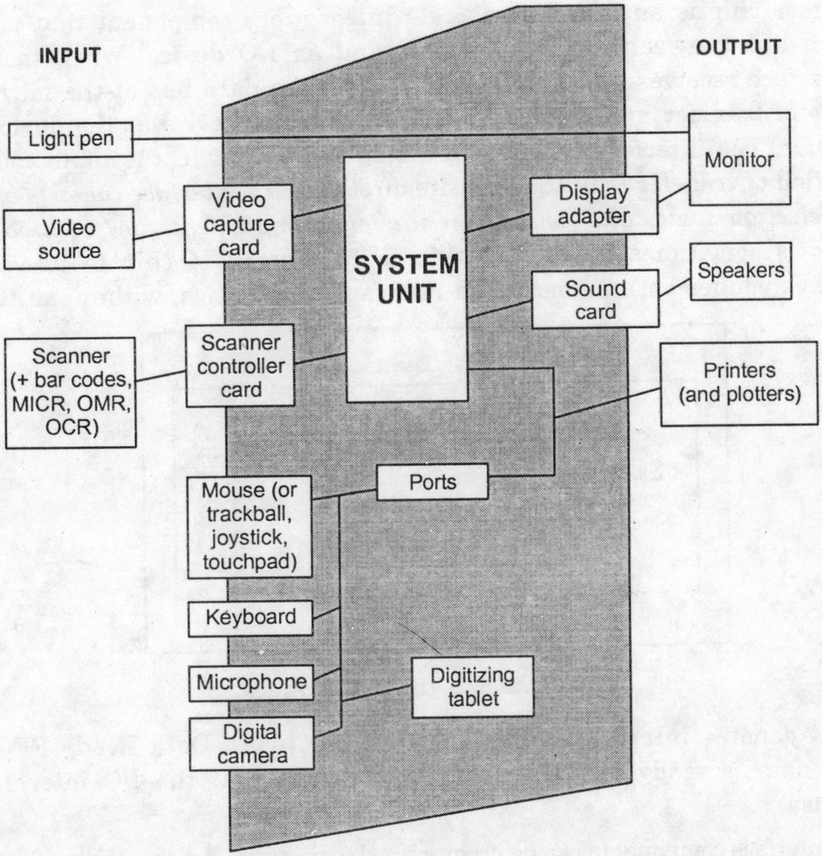


**Fig. 12.1:** Common input and output devices.

## 12.3 I/O INTERFACE

Input-output interface provides a method for transferring information between internal memory and I/O devices. Peripherals connected to a computer require special communication links for interfacing them with the central processing unit. The purpose of the communication link is to resolve the differences that exist between the central computer and each peripheral.

The main differences are given below:

(*i*) Peripherals are electro mechanical and electromagnetic devices and their way of operation differs from that of the CPU and memory, which are electronic devices. Therefore a conversion of signal values may be required.

(*ii*) The data transfer rate of peripherals in usually slower than the transfer rate of the CPU.

(*iii*) Data codes and formats in peripherals differ from the word format in the CPU and memory.

(*iv*) The operating modes of peripherals differ from each other.

An interface chip is an LSI (Large Scale Integration) component that provides the communication link between a microprocessor and an I/O device. When in the output mode, the interface receives binary information from the data bus at the microprocessor rate and mode of transfer and transmits it to an external device at the device rate and mode of transfer. The interface behaves in a similar manner in the input mode, except that the direction of transfer is in the opposite direction. *An interface consists of a number of registers, selection logic, and control circuits that implement the required transfers.* Interface logic is sometimes included within a RAM or ROM chip to provide an LSI component that includes both memory and interface capabilities, within one IC package.

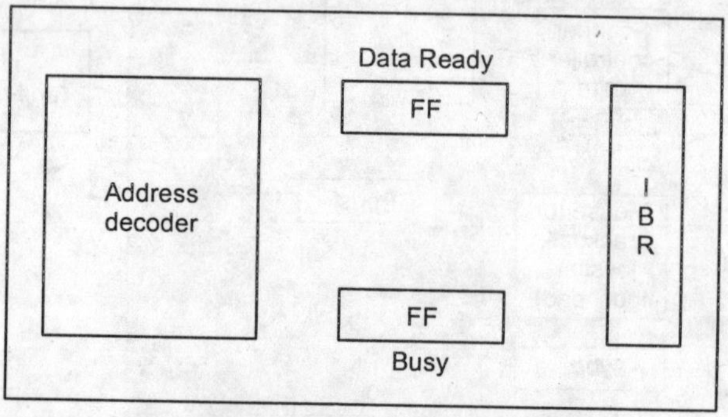


**Fig. 12.2:** I/O Interface unit.

Here, IBR denotes Interface Buffer Register (one byte). Data Ready FF (Flip-flop) indicates that data is ready in IBR. Busy FF indicates that the I/O interface unit is engaged (or busy).

Most LSI interface components can be programmed to accommodate a variety of combinations of operating modes. *The microprocessor, through program instructions, transfers a byte to a control register inside the interface unit. This control information puts the interface in one of the possible modes suitable for the particular device to which it is attached. By changing the control byte, it is possible to change the interface characteristics. For this reason, LSI interface units are often said to be programmable.* The instructions that transfer control information into a programmable interface are included in the microcomputer program and they initialize the interface for a particular mode of operation.

Manufacturers of microprocessors supplement their product with a set of interface chips suitable for communication between the microprocessor and a variety of standard input and output devices. Interface components are usually designed to operate with a particular microprocessor system bus with no additional logic besides address decoding. There are a variety of interface components in commercial use and each can be classified to be in one of four categories:

(i) A *parallel peripheral interface* transfers data in parallel between the microprocessor and a peripheral device.

(ii) A *serial communication interface* converts parallel data from the microprocessor into serial data for transmission and converts incoming serial data into parallel data for reception by the microprocessor.

(iii) A *special dedicated interface* is constructed to communicate with one particular input-output device, or can be programmed to operate with a particular device.

(iv) A *direct memory access (DMA)* interface is used for transferring data directly between an external device and memory. The bus buffers in the microprocessor are disabled and go into a high-impedance state during DMA transfer.

Commercial interface units may have different names from the ones given here. Moreover, the internal and external characteristics differ considerably from one commercial unit to another.

### 12.3.1 Device Controller and Interface Unit

Let us assume that an I/O device is associated with an "intelligent process" or a programmable unit to perform the three functions mentioned earlier.

We know that the I/O devices differ widely in their characteristics and in their operational principles. For uniform design of the I/O subsystem of a computer, it is better to *separate device dependent aspects from device independent aspects*. Thus, we introduce two terms: *device controller* and *interface unit*.

The *device controller* performs device-dependent electro-mechanical or electro-optical functions; whereas the *interface unit* performs the logic of communicating with the receiver of the input read or the sender of the output to be displayed. An I/O organisation based on this division of responsibilities is illustrated in Figure 12.3. A computer system contains many I/O devices and each of them will be assigned a unique address for the purpose of identification. The interface units of the various I/O devices are connected through a *bus* called *I/O bus* to the rest of the computer system as illustrated in Figure 12.3.

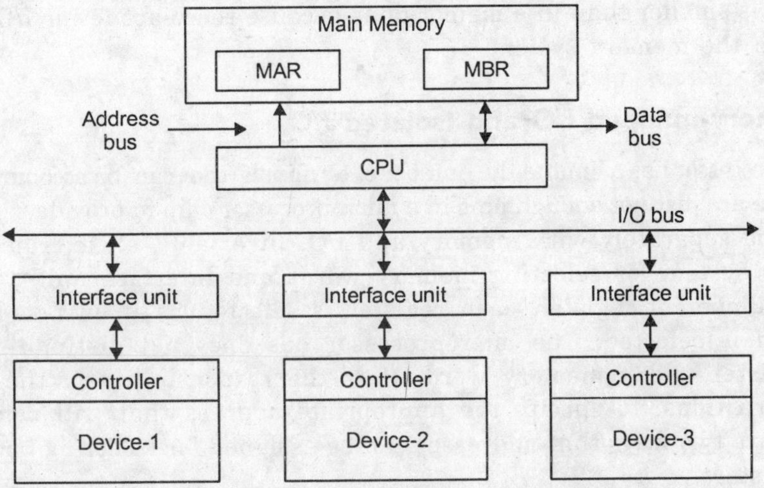


**Fig. 12.3:** Communication between CPU and I/O devices.

The interface unit should have the following features:

(*i*) ***Device Address Decoder:*** Each device has a unique address. When the CPU wants to send data to a device or receive data from it then it places the device's address on the I/O bus. This address is decoded by the address decoder in the interface unit. Some microcomputers have part of the memory address space being used for addressing I/O devices. This has the advantage of allowing access to I/O devices as though they are memory locations. Special I/O instructions need not be defined as a MOVE to or from one of these addresses will, by implication, move data to an I/O device or from an I/O rather than memory.

(*ii*) ***Data Register:*** The data to be moved to or from the memory is kept in this register. In some devices such as a teletype this may be a one byte register. In the case of faster peripheral devices such as magnetic disks it would be a one word register and there will be another register to store the number of words to be moved in or out of the device.

(*iii*) ***Status Register:*** This register is used to specify when the data from the device is ready to be read by the CPU or whether the device is ready to receive data from the memory. In the simplest case it will be just a flip-flop. This register is vital to synchronize the operation of devices with that of the CPU.

In Figure 12.3, we have illustrated one model of I/O organisation. It has one I/O bus to which all I/O devices, are connected regardless of whether it is slow like the keyboard or fast like a disk. Also, we have assumed in this model, that the I/O bus is connected to the CPU rather than to the memory. Although we have shown the I/O bus as a single entity for the sake of simplicity, it would normally be organized into a *data bus* and a *control bus*.

Large computers quite often use separate buses in the CPU to communicate with memory and I/O interface. An I/O bus in large computers consists of a *data bus*, and an *address bus* similar to the buses that communicate with memory. The I/O data bus transfers information to and from the external devices, and the I/O address bus is used to select a particular I/O device through its interface unit. The number of address lines in an I/O bus is smaller than in a memory bus because there are fewer I/O units to select than words in the memory system.

### 12.3.2 Memory-mapped I/O and Isolated I/O

A microprocessor has a limit to the number of terminals that can be accommodated in the IC package. These are just not enough pins in a microprocessor chip to provide separate buses for communicating separately with memory and I/O. Invariably, all microprocessors use a common bus system for selecting memory words and interface units. If an interface chip has a number of register, each register is selected by it own address just as a memory word is selected. The microprocessor bus does not distinguish between an interface register and a memory word. It is the responsibility of the user, through program instructions, to specify the appropriate address that will select one or the other. There are two ways that addresses can be assigned for selecting both memory and interface registers.

(*i*) Memory-mapped I/O and

(*ii*) Isolated I/O.

In the ***memory-mapped I/O method***, the microprocessor treats an interface register as being part of the memory system, The assigned addresses for interface registers cannot be used for memory words, thus reducing the memory space available. In a memory-mapped I/O organisation there are no input or output instructions because the microprocessor can manipulate I/O data residing in interface registers with the same instructions that are used to manipulate memory locations. Each interface is organized as a set of registers that respond to read and write commands in the normal address space of the microprocessor. Typically, a segment of the total address space is reserved for interface registers, but in general, they can be located at any address as long as there is not also a memory word that corresponds to that address.

The memory-mapped I/O organisation is very useful for systems that do not require all the memory space available from the address bus lines. A microprocessor with a 16-bit address bus that requires a memory of less than 32K bytes can use the other 32K addresses available on the bus to access interface registers. A specific configuration for a memory-mapped I/O can be implemented by modifying slightly the address connections.

With the ***isolated I/O*** organisation, the microprocessor itself specifies whether the address on the address bus is for a memory word or for an interface register. It is done by means of one or two additional control lines provided with the microprocessor. For example, a microprocessor may have an output control line labelled M/IO. When M/IO = 1, it is signifies that the address in the address bus is for a memory word. When M/IO = 0, the address is for an interface register. This control line must be connected to the chip select inputs of RAM, ROM, and interface chips.

In the isolated I/O organisation, the microprocessor must provide distinct input and output instructions, and each of these instructions must be associated with an address. When the microprocessor fetches and decodes the operation code of an input or output instruction, it reads the address associated with the instruction and places it on the address bus. At the same time it makes control line M/IO equal to 0 to inform the external components that this address is for an interface and not for memory. Thus, during a fetch cycle or a memory-reference execute cycle, the microprocessor enables the read or write control and sets the M/IO line to 1. During the execution of an input or output instruction, the microprocessor enables the read or write control and sets the M/IO line to 0.

The isolated I/O method isolates memory and I/O addresses so that memory space is not affected by the interface address assignment. Due to this isolation, the full address space available by the address bus is unaffected by interface addressing as in the memory-mapped I/O method.

## 12.4 I/O TECHNIQUES

Let us view the I/O operation as a process and the main computation performed in the CPU as another process and call them I/O process and *computation process* respectively. The state diagram shown in Figure 12.4 depicts the I/O process, which is explained ahead.

Let us assume a dedicated processor to be resident in a computer keyboard device that will constantly scan the rows of keys in a keyboard and do the following:

- Determine if any key is pressed.
- If a key is pressed then store the corresponding ASCII code in a "buffer storage".
- Request the CPU to read the buffer.
- Wait till the buffer is read and then go back to scanning the key board.

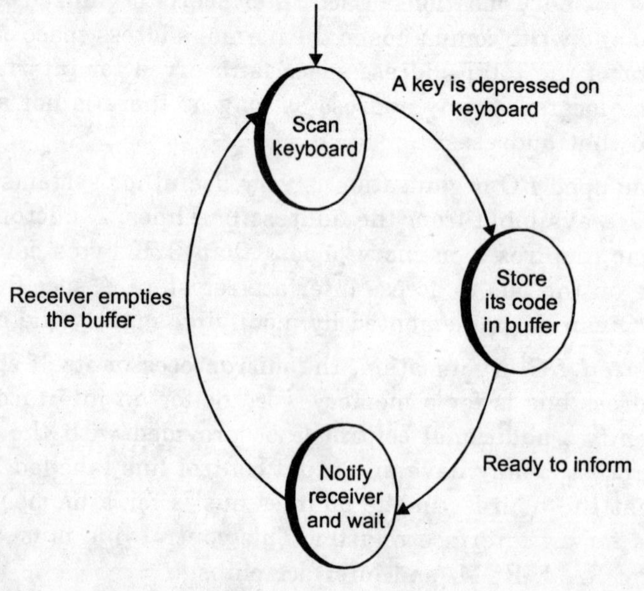


**Fig. 12.4:** A state diagram for the keyboard scanner.

Figure 12.4 shows the sequence of operations given above in the from of a state diagram. The set of keys in a keyboard are organized in the form of a matrix with several rows and columns. The scanner subsystem contains device dependent operations that perform the sub-operations such as, scan one row, check each column of that row, move to the next row, etc.

The two processes (I/O process and computation process) communicate with each other in order to exchange information, such as data, coded commands, control signals or status signals. The information transfer between them can take place in many ways. It is one of the major aspects of I/O organisation.

The two communicating processes namely, the I/O process and the computational process may communicate synchronously or asynchronously. We should remember that *the I/O process involves electro-mechanical, electro-optial or other physical systems and hence it is thousands of times slower than the electronically running computational process.*

The sequence of steps followed by a simple I/O organisation while transforming a single byte are given below. This organisation is called simple as CPU has the responsibility of synchronizing operations. Figure 12.5 illustrates this.

***Simple I/O Organisation***

Here, IBR: Interface Buffer Register (one byte).

Data-Ready: Flip-flop that indicates that data is ready in the IBR.

Busy: Flip-flop that indicates that the I/O interface unit is engaged (or busy).

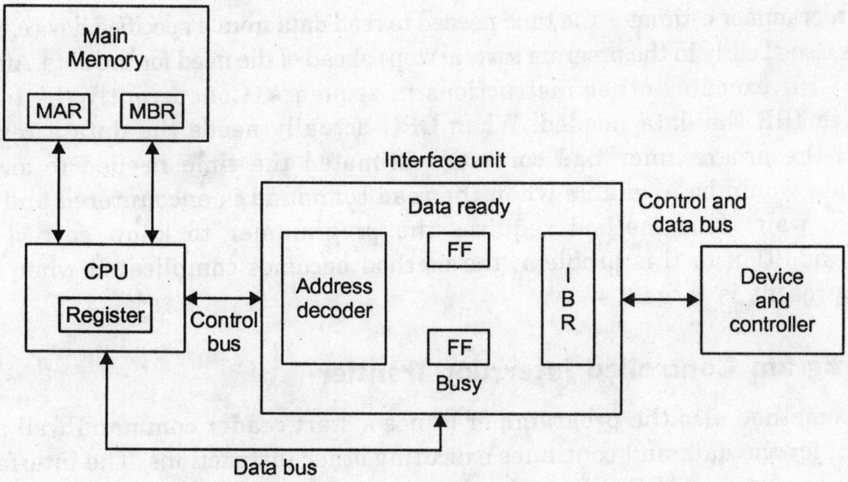


**Fig. 12.5:** Illustration of CPU-peripheral communication.

The reader should refer to Figure 12.5 before reading the steps given below:

- An I/O instruction is encountered in the program being executed. The instructions may be of the form: I/O operation code, device address, device command.
- The CPU sends on I/O bus the device address and command to be executed, namely, read or write.
- The device address on the I/O bus is recognized by the address decoder of the desired I/O device interface unit. (Make it sure that the device is free before issuing the command.)
- The interface unit commands (for a read command) the concerned device controller to assemble a word in the interface buffer register (IBR) and at the same time it turns on an *interface busy* flip-flop. As long as this busy flip-flop is set, the interface unit will not accept any other I/O requests. A data ready flip-flop in the interface unit is reset to 0.
- The device controller fills the IBR. When the data is ready in IBR, the data ready flip-flop of the device interface is set to 1.
- The CPU continually interrogates the data ready flip-flop in a wait loop. It gets out of the loop immediately when the data ready flip-flop is set to 1. Now the contents of IBR are transferred to the specified CPU register through the I/O bus.

This method of transfer of data from I/O to CPU is known as **program controlled ransfer.** In this method synchronization of I/O device and CPU is achieved by making

CPU wait till the data is assembled by the device. As I/O devices are normally much slower compared to CPU this method of synchronization is not desirable as it wastes CPU time. There are two ways in which the CPU waiting time can be reduced and these are discussed below.

### 12.4.1 Program Controlled I/O Technique

The programmer estimates the time needed to read data from a specified device. A start reader command is issued early in the program several steps ahead of the need for the data. After giving this command, CPU executes other instructions in sequence. Concurrently the interface unit assembles in IBR the data needed. When CPU actually needs the data a read command is given. If the programmer had correctly estimated the time needed to assemble data then the data would be available when the read command is encountered and CPU would not have to wait. This method requires the programmer to know correct instruction timings. In addition to this problem, the method becomes complicated when the number of devices present is large.

### 12.4.2 Program Controlled Interrupt Transfer

In this method also the programmer issues a start reader command well ahead of the requirement for the data and continues executing other instructions. The interface proceeds to assemble the data in IBR. When the data is ready, the interface unit sends a signal to the CPU and *interrupts* it. Observe that instead of the CPU trying to find out whether the data is ready, in this case the CPU is told that the data is ready by the interrupt signal. On interruption the CPU jumps to a special subroutine which reads the contents of IBR and stores it in the specified location in memory. This method is called **program controlled interrupt transfer** This method is better than the previous method as a programmer need not carry out detailed timing calculations. If many devices are active then the CPU will receive many interrupt signals and a method should be evolved to handle them systematically.

### 12.4.3 Direct Memory Access (DMA) I/O Technique

In both program controlled transfer and interrupt controlled transfer of data, data is transferred to or from I/O devices to the memory via a CPU register. This is a slow process as data is transferred byte by byte. For transferring each byte several instructions need to be executed by the CPU. Input or output of a block of data from a fast peripheral such as a disk is at high speed. These devices operate synchronously using their own internal clock and are independent of CPU. The combination of high speed of such devices and their synchronous operation makes it impractical to use program controlled transfer or interrupt controlled transfer via CPU to read or write data in such devices. Another method which uses a *Direct Memory Access (DMA)* interface eliminates the need to use CPU registers to transfer data from I/O units to memory or vice versa.

We could take DMA based I/O to be memory centred, that is, memory is the main entity for whose service both I/O and CPU compete. Of course, it is necessary for the DMA device to know from the CPU where in memory the data would be stored and how many bytes would have to be transferred. Thus, CPU is also connected to the DMA device as illustrated in Figure 12.6.

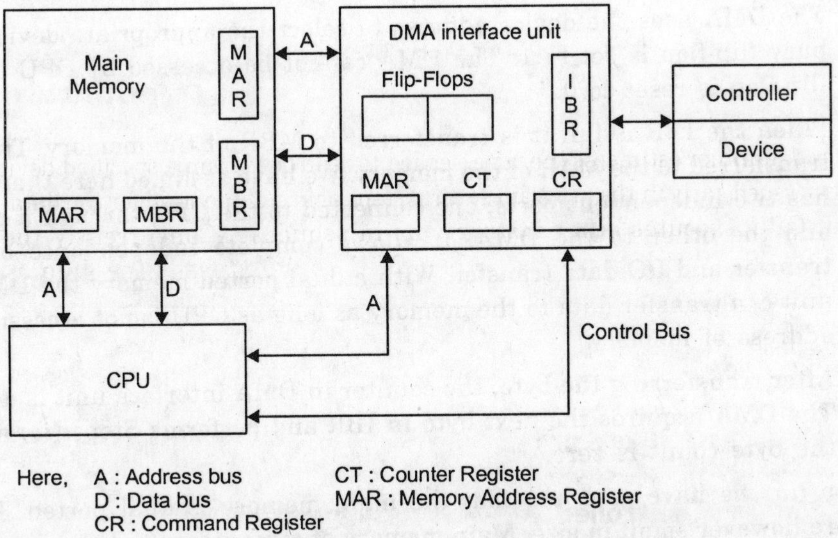


**Fig. 12.6:** Illustration of DMA interface.

The various registers of a DMA interface which facilitate direct data transfer from I/O devices to memory are given below:

- A Memory Address Register (MAR) which stores the address in memory to which data is to be transferred or from where data is to be received.
- A Memory Buffer Register (MBR) which stores the byte to be sent to memory or that received from memory.
- A counter register which contains the count of the number of bytes to be sent or received from memory. With the transfer of each byte the counter is decremented by 1.
- A status register indicating DMA busy/free, data ready and other status information.
- A register storing the I/O command to be carried out. This command is received from the CPU and stored in DMA to enable the DMA interface to carry out the command independent of CPU.

The configuration of the DMA interface unit and its connection to the CPU through buses is shown in Figure 12.6. The DMA interface functions as follows:

***DMA Operation***

(*i*) When an I/O instruction is encountered by the CPU it sends the device address and the I/O command to the DMA interface. The address in memory where a byte is to be stored or from where a byte is to be received is also sent to DMA by the CPU. If several bytes are to be stored or retrieved then the address of the first byte in the group and the count of the number of bytes is sent by CPU to the DMA interface. All the information sent by the CPU to the DMA interface is stored locally in the appropriate registers by the DMA interface unit.

(*ii*) After sending the above information to the DMA interface the CPU continues with the next instruction in the program. CPU resources are not needed hereafter.

(*iii*) The DMA uses the device address to select the appropriate device. The DMA busy flip-flop is set to 1. The DMA cannot be accessed by CPU till this busy flip-flop is reset to 0.

(*iv*) When the IBR is full it is transferred to MBR of the memory. The address is transferred to the MAR of the memory. We have assumed here that the memory has two independent ports, one connected to the CPU through a pair of buses and the other to the DMA. It allows complete independence of CPU data transfer and I/O data transfer. With a dual ported memory the DMA interface unit can transfer data to the memory as long as CPU is not accessing the same address of memory.

(*v*) After transferring the byte, the counter in DMA interface unit is decremented. The DMA acquires the next byte in IBR and performs Steps (*iv*) and (*v*) until the byte count is zero.

In Step (*iv*) we have assumed that the main memory is dual ported. Dual ported memories are however small in size. Main memory of computers are thus not dual ported. CPU and DMA interface must thus share MAR and MBR. Only one of them can access the main memory at a time. Thus if the DMA does not have access to a separate port of the main memory then it shares the MAR and MBR with CPU. In such cases when IBR in DMA interface unit is filled and ready to be transferred to memory, the DMA sends a signal to CPU. The CPU completes execution of the instruction it is currently carrying out and yields the next memory cycle to DMA. During this memory cycle IBR is sent to MBR of memory and the address to MAR and a byte is transferred to memory. After the byte is transferred, the counter in DMA is decremented. This method of transfer of a word from I/O to memory in which a memory cycle is taken away from CPU by DMA is known as *cycle stealing*. This procedure is shown in the flow chart of Figure 12.7.

Observe that this entire process of data transfer is performed by the hardware without any program intervention. In other words the programmer does not have to worry about the detailed transfer of data. In computer literature such hardware procedures which are hidden from or *not visible* to the programmer are called *transparent* to programmers. The choice of this term 'transparent' is not good as the dictionary meaning of this word is 'allowing light to pass through so that objects behind can be distinctly seen'. However the term transparent is a jargon which is universally used in computer literature.

This method of data transfer between I/O devices and memory is *non-program controlled*. The programmer must, however, give a read instruction sufficiently in advance so that the data is available in memory when required for use in the application program.

Let us compare DMA information transfer with transfer of information via CPU. The DMA transfer is faster and convenient to use. The CPU does not unnecessarily waste time. This advantage is gained by providing extra hardware in DMA and also by introducing extra information paths.

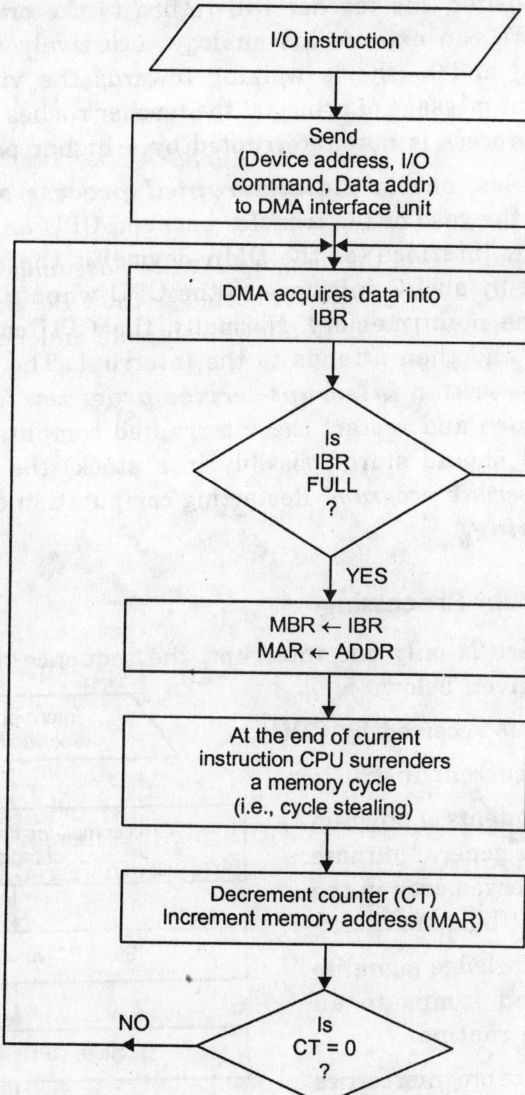


**Fig. 12.7:** DMA interface procedure (for I/O read).

## 12.5 INTERRUPT STRUCTURES

The information can be transferred between peripheral and CPU using an interrupt. The interrupt process may be compared to the action of a teacher when someone knocks at the door while he/she is present in the classroom. The teacher may have been teaching some interesting topic. He/she would then stop teaching and go to the door to attend the caller. After meeting the visitor, the teacher will return to the original job he/she was doing, namely, teaching. We can extend this analogy recursively. When the teacher is interrupted while teaching and he/she is walking towards the visitor to meet, if the college peon brings an urgent message of principal the teacher rushes to meet the principal. That is, the interrupting process is now interrupted by a higher priority event.

There are two processes, one is the ***interrupted process*** and the other is the ***interrupting process.*** In the case of I/O transfer between CPU and I/O the CPU is the interrupted process and I/O interface (or the DMA device) is the interrupting process. An interrupt signal is sent by an I/O interface to the CPU when it is ready to transfer information to (or from) the main memory. Normally, the CPU completes the current instruction it is executing and then attends to the interrupt. The interrupt request is serviced by executing a pre-written ***interrupt-service program***. After the interrupt is serviced, the CPU will return and restart the interrupted computation. For restarting the computation, the CPU should store (possibly in a stack) the *process state before branching to the interrupt service program.* Restarting computation can then be achieved by a simple ***process-switching.***

### 12.5.1 Single Level Interrupt Processing

If we assume that there is only one interrupt, the sequence of steps involved for interrupt processing is as given below:

(*i*) Interrupt signal is received by CPU.

(*ii*) CPU completes current instruction.

(*iii*) CPU stores the contents of program counter and other general purpose registers in a reserved area in the main memory of the computer.

(*iv*) CPU sends acknowledge signal to I/O interface and jumps to an interrupt service routine.

(*v*) The interrupt service program carries out the required transfer of data from or to I/O. The last instructions in the service program restores the contents of the general purpose registers. The content of the program counter is then restored to that stored in Step (*iii*) and CPU returns to execute the original program it was executing.

These steps are summarized in Figure 12.8(*a*). Figure 12.8(*b*) depicts the status of memory during interrupt processing.

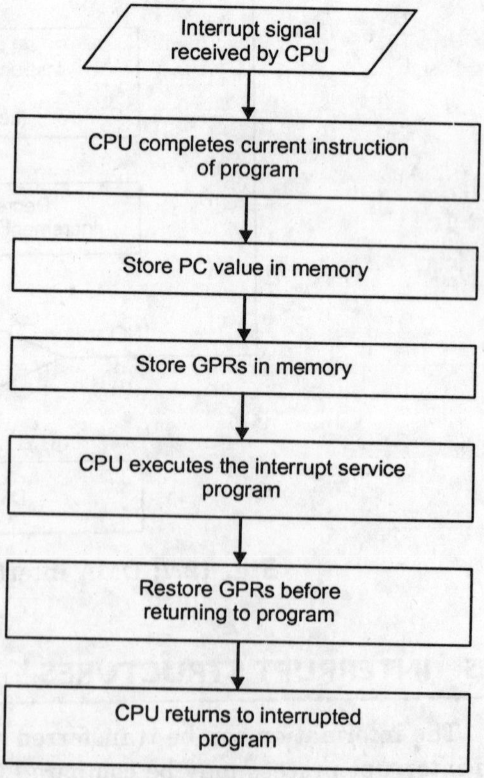


**Fig. 12.8(*a*):** Sequence of events in interrupt processing.

The assumption that only one interrupt occurs is not realistic. In practice CPU should handle a variety of interrupts from many I/O devices The order of importance or priority of these interrupts are different. Besides interrupts from device interface to transfer data from external devices, other interrupts are also generated. For example, the occurrence to an emergency condition such as power failure. When a sensor detects that power is about to fail, it sends an interrupt signal to the CPU. The CPU initiates a power failure service routine whose execution may be supported by a small battery backup power. This routine would store all important registers in non-volatile memory so that the program may be resumed when power returns. Interrupts caused by I/O devices and emergency events outside CPU's control are called *external interrupts*.

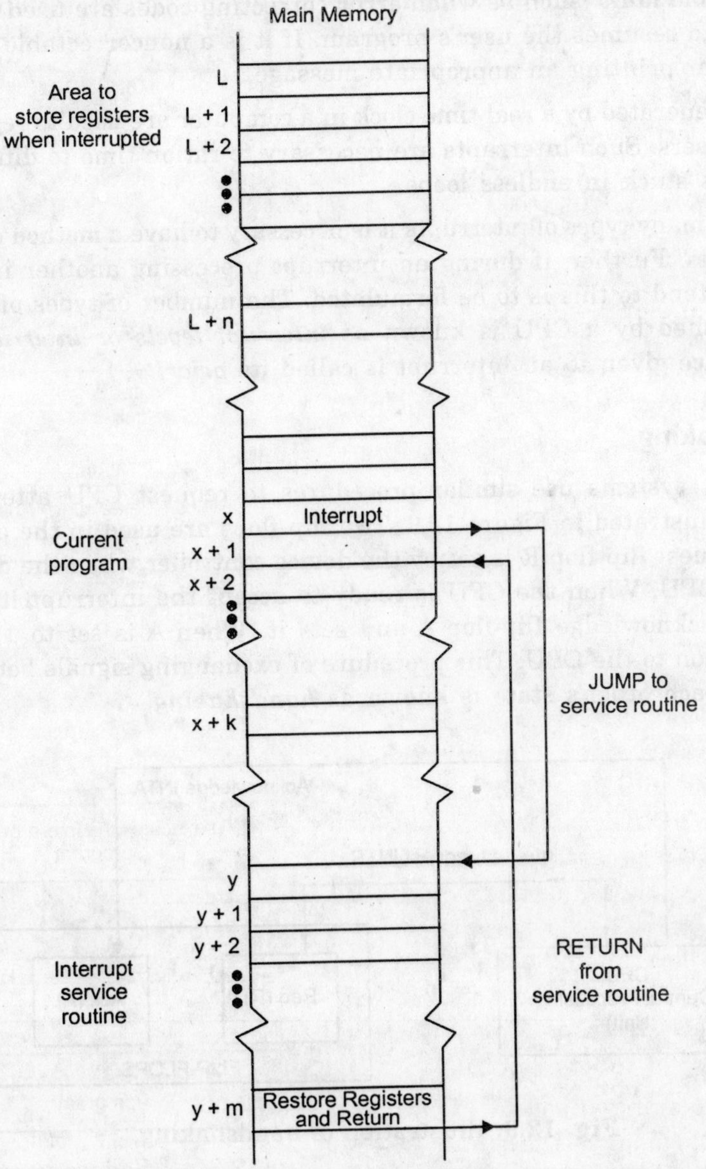


**Fig. 12.8(*b*):** Memory map in interrupt processing.

Another class of interrupts, *internal interrupts* (also known as *traps*) can occur when there is a mistake in a user's program. *Common mistakes which lead to traps are: attempt to divide by zero, accumulator overflow or use of an illegal operation code.* When such a mistake is detected by CPU it interrupts the user's program and branches to a trap routine which usually prints out the place where a trap occurred and the reason for the trap. The CPU may then resume the program if the mistake is not a serious one or suspend execution in case it is meaningless to continue with the interrupted program.

Another type of interrupt is caused if the hardware of a computer develops a fault. When the error detecting circuitry detects a fault the CPU is informed of the location and nature of the fault. The CPU then jumps to a fault service routine which determines if it is a correctable fault (such as when error correcting codes are used) and carries out the correction and resumes the user's program. If it is a noncorrectable fault, operation is suspended after printing an appropriate message.

Interrupts generated by a real time clock in a computer are used to regulate allocation of CPU time to users. Such interrupts are necessary to ration time to different users and to throw out jobs stuck in endless loops.

As there are many types of interrupts it is necessary to have a method of distinguishing types of interrupts. Further, if during an interrupt processing another interrupt occurs, a procedure to attend to this is to be formulated. The number of types of interrupts that can be distinguished by a CPU is known as *interrupt levels or interrupt classes.* The relative importance given to an interrupt is called its *priority.*

### 12.5.2 Handshaking

All interrupt systems use similar procedures to request CPU attention. A simple model of this is illustrated in Figure 12.9. Two flip-flops are used in the device interface. The interrupt request flip-flop R is set by the device controller when the device needs the attention of the CPU. When the CPU is ready to accept the interrupt it sends a signal to the interrupt acknowledge flip-flop A and sets it. When A is set to 1 the device can transfer information to the CPU. This procedure of exchanging signals between processes to communicate each other's state is known as *handshaking.*

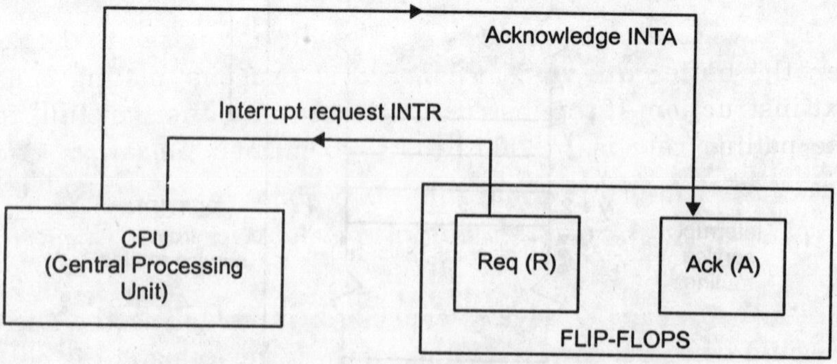


**Fig. 12.9:** Illustration of handshaking.

The model shown in Figure 12.9 is simplified and shows only one device. Let us suppose that several I/O devices of the same interrupt class are involved. Then two problems arise:

(*i*) How to connect the INTR (interrupt request) lines of these devices to the CPU?

(*ii*) How will the CPU determine which of the many devices has sent the interrupt so the INTA (interrupt acknowledge) can be given to the right device.

If many devices interrupt at the same time, there has to be an established priority in servicing them. When the set of all interrupts in a computer system is organized into several interrupt classes, priority assigned can be applied for each class, and again within each class.

### 12.5.3 Polling

Polling is a method in which a process periodically checks the status of an object. Usually the status is indicated by *status bit.* As long as the status bit does not change polling continues. When the status bit change a specified action is taken. This is illustrated by the algorithm given below:

```
                •
                •
                •
                •
LABEL_A :       Branch if buffer not full to : LABEL_A
                Next instruction
                •
                •
                •
```

Observe that when the instruction "branch if buffer not full" returns to itself if buffer-full bit = 0 (*i.e.,* buffer is not full). When the buffer becomes full, that is, buffer-full bit = 1 control branches to the next instruction. The above algorithm polls the buffer-full flip-flop. This flip-flop is set to 0 initially. It is set to 1 by I/O interface controller when the buffer fills up and when this happens, polling ends and control goes to the next instruction. If the instruction "branch if buffer not full" takes 200 nsec to execute. The polling rate is $1/(200 \times 10^{-9}) = 5$ million times per second.

*Polling techniques have many applications in computing. Besides its use in hardware, it is also used in system software design and in some applications. Its merit is simplicity. It is, however, not efficient.*

When there are several I/O devices capable of interrupting the CPU, one way to organize them would be to OR the INTR lines of these devices and the output of the OR gate can be used as a single interrupt request line to the CPU. When interrupt occurs, CPU knows that one of the I/O devices has interrupted. The interrupt service routine will *poll* INTR flags of the I/O devices cyclically one after another to determine which device has actually interrupted. If two or more I/O devices simultaneously interrupt the CPU, the *polling sequence* will determine the priority. A device which is polled earlier has a higher priority and gets CPU's attention first. The polling sequence may be fixed as a hardware or may be kept flexible in the interrupt service routine (software).

### 12.5.4 Device Address Posting

One way to improve the above I/O organisation is to reduce the time spent in interrupt service. Polling a large set of I/O devices to determine which device interrupted is time consuming. Let us suppose, each I/O device is assigned a unique *device address* and a *device address register* is included in the CPU. In the modified scheme, the interrupting device gains access to the address bus (see Figure 12.10—the address and databus are combined), and post its own address in the device address register. The interrupt service routine reads this register to determine which device has interrupted. This scheme is very flexible. The interrupt service routine of a device may selectively enable or disable further interrupts. It can be achieved by incorporating a *mask* bit (or register) in the CPU hardware design. Even though INTR is ON, the instruction sequence of CPU will not be interrupted if the *mask* bit is set to ON. Accordingly, there will be special CPU instructions to set this *mask* bit ON or OFF.

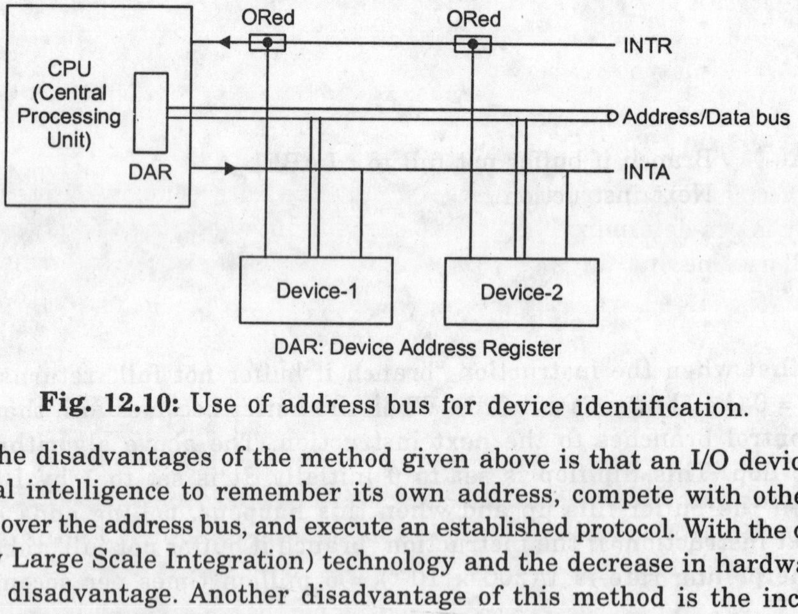


**Fig. 12.10:** Use of address bus for device identification.

One of the disadvantages of the method given above is that an I/O device must have adequate local intelligence to remember its own address, compete with other devices to obtain control over the address bus, and execute an established protocol. With the developments in VLSI (Very Large Scale Integration) technology and the decrease in hardware cost, this is no more a disadvantage. Another disadvantage of this method is the increase in the complexity of the interrupt service routine. The routine has to manage the *mask* bit, send INTA to the appropriate device etc.

### 12.5.5 Daisy Chaining

When several agents compete for a particular resource, we need some way of arbitration. Daisy chaining the agents is one scheme. For example, several I/O devices compete to get the INTA (interrupt acknowledge) from the CPU, and only one of them can have it at a time. The I/O devices can be *daisy chained* as shown in Figure 12.11. The highest priority device, D1 in Figure 12.11, is placed first in the chain. When the INTA signal is available from the CPU, the device D1, using its internal logic determines if it needs the interrupt services. If so, the device does not let INTA to propagate any further. It identifies itself to the CPU using the address lines. If it does not require the interrupt services, the device D1 lets the INTA signal propagate to the next device in the chain by closing the signal propagation gate G1 (Refer to Figure 12.11).

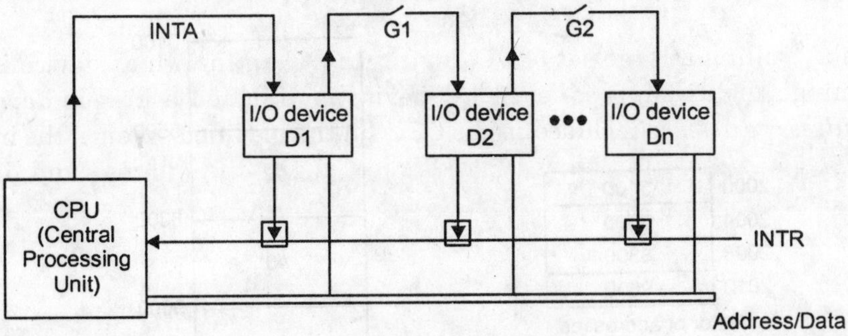


**Fig. 12.11:** Daisy chaining.

Daisy chaining is a simple means for arbitration but it does not ensure *fairness* of service to all devices. A low priority device further down in the chain will not get access, if higher priority devices in the chain keep requesting attention. Thus it may happen that a low priority device may never be attended.

### 12.5.6 Daisy Chaining Based I/O Arbitration

The sequence of events that take place in this scheme are as follows. Note that, in this scheme, priority is pre-determined as per the sequence in which the I/O devices are daisy chained. We will assume that the gates Gi are normally closed, and the interrupt services of a device can be interrupted by interrupts coming from devices of higher priority.

(*i*) When a device Di requires interrupt services, it sends an INTR signal and opens its gate Gi so that no other lower priority device can send the INTR.

(*ii*) The CPU recognizes the INTR and sends out the acknowledgement signal, INTA.

(*iii*) The device Di will receive INTA if no higher priority device has requested an interrupt service. When it receives the INTA, Di identifies itself to the CPU by posting its address on the bus. We assume the bus is always available.

(*iv*) The CPU starts executing the interrupt service routine that corresponds to the device Di. The execution of this routine can be interrupted by another device that has higher priority.

(*v*) At the end of the interrupt services, the switch Gi will be closed to enable communication with lower priority devices.

### 12.5.7 Vectored Interrupts

A major aim in I/O organisation is to reduce the overhead involved in interrupt handling. In step 3 above, we mentioned that the I/O device identifies itself to the CPU by posting its own address on the bus. This idea is extended in a more fruitful manner in *vectored interrupts*. Let us explain this with an example.

Suppose that there are 4 different I/O devices connected to a CPU. Assume that the system programmer or the operating system designer has written the interrupt service routines for each of these devices and stored these routines in the reserved area of memory as shown in Figure 12.12.

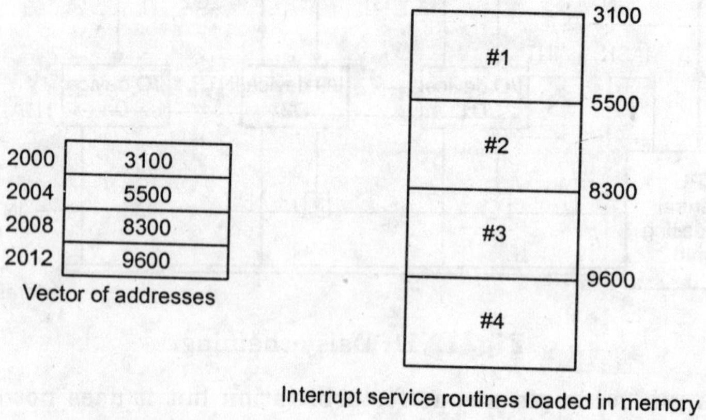


**Fig. 12.12:** Illustration of vector of addresses.

The *vector of addresses* stored starting from address 2000 in Figure 12.12, contain the starting addresses of the four interrupt service routines. Let us associate the vector of addresses (2000, 2004, 2008, 2012) with the four devices (#1, #2, #3, #4) respectively. When the I/O device #2 is ready it posts the code 2004 on the bus. This information can be used by the CPU to straight away branch to the corresponding interrupt service routine (using the concept of indirect addressing). The interrupt service routines may be relocated at some other areas of memory but the vector of addresses must reside in the same place; otherwise this method will not work correctly.

### 12.5.8 Multiple Interrupt Lines

Till now, we have considered models of interrupt systems in which we had only one interrupt request line entering the CPU and one interrupt acknowledge line leaving the CPU. If there are many devices, we assumed that the INTR of different devices are ORed together. We can extend this model to associate multiple pairs of (INTR, INTA) with the CPU. This model is illustrated in Figure 12.13. The INT register has one bit reserved for each INTR line which registers the interrupt requests from various lines. For example, the I/O devices may be grouped into 4 classes and connected through 4 separate INTR lines, as shown in Figure 12.13. In this scheme two or more simultaneous interrupt requests from different lines can be registered in the INT register. However, there is only one CPU and hence only one interrupt service routine can be executed at a time. Thus the CPU has to assign priorities among multiple requests and select one of them at a time for service. Such a selection may be made using hardware devices called *priority encoders* or by software means with the help of an interrupt analyzer software. In order to allow easy programming of priority selection, a *mask register* and a set of machine instructions to set or reset the bits of this register are introduced in the CPU. There is one bit in the MASK register corresponding to each bit in the INT register. If this bit is set (ON), the corresponding interrupt request is not selected or said to be masked until the bit is reset (OFF) at a later time by the interrupt analyzer software. The system programmer can alter the priority of selection by selectively turning the mask bits ON or OFF at different instances.

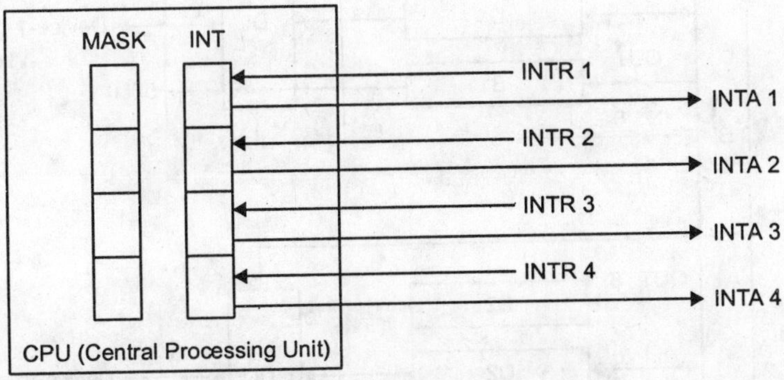


**Fig. 12.13:** Illustration of multiple interrupt lines.

### 12.5.9 Peripheral Interface Adapter

Peripheral Interface Adapter (PIA) is VLSI (Very Large Scale Integration) chip manufactured by the semiconductor company Motorola. It is intended for the modular design of I/O systems. Several other companies like INTEL also manufacture VLSI chips of this kind. A *simplified* block diagram of PIA is shown in Figure 12.14. Motorola has been producing a series of microprocessors MC 68000, 68020, 68040 etc. based on which several computer systems (Apple Macintosh, SUN 3/50) and UNIX workstations have been marketed. The PIA is designed to interface easily with the microprocessor bus and such interface details are not shown in Figure 12.14.

From Figure 12.14, we observe that two I/O devices can be connected through the device interface circuitry (DI). The interrupt requests generated by these two devices are marked as INTR-1 and INTR-2. The data lines are 8-bits wide. This particular PIA allows the programmer to designate each of the 8 data lines to be input (from the device) or output (to the device). The 8-bit data direction registers D1 and D2 are for specifying the direction. These registers can be loaded or read by the CPU. The output from the CPU to the device is buffered through the 8-bit buffer registers B1 and B2; but the input from the device is sent directly to the bus interface unit BI. The control and status register C1 and C2 are used to coordinate the I/O device functions with the CPU. The control and status register C1 is used for device-1 and C2 is for device-2. The register (8-bits) is divided into two parts, one part for controlling the device, that is, to specify the I/O operation to be performed and the other part is used for storing the status of the I/O device. Device operations in the case of a disk device could be SEEK, READ, WRITE, READ-WRITE-HEAD-UP or DOWN. The registers C1 and C2 are connected on the one side to an I/O device and on the other side to the CPU. All the registers shown in Figure 12.14 are accessible to the CPU via the bus interface unit. Each register will have an address allocated in I/O address space, or in the memory address space, if memory mapped I/O is used.

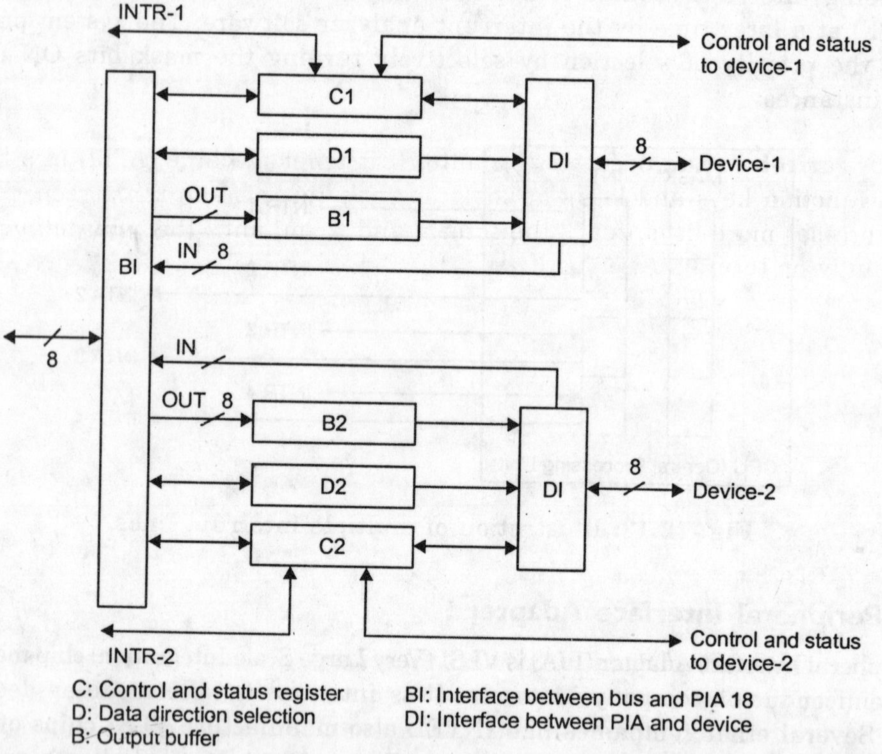


**Fig. 12.14:** A simplified block diagram of Motorola's PIA.

## 12.5.10 Interrupt Enable and Disable

We have seen earlier, how to selectively mask an interrupt using the mask register. In some situations or during some time intervals the CPU should ignore the interrupt requests totally but only for short intervals. For example, suppose the CPU is saving its own state in order to service an interrupt. While saving the state, we do not want another interrupt; otherwise it can go on recursively to an indefinite level of nesting. In some situations the CPU can execute a privileged instruction (ENABLE INTERRUPTS, DISABLE INTERRUPTS) to prevent further interruptions.

In the status register of a CPU, there is one bit that indicates if the interrupts are enabled or disabled in the system. This bit will be *set*, or *reset* by the ENABLE or DISABLE instructions. The interrupt hardware which recognizes any interrupt normally at the end of the current instruction execution, will do so only if the interrupt bit is set ON. The user should understand the correct execution of the matched pair (ENABLE, DISABLE) of instructions. The interrupt system of a computer can not be left disabled for "unacceptably long intervals" because the computer may be receiving interrupts from important and indispensable events occurring in the external world. For example, if the safety valve of an aeroplane in mid-air is stuck the computer has to take immediate corrective action. In safety critical systems like this, the computer designer has goals which are different from those used in designing a general purpose computer.

## 12.6 INPUT/OUTPUT OPERATION MODELS

All I/O actions are not of the same type. We will emphasize this with three scenarios:

**Scenario-I.** A user operating an automatic teller machine (ATM) in a bank, presses certain function keys and looks at the machine's response on the screen, following that he/she presses more keys, reads the screen, and so on, until the *transaction* is completed successfully or terminated unsuccessfully. In such online transaction processing (OLTP) applications, the *response time* is an important measure of performance. Also, the bank would like to have as many transactions processed as possible at an ATM counter. Thus, the *throughput* measured in so many OLTP's per second is also an indicator of performance measure.

A transaction in this case consists of an arbitrary but finite sequence of pairs (input, output). Each input or output is "small" in terms of the number of bytes read or written. The actual time elapsed between the machine's output and the user's input depends upon the user's think-time and user's machine-time.

**Scenario-II.** An organisation having 5,000 employees produces pay-slips every two weeks. A pay slip contains, an employee's name, address, personal identification number, total earnings, details of each deduction, total deductions, net pay for the period, etc. At the end of printing all the payslips, the payroll program has to produce a number of reports to be sent to the Taxation Office, Financial Officer, etc. For this purpose, the payroll program uses three files: (employee's details file, deductions file, earnings file). Each of these files will store several kilobytes or megabytes of data. The payroll program must have a good throughput. Every time the program reads a file, it can read a large chunk of data and keep them in its RAM. The time between two successive reads (or writes) will depend upon the processing needs and the size of the allocated buffer. The input/output in this scenario are **file based** whereas that in scenario-I are **transaction based.**

**Scenario-III.** A supercomputer performing computation-intensive calculations loads the program, reads the necessary data, and then goes into computational state. Data input are a few in this case. Majority of the execution time is spent in calculations and the volume of I/O is negligibly small. This scenario would correspond to "type-III" in Figure 12.15.

| | $\bar{t}$ | $\bar{w}$ |
|---|---|---|
| Type-I | small | small |
| Type-II | small | large |
| Type-III | large | small |
| Type-IV | large | large |

$\bar{t}$, $\bar{w}$ : average values

**Fig. 12.15:** I/O operation models.

We could follow the models used in the well known field of mathematics called queuing theory and represent the I/O activities in the above scenarios (see Figure 12.15). The time between two consecutive occurrences is denoted by 't' and the width or size of each occurrence is denoted by 'w'. Both 't' and 'w' are random variables, non-negative, and their maximum size is bounded. We can examine their statistics (average, standard deviation) and distribution. We have not stated whether the elements of Figure 12.15 are input items, output items, or I/O items. If we want to evaluate the input design and output design differently, then we can think of separate distributions for input and output.

## 12.7 INPUT-OUTPUT PROCESSOR

Instead of having each interface communicate with the CPU, a computer may have one or more external processors and assign them the task of communicating directly with all I/O devices. An input-output processor (IOP) may be classified as a processor with direct memory access capability that communicates with I/O devices. In this configuration, the computer system can be divided into a memory unit, and a number of processors comprised of the CPU and one or more IOPs. Each IOP takes care of input and output tasks, relieving the CPU from the housekeeping chores involved in I/O transfers. A processor that communicates with remote terminals over telephone and other communication media in a serial fashion is known as a data communication processor (DCP).

The IOP is similar to a CPU except that it is designed to handle the details of I/O processing. Unlike the DMA controller that must be set up entirely by the CPU, the IOP can fetch and execute its own instructions. IOP instructions are specifically designed to facilitate I/O transfers. In addition, the IOP can perform other processing tasks, such as arithmetic, logic, branching, and code translation.

The block diagram of a computer with two processors is illustrated in Figure 12.16.

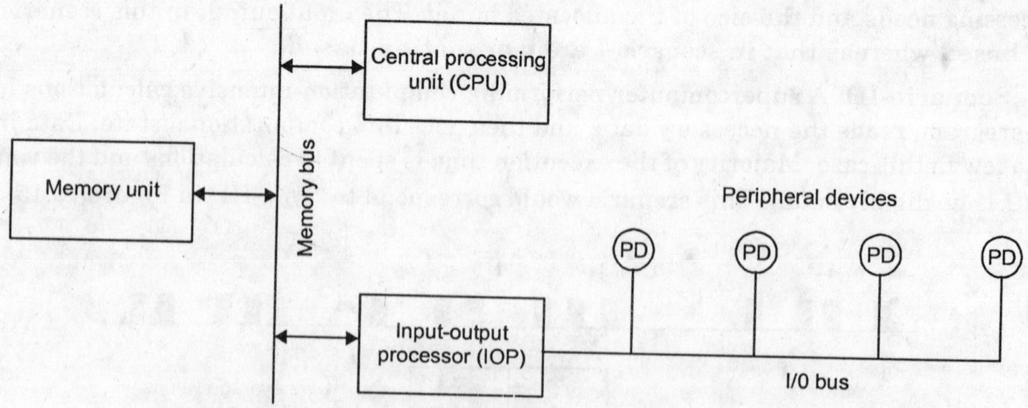


**Fig. 12.16:** Block diagram of a computer with I/O processor.

The memory unit occupies a central position and can communicate with each processor by means of direct memory access. The CPU is responsible for processing data needed in the solution of computational tasks. The IOP provides a path for transfer of data between various peripheral devices and the memory unit. The CPU is usually assigned the task of initiating the I/O program. From then on the IOP operates independent of the CPU and continues to transfer data from external devices and memory.

The data formats of peripheral devices differ from memory and CPU data formats. The IOP must structure data words from many different sources. For example, it may be necessary to take four bytes from an input device and pack them into one 32-bit word before the transfer to memory. Data are gathered in the IOP at the device rate and bit capacity while the CPU is executing its own program. After the input data are assembled into a memory word, they are transferred from IOP directly into memory by **"stealing"** one memory cycle from the CPU. Similarly, an output word transferred from memory to the IOP is directed from the IOP to the output device at the device rate and bit capacity.

The communication between the IOP and the devices attached to it is similar to the program control method of transfer. Communication with the memory is similar to the direct memory access method. The way by which the CPU and IOP communicate depends on the level of sophistication included in the system. In very-large-scale computers, each processor is independent of all others and any one processor can initiate an operation. In most computer systems, the CPU is the **master** while the IOP is a **slave processor.** The CPU is assigned the task of initiating all operations, but I/O instructions are executed in the IOP. CPU instructions provide operations to start an I/O transfer and also to test I/O status conditions needed for making decisions on various I/O activities. The IOP, in turn, typically asks for CPU attention by means of an interrupt. It also responds to CPU requests by placing a status word in a prescribed location in memory to be examined later by a CPU program. When an I/O operation is desired, the CPU informs the IOP where to find the I/O program and then leaves the transfer details to the IOP.

Instructions that are read from memory by an IOP are sometimes called *commands*, to distinguish them from instructions that are read by the CPU. Otherwise, an instruction and a command have similar functions. Commands are prepared by experienced programmers and are stored in main memory. The command words constitute the program for the IOP. The CPU informs the IOP where to find the commands in memory when it is time to execute the I/O program.

### 12.7.1 CPU-IOP Communication

The communication between CPU and IOP may take different forms, depending on the particular computer considered. In most cases the memory unit acts as a message center where each processor leaves information for the other. To appreciate the operation of a typical IOP, we will illustrate by a specific example the method by which the CPU and IOP communicate. This is a simplified example that omits many operating details in order to provide an overview of basic concepts.

The sequence of operations may be carried out as illustrated in the flowchart of Figure 12.17.

The CPU sends an instruction to test the IOP path. The IOP responds by inserting a status word in memory for the CPU to check. The bits of the status word indicate the condition of the IOP and I/O device, such as IOP overload condition, device busy with another transfer, or device ready for I/O transfer. The CPU refers to the status word in memory to decide what to do next. If all is in order, the CPU sends the instruction to star I/O transfer. The memory address received with this instruction tells the IOP where t find its program.

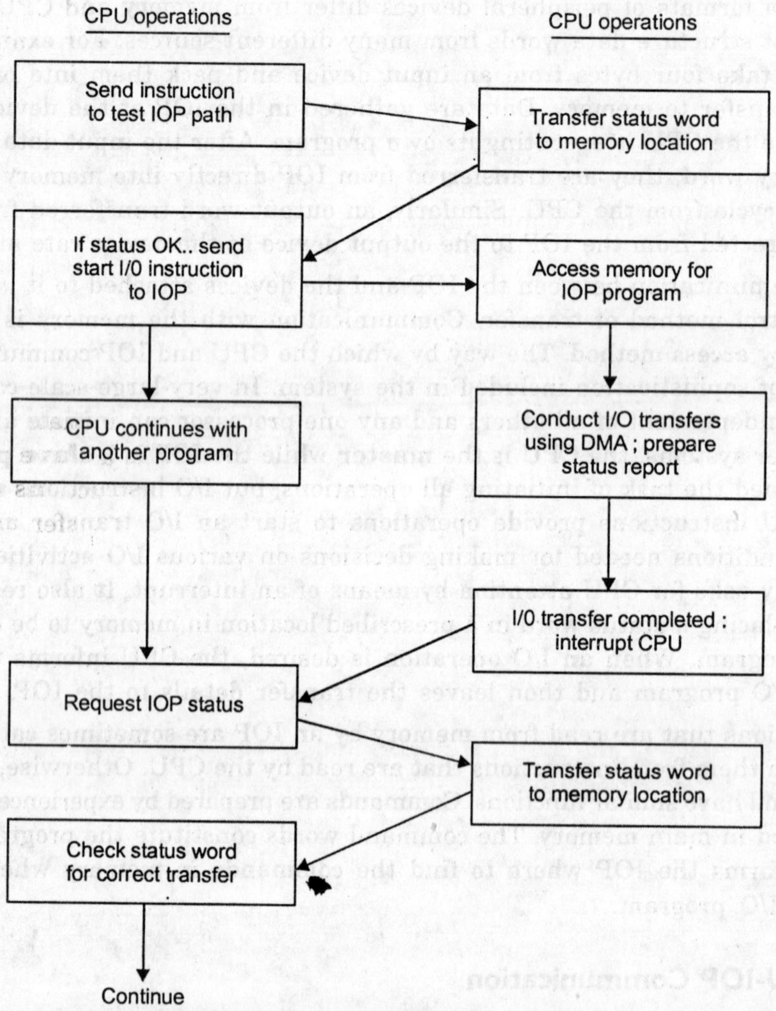


**Fig. 12.17: CPU-IOP Communication.**

The CPU can now continue with another program while the IOP is busy with the I O program. Both programs refer to memory by means of DMA transfer. When the IO terminates the execution of its program, it sends an interrupt request to the CPU. Th CPU responds to the interrupt by issuing an instruction to read the status from the IO The IOP responds by placing the contents of its status report into a specified memor location. The status word indicates whether the transfer has been completed or if an errors occurred during the transfer. From inspection of the bits in the status word, th CPU determines if the I/O operation was completed satisfactorily without errors.

The IOP takes care of all data transfers between several I/O units and the memor while the CPU is processing another program. The IOP and CPU are competing for th use of memory, so the number of devices that can be in operation is limited by the access time of the memory. It is not possible to saturate the memory by I/O devices in most systems, as the speed of most I/O devices is much slower than the CPU. However, some very fast units, such as magnetic disks, can use an appreciable number of the available memory cycles. In that case, the speed of the CPU may deteriorate because it will often have to wait for the IOP to conduct memory transfers.

### 12.7.2 IBM 370 I/O Channel

In the IBM 370 computer, the I/O processor computer is known as a channel. A typical computer system configuration has a number of channels with each channel attached to one or more I/O devices. There are three types of channels: *multiplexer, selector,* and *block-multiplexer*. The multiplexer channel can be connected to a number of slow- and medium-speed devices and is capable of operating with a number of I/O devices simultaneously. The selector channel is designed to handle one I/O operation at a time and is normally used to control one high-speed device. Block multiplexer channel combine the features of multiplexer and select channels.

The CPU communicates directly with the channels through dedicated control lines and indirectly through reserved storage areas in memory. Figure 12.18 illustrates the word formats associated with the channel operation. The I/O instruction format has three fields: *operation code, channel address*, and *device address*. The computer system may have a number of channels, and each is assigned an address. Similarly, each channel may be connected to several devices and each device is assigned an address. The operation code specifies one of eight I/O instructions: *start I/O, start I/O fast release, test I/O, clear I/O, halt I/O, halt device, test channel*, and *store channel identification*. The addressed channel responds to each of the I/O instructions and executes it. It also sets one of four condition codes in a processor register known as PSW (processor status word). The CPU can check the condition code in the PSW to determine the result of the I/O operation. The meaning of the four condition codes is different for each I/O instruction. But, in general, they specify whether the channel or the device is busy, whether or not it is operational, whether interruptions are pending, if the I/O operation had started successfully, and whether a status word was stored in memory by the channel.

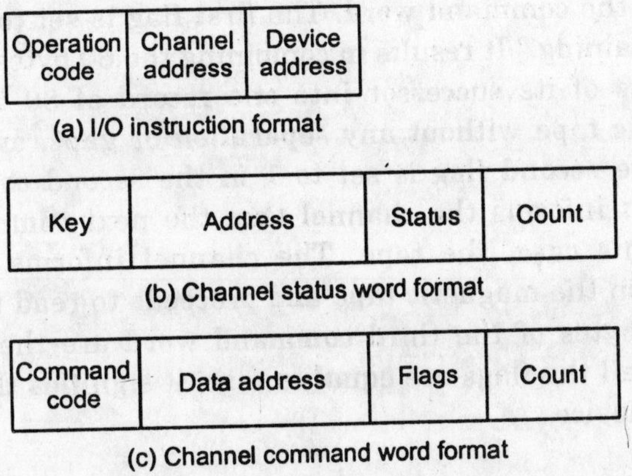


**Fig. 12.18:** Illustrating IBM 370 I/O related word formats.

The format of the channel status word is illustrated in Figure 12.18(*b*). It is always stored in location 64 in main memory. The key field is a protection mechanism used to prevent unauthorized access by one user to information that belongs to another user or to the operating system. The address field in the status word provides the addresses of the last command word used by the channel. The count field provides the residual count when the transfer was terminated. The count field will show zero if the transfer was completed successfully. The status field identifies the conditions in the device and the channel and any errors that occurred during the transfer.

The difference between the start I/O and start I/O fast release instructions is that the latter requires less CPU time for its execution. When the channel receives one of these two instructions, it refers to memory location 72 for the address of the first channel command word (CCW). The format of the channel command word is illustrated in Figure 12.18(*c*). The data address field specifies first address of a memory buffer and the count field gives the number of bits involved in the transfer. The command field specifies an I/O operation. The flag bits provide additional information for the channel. The command field corresponds to an operation code that specifies one of six basic types of I/O operations:

(*i*) *Write*. Transfer data from main memory to I/O device.

(*ii*) *Read*. Transfer data from I/O device to main memory.

(*iii*) *Read backwards*. Read magnetic tape with tape moving backward.

(*iv*) *Control*. Used to initiate an operation not involving transfer of data, such as rewinding of tape or positioning a disk-access mechanism.

(*v*) *Sense*. Informs the channel to transfer its channel status to memory location 64.

(*vi*) *Transfer in channel*. Used instead of a jump instruction. Here the data address field specifies the address of the next command word to be executed by the channel.

An example of a channel program is given in Table 12.1. It has three command words. The first causes a byte transfer into a magnetic tape from memory starting at address 5000. The next two command-words perform a similar function with a different portion of memory and byte count. The six flags in each control word specify certain interrelations between the command word. The first flag is set to 1 in the first command word to specify "data chaining." It results in combining the 60 bytes from the first command word with the 20 bytes of its successor into one record of 80 bytes. The 80 bytes are written on the magnetic tape without any separation or gaps, even though two memory sections were used. The second flag is set to 1 in the second command word to specify "*command chaining*." It informs the channel that the next command word will use the same I/O device, in this case, the tape. The channel informs the tape unit to start inserting a record gap on the magnetic tape and proceeds to read the next command word from memory. The 50 bytes of the third command word are then written on tape as a separate record. When all the flags are equal to zero, it signifies the end of I/O operations for the particular I/O device.

**Table 12.1: IBM-370 Channel Program Example**

| *Command* | *Address* | *Flags* | *Count* |
|---|---|---|---|
| Write tape | 5000 | 100000 | 60 |
| Write tape | 7000 | 010000 | 20 |
| Write tape | 4000 | 000000 | 50 |

A memory map showing all relevant information for I/O processing is shown in Figure 12.19. The operation takes place when the CPU program encounters a start I/O instruction. The IOP then goes to memory location 72 to obtain a channel address word. This word contains the starting address of the I/O channel program. The channel then proceeds to execute the program specified by the channel command words. The channel constructs a status word during the transfer and stores it in location 64. Upon interruption, the CPU can refer the memory location 64 for the status word.

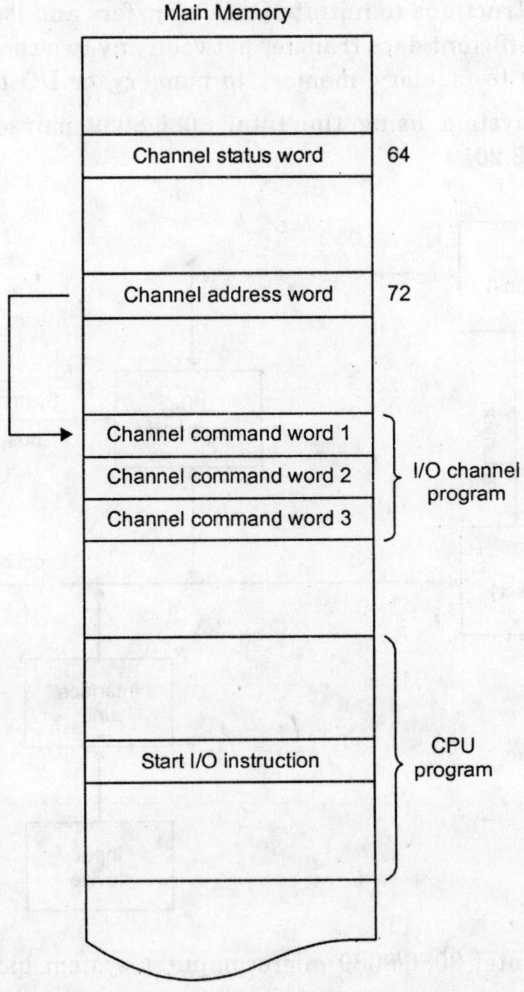


**Fig. 12.19:** Location of information in main memory for I/O operation in the IBM-370.

### 12.7.3 Intel 8089 IOP

The Intel 8089 I/O processor is contained in a 40-pin integrated circuit package. Within the 8089 are two independent units called **channels.** Each channel combines the general characteristics of a processor unit with those of a direct memory access controller. The 8089 is designed to function as an IOP in a microcomputer system where the Intel 8086 microprocessor is used as the CPU. The 8086 CPU initiates an I/O operation by building a message in memory that describes the function to be performed. The 8089 IOP reads the message from memory, performs the operation, and notifies the CPU when it has finished.

In contrast to the IBM 370 channel, which has only six basic I/O commands, the 8089 IOP has 50 basic instructions that can operate on individual bits, on bytes, or 16-bit words. The IOP can execute programs in a manner similar to a CPU except that the instruction set is specifically chosen to provide efficient input-output processing. The instruction set includes general data transfer instructions, basic arithmetic and logic operations, conditional and unconditional branch operations, and subroutine call and return capabilities. The set also includes special instructions to initiate DMA transfers and issue an interrupt request to the CPU. It provides efficient data transfer between any two components attached to the system bus, such as I/O to memory, memory to memory, or I/O to I/O.

A microcomputer system using the Intel 8086/8089 pair of integrated circuits is illustrated in Figure 12.20.

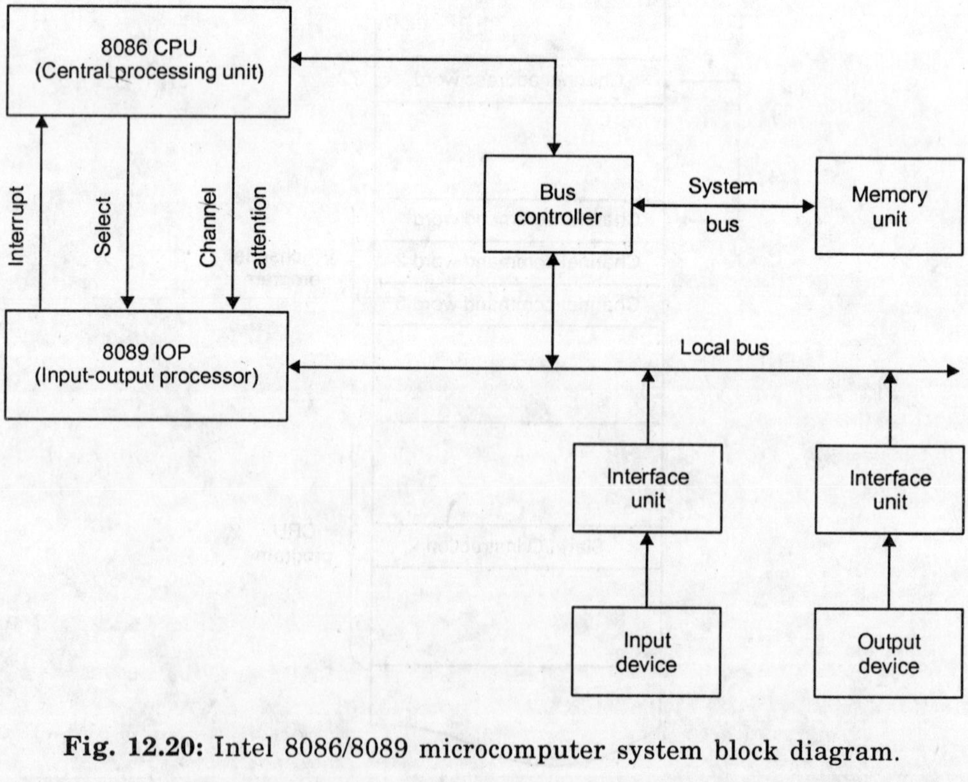


**Fig. 12.20:** Intel 8086/8089 microcomputer system block diagram.

The 8086 functions as the CPU and the 8089 as the IOP. The two units share a common memory through a bus controller connected to a system bus, which is called a "multibus" by Intel. The IOP uses a local bus to communicate with various interface units connected to I/O devices. The CPU communicates with the IOP by enabling the *channel attention* line. The *select* line is used by the CPU to select one of two channels in the 8089. The IOP gets the attention of the CPU by sending an interrupt request.

The CPU and IOP communicate with each other by writing messages for one another in system memory. The CPU prepares the message area and signals the IOP by enabling the channel attention line. The IOP reads the message, performs the required I/O functions, and executes the appropriate channel program. When the channel has completed its program, it issues an interrupt request to the CPU.

The communication scheme consists of program sections known as "blocks," which are stored in memory as illustrated in Figure 12.21.

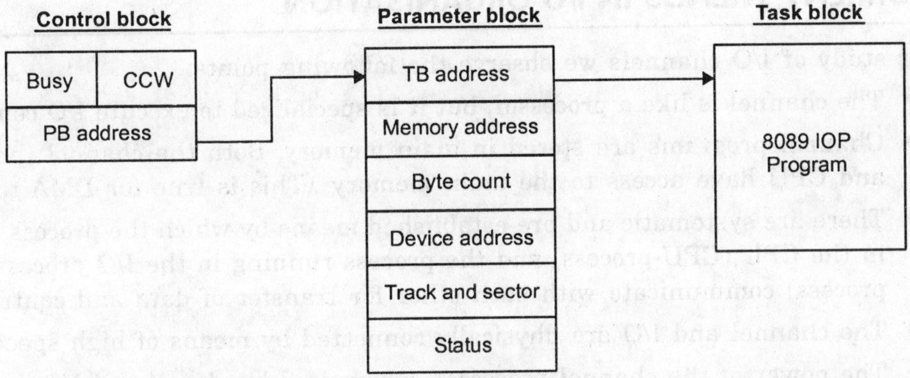


**Fig. 12.21** Location of information in memory for I/O operations in the Intel 8086/8089 microcomputer system.

Each block contains control and parameter information as well as an address pointer o its successor block. The address of the control block is passed to each IOP channel luring initialization. The busy flag indicates whether the IOP is busy or ready to perform new I/O operation. The CCW (channel command word) is specified by the CPU to ndicate the type of operation required from the IOP. The CCW in the 8089 does not have he same meaning as the command word in the IBM channel. The CCW here is more like n I/O instruction that specifies an operation for the IOP, such as start operation, suspend peration, resume operation, and halt I/O program. The parameter block contains variable lata that the IOP program must use in carrying out its task. The task block contains the ctual program to be executed in the IOP.

The CPU and IOP work together through the control and parameter blocks. The 'PU obtains use of the shared memory after checking the busy flag to ensure that the OP is available. The CPU then fills in the information in the parameter block and writes "start operation" command in the CCW. After the communication blocks have been set p, the CPU enables the channel attention signal to inform the IOP to start its I/O peration. The CPU then continues with some other program. The IOP responds to the hannel attention signal by placing the address of the control block into its program counter. The IOP refers to the control block and sets the busy flag. It then checks the operation in the CCW. The PB (parameter block) address and TB (task block) address are then transferred into internal IOP registers. The IOP starts executing the program in the task block using the information in the parameter block. The entries in the parameter block depend on the I/O device. The parameters listed in Figure 12.21 are suitable for data transfer to or from a magnetic disk. The memory address specifies the beginning address of a memory buffer (portion of main memory that can be directly accessed by the I/O devices). The byte count gives the number of bytes to be transferred. The device address specifies the particular I/O device to be used. The track and sector numbers locate the data on the disk. When the I/O operation is completed, the IOP stores its status bits in the status word location of the parameter block and interrupts the CPU. The CPU can refer to the status word to check if the transfer has been completed satisfactorily.

## 12.8 CURRENT TRENDS IN I/O ORGANISATION

After study of I/O channels we observe the following points:

- The channel is like a processor, but it is specialized to execute I/O commands.
- Channel programs are stored in main memory. Both the channel (processor) and CPU have access to the main memory. (This is true for DMA too.)
- There are systematic and pre-established means by which the process running in the CPU (CPU-process) and the process running in the I/O processor ((I/O process) communicate with each other for transfer of data and control.
- The channel and I/O are physically connected by means of high speed buses.
- The power of the channel processor, when used by slow speed I/O devices, is shared by multiple devices through multiplexing. This is to reduce the overall system cost.

When the channel organisation was introduced three decades ago, the cost of a processor and main memory were very high. As a result the I/O processor was specialized, multiplexed, and made to share expensive resources. This concept of sharing expensive resources is still valid. But the expensive resources are different now. A Pentium processor running at 100 MHz is not even one-tenth the cost of a high speed laser printer. Also semi-conductor RAMs have become chapter now. Thus, a local processor with megabytes of memory is nowadays used to control expensive I/O devices. Such computers have taken over the job of the channel processors we have studied in the previous section.

Now we have two processes, just as we had earlier, but they are technologically different. Let us call these two as *client* and *server*. The client process requests the services of a server process. In Figure 12.22, we have shown 2 server processes and 10 client processes. A client process requiring the printing of an object (a file) will transmit it and request the services of the print server. The object will have information about how it should be printed and this will be interpreted by the complex programs resident in the print server. A powerful processor which is part of the print server can be programmed to store such requests coming from multiple clients and carry them out appropriately. In a similar way disk server or file server will be used for reading or writing large files from disks.

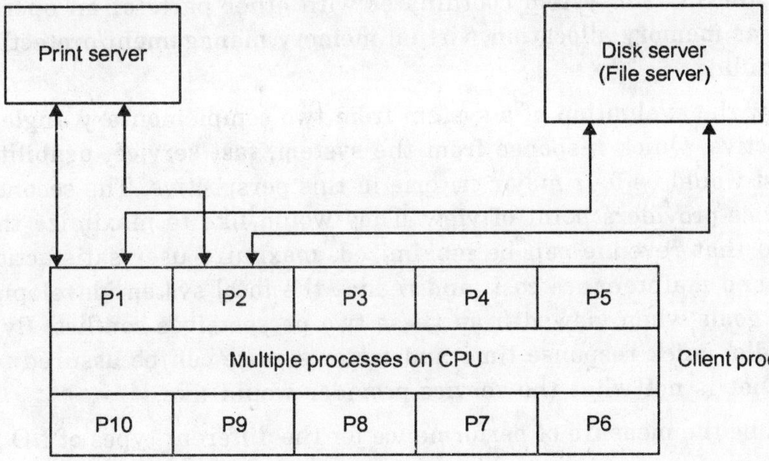


**Fig. 12.22:** Client-server computing.

The synchronization and communication between the two concurrent processes (client and server) are important. Because the server process doing the I/O operation is now more powerful than before (powerful CPU and more local memory), it has become possible to transmit larger chunks of data (when possible) and to implement complex control protocols. The bus connecting the two processors before was a standardized high speed I/O bus, but is now replaced by a local area network, such as Ethernet or Novell-Net. The same concept of client-server computing is useful for information processing. In such a case, a commonly used server is called a database server. It can accept queries from clients in high level query languages and return responses to those queries.

## 12.9 I/O ORGANISATION EVALUATION

Evaluation of a design is necessary to ensure that the design meets its specification and also to improve the design. It is hard to agree on a single "figure-of-merit" to evaluate the design of a complex system. We can use instruction mixes, kernels, and bench mark programs for evaluating the CPU of a computer system. Two factors, namely ***throughput*** and ***response time*** can also be used. A similar approach is followed in the evaluation of I/O design. Input-output design has to deal with a wide variety of issues. In particular we have to address the following:

- The variety of I/O devices that the design accommodates. How many such varieties are connected in the *configuration* being evaluated?
- The I/O types and their timing characteristics (we have arbitrarily divided the I/O types into four groups based on the time between two consecutive I/O requests (small and large) and the length of an I/O service (small and large). In practice these types would correspond to OLTP (small, small), computation intensive jobs (large, small), file transfers (large, large) and file-intensive (small, large).
- The I/O organisation, and the various ways in which devices, controllers, and buses are connected or shared.

- How the I/O subsystem coordinates with other parts of an operating system such as memory allocation, virtual memory management/protection, and CPU scheduling.

We can view the evaluation of a system from two complementary angles: One is the *end-user* perspective. Quick response from the system, fast service, usability or ease-of-use, and low cost would be four major criteria in this perspective. The second perspective is from the service-providers point of view. They would like to maximize the utilization of the system so that revenue can be maximized, maximize user satisfaction, minimize the operational and maintenance cost, and reduce the total system development cost. As we can see, the goals when viewed from these two perspectives conflict. By keeping the system mostly idle, quick response time and faster service can be assured to a specified end-user. But, that is not what the service-provider would like.

What could be the measure of performance for the different types of I/O given above?

| | |
|---|---|
| OLTP (on-line transaction processing) type: | • Throughput measured in terms of so many *typical transactions* per unit time. |
| | • Average response time. |
| | • Percentage transactions that have to wait for service beyond the acceptable time limit. |
| Computer-intensive type: | • Data throughput. |
| File-transfer type: | • Throughput measured in terms of so many *typical file accesses* per unit time. |

For assisting evaluation, *synthetic bench marks* have been developed to describe what is meant by a typical transaction or a typical file access. These synthetic bench marks take into account several variations. For example, a file may be a read only file, or read-write file; the number of read operations and write operations to a file may or may not be equal; the file size may be small (10 to 100s of kilobytes) or large (several megabytes); a file may be indexed in several different ways; etc. Similarly, a transaction also has a large number of characteristics: the number of disk accesses required per transaction; the number of bytes transferred; types of failure recovery required etc.

In the past, evaluation of I/O system has not been given the same importance as the evaluation of CPU or the instruction set design. The widespread use of computers and networking has created the need to recognize the importance of user interfaces to computer based systems. As a result of this, in future, interest in the evaluation of I/O system and user interfaces is likely to grow.

## SUMMARY

- I/O devices differ widely in their characteristics and in their operational principles.
- Input-outputs interface provides a method for transferring information between internal storage and external I/O devices.
- The I/O bus consists of data lines, address lines and control lines.

- The speed of information transfer of I/O devices is slow compared to that of a computer's main memory.
- The *device controller* performs device-dependent electro-mechanical or electro-optical functions.
- The *interface unit* performs the logic of communicating with the receiver of the input read or the sender of the output to be displayed.
- The information transfer between CPU and I/O devices can take place in several ways.
- The device address on the I/O bus is recognized by the address decoder of the desired I/O device interface unit.
- In *program controlled transfer* method synchronization of I/O device and CPU is achieved by making CPU wait till the data is assembled by the device.
- The I/O devices are normally much slower compared to CPU the method of synchronization is not desirable as it wastes CPU time.
- The *Direct Memory Access* (DMA) interface eliminates the need to use CPU registers to transfer data from I/O units to memory or vice versa.
- The method of transfer of a word from I/O to memory in which a memory cycle is taken away from CPU by DMA is known as *cycle stealing.*
- The DMA transfer is faster and convenient to use.
- Every I/O activity is initiated by I/O instruction written in the code.
- An interrupt generated internally by CPU is sometimes termed as *trap.*
- The number of types of interrupts that can be distinguished by a CPU is called *interrupt levels* or *interrupt classes.* The relative importance given to an interrupt is called its *priority.*
- The procedure of exchanging signals between processes to communicate each other's state is known as *hand shaking.*
- Hand shaking is a commonly used procedure and is not restricted to interface chips alone.
- There are three ways that computer buses can be used to communicate with memory and I/O:
  - Use two separate buses, one for the memory and the other for I/O.
  - Use one common bus for both memory and I/O but have separate control lines for each.
  - Use one common bus for memory and I/O with common control lines.
- Input/Output channels are also called IOPs, an abbreviation for I/O processors.
- The channel is like a processor, but it is specialized to execute I/O commands.
- The maximum capacity for data transfer for a channel is called the *channel band width.* It is expressed in bits per second.
- A multiplexer channel is used to connect several very slow speed I/O devices to the main memory and services each active I/O devices in a cyclic order.

- A *channel program* is a program written for the control operations of a channel and the instructions of a channel (computer) are known as *channel commands.*
- Channel programs are stored in main memory. Both the channel (processor) and CPU have access to the main memory. (It is true for DMA too.)
- The channel and I/O are physically connected by means of high speed buses.

## REVIEW QUESTIONS AND EXERCISES

1. What are the main functions which have to be performed by the computer system to handle I/O devices?
2. Describe the I/O interface with an example.
3. Write a short note on the following:
   (*i*) Memory mapped I/O
   (*ii*) Isolated I/O
4. Describe the following:
   (*i*) Program controlled transfer.
   (*ii*) Program controlled interrupt transfer.
5. Discuss the need of Direct Memory Access (DMA) interface.
6. What is an interrupt? What is the need of priority interrupt?
7. Describe interrupt structures.
8. What is hand shaking? Explain.
9. Distinguish between traps and external interrupts. What are the major differences in handling these in a computer system?
10. What is the need of I/O Processor? Explain.
11. What are the current trends in I/O organisation?
12. Describe the evaluation of I/O organisation.
13. What are different types of interface units? Explain in brief.
14. Why does DMA have priority over the CPU when both request a memory transfer?
15. Describe the IBM 370 I/O channel.
16. Describe the Intel 8089 IOP.
17. State True or False:
   (*i*) I/O interface gives a method for transferring information between internal memory and I/O devices.
   (*ii*) The data transfer rate of peripherals is usually faster than the transfer rate of the CPU.
   (*iii*) The *program controlled transfer* does not waste CPU time.
   (*iv*) A *direct memory access* (DMA) interface is used for transferring data directly between an external device and memory.

(v) A priority interrupt system is a communication of branch and loop techniques.

(vi) Internal interrupts (also known as *traps*) can occur when there is a mistake in a user's program.

(vii) The relative importance given to an interrupt is called its *big boss.*

(viii) Input/Output channels are also called IOPs.

18. Fill in the blanks:

(i) The speed of information transfer of I/O devices is .................. compared to that of a computer's main memory.

(ii) A .................. transfer data is parallel between the microprocessor and a peripheral device.

(iii) The entire process of data transfer performed by the hardware without any program intervention which is hidden from the programmer are called .................. to programmers.

(iv) The .................. transfer is fast and convenient to use.

(v) Interrupts caused by I/O devices and emergency events outside CPU's control are called .................. .

(vi) The number of types of interrupts that can be distinguished by a CPU is called .................. .

(vii) .................. channels are used for high speed I/O devices.

(viii) A channel has certain maximum capacity for data transfer, expressed in bits per second. It is called the .................. .

## ANSWERS

17. State True or False:

| | |
|---|---|
| (i) True | (ii) False |
| (iii) False | (iv) True |
| (v) False | (vi) True |
| (vii) False | (viii) True |

18. Fill in the blanks:

| | |
|---|---|
| (i) slow | (ii) parallel peripheral interface |
| (iii) transparent | (iv) DMA |
| (v) external interrupts | (vi) interrupt levels or interrupt classes |
| (vii) Selector channels | (viii) channel band width |

Chapter 13

# CISC AND RISC ARCHITECTURE

## 13.1 INTRODUCTION

The primary objective of processor designers is to improve performance. Performanc is defined as the amount of work that the processor can do in a given period of tim Different instructions perform different amounts of work.

To increase performance, you can either have the processor execute instructions i less time, or make each instruction it executes do more work. Increasing performance b executing instructions in less time means increasing the clock speed of the processo Making it do more work with each instruction means increasing the power and complexit of each instruction. Ideally you would like to do both, of course, but it is a design tradeof it is hard to make more complex instructions run faster.

This trade-off in basic instruction set design philosophy is reflected in the two mai labels given to instruction sets. **CISC** stands for **complex instruction set compute** and is the name given to processors that use a large number of complicated instruction to try to do more work with each one. **RISC** stands for **reduced instruction set compute** and is the generic name given to processors that use a small number of simple instruction to try to do less work with each instruction but execute them much faster.

## 13.2 CISC

CISC is an acronym for Complex Instruction Set Computer and are chips that ar easy to program and which make efficient use of memory. Since the earliest machin were programmed in assembly language and memory was slow and expensive, the CIS philosophy made sense, and was commonly implemented in such large computers as th PDP-11 and the DEC system 10 and 20 machines.

Most common microprocessor designs such as the Intel 80 × 86 and Motorola 68 series followed the CISC philosophy.

But recent changes in software and hardware technology have forced a re-examinatic of CISC and many modern CISC processors are hybrids, implementing many RISC principle

### 13.2.1 Advantages

At the time of their initial development, CISC machines used available technologies to optimize computer performance.

- *Microprogramming is as easy as assembly language to implement,* and much less expensive than hardwiring a control unit.
- The ease of microcoding new instructions allowed designers to make *CISC machines upwardly compatible* : a new computer could run the same programs as earlier computers because the new computer would contain a superset of the instructions of the earlier computers.
- As each instruction became more capable, *fewer instructions could be used* to implement a given task. This made more efficient use of the relatively slow main memory.
- Because microprogram instruction sets can be written to match the constructs of high-level languages, *the compiler does not have to be as complicated.*

### 13.2.2 Disadvantages

The CISC philosophy had its own problems, including:

- Earlier generations of a processor family generally were contained as a subset in every new version—so *instruction set and chip hardware become more complex with each generation of computers.*
- So that as many instructions as possible could be stored in memory with the least possible wasted space, individual instructions could be of almost any length—this means that *different instructions will take different amounts of clock time to execute,* slowing down the overall performance of the machine.
- *Many specialized instructions aren't used frequently* enough to justify their existence—approximately 20% of the available instructions are used in a typical program.
- *CISC instructions typically set the condition codes as a side effect of the instruction.* Not only does setting the condition codes take time, but programmers have to remember to examine the condition code bits before a subsequent instruction changes them.

## 13.3 RISC MACHINES

In the mid-1970's advances in semiconductor technology began to reduce the difference in speed between main memory and processor chips. As memory speed increased, and high-level languages displaced assembly language, the major reasons for CISC began to disappear, and computer designers began to look at ways computer performance could be optimized beyond just making faster hardware.

### 13.3.1 RISC Characteristics

- ***Simple Instruction Set.*** In a RISC machine, the instruction set contains simple, basic instructions, from which more complex instructions can be composed.

- ***Same Length Instructions.*** Each instruction is of the same length, so that it may be fetched in a single operation.
- ***1 machine-cycle Instructions.*** Most instructions complete in one machine cycle, which allows the processor to handle several instructions at the same time. This pipelining is a key technique used to speed up RISC machines.

### 13.3.2 Advantages

Implementing a processor with a simplified instruction set design provides several advantages over implementing a comparable CISC design:

- ***Speed.*** Since a simplified instruction set allows for a pipelined, superscalar design RISC processors often achieve 2 to 4 times the performance of CISC processors using comparable semiconductor technology and the same clock rates.
- ***Simpler Hardware.*** Because the instruction set of a RISC processor is so simple, it uses up much less chip space; extra functions, such as memory management units or floating point arithmetic units, can also be placed on the same chip. Smaller chips allow a semiconductor manufacturer to place more parts on a single silicon wafer, which can lower the per-chip cost dramatically.
- ***Shorter Design Cycle.*** Since RISC processors are simpler than corresponding CISC processors, they can be designed more quickly, and can take advantage of other technological developments sooner than corresponding CISC designs, leading to greater leaps in performance between generations.

### 13.3.3 RISC Instructions

The instruction set of a typical RISC processor is restricted to the use of load and store instructions when communicating between memory and CPU. All other instructions are executed within the registers of the CPU without referring to memory. A program for a RISC-type CPU consists of LOAD and STORE instructions that have one memory and one register address, and computational-type instructions that have three addresses with all three specifying processor registers. For example, the program to evaluate X = (A + B) × (C + D) using RISC instructions is as follows:

| | | |
|---|---|---|
| LOAD | R1, A | R1 ← M[A] |
| LOAD | R2, B | R2 ← M[B] |
| LOAD | R3, C | R3 ← M[C] |
| LOAD | R4, D | R4 ← M[D] |
| ADD | R1, R1, R2 | R1 ← R1 + R2 |
| ADD | R3, R3, R4 | R3 ← R3 + R4 |
| MUL | R1, R1, R3 | R1 ← R1 × R3 |
| STORE | X, R1 | M[X] ← R1 |

The load instructions transfer the operands from memory to CPU registers. The add and multiply operations are executed with data in the registers without accessing memory. Finally the result of the computations is stored in memory using a store instruction.

### 13.3.4 RISC Hazards

The transition from a CISC design strategy to a RISC design strategy isn't without its problems. Software engineers should be aware of the key issues which arise when moving code from a CISC processor to a RISC processor.

#### *Code Quality*

The performance of a RISC processor depends greatly on the code that it is executing. If the programmer (or compiler) does a poor job of instruction scheduling, the processor can spend quite a bit of time stalling : waiting for the result of one instruction before it can proceed with a subsequent instruction.

Since the scheduling rules can be complicated, most programmers use a high level language (such as C or C++) and leave the instruction scheduling to the compiler.

This makes the performance of a RISC application depend critically on the quality of the code generated by the compiler. Therefore, developers (and development tool suppliers such as Apple) have to choose their compiler carefully based on the quality of the generated code.

#### *Debugging*

Unfortunately, instruction scheduling can make debugging difficult. If scheduling (and other optimizations) are turned off, the machine-language instructions show a clear connection with their corresponding lines of source. However, once instruction scheduling is turned on, the machine language instructions for one line of source may appear in the middle of the instructions for another line of source code.

Such an intermingling of machine language instructions not only makes the code hard to read, it can also defeat the purpose of using a source-level compiler, since single lines of code can no longer be executed by themselves.

Therefore, many RISC programmers debug their code in an un-optimized, un-scheduled form and then turn on the scheduler (and other optimizations) and hope that the program continues to work in the same way.

#### *Code Expansion*

Since CISC machines perform complex actions with a single instruction, where RISC machines may require multiple instructions for the same action, code expansion can be a problem.

Code expansion refers to the increase in size that you get when you take a program that had been compiled for a CISC machine and re-compile it for a RISC machine. The exact expansion depends primarily on the quality of the compiler and the nature of the machine's instruction set.

Fortunately for us, the code expansion between a 68K processor used in the non-PowerPC Macintoshes and the PowerPC seems to be only 30–50% on the average, although size-optimized PowerPC code can be the same size (or smaller) than corresponding 68K code.

***System Design***

Another problem that faces RISC machines is that they require very fast memory systems to feed them instructions. RISC-based systems typically contain large memory caches, usually on the chip itself.

## 13.4 CISC VS. RISC

From the above discussion on CISC and RISC we conclude that the main characteristics of CISC microprocessors are:

- Extensive instructions.
- Complex and efficient machine instructions.
- Microencoding of the machine instructions.
- Extensive addressing capabilities for memory operations.
- Relatively few registers.

In comparison, RISC processors are more or less the opposite of the above:

- Reduced instruction set.
- Less complex, simple instructions.
- Hardwared control unit and machine instructions.
- Few addressing schemes for memory operands with only two basic instructions, LOAD and STORE
- Many symmetric registers which are oraganised into a register file.

The question of which of these two approaches to use in designing a processor has become one of the great arguments of the computer world. This is especially true because once a platform makes an instruction set decision, it tends to stick with it in order to ensure compatibility with existing software. Somewhat ironically, the line between RISC and CISC has become blurred in recent years, with each moving toward the middle ground in an attempt to improve performance. In addition, new ways to mixing RISC and CISC concepts have emerged through the use of *translating processors*.

## SUMMARY

- Microprogram sequencer sequences the microinstructions in control memory.
- CISC machines are more complex and less efficient.
- The aim of employing RISC design is to increase the computing speed by reducing the execution time of instructions.

## REVIEW QUESTIONS AND EXERCISES

1. What is a microprocessor? Give its various units.
2. Discuss the function of a CPU. What are the main sections of a CPU? Discuss the function of each section.
3. Describe the CISC and RISC machines.
4. Compare various CPU's features.
5. What is the purpose of using address mode techniques by a computer? Summarize the various addressing modes?
6. What are the advantages of microprogram control?
7. What are the advantages of CISC and RISC?

# REFERENCES


1. D. A. Patterson and J. L. Hennessey, "Computer organisation and design," Morgan Kaufmann, 2nd Ed.
2. J.P.Hayes, "Computer Architecture and Organisation"; McGraw-Hill.
3. Harvey G.Cragon, "Memory System and Pipelined processors"; Narosa Publication.
4. V.Rajaranam and C.S.R.Murthy, "Parallel computer"; PHI.
5. Andrews, "Computer Organisation", Computer Science Press.
6. D.Sima, T.Fountain, P.Kasuk, "Advanced Computer Architecture-A Design space Approach," Addison Wesley, 1997.
7. M.J. Flynn, "Computer Architecture, Pipelined and Parallel Processor Design"; Narosa Publishing.
8. Hwang and Briggs, "Computer Architecture and Parallel Processing"; MGH.
9. M. Ercegovac, T. Lang and L.J. Moreno, "Introduction to Digital Systems", Wiley, 2000.
10. C. H. Roth, "Digital System Design using VHDL", PWS Publishing.
11. J.F. Wakerly, "Digital Design-Principles and Practices", PHL.
12. William Stallings, "Computer Organisation & Architecture: *Designing for performance*", PHI, 7th Ed. 2006.
13. Barry B. Brey, "The Intel Microprocessors: Architecture, *Programming and Interfacing*, By Barry B. Brey, PHI 7th Ed., 2006.
14. S. Palnitkar, "HDL: Guide to Digital Design and Synthesis", Pearson Education Asia, 2003.
15. C. Hamacher, Z. Vranesic and S. Zaky, "Computer Organization", McGraw-Hill 5th Ed.
16. R.P. Jain, "Modern Digital Electronics", McGraw-Hill, 2006.
17. Marris Mano, "Computer System Architecture", Prentice-Hall.
18. M. Lacy, "Understanding Computer Architecture", BPB Publications, N.Delhi.
19. Rajaraman and Radhakrishanan, "An Introduction to Digital Computer Design", PHI.
20. M. Morris Mano, "Computer System Architecture", PHI.
21. Sanjay K. Bose, "Digital Systems", New Age International Publishers Ltd.

22. Madhulika Jain, Anita Rajdev and Satish Jain, "Principles of Electronics", BPB Publications, N.Delhi.
23. M.R. Bhujade, "Digital Computer Design Principles", Pitambar Pub. Co. Pvt. Ltd.
24. Salivahanan and Arivazhagan, "Digital Circuits and Design", Vikas Pub. House Pvt. Ltd.
25. Y. Chu, "Digital Computer Design Fundamentals", McGraw Hill.
26. Wickes, "Logic Design with Integrated Circuits", Wiley.
27. Hellerman, "Digital Computer System Principles", McGraw Hill.
28. Y. Chu, "Computer Organisation and Microprogramming", Englewood Cliffs: Prentice-Hall.
29. Bartee, Lebow and Reed, "Theory and Design of Digital Machines", McGraw-Hill.
30. Bell and Newell, "Computer structures: Readings and Examples", McGraw-Hill.
31. Barna and Porat, "Integrated Circuits in Digital Electronics", John wiley & Sons.
32. Richard, "Arithmetic Operations in Digital Computers", Van Nostrand, NY.
33. Whitesitt, "Boolean Algebra and Its Applications", Addison-Wesley.
34. Humhprey, "Switching Circuits with Computer Applications", McGraw-Hill.
35. McCluskey, "Introduction to the Theory of Switching Circuits", McGraw-Hill.
36. Kohavi, "Switching and Finite Automata Theory", McGraw-Hill.
37. Nagel, Carrol and Irwin, "An Introduction to Computer Logic", Prentice-Hall.
38. Rhyne, "Fundamentals of Diital Systems Design", Prentice-Hall.
39. Preatman, "The Design of Digital Systems", McGraw-Hill.
40. Friedman and Menon, "Theory and Design of Switching Circuits", Woodland Hills.
41. Blakeslee, "Digital Design with Standard MSI and LSI", John Wiley & Sons.
42. Marcus, "Switching Circuits for Engineers", Prentice-Hall.
43. Miller, "Switching Theory", John Wiley & Sons.
44. Krieger, "Basic Switching Circuit Theory", Macmillan Co.
45. Phister, "The Logical Design of Digital Computers", John Wiley & Sons.
46. Givone, "Introduction to Switching Circuit Theory", McGraw Hill.
47. Grinich and Jackson, "Introduction to Integrated Circuits", McGraw-Hill.
48. Kostopoulos, "Digital Engineering", McGraw-Hill.
49. Scott, "Electronic Computer Technology", McGraw-Hill.
50. Kline,"Digital Computer Design", Prentice-Hall.
51. Dietmeyer, "Logical Design of Digital Systems", Allyn and Bacon.
52. Malvino, "Digital Computer Electronics: An Introduction to Microcomputers", McGraw-Hill.
53. Lorin, "Introduction to Computer Organisation and Architecture", Wiley.
54. Kuck, "The Structure of Computers and Computations", Wiley.
55. Khabata, "Microprocessors/Microcomputers: Architecture, Software and System", Wiley.

# INDEX